The Definitive
TAGORE

The Definitive
TAGORE

RUPA

Published by
Rupa Publications India Pvt. Ltd 2017
161-B/4, Gulmohar House,
Yusuf Sarai Community Centre,
New Delhi 110049

Sales centres:
Bengaluru Chennai
Hyderabad Kolkata Mumbai

Edition copyright © Rupa Publications India Pvt. Ltd 2017

This is a work of fiction. Names, characters, places and incidents are
either the product of the author's imagination or are used fictitiously
and any resemblance to any actual person, living or dead,
events or locales is entirely coincidental.

All rights reserved.
No part of this publication may be reproduced, transmitted,
or stored in a retrieval system, in any form or by any means, electronic,
mechanical, photocopying, recording or otherwise,
without the prior permission of the publisher.

P-ISBN: 978-81-291-4818-6
E-ISBN: 978-81-291-4822-3

Fifth impression 2025

10 9 8 7 6 5

This edition is for sale in the Indian Subcontinent only.

Printed in India

This book is sold subject to the condition that it shall not,
by way of trade or otherwise, be lent, resold, hired out, or otherwise
circulated, without the publisher's prior consent, in any form of binding or
cover other than that in which it is published.

CONTENTS

The Nobel Prize Acceptance Speech / 1

My Boyhood Days / 11

The Post Office / 67

Chokher Bali / 91

Short Stories / 323
The Cabuliwallah / 324
The Hungry Stones / 332
The Victory / 344
Living or Dead? / 351
The Parrot's Training / 362

Gitanjali / 367

Home and the World / 405

Nationalism in India / 583

Glimpses of Bengal / 603

THE NOBEL PRIZE
ACCEPTANCE SPEECH

I am glad that I have been able to come at last to your country and that I may use this opportunity for expressing my gratitude to you for the honour you have done to me by acknowledging my work and rewarding me by giving me the Nobel Prize.

I remember the afternoon when I received the cablegram from my publisher in England that the prize had been awarded to me. I was staying then at the school Shantiniketan, about which I suppose you know. At that moment we were taking a party over to a forest near by the school, and when I was passing by the telegram office and the post office, a man came running to us and held up the telegraphic message. I had also an English visitor with me in the same carriage. I did not think that the message was of any importance, and I just put it into my pocket, thinking that I would read it, when I reached my destination. But my visitor supposed he knew the contents, and he urged me to read it, saying that it contained an important message. And I opened and read the message, which I could hardly believe. I first thought that possibly the telegraphic language was not quite correct and that I might have misread the meaning of it, but at last I felt certain about it. And you can well understand how rejoicing it was for my boys at the school and for the teachers. What touched me more deeply than anything else was that these boys who loved me and for whom I had the deepest love felt proud of the honour that had been awarded to him for whom they had a feeling of reverence, and I realized that my countrymen would share with me the honour which had been awarded to myself.

The rest of the afternoon passed away in this manner, and when the night came I sat upon the terrace alone, and I asked myself the question what the reason could be of my poems being accepted and honoured by the West—in spite of my belonging to a different race, parted and separated by seas and mountains from the children of the West. And I can assure you that it was not with a feeling of exaltation but with a searching of the heart that I questioned myself, and I felt humble at that moment.

I remember how my life's work developed from the time when I was very young. When I was about 25 years, I used to live in utmost seclusion in the solitude of an obscure Bengal village by the river Ganges in a boathouse. The wild ducks which came during the time of autumn from the Himalayan lakes were my only living companions, and in that solitude I seem to have drunk in the open space like wine overflowing with sunshine, and the murmur of the river used to speak to me and tell me the secrets of nature. And I passed my days in the solitude dreaming and giving shape to my dream in poems and studies and sending out my thoughts to the Calcutta public through the magazines and other papers. You can well understand that it was a life quite different from the life of the West. I do not know if any of your Western poets or writers do pass the greatest part of their young days in such absolute seclusion. I am almost certain that it cannot be possible and that seclusion itself has no place in the Western world.

And my life went on like this. I was an obscure individual—to most of my countrymen in those days. I mean that my name was hardly known outside my own province, but I was quite content with that obscurity, which protected me from the curiosity of the crowds.

And then came a time when my heart felt a longing to come out of that solitude and to do some work for my human fellow-beings, and not merely give shapes to my dreams and meditate deeply on the problems of life, but try to give expression to my ideas through some definite work, some definitive service for my fellow-beings.

And the one thing, the one work which came to my mind was to teach children. It was not because I was specially fitted for this work of teaching, for I have not had myself the full benefit of a regular education. For some time I hesitated to take upon myself this task, but I felt that as I had a deep love for nature I had naturally love for children also. My object in starting this institution was to give the children of men full freedom of joy, of life and of communion with nature. I myself had suffered when I was young through the impediments which were inflicted upon most boys while they attended school and I have had to go through the machine of education which crushes the joy and freedom of life for which children have such insatiable thirst. And my object was to give freedom and joy to children of men.

And so I had a few boys around me, and I taught them, and I tried to make them happy. I was their playmate. I was their companion. I shared their life, and I felt that I was the biggest child of the party. And we all grew up together in this atmosphere of freedom. The vigour and the joy of the children, their chats and songs filled the air with a spirit of delight, which I drank every day I was there. And in the evening during the sunset hour I often used to sit alone watching the trees of the shadowing avenue, and in the silence of the afternoon I could hear distinctly the voices of the children coming up in the air, and it seemed to me that these shouts and songs and glad voices were like those trees, which come out from the heart of the earth like fountains of life towards the bosom of the infinite sky. And it symbolized, it brought before my mind the whole cry of human life all expressions of joy and aspirations of men rising from the heart of Humanity up to this sky. I could see that, and I knew that we also, the grown-up children, send up our cries of aspiration to the infinite. I felt it in my heart of hearts.

In this atmosphere and in this environment I used to write my poems Gitanjali, and I sang them to myself in the midnight under the glorious stars of the Indian sky. And in the early morning and in the afternoon glow of sunset, I used to write these songs till a day came when I felt impelled to come out once again and meet the heart of the large world.

I could see that my coming out from the seclusion of my life among these joyful children and doing my service to my fellow creatures was only a prelude to my pilgrimage to a larger world. And I felt a great desire to come out and come into touch with the Humanity of the West, for I was conscious that the present age belongs to the Western man with his superabundance of energy.

He has got the power of the whole world, and his life is overflowing all boundaries and is sending out its message to the great future. And I felt that I must before I die come to the West and meet the man of the secret shrine where the Divine presence has his dwelling, his temple. And I thought that the Divine man with all his powers and aspirations of life is dwelling in the West.

And so I came out. After my Gitanjali poems had been written in Bengali I translated those poems into English, without having any desire to have them published, being diffident of my mastery of that language, but I had—the manuscript with me when I came out to the West. And you know that the British public, when these poems were put before them, and those who had the opportunity of reading them in manuscript before, approved of them. I was accepted, and the heart of the West opened without delay.

And it was a miracle to me who had lived for fifty years faraway from activity, faraway from the West, that I should be almost in a moment accepted by the West as one of its own poets. It was surprising to me, but I felt that possibly this had its deeper significance and that those years which I had spent in seclusion, separated from the life and the spirit of the West, had brought with them a deeper feeling of rest, serenity and, feeling of the eternal, and that these were exactly the sentiments that were needed by the Western people with their overactive life, who still in their heart of hearts have a thirst for the peace, for the infinite peace. My fitness was that training which my muse had from my young days in the absolute solitude of the beaches of the Ganges. The peace of those years had been stored in my nature so that I could bring it out and hold it up to the man of the West, and what I offered to him was accepted gratefully.

I know that I must not accept that praise as my individual share. It is the East in me which gave to the West. For is not the East the mother of spiritual Humanity and does not the West, do not the children of the West amidst their games and plays when they get hurt, when they get famished and hungry, turn their face to that serene mother, the East? Do they not expect their food to come from her, and their rest for the night when they are tired? And are they to be disappointed?

Fortunately for me I came in that very moment when the West had turned her face again to the East and was seeking for some nourishment. Because I represented the East I got my reward from my Eastern friends.

And I can assure you that the prize which you have awarded to me was not wasted upon myself. I as an individual had no right to accept it, and therefore I have made use of it for others. I have dedicated it to our Eastern children and students. But then it is like a seed which is put into the earth and comes up again to those who have sown it, and for their benefit it is producing fruits. I have used this money which I got from you for establishing and maintaining the university which I started lately, and it seemed to me, that this university should be a place where Western students might come and meet their Eastern brethren and when they might work together in the pursuit of truth and try to find the treasures that have lain hidden in the East for centuries and work out the spiritual resources of the East, which are necessary for all Humanity.

I can remind you of a day when India had her great university in the glorious days of her civilization. When a light is lighted it cannot be held within a short range. It is for the whole world. And India had her civilization with all its splendours and wisdom and wealth. It could not use it for its own children only. It had to open its gates in hospitality to all races of men. Chinese and Japanese and Persians and all different races of men, came, and they had their opportunity of gaining what was best in India, her best offering of all times and to all Humanity. And she offered it generously. You know the traditions of our country are never to accept any material fees from the students in return for the teaching, because we consider in India that he who has the knowledge has the responsibility to impart it to the students. It is not merely for the students to come and ask it from the master, but it is the master who must fulfil his mission of life by offering the best gift which he has to all who may need it. And thus it was that need of self expression, of giving what had been stored in India and offering the best thing that she has in herself that made it possible and was the cause and the origin of these universities that were started in the different provinces of India.

And I feel that what we suffer from in the present day is no other calamity but this calamity of obscurity, of seclusion, that we have missed our opportunity of offering hospitality to Humanity and asking the world to share the best things we have got. We lost our confidence in our own civilization for over a century, when we came into contact with the Western races with their material superiority over the Eastern Humanity and Eastern culture, and in the educational establishments no provision was made for our own culture. And for over a century our students have been brought up in utter ignorance of the worth of their own civilization of the past. Thus we did not only lose touch of the great which lay hidden in our own inheritance, but also the great honour of being able to contribute to the civilization of Humanity, to have opportunity of giving what we have and not merely begging from others, not merely borrowing culture and living like eternal schoolboys.

But the time has come when we must not waste our opportunities. We must try to do our best to bring out what we have, and not go from century to century, from land to land and display our poverty before others. We know what we have to be proud of, what we have inherited from our ancestors, and such opportunity of giving should not be lost—not only for the sake of our people, but for the sake of Humanity.

That is the reason, and that led me to the determination to establish an international institution where the Western and Eastern students could meet and share the common feast of spiritual food.

And thus I am proud to say that your awarding me the prize has made some contribution to this great object which I had in my mind. This has made me come out once again to the West, and I have come to ask you, to invite you to the feast which is waiting for you in the far East. I hope that my invitation will not be rejected. I have visited different countries of Europe, and I have accepted from them an enthusiastic welcome. That welcome has its own meaning, that the West has need of the East, as the East has need of the West, and so the time has come when they should meet.

I am glad that I belong to this great time, this great age, and I am glad that I have done some work to give expression to this great age, when the East and the West are coming together. They are proceeding towards each other. They are coming to meet each other. They have got their invitation to meet each other and join hands in building up a new civilization and the great culture of the future.

I feel certain that through my writing some such idea has reached you, even if obscurely through the translation, some idea which belongs both to the East and the West, some idea which proceeding from the East has been able to come to the West and claim its rest here, its dwelling, and to be able to receive its welcome, and has been accepted by the West. And if in my writings I have been fortunate enough to be able to interpret the voice of the need of the time I am deeply thankful to you for giving me this glorious opportunity. The acknowledgment I got from Sweden has brought me and my work before the Western public, though I can assure you that it has also given me some trouble. It has broken through the seclusion which I have been accustomed to. It has brought me out before the great public to which I have never been accustomed. And the adjustment has not been yet made. I shrink in my heart when I stand before the great concourse of Humanity in the West. I have not yet been accustomed to accept the great gift of your praise and your admiration in the manner in which you have given it to me. And I feel ashamed and shy when standing before you—I do so now. But I will only say that I am thankful to God that he has given me this great opportunity, that I have been an instrument to bring together, to unite the hearts of the East and the West. And I must to the end of my life carry on that mission. I must do all that I can. The feeling of resentment between the East and the West must be pacified. I must do something, and with that one object I have started this institution.

I do not think that it is the spirit of India to reject anything, reject any race, reject any culture. The spirit of India has always proclaimed the ideal of unity. This ideal of unity never rejects anything, any race, or any culture. It comprehends all, and it has been the highest aim of our spiritual exertion to be able to penetrate all things with one soul, to comprehend all things as they are, and not to keep out anything in the whole universe—to comprehend all things with sympathy and love. This is the spirit of India. Now, when in the present time of political unrest the children of the same great India cry for rejection of the West I feel hurt. I feel that it is a lesson which they have received from the West. Such is not our mission. India is there to unite all human races.

Because of that reason in India we have not been given the unity of races. Our problem is the race problem which is the problem of all Humanity. We have Dravidians, we have Mohammedans, we have

Hindoos and all different sects and communities of men in India. Therefore, no superficial bond of political unity can appeal to us, can satisfy us, can ever be real to us. We must go deeper down. We must discover the most profound unity, the spiritual unity between the different races. We must go deeper down to the spirit of man and find out the great bond of unity, which is to be found in all human races. And for that we are well equipped. We have inherited the immortal works of our ancestors, those great writers who proclaimed the religion of unity and sympathy, in say: He who sees all beings as himself, who realizes all beings as himself, knows Truth. That has once again to be realized, not only by the children of the East but also by the children of the West. They also have to be reminded of these great immortal truths. Man is not to fight with other human races, other human individuals, but his work is to bring about reconciliation and Peace and to restore the bonds of friendship and love. We are not like fighting beasts. It is the life of self which is predominating in our life, the self which is creating the seclusion, giving rise to sufferings, to jealousy and hatred, to political and commercial competition. All these illusions will vanish, if we go down to the heart of the shrine, to the love and unity of all races.

For that great mission of India I have started this university. I ask you now, when I have this opportunity, I invite you to come to us and join hands with us and not to leave this institution merely to us, but let your own students and learned men come to us and help us to make this university into a common institution for the East and the West, may they give the contributions of their lives and may we all together make it living and representative of the undivided Humanity of the world.

For this I have come to you. I ask you this and I claim it of you in the name of the unity of men, and in the name of love, and in the name of God. I ask you to come. I invite you.

26 May 1921, *Stockholm*

MY BOYHOOD DAYS

I

The Calcutta where I was born was an altogether old world place. Hackney carriages lumbered about the city raising clouds of dust, and the whips fell on the backs of skinny horses whose bones showed plainly below their hide. There were no trams then, no buses, no motors. Business was not the breathless rush that it is now, and the days went by in leisurely fashion. Clerks would take a good pull at the hookah before starting for office, and chew their betel as they went along. Some rode in palanquins, others joined in groups of four or five to hire a carriage in common, which was known as a 'share-carriage'. Wealthy men had monograms painted on their carriages, and a leather hood over the rear portion, like a half-drawn veil. The coachman sat on the box with his turban stylishly tilted to one side, and two grooms rode behind, girdles of yaks' tails round their waists, startling the pedestrians from their path with their shouts of 'Hey-yo!'

Women used to go about in the stifling darkness of closed palanquins; they shrank from the idea of riding in carriages, and even to use an umbrella in sun or rain was considered unwomanly. Any woman who was so bold as to wear the new-fangled bodice, or shoes on her feet, was scornfully nicknamed 'memsahib', that is to say, one who had cast off all sense of propriety or shame. If any woman unexpectedly encountered a strange man, one outside her family circle, her veil would promptly descend to the very tip of her nose, and she would at once turn her back on him. The palanquins in which women went out were shut as closely as their apartments in the house. An additional covering, a kind of thick tilt, completely enveloped the palanquin of a rich man's daughters and daughters-in-law, so that it looked like a moving tomb. By its side went the durwan carrying his brass-bound stick. His work was to sit in the entrance and watch the house, to tend his beard, safely to conduct the money to the bank and the women to their relatives' houses, and on festival days to dip the lady of the house into the Ganges, closed palanquin and all. Hawkers who came to the door with their array of wares would grease Shivnandan's palm to gain admission, and the drivers of hired carriages were also a source of profit to him. Sometimes, a man who was unwilling to fall in with this idea of going shares would create a great scene in front of the porch.

Our 'jamadar' Sobha Ram, who was a wrestler, used to spend a good deal of time in practising his preparatory feints and approaches, and in brandishing his heavy clubs. Sometimes he would sit and grind hemp for drink, and sometimes he would be quietly eating his raw radishes, tender leaves and all, when we boys would creep upon him and yell 'Radhakrishna!' in his ear. The more he waved his arms and protested the more we delighted in teasing him. And perhaps—who knows?—his protests were merely a cunning device for hearing repeated the name of his favourite god.

There was no gas then in the city, and no electric light. When the kerosene lamp was introduced, its brilliance amazed us. In the evening the house-servant lit castor oil lamps in every room. The one in our study-room had two wicks in a glass bowl.

By this dim light, my master taught me from Peary Sarkar's First Book. First I would begin to yawn, and then, growing more and more sleepy, rub my heavy eyes. At such times I heard over and over again of the virtues of my master's other pupil Satin, a paragon of a boy with a wonderful head for study, who would rub snuff in his eyes to keep himself awake, so earnest was he. But as for me—the less said about that the better! Even the awful thought that I should probably remain the only dunce in the family could not keep me awake. When nine o'clock struck I was released, my eyes dazed and my mind drugged with sleep.

There was a narrow passage, enclosed by latticed walls, leading from the outer apartments to the interior of the house. A dimly burning lantern swung from the ceiling. As I went along this passage, my mind would be haunted by the idea that something was creeping upon me from behind. Little shivers ran up and down my back. In those days, devils and spirits lurked in the recesses of every man's mind, and the air was full of ghost stories. One day it would be some servant girl falling in a dead faint because she had heard the nasal whine of *Shañk-chunni*. The female demon of that name was the most bad-tempered devil of all, and was said to be very greedy of fish. Another story was connected with the thick-leaved *bādām* tree at the western corner of the house. A mysterious Shape was said to stand with one foot in its branches and the other on the third storey cornice of the house. Plenty of people declared that they had seen it, and there were not a few who believed them. A friend of my elder brother's laughingly made light of the story, and the servants looked upon him as lacking in all piety, and said that his neck would surely be wrung one day and his pretensions exposed. The very atmosphere was so enmeshed in ghostly terrors that I could not put my feet into the darkness under the table without them getting the creeps.

There were no water-pipes laid on in those days. In the spring months of *Māgh* and *Fālgoon* when the Ganges water was clear, our bearers would bring it up in brimming pots carried in a yoke across their shoulders. In the dark rooms of the ground floor stood rows of huge water jars filled with the whole year's supply of drinking water. All those musty, dingy, twilit rooms were the home of furtive 'Things'—which of us did not know all about those 'Things'? Great gaping mouths they had, eyes in their breasts, and ears like winnowing fans; and their feet turned backwards. Small wonder that my heart would pound in my breast and my knees tremble when I went into the inner garden, with the vision of those devilish shapes before me.

At high tide, the water of the Ganges would flow along a masonry channel at the side of the road. Since my grandfather's time an allowance of this water had been discharged into our tank. When the sluices were opened the water rushed in, gurgling and foaming like a waterfall. I used to watch it fascinated, holding on by the railings of the south verandah. But the days of our tank were numbered, and finally there came a day when cartload after cartload of rubbish was tipped into it. When the tank no longer reflected the garden, the last lingering illusion of rural life left it. That *bādām* tree is still standing near the third storey cornice, but though his footholds remain, the ghostly shape that once bestrode them has disappeared forever.

II

The palanquin belonged to the days of my grandmother. It was of ample proportions and lordly appearance. It was big enough to have needed eight bearers for each pole. But when the former wealth and glory of the family had faded like the glowing clouds of sunset, the palanquin bearers, with their gold bracelets, their thick earrings, and their sleeveless red tunics, had disappeared along with it. The body of the palanquin had been decorated with coloured line drawings, some of which were now defaced. Its surface was stained and discoloured, and the coir stuffing was coming out of the upholstery. It lay in a corner of the counting house verandah as though it were a piece of commonplace lumber. I was seven or eight years old at that time.

I was not yet, therefore, of an age to put my hand to any serious work in the world, and the old palanquin on its part had been dismissed from all useful service. Perhaps it was this fellow-feeling that so much attracted me towards it. It was to me an island in the midst of the ocean, and I on my holidays became Robinson Crusoe. There I sat within its closed doors, completely lost to view, delightfully safe from prying eyes.

Outside my retreat, our house was full of people, innumerable relatives and other folk. From all parts of the house I could hear the shouts of the various servants at their work. Pari the maid is returning from the bazaar through the front courtyard with her vegetables in a basket on her hip. Dukhon the bearer is carrying in Ganges water in a yoke across his shoulder. The weaver woman has gone into the inner apartments to trade the newest style of saries. Dinu the goldsmith, who receives a monthly wage, usually sits in the room next to the lane, blowing his bellows and carrying out the orders of the family; now he is coming to the counting house to present his bill to Kailash Mukherjee, who has a quill pen stuck over his ear. The carder sits in the courtyard cleaning the cotton mattress stuffing on his twanging bow. Mukundalal the durwan is rolling on the ground outside with the one-eyed wrestler, trying out a new wrestling fall. He slaps his thighs loudly, and repeats his 'physical jerks' twenty or thirty times, dropping on all fours. There is a crowd of beggars sitting waiting for their regular dole.

The day wears on, the heat grows intense, the clock in the gate-house strikes the hour. But inside the palanquin the day does not acknowledge the authority of clocks. Our midday is that of former days, when the drum at the great door of the king's palace would be beaten for the breaking-up of the court, and the king would go to bathe in sandal-scented water. At midday, on holidays, those in charge of me have their meal and go to sleep. I sit on alone. My palanquin, outwardly at rest, travels on its imaginary journeys. My bearers, sprung from 'airy nothing' at my bidding, eating the salt of my imagination, carry me wherever my fancy leads. We pass through far, strange lands, and I give each country a name from the books I have read. My imagination has cut a road through a deep forest. Tigers' eyes blaze from the thickets, my flesh creeps and tingles. With me is Biswanath the hunter; his gun speaks—Crack! Crack!—and there, all is still. Sometimes my palanquin becomes a peacock-boat, floating far out on the ocean till the shore is out of sight. The oars fall into the water with a gentle plash, the waves swing and swell around us. The sailors cry to us to beware, a storm is coming. By the tiller stands Abdul the sailor, with his pointed beard, shaven moustache and close-cropped head. I know him, he brings hilsa fish and turtle eggs from the Padma for my elder brother.

Abdul has a story for me. One day at the end of *Chaitra*[1] he had gone out in a dinghy to catch fish when suddenly there arose a great *Vaisākh* gale.[2] It was a tremendous typhoon and the boat sank lower and lower. Abdul seized the tow-rope in his teeth, and jumping into the water swam to the shore, where he pulled his dinghy up after him by the rope. But the story comes to an end far too quickly for my taste, and besides, the boat is not lost, everything is saved—that isn't what I call a story! Again and again I demand, 'What next?' 'Well,'

---

[1] March-April.
[2] Nor-wester, a very common phenomenon in Bengal in the beginning of the hot weather.

says Abdul at last, 'after that there were great doings. What should I see next but a panther with enormous whiskers! During the storm he had climbed up a *pākur* tree on the village ghat on the other side of the river. In the violent wind the tree broke and fell into the Padma. Brother Panther came floating down on the current, rolled over and over in the water and reached and climbed the bank on my side. As soon as I saw him, I made a noose in my tow-rope. The wild beast drew near, his big eyes glaring. He had grown very hungry with swimming, and when he saw me saliva dribbled from his red, lolling tongue. But though he had known many other men, inside and out, he did not know Abdul. I shouted to him, "Come on old boy", and as soon as he raised his fore-feet for the attack, I dropped my noose round his neck. The more he struggled to get free the tighter grew the noose, until his tongue began to loll out...' I am tremendously excited. 'He didn't die, did he Abdul?' I ask. 'Die?' says Abdul, 'He couldn't die for the life of him! Well, the river was in spate, and I had to get back to Bahadurganj. I yoked my young panther to the dinghy and made him tow me fully for forty miles. Oh, he might roar and snarl, but I goaded him on with my oar, and he carried me a ten or fifteen hours' journey in an hour and a half! Now, my little fellow, don't ask me what happened next, for you won't get an answer.'

'All right,' say I, 'so much for the panther; now for the crocodile?' Says Abdul, 'I have often seen the tip of his nose above the water. And how wickedly he smiles as he lies basking in the sun, stretched at full length on the shelving sandbanks of the river. If I'd had a gun I should have made his acquaintance. But my license has expired.'

'Still, I can tell you one good yarn. One day Kanchi the gypsy woman was sitting on the bank of the river trimming bamboo with a bill-hook, with her young goat tethered nearby. All at once the crocodile appeared on the surface, seized the billy-goat by the leg and dragged it into the water. With one jump the gypsy woman landed astride on its back, and began sawing with her sickle at the throat of the "demon lizard", over and over again. The beast let go of the goat and plunged into the water.'

'And then? And then?' comes my excited question. 'Why,' says Abdul, 'the rest of the story went down to the bottom of the river with the crocodile. It will take some time to get it up again. Before I see you again I will send somebody to find out about it, and let you know.' Abdul has never come again; perhaps he is still looking for news.

So much, then, for my travels in the palanquin. Outside the palanquin there were days when I assumed the role of teacher, and the railings of the verandah were my pupils. They were all afraid of me, and would cower before me in silence. Some of them were very naughty, and cared absolutely nothing for their books. I told them with dire threats that when they grew up they would be fit for nothing but casual labour. They bore the marks of my beatings from head to foot, yet they did not stop being naughty. For it would not have done for them to stop, it would have made an end of my game.

There was another game too, with my wooden lion. I heard stories of poojah sacrifices and decided that a lion sacrifice would be a magnificent thing. I rained blows on his back—with a frail little stick. There had to be a 'mantra', of course, otherwise it would not have been a proper poojah:

'Liony, liony, off with your head,
Liony, liony, now you are dead.
Woofle the walnut goes clappety clap,
Snip, snop, SNAP!'

I had borrowed almost every word in this from other sources; only the word walnut was my own. I was very fond of walnuts. From the words 'clappety clap' you can see that my sacrificial knife was made of wood. And the word 'snap' shows that it was not a strong one.

III

The clouds have had no rest since yesterday evening. The rain is pouring incessantly. The trees stand huddled together in a seemingly foolish manner; the birds are silent. I call to mind the evenings of my boyhood.

We used then to spend our evening in the servants' quarters. At that time English spellings and meanings did not yet lie like a nightmare on my shoulders. My third brother used to say that I ought first to get a good foundation of Bengali and only afterwards to go on to the English superstructure. Consequently, while other school-boys of my age were glibly reciting 'I am up', 'He is down', I had not even started on B, A, D, bad and M, A, D, mad. In the speech of the nabobs the servants' quarters were then called 'tosha-khana'. Even though our house had fallen far below its former aristocratic state, these old high-sounding names, 'tosha-khana', 'daftar-khana', 'baithak-khana', still clung to it.

On the southern side of this 'tosha-khana', a castor oil lamp burned dimly on a glass stand in a big room; on the wall was a picture of Ganesh and a crude country painting of the goddess Kali, round which the wall lizards hunted their insect prey. There was no furniture in the room, merely a soiled mat spread on the floor.

You must understand that we lived like poor people, and were consequently saved the trouble of keeping a good stable. Away in a corner outside, in a thatched shed under a tamarind tree, was a shabby carriage and an old horse. We wore the very simplest and plainest clothes, and it was a long time before we even began to wear socks. It was luxury beyond our wildest dreams when our tiffin rations went beyond Brajeswar's inventory and included a loaf of bread, and butter wrapped in a banana leaf. We adapted ourselves easily to the broken wrecks of our former glory.

Brajeswar was the name of the servant who presided over our mat seat. His hair and beard were grizzled, the skin of his face dry and tight-drawn; he was a man of serious disposition, harsh voice, and deliberately mouthed speech. His former master had been a prosperous and well known man, yet necessity had degraded him from that service to the work of looking after neglected children like us. I have heard that he used to be a master in a village school. To the end of his life he kept this school-masterly language and prim manner. Instead of saying 'The gentlemen are waiting', he would say 'They await you', and his masters smiled when they heard him. He was as finicky about caste matters as he was conceited. When bathing he would go down into the tank and push back the oily surface water five or six times with his hands before taking a plunge. When he came out of the tank after his bath, Brajeswar would edge his way through the garden in so gingerly a way that one would think he could only keep caste by avoiding all contact with this unclean world that God has made. He would talk very emphatically about what was right and what was wrong in manners and behaviour. And besides, he held his head a little on one side, which made his words all the more impressive.

But with all this there was one flaw in his character as *guru*. He cherished secretly a suppressed greed for food. It was not his method to place a proper portion of food on our plates before the meal. Instead, when we sat down to eat he would take one *luchi*[1] at a time, and dangling it at a little distance ask, 'Do you want any more?' We knew by the tone of his voice what answer he desired, and I usually said that I didn't want any. After that he never gave us an opportunity to change our minds. The milk bowls also had an irresistible attraction for him—an attraction which I never felt at all. In his room was a small wired foodsafe with shelves in it. In it was a big brass bowl of milk, and *luchis* and vegetables on a wooden platter. Outside the wire-netting, the cat prowled longingly to and fro sniffing the air.

From my childhood upwards these short commons suited me very well. Small rations cannot be said to have made me weak. I was, if anything, stronger, certainly not weaker, than boys who had unlimited food. My constitution was so abominably sound that even when the most urgent need arose for avoiding school, I could never make myself ill by fair means or foul. I would get wet through shoes, stockings

---

[1] Fried pancake known in Hindusthani as *puri*.

and all, but I could not catch cold. I would lie on the open roof in the heavy autumn dew; my hair and clothes would be soaked, but I never had the slightest suspicion of a cough. And as for that sign of bad digestion known as stomachache, my stomach was a complete stranger to it, though my tongue made use of its name with mother in time of need. Mother would smile to herself and not feel the least anxiety; she would merely call the servant and tell him to go and tell my teacher that he should not teach me that evening. Our old fashioned mothers used to think it no great harm if the boys occasionally took a holiday from study. If we had fallen into the hands of these present-day mothers, we should certainly have been sent to the teacher, and had our ears tweaked into the bargain. Perhaps with a knowing smile they would have dosed us with castor oil, and our pains would have been permanently cured. If by chance I got a slight temperature no one ever called it fever, but 'heated blood'. I had never set eyes on a thermometer in those days. Dr Nilmadhav would come and place his hand on my body, and then prescribe as the first day's treatment castor oil and fasting. I was allowed very little water to drink, and what I had was hot, with a few sugar-coated cardamoms for flavouring. After this fast, the *mouralā fish* soup and soft-boiled rice which I got on the third day seemed a veritable food for the gods.

Serious fever I do not remember, and I never heard the name of malaria. I do not remember quinine—that castor oil was my most distasteful medicine. I never knew the slightest scratch of a surgeon's knife; and to this very day I do not know what measles and chickenpox are. In short, my body remained obstinately healthy. If mothers want their children to be so healthy that they will be unable to escape from the school master, I recommended them to find a servant like Brajeswar. He would save not only food bills but doctor's bills also, especially in these days of mill flour and adulterated ghee and oil. You must remember that in those days chocolate was still unknown in the bazaar. There was a kind of rose lollipop to be had for a pice. I do not know whether modern boy's pockets are still made sticky by this sesamum-covered sugar-lump, with its faint scent of roses. It has certainly fled in shame from the houses of the respectable people of today. What has become of those cone shaped packets of fried spices?

And those cheap sesamum sweetmeats? Do they still linger on? If not, it is no good trying to bring them back.

Day after day, in the evenings, I listened to Brajeswar reciting the seven cantos of Krittibas' *Rāmāyanā*. Kishori Chatterjee used to drop in sometimes while the reading was going on. He had by heart *Pānchāli*[1] versions of the whole *Rāmayanā*, tune and all. He took possession at once of the seat of authority, and superseding Krittibas, would begin to recite his simple folk-stanzas in great style:

> 'Lakshman O hear me
> Greatly I fear me
> Dangers are near me.'

There was a smile on his lips, his bald head gleamed, the song poured from his throat in a torrent of sound, the rhymes jingled and rang verse after verse, like the music of pebbles in a brook. At the same time, he would be using his hands and feet in acting out the thought. It was Kishori Chatterjee's greatest grief that Dadabhai, as he called me, could not join a troupe of strolling players and turn such a voice to account. If I did that, he said, I should certainly make my name.

By and by it would grow late and the assembly on the mat would break up. We would go into the house, to Mother's room, haunted and oppressed on our way by the terror of devils. Mother would be playing cards with her aunt, the inlaid parquet floor gleamed like ivory, a coverlet was spread on the big divan. We would make such a disturbance that Mother would soon throw down her hand and say, 'If they are going to be such a nuisance, auntie, you'd better go and tell them stories.' We would wash our feet with water from the pot on the verandah outside, and climb on to the bed, pulling 'Didima' with us. Then it would begin—stories of the magical awakening of the princess and her rescue from the demon city. The princess might wake, but who could waken me?... In the early part of the night the jackals would begin to howl, for in those days they still haunted the basements of some of the old houses of Calcutta with their nightly wail.

---

[1] A kind of folk-version very popular in Bengal.

IV

When I was a little boy Calcutta city was not so wakeful at night as it is now. Nowadays, as soon as the day of sunlight is over, the day of electric light begins. There is not much work done in it, but there is no rest, for the fire continues, as it were, to smoulder in the charcoal after the blazing wood has burnt itself out. The oil mills are still, the steamer sirens are silent, the labourers have left the factories, the buffaloes which pull the carts of jute bales are stabled in the tin-roofed sheds. But the nerves of the city are throbbing still with the fever of thought which has burned all day in her brain. Buying and selling go on as by day in the shops that line the streets, though the fire is a little choked with ash. Motors continue to run in all directions, emitting all kinds of raucous grunts and groans, though they no longer run with the zest of the morning. But in those old times which we knew, when the day was over whatever business remained undone wrapped itself up in the black blanket of the night and went to sleep in the darkened ground floor premises of the city. Outside the house, the evening sky rose quiet and mysterious. It was so still that we could hear, even in our own street, the shouts of the grooms from the carriages of those people of fashion who were returning from taking the air in Eden Gardens by the side of the Ganges.

In the hot season of *Chaitra* and *Vaishākh* the hawkers would go about the streets shouting 'I-i-i-ce'. In a big pot full of lumps of ice and salt water were little tin containers of what we called 'kulpi' ice—nowadays ousted by the more fashionable ices or 'ice cream'. No one but myself knows how my mind thrilled to that cry as I stood on the verandah facing the street. Then there was another cry, *'Bela* flowers'. Nowadays for some reason one hears little of the gardeners baskets of spring flowers—I do not know why. But in those days the air was full of the scent of the thickly strung *bel* flowers which the women and girls wore in their hairknots. Before they went to bathe the women would sit outside their rooms with a hand mirror set up before them, and dress their hair. The knot would be skilfully bound with the black hair-braid into all sorts of different styles. They wore black-bordered Chandernagore saries, skilfully crinkled before use by pleating and twisting after the fashion of those days. The barber's wife would come to scrub their feet with pumice and paint them with red lac. She and her like were the gossipmongers of the women's courts.

The crowds returning from office or from college did not then, as they do now, rush to the football fields, clinging in swarms to the foot-boards of the trams. Nor did they crowd in front of cinema halls as they returned. There was some active interest shown in drama, but alas! I was only a child then.

Children of those times got no share in the pleasures of the grown-ups, even from a distance. If we were bold enough to go near, we should be told, 'Off with you, go and play.' But if we boys made the amount of noise appropriate for proper play, it would then be, 'Be quiet, do.' Not that the grown-ups themselves conducted their pleasures and conversation in silence, by any means; and now and again we would stand on the fringe of their far-flung jubilations, as though sprinkled by the spray of a waterfall. We would hang over the verandah on our side of the courtyard, staring across at the brilliantly lit reception-room on the other side. Big coaches would roll up to the portico one after another. Some of our elder brothers conducted the guests upstairs from the front door, sprinkling them with rose water from the sprinkler, and giving each one a small buttonhole or nosegay of flowers. As the dramatic entertainment proceeded, we could hear the sobs of the 'highcaste *kulin* heroine', but we could make out nothing of their meaning, and our longing to know grew intense. We discovered later that though the sobber was certainly highcaste, 'she' was merely our own brother-in-law. But in those days grown-ups and children were kept apart as strictly as men and women with their separate apartments. The singing and dancing would go on in the blaze of the drawing room chandeliers, the men would pull at the hookah, the women of the family would take their betel boxes and sit in the subdued light behind their screen, the visiting ladies would gather in these retired nooks, and there would be much whispering of intimate domestic gossip. But we children were in bed by this time, and lay listening as our maidservants Piyari or Sankari told us stories—'In the moonlight, expanding like an opening flower...'

V

A little before our day it was the fashion among wealthy householders to run *jātrās* or troupes of actors. There was a great demand for boys with shrill voices to join these troupes. One of my uncles was patron of such an amateur company. He had a gift for writing plays, and was very enthusiastic about training the boys. All over Bengal, professional companies were the rage, just as the amateur companies were in aristocratic circles. Troupes of players sprang up like mushrooms on all sides, under the leadership of some well known actor or other. Not that either patron or manager was necessarily of high family or good education. Their fame rested on their own merits. *Jātrā* performances used to take place in our house from time to time. But we children had no part in them, and I managed to see only the preliminaries. The verandah would be full of members of the company, the air full of tobacco smoke. There were the boys, long-haired, with dark rings of weariness under their eyes, and, young as they were, with the faces of grown men. Their lips were stained black with constant betel chewing. Their costumes and other paraphernalia were in painted tin boxes. The entrance door was open, people swarmed like ants into the courtyard, which, filled to the brim with the seething, buzzing mass, spilled over into the lane and beyond into the Chitpore Road. Then nine o'clock would strike, and Shyam would swoop down on me like a hawk on a dove, grip my elbow with his rough, gnarled hand, and tell me that Mother was calling me to go to bed. I would hang my head in confusion at being thus publicly dragged away, but would bow to superior force and go to my bedroom. Outside all was tumult and shouting, outside flared the lighted chandeliers, but in my room there was not a sound and a brass lamp burned low on its stand. Even in sleep, I was dimly conscious of the crash of the cymbals marking the rhythm of the dance.

The grown-ups usually forbade everything on principle, but on one occasion for some reason or other they decided to be indulgent, and the order went forth that the children also might come to the play.

It was a drama about Nala and Damayanti. Before it began we were sent to bed till half-past eleven. We were assured again and again that when the time came we should be roused, but we knew the ways of the grown-ups, and we had no faith at all in these promises—*they* were adults, and *we* were children!

That night, however, I did drag my unwilling body to bed. For one thing, Mother promised that she herself would come and wake me. For another thing, I always had to pinch myself to keep myself awake after nine o'clock. When the time came, I was awakened and brought outside, blinking and bewildered in the dazzling glare. Light streamed brightly from coloured chandeliers on the first and second storeys, and the white sheets spread in the courtyard made it seem much bigger than usual. On one side were seated the people of importance, senior members of the family, and their invited guests. The remaining space was filled with a motley crowd of all who cared to come. The performing company was led by a famous actor wearing a gold chain across his stomach, and old and young crowded together in the audience. The majority of the audience were what the respectable would call 'riff-raff'. The play itself had been written by men whose hands were trained only to the villager's reed pen, and who had never practised on the letters of an English copy book. Tunes, dances, and story had all sprung from the very heart of rural Bengal, and no pundit had polished their style.

We went and sat by our elder brothers in the audience, and they tied up small sums of money in kerchiefs and gave them to us. It was the custom to throw this money on to the stage at the points where applause was most deserved. By this means the actors gained some extra profit and the family a good reputation.

The night came to an end, but the play would not. I never knew whose arms gathered up my limp body, nor where they carried me. I was far too much ashamed to try to find out. I, a fellow who had been sitting like an equal among the grown-ups and doling out *baksheesh*, to be disgraced in this way before a whole courtyard full of people! When I woke up I was lying on the divan in my mother's room; it was very late, and already blazing hot. The sun had risen, but I had not risen!—Such a thing had never happened before.

Nowadays, the city's pleasures flow on in an unbroken stream.

There is always a cinema show somewhere, and whoever pleases may see it for a trifling sum. But in those days entertainments were few and far between, like water holes dug in the sandy bed of a dried up river, three or four miles apart. Like these too they lasted only a few hours, and the wayfarers hastily gathered round, drinking from their cupped hands to quench their thirst.

The old days were like a king's son who, from time to time on festive occasions, or according to his whim, distributes rich and royal gifts to all within his jurisdiction. Modern days are like a merchant's son, sitting at the crossroads on some great highway with many kinds of cheap and tawdry goods spread glittering before him, and drawing his customers by highway and byway from every side.

VI

Brajeswar was the head servant, and his second-in-command was called Shyam. He came from Jessore, and he was a real countryman, speaking in a dialect strange to Calcutta. He would say 'tenārā' and 'onārā' for 'tārā' and 'orā', 'jāti' and 'khāti' for 'jete' and 'khete'. He used to call us affectionately 'Domani'. He had a dark skin, big eyes, long hair glistening with oil, and a strong, well built body. He was really good at heart, and affectionate and kind to children. He used to tell us stories of dacoits. Dacoity stories filled men's houses then as universally as the fear of ghosts filled their minds. Even today dacoity is not uncommon; murder, assault and looting still take place, and the police still do not catch the right man. But nowadays this is only a news-item, it has none of the fascination of romance. In those days dacoities were woven into stories, and passed from mouth to mouth for long periods. In my childhood, men were still to be met with who in their prime had been members of dacoit gangs. They were all pastmasters in the science of the *lathi*, and were surrounded by disciples eager to learn the art of single-stick. Men salaamed at the very mention of their names. Dacoity then was usually not a mere matter of rash, headstrong bloodshed. As bodily strength and skill played their part, so did a generous, gallant mind. Moreover, gentlemen's houses often contained an exercise-ground for the practice of *lathi*-fighting, and those who made a name on these grounds were acknowledged as masters even by dacoits, who gave them a wide berth. Many zemindars made a profession of dacoity. There was a story of a man of this class who had stationed his desperadoes at the mouth of a river. It was new moon, and poojah night, and when they returned, carrying a severed head to the temple in honour of Kali Kankali[1], the zemindar clapped his hands to his head and cried out, 'What have you done? It's my son-in-law!'

We heard also about the exploits of the dacoits Raghu and Bishu. They used to give notice before they attacked, and there was nothing

---

[1] The destructive aspect of the goddess Kali, pictured with a necklace of skulls.

underhand in their dacoity. When their rallying-cry was heard in the distance, the blood of the villagers ran cold. But their code forbade them to lay hands on women. On one occasion, in fact, a woman even succeeded in 'robbing the robbers', by appearing to them dressed as Kali, brandishing the goddess's heavy curved blade, and claiming their devout offerings.

One day there was a display of dacoits' wrestling feats in our house. They were all strong young fellows, big-made, dark-skinned, and long-haired. One man tied a cloth round a heavy grain-pounder, seized the cloth in his teeth, and then flung the pounder upwards and backwards over his shoulder. Another got a man to grasp him by his shaggy hair, and then whirled him round and round by a mere turn of his head. Using a long pole as support and lever, they leaped up to the second storey. Then one man stood with his hands clasped above his bent head, and others shot through the aperture like diving birds. They also showed how it was possible for them to manage a dacoity twenty or thirty miles away, and the same night be found sleeping peacefully in their beds like law-abiding citizens. They had a pair of very long poles with a piece of wood lashed cross-wise in the middle of each as a foot-rest. These poles were called *rang-pā* (stilts). When walking with the tops of the poles held in the hands, and the feet on these footholds, one stride had the value of ten ordinary steps, and a man could run faster than a horse. I used to encourage boys at Santiniketan to practise stilt-walking—though without any idea of committing dacoity! My imagination mingled such pictures of dacoity feats with Shyam's stories with gruesome effect, so that I have often spent the evening with my arms huddled against my pounding heart!

Sunday was a holiday. On the previous evening the crickets were chirping in the thickets outside in the south garden, and the story was about Raghu the highwayman. My heart went pit-a-pit in the dim light and flickering shadows of the room. The next day in my holiday leisure I climbed into the palanquin. It began to move unbidden, its destination unknown, and my mind, enthralled still by the magic of the previous night's romance, knew a thrill of delicious fear. In the silent darkness, my pulses attuned themselves to the rhythmic shouts of the bearers, and my body grew numb with terrified anticipation.

On the boundless expanse of plain the air quivers in the heat, in the distance glistens the Kali tank; the sand sparkles, the wide-spreading *pākur* tree leans from the bank of the river over the cracked, ruined *ghāt*. My romance-fed terrors are concentrated on that thick clump of reeds, and in the shade of the tree on that unknown plain. Nearer and nearer we approach, quicker and quicker beats my heart. Above the reeds can be seen the tips of one or two stout bamboo staves. The bearers will stop there to change shoulders. They will drink, and wind wet towels round their heads. And then?...

Then with a blood-curdling shout, the dacoits are upon us...

VII

From morning till night the mills of learning went on grinding. To wind up this creaking machinery was the work of *Shejadādā*,[1] Hemendranath. He was a stern taskmaster, but it is useless now to try to hide the fact that the greater part of the cargo with which he sought to load our minds was tipped out of the boat and sent to the bottom. My learning at any rate was a profitless cargo. If one seeks to key an instrument to too high a pitch, the strings will snap beneath the strain.

Shejadādā made all arrangements for the education of his eldest daughter. When the time came, he got her admitted into the Loreto Convent School, but even before that she had been given a foundation in Bengali. He also gave Protibha a thorough training in western music, which, however, did not cause her to lose her skill in Indian music. Among the gentlemen's families of that time, she had no equal in Hindustani songs.

It is one merit of western music that its scales and exercises demand diligent practice, that it makes for a sensitive ear, and that the discipline of the piano allows of no slackness in the matter of rhythm.

Meanwhile, she had learnt Indian music from her earliest years from our teacher Vishnu. In this school of music I also had to be entered. No present-day musician, whether famous or obscure, would have consented to touch the kind of songs with which Vishnu initiated us. They were the very commonest kind of Bengali folk songs. Let me give you a few examples:

> 'A gypsy lass is come to town
> To paint tattoos, my sister.
> The painting's nothing, so they tell,
> Yet she on me has cast a spell,
> And makes me weep and mocks me well,
> By her tattoos, my sister.'

---

[1]Third elder brother.

I remember also a few fragmentary lines, such as:

> 'The sun and moon have owned defeat,
> the firefly's lamp lights up the stage;
> the Moghul and the Pathan flag,
> the weaver reads the Persian page.'

and:

> 'Your daugher-in-law is the plantain tree,
> Mother of Ganesh, let her be.
> For if but one flower should blossom and grow
> She will have so many children you won't
> know what to do.'

Lines too come back to me in which one can catch a glimpse of old forgotten histories:

> 'There was a jungle of thorn and burr,
> Fit for the dogs alone;
> There did he cut for himself a throne...'

The modern custom is first to practise scales—*sā- re-ga-ma,* etc., on the harmonium, and then to teach some simple Hindu songs. But the wise supervisor who was then in charge of our studies understood that boyhood has its own childish needs, and that these simple Bengali words would come much more easily to Bengali children than Hindi speech. Besides this, the rhythm of this folk music defied all accompaniment by *tabla*. It danced itself into our very pulses. The experiment thus made showed that just as a child learns his first enjoyment of literature from his mother's nursery rhymes, he learns his first enjoyment of music also from the same source.

The harmonium, that bane of Indian music, was not then in vogue. I practised my songs with my *tamburā* resting on my shoulder, I did not subject myself to the slavery of the keyboard.

It was no one's fault but my own, that nothing could keep me for many days together in the beaten track of learning. I strayed at will, filling my wallet with whatever gleanings of knowledge I chanced upon. If I had been disposed to give my mind to my studies, the musicians of these days would have had no cause to slight my work, for I had plenty of opportunity. As long as my brother was in charge of my education, I repeated Brahmo songs with Vishnu in an absent-minded fashion. When I felt so inclined I would sometimes hang about the doorway while *Shejadādā* was practising, and pick up the song that was going on. Once he was singing to the *Behāg* air, 'O thou of slow and stately tread'. Unobserved I listened and fixed the tune in my mind, and astounded my mother—an easy task—by singing it to her that evening. Our family friend Srikantha Babu was absorbed in music day and night. He would sit on the verandah, rubbing *chāmeli* oil on his body before his bath, his *hookāh* in his hand, and the fragrance of amber-scented tobacco rising into the air. He was always humming tunes, which attracted us boys around him. He never *taught* us songs, he simply sang them to us, and we picked them up almost without knowing it. When he could no longer restrain his enthusiasm, he would stand up and dance, accompanying himself on the *sitār*. His big expressive eyes shone with enjoyment, he burst into the song, *Mai chhōrō brajaki bāsari,* and would not rest content till I joined in too.

In matters of hospitality, people kept open house in those days. There was no need for a man to be intimately known before he was received. There was a bed to be had at any time, and a plate of rice at the regular meal times for any who chanced to come. One day, for example, one such stranger guest, who carried his *tamburā* wrapped in a quilt on his shoulder, opened his bundle, sat down, and stretched his legs at ease on one side of our reception room, and Kanai the *hookāh*-tender offered him the customary courtesy of the *hookāh*.

Pān, like tobacco, played a great part in the reception of guests. In those days, the morning occupation of the women in the inner apartments consisted in preparing piles of *pān* for the use of those who visited the outer reception room. Deftly they placed the lime on the leaf, smeared catechu on it with a small stick, and putting in the appropriate amount of spice folded and secured it with a clove. This prepared *pān* was then piled into a brass container, and a moist piece of cloth, stained with catechu, acted as cover. Meanwhile, in the room under the staircase outside, the stir and bustle of preparing tobacco would be going on. In a big earthenware tub were balls of charcoal covered with ash, the pipes of the *hookāhs* hung down like snakes of *N*āgaloka, with the scent of rose water in their veins. This amber scent of tobacco was the first welcome extended by the household to those who climbed the steps to visit the house. Such was the invariable custom then prescribed for the fitting reception of guests. That overflowing bowl of *pān* has long since been discarded, and the caste of *hookāh*-tenders have thrown off their liveries and taken to the sweetmeat shops, where they knead up three-day-old *sandesh* and refashion it for sale.

That unknown musician stayed for a few days, just as he chose. No one asked him any questions. At dawn I used to drag him from his mosquito curtains and make him sing to me. (Those who have no fancy for regular study revel in study that is irregular). The morning melody of *Bansi hāmāri re...*would rise on the air.

After this, when I was a little older, a very great musician called Jadu Bhatta came and stayed in the house. He made one big mistake in being determined to teach me music, and consequently no teaching took place. Nevertheless, I did casually pick up from him a certain amount of stolen knowledge. I was very fond of the song *Ruma jhuma barakh*ā *āju bādara* ā*...*which was set to a *Kāfi* tune, and which remains to this day in my store of rainy season songs. But unfortunately just at this time another guest arrived without warning, who had a name as a tiger-killer. A Bengali tiger-killer was a real marvel in those days, and it followed that I remained captivated in his room for the greater part of the time. I realize clearly now what I never dreamed of then, that the tiger whose fell clutches he so thrillingly described could never have bitten him at all; perhaps he got the idea from the snarling jaws of the stuffed Museum tigers. But provision of *pān* and tobacco for this hero, while the distant strains of *kānārā* music fell faintly on my indifferent ears.

So much for music. In other studies, the foundation provided by *Shejadādā* was equally generously laid. It was the fault of my own nature that no great matter came of it. It was with people like me in view that Ramprosad Sen wrote, 'O Mind, you do not understand the art of cultivation.' With me, the work of cultivation never took place. But let me tell you of a few fields where the ploughing at least was done.

I got up while it was still dark and practised wrestling—on cold days I shivered and trembled with cold. In the city was a celebrated one-eyed wrestler, who gave me practice. On the north side of the outer room was an open space known as the 'granary'. The name clearly had survived from a time when the city had not yet completely crushed out all rural life, and a few open spaces still remained. When the life of the city was still young, our granary had been filled with the whole year's store of grain, and the *ryots* who held their land on lease from us brought to it their appointed portion. It was here that the lean-to shed for wrestling was built against the compound wall. The ground had been prepared by digging and loosening the earth to a depth of about a cubit and pouring over it a maund of mustard oil. It was mere child's play for the wrestler to try a fall with me there, but I would manage to get those days. I busied myself eagerly in the liberal well smeared with dust by the end of the lesson, when I put on my shirt and went indoors.

Mother did not like to see me come in every morning so covered with dust—she feared that the colour of her son's skin would be darkened and spoiled. As a result, she occupied herself on holidays in scrubbing me. (Fashionable housewives of today buy their toilet preparations in boxes from western shops; but then they used to make their unguent with their own hands. It contained almond paste, thickened cream, the rind of oranges and many other things which I forget. If only I had learnt and remembered the receipt, I might have set up a shop and sold it as 'Begum Bilash' unguent, and made at least as much money as the *sandesh-wāllāhs*.) On Sunday mornings there was a great rubbing and scrubbing on the verandah, and I would begin to grow restless to get away. Incidentally a story used to go about among our school fellows that in our house babies were bathed in wine as soon as they were born, and that was the reason for our fair European complexions.

When I came in from the wrestling ground, I saw a Medical College student waiting to teach me the lore of bones. A whole skeleton hung on the wall. It used to hang at night on the wall of our bedroom, and the bones swayed in the wind and rattled together. But the fear I might otherwise have felt had been overcome by constantly handling it, and by learning by heart the long, difficult names of the bones.

The clock in the porch struck seven. Master Nilkamal was a stickler for punctuality, there was no chance of a moment's variation. He had a thin, shrunken body, but his health was as good as his pupil's, and never once, unluckily for us, was he afflicted even by a headache. Taking my book and slate I sat down before the table, and he began to write figures on the blackboard in chalk. Everything was in Bengali, arithmetic, algebra and geometry. In literature, I jumped at one bound from *Sitār Banabās*[1] to *Meghnādbadh Kābya*[2]. Along with this there was natural science. From time to time Sitanath Datta would come, and we acquired some superficial knowledge of science by experiments with familiar things. Once Heramba Tattvaratna, the Sanskrit scholar, came; and I began to learn the Mugdhabodh Sanskrit grammar by heart, though without understanding a word of it.

In this way, all through the morning, studies of all kinds were heaped upon me, but as the burden grew greater, my mind contrived to get rid of fragments of it; making a hole in the enveloping net, my parrot-learning slipped through its meshes and escaped—and the opinion that Master Nilkamal expressed of his pupil's intelligence was not of the kind to be made public.

In another part of the varandah is old tailor, with his thick-lensed spectacles on his nose, sitting bent over his sewing, and ever and anon, at the prescribed hours, going through the ritual of his Namāz.[3] I watch him and think what a lucky fellow Niāmat is. Then, with my head in a whirl from doing sums, I shade my eyes with my slate, and looking down see in front of the entrance porch Chandrabhān the *durwan* combing his long beard with a wooden comb, dividing it in two and looping it round each ear. The assistant *durwan*, a slender

---

[1] 'Sita in the Forest,' by Iswarchandra Vidyasagar.
[2] An Epic on the death of Meghnād (son of Rāvana in *Rāmāyana*) by Michael Madhusudan Dutta.
[3] Muslim devotional exercises.

boy, is sitting nearby, a bracelet on his arm, and cutting tobacco. Over there the horse has already finished his morning allowance of gram, and the crows are hopping round pecking at the scattered grains. Our dog Johnny's sense of duty is aroused and he drives them away barking.

I had planted a custard-apple seed in the dust which continual sweeping had collected in one corner of the verandah. All agog with excitement, I watched for the sprouting of the new leaves. As soon as Master Nilkamal had gone, I had to run and examine it, and water it. In the end my hopes went unfulfilled—the same broom that had gathered the dust together dispersed it again to the four winds.

Now the sun climbs higher, and the slanting shadows cover only half the courtyard. The clock strikes nine. Govinda, short and dark, with a dirty yellow towel slung over his shoulder, takes me off to bathe me. Promptly at half past nine comes our monotonous, unvarying meal—the daily ration of rice, *dāl* and fish curry—it was not much to my taste.

The clock strikes ten. From the main street is heard the hawker's cry of 'Green Mangoes'—what wistful dreams it awakens! From further and further away resounds the clanging of the receding brass-peddler, striking his wares till they ring again. The lady of the neighbouring house in the lane is drying her hair on the roof, and her two little girls are playing with shells. They have plenty of leisure, for in those days girls were not obliged to go to school, and I used to think how fine it would have been to be born a girl. But as it is, the old horse draws me in the rickety carriage to my Andamans, in which from ten to four I am doomed to exile.

At half past four I return from school. The gymnastic master has come, and for about an hour I exercise my body on the parallel bars. He has no sooner gone that the drawing master arrives.

Gradually, the rusty light of day fades away. The many blurred noises of the evening are heard as a dreamy hum resounding over the demon city of brick and mortar. In the study room an oil lamp is burning. Master Aghor has come and the English lesson begins. The black-covered reader is lying in wait for me on the table. The cover is loose; the pages are stained and a little torn; I have tried my hand at writing my name in English in it, in the wrong places, and all in capital letters. As I read I nod, then jerk myself awake again with a start, but miss far more than I read. When finally I tumble into bed I have at last a little time to call my own. And there I listen to endless stories of the king's son travelling over an endless, trackless plain.

VIII

When I see the roofs of modern houses, uninhabited by either men or ghosts, I realize vividly the change that has taken place between those times and these. I have already mentioned how the *brahma-daitya*[1] of the *bādām* tree has fled, unable to endure the modern atmosphere of excessive learning. On the cornice where rumour had it that he had rested his foot, the crows snatch and squabble over our discarded mango stones. And men too restrict themselves nowadays to the confined, boxed-in rooms of the lower storeys, and pass their time within four walls.

My mind goes back to the parapet-surrounded roof of the inner apartments. It is evening, and Mother has spread her mat and seated herself, with her friends gossiping round her. Their talk has no need of authentic information, it is only a means of passing the time. There was then no regular supply of valuable and varied ingredients to fill the day, which was not, as now, a closely woven mesh, but like a net of loose texture, full of holes. And therefore, stories and rumours, laughter and jokes, all in the lightest vein, filled both the social gatherings of the men and the women's assemblies. Among Mother's friends, the first in importance was Braja Acharji's sister, who was called 'Acharjini'. She was the daily purveyor of news to the company. Almost every day she picked up, (or made up!) and brought with her, every item of fantastic, ominous news in the country. By this means expenditure on all ceremonies calculated to avert impending calamity or the evil eye, was greatly increased.

Into this assembly I imported from time to time my recently acquired book-learning. I informed them that the sun is nine crores of miles distant from the earth. From the second part of my *Rju-Pāth* I recited a portion of Valmiki's *Rāmāyana* in the original complete with Sanskrit terminations. Mother was no judge of the accuracy of her son's pronunciation, but the range of his learning filled her with

---

[1] A class of formidable ghosts believed to be the spirits of departed Brahmins.

awe, and seemed to her far to outrun the nine crore miles journey of light. Who would have thought that any except Naradmuni himself could recite all these *slōkas*?

This inner apartment roof was entirely the women's domain, and had a close connection with the store room. The sun's rays fell full upon it, so it was used for preparing lemons for pickle. The women used to sit there with brass vessels full of *kalāi* paste, and while their hair was drying they made pulse-balls with their deft, quick fingers. The maidservants who had washed the soiled linen came here to spread it in the sun, for the *dhoby* had little work in those days. Green mangoes were cut in slices and dried into āmsi. The mango juice was poured layer after layer into black stone moulds of all sizes and all patterns.[1] A pickle of young jack-fruit stood there to season in sun-warmed mustard oil. Catechu, scented with the fragrant screw-pine, would be prepared with great care.

I had a special reason for remembering this item. When my schoolmaster informed me that he had heard the fame of my family's screw-pine catechu, it was not difficult to understand his meaning. What he had heard of, he wished to become acquainted with. So to preserve the good name of my family, I occasionally climbed secretly to the roof containing the screw-pine catechu, and—what shall I say? 'Appropriated' a piece or two sounds better than 'stole'. For even kings and emperors may make 'appropriations' when need arises, or indeed even if it does not, but vulgar 'stealing' is punished by prison or impaling.

In the pleasant sunlight of the cold weather it was the family tradition for the women to sit on the roof gossiping, driving off crows and passing the time of day. I was the only younger brother-in-law in the house, the guardian of my sister-in-law's 'āmsatta', and her friend and ally in many other trival pursuits. I used to read to them from *Bangādhipa Parājaya*.[2] From time to time the duty of cutting up betel-nut would devolve on me. I could cut betel very finely. My sister-in-law would never admit that I had any other good quality,

---

[1] This preparation is called āmsatta.
[2] "The Defeat of the King of Bengal."

so much so that she even made me angry with God for giving me such a faulty appearance. But she found no difficulty in speaking in exaggerated fashion of my skill in cutting betel. Therefore, the work of betel-cutting used to go on at a fine pace. But for a long time now, for want of anyone to encourage me, the hand that was so skilled in fine betel-cutting has perforce busied itself in other fine work.

Around all this women's work spread on the roof there lingered the aroma of village life. These occupations belonged to the days when there was a pounding-room in the house, when confectionery balls were made, when the maidservants sat in the evening rolling on their thighs the cotton wicks for the oil lamps, when invitations came from neighbours' houses to the ceremonies of the eighth day after birth. Modern children do not hear fairy stories from their mothers' lips, they read them for themselves in printed books.

Pickles and chutney are bought from the Newmarket by the bottleful, each bottle corked and sealed with wax.

Another relic of a bygone village life was the *chandimandap,* the outer verandah where the school was held. Not only the boys of the house, but those of the neighbourhood, also, made there their first attempt to search letters on palm-leaves. I suppose that I too must have traced out my first laborious letters on that verandah, but I have no clear memory of the child I then was, who seems as far removed as the farthest planet of the solar system, and I possess no telescope which can bring him into view.

The first thing I remember about reading after this is the terrible story of Sanāmārka Muni's school, and of the *avatār* Narasimha tearing the bowels of Hiranyakaśipu; I think also that there was a lead-plate engraving of it in the same book—and I remember also reading a few *slōkas* of Chānakya.

My chief holiday resort was the unfenced roof of the outer apartments. From my earliest childhood till I was grown up, many varied days were spent on that roof in many moods and thoughts. When my father was at home his room was on the second floor. How often I watched him at a distance, from my hiding place at the head of the staircase. The sun had not yet risen, and he sat on the roof silent as an image of white stone, his hands folded in his lap. From time to time he would leave home for long periods in the mountains, and then the journey to the roof held for me the joy of a voyage through the seven seas. Sitting on the familiar first floor verandah, I had daily watched through the railings the people going about the street. But to climb to that roof was to be raised beyond the swarming habitations of men. When I went on to the roof, my mind strode proudly over prostrate Calcutta to where the last blue of the sky mingled with the last green of the earth; my eye fell on the roofs of countless houses, of all shapes and sizes, high and low, with the shaggy tops of trees between.

I would go up secretly to this roof, usually at midday. The midday hours have always held a fascination for me. They are like the night of the daytime, the time when the *Sannyāsi* spirit in every boy makes him long to quit his familiar surroundings. I put my hand through the shutter and drew the bolt of the door. Right opposite the door was a sofa, and I sat there in perfect bliss of solitude. The servants who acted as my warders had eaten their fill and become drowsy, and yawning and stretching had betaken themselves to sleep on their mats. The afternoon sunlight deepened into gold, and the kite rose screaming into the sky. The bangle seller went crying his wares down the opposite lane. His sudden cry would penetrate to where the housewife lay with her loosened hair falling over her pillow, a maidservant would bring him in, and the old bangle seller dexterously kneaded the tender fingers as he fitted on the glass bangles that took her fancy. The hushed pause of that old world midday is now no more, and the hawkers of the silent time are heard no longer. The girl who in those days had married status, nowadays has still not attained it, she is learning her lessons in the second class. Perhaps the bangle seller runs, pulling a rickshaw, down that very lane.

The roof was like what I imagined the deserts of my books to be, a sheer expanse of quivering haze. A hot wind ran panting across it, whirling up the dust, the blue of the sky paled above it. Moreover, in this roof desert there appeared an oasis. Nowadays, the pipe water does not reach the upper floors, but then it ran even up to the second floor rooms. Like some young Livingstone of Bengal, alone and unaided, I secretly sought and found a new Niagara, the private bathroom. I would turn on the tap, and the water would run all over my body. I then took a sheet from the bed and dried myself, looking the picture of innocence.

Gradually the holiday drew towards its close, and four struck on the gateway clock. The face of the sky on Sunday evenings was always very ill-favoured. There fell across it the shadow of the coming Monday's gaping jaws, already swallowing it in dark eclipse. Below, at last, a search had been instituted for the boy who had given his guards the slip, for now it was tiffin time. This part of the day was a red-letter time for Brajeswar. He was in charge of buying the tiffin. In those days the shopkeepers did not make thirty or forty per cent profit on the price of *ghee,* and in odour and flavour the tiffin was still unpoisoned. When we were lucky enough to get them, we lost no time in eating up our *kochuri, singārā,* or even *ālur dom.* But when the time came round and Brajeswar, with his neck still further twisted, called to us, 'Look *babu,* what I have brought you today', what was usually to be found in his cone of paper was merely a handful of fried groundnuts. It was not that I did not like this, but its attractiveness lay in its price. I never made the least objection, not even on the days when only sesamum *gojā* came out of the palm-leaf wrapper.

The light of day begins to grow murky. Once more with a gloomy spirit, I make the round of the roof. I gaze down at the scene below, where a procession of geese has climbed out of the tank. People have begun to come and go again on the steps of the *ghāt,* the shadow of the banyan tree lengthens across half the tank, the driver of a carriage and pair is yelling at the pedestrians in the street.

IX

In this way the days passed monotonously on. School grabbed the best part of the day, and only fragments of time in the morning and evening slipped through its clutching fingers. As soon as I entered the classroom, the benches and tables forced themselves rudely on my attention, elbowing and jostling their way into my mind. They were always the same—stiff, cramping, and dead. In the evening I went home, and the oil lamp in our study-room, like a stern signal, summoned me to the preparation of the next day's lessons. There is a kind of grasshopper which takes the colour of the withered leaves among which it lurks unobserved. In like manner, my spirit also shrank and faded among those faded, drab-coloured days.

Now and again there came to our courtyard a man with a dancing bear, or a snake charmer playing with his snakes. Now and again the visit of a juggler provided some little novelty. Today, the drums of the juggler and snake-charmer no longer beat in our Chitpore Road. From afar they have salaamed to the cinema, and fled before it from the city. Games were few and of very ordinary kinds. We had marbles, we had what is called 'bat-ball,' a very poor distant relation of cricket, and there were also top-spinning and kite flying. All the games of the city children were of this same lazy kind. Football, with all its running and jumping about on a big field, was still in its overseas home. And so I was fenced in by the deadly sameness of the days, as though by an imprisoning hedge of lifeless, withered twigs.

In the midst of this monotony there played one day the flutes of festivity. A new bride came to the house, slender gold bracelets on her delicate brown hands. In the twinkling of an eye the cramping fence was broken, and a new being came into view from the magic land beyond the bounds of the familiar. I circled around her at a safe distance, but I did not dare to go near. She was enthroned at the centre of affection, and I was only a neglected, insignificant child.

The house was then divided into two suites of rooms. The men lived in the outer, and the women in the inner apartments. The ways of the nabobs obtained there still. I remember how my elder sister was walking on the roof with the new bride at her side, and they were exchanging intimacies freely. As soon as I tried to go near, however, I brought reprimand on my head, for these quarters were outside the boundaries laid down for boys. I saw myself obliged to go back crestfallen to my shabby retreat of former days.

The monsoon rain, rushing down suddenly from the distant mountains, undermines the ancient banks in a moment, and that is what happened now. The new mistress brought a new régime into the house. The quarters of the bride were in the room adjoining the roof of the inner suite. That roof was under her complete control. It was there that the leaf-plates were spread for the dolls' weddings. On such feast days, boy as I was, I became the guest of honour. My new sister-in-law could cook well, and enjoyed feeding people, and I was always ready to satisfy this craving for playing the hostess. As soon as I returned from school, some delicacy made with her own hands stood ready for me. One day, she gave me shrimp curry with yesterday's soaked rice, and a dash of chillies for flavouring, and I felt that I had nothing left to wish for. Sometimes when she went to stay with relatives and I did not see her slippers outside the door of her room, I would go in a temper and steal some valuable object from her room, and lay the foundation of a quarrel. When she returned and missed it, I had only to make such a remark as 'Do you expect *me* to keep an eye on your room when you go away? Am I a watchman?' She would pretend to be angry and say, 'You have no need to keep an eye on the room. Watch your own hands.' Modern women will smile at the *nad'veté* of their predecessors who knew how to entertain only their own brothers-in-law, and I daresay they are right. People today are much more grown-up in every way than they were then. Then we were all children alike, both young and old.

X

And so began a new chapter of my lonely Bedouin life on the roof, and human company and friendship entered it. Across the roof kingdom a new wind blew, and a new season began there. My brother Jyotidada played a large part in this change. At that time my father finally left our home at Jorasanko. Jyotidada settled himself into that outside second-floor room, and I claimed a little corner of it for my own.

No *purdah* was observed in my sister-in-law's apartments. That will strike no one as strange today, but it then sounded an unimaginable depth of novelty. A long time even before that, when I was a baby, my second brother had returned from England to enter the Civil Service. When he went to Bombay to take up his first post, he astonished the neighbourhood by taking off his wife with him before their very eyes. And as if it was not enough to take her away to a distant province, instead of leaving her in the family home, he made no provision for proper privacy on the journey. That was a terrible breach of propriety. Even the relatives felt as if the sky had fallen on their heads.

A style of dress suitable for going out was still not in vogue among women. It was this sister-in-law who first introduced the manner of wearing the *sari* and blouse which is now customary. Little girls had not then begun to wear frocks or let their hair hang in plaits—at least not in our family. The little ones used to wear the tight Rajput pyjamas instead of the traditional *sari*. When the Bethune School was first opened my eldest sister was quite young. She was one of the pioneers who made the road to education easy for girls. She was very fair, uniquely so for this country. I have heard that once when she was going to school in her palanquin the police detained her, thinking her in her Rajput dress to be an English girl who had been kidnapped.

I said before that in those days there was no bridge of intimacy between adults and children. Into the tangle of these old customs Jyotidada brought a vigorously original mind. I was twelve years younger than he, and that I should come to his notice in spite of such a difference in age is in itself surprising. What was more surprising is that in my talks with him he never called me impudent or snubbed me. Thanks to this, I never lacked courage to think for myself. Today I live with children, I try all kind of subjects of conversation, but I find them dumb. They hesitate to ask questions. They seem to me to belong to those old times when the grown-ups talked and the children remained silent. The self-confidence that doubts and questions is the mark of the children of the new age; those of the former age are known by a meek and docile acceptance of what they are told.

A piano appeared in the terrace room. There came also modern varnished furniture from Bowbazar. My breast swelled with pride, as the cheap grandeur of modern times was displayed before eyes inured to poverty. At this time the fountain of my song was unloosed. Jyotidada's hands would stray about the piano as he composed and rattled off tunes in various new styles, and he would keep me by his side as he did so. It was my work to fix the tunes which he composed so rapidly by setting words to them then and there.

At the end of the day, a mat and pillow were spread on the terrace. Nearby was a thick garland of *bel* flowers on a silver plate, in a wet handkerchief, a glass of iced water on a saucer, and some *chhānchi pān* in a bowl. My sister-in-law would bathe, dress her hair and come and sit with us. Jyotidada would come out with a silk *chaddar* thrown over his shoulders, and draw the bow across his violin, and I would sing in my clear treble voice. For providence had not yet taken away the gift of voice it had given me, and under the sunset sky my song rang out across the house-tops.

The south wind came in great gusts from the distant sea, the sky filled with stars.

My sister-in-law turned the whole roof into a garden. She arranged rows of tall palms in barrels and beside and around them *chāmeli, gandharāj, rajanigandhā, karabi* and *dolan-champā*. She considered not at all the possible damage to the roof—we were all alike unpractical visionaries.

Akshay Chaudhuri used to come almost every day. He himself knew that he had no voice, other people knew it even better. In spite of that nothing could stop the flow of his song. His special favourite was the *Behāg* mode. He sang with his eyes shut, so he did not see the expression on the faces of his hearers. As soon as anything capable of making a noise came to hand, he took it and turned it into a drum, beating it in happy absorption, biting his lips with his teeth in his earnestness. Even a book with a stiff binding would do very well. He was by nature a dreamy kind of man, one could see no difference between his working days and his holidays.

The evening party broke up, but I was a boy of nocturnal habits. All went to lie down, I alone would wander about all night with the *Brahma-daitya*. The whole district was steeped in silence. On moonlight nights, the shadows of the lines of palm trees on the terrace lay in dream-patterns on the floor. Beyond the terrace the top of the *sishu* tree swayed and tossed in the breeze, and its leaves gleamed as they caught the light. But for some reason, what caught my eye more than anything was a squat room with a sloping roof built over the staircase of the sleeping house on the opposite side of the lane. It stood like a finger pointing forever towards I knew not what.

It may have been one or two in the morning, when in the main street in front a wailing chant arose—*Bolō-Hari Hari-bōl.*[1]

---

[1] Funeral chant of the Hindus.

XI

It was the fashion then in every house to keep caged birds. I hated this, and the worst thing of all to me was the call of a *koel* imprisoned in a cage in some house in the neighbourhood. *Bouthākrun*[1] had acquired a Chinese *shyama*. From under its covering of cloth its sweet whistling rose continuously, a fountain of song. Besides this there were other birds of all kinds, and their cages hung in the west verandah. Every morning a bird-seed and insect hawker provided the birds' food. Grasshoppers came from his basket, and gram flour for the grain-eating birds.

Jyotidada gave me proper answers in my difficulties, but as much could not be expected from the women. Once *Bouthākrun* took a fancy for keeping pet squirrels in cages. I said it wasn't right, and she told me not to set myself up to be her teacher. That could hardly be called a reasoned reply, and consequently, instead of wasting time in bickering, I privately set two of the little creatures free. After that too I had to listen to a certain amount of scolding, but I made no retort.

There was a permanent quarrel between us which was never made up, which was as follows.

There was a smart fellow called Umesh. He used to go the rounds of the English tailoring shops and buy up for an old song all their scraps, remnants and strips of many coloured silk, and make up women's garments from them with the addition of a bit of net and cheap lace. He would open his paper parcel and spread them carefully out before the eyes of the women, extolling them as 'the very latest fashion'. The women could not resist the attraction of such a *mantra*, but I disliked it all intensely. Again and again, unable to contain myself, I made known my objections, but all the answer I got was 'Don't be cheeky'. I used to tell *Bouthākrun* that the old-fashioned black-bordered white saries, and the Dacca ones, were far better and more tasteful than these. I sometimes wonder, do modern brothers-in-law never open their mouths when they see their *Boudidis* robed in these modern

---

[1] Sister-in-law.

georgette saries, with their faces painted like dolls? Even *Bouthākrun* decked out in Umesh's handiwork was not as bad as they are. Ladies then were at least not so guilty of forgery in dress or complexion.

I was, however, always beaten by *Bouthākrun* in argument, because she would never deign to give a logical answer; and I was beaten too in chess, in which she was an expert.

As I have referred to Jyotidada I ought to give a little more information about him, to make him better known. To do that I must go back to rather earlier days.

He had to go very often to Shelidah to see after the business of the zemindari. Once when he was travelling for this purpose he took me also with him. This was quite contrary to custom in those days, in fact it was what people would have called 'altogether *too* much'. He certainly considered that this travelling away from home was a kind of peripatetic schooling. He realized that my nature was attuned to ramblings in the open air, that in such surroundings it nourished itself spontaneously. A little later, when I was more mature, it was in Shelidah that my nature developed.

The old indigo factory was still standing, with the river Padma in the distance. The zemindari office was on the ground floor, and our living quarters on the upper floor. In front of them was a very large terrace. Beyond were tall casuarina trees, which had grown in stature with the growing prosperity of the indigo-trading sahebs. Today, the blustering shouts of the sahebs are completely silent. Where is now the indigo factory's steward, that 'messenger of death'? Where the troop of bailiffs, loins girded up and *lāthis* on shoulder? Where is the dining hall with its long tables, where the sahebs rode back from their business in the town and turned night into day? The feasting reached its height, the dancing couples whirled round the room, the blood coursed madly through the veins in the swelling intoxication of champagne—and the authorities never heard the appealing cries of the wretched *ryots*, whose weary journey took them only to the District Jail. All traces of those days have vanished, save one record alone—the two graves of two of the sahebs. The high casuarina trees bend and sway in the wind, and sometimes at midnight the grandsons and granddaughters of the former *ryots* see the ghosts of the sahebs wandering in the deserted waste of garden.

Here I revelled in my solitude. I had a little corner room, and my days of ample leisure were spacious as the wide-spreading terrace. It was the leisure of a strange and unknown region, unfathomable as the dark waters of some ancient tank. The *bou-kathā-kao*[1] calls incessantly, my fancy unweariedly takes wing. Meantime my notebook is gradually filled with verses. They were like the blossoms of the mango tree's first flowering in the month of *Māgh*, destined like them to wither forgotten.

In those days if a young boy, or still more a young girl, laboriously counted out the fourteen syllables and wrote two lines of verse, the wise critics of the country used to hail it as a unique and unparalleled achievement.

I saw in the papers and magazines the names of these girl-poets, and their verses also were published. Nowadays, these carefully constructed metres and crude rhyming platitudes have vanished along with the names of their authors, and the names of countless modern girls have appeared in their stead.

Boys are less bold and far more self-conscious than girls. I do not remember any young boy-poet writing verse in those days, except myself. My sister's son, who was older than I, explained to me one day that if one poured words into a fourteen-syllable mould, they would condense into verse. I soon tried this magic formula for myself. The lotus of poetry blossomed in no time in this fourteen-syllabled form and even the bees found a foothold on it. The gulf between me and the poets was bridged, and from that time on I have struggled to overtake them.

I remember how, when I was in the lowest class of the *chhātra britti*[2] our superintendent Govinda Babu heard a rumour that I wrote poetry. He thereupon ordered me to write, thinking that it would redound to the credit of the Normal School. There was nothing for it but to write, to read my work before my classmates, and to hear

---

[1] Also called 'makwa-pāko', an Indian species of cuckoo. Both names are imitations of the call.

[2] This corresponds roughly to the modern transition from 'primary' to 'secondary' education.

the verdict—'this verse is assuredly stolen goods'. The cynics of that day did not know that when I increased in worldly wisdom I should grow shrewd in stealing, not words but thoughts. Yet it is these stolen goods which are valuable.

I remember once composing a poem in the *Payār* and *Tripadi* metres, in which I lamented that as one swims to pluck the lotus it floats further and further away on the waves raised by one's own arms, and remains always out of reach. Akshay Babu took me round to the houses of his relatives and made me recite it to them. 'The boy has certainly a gift for writing', they said.

Bouthākrun's attitude was just the opposite. She would never admit that I should ever make a success of writing. She would say mockingly that I should never be able to write like Bihari Chakravarti. I used to think despondently that even if I were placed in a far lower class than he, she would then be prevented from so disregarding her little poet-brother-in-law's disapprobation of women's fashions.

Jyotidada was very fond of riding. He actually took even *Bouthākrun* riding along Chitpore Road to the Eden Gardens. In Shelidah, he gave me a pony, a beast that was no mean runner. He sent me to give the pony a run on the open *rath-talā* field.[1] I did as I was bidden, in continual imminent danger of a fall on that uneven ground. That I did not fall was solely because he was so determined that I should *not* do so. Shortly afterwards Jyotidada sent me out riding on the roads of Calcutta also. Not on the pony, but on a high-spirited thoroughbred. One day it galloped straight in through the porch, with me on its back, to the courtyard where it was accustomed to be fed. From that day on I had nothing more to do with it.

I have referred elsewhere to the fact that Jyotidada was a practised shot. He was always eager for a tiger-hunt. One day, the *shikāri* Visvanath brought news that a tiger was living in the Shelidah jungle, and Jyotidada at once furbished up his gun and prepared for sport. Surprising to say, he took me with him. It never seemed to occur to him that there could be any danger.

Visvanath was indeed an expert *shikāri*. He knew that there was

---

[1] The field reserved in a Bengali village for the celebration of the car-festival.

nothing manly about hunting from a *māchān*. He would call the tiger out and shoot face to face, and he never missed his aim.

The jungle was dense, and in its lights and shadows the tiger refused to show himself. A rough kind of ladder was made by cutting footholds in a stout bamboo, and Jyotidada climbed up with his gun ready to hand. As for me, I was not even wearing slippers, I had not even that poor instrument with which to beat and humiliate the tiger. Visvanath signed to us to be on the alert, but for some time Jyotidada could not even see the tiger. After long straining of his bespectacled eyes, he at last caught a glimpse of one of its markings in the thicket. He fired. By a lucky chance the shot pierced the animal's backbone, and it was unable to rise. It roared furiously, biting at all the sticks and twigs within reach, and lashing its tail. Thinking it over, I know that it is not in the nature of tigers to wait so long and patiently to be killed. I wonder if someone had had the forethought to mix a little opium with its feed on the previous night? Otherwise, why such sound sleep?

There was another occasion when a tiger came to the jungles of Shelidah. My brother and I set out on elephants to look for him. My elephant lurched majestically on, uprooting cane from the sugarcane fields and munching as he went, so that it was like riding on an earthquake. The jungle lay ahead of us. He crushed the trees with his knees, pulled them up with his trunk and cast them to the ground. I had previously heard tales of terrible possibilities from Visvanath's brother Chamru, how sometimes the tiger leaps on to the elephant's back and clings there, digging in his claws. Then the elephant trumpeting with pain, rushes madly through the forest, and whoever is on his back is dashed against the trees till arms, legs and head are crushed out of all recognition. That day, as I sat on my elephant, the image of myself thus being pounded to a jelly filled my imagination from first to last. For very shame I concealed my fear, and glanced from side to side in nonchalant fashion, as though to say, 'Let me but catch a glimpse of the tiger, and then!...' The elephant entered the densest part of the jungle, and coming to a certain place, suddenly stood stock-still. The *māhout* made no attempt to urge it forward. He had clearly more respect for the tiger's powers as a *shikāri* than for my brother's. His great anxiety was undoubtedly that Jyotidada should so wound the tiger as to drive it to desperation. Suddenly the tiger leaped from the jungle, swift as the thunder-charged storm from the cloud. We are accustomed to the sight of a cat dog, or jackal, but here were shoulders of terrific bulk and power, yet no sense of heaviness in that perfectly proportioned strength. It crossed the open fields at a canter in the full blaze of the midday sun. What loveliness, ease and speed of motion! The land was empty of crops; here indeed was a setting in which to feast one's eyes on the running tiger, this wide stretch of golden stubble drenched in the noonday sunlight.

There is one more story that may prove amusing. In Shelidah, the gardener used to pluck flowers and arrange them in the vases. I took a fancy to write poetry with a pen dipped in the coloured essences of flowers. But the moisture that I could obtain by squeezing was not sufficient to wet the tip of my pen. I decided that it must be done by machinery. It would do, I thought, if I had a cup-shaped wooden sieve and a pestle revolving in it. It could be turned by an arrangement of ropes and pulleys. I made known my wants to Jyotidada. It may be that he smiled to himself, but he gave no outward sign. He issued instructions, and the carpenter brought wood. The machine was ready. I filled the wooden cup with flowers, but turn the ropes of the pestle as I would, the flowers merely turned to mud and not a drop of essence ran out. Jyotidada saw that the essence of flowers was incompatible with the grinding of machinery, yet he never laughed at me.

This was the only occasion in my life on which I tried my hand at engineering. It is said in the *sāstras* that there is a god who compasses the humiliation of those who ignore their own limitations. That god cast a mocking glance that day upon my engineering, and from that time I have not so much as laid hands on any kind of instrument, not even on a *sitār* or an *esrāj*.

I described in my *Reminiscences* how Jyotidada went bankrupt in his attempt to run a *swadeshi* steamer company on the rivers of Bengal in competition with the Flotilla Company. *Bouthākrun's* death had taken place before then. Jyotidada gave up his rooms on the third storey and finally built himself a house on a hill at Ranchi.

XII

A new chapter in the life of the third storey room now opened, as I took up my abode there. Up to that time it had been merely one of my gypsy haunts, like the palanquin and the granary, and I roamed from one to another. But when *Bouthākrun* came a garden appeared on the roof, and in the room a piano was established. Its flow of new tunes symbolized the changed the tenor of my life.

Jyotidada used to arrange to have his coffee in the mornings in the shade of the staircase room on the eastern side of the terrace. At such times he would read to us the first draft of some new play of his. From time to time I also would be called upon to add a few lines with my unpractised hand. The sun's rays gradually invaded the shade, the crows cried hoarsely to each other as they sat on the roof keeping an eye upon the breadcrumbs. By ten o'clock, the patch of shade had dwindled away and the terrace grew hot.

At midday Jyotidada used to go down to the office on the ground floor. *Bouthākrun* peeled and cut fruit and arranged it carefully on a silver plate, along with a few sweetmeats made with her own hands, and strewed a few rose petals over it. In a tumbler was coconut milk or fruit juice or *tāl shāns* (fresh palmyra kernels), cooled in ice. Then she covered it with a silk kerchief embroidered with flowers, put it on a Moradabad tray, and despatched it to the office at tiffin time, about one or two o'clock.

Just then *Bangadarśan*[1] was at the height of its fame, and *Suryamukhi* and *Kundanandini*[2] were familiar figures in every house. The whole country thought of nothing else but what had happened and what was going to happen to the heroines.

When *Bangadarśan* came there was no midday nap for anyone in the neighbourhood. It was my good fortune not to have to snatch for

---

[1] A famous Bengali magazine edited by the well known Bengali novelist, Bankim Chandra Chatterji.
[2] Characters in Bankim Chandra's novel.

it, for I had the gift of being an acceptable reader. *Bouthākrun* would rather listen to my reading aloud than read for herself. There were no electric fans then, but as I read I shared the benefits of *Bouthākrun's* hand fan.

XIII

Now and again Jyotidada used to go for change of air to a garden house on the bank of the Ganges. The Ganges shores had then not yet lost caste at the defiling touch of English commerce. Both shores alike were still the undisturbed haunt of birds, and the mechanized dragons of industry did not darken the light of heaven with the black breath of their upreared snouts.

My earliest memory of our life by the Ganges is of a small two-storey house. The first rains had just fallen. Cloud shadows danced on the ripples of the stream, cloud shadows lay dark upon the jungles of the further shore. I had often composed songs of my own on such days, but that day I did not do so. The lines of Vidyapati came to my mind, *e bharā bādara māha bhādara śūnya mandira mōr.*[1] Moulding them to my own melody and stamping them with my own musical mood, I made them my own. The memory of that monsoon day, jewelled with that music on the Ganges shore, is still preserved in my treasury of rainy season songs. I see in memory the tree-tops struck ever and again by great gusts of wind, till their boughs and branches were tangled together in an ecstasy of play. The boats and dinghies raised their white sails and scudded before the gale, the waves leaped against the *ghāt* with sharp, slapping sounds. *Bouthākrun* came back and I sang my song to her. She listened in silence and said no word of praise. I must then have been sixteen or seventeen years old. We used to have arguments even then about various matters, but no longer in the old spirit of childish wrangling.

A little while after we removed to Moran's Garden. That was a regular palace. The rooms, of varying heights, had coloured glass in their windows, the floors were of marble, and steps led down from the long verandah to the very edge of the Ganges. Here a fit of wakefulness by night came upon me, and I used to pace to and fro, as I did later

---

[1]Brimmed with rain is the month of Bhadra (August-September), empty my spirit's dwelling stands.

on the banks of the Sabarmati. That garden is no longer in existence, the iron jaws of the Dundee Mills have crushed and swallowed it.

At the mention of Moran's Garden there comes back the memory of our occasional picnics under the *bakul* tree. The food owed its flavour not to spices but to the hands that prepared it. How I remember our sacred-thread ceremony, when we two boys were fed by *Bouthākrun* with the ceremonial rice and fresh ghee! For those three days we had our fill of tasty and savoury dishes.

It was a great annoyance to me that it was so difficult for me to fall ill. All the other boys in the house could manage it, and then they would enjoy *Bouthākrun's* personal care. Not only did they enjoy her care, but they took up all her time, and my own share of it was correspondingly diminished.

So came to an end that page of the history of the third storey, and with it *Bouthākrun* also passed away. After that the second floor became my own domain, but it was no longer as in the old days.

I have wandered in my story up to the very gateway of my young manhood. I must return to the territory of my boyhood once more.

Now I must give some account of my sixteenth year. At its very entrance stands *Bhārati*.[1] Nowadays, the whole country seethes with the excitement of bringing out papers, and I can well understand the strength of that passion when I look back on my own madcap escapades. That a boy like me, with neither learning nor talents, should succeed in establishing himself in that *salon,* or at least in escaping reprimand there, shows what a youthful spirit was abroad everywhere. *Bangadarśan* was then the only magazine in the country controlled by a mature hand. As for ours, it was a medley of the mature and the crude. Badadada's contributions were as difficult to understand as they were to write; and side by side with them stood a story of mine, the raw verbosity of whose style I was too young to appraise, nor did others apparently possess the critical judgment to do so.

The time has come to say something of Badadada. Jyotidada held

---

[1] Monthly magazine founded by Jyotidada (Jyotirindranath Tagore) and first edited by the Poet's eldest brother Dwijendranath Tagore, referred to here as Badadada. It ran for about half a century.

court in that third storey room, and Badadada in our south verandah. At one time he plunged into the deepest problems of metaphysics, far outside the range of our comprehension. There were few to listen to what he wrote and thought, and he would not lightly let any man go who showed himself willing to be audience. Nor would the man himself soon relinquish Badadada, but what he claimed from him was not alone the privilege of listening to metaphysics. One such man attached himself whose name I do not remember, but everyone called him 'The Philosopher'. My other brothers made great fun of him, not only about his love for mutton chops, but about his endless stream of varied and urgent necessities. Besides philosophy, Badadada then began to take great interest in the construction of mathematical problems. The verandah would be full of papers, covered with figures, flying about in the south wind. Badadada could not sing, but he used to play an English flute, not for the sake of the music, but in order to measure mathematically the notes of each scale. After that he occupied himself for a time in writing *Svapm-Prayāna*. To start with, he began to experiment in verse-making, weighing the sound-values of Sanskrit words in the scales of Bengali rhythm, and so creating new forms. Many of these attempts he retained, but many he threw away, and torn pages were scattered everywhere. After that he started to write his book of poems, but he rejected far more than he kept, for he was not easily satisfied with his work. We had not the sense to pick up and keep all these discarded lines. As he wrote he would read his work, and people would gather round him to listen. Our whole household was intoxicated with this wine of poetry. Sometimes in the midst of his reading, he would burst into a great shout of laughter. His laughter was ample and generous as the skies, but woe betide the man who sat within reach when the fit took him; he received slaps on the back to shake his very soul. The south verandah was the living fountain of the life of Jorasanko, but the fountain dried up when Badadada went to live at the Santiniketan *asrama*. I remember, however, times spent in the garden opposite that south verandah, when with mind made listless by the touch of the autumn sun I composed and sang a new song: 'Today in the autumn sun, in my dreams of dawn, a nameless yearning fills my soul.' I remember also a song made in the quivering heat of one blazing noon: 'In this listless abandon of spirit, I know not what games I kept on playing with my own self.'

Another striking thing about Badadada was his swimming. He would swim backwards and forwards across our tank at least fifty times. When he lived at Panihati Garden he used to swim far out into the Ganges. With his example before us we also learned to swim as boys. We started to learn by ourselves. We would wet our pyjamas and then pull them up tight so as to fill them with air. In the water they swelled out round our waists like balloons, and we could not possibly sink. When I was older and stayed on the river-lands[1] of Shelidah, I once swam across the Padma. This was not as wonderful an achievement as it sounds. The Padma was full of alluvial islands which broke the force of its current, so that the feat was not worthy of any great respect. Still, it was certainly a story with which to impress others, and I have used it so many times. When I went as a boy to Dalhousie, my father never forbade me to wander about by myself. With an alpenstock in my hand I traversed the footpaths, climbing one hill after another. It was most amusing to scare myself with my own make-believe. Once while going steeply downhill, I stepped on a heap of withered leaves at the foot of a tree. My foot slipped a little and I saved myself with my stick. But perhaps I might not have been able to stop myself! I wondered how long it would have taken to roll down the steep slope and fall into the waterfall far below. I described to Mother with picturesque inventiveness all that might have happened. Then, wandering in the deep pinewoods, I might suddenly have come upon a bear that also was certainly something worth talking about. As nothing ever really happened I stored up all these imaginary adventures in my mind. The story of my swimming across the Padma was much of a piece with this class of romances.

When I was seventeen, I had to leave the editorial board of *Bhārati*, for it was then decided that I should go to England. Further, it was considered that before sailing I should live with *Mejadādā*[2] for a time

---

[1] Tracts of rich alluvial land often found as islands in the great rivers (Beng. *Char*).

[2] Second brother, Satyendranath Tagore.

to get some grounding in English manners. He was then a judge in Ahmedabad, and *Meja-Bouthākrun* and her children were in England, waiting for *Mejadādā* to get a furlough and join them.

I was torn up by the roots and transplanted from one soil to another, and had to get acclimatized to a new mental atmosphere. At first my shyness was a stumbling-block at every turn. I wondered how I should keep my self-respect among all these new acquaintances. It was not easy to habituate myself to strange surroundings, yet there was no means of escape from them; in such a situation a boy of my temperament was bound to find his path a rough one.

My fancy, free to wander, conjured up pictures of the history of Ahmedabad in the Moghul period. The judge's quarters were in Shahibag, the former palace grounds of the Muslim kings. During the daytime *Mejadādā* was away at his work, the vast house seemed one cavernous emptiness, and I wandered about all day like one possessed. In front was a wide terrace, which commanded a view of the Sabarmati river, whose knee-deep waters meandered along through the sands. I felt as though the stone-built tanks, scattered here and there along the terrace, held locked in their masonry wonderful secrets of the luxurious bathing-halls of the Begums.

We are Calcutta people, and history nowhere gives us any evidence of its past grandeur there. Our vision had been confined to the narrow boundaries of these stunted times. In Ahmedabad I felt for the first time that history had paused, and was standing with her face turned towards the aristocratic past. Her former days were buried in the earth like the treasure of the *yakshas*.[1] My mind received the first suggestion for the story of *Hungry Stones*.

How many hundred years have passed since those times! Then in the *nahabat-khānā*, the minstrel's gallery, an orchestra played day and night, choosing tunes appropriate to the eight periods of the day. The rhythmic beat of horses' hoofs echoed on the streets, and great parades were held of the mounted Turkish cavalry, the sun glittering on the points of their spears. In the court of the Pādshāh whispered conspiracies were ominously rife. Abyssinian eunuchs, with drawn

---

[1] Demons who guard treasure.

swords, kept guard in the inner apartments. Rose water fountains played in the *hamāms* of the Begums, the bangles tinkled on their arms. Today Shahibag stands silent, like a forgotten tale; all its colour has faded, and its varied sounds have died away; the splendours of the day are withered and the nights have lost their savour.

Only the bare skeleton of those old days remained, its head a naked skull whose crown was gone. It was like a mummy in a museum, but it would be too much to say that my mind was able fully to re-clothe those dry bones with flesh and blood and restore the original form. Both the first rough model, and the background against which it stood, were largely a creation of the fancy. Such patch-work is easy when little is known and the rest has been forgotten. After these eighty years even the picture of myself that comes before me does not correspond line for line with the reality, but is largely a product of the imagination.

After I had stayed there for some time, *Mejadādā* decided that perhaps I should be less homesick if I could mix with women who could familiarize me with conditions abroad. It would also be an easy way to learn English. So for a while I lived with a Bombay family. One of the daughters of the house was a modern educated girl who had just returned with all the polish of a visit to England. My own attainments were only ordinary, and she could not have been blamed if she had ignored me. But she did not do so. Not having any store of book-learning to offer her, I took the first opportunity to tell her that I could write poetry. This was the only capital I had with which to gain attention. When I told her of my poetical gift, she did not receive it in any carping or dubious spirit, but accepted it without question... She asked the poet to give her a special name, and I chose one for her which she thought very beautiful. I wanted that name to be entwined with the music of my verse, and I enshrined it in a poem which I made for her. She listened as I sang it in the *Bhairavi* mode of early dawn, and then said, 'Poet, I think that even if I were on my death-bed your songs would call me back to life.' There is an example of how well girls know how to show their appreciation by some pleasant exaggeration. They simply do it for the pleasure of pleasing. I remember that it was from her that I first heard praise of my personal appearance,—praise that was often very delicately given.

For example, she asked me once very particularly to remember one thing, 'You must never wear a beard. Don't let anything hide the outline of your face.' Everyone knows that I have not followed that advice. But she herself did not live to see my disobedience proclaimed upon my face.

In some years, birds strange to Calcutta used to come and build in that banyan tree of ours. They would be off again almost before I had learnt to recognize the dance of their wings, but they brought with them a strangely lovely music from their distant jungle homes. So, in the course of our life's journey, some angel from a strange and unexpected quarter may cross our path, speaking the language of our own soul, and enlarging the boundaries of the heart's possessions. She comes unbidden, and when at last we call for her she is no longer there. But as she goes, she leaves on the drab web of our lives a border of embroidered flowers, and forever and ever the night and day are for us enriched.

XIV

The Master-Workman, who made me, fashioned his first model from the native clay of Bengal. I have described this first model, which is what I call my boyhood, and in it there is little admixture of other elements. Most of its ingredients were gathered from within, though the atmosphere of the home and the home people counted for something too. Very often the work of moulding goes no further than this stage. Some people get hammered into shape in the book-learning factories, and these are considered in the market to be goods of a superior stamp.

It was my fortune to escape almost entirely the impress of these mills of learning. The masters and pundits who were charged with my education soon abandoned the thankless task. There was Jnanachandra Bhattacharya, the son of Anandachandra Vedāntabāgish, who was a B.A. He realized that this boy could never be driven along the beaten tract of learning. The teachers of those days, alas! were not so strongly convinced that boys should all be poured into the mould of degree-holding respectability. There was then no demand that rich and poor alike should all be confined within the fenced-off regions of college studies. Our family had no wealth then, but it had a reputation, so the old traditions held good, and they were indifferent to conventional academic success. From the lower classes of the Normal School we were transferred to De Cruz's Bengal Academy. It was the hope of my guardians that even if I got nothing else, I should get enough mastery of spoken English to save my face. In the Latin class I was deaf and dumb, and my exercise books of all kinds kept from beginning to end the unrelieved whiteness of a widow's cloth. Confronted by such unprecedented determination not to study, my class teacher complained to Mr De Cruz, who explained that we were not born for study, but for the purpose of paying our monthly fees. Jnana Babu was of a similar opinion, but found means of keeping me occupied nevertheless.

He gave me the whole of *Kumārsambhava*[1] to learn by heart. He shut me in a room and gave me *Macbeth* to translate. Then Pundit Ramsarbaswa read *Sakuntalā* with me. By setting me free in this way from the fixed curriculum, they reaped some reward for their labours. These then were the materials that formed my boyish mind, together with what other Bengali books I picked up at random.

I landed in England, and foreign workmanship began to play a part in the fashioning of my life. The result is what is known in chemistry as a compound. How capricious is Fortune!—I went to England for a regular course of study, and a desultory start was made, but it came to nothing. *Meja-Bouthān* was there, and her children, and my own family circle absorbed nearly all my interest. I hung about around the school room, a master taught me at the house, but I did not give my mind to it.

However, gradually the atmosphere of England made its impression on my mind, and what little I brought back from that country was from the people I came in contact with. Mr Palit finally succeeded in getting me away from my own family. I went to live with a doctor's family, where they made me forget that I was in a foreign land. Mrs Scott lavished on me a genuine affection, and cared for me like a mother. I had then been admitted to London University, and Henry Morley was teaching English literature. His teaching was no dry-as-dust exposition of dead books. Literature came to life in his mind and in the sound of his voice, it reached to our inner being where the soul seeks its nourishment, and nothing of its essential nature was lost. With his guidance, I found the study of the Clarendon Press books at home to be an easy matter and I took upon myself to be my own teacher. For no reason at all Mrs Scott would sometimes fancy that I did not look well, and would become very worried about me. She did not know that the portals of sickness had been barred against me from childhood. I used to bathe every morning in ice-cold water—in fact, in the opinion of the doctors, it was almost a sacrilege that I should survive such flagrant disregard of the accepted rules!

I was able to study in the University for three months only, but I

---

[1] A work of Kalidasa.

obtained almost all my understanding of English culture from personal contacts. The artist who fashions us takes every opportunity to mingle new elements in his creation. Three months of close intimacy with English hearts sufficed for this development. Mrs Scott made it my duty each evening till eleven o'clock to read aloud from poetic drama and history by turn. In this way, I did a great deal of reading in a short space of time. It was not prescribed class study, and my understanding of human nature developed side by side with my knowledge of literature. I went to England but I did not become a barrister. I received no shock calculated to shatter the original framework of my life—rather East and West met in friendship in my own person. Thus it has been given me to realize in my own life the meaning of my name.[1]

---

[1] The poet's name *Rabi* means the sun, which does not distinguish between East and West.

THE POST OFFICE

THE CHARACTERS

Madhav
Amal, His Adopted Child
Sudha, A Little Flower-girl
The Doctor
Dairyman
Watchman
Gaffer
Village Headman, A Bully
King's Herald
Royal Physician

ACT I

(Madhav's House)

Madhav. What a state I am in! Before he came, nothing mattered; I felt so free. But now that he has come, goodness knows from where, my heart is filled with his dear self, and my home will be no home to me when he leaves. Doctor, do you think he…

The Doctor. If there's life in his fate, then he will live long. But what the medical scriptures say, it seems…

Madhav. Great heavens, what?

The Doctor. The scriptures have it: 'Bile or palsy, cold or gout spring all alike.'

Madhav. Oh, get along, don't fling your scriptures at me; you only make me more anxious; tell me what I can do.

The Doctor (Taking snuff). The patient needs the most scrupulous care.

Madhav. That's true; but tell me how.

The Doctor. I have already mentioned, on no account must he be let out of doors.

Madhav. Poor child, it is very hard to keep him indoors all day long.

The Doctor. What else can you do? The autumn sun and the damp are both very bad for the little fellow for the scriptures have it:

"In wheezing, swooning, or in nervous fret,

In jaundice or leaden eyes…"

Madhav. Never mind the scriptures, please. Eh, then we must shut the poor thing up. Is there no other method?

The Doctor. None at all, for 'In the wind and in the sun…'

Madhav. What will your 'in this and in that' do for me now? Why don't you let them alone and come straight to the point? What's to be done, then? Your system is very, very hard for the poor boy; and he is so quiet too with all his pain and sickness. It tears my heart to see him wince, as he takes your medicine.

The Doctor. The more he winces, the surer is the effect. That's why the sage Chyabana observes, 'In medicine as in good advice, the least palatable is the truest.' Ah, well! I must be trotting now.

[Exit

(Gaffer enters)

Madhav. Well, I'm jiggered, there's Gaffer now.
Gaffer. Why, why, I won't bite you!
Madhav. No, but you are a devil to send children off their heads.
Gaffer. But you aren't a child, and you've no child in the house; why worry, then?
Madhav. Oh, but I have brought a child into the house.
Gaffer. Indeed, how so?
Madhav. You remember how my wife was dying to adopt a child?
Gaffer. Yes, but that's an old story; you didn't like the idea.
Madhav. You know, brother, how hard all this getting money in has been. That somebody else's child would sail in and waste all this money earned with so much trouble...oh, I hated the idea. But this boy clings to my heart in such a queer sort of way...
Gaffer. So that's the trouble! And your money goes all for him and feels jolly lucky it does go at all.
Madhav. Formerly, earning was a sort of passion with me; I simply couldn't help working for money. Now, I make money, and as I know it is all for this dear boy, earning becomes a joy to me.
Gaffer. Ah, well, and where did you pick him up?
Madhav. He is the son of a man who was a brother to my wife by village ties. He has had no mother since infancy; and now the other day he lost his father as well.
Gaffer. Poor thing! And so he needs me all the more.
Madhav. The doctor says all the organs of his little body are at loggerheads with each other, and there isn't much hope for his life. There is only one way to save him and that is to keep him out of this autumn wind and sun. But you are such a terror! What with this game of yours at your age, too, to get children outdoors!
Gaffer. God bless my soul! So I'm already as bad as autumn wind and sun, eh! But, friend, I know something, too, of the game of keeping

them indoors. When my day's work is over I am coming in to make friends with this child of yours.

[*Exit*

(Amal enters)

Amal. Uncle, I say, Uncle!
Madhav. Hello! Is that you, Amal?
Amal. Mayn't I be out of the courtyard at all?
Madhav. No, my dear, no.
Amal. See there, where Auntie grinds lentils in the quern, the squirrel is sitting with his tail up and with his wee hands he's picking up the broken grains of lentils and crunching them. Can't I run up there?
Madhav. No, my darling, no.
Amal. Wish I were a squirrel! It would be lovely. Uncle, why won't you let me go about?
Madhav. Doctor says it's bad for you to be out.
Amal. How can the doctor know?
Madhav. What a thing to say! The doctor can't know and he reads such huge books!
Amal. Does his book-learning tell him everything?
Madhav. Of course, don't you know!
Amal (With a sigh). Ah, I am so stupid! I don't read books.
Madhav. Now, think of it; very, very learned people are all like you; they are never out of doors.
Amal. Aren't they really?
Madhav. No, how can they? Early and late they toil and moil at their books, and they've eyes for nothing else. Now, my little man, you are going to be learned when you grow up; and then you will stay at home and read such big books, and people will notice you and say, 'He's a wonder.'
Amal. No, no, Uncle; I beg of you, by your dear feet—I don't want to be learned; I won't.
Madhav. Dear, dear; it would have been my saving if I could have been learned.
Amal. No, I would rather go about and see everything that there is.

Madhav. Listen to that! See! What will you see, what is there so much to see?

Amal. See that faraway hill from our window—I often long to go beyond those hills and right away.

Madhav. Oh, you silly! As if there's nothing more to be done but just get up to the top of that hill and away! Eh! You don't talk sense, my boy. Now listen, since that hill stands there upright as a barrier, it means you can't get beyond it. Else, what was the use in heaping up so many large stones...to make such a big affair of it, eh!

Amal. Uncle, do you think it is meant to prevent us from crossing over? It seems to me because the earth can't speak, it raises its hands into the sky and beckons. And those who live far off and sit alone by their windows can see the signal. But I suppose the learned people...

Madhav. No, they don't have time for that sort of nonsense. They are not crazy like you.

Amal. Do you know, yesterday, I met someone quite as crazy as I am.

Madhav. Gracious me, really, how so?

Amal. He had a bamboo staff on his shoulder with a small bundle at the top, and a brass pot in his left hand, and an old pair of shoes on; he was making for those hills straight across that meadow there. I called out to him and asked, 'Where are you going?' He answered, 'I don't know; anywhere!' I asked again, 'Why are you going?' He said, 'I'm going out to seek work.' Say, Uncle, have you to seek work?

Madhav. Of course I have to. There's many about looking for jobs.

Amal. How lovely! I'll go about like them too, finding things to do.

Madhav. Suppose you seek and don't find. Then...

Amal. Wouldn't that be jolly? Then I would go farther! I watched that man slowly walking on with his pair of worn out shoes. And when he got to where the water flows under the fig tree, he stopped and washed his feet in the stream. Then he took out from his bundle some gram flour, moistened it with water and began to eat it. Then he tied up his bundle and shouldered it again; tucked up his cloth above his knees and crossed the stream. I've asked Auntie to let me go up to the stream, and eat my gram flour just like him.

Madhav. And what did your Auntie say to that?

Amal. Auntie said, 'Get well and then I'll take you over there.' Please,

Uncle, when shall I get well?

Madhav. It won't be long, dear.

Amal. Really, but then I shall go right *away* the moment I'm well again.

Madhav. And where will you go?

Amal. Oh, I will walk on, crossing so many streams, wading through water. Everybody will be asleep with their doors shut in the heat of the day but I will tramp on and on seeking work far, very far.

Madhav. I see! I think you had better be getting well first; then...

Amal. But then you won't want me to be learned, will you, Uncle?

Madhav. What would you rather be, then?

Amal. I can't think of anything just now; but I'll tell you later on.

Madhav. Very well. But mind you, you aren't to call out and talk to strangers again.

Amal. But I love to talk to strangers!

Madhav. Suppose they had kidnapped you?

Amal. That would have been splendid! But no one ever takes me away. They all want me to stay in here.

Madhav. I am off to my work but, darling, you won't go out, will you?

Amal. No, I won't. But, Uncle, you'll let me be in this room by the roadside.

[Exit Madhav

Dairyman. Curds, curds, good nice curds.

Amal. Curdseller, I say, Curdseller.

Dairyman. Why do you call me? Will you buy some curds?

Amal. How can I buy? I have no money.

Dairyman. What a boy! Why call out then? Ugh! What a waste of time!

Amal. I would go with you if I could.

Dairyman. With me?

Amal. Yes, I seem to feel homesick when I hear you call from far down the road.

Dairyman (lowering his yoke pole). Whatever are you doing here, my child?

Amal. The doctor says I'm not to be out, so I sit here all day long.

Dairyman. My poor child, whatever has happened to you?

Amal. I can't tell. You see, I am not learned, so I don't know what's

the matter with me. Say, Dairyman, where do you come from?
Dairyman. From our village.
Amal. Your village? Is it very far?
Dairyman. Our village lies on the river Shamli at the foot of the Panch-mura hills.
Amal. Panch-mura hills! Shamli river! I wonder. I may have seen your village. I can't think when, though!
Dairyman. Have you seen it? Been to the foot of those hills?
Amal. Never. But I seem to remember having seen it. Your village is under some very old big trees, just by the side of the red road—isn't that so?
Dairyman. That's right, child.
Amal. And on the slope of the hill cattle grazing.
Dairyman. How wonderful! Cattle grazing in our village! Indeed there are!
Amal. And your women with red sarees fill their pitchers from the river and carry them on their heads.
Dairyman. Good, that's right! Women from our dairy village do come and draw their water from the river; but then it isn't everyone who has a red saree to put on. But, my dear child, surely you must have been there for a walk some time.
Amal. Really, Dairyman, never been there at all. But the first day doctor lets me go out, you are going to take me to your village.
Dairyman. I will, my child, with pleasure.
Amal. And you'll teach me to cry curds and shoulder the yoke like you and walk the long, long road?
Dairyman. Dear, dear, did you ever? Why should you sell curds? No, you will read big books and be learned.
Amal. No, I never want to be learned. I'll be like you and take my curds from the village by the red road near the old banyan tree, and I will hawk it from cottage to cottage. Oh, how do you cry, 'Curds, curds, fine curds.' Teach me the tune, will you?
Dairyman. Dear, dear, teach you the tune; what a notion!
Amal. Please do. I love to hear it. I can't tell you how queer I feel when I hear you cry out from the bend of that road through the line of those trees! Do you know I feel like that when I hear the shrill cry

of kites from almost the end of the sky?
Dairyman. Dear child, will you have some curds? Yes, do.
Amal. But I have no money.
Dairyman. No, no, no, don't talk of money! You'll make me so happy if you take some curds from me.
Amal. Say, have I kept you too long?
Dairyman. Not a bit; it has been no loss to me at all; you have taught me how to be happy selling curds.

[Exit

Amal (intoning). Curds, curds, fine curds...from the dairy village... from the country of the Panch-mura hills by the Shamli bank. Curds, good curds; in the early morning, the women make the cows stand in a row under the trees and milk them, and in the evening they turn the milk into curds. Curds, good curds. Hello, there's the watchman on his rounds. Watchman, I say, come and have a word with me.
Watchman. What's all this row about? Aren't you afraid of the likes of me?
Amal. No, why should I be?
Watchman. Suppose I march you off, then?
Amal. Where will you take me to? Is it very far, right beyond the hills?
Watchman. Suppose I march you straight to the King?
Amal. To the King! Do, will you? But the doctor won't let me go out. No one can ever take me away. I've got to stay here all day long.
Watchman. Doctor won't let you, poor fellow! So I see! Your face is pale and there are dark rings round your eyes. Your veins stick out from your poor thin hands.
Amal. Won't you sound the gong, Watchman?
Watchman. Time has not yet come.
Amal. How curious! Some say time has not yet come, and some say time has gone by! But surely your time will come the moment you strike the gong!
Watchman. That's not possible; I strike up the gong only when it is time.
Amal. Yes, I love to hear your gong. When it is midday and our meal is over, Uncle goes off to his work and Auntie falls asleep reading her *Ramayana,* and in the courtyard under the shadow of the wall

our doggie sleeps with his nose in his curled-up tail; then your gong strikes out, 'Dong, dung, dong!' Tell me, why does your gong sound?
Watchman. My gong sounds to tell the people, time waits for none, but goes on forever.
Amal. Where, to what land?
Watchman. That none knows.
Amal. Then I suppose no one has ever been there! Oh, I do wish to fly with the time to that land of which no one knows anything.
Watchman. All of us have to get there one day, my child.
Amal. Have I too?
Watchman. Yes, you too!
Amal. But doctor won't let me out.
Watchman. One day the doctor himself may take you there by the hand.
Amal. He won't; you don't know him. He only keeps me in.
Watchman. One greater than he comes and lets us free.
Amal. When will this great doctor come for me? I can't stick in here anymore.
Watchman. Shouldn't talk like that, my child.
Amal. No. I am here where they have left me—I never move a bit. But, when your gong goes off, dong, dong, dong, it goes to my heart. Say, Watchman?
Watchman. Yes, my dear.
Amal. Say, what's going on there in that big house on the other side, where there is a flag flying high up and the people are always going in and out?
Watchman. Oh, there? That's our new Post Office.
Amal. Post Office? Whose?
Watchman. Whose? Why, the King's, surely!
Amal. Do letters come from the King to his office here?
Watchman. Of course. One fine day there may be a letter for you in there.
Amal. A letter for me? But I am only a little boy.
Watchman. The King sends tiny notes to little boys.
Amal. Oh, how splendid! When shall I have my letter? How do you know he'll write to me?
Watchman. Otherwise why should he set his Post Office here right in

front of your open window, with the golden flag flying?
Amal. But who will fetch me my King's letter when it comes?
Watchman. The King has many postmen. Don't you see them run about with round gilt badges on their chests?
Amal. Well, where do they go?
Watchman. Oh, from door to door, all through the country.
Amal. I'll be the King's postman when I grow up.
Watchman. Ha! Ha! Postman, indeed! Rain or shine, rich or poor, from house to house delivering letters…that's very great work!
Amal. That's what I'd like best. What makes you smile so? Oh, yes, your work is great too. When it is silent everywhere in the heat of the noonday, your gong sounds, dong, dong, dong, and sometimes when I wake up at night all of a sudden and find our lamp blown out, I can hear through the darkness your gong slowly sounding, dong, dong, dong!
Watchman. There's the village headman! I must be off. If he catches me gossiping, there'll be a great to-do.
Amal. The headman? Whereabouts is he?
Watchman. Right down the road there; see that huge palm leaf umbrella hopping along? That's him!
Amal. I suppose the King's made him our headman here?
Watchman. Made him? Oh, no! A fussy busybody! He knows so many ways of making himself unpleasant that everybody is afraid of him. It's just a game for the likes of him, making trouble for everybody. I must be off now! Mustn't keep work waiting, you know! I'll drop in again tomorrow morning and tell you all the news of the town.

[Exit

Amal. It would be splendid to have a letter from the King every day. I'll read them at the window. But, oh! I can't read writing. Who'll read them out to me, I wonder! Auntie reads her *Ramayana;* she may know the King's writing. If no one will, then I must keep them carefully and read them when I'm grown up. But if the postman can't find me? Headman, Mr Headman, may I have a word with you?
Headman. Who is yelling after me on the highway? Oh, it's you, is it, you wretched monkey?

Amal. You're the headman. Everybody minds you.
Headman (Looking pleased). Yes, oh yes, they do! They must!
Amal. Do the King's postmen listen to you?
Headman. They've got to. By Jove, I'd like to see...
Amal. Will you tell the postman it's Amal who sits by the window here?
Headman. What's the good of that?
Amal. In case there's a letter for me.
Headman. A letter for you! Whoever's going to write to you?
Amal. If the King does.
Headman. Ha! Ha! What an uncommon little fellow you are! Ha! Ha! The King, indeed; aren't you his bosom friend, eh! You haven't met for a long while and the King is pining for you, I am sure. Wait till tomorrow and you'll have your letter.
Amal. Say, Headman, why do you speak to me in that tone of voice? Are you cross?
Headman. Upon my word! Cross, indeed! You write to the King! Madhav is a devilish swell nowadays. He's made a little pile; and so kings and padishahs are everyday talk with his people. Let me find him once and I'll make him dance. Oh, you...you snipper-snapper! I'll get the King's letter sent to your house...indeed I will!
Amal. No, no, please don't trouble yourself about it.
Headman. And why not, pray! I'll tell the King about you and he won't be long. One of his footmen will come presently for news of you. Madhav's impudence staggers me. If the King hears of this, that'll take some of his nonsense out of him.

[Exit

Amal. Who are you walking there? How your anklets tinkle! Do stop a while, won't you? *(A Girl enters)*
Girl. I haven't a moment to spare; it is already late!
Amal. I see you don't wish to stop; I don't care to stay on here either.
Girl. You make me think of some late star of the morning! Whatever's the matter with you?
Amal. I don't know; the doctor won't let me out.
Girl. Ah me! Don't go, then! You should listen to the doctor. People will be cross with you if you're naughty. I know, always looking out

and watching must make you feel tired. Let me close the window a bit for you.

Amal. No, don't, only this one's open! All the others are shut. But will you tell me who you are? I don't seem to know you.

Girl. I am Sudha.

Amal. What Sudha?

Sudha. Don't you know? Daughter of the flower seller here.

Amal. What do *you* do?

Sudha. I gather flowers in my basket.

Amal. Oh, flower-gathering! That is why your feet seem so glad and your anklets jingle so merrily as you walk. Wish I could be out too. Then I would pick some flowers for you from the very topmost branches right out of sight.

Sudha. Would you really? Do you know as much about flowers as I?

Amal. Yes, I do, quite as much. I know all about Champa of the fairy tale and his six brothers. If only they let me, I'll go right into the dense forest where you can't find your way. And where the honey-sipping hummingbird rocks himself on the end of the thinnest branch, I will blossom into *a champa*. Would you be my sister Parul?

Sudha. You are silly! How can I be sister Parul when I am Sudha and my mother is Sasi, the flower seller? I have to weave so many garlands a day. It would be jolly if I could lounge here like you!

Amal. What would you do then, all the day long?

Sudha. I could have great times with my doll Benay the bride, and Meni the pussycat, and...but I say, it is getting late and I mustn't stop, or I won't find a single flower.

Amal. Oh, wait a little longer; I do like it so!

Sudha. Ah, well...now you don't be naughty. Be good and sit still, and on my way back home with the flowers I'll come and talk with you.

Amal. And you'll let me have a flower, then?

Sudha. No, how can I? It has to be paid for.

Amal. I'll pay when I grow up—before I leave to look for work out on the other side of that stream there.

Sudha. Very well, then.

Amal. And you'll come back when you have your flowers?

Sudha. I will.

Amal. You will, really?

Sudha. Yes, I will.

Aural. You won't forget me? I am Amal, remember that.

Sudha. I won't forget you, you'll see.

[*Exit*

(A Troop of Boys enter)

Amal. Say, brothers, where are you all off to? Stop here a little.

A Boy. We're off to play.

Amal. What will you play at, brothers?

A Boy. We'll play at being ploughmen.

Another Boy (showing a stick). This is our ploughshare.

Another Boy. We two are the pair of oxen.

Amal. And you're going to play the whole day?

A Boy. Yes, all day long.

Amal. And you will come home in the evening by the road along the river bank?

A Boy. Yes.

Amal. Do you pass our house on your way home?

A Boy. Come out and play with us; yes, do.

Amal. Doctor won't let me out.

A Boy. Doctor! Do you mean to say you mind what the doctor says? Let's be off; it is getting late.

Amal. Don't go. Play on the road near this window. I could watch you, then.

A Boy. What can we play at here?

Amal. With all these toys of mine that are lying about. Here you are; have them. I can't play alone. They are getting dirty and are of no use to me.

Boys. How jolly! What fine toys! Look, here's a ship. There's old mother Jatai. Isn't this a gorgeous sepoy? And you'll let us have them all? You don't really mind?

Amal. No, not a bit; have them by all means.

A Boy. You don't want them back?

Amal. Oh, no, I shan't want them.

A Boy. Say, won't you get a scolding for this?

Amal. No one will scold me. But will you play with them in front of our door for a while every morning? I'll get you new ones when these are old.

A Boy. Oh, yes, we will. I say, put these sepoys into a line. We'll play at war; where can we get a musket? Oh, look here, this bit of reed will do nicely. Say, but you're off to sleep already.

Amal. I'm afraid I'm sleepy. I don't know, I feel like it at times. I have been sitting a long while and I'm tired; my back aches.

A Boy. It's hardly midday now. How is it you're sleepy? Listen! The gong's sounding the first watch.

Amal. Yes, dong, dong, dong; it tolls me to sleep.

A Boy. We had better go, then. We'll come in again tomorrow morning.

Amal. I want to ask you something before you go. You are always out. Do you know of the King's postmen?

Boys. Yes, quite well.

Amal. Who are they? Tell me their names.

A Boy. One's Badal.

Another Boy. Another's Sarat.

Another Boy. There's so many of them.

Amal. Do you think they will know me if there's a letter for me?

A Boy. Surely, if your name's on the letter they will find you out.

Amal. When you call in tomorrow morning, will you bring one of them along so that he'll know me?

A Boy. Yes, if you like.

Curtain

ACT II

(Amal in Bed)

Amal. Can't I go near the window today, Uncle? Would the doctor mind that too?
Madhav. Yes, darling; you see you've made yourself worse squatting there day after day.
Amal. Oh, no, I don't know if it's made me more ill, but I always feel well when I'm there.
Madhav. No, you don't; you squat there and make friends with the whole lot of people round here, old and young, as if they are holding a fair right under my eaves—your flesh and blood won't stand that strain. Just see, your face is quite pale.
Amal. Uncle, I fear my fakir will pass and not see me by the window.
Madhav. Your fakir; whoever's that?
Amal. He comes and chats with me of the many lands where he's been. I love to hear him.
Madhav. How's that? I don't know of any fakirs.
Amal. This is about the time he comes in. I beg of you, by your dear feet, ask him in for a moment to talk to me here.
(Gaffer enters in a Fakir's guise)
Amal. There you are. Come here, Fakir, by my bedside.
Madhav. Upon my word, but this is...
Gaffer (winking hard). I am the Fakir.
Madhav. It beats my reckoning what you're not.
Amal. Where have you been this time, Fakir?
Gaffar. To the Isle of Parrots. I am just back.
Madhav. The Parrots Isle!
Gaffer. Is it so very astonishing? I am not like you. A journey doesn't cost a thing. I tramp just where I like.
Amal (clapping). How jolly for you! Remember your promised to take me with you as your follower when I'm well.
Gaffer. Of course, and I'll teach you so many travellers secrets that

nothing in sea or forest or mountain can bar your way.

Madhav. What's all this rigmarole?

Gaffer. Amal, my dear, I bow to nothing in sea or mountain; but if the doctor joins in with this uncle of yours, then I with all my magic must own myself beaten.

Amal. No. Uncle won't tell the doctor. And I promise to lay quiet; but the day I am well, off I go with the Fakir, and nothing in sea or mountain or torrent shall stand in my way.

Madhav. Fie, dear child, don't keep on harping upon going! It makes me so sad to hear you talk so.

Amal. Tell me, Fakir, what the Parrots Isle is like.

Gaffer. It's a land of wonders; it's a haunt of birds. No men are there; and they neither speak nor walk, they simply sing and they fly.

Amal. How glorious! And it's by some sea?

Gaffer. Of course. It's on the sea.

Amal. And green hills are there?

Gaffer. Indeed, they live among the green hills; and at the time of sunset, when there is a red glow on the hillside, all the birds with their green wings go flocking to their nests.

Amal. And there are waterfalls!

Gaffer. Dear me, of course; you don't have a hill without its waterfalls. Oh, it's like molten diamonds; and, my dear, what dances they have! Don't they make the pebbles sing as they rush over them to the sea! No devil of a doctor can stop them for a moment. The birds looked upon me as nothing but a man, merely a trifling creature without wings and they would have nothing to do with me. Were it not so I would build a small cabin for myself among their crowd of nests and pass my days counting the sea-waves.

Amal. How I wish I were a bird! Then…

Gaffer. But that would have been a bit of a job; I hear you've fixed up with the dairyman to be a hawker of curds when you grow up; I'm afraid such business won't flourish among birds; you might land yourself into serious loss.

Madhav. Really this is too much. Between you two, I shall turn crazy. Now, I'm off.

Amal. Has the dairyman been, Uncle?

Madhav. And why shouldn't he? He won't bother his head running errands for your pet fakir, in and out among the nests in his Parrots Isle. But he has left a jar of curds for you saying that he is busy with his niece's wedding in the village, and has to order a band at Kamlipara.
Amal. But he is going to marry me to his little niece.
Gaffer. Dear me, we are in a fix now.
Amal. He said she would be my lovely little bride with a pair of pearl drops in her ears and dressed in a lovely red saree; and in the morning she would milk with her own hands the black cow and feed me with warm milk with foam on it from a brand new earthen cruse; and in the evenings, she would carry the lamp round the cowshed, and then come and sit by me to tell me tales of Champa and his six brothers.
Gaffer. How charming! It would even tempt me, a hermit! But never mind, dear, about this wedding. Let it be. I tell you that when you marry there'll be no lack of nieces in his household.
Madhav. Shut up! This is more than I can stand.

[Exit

Amal. Fakir, now that Uncle's off, just tell me, has the King sent me a letter at the Post Office?
Gaffer. I gather that his letter has already started; it is on the way here.
Amal. On the way? Where is it? Is it on that road winding through the trees which you can follow to the end of the forest when the sky is quite clear after rain?
Gaffer. That is where it is. You know all about it already.
Amal. I do, everything.
Gaffer. So I see, but how?
Amal. I can't say; but it's quite clear to me. I fancy I've seen it often in days long gone by. How long ago I can't tell. Do you know when? I can see it all: there the King's postman coming down the hillside alone, a lantern in his left hand and on his back a bag of letters; climbing down for ever so long, for days and nights, and where at the foot of the mountain the waterfall becomes a stream, he takes to the footpath on the bank and walks on through the rye; then comes the sugarcane field and he disappears into the narrow lane cutting through the tall stems of sugarcanes; then he reaches the open meadow where

the cricket chirps and where there is not a single man to be seen, only the snipe wagging their tails and poking at the mud with their bills. I can feel him coming nearer and nearer and my heart becomes glad.
Gaffer. My eyes are not young; but you make me see all the same.
Amal. Say, Fakir, do you know the King who has this Post Office?
Gaffer. I do; I go to him for my alms every day.
Amal. Good! When I get well I must have my alms too from him, mayn't I?
Gaffer. You won't need to ask, my dear; he'll give it to you of his own accord.
Amal. No, I will go to his gate and cry, 'Victory to thee, O King!' and dancing to the tabor's sound, ask for alms. Won't it be nice?
Gaffer. It will be splendid, and if you're with me I shall have my full share. But what will you ask?
Amal. I shall say, 'Make me your postman that I may go about, lantern in hand, delivering your letters from door to door. Don't let me stay at home all day!'
Gaffer. What is there to be sad for, my child, even if you were to stay at home?
Amal. It isn't sad. When they shut me in here first I felt the day was so long. Since the King's Post Office was put there, I like more and more being indoors, and as I think I shall get a letter one day, I feel quite happy and then I don't mind being quiet and alone. I wonder if I shall make out what'll be in the King's letter?
Gaffer. Even if you didn't, wouldn't it be enough if it just bore your name?

(Madhav enters)

Madhav. Have you any idea of the trouble you've got me into, between you two?
Gaffer. What's the matter?
Madhav. I hear you've let it get rumoured about that the King has planted his office here to send messages to both of you!
Gaffer. Well, what about it?
Madhav. Our headman Panchanan has had it told to the King anonymously!

Gaffer. Aren't we aware that everything reaches the King's ears?
Madhav. Then why don't you look out? Why take the King's name in vain? You'll bring me to ruin if you do.
Amal. Say, Fakir, will the King be cross?
Gaffer. Cross, nonsense! And with a child like you and a fakir such as I am? Let's see if the King be angry, and then won't I give him a piece of my mind!
Amal. Say, Fakir, I've been feeling a sort of darkness coming over my eyes since the morning. Everything seems like a dream. I long to be quiet. I don't feel like talking at all. Won't the King's letter come? Suppose this room melts away all on a sudden, suppose...
Gaffer (fanning Amal). The letter's sure to come today, my boy.

(Doctor enters)

Doctor. And how do you feel today?
Amal. Feel awfully well today, Doctor. All pain seems to have left me.
Doctor (aside to Madhav). Don't quite like the look of that smile. Bad sign that, his feeling well! Chakradhan has observed...
Madhav. For goodness' sake, Doctor, leave Chakradhan alone. Tell me what's going to happen?
Doctor. Can't hold him in much longer, I fear! I warned you before—this looks like a fresh exposure.
Madhav. No! I've used the utmost care, never let him out of doors; and the windows have been shut almost all the time.
Doctor. There's a peculiar quality in the air today. As I came in, I found a fearful draught through your front door. That's most hurtful. Better lock it at once. Would it matter if this kept your visitors off for two or three days? If someone happens to call unexpectedly—there's the back door. You had better shut this window as well; it's letting in the sunset rays only to keep the patient awake.
Madhav. Amal has shut his eyes. I expect he is sleeping. His face tells me—Oh, Doctor, I bring in a child who is a stranger and love him as my own, and now I suppose I must lose him!
Doctor. What's that? There's your headman sailing in! What a bother! I must be going, brother. You had better stir about and see to the doors being properly fastened. I will send on a strong dose directly

the moment I reach home. Try it on him—it may save him at last, if he can be saved at all.

[Exit Madhav and Doctor)

(The Headman enters)

Headman. Hello, urchin!...
Gaffer (rising hastily). 'Sh, be quiet.
Amal. No, Fakir, did you think I was asleep? I wasn't. I can hear everything; yes, and voices faraway. I feel that mother and father are sitting by my pillow and speaking to me.

(Madhav enters)

Headman. I say, Madhav, I hear you hobnob with bigwigs nowadays.
Madhav. Spare me your jokes, Headman; we are but common people.
Headman. But your child here is expecting a letter from the King.
Madhav. Don't you take any notice of him, a mere foolish boy!
Headman. Indeed, why not! It'll beat the King hard to find a better family! Don't you see why the King plants his new Post Office right before your window? Why, there's a letter for you from the King, urchin.
Amal (starting up). Indeed, really!
Headman. How can it be false? You're the King's chum. Here's your letter *(showing a blank slip of paper)*. Ha, ha, ha! This is the letter.
Amal. Please don't mock me. Say, Fakir, is it so?
Gaffer. Yes, my dear. I as Fakir tell you it is his letter.
Amal. How is it I can't see? It all looks so blank to me. What is there in the letter, Mr Headman?
Headman. The King says, 'I am calling on you shortly; you had better have puffed rice for me. Palace fare is quite tasteless to me now.' Ha! Ha! Ha!
Madhav (with folded palms). I beseech you, Headman, don't you joke about these things...
Gaffer. Joking indeed! He would not dare.
Madhav. Are you out of your mind too, Gaffer?
Gaffer. Out of my mind; well then, I am. I can read plainly that the King writes he will come himself to see Amal, with the State Physician.

Amal. Fakir, Fakir, 'sh, his trumpet! Can't you hear?
Headman. Ha! Ha! Ha! I fear he won't until he's a bit more off his head.
Amal. Mr Headman, I thought you were cross with me and didn't love me. I never could have believed you would fetch me the King's letter. Let me wipe the dust off your feet.
Headman. This little child does have an instinct of reverence. Though a little silly, he has a good heart.
Amal. It's hard on the fourth watch now, I suppose. Hark, the gong, 'Dong, dong, ding, dong, dong, ding.' Is the evening star up? How is it I can't see...
Gaffer. Oh, the windows are all shut; I'll open them.

(A knocking outside)

Madhav. What's that? Who is it? What a bother!
Voice (from outside). Open the door.
Madhav. Headman, I hope they're not robbers.
Headman. Who's there? It is Panchanan, the headman, who calls. Aren't you afraid to make that noise? Fancy! The noise has ceased! Panchanan's voice carries far. Yes, show me the biggest robbers!
Madhav (peering out of the window). No wonder the noise has ceased. They have smashed the outer door. *(The King's Herald enters)*
Herald. Our Sovereign King comes tonight!
Headman. My God!
Amal. At what hour of the night, Herald?
Herald. On the second watch.
Amal. When my friend the watchman will strike his gong from the city gates, 'Ding dong ding, ding dong ding' then?
Herald. Yes, then. The King sends his greatest physician to attend on his young friend. *(State Physician enters)*
State Physician. What's this? How close it is here! Open wide all the doors and windows. *(Feeling Amal's body.)* How do you feel, my child?
Amal. I feel very well, Doctor, very well. All pain is gone. How fresh and open! I can see all the stars now twinkling from the other side of the dark.
Physician. Will you feel well enough to leave your bed when the King comes in the middle watches of the night?

Amal. Of course, I'm dying to be about for ever so long. I'll ask the King to find me the polar star. I must have seen it often, but I don't know exactly which it is.

Physician. He will tell you everything. *(To Madhav.)* Arrange flowers through the room for the King's visit. *(Indicating to the Headman.)* We can't have that person in here.

Amal. No, let him be, Doctor. He is a friend. It was he who brought me the King's letter.

Physician. Very well, my child. He may remain if he is a friend of yours.

Madhav (whispering into Amal's ear). My child, the King loves you. He is coming himself. Beg for a gift from him. You know our humble circumstances.

Amal. Don't you worry, Uncle. I've made up my mind about it.

Madhav. What is it, my child?

Amal. I shall ask him to make me one of his postmen that I may wander far and wide, delivering his message from door to door.

Madhav (slapping his forehead). Alas, is that all?

Amal. What'll be our offerings to the King, Uncle, when he comes?

Herald. He has commanded puffed rice.

Amal. Puffed rice. Say, Headman, you're right. You said so. You knew all we didn't.

Headman. If you would send word to my house I could manage for the King's advent really nice...

Physician. No need at all. Now be quiet, all of you. Sleep is coming over him. I'll sit by his pillow; he's dropping asleep. Blow out the oil lamp. Only let the starlight stream in. Hush, he sleeps.

Madhav (addressing Gaffer). What are you standing there for like a statue, folding your palms? I am nervous. Say, are there good omens? Why are they darkening the room? How will starlight help?

Gaffer. Silence, unbeliever!

(Sudha enters)

Sudha. Amal.

Physician. He's asleep.

Sudha. I have some flowers for him. Mayn't I give them into his own hand?

Physician. Yes, you may.
Sudha. When will he be awake?
Physician. Directly the King comes and calls him.
Sudha. Will you whisper a word for me in his ear?
Physician. What shall I say?
Sudha. Tell him Sudha has not forgotten him.

Curtain

CHOKHER BALI

TRANSLATOR'S NOTE

Translations are never easy, since no two languages are truly equivalent in anything except the simplest terms. This is where translation into another language becomes most arduous, and this difficulty gets compounded when confronted with the works of someone like the colossal Rabindranath. Translations then seem almost like an effrontery. It is in this context that I have opted to be as faithful to his text as was possible, since I did not think I ought to tamper with Tagore's language or thoughts. Even so, some liberties had to be taken by excisions where no acceptable translations were possible to convey with any degree of fidelity the nuances of the original language. There are also some minor deletions, which were basically digressions and not relevant to the story.

SUKHENDU RAY

ONE

Harimati laid almost a siege at her friend Rajlakshmi's door, pleading to get her daughter Binodini married to Rajlakshmi's son Mahendra. Rajlakshmi and Harimati were neighbours in the same village, and were playmates as children.

Eventually, Rajlakshmi decided to speak to her son. 'Mohin (that was how Mahendra was called by his mother and by his close relations and friends), we ought to help my old friend Harimati. She is most keen to get her daughter married to you. I believe she is a very pretty girl, as well as well-educated. A foreign lady teacher had tutored her. Should suit well modern young men like you.'

'There are many modern young men besides myself,' was Mahendra's disinterested response.

'There you go again, at your old game,' complained his mother, 'You never take me seriously whenever I raise the topic of your marriage.'

'Surely, mother, there are other more serious issues in life than the question of my marriage,' Mahendra said. 'Don't fault me if I can't see my marriage as a priority.'

Having lost his father very early in his childhood, the affinity between Mahendra and his mother was deeper than the normal mother and son kinship. He was nearly twenty-two years of age, and after a Master's degree, he was now in Medical College to qualify as a doctor. Though grown up, there was no end to his many juvenile demands on his mother. He could do nothing without mother's help, and the mother completely overshadowed his life. She sheltered him like a kangaroo cub in its mother's pouch.

When his mother became very insistent on the question of his marriage to Binodini, he reluctantly agreed to have a look at the girl. The day he was supposed to meet Binodini, he abandoned the idea. 'Just what is the point,' was his argument to his mother, 'of my meeting this girl? I have agreed to marry her just to please you, so how does it matter what sort of a girl she is?'

If the mother suspected a note of dissatisfaction in his voice, she decided to overlook it. She was convinced, more or less, that after the marriage the son would have no reason to be unhappy with her choice. Rajlakshmi went ahead confidently to fix a firm date for the wedding, but as the day drew nearer, Mahendra exhibited increasing signs of edginess, so much so, that shortly before the due date he stumped his mother by telling her firmly, 'No mother, I can't go through this marriage.'

The trouble with Mahendra was that immoderately pampered as he was in all manners since his young days, he grew up an extremely self willed person. He hated to be pressurised in doing anything that he did not initiate himself. This marriage was not his choice. He gave his consent to oblige someone else, to wit his mother. He resented being forced into this marriage, and this resentment progressively magnified with the passing time until he found it too suffocating, when he rebelled against the idea.

Rajlakshmi found herself placed in a most awkward position. At this critical moment she thought of Bihari, a long time devoted friend of Mahendra. Bihari regarded Mahendra as a sort of an elder brother and looked upon Mahendra's mother as his own. The mother, though fond of him, took Bihari granted as a useful and necessary appendage to her son. Rajlakshmi caught hold of Bihari and told him, 'Please, son, you must take Mahendra's place and marry this poor girl, otherwise...'

Bihari, in all humility, begged to be excused. 'Ma, I am afraid, this I cannot do. On many an occasion in the past you had offered me sweets declined by your son, which I had happily consumed, but marriage is altogether a far more serious issue. In any case, I find it most inappropriate to accept a bride whom you had intended for Mahendra.'

Rajlakshmi was well aware that Bihari's life revolved round Mahendra's and that marriage was the last priority in his mind. This renewed evidence of his attachment to her son raised her fondness for Bihari by a notch, albeit mixed with a degree of condescension.

Binodini's father was not exactly a man of means; nevertheless, he did not stint engaging a foreign missionary lady to educate his daughter, which included lessons in arts and crafts. Unfortunately, he failed to notice that the daughter was growing up and in due course reached the age of marriage. His premature death left the widowed mother frantically searching for a suitable husband for the daughter—a task not made easy when her means were also straitened.

A harried Rajlakshmi finally located a distant nephew of hers in a village in Barasat, and Binodini was married off to him. This marriage did not last, and Binodini found herself a widow almost in no time. Mahendra gave a sarcastic laugh on receiving this information. 'What a lucky escape! Good thing I did not marry her, or how would I have survived her widowhood?'

Three years down the line Rajlakshmi confronted her son. 'Look, son, I am getting a bad name.'

'Why, Mother, I had no idea that you had harmed anyone,' Mahendra said playfully.

'The talk goes round that I am not deliberately getting you married for fear that your wife will dislodge me from your affection.'

'A very valid ground for fear,' Mahendra said. 'If I were a mother I would not have, for whatever it is worth, marry off a son. I fully concur with the comments of the people whoever they may be.'

Mother laughed. 'What a silly boy you are.'

'Look, Mother,' Mahendra continued, 'it is a fact of life that a son's wife enslaves the son, and the mother, that dear and beloved mother who had gone through so much pains to bring up the son, is lost. I can hardly believe that you would really care for this, but I certainly cannot agree.'

Though delighted in her heart of hearts, Rajlakshmi decided to talk to her sister-in-law, Annapurna, widow of her husband's brother. 'Do you know what Mohin, that silly boy, says? He says he does not wish to get married for fear that he might lose his mother to his wife. Can you believe it?'

Annapurna cautioned the mother, 'You must not encourage this. What has to be done must be done at the proper time, and it is time for Mohin to get a wife and live his own life. He ought not to cling to his mother like a child. This is not at all appropriate.'

Annapurna's reaction clearly did not please Rajlakshmi, and her response was none too friendly. 'Why should it bother you if my son is excessively attached to me? Perhaps not being a mother, you cannot appreciate this.' Nothing but a childless widow's envy for a mother blessed with a son—that was Rajlakshmi's unfeeling thought.

Annapurna said, 'You see, it is you who brought up the topic of your son's marriage, or else why should I come into this?'

'I don't understand why it should affect you anyway if my son refuses to marry. If I have been able to look after him until now, I can continue to do so. I shan't need anybody's help.'

Annapurna left in tears, and Mahendra found this most distressing. He returned early from college and went straight to his aunt's room. He knew well that whatever the aunt said was out of her deep affection for him. He also knew that his aunt had a niece, her sister's daughter, who had lost both her parents early in her life, and the aunt had been nursing a hope if she could get her niece married to Mahendra. To see her niece happily married was a natural enough anxiety, Mahendra conceded, even though the aunt was well aware of his disinclination to marry.

It was late in the afternoon when Mahendra reached his aunt's room. He found her looking depressed. Her midday food was still there, untouched. This upset him. He tenderly called, '*Kakima?*'

Annapurna, trying to look cheerful, said, 'Oh, is it you Mohin? Come in.'

'I am famished, do give me something to eat, maybe some leftovers from your food.'

She understood well that it was a ruse of Mahendra's to make her eat. With some effort she suppressed her flowing tears, ate herself and fed Mahendra.

Mahendra's heart was still full of tenderness for the aunt. Suddenly, and no doubt impulsively, perhaps only to please his aunt, he said, 'The other day you spoke about your niece. Aren't you going to present her before us?'

Annapurna smiled. 'Since when did your thoughts turn to marriage?'

'No, no, not for me,' Mahendra quickly replied. 'I am speaking for Bihari. He is willing. Do fix a date when we can meet your niece.'

This unexpected proposal was beyond Annapurna's dream. Much moved, she said, 'How wonderful! How fortunate she must be to get a husband like Bihari.'

Mahendra left and just outside the door he met his mother. She asked suspiciously, 'What were the two of you talking about?' 'Nothing really. I just wanted some pawn.'

'But your pawn is kept as usual in my room.'

She barged into Annapurna's room and observing her tearstained eyes, jumped to uncharitable conclusions. She burst out, 'I presume you were complaining to my son against me,' and rushed out without waiting for a reply.

TWO

Mahendra had quite forgotten his proposal to his aunt, but the aunt had not. After Mahendra spoke to her, she promptly shot off a letter to the guardian of her niece, her father's elder brother, suggesting a date for meeting the girl. As soon as Mahendra was told this, he said, 'But what was the rush? I haven't had any opportunity to speak to Bihari yet.'

This put Annapurna in a delicate position. She said, 'But how can I now postpone it? What will the girl's people think if we call it off now?'

Mahendra had now no option but to speak to Bihari. 'There can be no harm in just seeing the girl,' Mahendra told Bihari by way of placating him. 'You are under no obligation if you don't approve of the girl.'

Bihari strongly protested. 'I can no way reject Kakima's niece after meeting her. I am sorry, I cannot do that.'

'That's fine. Then there's no problem,' Mahendra appeared relieved.

'What you did, Mohin, was most unfair,' Bihari said, taking exception, 'unscrupulous of you to duck your obligation and pass it on to another. To hurt Kakima will be extremely painful.'

Mahendra was abashed as well as annoyed. 'Then what do you suggest that we should do?'

'Since you have raised some expectation in Kakima's mind then I will have to marry her niece. There is, therefore, little point in this pretence of going to have a look at the girl.' Bihari had the highest regard for Annapurna, almost deifying her.

When Annapurna was told about Bihari's stand, she spoke to him, 'No, son, I can't allow this. You cannot commit yourself before you meet my niece. If you do not find her suitable, you will be under no obligation to marry her. I give you my word.'

On the day fixed for their visit to the girl's home, Mahendra asked his mother when he returned from college, 'Mother, can you please take out my silk kurta and my fine crimpled dhoti.'

'Why, where are you going?' asked the mother in surprise.

'I'll tell you later, Mother. Just lay those out, please.

Although the proposed call at the girl's place was not for Mahendra himself, he nevertheless, could not resist taking some care over his toilet. At the prospect of meeting a young girl, a young man's fancies turn to sprucing himself up, carefully grooming his hair, and dabbing himself with a few drops of perfume. Toilet completed, the two friends set out on their expedition.

The girl's uncle Anukul-babu's home was in the locality of Shyambazar where he had built a fine three-storeyed house. When his younger brother died, he took care of the orphaned child. Annapurna was willing to keep the niece with her, which was an economic option for the uncle, but conscious of the social loss of face that might ensue, the uncle took the child under his wings.

The child grew up and in due course reached the age of marriage. And, that was of some concern to the uncle as marriages entailed expense. If the question of dowry ever cropped up from prospective proposals, the uncle moaned, 'I have also my own daughters to worry about, so how can I manage all these expenses all by myself?' And so, time flew and the niece remained unmarried. It is at this point of time that the two friends, well-groomed and perfumed, entered the stage.

It was an afternoon in the month of Chaitra when the sun was just about to go down. The south verandah of the first floor was paved with shiny decorative ceramic tiles. At one end a table was set up with various refreshments on silver plates and tumblers of iced water. Mahendra and Bihari took their seats, and hesitantly helped themselves with the refreshments offered. Down below the gardener was watering the plants, and the breeze from the south carrying the whiff of the wet earth created an agreeable ambience. Through the chinks in the door and the windows could be heard suppressed laughter, whispered voices and tinkling of ornaments.

Refreshments over, Anukul-babu gave a call, 'Chuni, can you get the paan, please?' A door opened, out came a girl, nervous, carrying a container with paan, and stood facing Anukul-babu, who told her, 'No need to be shy, child, put the paan down for the guests.' The girl with trembling hands did so. The dying rays of the sun caught the girl's face, and at that very instant the vision of a timorous young face flashed through Mahendra's eyes.

As the girl was about to leave, Anukul-babu asked her to wait. Addressing Bihari, he said, 'Bihari-babu, she is my younger brother Apurba's daughter. Apurba has gone, and she has no one other than me to take care of her.' Then he took a deep long sigh. It stirred Mahendra's heart, and he once again looked at the poor girl.

It was not very clear how old she was. Vaguely, some relations claimed she was around twelve or thirteen years of age, meaning thereby she was more likely to be fourteen or fifteen years old. Brought up in conditions of charity she grew up a melancholic and withdrawn person, which effectively concealed the burgeoning of the first flush of her youth.

Mahendra asked kindly, 'Tell us your name.'

'Come, no need to feel shy, tell the gentlemen your name,' encouraged the uncle. And the girl, used to compliance, answered, with her head bowed, 'Ashalata is my name.'

Asha! Hope! Not a very appropriate name for her, and the voice was also morose. Poor helpless girl! Mahendra felt truly sorry for her.

On their way back Mahendra told Bihari, 'You must not let this girl slip out of your hand.'

Bihari, instead of giving a direct answer, observed rather solemnly, 'From the look of this girl I get the impression that she might be a gentle soul like her aunt.'

'Ah, the onus that I imposed on YOU is then not all that heavy, is it?' Mahendra teased Bihari.

Bihari smiled, 'Yes, I think I shall be able to carry it.'

'Equally, if you are not keen, then you do not have to go for it,' said Mahendra rather unexpectedly. 'I am prepared to take on myself your burden. What do you say to that?'

Bihari appeared grave as he looked at Mahendra. 'Are you serious? If you are, you must make up your mind immediately. I believe our aunt will feel much happier if you marry her, and in that case she will also have her niece near her.'

'Are you mad?' Mahendra said, 'If I had any intention to marry her, I could have done so earlier.'

After parting from Bihari, Mahendra did not go home immediately. He deliberately tarried, and returned home late. His mother was busy cooking, and the aunt had still not returned from her niece's place.

Mahendra went straight up to the roof and lay down on a reed mat. A bright moon was up, casting its magic spell on the city mansions as well as in his heart. When his mother sent word that food was ready, he told his mother, 'I am very comfortable here, don't feel like getting up.'

'Then I will take the food up there,' his mother suggested.

'I already had something to eat, and don't feel too hungry at the moment.'

'But where did you have this food?' asked the surprised mother.

'That I'll tell you later, mother, it is a long story,' Mahendra shot back.

Most unusual, the mother thought. Mahendra then changed his mind, and perhaps to divert his mother's curiosity, told her to send his food up.

'But if you are not hungry, then what is the point?' the mother said tersely.

After a great deal of cajoling and humouring between the mother and the son, Mahendra eventually sat down to his meal.

THREE

Mahendra did not sleep well that night, and very early in the morning he called on Bihari at the latter's home. He told Bihari, 'Look, I had given this matter some thought, and I believe that in her heart of hearts my aunt really wishes me to marry her niece.'

'Nothing new in it. Your aunt had been indicating this in many ways,' Bihari observed.

'That is true. I feel she will be tremendously upset if I don't marry Asha.'

'That is possible.'

'In that case,' Mahendra added, 'will it not be extremely wrong if I do not fall in line with her wishes?'

Bihari, with a show of unexpected eagerness, said, 'Well, it is fine then. There should be no problem if you agree to marry her, but really, you should have thought of this yesterday.'

'Surely, a day's delay is not likely to make much difference,' Mahendra said petulantly.

Once Mahendra settled his mind on marrying Asha, he found it difficult to rein in his patience. There was no need to waste any more time in talks; he wished the formalities of marriage over as soon as possible.

He spoke to his mother, 'I am prepared to get married since you wish it.'

Rather strange, the mother felt. Was that why Annapurna went the other day to visit her niece, the same day that Mahendra also went out after a careful toilet? The fact that Annapurna's machinations succeeded against her many pleadings with her son made her acutely bitter. Nevertheless, concealing her feelings she told her son, 'That is wonderful. I shall now be on the lookout for a suitable bride for you.'

Mahendra told his mother, 'No need for that really. I have decided to get married to Asha.'

Rajlakshmi saw red, and spoke with considerable vehemence, 'That I cannot allow, let me make that quite clear to you.'

'But why not, Mother? Asha is quite a nice girl,' Mahendra tried to sound not too eager.

Rajlakshmi was adamant. 'She is an orphaned child with no social standing. To me it is not a suitable connection.'

'That is immaterial, Mother. I like this girl,' Mahendra told his mother firmly.

The son's insistence hardened her determination to prevent this marriage at any cost. She accosted Annapurna and accused her, 'So you wish to ruin me? You are scheming to take my only son away from me by marrying him to your orphaned and ill-starred niece. How mischievous can you get?'

Annapurna broke down in tears, 'But I never did propose Mahendra's marriage with my niece. I have no idea what he told you.'

Mahendra's mother did not believe a word of hers. Annapurna, sorely tried, spoke to Bihari, 'I had proposed my niece's marriage with you, how then was this decision changed? Please Bihari, you must marry my niece, otherwise I shall find myself in a most awkward situation. My niece is a very good natured girl, and will suit you in every respect.'

Bihari replied, 'I know all that, Kakinia. There can hardly be any question of my disapproval since she is your niece. But...you see... Mahendra...'

Annapurna quickly intercepted, 'Mahendra can in no way marry my niece. I will feel very comfortable if you marry her, and I truly believe that I cannot permit her marriage with Mahendra.'

'Well, *Kakima*, if you don't agree to Mahendra, then there is nothing more to be said.'

Bihari saw Rajlakshmi later and told her, 'Ma, my marriage with *Kakima's* niece is now fixed. As I have no female relation, I had to come and shamelessly give you this information myself.'

'Is that true?' Rajlakshmi almost gushed. 'How delightful! I am, indeed, most happy for you. Do not let this proposal slip out of your hands.'

'There is no reason why I should. After all, Mohin has himself selected this girl for me,' Bihari responded happily.

These new obstructions to his aspiration only added fuel to

Mahendra's fury, and disgusted with both his mother and aunt, he banished himself from home to a clingy hostel for students. Rajlakshmi was desolated and ran to Annapurna in desperation. With tears in her eyes she begged her sister-in-law, 'My son has deserted me frustrated and discontent. Please do something to bring him back.'

Annapurna counselled Rajlakshmi, 'Didi, have patience. He will get over his disappointment in a few days and return home.'

'You do not know him,' moaned Rajlakshmi. 'He tends to get out of control if he is denied what he wants. You have somehow to arrange for your niece's marriage with my son.'

'But how can I do so? She is engaged to be married to Bihari,' Annapurna said.

Rajlakshmi, inconsolable, suggested, 'It is surely not impossible to break this engagement.' Then she sent for Bihari and told him, 'Look, you have to sacrifice Ashalata. In any case, I do not think she will suit you at all. I will find a better bride for you.'

Bihari was reluctant. He said, 'No, Ma, this I cannot do. All arrangements have been made for my marriage.'

Rajlakshmi rushed back to Annapurna and pitifully pleaded with her, 'I beg of you, if you speak to Bihari he might relent.'

Unhappy and unwilling though she was, Annapurna was obliged to confront Bihari. 'I find it extremely difficult to suggest this to you, but I am helpless. I would have been most happy if Asha were married to you, but you will no doubt appreciate the present circumstances...'

'Yes, *Kakima*, I do appreciate. I will do as you wish, but please do not ever in future try to get me married.'

Annapurna's eyes filled with tears after Bihari left, but she reasoned in her heart, perhaps, what happened had happened for the best.

Thus, in this somewhat heartless fashion, with strifes and tensions assailing Annapurna, Rajlakshmi and Mahendra, the day of the wedding dawned. With bright lights and much pomp, with sweet music poured forth by the shehnai, lavish feasts nothing was lacking for the occasion, amidst a great show, Mahendra brought home his new bride.

Asha decked in fineries and looking enchanting stepped into her new home, rapturously but diffidently. Little did her timorous heart suspect that there could be any thorns in her new nest. On the other hand, whatever apprehensions, whatever misgivings she had, were swept away by the reassuring proximity of her aunt Annapurna, who was like a second mother to her.

Some days after the marriage Rajlakshmi proposed to her son, 'I suggest that my daughter-in-law should go back to her uncle and stay there for sometime.'

'Why must she, Mother?'

'Your examinations are very near, and her presence might disrupt your preparations,' replied the mother.

Mahendra protested. 'Really Mother, do you think I am a child who does not know what is good for him?'

Rajlakshnii still insisted, 'Whatever it may be, it will be no more than a year.'

Mahendra demurred. 'If my wife had her parents alive I could have considered sending her back to them, but I cannot agree to her going back to her uncle.'

So that is how it was, Rajlakshmi thought to herself. The husband was now the lord and master and the mother-in-law did not count. In her times husbands were not so attached to the apron strings of the wives, nor were they so devoid of modesty!

Mahendra assured his mother very firmly, 'Do not be agitated, Mother. My preparations will not suffer.'

FOUR

Rajlakshmi devised her own strategies to keep the daughter-in-law away from the son. With great energy she commenced training Asha in all aspects of the household affairs. Throughout the day she was kept entrapped variously in the kitchen or the store room or the puja room, and at night she would take Asha to her own bedroom, in the feigned kindly thought that by doing so she was assuaging her pangs of separation from her natal family. Annapurna deliberately kept her distance from the niece.

For Mahendra the situation was getting increasingly insufferable. His situation was like the little boy who watched hopelessly but covetously a more powerful person sucking the sugarcane dry and leaving nothing for him. To see before his eyes his young and lovely wife crushed by the weight of housework, wringing out all her grace and charm, was too much for him to bear.

Not daring to approach his mother, Mahendra went to his aunt. '*Kakima*, the way my mother is working my wife to the bones is more than I can stand.'

Annapurna was well aware that Rajlakshmi had been wilfully keeping her daughter-in law in hard grind, and was not willing to lend her ears to Mahendra's grievance. She said, 'What is wrong with it, Mohin? The young wife is being taught the ropes of running a home, and that is how it should be. Surely, it is not right to imitate modern girls who appear to while away their time doing nothing except reading frivolous romances or idle needlework.'

Mahendra became agitated. 'Well for better or worse, modern girls will be modern girls. If my wife enjoys literature as I do, I do not see why should this invite censure or ridicule.'

Rajlakshmi, who heard voices coming from Annapurna's room, barged in there and found Mahendra and Annapurna talking. She asked suspiciously, 'May I know what you two are discussing?'

Mahendra, who was still in his rebellious frame of mind, said, 'We were discussing nothing. I just happened to mention to *Kakima* that I cannot stand any longer the way my wife is made to work like a slave.'

Intensely outraged though she was, Rajlakshmi managed to hold herself in check and spoke quite calmly, 'What then are you proposing to do with her?'

Mahendra replied equally calmly, 'I intend to educate her.'

The mother rustled out without another word and returned almost immediately, dragging the daughter-in-law with her. Setting her in front of Mahendra, she said, 'Here is your wife, take her away and educate her.' Then turning to Annapurna she spoke in mock humbleness, and with folded hands, 'Please forgive me, sister-in-law. I did not quite appreciate the standing of your niece, so I did soil her precious hands with dirty housework. Do please cleanse them up, doll her up like a modern girl of fashion, and let Mahendra take charge of her education. As for the housework I will be the drudge, no problem.' And, she stormed out of the room.

Annapurna sank with a deep sense of mortification, and Asha, who had no clue to this domestic upheaval, trembled with alarm. Mahendra, furious with his mother, decided that enough was enough, and that it was high time that he took charge of his wife in his own hands. It would otherwise be most unfair for her.

Mahendra's personal aspirations for his wife clashing with his other commitments took the most adverse turns. He neglected his own studies oblivious of the forthcoming examinations, sacrificed his friends, and ignored his social obligations. He seriously applied himself in improving his wife's mind, and had no time for his own work or for other people.

Rajlakshmi, her ego bruised, decided never to forgive her son, nor to see him even if he came to her profoundly penitent. She would watch and see how long could he carry on with his wife at the cost of the mother.

Days passed, but no contrite footfalls were heard at the mother's doorstep. Rajlakshmi then decided that if her son did, indeed, come to beg her forgiveness, she would overlook his transgression and condone it. After all, her refusal to do so would cause her son much pain. No plea for mercy reached her. Rajlakshmi had further ideas. She thought of approaching Mahendra on her own and telling him that all was forgotten and forgiven. If a son sulks with unhappiness, it will not be proper for a mother to reciprocate a similar attitude.

The attic on the second floor roof was both Mahendra's bedroom as well as his study. For some days, she had deliberately not paid any attention to his room or his needs. This neglect of the mother's usual loving chores for the son had been tormenting her. One afternoon she decided to go up to his room, when Mahendra would normally be away in college, and tidy up the room. Upon his return, Mahendra would surely not fail to recognize the touch of the loving hands of the mother which had done up his room!

She climbed to the roof and approached Mahendra's room. She found the door open, and immediately recoiled from what caught her eyes through the open door. Mahendra was asleep, and his wife, her back to the door, was tenderly caressing her husband's feet. This brazen display of conjugal ardour, in open daylight, revolted and sickened her. She quickly ran down, deeply traumatized.

FIVE

Asha blossomed forth as a watered flower, like the yellowing drought-affected crops that revive as soon as rains drench them. She had gained her place and firmly established her position at a new home with which she had no earlier kinship bond.

Asha had now discovered her closest bond and secured her undisputed privileges, without even asking for them. And, when her doting husband crowned an orphan, who grew up without any love, as the queen of his heart, she readily assumed her elevated status. She lost no time tossing away the inhibitions and reticence of a new bride, and ascended the throne her husband had created for her in her exalted capacity of a beloved wife.

On that fateful afternoon when Rajlakshmi discovered a newly arrived girl from an unrelated family majestically occupying this throne, as if born to it, she ran down to her room in utter revulsion. She found a scapegoat in Annapurna on whom she unleashed a verbal assault. She told her, 'Go and have a look at your darling princess, the sort of training she has received from her royal family. If only men like our husbands were around...'

Annapurna, though unfairly impeached, spoke humbly, 'Didi, she is your daughter-in-law, it is for you to teach her, discipline her. Why do you come and tell me?'

Rajlakshmi flared up, 'Do you believe that with a counsellor like you at hand, she would heed me at all?'

Unable to take it anymore, Annapurna went up, and surprising both the husband and the wife, entered their room. She sternly upbraided her niece, 'Must you put me to shame by your irresponsible conduct? Have you lost all sense of decency that you spend all your time here, ignoring your elderly mother-in-law and leaving to her all the housework? Curse my fate that I brought you to this home.'

Annapurna had been copiously shedding tears as she spoke, and Asha, thus scolded also started to weep. Mahendra spoke up for his wife, 'Kakima, why are you unjustly taking my wife to task? She is not to be blamed, it is I who keep her detained here.'

'Do you think you are doing the right thing?' Annapurna said with some asperity. 'She is a young, immature girl, an orphan who never had a mother to instruct her about her obligations. How would she know what is right or wrong? And what, if I may ask, is she learning from you?'

Unruffled Mahendra said, 'Come and see for yourself. I have procured books for her, writing materials, slates and pencils. I wish to make her literate, I want to educate her, and I am not bothered about people's disapproval or your indignation.'

Annapurna hurled back, 'Surely, it is not necessary to keep her engaged in her lessons the whole day. An hour or so in the evening ought to be adequate.'

'It is not all that easy. One needs a great deal of time to devote to studies,' was Mahendra's unconcerned reply.

Annapurna left thoroughly disgusted. Asha was about to follow her out when Mahendra restrained her. He had no patience to heed her pathetic pleas or her tears. He told her firmly, 'Let us not forget that we lost some time when I slept, and we must make up for this loss.'

Asha herself was not overtly confident that she would make much progress in her husband's scheme of education for her, but yielded as an obedient and loyal wife. Nevertheless, she did apply herself diligently to learn her lessons. Occupying one end of the bed, with her books, she made strenuous efforts to cram what she had been taught. At another corner of the room, sitting at a desk, Asha's tutor, with an open medical text in front of him, kept continuously casting his eyes towards his pupil to ensure that she did not relax. Then, unexpectedly, he would tell Asha, 'Chuni, come here, let me check your progress.'

Such summons made Asha nervous, in case her teacher decided to test her, which she was well aware she was likely to flunk. Her primer, Charupath, held very little charm for her. The piece on ant heaps in that book made little or no sense to her, and all that she saw were the printed letters crawling in a row like black ants.

At the command of her teacher, Asha picked up her book and presented herself to him, jittery like an ill-prepared student. Mahendra, immediately, put his arm round her waist, squeezed her tightly, and taking her book in the other hand, asked, 'Now, let me see where you are.' Asha indicated to him the point she had reached, at which Mahendra exclaimed, 'Really? Have you covered so much, indeed? Now, come and look at my progress.' Opening his textbook at a page he showed her the chapter heading, meaning that was the sum total of his progress. Asha, with wide-eyed surprise, asked, 'Then, what have you been doing all this time?' Mahendra lovingly lifted her face by her chin and said, 'I was thinking of someone, and that someone at that time was heartlessly beguiled by the antics of termites described in her printer.' She possibly could have answered back this unfounded allegation, but because of her introvert nature, she conceded defeat in this unequal game of love. Clearly, Mahendra's school did not observe the rules of conventional schools, either public or private.

Mahendra's pranks retarded instead of advancing Asha's progress. Once when Mahendra was out somewhere, Asha was trying to concentrate on her lessons. Mahendra returned unexpectedly, came stealthily from behind and closed Asha's eyes. Snatching away her book, he moaned, 'How heartless can you get? When I am away, you keep busy with your books instead of thinking of me! How cruel!'

'Is it your wish that I remain an illiterate?' Asha groaned.

Promptly retorted Mahendra, 'No, it is not, but thanks to you, I am hardly making any advance in my Studies.'

This struck Asha as ominous. 'In what way have I interfered with your preparations?'

Mahendra took her hand in his and said gravely, 'Yes, how could you ever know that? You may well be able to learn your lessons away from me, but I can't do so without you by my side.'

A most serious allegation, indeed. A natural outcome of this was a surge of tears, albeit of short duration like an autumn shower, and soon thereafter all traces vanished in the bright sunshine of the crushing grip of love.

If the teacher himself happened to be the chief obstacle to learning, how could a helpless student then wend her way through an unmarked labyrinth? Recalling her aunt's reprimand, Asha was often uneasy in her mind. Whenever she met her mother-in-law, she was gripped with an overpowering sense of discomfiture. The mother-in-law herself kept a studied distance and never asked Asha for any help, nor did she, on her own, volunteer any counsel or advice. If on occasions Asha offered her services, her mother-in-law, with an excessive show of concern, dismissed her, 'No, there is no need for you to do anything. You must not waste your time at the cost of your education.'

Watching Mahendra and Asha for some days, Annapurna's patience gave out. She told her niece, 'I can well guess the extent of progress in your education, but are you determined to stop Mahendra from qualifying as a doctor?'

The aunt's warning prodded Asha into action. She told her husband, 'I don't think the preparations for your examinations are going as well as they ought to. I am proposing to move into my aunt's room for the time being.'

What a hard unromantic decision at this tender age! A self-inflicted banishment from her own bedroom to her aunt's! Did her eyes turn misty when she announced her decision, was there a faint suspicion of quiver animating her unruly lips, did her voice falter when she spoke?

'A splendid idea,' said Mahendra, 'let us both move to *Kakima's* room. Of course, in that case *Kakima* will have to shift to our room.'

That her well-meant proposal was treated by her husband so casually annoyed her no end. Mahendra came out with another idea. He said, 'I suggest, instead, that you keep a strict vigil on me to ensure that I apply myself rigorously to my preparations.' Easily said. That this plan did not work out in practice hardly need to be iterated. Not unexpectedly, Mahendra failed his tests that year, and Asha's struggles with her primer made not much headway either.

This eccentric system of education was not calculated to run smoothly, and on top of that it was frequently interrupted by Bihari's invasions. Bihari not only disrupted their life, he often dragged Mahendra out of his room and soundly admonished him for neglecting his studies. To Asha he said by way of forewarning her, '*Bouthan*, prerequisite to proper digestion is to chew your food slowly, not gulp it down. That is what you both are doing, greedily swallowing your food wholesale, and later you will not find enough digestive palliates to help you.'

Mahendra contemptuously waved Bihari away and told Asha, 'Don't believe what he says. He is just jealous of our idyllic life.'

'Your happiness is in your hand, so enjoy it without frittering it away by exercising no restraint. And why, at any rate, invite jealousy from others?' Bihari said with feeling.

Mahendra retorted facetiously, 'Provoking jealousy in others can be rather fun, don't you know? But, Chuni, at one point of time, like an idiot, I had almost lost you to Bihari.'

Bihari went red in the face, and asked Mahendra to shut up.

Asha was not particularly well disposed to Bihari. She was well aware that early on a proposal for her marriage to Bihari was almost fixed. She also found annoying the way Bihari talked.

Rajlakshmi often unburdened her unhappiness to Bihari, and Bihari in turn tried to console her. He would tell her, 'A worm in a cocoon is not so harmful, but when as a moth it flies away, that is when the trouble starts. It is difficult to bring it back.'

Rajlaksluni flared up and raged like bush fire when told of Mahendra's failure in his examination, but it was Annapurna who bore the brunt of her fury.'

SIX

On a rain washed day, heralding the onset of the season of rains, Mahendra returned home early in the evening, pleasurably anticipating a cosy romantic tryst with his wife. He had attired himself for the occasion; he had donned a silk robe, perfumed himself liberally, and put round his neck a thick garland of fragrant jasmines. He tiptoed softly to surprise the unsuspecting Asha. As he entered the room, he was startled to find a strong breeze dribing the rain into the room through sin open window, which no one had taken care to close. The lamp had also gone out. Then, to his consternation, he discovered Asha huddled on the bed, sobbing her heart out uncontrollably.

Mahendra went quickly to her side and asked gently, 'Why, what is wrong, dearest?'

Mahendra's voice intensified her agony. After patiently listening to Asha's not altogether coherent tale, Mahendra was able to piece together the cause of Asha's distress. Annapurna, unable to take any more of Rajlakshmi's vicious persecution, had left their home and moved to a cousin's place.

Mahendra was very annoyed with the aunt. If she had to go, then why did she choose to go this evening of all evenings to upset his romantic plan? Realizing that the root of the trouble was his mother, his wrath was directed against her. Impulsively, as his nature was, he promptly decided that they would also leave home and join Annapurna, if only to teach his mother a lesson.

With great energy and a great deal of commotion, Mahendra started packing. Rajlakshmi was shrewd enough to guess his intentions. She asked him, 'And, where do you think you are going?'

Mahendra chose not to answer her, but when the question was repeated he replied curtly, 'To be with our *Kakima*.'

'You don't have to go anywhere,' said Rajlakshmi, 'I will get her back.'

She sent for her palanquin, ascended it and went to see Annapurna. With folded palms, with a show of much humility, she pleaded with

Annapurna, 'Please, sister-in-law, have mercy on me. Do forgive me.' Her manner was anything but agreeable.

Considerably flustered, Annapurna touched Rajlakshmi's feet, and in a strained voice said, 'Please, *didi*, don't make me feel guilty. Just tell me what you wish me to do, and I will gladly obey you.'

Rajlakshmi told her, more or less accusing her, 'Because you left home, my son and his wife have also decided to abandon me.' As she spoke, she broke down in a vile mood of humiliation and resentment.

Annapurna came home with Rajlakshmi. By the time she reached Mahendra's room, Ashalata's tears had dried, and Mahendra was trying in various ways to avulse her. As the rains resumed, it pleased Mahendra that, after all, his dream evening might not be totally ruined.

Annapurna charged her niece, 'Tell me, Chuni, what am I supposed to do? By your conduct you make my life difficult to live in peace here, and at the same time neither will you allow me to go away. Do I not deserve some consideration for me to live in peace?'

Asha reacted like a wounded creature. Mahencra, terribly annoyed with the aunt, grumbled, 'But what has Chuni done that you are so severe with her?'

Annapurna explained her stand. 'I could not abide such shameless conduct of a young wife of the family, and that is why I left. But, why did you, you accursed girl, get me back by making your mother-in-law so unhappy?'

Mahendra was thoroughly disgusted. He hardly could contemplate that a mother and an aunt could be of such a hindrance to their conjugal bliss!

The following day Rajlakshmi spoke to Bihari, 'I have not been back to my old home for a long time. Will you please tell Mohin that I wish to visit Barasat?'

Bihari said, 'Ma, if you have not visited your natal home for many years since, then why do you wish to go there now? I will certainly speak to Mohin, but I doubt if he will agree.'

Bihari did speak to Mahendra, and to Bihari's surprise, Mahendra took it very calmly. He said, 'It is quite a natural desire to re-visit one's birth place, but tell her that she ought not to tarry there long. The season of monsoon is not exactly salubrious in the villages.'

Bihari could hardly believe that Mahendra would so readily agree to his mother's proposed visit to Barasat. Though rather upset, he told Mahendra, 'But she ought not to go alone. I suggest you ask your wife to accompany her.'

Mahendra saw through the mild rebuke implicit in Bihari's suggestion, but demurred. 'I don't think that will be possible.'

The matter ended there, but Bihari's intrusion in their life induced in Asha an antagonism against Bihari. Bihari, on the other hand, oddly enough, derived some sort of a perverse satisfaction from Asha's indignation.

Rajlakshmi, in reality, was not overly keen to visit her ancestral home. She was merely testing water. Her primary objective was to plumb the depth of their mother and son relationship, the way boatmen, during the hot summer days when rivers are shallow, try to fathom the depth of the river by driving long poles into the water. This unexpectedly swift consent of her son to her none too serious proposal laid bare the shallowness of their current bond. The contrast between her son's attitude when Annapurna went away and the attitude when she, the mother, proposed to leave stood out sharply. There was clearly a gulf of difference, with Annapurna. Well, she pondered ruefully, Annapurna was a witch and knew how to cast a spell, while she was merely a mother. The hint was clear; she must go away, she concluded.

It took Annapurna no time to grasp what was bothering Rajlakshmi, and she did not like the shape of things. She approached Mahendra and told him, 'If *Didi* goes, then I must also leave. I cannot continue here.'

Mahendra in turn reported this to his mother. 'If *Kakima* goes, then who is going to run this house?'

Embittered with a sense of extreme jealousy, Rajlakshmi told Annapurna, 'How can you go away now? You are indispensable in this home, or else who will look after this place?'

Rajlakshmi was now too impatient to go away, and by noon the following day, she was ready to leave. It was assumed that Mahendra himself would escort his mother, but instead he had arranged for some of his employees to travel with her. Bihari did not like this at all. He asked, 'How is it that you are not going with your mother?'

Mahendra replied, somewhat put out of countenance, 'You see, with college...'

'Yes, I see,' said Bihari. 'You need not go. I will take her.'

Mahendra did not take to this kindly. On the contrary, he was most annoyed. He told Asha later, 'Bihari is increasingly going out of hand. He acts as if he is more concerned about mother than I am.'

Annapurna was obliged to stay back, and smarting under a sense of anguish, mortification and irritation, she withdrew herself. Mahendra found the aunt's aloofness sorely trying, and Asha found the situation most painful.

SEVEN

Bihari had planned to return after seeing Rajlakshmi to her old home, but after he saw the chaotic condition there he decided he could not. Her parental home had long remained uncared for; wild vegetation had engulfed the surrounding area, the water tank was shrouded with a film of green slime and howls of wild jackals were heard even during daytime. All these were driving Rajlakshmi crazy.

Bihari said to her, 'Ma, this may be your place of birth, but I can hardly describe this place as 'more glorious than the heavens' as the saying goes. I can't leave you alone here. I suggest we go back.'

Rajlakshmi was by then pretty desperate and disturbed, and was ready to fall in line with Bihari's suggestion, when unexpectedly arrived Binodini and took charge of her. Binodini, it will be recalled, was once set to marry Mahendra, and later Bihari, but none of these proposals finally came through. The man who did become her husband was congenitally afflicted with an enlarged spleen, and it was this enlarged spleen that precipitated his untimely exit from this world, almost immediately after the marriage.

Ever since, Binodini was consigned to live in that wasteland, like a wild flower, leading a joyless existence. She came to meet Rajlakshmi, her aunt-in-law, devotedly touched her feet, and before anyone knew, she took charge of looking after Rajlakshmi. She dedicated herself wholeheartedly in taking care of Rajlakshmi. She was never idle for a moment, supremely efficient in everything she did, an excellent cook, and above all, a girl of engaging temperament.

If Rajlakshmi urged her to go and eat as it was getting too late, Binodini would wave it away and, instead, sit up with a hand fan until the aunt fell asleep. If Rajlakshmi admonished her that she might fall sick if she continued to work so hard, Binodini would laugh it away and say, 'Our sort of hard and dreary life does not succumb so easily to sickness. Here you are, back at your ancestral home after such a long gap, and we here are too ill-equipped to do you adequate honour.'

Bihari, meanwhile, became quite well known and friendly with the local people. He was hugely in demand for consultation on wide ranging issues that usually trouble rural people. Some came seeking help for treatment of their illness, some sought advice on matters of litigation, some others needed assistance in composing applications, and a few soliciting job recommendations for their unemployed sons. Be it at sessions of cards or chess of elderly residents or at drinking sessions of the lower orders—he romped everywhere with equal felicity, equally welcome everywhere and by everyone.

From behind the scene, Binodini did her best to make Bihari's life agreeable—a young man on self-exile from Calcutta. On return from his various outings, Bihari invariably found someone had tidied up his room, occasionally placed a nosegay of flowers, volumes of works by Bakimchandra and Dinabandhu next to his bed. On the fly leaves of the books, he found Binodini's name neatly inscribed in practised hand.

This sort of care and attendance was virtually unexpected in a village society. When talking to Rajlakshmi, Bihari extolled Binodini's virtues. Rajlakshmi lamented, 'And, it is this girl that both of you rejected.'

Bihari agreed, with a weak smile, 'We made a mistake, but perhaps it is better to make a mistake before than after marriage.'

Whenever Rajlakshmi brought up the question of returning to Calcutta, Binodini protested most unhappily. 'Why must you go away so soon? When you were not here, I got used to my life here whatever it was, but what do I do now when you go away?'

The brooding thoughts which Rajlakshmi had been nursing in her heart, erupted, 'Only if you came to me as my daughter-in-law, you would have reigned as a queen in both my heart and my home.'

This was far too awkward for Binodini, who ran away to escape the embarrassment.

For some days, Rajlakshmi had been avidly expecting a letter from her son, desperately praying for her return. This was the very first occasion when the mother and the son had been living apart. She doubted not that this long separation must have made her son restless, looking forward to her return.

A letter did arrive from Mahendra, but it was for Bihari, not for her. Mahendra wrote, as Bihari read, 'I presume Mother must be having a great time in her old home, which she had not visited for a long time.' Rajlakshmi interpreted this as her son's brooding complaint. How can she have a great time without her darling son?

'Now, tell me, what else does he say in his letter?' the mother asked expectantly.

'Oh, nothing much,' Bihari then crumpled the letter and threw it in a corner of the room.

Rajlakshmi was most upset. Her fluttering heart raced in high gears with imaginations and apprehensions. Mahendra must be extremely cross with his mother for being away so long, and Bihari deliberately avoided telling her so not to make her unhappy. The belief that her continued absence was unbearable to the son filled her with an upsurge of motherly love. She found it possible to forgive him. He was happy with his wife, so let him be, reasoned the mother. That was all she wanted for her son, for him to be happy, and she magnanimously decided she would give her son no cause for unhappiness on account of his wife. Poor boy, he must be so miserable because he was unused to separation from the mother. This very thought opened a floodgate of tears.

Suddenly, for no apparent reason, Rajlakshmi displayed unusual concern for Bihari. 'You seem to have got into an irregular way of life. I suggest, go and have your bath now,' she told him.

Bihari found this concern of Rajlakshmi's rather odd. In any case he had no inclination to go for an immediate bath. He told Rajlakshmi, 'Do you not know that irregularity is the natural make-up of worthless fellows like me? So, why bother?'

Nevertheless, Rajlakshmi continued to press, and Bihari ultimately gave in. As soon as Bihari left the room, Rajlakshmi picked up the crumpled letter and asked Binodini to read the letter to her.

The letter contained nothing more about the mother than what Bihari had already told her. The rest of the letter was full of Asha and Asha only. Mahendra was completely absorbed in her, totally besotted with her. Binodini found the letter much too embarrassing to go on, and told Rajlakshmi, 'Really, you do not want to know all this.'

Rajlakshmi who, heart filled with love for her son, had been anxiously looking forward to what her son had written about herself, now congealed with pain. She went speechless for a while and then told Binodini, 'No, I do not.' She left the room, and Binodini carrying the letter to her room started reading it all over again.

What charm Binodini found in this letter only she knew. It was not exactly a letter that could be regarded as amusing, yet she read the letter over and over again till her eyes glowed like burning embers and her deep laboured breaths blew hot like the desert wind.

What kind of a person was Mahendra? And Asha? How intense was their love life? These speculations obsessed Binodini. Clutching the letter she sat there, deeply wrapped in her thoughts. If Bihari ever tried to retrieve Mahendra's letter that he had cast away, he certainly never found it.

The same day, in the afternoon, Annapurna landed there, unannounced, surprising everyone. Fearful of some disaster Rajlakshmi, her face ashen, stared nervously at Annapurna. Annapurna, dispelling her anxiety, said, 'Have no worry, *didi*, all is well in Calcutta.'

'Then what brings you here?' asked Rajlakshmi.

'*Didi*, I seriously feel that you should go back and take charge of your home,' Annapurna said in reply, 'I have now decided to renounce domestic life to retire at Kashi. I came here to seek your blessings. If I gave you any cause for offence, do please forgive my sins. As for your daughter-in-law,' tears rolled down as she said this, 'she is just a child who has no mother. She may have been delinquent, but she is still yours and yours only, like a daughter.' Her voice had by then choked.

Bihari came running when the news reached him. After touching Annapurna's feet, he groaned, 'But, Kakima, how can you be so heartless, deserting us in this fashion?'

Annapurna, trying to stem her tears, said, 'Do not stop me, Bihari. You will be all fine without me, I have no doubt, and for myself I see no problem.'

Bihari kept quiet for a while and then spoke, 'How could Mohin at all agree to part with you, I wonder? Most unfortunate for him.'

Unhappy with Bihari's remark she promptly rebutted him. 'You must never say so. Mohin has given me no cause for offence. To retire to Kashi is entirely my personal decision. I have a feeling that my presence in that home will bode no good for anyone.'

A little later Annapurna brought out a pair of gold bangles which she gave to Bihari. 'Give them to your wife when you marry. Tell her that they are *Kakima's* blessings for her.'

Bihari accepted *Kakima's* blessing with both hands, and with much veneration he raised the bangles to his head. He then ran out of the room with his eyes welling with tears.

When the time for departure came, Annapurna told Bihari, 'Please keep an eye on my Mohin and Asha.' She then passed a piece of paper to Rajlakshmi and told her, 'This is a deed of gift. I have gifted my share of the inheritance from my father-in-law in Mohin's favour. Please arrange to send fifteen rupees each month to me, which should be adequate for my needs.' Then she left.

EIGHT

An uncommon sense of fright gripped Asha. What did go wrong? First, her mother-in-law left home, the aunt then followed her. Was their euphoric life driving them away one after another? Was it going to be her turn next? In this deserted, empty mansion, their conjugal rapture seemed so incongruous to her.

Romantic ardour, if isolated from mundane obligations of everyday life, does not survive long and wilts like cut flowers. Signs of erosion in their idyllic existence became increasingly evident to Asha. Their uninterrupted togetherness was in danger of losing its vigour through lassitude; their bond of love tended to flag, lacking the normal familial support system. Love needed to be rooted in life's labour, otherwise ecstasy would never be profound and enduring.

Turning himself totally blind and deaf to the ominous deterioration and disorder in his home, Mahendra continued deeply engrossed in his life of romance that he vigorously pursued with all the ardours that he could command. Observing occasionally Asha's drooping fervour he would complain to her, 'I don't know what is troubling you. Your aunt has left us, so what? Why must it make you so morose? Surely, our love and our life together is all that is supreme to us, dislodging other attachments.'

Mahendra's remarks set another strain of thought in Asha's mind. Am I, she asked herself, failing fully to reciprocate my husband's love for me? She often did think of her absent mother-in-law and the absent aunt, and almost immediately tried to banish such renegade thoughts for her husband's sake.

Meanwhile, lacking a strong controlling hand and strict supervision, the domestic staff tended to relax and take life easy. One of the maidservants malingered for days; the cook on a drunken bout remained traceless. Asha was at sea, not knowing how to cope. But Mahendra was unperturbed; indeed, he rejoiced in the situation. 'What fun,' he exclaimed to his wife, 'we shall, you and I, do the cooking.'

Mahendra called for his carriage and went all the way to New

Market on a shopping spree. He had, of course, no idea at all what they needed or how much of anything was needed, and so he returned home in a joyous frame of mind bringing home basketfuls of a variety of foodstuff. Asha was out of her depth with no clue of what to do with all the foodstuff that Mahendra had collected. Mahendra's experiments with cooking continued till late in the afternoon, well past the usual time of their meal. He found an enormous load of fun in innovating many exotic but inedible dishes. Asha could not share at all in his sense of fun; on the contrary, she was dying with a feeling of mortal shame for her inadequacy and incompetence.

Utter disorder now reigned everywhere, so much so, that it was not easy to locate things that one needed. Mahendra's surgical lancet used as a vegetable cutting knife was lost in the garbage heap. On another occasion, one of his class notebooks, used as a hand fan in the kitchen, was accidentally consumed by fire. All these bizarre instances of mismanagement were a source of much amusement to Mahendra but despaired Asha. No woman can condone such wilful and wayward state of affairs in a home, and neither could Asha. To her, the conditions were nothing short of a frightful nightmare.

One evening the two of them were relaxing in their favourite corner of the covered terrace. A shower of rain had earlier washed away the clouds, and the city was basking in bright moonlight. Asha had collected a supply of flowers from the garden and was trying to string then into a garland. This was not acceptable to Mahendra, and he tried to disrupt her work, interfered with her, picked holes in her effort, and in so many ways provoked her. If Asha made any show of protest, he shut her up by putting his hand on her mouth.

A caged *koel* of a neighbour's decided just then to break into song. Both Asha and Mahendra looked up at the swinging cage that was the home of their *koel*, which never failed to answer the neighbour's *koel* back with its own dulcet music. But not this evening. Anxiously Asha said, 'What is wrong with our bird? Why is it silent?'

'Perhaps your musical voice has shamed it into silence,' Mahendra teased her.

Still much concerned, she admonished her husband. 'No clowning, please. Go and have a look at the bird.'

Mahendra reluctantly got up and brought the cage down. When he removed the cover, they found the bird dead. After Annapurna left, no one had taken any notice of the bird.

Asha was terribly upset. She lost interest in her garland and cast away the flowers. Mahendra was also unhappy but he was unwilling to ruin their evening by this unfortunate accident. He said jokingly to Asha, 'In a sense what has happened has happened for the best. When I am away in the college, this bird will no longer tease you by its needless cooing to remind you of my absence.'

Mahendra tried to take Asha in his arms, but she extricated herself. 'No, I cannot take it any longer,' she cried, 'Please go and fetch mother back, immediately. We have treated her shamefully.'

NINE

Asha moaned about her absent mother-in-law and was urging her husband to bring her back home, when they heard someone shout below stairs, 'Mohin, are you home,' and of footsteps climbing up. It was Bihari's voice. After a long break, Bihari's arrival made Mahendra unusually happy. He welcomed him back very warmly. After his marriage, Bihari's frequent visits to them appeared to Mahendra as unwarranted invasions on their privacy, but his unannounced arrival this evening came as an opportune interruption.

To Asha, Bihari's arrival came as an agreeable relief. She quickly covered her head and was about to go, when Mahendra stopped her, 'Why are you running away? It is only Bihari.'

Asha said, 'I am just going to get some refreshments for your friend.' She was actually looking forward to a pretext to do something, just to have a break from her otherwise idle existence. Asha, however, did not step out immediately. She waited for news of her mother-in-law. Till now Asha had not spoken directly to Bihari.

As soon as Bihari stepped in, he took in the scene and exclaimed, 'How devastating! Have I broken up your romantic tryst? But have no fear, *Bouthan*, I will make myself scarce immediately.'

Nudged by Asha, Mahendra asked, 'How is mother?'

'This is not the moment to ask about mothers and aunts,' Bihari shot back, 'there's time enough for that. Such a night was not made for sleep, nor for mothers and aunts.'

Mahendra forced him back as Bihari turned away to leave. Bihari impishly pleaded with Asha, '*Bouthan*, mea not culpa. Mahendra has forced me back. If it is wrong then Mahendra is at fault, and I ought to be spared your curses.'

It had always irritated Asha that she could never answer Bihari back, and Bihari, well aware of this weakness of Asha, deliberately teased her.

Suddenly, Bihari observed, 'As I came up I could not help noticing the scandalous state of your home. Don't you think it is time for you to ask your mother to return?'

Mahendra replied, 'Yes, I agree with you, and we are waiting for her return.'

'In that case why do you not write telling her to do so? It will not take much time to pen a few lines, and this will make her extremely happy. *Bouthan*, can you spare Mahendra for a few minutes, I beg of you?'

Asha left, quite irate, almost tearful. Mahendra commented, 'It must have been an ill-starred moment when the two of you first met. Neither of you get along with each other, skirmishes always.'

Bihari said, 'All your life you have been thoroughly spoilt by your mother, and now you are being ruined by your wife. I cannot always hold myself in check and speak out in protest.'

'How does it help anyone?' Mahendra asked.

'Not you perhaps, but does me in some ways,' Bihari replied laconically.

TEN

Bihari succeeded in extracting a letter from Mahendra to his mother, and armed with this letter he left to bring Rajlakshmi back. It was not easy to fool Rajlakshmi, who clearly saw through Bihari's hand in it. Nevertheless, she decided to return as she had been dying to do, and she took Binodini with her.

The untidy and chaotic state of her home that greeted her on her arrival added to her bitterness towards her daughter-in-law. But a great surprise awaited her—a completely transformed daughter-in-law. Asha, an altogether new person, was constantly at the side of the mother in law, almost like her shadow, helping her in all household chores, offering to assist when not even asked. Rajlakshmi did not take all this very kindly and often discouraged her by asking her to desist, 'Leave that alone. Why try to do something that you know nothing about? You will only spoil it.'

Rajlakshmi, in fact, was wary about her son. He was probably cursing his mother that with her return he had lost his wife, who was kept engaged by the mother in all manners of domestic work. She would fare unfavourably, she contemplated, in contrast with Annapurna who, during her regime, made no demands on Asha, and the two were left undisturbed. There was no point, she decided, in courting the son's displeasure.

These days, if Mahendra sent for his wife, Asha hesitated, but Rajlakshmi admonished her, 'Can't you hear that Mahendra is calling you? Too spoilt by your husband, that is your problem. Go now, no point in worrying about the cooking.'

Back once more to the make believe pretence with slates and pencils and primers! Usual lovers' tiff on baseless mutual allegations! Violent and pointless arguments on whose love was the more intense! Their wrangles often reached the heights of absurdities. They tried to shake off the encroaching ennui and weariness, the inevitable outcome of over-indulgence in their passion. There was little or no impetus to change their way of life even when their togetherness did not always bring them any real joy. Ecstasy, alas, seldom endures, but a bond, which has become a second nature, is too formidable to break.

Just at this critical point appeared Binodini in their life. Binodini herself accosted Asha, and warmly embracing her said, 'Let your good fortune smile on you forever, but must you not ever look at me just because my life is dogged by misfortune?'

Raised as an orphan since she was a child, Asha grew into an introvert. By nature she was always too nervous of being scorned by others. When Binodini, with her impeccable good looks and her flaming youth, appeared in their home, Asha was too diffident to get to know her.

Gradually, Asha came to discover the many accomplishments of Binodini. Her dealings with Rajlakshmi were on unbelievably free and easy terms, and Rajlakshmi, perhaps deliberately to put down Asha, displayed a great deal of regard for Binodini and heaped encomiums on her. Binodini was adept in every sort of housework, leadership was instinctive to her, she had no qualms ordering the servants about, setting their tasks, and disciplining them when necessary. Asha considered herself despicably insignificant in contrast to Binodini.

When this uniquely superlative Binodini on her own came to seek her friendship, Asha, despite her diffidence, was exultant, and like the magic tree, her love for Binodini took roots, sprouted leaves and blossomed instantaneously. Flushed with happiness Asha suggested they must give their friendship a name.

Binodini smiled indulgently, 'What sort of a name?' Asha thought of a variety of names, then popular for bonding women, but Binodini rejected all of them. 'These names are too old fashioned. These adorable names have fallen into disfavour.'

'Then, what would you suggest?' Asha asked.

Bindoni smiled once again and proposed, 'How about *Chokher Bali*—a mote in the eye?'

Asha would have preferred a more pleasant sounding term for their friendship, but acceded to Binodini's proposal of this odd but amusing appellation. She called Binodini sweetly, '*Chokher Bali*,' and went into a spate of childlike giggles.

ELEVEN

Asha badly needed a female friend and companion. Celebration of love lacks repletion when confined to two partners only. Happiness needs to be shared. Binodini on her own part avidly drank in the love tales of a young bride. Her arid and thirsty heart vicariously sought to quench her unsatisfied passion like an inebriate, imbibing strong and heady wine. The drink went into her head and incited her body.

In the afternoons, it is quiet all round when everyone rests. Rajlakshmi retires to her room, the domestic staff after the morning's labour are off duty, Mahendra is away at college when persuaded to do so, an odd solitary kite occasionally flies round the sun-drenched sky with its shrill calls piercing the air. That is the time for Asha to go into her own sanctum, where she lies flat on her bed, with her long tresses fanning out. And, it is also the time for Binodini to join Asha, when she rests on her stomach hugging a cushion. It is the time for Binodini to listen absorbingly to the chronicles of Asha's amours. Her ears would turn purple with excitement and her breathing heavy and rapid.

Binodini was never satisfied. She pumped Asha again and again for the most trivial of details, never tired of repetitions of the same tales, and when there was nothing more to say, her supercharged imagination explored absurdities. 'Tell me, if something like this had happened, what would you have done?' or 'Assuming it did not go like this, then how would you have coped with it?' and so on and so forth. She held Asha captive with such wild fancies, which thrilled Asha, as they also helped in giving a new lease of life to their intimate exchanges.

Binodini one day caught Asha unawares when she popped the question, 'Now, *Chokher Bali*, suppose you were married to Bihari, then ...?'

'No, no, you must never say this,' Asha quickly protested, 'it is most embarrassing for me. But you, yourself, could have been married to Bihari. I believe there was some such proposal once.'

'Come off it,' Binodini reacted, 'I had so many other proposals.

So what, that I did not get married to Bihari? I am fine as it is.'

Asha did not agree. How could Binodini be happy with her present life? 'Just imagine if my husband had married you. It did almost happen, did it not?' she blurted out innocently.

Yes, that could have happened, and why did it not? This room, this bed, which now belonged to Asha, could have been rightfully hers, and Binodini never allowed herself to forget this loss. Today she was a mere guest, and tomorrow she might be asked to leave!

For some days now, Binodini had offered to dress Asha's hair, which she did with great artistry. She would also deck Asha out in her fineries before dispatching her to meet her husband. Binodini's own subconscious fantasizing followed in the wake of Asha's footsteps to her tryst with her besotted husband. There were days when Binodini intentionally held Asha back. 'Please, be with me a little longer. After all, your husband is not running away. In any case, he is not the elusive deer of the Ramayama, he is your captive creature.'

Mahendra fumed. 'Your friend seems to be permanently settled here. When does she intend to go back to her own place?'

Asha rose in support of her friend. 'Please don't be so hard on her. You have no idea how very interested she is to talk about you. She takes such pains over my toilet before I come to you.'

Rajlakshmi had assiduously discouraged Asha to get involved in chores in the house, but Binodini convinced Rajlakshmi to change her mind. Binodini worked tirelessly the whole day, and kept Asha engaged with her, giving her no respite. She devised a routine of work, which made it almost impossible for Asha to get away. The thought of Asha's husband impatiently waiting for her gave Binodini a diabolical pleasure.

Asha anxiously pleaded with Binodini, 'Let me go now, or my husband will be most annoyed.' Binodini still detained her. 'Only a few more minutes, let us just finish this job, it won't take much time.' A little later a restless Asha would say, 'I must go now, or else my husband will be really very cross.' Binodini, much amused, would tease her, 'How does it matter? Love turns bland if not seasoned with a touch of pique, like cooking without spices.'

Binodini assuredly knew what spices could do. Her whole body was feverish, and all her nerves tingled with desire. Her eyes emitted fiery sparks. This happy home with such a loving husband, all these could have been mine, she contemplated. My husband would have been my slave, and I would have reigned as a queen. It would have been altogether another world, and he another kind of a man. And, what has he instead? An ignoramus juvenile in my place!

She would impulsively embrace Asha and ask her, 'Tell me, dear *Chokher Bali*, what did you talk, the two of you, last night? I get so engrossed when you speak to me about your tender passion, that I forget myself and go into another world.'

TWELVE

Mahendra confronted his mother with a great deal of annoyance, 'I cannot understand, Mother, why are you keeping a young widow in our home? She does not belong to our family. It is fraught with risk. I must say I don't like it all.'

Rajlakshmi replied, 'But she is not a stranger, she is the widow of my nephew Bipin.'

Mahendra insisted, 'No Mother, I cannot approve of this. In my view it is not right to keep her with us.'

Rajlakshmi knew well that it would be difficult to go against her son. She decided to seek Bihari's help. 'Bihari, my son, please will you reason with Mahendra. It is because of Bipin's widow that in this advanced years of my life I enjoy some comforts. She may not be a near relation, but the truth is that I have never received so much care and attention in my life, certainly not from any of our near relations.'

Bihari immediately went to see Mahendra and asked him, 'Mohin, have you given any thought to Binodini?'

Mahendra gave a dry laugh. 'Have I given any thought to Binodini? A jolly good question. In fact, you can say I am literally obsessed with her thoughts so much so that she has driven away everything else from my mind.'

Behind her veil, Asha made a gesture of silent admonition to her husband.

'Really, is it so?' Bihari said, 'Is it another enactment of Bankimchandra's novel *Bishabriksha*?'

'Absolutely,' said Mahendra, 'Chuni can't wait to get rid of her.'

Another silent admonition from behind the veil!

Bihari commented, 'Even if you get rid of her she may still return. Better marry off the widow. The poison fang will then be de-venomed permanently.'

'Wasn't the widow Kunda of *Bishabriksha* also re-married?' reminded Mahendra.

'Leave aside *Bishabriksha* for the moment,' Bihari told Mahendra,

'I have also worries about Binodini. She really cannot stay here all her life; equally, it will be unfair to send her back to that god-forsaken habitat which I have seen. Banishment for life to that wilderness will, indeed, be a severe punishment for her.'

Binodini had not so far, as the custom was, showed up in Mahendra' presence, but Bihari had seen her. Bihari was clear in his mind that a woman like Binodini ought not be sent away to her old place, but he was at the same time deeply nervous that a flame that illuminates a home could also burn it down.

Mahendra treated this apprehension of Bihari as a huge joke, and pulled his legs in good fun. Bihari outwardly joined in this fun, but deep inside his consciousness he knew well that this woman could not be treated as a plaything, and that she could also not be brushed aside.

Rajlakshmi, who had been watching Binodini, cautioned her, 'Look child, don't get too involved with my daughter-in-law. Your background is of a rural culture, you have no idea about the ways of the modern society. You are a person of intelligence, so I need not tell you more. I am sure you will watch your steps.'

Thereafter, Binodini punctiliously kept herself aloof from Asha. To her she said, 'Look, I am a small fry, a person of inferior status, who has to conduct herself carefully to avoid creating unpleasant situations.'

Asha pleaded with her, cried her heart out, but Binodini remained firm in her decision. Asha was dying to unbosom her tender tales but Binodini denied her that pleasure.

A low depression was meanwhile making inroads into the conjugal life. Mahendra's once delirious embraces had perhaps gone a trifle slack, and there was possibly a touch of weariness in his adoring eyes. The wild and unbridled torrid days that he earlier found so exciting now appeared to him relatively tiresome. Asha's ineptness in domestic chores of which he was so long unconcerned was beginning to annoy him, though he did not tell her so. Asha herself was also beginning to grasp the truth. Their earlier frenzied love life was losing its charm, and a chord of disharmony appeared to mar Mahendra's ardour—an ardour that, seemingly now, was contrived and not real.

Asha was in a quandary. Her feminine instinct told her to leave Mahendra alone, and she tried to do that as much as she could do decently. But where then could she find refuge except with Binodini?

Mahendra now woke up to the realities of life and began to take a renewed interest in his studies. He dusted his medical texts and called for his college uniforms to be aired and pressed.

THIRTEEN

When Binodini refused to yield to Asha's many pleadings to resume their relationship, Asha conceived a stratagem. She reproached Binodini, 'Tell me, what prevents you from meeting my husband? Why do you keep eluding him?'

'Because it is not the done thing,' Binodini said firmly.

'Why? I understand from my mother-in-law that you are not at all unrelated to us,' said Asha.

Binodini turned a little sombre. 'Look, it is all illusory distinctions that we try to make between who is your own and who is not. It is all a question of attitude and belief. A person who considers himself to be your own becomes one even though not related. Conversely, even a close relation ceases to be one if he distances himself.'

Asha had no reply to this. She knew that her husband was most unfortunately ill-disposed towards Binodini, was blatantly unfair to her, and her presence at home irritated him. The same evening she insisted that her husband should meet and get to know her *Chokher Bali*.

'Rather brave of you to suggest this,' said Mahendra displaying total disinterest.

'Why? What is there to be afraid of?' Asha asked.

The way you go ecstatic over your friend's looks, I don't think it will be very safe for me to know her,' said Mahendra in jest.

'I'll take care of that,' Asha said, 'but jokes apart, tell me, would you agree to meet her or not?'

Not that Mahendra was not keen to meet Binodini; in fact, just the contrary. He, however, was afraid that his eagerness could be misunderstood as an improper curiosity. His ideas of what was morally right and what was not were rigid and orthodox. His earlier reluctance to marry stemmed from the same moral consideration that his marriage might dilute his mother's authority at home. Similarly, after his marriage he was meticulous in protecting his relationship with Asha by shutting out thoughts of any other woman. It was a matter of considerable gratification to him that his love for Asha was absolute and unsullied.

He regarded his friendship with Bihari on a similar footing. There was no place in his heart of a second friendship of the same intimacy. He went to the length of humbling anyone who attempted to get close to him. To Bihari, he articulated his profound disdain for such tiresome characters. If Bihari was critical of his insensitive attitude, his reply invariably was, 'I know you make friends easily, but I am not made like that. I confess I am choosy where friendship is concerned.'

When Mahendra discovered that he was getting increasingly curious about this stranger, he felt correspondingly small by his own moral standards. This was beginning to trouble him so much that he started putting pressure on his mother to get rid of Binodini.

'No, please don't insist,' he told Asha, 'and in any case I would hardly have any time to spare for your friend. My studies will keep me occupied a great deal, and when I am free, I prefer to be with you. So, where will you fit in your friend?'

Asha assured him, 'Have no fear. No one will interrupt your studies. I will share my time with her.'

Mahendra laughed, 'You may but why should I allow it?'

Mahendra, so it would seem, resented Asha's affection for Binodini. He detected in this a threat to Asha's attachment to him. He bragged to his wife, 'The love that you have for me is not so single minded as mine for you,' which Asha, of course, never conceded, leading to disputes and dissentions, tiffs and tussles, ultimately leaving Asha in tears. But then, Asha never could best her husband in exchanges.

Mahendra took pride in the fact that he never wished to cede even the minutest of space to Binodini in their life, but Asha found such conceit disagreeable. Nevertheless, she yielded to her husband and in desperation told him, 'Fair enough, but the least you can do for me is to meet her just once for my sake.'

Having won the battle of demonstrating to Asha that his love was comparatively superior and unswerving, he finally condescended to meet Binodini, with the rider, 'Do take care that your friend has the discretion of not disturbing us too often.' The following morning Asha saw Binodini and gave her a fond hug. Binodini exclaimed, 'I say, what's up? How is it that the little bird has flown its celestial coop and landed amongst the ordinary mortals?'

Asha said, 'Spare me your poetical allusions. It is like casting pearls before the swine. Rather, save them for someone who can give you an appreciative response.'

'Really? Who is this great person of discernment?' asked Binodini with a twinkle in her eyes.

'None other than my husband, and in a way he also happens to be your brother-in-law. I am serious, not joking. He is really keen to meet you.'

So, the summons was at the wife's behest. That much was quite clear to Binodini, but she was not going to make herself cheap and jump at the opportunity. Asha's persistence failed to persuade Binodini, and poor Asha lost face with her husband.

Binodini's refusal infuriated Mahendra. By refusing to see him, she was treating Mahendra like any other male stranger, which Mahendra felt was latterly ridiculous. He, however, found comfort in the thought that had it been any other male, he would have invented excuses to get to know her. Had she pondered, she would have known how different a person he was from the usual run of men.

On her part Binodini had also cause for grievance against Mahendra. Was it not strange that he never expressed any wish to meet her although she had been in his home for quite some time? She had not failed to observe that he pompously avoided visiting his mother if she happened to be in the mother's room. What was behind this calculated disdain? Was she not a live human being? Why treat her like an inanimate object? She was also a woman, and had he cultivated her, he would have appreciated the gulf of difference between herself and his adorable Chuni!

A desperate Asha finally had a suggestion for her husband, 'I will invite her to our room on the pretext that you are away in college, and then you will return unexpectedly. That will teach her a lesson.'

'What is her heinous offence that you sentence her to this harsh punishment?' commented Mahendra dryly.

'I am thoroughly disgusted with her,' Asha said. 'How can she refuse to meet you? I am determined to break her back.'

Mahendra demurred. 'But I am not dying to meet your dear friend, and in any case certainly not clandestinely.'

Asha seized her husband's hand and pleaded earnestly with him, 'Please, for my sake, do agree to my request, even if it is just for once only. I want to deflate her vanity, and thereafter it is up to you to do whatever you wish to.'

Mahendra was still unresponsive when Asha repeated her plea, 'Please, just for once.'

Mahendra's fervour to meet Binodini was all this while gathering momentum. He finally gave in, but not before showing an excessive degree of disinterest.

On a tranquil autumn afternoon, in Asha's room, Binodini was teaching her how to knit carpet slippers. Asha, distracted by her constant watchful glances towards the door, kept dropping stitches, revealing her prodigious ineptness. At the end of her patience, Binodini snatched away from Asha the unfinished knitting and told her, 'I don't think you can do it. Anyway, I must run now, too much to do.'

'Please, give me some more time. I promise you I shan't make anymore mistakes,' Asha appealed to Binodini anxiously, and resumed her knitting.

Soon thereafter, in walked Mahendra, on tiptoe, through a door behind Binodini. Asha, who was expecting him, broke into a grin without lifting her face. Binodini noticed this and asked, 'What amuses you?' Unable to restrain herself any longer, Asha flung away the knitting and declared, 'You are quite right, this work is not for me,' and then unexpectedly hugging Binodini, went into hysterics.

Puzzled by Asha's restlessness and her odd manners, Binodini did wonder if something was in the air, when Mahendra silently came in and stood behind her. Surprisingly, she fell into this amateurish trap of Asha like a simpleton.

Mahendra broke the silence. 'Can I not share in the joke that makes you so merry?'

Binodini, startled, tried hastily to cover her head but Asha restrained her. Unlike other women, Binodini did not resist Asha.

Mahendra sheepishly smiled and said, 'Either you stay on and I go out, or both of us remain here.'

'I will stay on since you ask me but don't please curse me later,' said Binodini, very calm.

Mahendra took her up. 'Yes, I probably will, but that will be a spell to immobilize you here.'

Binodini laughed. 'Fine, I am not exactly terrified because your curse or spell is unlikely to work. In any case, my time is up, I must leave now.' Asha held her back, 'For heaven's sake, tarry a little longer.'

FOURTEEN

'Be honest. Tell me what do you think of my *Chokher Bali*?' Asha anxiously asked her husband.

'Not too bad, not too bad,' was Mahendra's laconic answer. 'Is that all? Clearly, you don't seem to like anyone.' Asha was decidedly aggrieved.

'Except one particular person,' Mahendra solemnly observed.

'Never mind,' Asha said hopefully, 'when you get to know her better, we will see if you like her or not.'

'Get to know her better?' Mahendra said with apparent consternation, 'Surely, we are not going to carry on in this fashion?

'And, why not?' Asha replied. 'Do you not believe in observing decorum? For the sake of decorum, people do talk to each other. If you cut her off after your first meeting, how do you think my *Chokher Bali* would feel? You really are a most peculiar person. Anyone else in your place would die to meet someone like my friend, but the way you behave as if she were a monster.'

It tickled Mahendra enormously that his wife regarded him so superior to other men. He said, 'Agreed. I will not refuse to speak to her, but equally, there is no need to go headlong about it. After all, I am not running away, and from the present outlook, it does not appear your friend has any plans to leave us soon, in which case we cannot avoid corning across each other. But have no concern, I assure you. Your husband has sense enough to observe what you call decorum.'

Mahendra firmly believed that Binodini on her own would find excuses to meet him, but she proved him wrong. She made herself absolutely scarce; they did not even meet accidentally.

Mahendra deliberately never raised the topic of Binodini with his wife to avoid revealing his mounting frustration. His suppressed desire to meet Binodini progressively incited his yearning, and to cap it Binodini's indifference added fuel to the fire of his passion.

Soon after their meeting, Mahendra asked Asha, 'You never told me how your friend viewed your worthless husband?' Mahendra had confidently expected a glowing account from Binodini of their meeting, but with no such report forthcoming, he was likable to hold back his patience and playfully brought up this topic.

Asha also felt awkward that her friend had said nothing at all, and that was a cause of her own unhappiness. She told her husband, 'Give her some time. The two of you met very briefly, hardly talked to each other. I am sure she will have something to say when both of you come to know each other better.'

This answer considerably dampened Mahendra's spirit, and it became even more painful for him to remain cool towards Binodini. Bihari walked in while they were talking, and since he had no idea what they were talking about, he teased them, 'Another lovers' tiff, is it? What is it about?'

Mahendra replied, 'Just listen to this funny tale. Your *Bouthan* has a friend here, Kumudini or Promodini or some such name, and they call each other by another absurd name. Asha insists that I have to be her friend as well and assume an equally absurd name. Can you believe it?'

Beneath her veil Asha silently demonstrated her displeasure.

Bihari looked at them and laughed. He said, '*Bouthan*, the signs are ominous. All that he says now is just to mislead you. I have seen your *Chokher Bali*, and I can swear that if I chance to meet her often I shall not regard that as tragic. All these protests by Mohin look very suspicious, I must say.'

To Asha this inane statement of Bihari sounded as a renewed assurance of the contrast between her noble-minded husband and Bihari.

There was a time when Mahendra actively pursued the hobby of photography. He suddenly decided to resume this hobby. He brought out his old camera, had it cleaned and bought plates and chemicals. With a burst of energy he set about taking pictures of everyone including the domestic staff.

Asha suggested that Mahendra should take a picture of Binodini. Mahendra readily assented, but Binodini firmly declined to be photographed. Asha decided to trick her friend though she knew it would not be easy to deceive Binodini, who could always uncannily read Asha's moves.

Asha's plan was to invite Binodini to her room and then induce her to take a siesta, when Mahendra would walk in and surreptitiously take her photograph. Binodini did not normally nap in the afternoons, but strangely enough this afternoon she felt extremely drowsy and fell asleep. Covered with a red shawl and her face turned to the window she slept resting on her hand, presenting such an irresistible picture, that Mahendra thought she had deliberately assumed this pose to be photographed.

Mahendra tiptoed into the room with his camera. He studied Binodini from many angles to decide which composition would be right. In the interest of artistic perfection he even rearranged discretely some loose strands of her locks. Then, he whispered to his wife, 'Just shift the shawl a little to the left near her feet.'

Inept as she was, Asha whispered back, 'No, I dare not. I may wake her up. Better do it yourself.' Mahendra happily obliged.

Mahendra inserted the photographic plate inside the camera and was almost ready to click, when unexpectedly Binodini woke up and quickly sat up. Asha burst out in laughter, but Binodini was terribly annoyed. Her eyes blazing and flashing fire, she told Mahendra, 'This is most improper.'

Mahendra conceded. He said, 'Absolutely, you are quite right. But what will happen to me now? I was trying to steal, but have not succeeded in gaining any stolen goods. Please suspend your judgment after my misdeeds are over.'

Asha added her own persuasions. Finally, pictures were taken. The first shot apparently did not turn out well. The photographer insisted on further tries the next day. Binodini could not refuse the proposal of the two friends being photographed together as a permanent token of their friendship. Binodini declared that this must be absolutely the last picture, at which declaration, the photographer committed intentional mistakes. So, further sessions were needed; and thus through the process of such repeated sessions, the acquaintance between Binodini and Mahendra deepened.

FIFTEEN

Dying embers find new life when stirred. Similarly, the fading ardour of the newly married Asha and Mahendra received a new lease of life by the appearance of a third force in their midst. Asha, sadly, lacked a sense of wit and humour, but Binodini was abundantly endowed with this talent. Not surprisingly, Asha found a comfortable refuge in Binodini.

The frenzied love life of Asha and Mahendra tended to flag through reckless excesses. The symphony of their love had started on a high note instead of gradually building it to a crescendo, and unknown to them their marriage was eroding at its root. A sense of fatigue follows a hangover, and that fatigue then needs a new intoxicant. Asha could in no way provide this intoxicant. Just at this critical point in came Binodini who helped Asha with fresh and bracing recipes to revive Mahendra's spirit, much to Asha's relief.

Asha herself was now a happy creature. When Mahendra and Binodini engaged in light banters Asha would join in the fun with her hearty laugh. When in games of card Mahendra cheated her, Asha complained to Binodini to seek redress. When Mahendra teased her or made adverse comments, she expected Binodini to reply suitably on her behalf. The twosome thus became threesome.

In spite of her changed life, Binodini never neglected her regular domestic assignments. The kitchen, the housework, taking care of Rajlakshmi, everything went on like clockwork. It was only when all her work was over that Binodini participated in their evening get-together. If ever Binodini was late, Mahendra got irritated, 'It seems you are determined to spoil the servants by doing everything yourself.' Binodini's routine reply was, 'I prefer it this way.'

Binodini thus was getting increasingly involved in their life. There were days when she chased Mahendra. 'Isn't it time for you to get ready for your college?' Mahendra looked desperately at the sky, 'Looks like rain...'

'No excuses please, get ready. Your carriage is waiting. You can't bunk college.'

'But I had left instructions that I would not need the carriage this morning.'

'I countermanded it,' she said calmly and brought out Mahendra's college outfit.

Mahendra, outsmarted, moaned, 'You should have born a Rajput, whose women attired their men in armour before sending them out to the battlefield.'

Binodini with her firm hands guided back Mahendra to attend to his studies and stopped him playing truant from college. Irresponsible relaxations during the day were strongly discouraged during her regime, and so Mahendra looked forward to the evenings like a starved soul.

There had been days earlier when food was not ready in time, and on that pretext Mahendra merrily bunked college. With Binodini in command, his meal was unfailingly ready in time, and his carriage drawn at the door to take him to college as soon as he finished eating. His clothes presently were well laundered and pressed. He did not have to rummage through his wardrobe to find the right clothes.

In the beginning, Binodini used mildly to censure Asha, albeit benignly, for the chaotic state of their room. Mahendra joined her with affectionate indulgence at the poor girl's helpless ineptitude. In the end, for the sake of her love for her friend, Binodini took upon herself the complete charge of their room, which now looked totally transformed—considerably more bright and cheerful.

If Asha struggled helplessly with a missing button from Mahendra's jacket, Binodini would rush in to Asha's rescue and quickly stitch on a new button. If on occasions something went wrong with Mahendra's food leaving Asha clueless to deal with it, Binodini would run to the kitchen and dish up fresh supplies in no time, confounding Asha.

Mahendra could now see Binodini's increasingly active hands behind everything that concerned him—his food, his clothes, his work, his leisure. Woollen slippers and woollen scarves, knitted by Binodini, gave Mahendra the pleasurable feeling of a tender association with her. As for Asha, Binodini now took over her toilet, and dressed elegantly and perfumed delicately she went to meet her husband in the evenings. Binodini's repressed yearnings, in effect, found a proxy in

Asha, vicariously sharing in her ecstatic bliss in union with her husband!

Bihari was less frequently seen these days at Mahendra's place. He was no longer the favoured friend that he once was. Bihari wrote to Mahendra inviting himself to lunch the following Sunday to relish his mother's cooking. To Mahendra this spelt an unwarranted interference with his life. He did not wish his Sunday to be ruined, and so he wrote back saying he would be away from home that Sunday on some special assignment.

Bihari did not come for lunch but decided to call at Mahendra's home later in the afternoon. On being told that Mahendra was home, Bihari made straight for his room, announcing himself loudly from the staircase. Caught napping, Mahendra pleaded a nasty headache. Worried about her husband, poor Asha anxiously looked at Binodini seeking help. Binodini, of course, had seen through the game, but deliberately displayed some concern and suggested, 'Better lie down. I will presently get some eau de cologne.'

Mahendra hastily said, 'There's no need for that.' Binodini paid no heed, went out and returned almost immediately with a cup of iced water mixed with eau de cologne. She dipped a handkerchief into the cup and gave it to Asha, telling her to stretch it tightly on Mahendra's brow. Mahendra continued to protest, and Bihari watched this drama with suppressed amusement. Mahendra, meanwhile, was pretty pleased with himself that Bihari was there to see how important a person he was, being looked after by two women!

Asha, made nervous by Bihari's presence, fumbled with the handkerchief. Binodini came to her help. She neatly stretched the handkerchief on Mahendra's brow, and wetting another piece of cloth with the eau de cologne used it as a drip to keep the handkerchief damp.

Binodini asked Mahendra, 'Is there any relief?'

Binodini chanced to look at Bihari, and was confronted by a pair of impishly amused eyes. She understood instinctively that it wouldn't be easy to throw dust in his eyes. He recognized the entire episode was a play-acting as it indeed was. Nothing escaped his eyes.

Bihari remarked playfully, 'But, *Bouthan*, I am afraid your sort of nursing will only aggravate his malady, not cure it.'

'But how would I know, being an ignorant woman? Is that what your medical science says?' asked Binodini, most innocent.

'Yes it does, indeed,' said Bihari. 'I am almost tempted by your devoted nursing to catch a headache, but sadly I shall have to get well on my own without the benefit of any tender care. Not so fortunate as Mahendra.'

Binodini threw away the wet piece of cloth she had in her hand, and said, 'That lets me out then. Perhaps, it is better that a medically knowledgeable friend takes in hand the treatment of his friend.'

Bihari found exceedingly distasteful what he saw. Of late, he had been fairly occupied with his own studies and was not able to look up his friend. He had, therefore, no idea that in the meantime the three of them—Binodini, Asha and Mahendra—had tied themselves up in a vicious knot. For the first time, on this occasion, both Binodini and Bihari were able to take a measure of each other.

Bihari said, a little gruffly, 'Maybe, you are right. I will treat my friend. I caused this headache and I will remove it. Please, don't uselessly waste your precious eau de cologne.' He looked at Asha and said, 'It is better to prevent a sickness than try to cure it.'

SIXTEEN

Bihari was deeply disturbed when he left. It would not be morally right to allow these three to carry on in this fashion. He must somehow intervene, he decided, knowing too well that he would not be welcome. Even so, he must.

Bihari did not wait for any invitation, and on his own mounted as assault on Mahendra's citadel. To Binodini he said, '*Bouthan*, you see this young man,' pointing to Mahendra, 'he has been thoroughly spoilt by his mother, by his friend, namely, myself, and now by his wife. Do not, I beseech you, join this tribe, do something new, carve out a new path.'

'Meaning thereby?' Mahendra was curious.

'Meaning?' Bihari shot back. 'Take for instance someone like me about whom no one had ever bothered...'

'Ah, I see. You also wish to be spoilt, is that so? But, my friend, it is not all that easy. Mere appeals to be spoilt will take you nowhere!

'That requires some special acumen,' Binodini smiled and looked at Bihari when she said this.

'Perhaps so,' Bihari promptly came back. 'I may lack this particular attribute, but your own expertise, I suppose, can still do the trick. Why do you not indulge me for a change?'

'Because it is not possible to spoil one who is prepared to be spoilt,' observed Binodini solemnly, 'in fact, one must be caught totally unawares. But I say, my *Chokher Bali*, why do you not take charge of this brother-in-law of yours to spoil him?'

Asha protested by giving her a shove. Bihari ignored this badinage. It suddenly occurred to Binodini that Bihari was apparently very sensitive where Asha was concerned. He was evidently very respectful towards Asha, but gave her, Binodini, hardly any weight. This to Binodini was most offensive.

Binodini spoke to Asha once again. 'Look, this brother-in-law of your's is too anxious to be pandered by you. He is merely using me as a pretext. Do be kind to him.'

Asha was getting increasingly irked by Binodini's talk, and so was Bihari, but he pretended to laugh it off. He said, 'When it comes to me, you propose to palm it off to another, but when it is Mahendra, you prefer to deal directly with him.'

The danger signal was up, that was quite evident to Binodini. One must be wary of Bihari, he was out to wreck her life.

Bihari was also getting on Mahendra's nerves. He spoke sharply to Bihari, 'I don't need to get into any deals with anyone. I am happy as it is.'

Commented Bihari, 'You may not seek for deals yourself, but one never knows how the tides of fortune flood the favourite even if fortuitously.'

Binodini chaffed Bihari, 'Aha, so do I take it that you are anticipating some tide of fortune to turn your way, and if so, from which direction do you think this tide will flow?' She gave Asha a prod as she said this, and Asha, now utterly disgusted with Binodini, left the room. Bihari, thus outsmarted, went sullenly quiet. As he was about to leave, Binodini stopped him, 'Please don't be so desolate; I'll presently send Asha back here.'

Binodini's departure added to Mahendra's displeasure. Bihari noticed it but he allowed his repressed feelings to erupt. He warned his friend. 'If you wish to ruin yourself, do so by all means. This will not surprise me, because I happen to know your nature. All I am asking you is that, for heaven's sake, do not ruin the life of a simple hearted young woman who clings to you with utter devotion and love. I repeat, do not ruin her life.' Bihari's voice almost choked when he spoke.

Mahendra was furious. 'Talk plainly Bihari, not in riddles. I have no idea what you are hinting at.'

And Bihari, no less furious, said, 'Fair enough, I'll speak plainly. What I am trying to tell you is that Binodini is leading you by the nose, and you, in your ignorance, are following her headlong to your disgrace and ruin.'

Mahendra, now extremely angry, shouted at Bihari, 'A tissue of lies; that is what it is. If you chose to cast aspersions in this manner on a decent woman, then in my view you ought to keep yourself away from our inner quarters.'

Before Bihari could react to this, Binodini came in with a plate of refreshments. A surprised Bihari said, 'What is this in aid of? But I am not really hungry at the moment.'

There was no deterring Binodini, who insisted. 'No way, you have to have something.'

Bihari said in fun, 'Ah! Do I take it that my supplication has found favour, and hence this cordial treatment?'

With an enigmatic smile Binodini said, 'As a brother-in-law, you have your rightful claims, so why should you be a supplicant? All you have to do is to grab your dues. Now, what do you say to this?' The question was to Mahendra, who by now was so indignant that he went speechless.

Binodini noticed that Bihari was not eating at all. 'What is your problem?' she asked. 'Are you just displeased or is it some sort of shyness that holds you back? Or perhaps, I should get someone back here.'

Bihari said hastily, 'There is no need for it. What I have is more than enough.'

'Jesting again, are you?' said Binodini, 'I am afraid, I am no match for you when it comes to talking. Even tempting you with refreshments can't shut you up.'

Later the same night Asha complained to Mahendra against Bihari, about her displeasure with him. Mahendra for once agreed with her instead of dismissing her allegations as he used to do before.

Early the following morning Mahendra called on Bihari at his home. He told Bihari, 'I have noticed that you upset Binodini whenever you meet her. Do remember, she is not a member of our family.'

'Is that so?' Bihari was genuinely surprised. 'Then I have committed a grievous breach of conduct. If I do indeed annoy her, then I must make it a point not to see her.'

Mahendra was relieved that this disagreeable task was so easily resolved. Mahendra, in truth, held Bihari in some awe.

The very same day Bihari went to Mahendra's place. When he saw Binodini, he told her, 'Mahendra tells me that you do not approve of my meeting you. I am here specifically to ask you to forgive me if I have given you any cause for offence. I am truly penitent.'

Binodini was dismayed. 'Not at all. I do not know what your friend told you. I am just a temporary visitor here, so why must you stop coming here because of me? Had I known I could cause so much trouble, I would not have come here at all.' She left abruptly, trying to check her tears.

Bihari was not now sure if Mahendra had really told him the truth, in which case he had unfairly suspected Binodini and hurt her.

In the evening a distraught Rajalaksmi saw her son and told him, 'Bipin's wife wants to return to her home.'

Mahendra asked blandly, 'Why, Mother, is she not comfortable here?'

'It is not that. She feels that a long stay by a young widow like her in someone else's home may attract adverse comments.'

'Surely, that cannot be applicable to our sort of home,' Mahendra sounded aggrieved. He gave Bihari, who was present there, a black look.

Bihari was bothered that perhaps, by his comments, he might have ruffled Binodini's feathers, and hastened her decision to leave. Meanwhile, both Asha and Mahendra were extremely upset with Binodini. 'So, after all these days, we are nobody to you,' both of them charged Binodini.

Binodini said demurely, 'Surely, you do not expect me to stay here all my life?'

'How can we dare to do so?' sulked Mahendra.

'Then, why did you endear yourself to us?' moaned Asha.

Binodini looked at both of them dolefully and said, 'It will be wiser to break away now before the tie gets too strong.'

Bihari came the next day to talk to Binodini. '*Bouthan*, why are you proposing to go away? Is it because something I had said or done? So, am I to be punished?'

Binodini said, 'It has nothing at all to anything with you. It is just my destiny.'

'Well, if you leave, I shall always blame myself.'

Binodini looked piteously. He really could not advise her to stay on. He decided to skirt the issue by telling her, 'I know you will eventually have to go away some day, but why not carry on a little longer? No harm in it, is there?'

Binodini replied, with her eyes cast down, 'All of you make it very difficult for me to leave defying the wishes of you all, but I feel you are all making a serious mistake.'

When she said this, her eyes surged with tears that flowed through her thick long lashes.

Distressed by this silent deluge, Bihari spoke softly to her, 'During your brief stay here you have won all over by your charm. No one wishes to lose you. Don't get me wrong, but who will willingly sacrifice such a graceful person like you?'

Asha who was present there, with her face covered, was seen wiping away her own tears. Binodini never brought up the question of her leaving thereafter.

SEVENTEEN

In order to erase the memory of this unpleasant interlude, Mahendra proposed that they should go on a picnic the next Sunday at their garden house in Dumdum. Asha was inordinately enthused but Binodini declined the invitation to join. Her refusal considerably dampened the interest of both Asha and Mahendra. They felt Binodini was deliberately trying to keep a distance from them.

When she met Bihari in the evening, Binodini told him about the proposed picnic. 'Both Mahendra and Asha are very upset because I refused to go with them,' she told Bihari.

'Justifiably so,' Bihari told her. 'Can you imagine the effect of your absence? It will completely ruin their fun, and that you do not wish to happen even to your worst enemy.'

Binodini said, 'Oh, is that so? It never occurred to me. Why do you not also join then, in which case I might also change my mind.'

'An excellent idea,' agreed Bihari. 'It all depends on the lord and the master. What does he say?'

The lord and master did not at all appreciate the proposal to include Bihari in the party, and both he and Asha did not take kindly to Binodini's intervention to invite Bihari. Mahendra had persistently tried to imprint on his friend's mind that Binodini resented his presence amongst them, and how would he now continue with this pretence?

Mahendra had no option but to accede. He said, disinterestedly, 'Why, not? Do come with us, but the problem with you is that wherever you go you get into some kind of a mess. Either a bunch of local boys that you will collect round yourself for your sense of fun, or get into a scrap with a British soldier one never knows what you will be up to!'

Bihari had no illusion that Mahendra thoroughly disapproved of his inclusion in his picnic party. His reply to Mahendra was, 'True, one does not know what might turn up. That is where the fun lies, in unpredictability. One can never tell what lurking hazards await us, or how will our outing go. *Bouthan*, we shall have to make an early start in the morning, so do be ready. I shall be here in time.'

The designated Sunday dawned. A third class hackney carriage was engaged to carry the servants and the supplies, and a second class for the masters. Bihari arrived early, carrying, surprisingly, a large package with him. It irritated Mahendra. 'Now, what is that for? I don't think there is any room in the servants' carriage.'

Bihari assured him, 'No need for you to worry. I'll take care of it.' Binodini and Asha took their seats in the carriage, and Mahendra with them. He was worried where to accommodate Bihari, but Bihari solved his dilemma. He put his large package on the roof of the carriage and dumped into the seat next to the coachman, much to Mahendra's relief. He was not keen at all for Bihari to sit with them inside the carriage.

Binodini asked anxiously, 'Are you alright, Bihari-*babu*? No fear of your falling down, is there?' To which Bihari replied jokingly, 'No such fear; my role in this drama does not call for my fall and collapse!'

As soon as the carriages rolled out, Mahendra suddenly declared, 'I think I should go up and send Bihari to take my place.'

Asha strongly protested, 'No way can you go up. I won't allow you to.'

'You are not used to it, and may fall down,' Binodini added to Asha's protest.

'Fall down? Why should I? Never,' Mahendra was most indignant. He was almost on the verge of jumping out of the carriage, when Binodini spoke, thoroughly disgusted, 'Honestly! You accuse Bihari-*babu* of creating trouble, but you seem to be the lead actor in this game.'

Mahendra took umbrage at this comment. With a sour face he said, 'I have another plan. Let me engage another carriage which I will use, and Bihari can then replace me in this carriage.'

'If you do that, then I shall also travel with you,' declared Asha firmly.

'What about me, then? What do you expect me to do? Take a running jump out of the carriage?' said Binodini tersely. That effectively put paid to this bizarre idea of Mahendra, who remained silent with a long face all through the journey. When they reached the Dumdum house, there was no trace of the other carriage, with the servants, which had started earlier.

The autumn morning turned out to be most clement. The overnight dew had evaporated with the rising sun, and the trees in the garden sparkled in the clear bright light. Lined up against the wall were rows of *sefali* shrubs, the ground beneath them strewn with shed blooms, and the air redolent with their fragrance.

Away from the brick and mortar confinement of her city home, Asha, out in the open garden, was excited like a wild doe. With Binodini in tow, she collected heaps of flowers, plucked a ripe custard apple from a tree and relished it sitting under a tree. The two friends took a long soak in the pond, and between the two of them, in their unbridled sense of freedom and joy, they enlivened the whole ambience around them. The shade under the trees, the filtering light through the leaves, the clear water of the pond, the flowering shrubs of the garden everything turned lively and cheerful by the magic wand of their bursting energy.

When they returned after their bath, the servants' carriage was still missing. Mahendra, sitting by himself in the verandah, was wearily scanning a foreign catalogue.

Binodini asked Mahendra, 'Where is Bihari-*babu*?'

Mahendra, who could not care less where Bihari was, said in an offhand manner that he had no idea.

'Then, let us go and look for him,' suggested Binodini.

With ill-concealed humour, Mahendra said, 'I see no need for that. He is not going to get lost, nor is he going to be kidnapped.'

'You never know, he may be worried to death about you. We ought to relieve him of his misery,' Binodini chaffed Mahendra.

Near the edge of the water tank was a large banyan tree with a built-in circular base. It was there that Bihari had unpacked his package and was boiling water for tea on a stove. As soon as everybody assembled there, he handed each a cup of steaming tea and some eats.

'It was god-send that Bihari-babu on his own initiative had everything organized, which has saved the day for all of us. Or else, what would have happened to Mahendra-babu without his cup of tea?' quipped Binodini.

Mahendra was looking forward to his tea, no question, but still churlishly observed, 'Bihari has to overdo in whatever he does. We are here for a picnic, and Bihari has come fully prepared. Half the fun is lost that way.'

Bihari made fun of him. 'Well, if that is how you feel, leave your cup of tea. Have your fun by not drinking it, and we won't stop you.'

The day advanced but still no trace of the servants. Bihari, meanwhile, had magically brought out all manners of ingredients needed for cooking. There were rice and lentils, variety of vegetables, small bottles containing spices of all sorts. Binodini was genuinely impressed. 'I must say, Bihari-babu, you have outdone us women. With no wife to help, how did you learn all this?'

'The imperative need to keep alive, that's how,' Bihari replied. 'Or else, who will look after me if I don't?'

Bihari deliberately made light of his efforts, but it filled Binodini's heart with a great sense of pity for Bihari. Binodini and Bihari then put their hands jointly in preparing the food. Asha mildly offered to help, but Bihari waved her away. Mahendra, of course, lent no hand at all. He sat leaning against a tree, presumably watching the play of sunlight on the tree leaves.

The servants had arrived by then. They had a breakdown on the way, which delayed them. The afternoon had already rolled in. Cooking was almost over when Binodini spoke to Mahendra, I don't think you will ever get to the end of it if you are trying to count the tree leaves. Better get up, and have your bath.'

After the meal was over there was a proposal to play cards, hut Mahendra was in no mood for that. Shortly he fell asleep under the banyan tree. Asha went inside to rest.

Binodini, trying to cover her head, said, 'I think I should also retire now.'

'But why?' said Bihari, 'why not let us talk? Tell me about yourself, about the time when you were a small child, of your young days.'

The warm afternoon breeze blew round the trees, fluttering their leaves. A *koel* kept cooing somewhere on a tree. Binodini talked about her young days, of her parents, of her childhood friends. The sari covering her head slipped down as she talked. Her sharp youthful looks softened as she recounted tales of her early days. Binodini's penetrating eyes, playful yet curious, had earlier sown seeds of many misgivings and reservations in Bihari's mind. As the bright sparks mellowed to a serene glow when she kept talking, a new personality emerged in Bihari's eyes. He now perceived that at the core of this radiant person lay a heart tender with love and care. Her unsatisfied burning desires, her deprivations of a normal pleasurable life, had not dried up the essential woman in her. Until now, Bihari could not have conceived Binodini as a dutiful and devoted wife or a doting and caring mother hugging a child in her arms. The backdrop of a stage, as it were, had temporarily shifted revealing a behind-the-scene slice of reality. To the world outside, she might appear like a fun loving young woman, but deep inside her dwelt a serious and devout woman.

Bihari wished their talk to continue. He kept shooting questions to her to sustain the conversation. Binodini had no occasion until now to open her mind to anyone, but this talk with Bihari, the uninhibited flow of her thoughts, brought her a rare contentment.

Mahendra woke up late in the afternoon, perhaps to make up for the loss of sleep having had to get up early in the morning. He appeared still sore and grumpy. 'Let us pack up and go back,' he barked.

Binodini pleaded, 'Can we not stay a little longer?'

'No, we cannot,' Mahendra would not relent, 'we may get into trouble with drunken soldiers later.'

Darkness was setting in by the time everything was packed, when a servant came in to report that some white soldiers had taken their hired carriages away forcibly to take them to the railway station. The servant was sent back to engage fresh carriages. Meanwhile, Mahendra's irritation continued to aggravate; the day was ruined for him; he made little attempt to hide his dissatisfaction.

The moon slowly rose from behind the trees, weaving a kind of dream world in that silent garden. In this dream world, Binodini experienced an unprecedented ecstasy, and surprising Asha, hugged her warmly. Asha noted with alarm tears flowing down Binodini's face. She asked unhappily, *'My Chokher Bali*, what has gone wrong? Why are you crying?'

'Don't worry please. I am fine,' Binodini tried to reassure Asha.

'These are tears of happiness. It has been such a wonderful day for me.'

'Really, in what way?' Asha asked.

Binodini had a strange answer. 'You see, it was as if I had died and that I had reached the world beyond where, finally, I achieved my heart's desire.'

All this was beyond poor Asha's comprehension, except that she understood there was some reference to death, which troubled her. She said, with much agitation, 'Please, *Chokher Bali*, you must not speak of such sad things.'

Fresh carriages were hired, and Bihari as before climbed next to the coachman. During the journey, Binodini kept looking out and said not a word. Out there, the trees lining the roadsides receded, as they sped along, like fleeting stream of shadows under a clear and bright moonlight. Asha went to sleep in a corner, and Mahendra continued glum throughout the journey.

EIGHTEEN

After the picnic expedition, Mahendra discovered renewed interest in Binodini. He was keen to get her in his grip, but there was a hiatus as Rajlakshmi went down with fever. It was not serious, nevertheless she was ill and weak, and Binodini took complete charge of her and nursed her tirelessly.

Mahendra warned her, 'Look, if you go on like this you may yourself fall sick. Let me find someone else who can look after mother.'

Bihari dissuaded him. 'You must not do so. Let Binodini continue to nurse mother. There is no one who can replace her, and there is no reason to worry about her.'

Mahendra started visiting his mother frequently and regularly, which Binodini found extremely trying. He was of no use to her at all in the sick room. At the end of her patience, she told him one day, 'Mahendra-*babu*, how does your presence help your mother? Why do you, on this account, needlessly keep away from your college? What is the point?'

That Mahendra sought out her company was certainly gratifying and it did feed her vanity as well. Nevertheless, she found Mahendra's desire for her unbecoming, of all places in his mother's sick room. Being scrupulously conscious of her duties and responsibilities, she could nor stand any obtrusions in her way, and Mahendra's pursuit of her she found particularly obnoxious, when she was engaged in nursing his mother.

Bihari came regularly, though very briefly, to enquire about Rajlakshmi. He had the uncanny knack, without being told, of discovering if anything was missing or something more needed to be done, and he would fix it almost immediately. In this process Binodini came to appreciate that Bihari had developed some regard for her for the manner in which she was taking care of Rajlakshmi.

Mahendra, thus rebuffed, resumed his college attendance with rigorous discipline. He appeared, though, in a perpetual sour temper, which was not helped by Asha's incompetence. His food was seldom ready in time, his coachman went missing when he needed him, and the holes in his socks remained unattended. Used to be pampered in every way, he was now missing that orderly life. He no longer could smile benignly at Asha's ineptitudes.

He berated Asha, 'Chuni, how often have I told you that you must keep my clothes ready before I go for my bath. To put the studs in my shirt to lay out my trousers and jacket—but you never do it in time. I spend, hours after I come out from my bath in looking for my clothes, and in trying to insert studs in my shirt.'

She died with shame when rebuked in this way, and when by way of explanation she told her husband, 'But I did instruct the servant,' she only succeeded in adding to Mahendra's annoyance.

'Why must you tell the servant? Why could you not do it yourself? Is there nothing that you can do properly?'

She had never been so sharply reprimanded, yet it never occurred to her to answer back that it was he who had always discouraged her from doing any work at home. She firmly believed that her incompetence stemmed from her lack of skill and intelligence, not through lack of experience. When Mahendra, forgetting himself, censured her by comparing her unfairly with Binodini, she meekly accepted it with humility and with no sense of rancour.

Periodically Asha went to visit her mother-in-law, but waited hesitantly outside the door. She wanted to make herself useful, she wanted to do something, but no one wanted her help. She simply had no idea how to create her own space in the family, how to get involved in the routine of chores that were required in a home. Sensitive to her incapability, she never could break through the barrier. A gnawing pain kept tormenting her, but she had no clear understanding of what was the nature of her agony, the undefined qualms. She often felt like crying her heart out, denouncing her own incompetence, her lack of intelligence.

In those early happy days Asha and Mahendra spent long hours together in each other's company, but now, if Binodini was not with them, Mahendra felt fidgety and did not find it easy to talk to Asha. Neither was Mahendra very comfortable with himself to remain quiet.

Some days later Mahendra discovered a servant carrying a letter.

When asked, the servant said it was a letter for Bihari-*babu* from *Bohuthakurunee*, meaning Binodini.

'Let me have a look,' Mahendra said and took the letter from the servant. He was most keen to open the letter and to see what was in it. However, he did not open it and restored the letter to the servant. Had he actually read the letter, he would have been disappointed. The letter was about Mahendra's mother, telling Bihari that she was refusing her prescribed nourishment of sago and barley water, and went on to ask Bihari if she could instead be allowed lentil soup. Binodini never spoke to Mahendra about his mother's illness, and relied entirely on Bihari.

Mahendra's unpleasant mood continued. He discovered one day a picture in their room, hanging aslant on the wall, on a string gone almost threadbare. He charged Asha, 'Don't you ever notice anything? That is why everything is going to pots in this house.' On another occasion, he noticed the flowers that were collected by Binodini from the Dumdum garden on the day of the picnic and placed in a vase were still there, but dead and withered. Once again, Asha was the victim. He told her, unkindly, 'I suppose unless Binodini throws them away they will still remain here.' In a foul temper, he hurled the vase away, which rolled down the steps making a horrendous clang.

Why was Asha not shaping up to his expectation bothered Mahendra. He felt her slipshod ways, her imperfections, stood in the way of holding their life together. As he cogitated on Asha's shortcomings, he suddenly noticed that she had gone unusually pale, and her unruly lips quivering in intense emotional anguish. Before he could speak, she rushed out of the room.

Remorse gripped Mahendra. He ran down the steps and retrieved the vase. He sat down at his work-table, his head resting on his arms. The evening advanced, lamps were lit, but Asha remained invisible. Impatiently, Mahendra paced up and down on the roof, waiting for her. Late into the night the house went quiet and silent, and yet no signs of Asha. Mahendra's patience gave out, and he sent for Asha. She arrived, stood hesitantly at the entrance of the roof. Mahendra went to her and hugged her intimately. This made Asha break down in relentless sobs, her tears flowing ceaselessly. Mahendra held her tightly, kissed her tresses—and up there in the sky, the stars mutely witnessed this scene.

Later, in bed, Mahendra informed Asha, 'I shall have to be continuously on night duty at the hospital for sometime. I may have to find a place near the hospital and shift there temporarily.'

This sounded ominous to Asha. She immediately concluded that her husband was still terribly unhappy with her, and so he wished to move away. It was her folly, she assumed, that was driving him away from home. She wished she were dead.

There was, however, no trace of displeasure in Mahendra's conduct. On the contrary, he displayed over-abundance of love for his wife. He held her in close embrace for a long time, playing with her hair till he loosened her bun. Mahendra had done this before to great chagrin of Asha, who did not like her hair being messed up. Not tonight, though. Tonight she was in the throes of ecstatic bliss. When a drop of tear fell on Mahendra's forehead, he looked up affectionately at Asha and called her sweetly, 'Chuni!' Asha said nothing and clung on to her husband. Mahendra, by now deeply contrite, said, 'I have treated you very badly. Do please forgive me.' Asha quickly covered her husband's mouth with her delicate palms and said, 'You must never say so. No fault of yours, it is all mine. You have to discipline me as you do your servants. You must train me to serve you better.'

The next morning before they left their bed, Mahendra told Asha, 'Remember this, Chuni, you are the jewel of my heart, above everybody else. You will reign there, always. No one can dislodge you from my heart.'

Asha, in her turn, swore she was prepared to make any sacrifices for her husband. She pleaded with her husband, 'Please, when you are away, do promise to write to me everyday.'

Mahendra replied, 'And so will you, I hope.'

'But how can I? I can hardly write,' Asha moaned.

Mahendra, playfully, pulled her by her hair, and said, 'Of course, you can. Surely, you cannot have forgotten your *Charupath* lessons?'

'Come, you must not rag me,' said Asha.

Asha started to pack for Mahendra with great energy. His thick winter clothes were difficult to fold and even more difficult to pack in.

However, the two of them struggled with the packing, and eventually, what should have gone into one trunk, they managed to squeeze into two. Leftovers were found room in a number of separate packages. Once again, Asha felt put out by further instances of her incompetence. Nevertheless, the two working together, getting into each other's hair, finding fault with each other—the whole exercise was such fun. Asha was transported back to their earlier happy days. She almost overlooked the fact that all this preparation was a prelude to their separation!

Frequent reminders that the carriage was ready to take Mahendra away went unheeded. He continued to procrastinate. The morning rolled into afternoon, the afternoon into evening. It was then that realization dawned on them that they have to part, and after numerous caveats to each other to take care, after mutual promises to write regularly, they parted with heavy heart.

Mahendra went to see his mother to take her leave. Rajlakshmi, by now recovered, and having covered herself with a thick shawl, was engaged in a game of cards with Binodini.

Mahendra ignored Binodini, and told his mother, 'I will now have continuous night duties at the hospital, so I have decided to move out to a place near my college. I will be there from tonight.'

The mother was none too pleased with the son not telling her earlier of his plan. She said, lifelessly, 'You must if you have to. How can we let your work suffer?'

Until now Rajlakshmi was fine, but as soon as her son told her that he was leaving home, she promptly imagined herself too unwell and feeble. Mahendra anxiously touched her temple to see if she had any temperature, and was about to take her pulse, when she withdrew her hand in a huff and said, 'As if the pulse can always tell you the truth. Just don't worry about me, I will be fine.' She turned her face to the wall, feigning much weakness. Mahendra touched his mother's feet before he left, and said not a word to Binodini.

NINETEEN

Mahendra's apparent indifference to her left Binodini with food for thought. What was he trying to do? Was it a demonstration of sulking, or annoyance, or was it just frustration? Was it a message to me, Binodini pondered, that he could not care less for me, and so he wished to be away, elsewhere? Let me see how long can he stick there.

But Binodini herself was troubled, with a gnawing sense of unrest in her mind. All these days, she had been laying traps for Mahendra and darting flirtatious arrows at him. His absence left Binodini utterly restless. She was sorely deprived of her source of intoxication, and Asha without Mahendra was too bland for her taste. In Mahendra's torrid love for Asha she had found a vicarious excitement that captivated her loveless and deprived heart. It was this Mahendra who had capriciously denied her a resplendent life, sacrificed such a jewel among women like herself for a creature like Asha, immature and of poor intellect.

Binodini was in two minds—ought she to love Mahendra or loathe him? Should she surrender herself to him, or should she severely maul him? There was no denying that Mahendra had incited a burning pain in her heart, but she was still undecided if that pain was a mask of jealousy or of love, or was it a mixture of both. Was there ever a woman, she bitterly contemplated, who was so plagued by such a dilemma that she was not sure if she wished to prolong this life or preferred death? Whatever it might be, Mahendra was essential to her life, whether to be scorched by him or to scorch him. Who else could be the target of her poison-tipped fiery arrows? 'He will return to me, he must, for he is mine, and mine only,' murmured Binodini with deep sighs.

On the pretext of cleaning and tidying up Mahendra's study, Asha picked up various articles of Mahendra's daily use, handled them, dusted them, and in this way associated herself with her absent husband on a lovelorn lonely evening. Binodini walked in silently and stood near Asha. Embarrassed by Binodini's unexpected presence, she pretended as if she was looking for a lost object.

Binodini asked her solemnly, 'What have you lost?'

'Oh, nothing really,' Asha tried to smile it away.

Binodini put her arms round Asha and asked her, 'Tell me, why did your husband leave home in this peculiar fashion?'

Asha was a child of simple nature, and the way Binodini questioned her probably sowed some seeds of alarm and misgiving in her mind. She quickly replied, 'But you do know that he is occupied with night duties in the hospital, that is why.'

Binodini lifted Asha's face by her chin and looked at her intently, with poignant glances, as if her heart was melting for Asha, and at the same time drawing deep breaths.

Asha regarded Binodini as an extraordinarily intelligent person, and herself as total ignoramus. Her world suddenly turned bleak and dismal by Binodini's strange conduct. She was in the depth of despair, but at the same time she was afraid to question Binodini. She sat down on a sofa, and Binodini sitting next to her held her friend in tight embrace. There was no holding Asha back now, she collapsed into uncontrolled bouts of sobs.

Bihari, who came in looking for Mahendra, chanced upon this unusual scene of Asha crying her heart out, and Binodini comforting her. He quickly removed himself to another room. He was positively troubled about Asha. Why was she crying so heartbreakingly? She was such an innocent girl who gave no one any cause for offence, who could then be such a monster to reduce her to tears? His heart warmed to Binodini for her tender ministration to Asha. 'What a mistake we made about her. She is nothing short of an angel on earth,' he reminded himself.

Bihari waited to give some time to Asha and Binodini, and then went back, announcing himself with a gentle cough. As soon as Asha saw Bihari, she covered her head and ran out of the room. Something that Binodini noticed in Bihari's face alarmed Binodini. 'What is wrong with you, Bihari-*babu*? Are you not well?' she asked solicitously.

Bihari denied that anything was wrong with him, and when Binodini asked, 'Then, why are your eyes so red?' Bihari evaded her question, and instead asked her, 'Where is Mahendra?'

'I understand he has work at the hospital, so he had shifted to a place near the hospital.' Her voice sounded grim.

Bihari stopped her as she was about to leave. He said to her, 'Please *Bouthan*, do take care of Asha. She is an innocent simple-minded girl. She is incapable of hurting anyone; she is equally incapable of protecting herself from getting hurt.'

Bihari could not see her face in the dark, but were he able to do so he would have seen a face embittered with intense resentment. Bihari's heart was full of compassion and concern for Asha, but what about Binodini? She was nobody, just did not count. She came to this world, apparently, to be of service Asha, to protect her, to ease her path by removing all obstacles, to ensure her happiness. The illustrious Mahendra-*babu* wished to wed Asha, so she, Binodini, was forced into the wilderness of Barasat to make her home with an uncivilized creature. Equally illustrious Bihari-*babu* was unable to abide Asha's tears, so Binodini must at all times be ready to wipe her tears. Just you wait, Mahendra-*babu*, and you Bihari-*babu* as well, Binodini by demolishing both of you would open your eyes to the gulf of difference that was between herself and Asha. They would then know the true worth of Binodini. An adverse turn of fate had denied Binodini the opportunity of winning any man's heart by the use of her talents, so she must assume the role of the predator, armed with deadly missiles!

Binodini turned to Bihari, and told him most engagingly, 'Don't, please, trouble unnecessarily on Asha's account.'

TWENTY

Very shortly after his arrival at his new place Mahendra received a letter, with his address written in a familiar handwriting. He had a lot of pending work, so he did not open the letter immediately, and consigned it to his pocket. During lectures in the college, during his rounds in the hospital, he exulted in the feeling that a little lovebird was nestling next to his heart. When, in due course, he stirred it up, its dulcet trills would resonate in his ears.

Later in the evening, when he was back in his rooms, Mahendra settled himself comfortably in a chair. He took out the letter, by then warm from his body heat, but instead of opening it he cast his eyes adoringly on the address inscribed by a loving hand. It was not that Mahendra had much expectation from the letter itself. No way was it possible for Asha to give expressions to her emotions in written words. He would have to give free rein to his imagination to extract her feelings from her immature writing. For the moment, even his name inscribed in Asha's hand was enough to lend magic to his life.

These two days of separation were long enough to drive off the ennui induced earlier by continuous togetherness, now replaced by the resurgence of love for his naive and simple wife. Of late, the nitty-gritties of domestic life had begun to wear him down. He was now free of them. Presently, a bright and shining image of Asha occupied his heart, rejuvenated by a new emerging love.

Gently he tore open the cover and extracted the letter. He tenderly caressed the letter by patting it against his cheeks. The familiar scent of the perfume that he had once gifted Asha radiated from the letter to heighten his desolation and restlessness.

He started reading the letter, but it took him by surprise. The script was childish, indeed so, but the language? Immature handwriting, yes; but not the expressions! This is what she wrote:

'My dearest, why shall I remind you of one whom you wish to forget, whom you have abandoned? The climbing plant that you uprooted and cast away with disdain, how can the same plant take root again and climb back? Better for it to disintegrate!

'It cannot hurt you much if you think of me, even for an instant. You lose nothing by it, but I gain. Your indifference has sunk deep in my heart and pricks like a painful thorn. Day and night, night and day, in all my thoughts, in all my waking moments, wherever I turn to, the pain of your indifference shadows me.

'Dearest, is it my crime that you loved me? Did I ever dream of such good fortune smiling on me? What was I? A mere nobody. I came from nowhere. Would I have ever faulted you even if you never looked at me, even if I were just an unpaid slave in your home? No, I never could. I cannot in the least fathom what attracted me to you that you enriched my life so much with your abundant love. Now that, out of a clear sky, a thunderbolt has struck me, why did it merely singe me and not reduce me to cinders?

'For the last two days, I have been through a lot of pain and agony. I thought about it a great deal, but found no answer. Was it not possible for you to remain at home and just ignore me? Do I occupy so much of your thoughts that forced you to leave home? Why, indeed, why did you have to go away? I could have gone instead. I was carried in by a wave, and another wave would have cast me out.'

It was Mahendra's turn to be thunderstruck. What an amazing letter! Who could have composed it? He made a shrewd guess, but the letter left him in a daze. He was stunned, as it were, by the aftermath of a violent railway accident.

Mahendra pondered over this letter for some length of time; he read and re-read the letter a number of times. A faint earlier suspicion was now manifesting in clearer contours. The hint of a comet that appeared as a shadow in a corner of his firmament was now fully visible blazing its fiery tail!

Binodini was, indeed, the author of these letters. Asha had merely put down what Binodini dictated, simple-minded as she was. Thoughts, which had never occurred to Asha earlier, were taking shape in her mind when she followed Binodini's promptings for the letter to her husband. Borrowed ideas now became her own. She could not have expressed her feelings so poignantly without Binodini's help. It amazed Asha how did her friend so precisely read her mind, in what wonderful language did she put down Asha's own thoughts. She now clung more adhesively to her friend since there was no one else who could find the language to articulate her agonies.

Mahendra was terribly disturbed. Initially, he was extremely annoyed with Binodini, realizing that it was her hands behind the letter, and then with Asha. How foolish of Asha, he thought, to put her husband to such a ridiculous spot with her friend. He decided to read the letter once again, and to his surprise, the letter now excited him with a strange feeling of elation. He wanted to convince himself that the letter was, indeed, Asha's, even though he could not reconcile the style with Asha's. Why then just a few lines of this letter thrilled him with a touch of exhilaration, bubbling over like sparkling wine? Was there a hint in this letter of an ardour—veiled yet implied, forbidden yet intimate, noxious yet delicious, offered but unrequited? The very thought made Mahendra delirious, and immediately he was assailed with a feeling of guilt. He must exorcise this unbecoming rapture, he ardently wished to divest his mind of these disturbing thoughts, and he wanted to be distracted, somehow, at any cost. He leapt from his chair, thumped the desk hard, decided to burn the letter, but did not. The following day his servant discovered a pile of burnt paper ash, but it was not of Asha's letter, but of Mahendra's many futile attempts to pen a suitable reply to Asha.

TWENTY-ONE

Another letter arrived from Asha:
'I had no reply to my letter. Rightly so, perhaps. When a devotee prays to her deity, the deity never responds. I do hope the offering of this wretched creature has been accepted. But, lord of my heart, if my prayers interrupt your meditation, then please do not take it too harshly against me. You may or may not have any time for me, you may or may not grant my prayers, but this devotee will continue to worship at the altar of her deity. That is why I had to write this note, albeit short. My stony hearted God, may you remain unperturbed.'

Mahendra sat down once again to pen a reply, but it was Binodini's image, which loomed in his heart, not Asha's. He was incapable of camouflaging his thoughts, so he destroyed many drafts before he finally settled on one. As he was about to write Asha's name on the cover, his conscience rebelled. How could he be so wicked to deceive a true and loyal girl in this fashion? He shredded the letter, and sat up the whole night at his desk, sleepless.

A third letter from Asha followed:
'Is one capable of love if one is not sensitive? If I am unable to protect and preserve my love in the face of indifference and apathy, then how can I offer you my love? Perhaps, I never came to know you well enough, which may account for my audacity. So when you left me behind, I decided, on my own, to write to you. I have revealed my heart to you, even though you have chosen to remain silent. If I judged you wrong, is that my fault? Just try to recall everything that happened to us from the very beginning. Is it not true that whatever I learnt, I learnt at your feet?

'Be that as it may, right or wrong, whatever I had written cannot now be expunged. That is my tragedy. What a shameful fate for a woman! But, do not for a minute imagine that one who really loves will allow that love to be undermined. If you do not wish to write, if you do not wish to reply, in that case I have nothing more to say...'

After this Mahendra could not hold back, and decided to return home, but in anger, bristling against Binodini. Did Binodini think that he left home just to escape from her? What impudence? His decision to return was to confront Binodini and answer her insolence.

Unexpectedly, Bihari called on him, and Mahendra welcomed him with more than usual pleasure. Of late, their relationship had been strained, with Mahendra nursing many grievances against Bihari. All these grievances were banished for the moment with Mahendra's pronounced happiness in seeing Bihari. Up he stood from his chair, grabbed Bihari's hand and pushed him on to a chair.

Bihari looked melancholic. Mahendra assumed that he, probably, had been rebuffed by Binodini. He asked his friend, 'Have you recently been to my home?'

'I came here straight from your home,' Bihari said. He sounded disturbed. Mahendra jumped to the conclusion that his friend's scrappy mood must be due to his frustration, denied the love of any woman. In his weird sense of humour Mahendra unaccountably drew some satisfaction from his friend's misfortune.

He asked, 'Did you meet anyone there? Is all well there?'

Instead of answering him, Bihari asked Mahendra, 'Why did you have to leave home?'

'There is such a load of night duties. Difficult to attend from home.'

'You have had night duties before, but you did not leave home then?'

Mahendra smiled, 'Are you insinuating anything?' Bihari said, 'Forget your jokes. Come home with me.'

Mahendra who had, earlier decided to go home deliberately treated Bihari's suggestion with calculated nonchalance. He said, very solemnly, 'No, Bihari, that is not possible. I will lose a year if I do.'

Bihari reacted, with some asperity, 'Look Mohin, do not try to hoodwink me. I have known you for years. What you are doing is abominably wrong, and you know it.'

'And, whom am I wronging, Mr justice?' bantered Mahendra.

Bihari was getting nettled. 'You always brag about the largeness of your heart. Where have you consigned that heart now?'

'Presently at the college hospital,' Mahendra answered gruffly.

Bihari lost his cool. He admonished Mahendra, 'Stop your clowning.

Enough is enough. You may have your fun and games here, but there, in your home, poor Asha desolately cries her heart out in your absence.'

This report about Asha's lament was sort of a setback for him. In his smug self-absorption there was no place for the feelings of others. Surprised, he asked, 'But why must Asha cry?'

Intensely indignant, Bihari said, 'You may not know the answer, but I do.'

'If I am not omnipotent, then do not curse me, blame the creator.'

Bihari then recounted in detail the tragic scene he accidentally came upon when he found Asha bathed in tears and locked in embrace by Binodini who was trying to comfort her. Bihari appeared upset as he told his tale.

Mahendra did not fail to notice that Bihari was upset, which surprised him. He was always under the impression that Bihari was born without a heart. So, when did he find one? Probably, Mahendra hazarded a guess, the day they both went to see Asha. Poor, poor, Bihari. No, Mahendra was not exactly sad for his friend, instead he was vastly amused. He knew very well where Asha's heart was firmly moored. He had always candidly believed that what others coveted avidly as their heart's desire but could not attain came on their own to him without asking.

Mahendra agreed to go back with Bihari.

TWENTY-TWO

When Asha met her husband, soon after he stepped into the house, all her qualms and misgivings dispelled, like the thin film of mist. She was, on the other hand, dying with shame recalling the letters she wrote him. To make matters worse, Mahendra's first words were to chide her, 'How could you write to me brimming with such accusations?'

Mahendra extracted the three letters from his pocket, the letters that he had read many times over. Asha, now frightfully distraught, begged her husband pitifully to destroy the letters. She even attempted to snatch the letters from Mahendra, which Mahendra successfully repelled and restored the letters to his pocket.

'I left home in the interest of my work, but you chose to misunderstand me. You suspected my motives.' That was Mahendra's charge against his wife.

Asha, almost in tears, moaned, 'Please forgive me. I promise you I will never do it again.'

'Never?' Mahendra looked at her.

'No, never,' Asha assured him.

Mahendra tenderly drew her close and showered her with kisses. Ecstatic Asha once again appealed to him, 'Please, destroy those letters,' but Mahendra did not relent. Asha was left with the impression that her husband retained the letters as a token of her punishment.

These letters became a sore issue to turn Asha's mind against Binodini. She did not rush to her friend to tell her of her happy reunion with her husband, as Binodini had expected. On the contrary she, so it appeared, was deliberately avoiding meeting Binodini. Binodini was sharp enough to notice this, and kept herself aloof from both of them.

All this came as a bit of shock to Mahendra. He had expected that he would now have the opportunity of getting to know Binodini better, but it was just the reverse. Most strange, he felt. What then was the message of those letters?

At some point of time, early in his life, Mahendra had reached the conclusion that it was futile to plumb the mysteries of women's heart. It was in that context he had decided that if Binodini sought him out, he would keep away. All his speculations appeared to have gone awry. This was not what he had expected. Was there some kind of a mental aberration amongst all of thetas, he wondered? He decided to abandon his earlier resolution to keep away from Binodini, and instead thought it would be a good idea to break through this sultry atmosphere by evolving a free and easy relationship with Binodini on his own initiative.

To Asha, Mahendra said, 'It seems that I am your friend's *Chokher Bali*—her eyesore. We hardly see her these days.'

Asha replied impassively, 'I really don't know what is bothering her.'

Rajlakshmi came running to her son, almost in tears. 'I can't detain Bipin's wife any longer here.'

'Why, Mother, what has gone wrong?' Mahendra was disturbed but tried not to show it.

'I have no idea,' said Rajlakshmi. 'She insists that she must return to her village. Unfortunately, you take no notice of her any one. After all, she is our guest from another family, and if you ignore her why should she stay here?'

Binodini was in her room busy with sewing. Mahendra went straight to her and called her 'Bali'—the name used by his wife.

Binodini looked up and said formally, 'Hello, Mahendra-*babu*.'

Mahendra said, 'How terrible! Since when did I become a babu to you?'

Binodini said without lifting her eyes from her sewing, 'How then must I address you?'

'By the name that you use for your friend—*Chokher Bali*,' suggested Mahendra.

Binodini went on with her sewing and made no attempt to respond. Mahendra did a tentative exploring, 'I suppose I do not qualify for that relationship.'

Binodini snipped the thread with her teeth, and then said, 'I am sorry, I cannot answer that. May be you can.' To change the trend of this talk, she added, speaking in a sombre tone, 'What made you return home so unexpectedly?'

'How long can I go on dissecting cadavers?' answered Mahendra.

Once again Binodini snipped the thread, and without looking up remarked, So, now you need live creatures to dissect.'

Mahendra had decided earlier that he would make an effort to bring their association to an easy and natural footing through casual exchanges. He failed to do so as he discovered that he had unwittingly turned rather serious and could not induce a mood of levity. Her aloofness also deterred him. It was obvious that she was determined to keep her distance. This made him doubly keen to get close to her and break this barrier between them. Instead of rising to her biting remark, he sat down near her and asked, 'I understand you wish to leave us. Have we in any way offended you?'

Binodini now looked up from her sewing. Fixing her two large and luminous eyes on Mahendra, she said in an affectedly cold manner, 'Everyone has eventually to think of his or her normal obligations. When you went away to be near your college, was it because someone gave you cause for offence? Likewise, I will also have to go. I have also my field of responsibilities and obligations.'

Mahendra could not find a suitable answer to this. He just asked, 'But what are these pressing obligations that cannot wait?'

Binodini was trying to thread a needle then. 'How can I give you a list of my obligations? One instinctively recognizes them.'

Mahendra turned his face towards the window, looking idly at a coconut tree. An awkward silence reigned in the room. No one spoke. The silence was broken by Mahendra, abruptly, which so startled Binodini that she pricked her finger with the needle.

'Is there no way that we can persuade you to stay back?' pleaded Mahendra.

Binodini sucked the blood from the pricked finger, and then replied, 'Why must you persuade me, really? How is it material whether I stay or go? And, in any case, how does it affect you?'

Did she sound a trifle dejected as she spoke? Were her eyes moist with traces of tears lining her lower eyelashes? The afternoon melted into evening darkness. She sat there trying not to show her emotions.

Forgetting himself, Mahendra did something then that breached the norms of decorum. He jumped from his chair, seized Binodini's hands unawares to her, and spoke in an afflicted voice, 'If it does affect me, will you then promise to stay back?'

Binodini quickly withdrew her hand, and Mahendra, with a shock, sobered up. What he said to Binodini echoed in his mind as a terrible indiscretion. He cursed his runaway tongue and fell silent.

Asha walked into this silence, and immediately Binodini spoke up, as if she was continuing an ongoing conversation. 'Well, if all of you decide to pamper me, then I suppose I ought to concede to your pleas. I agree to stay on until I am asked to leave.'

Highly elated by what she assumed to be a case of her husband's brilliant success, Asha warmly hugged her friend.

'Wonderful,' she said, 'it is all fixed then. To make your promise binding, repeat it three tinges.'

Binodini obliged and repeated as asked her promise. Asha petulantly complained, 'Tell me, *Chukher Bali*, why did you need to play so hard to get at? You had ultimately to concede defeat to my husband.'

Binodini smiled, addressing her remark to Mahendra, 'Tell her, *Thakurpu*, who lost, you or me?'

All this while Mahendra sat there like a lost man. His overpowering feeling of guilt, it appeared to him, had vitiated the entire atmosphere of the room, and he was so shaken by his mortification that lie found difficult to regain his calmness. The devilry that had seized him was beyond the pale of his control, as he came to realize. He came to life when spoken to by Binodini. He answered in a solemn mood, 'Yes, it is I who lost,' and then promptly left the room.

And, he came back, almost immediately. He spoke to Binodini, 'Please, do forgive me.'

Binodini smiled and said, 'For what? What have you done?'

Mahendra was not quite sure what he wanted to say. He came out finally with this. 'We have no right to force you to stay here.'

Binodini smiled again, 'Force? I saw no signs of force applied to me. On the other hand, you spoke to me kindly, considerately. Surely, that was not forcing me.' She then turned to Asha, 'Would you say, Chokher Bali, that there is no difference between love and force?'

Asha readily agreed with her and said, 'Of course, there is.'

'I am really most fortunate that you wish me to stay on,' she told

Mahendra, 'otherwise you will be very upset. How many such friends and well-wishers can one find in life? When I have been favoured with a friend like yourself who shares my joys and sorrows, then why should I be anxious to desert him?' Observing her husband's embarrassment, Asha said a little ruefully, 'There you are. Who can match you in wits? My poor husband has already admitted defeat, do spare him now.'

Mahendra once again rushed out of the room and came across Bihari who, after calling on Rajlakshmi, was looking for Mahendra. Mahendra pathetically cried out to him, 'Bihari, I am a villain, the vilest in the world,' leaving Bihari stunned. He spoke so loudly that he was heard distinctly inside the room. From the room came a call, 'Bihari-babu, can you come in for a moment, please?

'Shortly, *Bouthan*,' Bihari answered.

'No, now, please,' Binodini implored.

Asha quickly covered her head, and from the little that Bihari could see of her face, he saw no signs of distress. Binodini detained Asha as she was trying to leave them. She spoke to Bihari, 'Tell me, what is the problem between yourself and my *Chokher Bali*? You two behave as if you share a husband and so cannot stand each other. Why does Asha run away whenever she sees you?'

A very discomfited Asha strongly remonstrated.

Bihari replied with a benign smile, 'Could be because the good God has denied me agreeable looks.'

Binodini laughed. 'Did you notice, Asha, how cleverly he sidesteps? He found no fault in you, but blamed the Creator. How did you overlook to cultivate such a perfect brother-in-law, modelled on the lines of the legendary Lakshman?'

Asha could not be held back. She wrenched herself free from Binodini's grip and left. Bihari was also about to leave, when Binodini asked him, 'Can you tell me what is troubling Mahendra-babu?'

Bihari also had his doubts. He said, 'Why, have you noticed anything disturbing?'

'I don't know, but I am nervous.'

Bihari sat down, clearly worried. Expecting to be told more he looked anxiously at Binodini, but she had apparently nothing more to say and resumed her sewing.

'Tell me, have you noticed anything odd in Mahendra's conduct recently?' asked Bihari after a pause.

Binodini answered in a most matter of fact fashion, 'I really do not know, but I am truly concerned about my *Chokher Bali*.' With a deep sigh she left aside her sewing and was about to leave.

Bihari, uneasy in his mind, detained Binodini, 'Please, do not go yet. I wish to talk to you.'

Binodini got up, opened wide all the doors and windows, turned up the oil lamp, and picking up her sewing, positioned herself at the far end of her bed. She looked at Bihari and said, 'Look, I am not going to be here all my life. Please, will you promise me, to keep an eye on her when I am not here to look after her? She will need protection.' She turned her face away as if she was trying to hide her emotions.

'No, *Bouthan*, you will have to be here,' Bihari almost appealed to her. 'You have no one of your own, so why should you go away? You have, I beg of you, to take charge of this innocent and helpless girl. If you abandon her, I see no other alternative.'

'But you know the ways of the world,' Binodini observed, 'If I stay here permanently, questions will be raised, unsavoury comments made, innuendos hinted.'

Bihari waved it away as insignificant. 'Let people say whatever they wish to, just don't need them. You are divinely inspired, so it is only fitting that you should shelter this helpless girl from the inhumanities of the world. Early on, I had misunderstood you for which I am truly repentant. Like other narrow-minded persons, I too had formed the most unfair impressions about you, to the extent that I had once imagined that you grudged Asha her happiness. But enough of that! I now realize how large hearted and generous you are, and I have the deepest respect for you.'

What Bihari never saw through was that all Binodini's talk was motivated and calculated. Nevertheless, Bihari's sincere appreciation exulted her, and she accepted them as genuine tribute. She never had such appreciation from any source. For an instant, perhaps, she was deluded into believing that she was probably a superior being, and out of some undefined compassion for Asha her eyes became moist, which she did not attempt to conceal from Bihari. By her action she succeeded eminently in creating an illusion about herself in Bihari's mind.

Bihari, now much moved, went to seek out Mahendra to speak to him. He was puzzled why Mahendra behaved in that odd manner, but he could not sleet him as Mahendra had gone out.

Meanwhile, Binodini got Asha to come to her room. 'Dear *Chokher Bali*, I am afraid I am a very ill-starred woman. I only bring misfortune wherever I am. Please, Bali, don't insist on my staying here. Let me go.'

Asha lifted Binodini's face by her chin and said, 'What nonsense? You must not talk so silly. ill-starred, indeed! I cannot positively live without you. I don't know what suddenly made you change your mind to think of leaving us.'

Hoping that he might catch Mahendra, Bihari returned once again and went to see Binodini to get a clearer picture of her fears for Mahendra and Asha. As he called out, '*Bouthan*,' he stopped short when he discovered Asha and Binodini locked in tearful embrace. Bihari's unexpected appearance disturbed Asha. She immediately concluded that Bihari must have said something unpleasant to her friend, and that is why her friend talked about going away. This soured Asha's mind against Bihari. He was clearly not a nice person who had upset her friend. She went out, disgusted with Bihari, and Bihari after making some polite noises also left.

Later that evening Mahendra told Asha, 'Chuni, I have decided to go to Kashi by the morning train tomorrow.'

Asha had a shock. 'Why?' she asked.

'To see my aunt. Have not seen her for such a long time.'

Asha was put to shame, because all these days she had hardly ever thought of her aunt. She had shamelessly neglected her, but Mahendra did not. He was actually proposing to visit this self-exiled saintly person. Asha felt very small.

Mahendra said, 'You are very precious to her, and she left you in my hands. I feel awful neglecting her so long.'

Mahendra appeared to be emotionally carried away when he said this. With great tenderness and love, he stroked his wife's hair and face, as if in a trance. Asha could not grasp the significance of this impulsive outburst of love. She recalled Binodini's touchingly loving words to her this evening. If there were any correlation between the two outpourings of love and affection, it was, of course, beyond the conception of such a simple-minded girl like Asha. Nevertheless, she had a premonition that it was casting an ominous shadow, whether for good or for worse, she could not tell.

With a degree of alarm Asha firmly clung to Mahendra, and Mahendra in some way sensed her unease. He said to her, 'Chuni, have no fear. You are fortified by your aunt's blessings, and nothing untoward can happen to you.'

Thus comforted, Asha dismissed all thoughts of her apprehensions from her mind, and accepted her husband's assurances as a protective amulet. She kept remembering her aunt and sent out her prayers to her, 'My dear aunt, my mother, let your benediction always safeguard my husband.'

Mahendra left the next day without speaking to Binodini. She was amused. The man misbehaved and yet wanted to turn the table against her. How noble, how righteous! Let us see how long his principles sustain, she pondered.

TWENTY-THREE

Annapurna was naturally delighted to see Mahendra arrive unexpectedly, but she was at the same time somewhat nervous about Asha. She was anxious that Asha was not in trouble again with her mother-in-law. That could be a reason for Mahendra's sudden visit, as he was likely to seek her advice. Ever since he was a small boy, Mahendra had always run to his aunt whenever he was in trouble or had grievances. She had been able to counsel him, comfort him, and relieve him of his worries. But to resolve any crisis that concerned his married life was outside her scope. She had, detected signs of unacceptable developments early enough, where she could not have helped. It was then that she decided to retire from domestic commitments and courted her exiled life. Presently, absorbed in her spiritual pursuits, she had, by and large, succeeded in detaching herself from worldly concerns. This unexpected arrival of Mahendra, not unnaturally, considerably agitated her.

Mahendra, however, never for once, said anything about trouble between his wife and his mother. Which, in turn, raised another sort of fear in Annapurna's mind. Why was Mahendra here leaving his wife behind, the wife on whose account he merrily cut college day after day? Was there any trouble between the husband and the wife? Had their deep attachment suffered a setback? Surely, Mahendra was not here purely for the pleasure of being with his aunt? Such were the disturbing thoughts that ran through her mind.

She anxiously asked Mahendra, 'Tell me the truth, is my Chuni all right?'

'She is fine, *Kakima*,' Mahendra assured her.

'How does she keep herself occupied these days? Are you still living in your childish dream world, or are you now more serious about the practical life?'

Mahendra told her, 'No *Kakima*, we have put behind all our childish ways. Do you recall the root of all our trouble Charupath, the primer? It is now lost, lost beyond recovery, disappeared, vanished! You will be happy to see your Chuni now; she is whole-heartedly devoted to neglecting her studies.'

'And Bihari, how is he and what is he doing?'

'Ah, almost everybody else's work except his own,' said Mahendra. 'His employees look after his estate, how well I have no idea. That is Bihari all over. He minds other peoples' affairs, other people take care of his.'

'Is he contemplating marriage, at all?' asked Annapurna.

Mahendra smiled. 'So far, I have seen no signs.'

For Annapurna it had been a sensitive issue, and it continued to haunt her. It was no secret to her that Bihari was smitten by Asha when he and Mahendra went to see her. Bihari was quite ready to marry her, but his wish was thwarted by a most unprincipled last minute decision. She recalled Bihari's words to her, '*Kakima*, never ever ask me to marry.' Those woebegone words kept ringing in her ears. She was full of remorse that she had abandoned her very devoted Bihari with no words of comfort for him. The thought that Bihari might still be drawn towards Asha also worried her.

Mahendra, half seriously and half-jokingly, related to his aunt the latest accounts of their life in Calcutta, except that he said not a word about Binodini. This was not a vacation time for Mahendra, yet he lingered on in Kashi. He felt invigorated, in the company of his aunt, like a convalescent patient in a salubrious climate, enjoying every minute of his stay there. The inner conflict that had been troubling him for sometime appeared to have resolved, restoring him to the tranquillity that he had missed. Being in constant association with a pious and spiritual person like Annapurna, living under her loving care, the duties and obligations of life now looked to him both pleasant and uncomplicated. Memories of his past abhorrence for domesticity he now dismissed as ridiculous. Surprisingly, Binodini ceased to matter him; he hardly ever thought of her. He persuaded himself to believe strongly that no one could displace Asha even an inch from his heart.

Eventually, practicalities of life caught up with Mahendra. He told Annapurna, '*Kakima*, I have now missed college for many days. It is time I went back. Allow me to leave you now, but permit me to visit you time to time to sit at your august feet.'

Fond memories of her aunt brought tears to Asha's eyes when Mahendra, on returning home, passed on to her Annapurna's gifts of a box of vermilion powder and a small stoneware jar. Thoughts of how they, particularly her mother-in-law, had ill-treated Annapurna, depressed her. She told her husband, 'I would also love to go and see my aunt. Do you think that would be possible at all?'

Mahendra was sympathetic, but was not keen to miss his college again so soon to take her to Kashi. Asha, however, had an answer. Her elder uncle and his wife were planning to visit Kashi shortly. 'If it is no problem, then I can travel with them,' she suggested.

Mahendra spoke to his mother, 'Your daughter-in-law wishes to go and see her aunt in Kashi.'

Rajlakshmi sneered, 'Well, if she wishes to go, then of course, she must go. Take her there then.'

Mahendra said, 'I can't take her myself, cannot afford to miss college anymore. She will travel with her elder uncle.'

'How wonderful,' said Rajlakshmi pouring more venom in her voice. 'Her elder uncle is such an eminent person, so eminent that he does not condescend even by mistake to step into our poor home. It will be such a privilege for your wife to be in the company of her uncle.'

His mother's continuous malignant barbs put Mahendra's back up against his mother. He was now determined to send Asha to Kashi.

When Bihari saw Rajlakshmi, she lost no time to tell him, 'Have you heard, Bihari, that my daughter-in-law wishes to visit Kashi?'

Somewhat puzzled, Bihari asked, 'Is Mohin proposing to miss college again to take his wife to Kashi?'

Rajlakshmi said with a bitter smile, 'Not at all. That is not the way of a modern woman. Mohin will stay back, and she will go with her great elder uncle. Everyone seems to follow the ways of *sahibs* and *bibis* these days.'

Bihari left Rajlaksluni with a degree of anxiety in his mind—his concern had nothing to do with the modern trend of anglicized manners, so despised by Rajlakshmi! His worry was on account of his friend and his wife. Had something gone wrong somewhere? When Mahendra went to Kashi he left Asha behind, and as soon as Mahendra returned Asha was proposing to visit her aunt in Kashi. Most odd was there any serious hitch between the husband and the wife, he wondered. If there was any, should this be allowed to continue? Should he not as their friend intervene to help, or must he stand back and watch the rot getting deeper?

Extremely annoyed by his mother's inexcusable behaviour, Mahendra had escaped to his bedroom. Since his return he and Binodini had not met, and in an adjacent room Asha was urging Binodini to go with her and meet her husband. Just then Bihari came in and asked Mahendra, 'Is *Bouthan's* plan to visit Kashi finally fixed?'

'Why should it not be?' Mahendra shot back, 'do you see any problem there?'

Bihari hurriedly replied, 'I was not thinking so much of any problem. I merely wondered why this sudden whim of *Bouthan*.'

'The anxiety to meet one's aunt, the wish to see one's dear relation who lives far away, is not exactly an abnormal trait in human nature,' was Mahendra's terse remark.

Ignoring Mahendra's sarcasm, Bihari asked, 'Are you planning to take her there?'

Mahendra assumed that Bihari disapproved of the idea of sending Asha with her elder uncle. To avoid getting provoked, Mahendra decided to stop this discussion and curtly said, 'No.'

Bihari knew Mahendra well, and saw that he was getting into a bad temper. It was very difficult to dissuade Mahendra once he was obsessed with anything. He, therefore, decided not to press the issue of Asha's escort. As he was still concerned about Asha, he wondered if it might not be a good idea to persuade Binodini to go with her—she could at least hold Asha's hands to comfort her in case she was for some reason miserable. He suggested gingerly. 'How about Binodini going with her?'

There was no holding back Mahendra now. He flared up and shouted at Bihari. 'Come clean, come out openly with what is in your mind. No need to play games with me. Yes, I do know. You suspect that I am in love with Binodini. What absolute rot. I am not in love with Binodini, and for heaven's sake, you don't have to be my watchdog. On the other hand, I warn you to be on guard. If your friendship was transparent and uncomplicated, I am sure you would have confessed your feelings to me much earlier. You did not. Allow me to be outspoken. I accuse you of being in love with Asha.'

When one is hurt where one is most vulnerable, the injured person tends to react instantly and thoughtlessly to counterattack the assailant. Bihari rose, pale and shaking, from his chair and impulsively rushed towards Mahendra. With some difficulty he restrained himself. He spoke gravely to Mahendra, 'May the good Lord forgive you,' and tottered out of the room.

Binodini emerged from the adjacent room and accosted Bihari. She told him, 'I am prepared to go to Kashi with Asha.'

'No, *Bouthan*, do not do anything rash, just because I suggested it,' Bihari protested. 'I am nobody here, and neither have I any wish to interfere in affairs here. This will do no good to anyone. As a person of saintly disposition, I am sure you will do what you think fit. I will take your leave now.'

Binodini appealed to him, 'Please, do listen to me. I am no saint as you think, and if you abandon this family out of pique, it will harm everyone. Don't blame me later for not warning you.'

Bihari left. Binodini gave Mahendra a stern scorching look before going back to Asha, who was still in the room, shaken to the core and dying with shame. She was devastated when she heard Mahendra charging Bihari of being in love with her. Binodini, though, had no remorse in her heart for Asha. Indeed, had Asha looked at her intently she would have been unnerved. Binodini was in a murderous mood. It was a lie, was it not, that Mahendra did not love her; and that everyone was in love with this lifeless doll, Asha.

Ever since his impulsive outburst when he told Bihari what an unmitigated villain he, Mahendra, was, Mahendra found it very uncomfortable to look Bihari straight in the face. He was horrified that he had betrayed his feelings by this explosion. He was certainly upset with Bihari for suspecting him of being in love with Binodini, which he felt was not true. Every time he faced Bihari he was obsessed with the belief that Bihari was incisively probing into his mind to extract the truth. His resentment towards Bihari was gradually mounting, so much so, that it reached a breaking point today when at the slightest of provocations he erupted.

To Mahendra it was unbelievable the way Binodini rushed out of the other room and, confronting Bihari, told him that she was prepared to go to Kashi with Asha as recommended by Bihari. It shattered Mahendra. He certainly did declare that he was not in love with Binodini, but what he saw, what he heard now, made him utterly miserable. He felt asphyxiated. He kept recalling with futile penitence that Binodini had heard with her own ears his denial of any tender sentiments for her!

TWENTY-FOUR

Mahendra was now much troubled in his mind. He had, unfortunately, pronounced rather loudly that he did not love Binodini. To say one did not love someone could be hurting. He decided to make amends, somehow. Naturally, he could not tell her that he loved her, but he could soften the blow in some manner. It would be unfair to allow Binodini nurse a wrong belief.

Mahendra took out the three letters that he had received from Asha, and re-read them. He was convinced, once again, that Binodini was indeed in love with him. In that case, why did she confront Bihari yesterday in that fashion? Was it her way of protest against her unrequited love for him? Mahendra perceived a danger signal here. Jilted by him, Binodini might turn to Bihari. The very prospect frightened Mahendra, and made him jittery. Binodini now knew the truth that Mahendra did not love her, and in her frustration she might turn against him. In his agitation, groping in the dark, like a storm-tossed boat, he sought to anchor himself more firmly to Asha.

That night Mahendra drew Asha close to him, and asked, 'Answer me truthfully, Chuni, how deep is your love for me?' What an odd question, thought Asha. Was it because of his suspicion of Bihari's feelings for her? She was outraged. 'How could you ever think of asking me this? Tell me, have you noticed anything wanting in my love for you?'

Mahendra pressed her closer to him. 'Then, why do wish to go to Kashi leaving me?' He wanted to test the intensity of his wife's love.

So, that was it. Asha quickly said, 'No, I have no desire to visit Kashi. Nowhere else either.'

'But you did,' Mahendra reminded her, not very kindly.

Asha was very upset, 'But you know why.'

Mahendra continued to rub Asha unfeelingly. 'I am sure you will have great time with your aunt in my absence.'

'Never. I did not propose to visit my aunt just for the sake of my pleasure.'

'I am quite certain, Asha, that you would have been happier married to someone else.' Another thoughtless remark from Mahendra.

Unable to take it any longer, Asha detached herself from her husband and sinking her face in a cushion, went stiff like a log. Almost instantly, she broke down with spasms of sobs. Mahendra made some efforts to comfort her by drawing her close, but she hung on to the cushion. This demonstration of Asha, which Mahendra regarded as an expression of her love for him, worked as a stupendous ego booster for him. He was now prepared to concede to some degree of unhappiness for her distress.

Incalculable but incipient broodings had been nagging all of them for some time, and now, being blatantly exposed, created a measure of turmoil in each of them. Binodini was surprised that Bihari let go unchallenged the serious allegations of Mahendra's. She would have been happy had Bihari made some show of protest even if the allegations might not have been wholly misplaced. Bihari was perhaps asking for this rap from Mahendra, but was it not unbelievable that such a high-minded person like Bihari could fall in love with Asha? Nevertheless, Binodini was not too unhappy about the breach that episode did bring about between Mahendra and Bihari.

Bihari's tortured face, drained of blood and stricken with pain, kept haunting Binodini. The caring and nurturing woman in her mourned for this unhappy soul. She wanted to take care of him as a mother did for a sick child, to revive Bihari back to his cheerful and smiling self.

Binodini waited for two days, distraught, amidst all her work, and then wrote to Bihari, 'After you left that day in such distress, I have been praying each day to see you restored to your normal and sunny disposition. I am dying once again to see your cheerful face and listen to your kindly voice. Do write telling us how you are.'

She dispatched the letter through a servant.

In the meantime, Bihari was revisiting everything. The crude and perverse attack by Mahendra, indicting him that he was in love with Asha, shook him. How could Mahendra do so? It was so vile, so baseless, so preposterous. Bihari was incensed with Mahendra.

Nevertheless, was there not a grain of truth in that charge? Could Bihari so facilely wave away Mahendra's imputation? Bihari recalled that day, the day he and Mahendra had gone to Asha's uncle to see her as a prospective bride for himself. The picture of a shy and innocent girl kept recurring in his mind, the girl he first met in the ambience of a twilight evening redolent with the fragrance of flowers. He had looked at the girl with adoration, who he assumed was going to be his. A feeling of pain constricted his heart, and an unspoken agony overtook him. During long sleepless nights, through aimless walks on the streets, what was latent so long suddenly seized Bihari's mind. What was kept in check until now came frightfully alive. What was a mild flicker of a lamp was fanned into a blaze by Mahendra's explosive statement.

Bihari now believed himself to be morally guilty. He felt that he had no grounds to feel aggrieved. After that disgraceful episode, Bihari was convinced that Mahendra was a cad. He now regretted this. How can he sit in judgment over him? Bihari decided to confess his infraction to Mahendra and ask for his forgiveness.

Soon, one evening, Bihari strolled into Mahendra's house. He had assumed that by then Asha must have left for Kashi. The first person he saw was Sadhucharan, a distant uncle of Rajlakshmi, whom he asked, 'Is all well here, Sadhu-da? I have not been around here for some days.' Upon being assured by Sadhucharan that all was well, he asked again, 'I suppose *Bouthan* must have left for Kashi.' When told by Sadhucharan that Asha had not gone to Kashi and was very much there, Bihari's first instinct was to rush and meet the family, but he restrained himself. He realized that he would now find it difficult to be free and easy with them as in his earlier days. He suddenly turned back and told Sadhucharan that he had some other engagements and that he would return another day. He hurried away and later, the same day, he left town.

The servant who had been dispatched with Binodini's letter returned without delivering it as he did not find Bihari at home. Mahendra who was then out in the garden saw the servant return and asked him whose letter was it. On being told, he took possession of the letter.

He decided to go and hand over the letter personally to Binodini. He was convinced that the letter contained some guilty secrets. He merely wished to look at the brazen-faced delinquent, and not speak to her. He recalled the earlier occasion when he had intercepted a letter from Binodini to Bihari, although he had not read that letter. He was now most curious to find what this present letter was about. As a justification he argued in his mind that Binodini was living under his protection, and he was morally responsible for her. He persuaded himself that it was his obligation to read this letter in order to save Binodini from falling into evil ways.

Thus convincing himself Mahendra tore open the letter and read it. It was a brief letter, written in simple and unambiguous language, expressing her genuine concern for Bihari. The letter puzzled him as it gave him no clue to Binodini's attitude. To whom was she inclined? It was Mahendra's persistent panic that being spurned by him, a jilted Binodini in desperation might look for consolation elsewhere. Binodini, he was certain, was mad at him and had given him up.

Mahendra's assumption made him extremely tense. He found it impossible to contain himself. He was haunted by the nightmarish thought that Binodini, who had almost surrendered to him and whom he had lost by a momentary lapse of discretion, had now escaped his grip. If Binodini, pondered Mahendra, cared to love him, she would be in a position of advantage. At least she would be safely anchored. Being a man of principle, he would never wrong her; in fact, she would be well protected. After all, he had Asha to whom he was wholly devoted, and therefore Binodini was safe with him. On the other hand, if she turned to someone else, this could lead to her utter ruination. Mahendra made up his mind. Without yielding himself, he would try to win her back.

Mahendra went in and saw Binodini waiting impatiently for someone. He mocked her, 'All this waiting of yours is futile. You won't see him. Here is your letter, returned.'

'But the letter is open,' Binodini was surprised.

Mahendra left without answering her. Binodini inferred that Bihari had contemptuously returned her letter after reading it, and not bothered to write a reply. This made here furious. She looked for the servant who had taken the letter, but he could not be located immediately.

Back in her room, all her pent up pains and agonies unlocked in a gush of unbridled torrent of tears. She viciously shredded her letter, but that was not enough to mitigate her rage. She wished she could dematerialize the letter, as if it had never existed. An irate queen bee stings everyone that comes in her path, and similarly an irate Binodini was prepared to destroy everyone around her. Obstacles, and nothing but obstacles, that is what she had faced all her life. Was there no way that she could find some satisfaction, some amelioration? If she could find no happiness, then whoever stood in her way to frustrate her, whoever was instrumental in depriving her from all that she deserved, whoever conspired to deny her what were her rightful dues, would be mercilessly crushed and humbled. Vengeance would be hers.

TWENTY-FIVE

Early in the spring, with its balmy south breeze, Asha spread a reed mat on the roof and was engrossed in a magazine. She was absorbed in a story where the hero while returning home for the puja holidays was abducted by bandits, and at that particular moment the heroine woke up after a nightmare dream. Poor Asha, she was so upset that she could not help breaking out in tears. Asha was exceedingly addicted to Bengali magazine stories and a lavish admirer of pulp fiction. Each story she read was unequalled. She would tell Binodini, '*Chokher Bali*, for my sake, do read this story. It is so divine. I could not stem my tears.' Binodini never took any trouble to read those stories, and unfeelingly ridiculed her ardour.

When Mahendra came in, Asha was most keen to get him to read the story that she had read that evening, but a look at Mahendra alarmed her. Mahendra with contrived cheerfulness teased her, 'May I ask who is that fortunate person in whose thought you are so deeply engrossed, secluded all by yourself on this rooftop?'

By then Asha had forgotten about her hero and heroine, and asked her husband, 'What is wrong with you? Are you not feeling well?'

'No, I am fine.'

'Is something bothering you, then? Tell me, please.'

Mahendra casually picked up a pawn from Asha's silver container, and putting it in his mouth said, 'I was just wondering about your aunt. She has not seen you for a long time, and I am sure it will make her enormously happy if you surprise her by a visit.'

Asha, unable to follow the trend of Mahendra's mind, looked blankly at him. Mahendra misunderstood her silence. 'Is it that you do not wish to go?' he asked.

A very difficult conundrum. She was certainly most keen to see her aunt again, but she was, equally, reluctant to leave Mahendra behind. She attempted a tentative reply, 'We shall both go together during your college vacation.'

Mahendra demurred. 'I doubt if I can take off during the next vacation. I'll need to work for my exams.'

'In that case let us postpone our visit for the time being,' Asha said.

'But why? You did once wish to go, so why do you not go on your own?'

Asha was firm. 'No, I shall not go now.'

'Only the other day you were very keen, what has changed your mind now?' Mahendra almost grumbled.

Asha remained quiet. Mahendra was getting increasingly restive recently to find an unobstructed opportunity to make peace with Binodini and to get to know her. Asha's recalcitrance loomed as an undesirable hitch to his plan, which annoyed him. 'Surely, you do not foster any suspicion about me that you wish to keep an eye on me.' He was distinctly petulant.

Mahendra now found insufferable Asha's usual modest and unassuming disposition. What was she trying to do? If she wished to visit her aunt, why did she not say so and ask to be taken there? What was the point in this silly vacillation—yes, and then followed by a no. Utterly incomprehensible.

Asha was simultaneously bewildered and unnerved by Mahendra's unexpected vehemence. She racked her brain but found no answer. She could never make out how Mahendra could by turn be such an adoring person and then treat her so unkindly. The more inscrutable Mahendra grew, the more tenuously her insecure heart clutched on to him, generating in her intense devotion as well as acute misapprehension.

She was unable to conceive how Mahendra could allege that she nursed misgivings about her husband, and that was why she wanted to keep a watchful eye on him. This was so absurd. Did he seriously mean it or was it a heartless prank? Should she vehemently deny the allegation or should she take it lightly and smile it away?

Mahendra could take no more of Asha's silence and rapidly strode away, thoroughly disgusted. Her literary magazine, her troubled hero and heroine, all melted away from Asha's thought. The sun dipped and the dark night took over. The earlier spring breeze turned into a chill wind. Poor Asha lay prostrate on the reed mat.

Much later when Asha went to their bedroom, she found Mahendra already asleep. He never even sent for her. She assumed her husband was displeased with her because of her apparent indifference to her aunt. Asha silently clasped his feet and rested her face there. Mahendra, now moved with pity, tried to pull her to him but Asha remained transfixed there. Remorsefully she said, 'If I have offended you in any way, do please forgive me.'

Mahendra had sufficiently softened by then. He told her, 'No, Chuni, you have done no wrong. I am really a heartless person to hurt you needlessly.' He raised himself and took Asha in his arms. After Asha had collected herself, she said, 'It is not that I do not wish to see my aunt, but at the same time I cannot bear leaving you behind. That is why I refused to go. Please do not misunderstand me.'

'No, I must go,' Asha insisted surprisingly.

'Why?'

'Because you thought that in my heart I do not fully trust you. On that ground alone I must be away for sometime, even if briefly.'

Mahendra said, 'Very strange. It is I who wronged you, but it is you who must pay the penalty for it?'

'That I cannot answer,' Asha said. 'All I know is that somehow somewhere there must have been lapses on my part, how otherwise could such absurd ideas occur in your mind? Why else should I be admonished for offences that are beyond my imagination?'

'Because you have no idea what a vile person I am,' Mahendra appeared genuinely contrite.

'Please, never say that again,' Asha protested. 'I am, nevertheless, determined to visit Kashi.'

Mahendra smiled, 'If you must, you must then. But what will you do if your husband goes astray once you take your eyes off him?'

'Come, you do not have to scare me,' Asha said calmly. 'I am, not exactly dying with worry on that score.'

'But you ought to worry,' Mahendra said, 'if because of your carelessness your husband slides down the slippery path, whom would you then blame?'

'Not you, I promise,' Asha said with a new found sense of assurance.

'Would you then admit it was your fault?'

Asha was firm in her reply. 'Decidedly.'

Mahendra now gave his consent for Asha to go to Kashi. 'I will see your elder uncle tomorrow to fix all arrangements. It is quite late now, let us go to sleep.'

Almost immediately Mahendra turned and spoke, 'I say, Chuni, drop this idea of going to Kashi.'

Asha reacted weakly, 'Why are you dissuading me again? Unless I go away, at least for once, your suspicion of me will always haunt me. Let me go, just for a few days.'

Mahendra conceded.

Asha met Binodini the day before she left for Kashi. 'Dear *Chokher Bali*, you must do me a favour.'

Binodini fondly pinched Asha's cheek and said, 'When have I refused to oblige you?'

'Oh, I don't know. You have changed a great deal,' Asha said despondently. 'You appear painstakingly to avoid meeting my husband these days.'

Binodini parried her. 'But surely, you must know why? You heard with your own ears the exchange between Bihari and your husband, and the allegations and the counter allegations. Tell me, would it be appropriate for me to meet them after this?'

Asha knew very well that it would not be. She knew how shameful that episode was. She herself was a victim. Even so, she argued with Binodini, 'People do talk irresponsibly. We have to shake them off. In the interest of our mutual affection we must disregard such foolish remarks. You must ignore them.'

'If you say so, I will,' Binodini agreed.

'I am off to Kashi tomorrow. Please, will you keep an eye on my husband?' Asha pleaded with Binodini. 'See that he is not inconvenienced in any way. You must not keep running away from him.'

Binodini kept quiet. Asha pressed her, 'For my sake, do give me your promise.'

Binodini nodded, 'Yes, I promise.'

TWENTY-SIX

The sun rises when the moon goes down, but Binodini remained invisible yet to Mahendra even after Asha left. Mahendra went round the house aimlessly, on odd pretexts, made forays into his mother's room, but Binodini continued to elude him.

Rajlakshmi noticed her son's restlessness. She assumed it must be due to his wife's absence. It hurt her to discover how redundant the mother had become in the son's life after his marriage. Nevertheless, his lugubrious air pained her. She spoke to Binodini, 'Look, after that illness of mine I have breathing trouble, I cannot run up and down the stairs to look after Mohin. Can I ask you to take charge of his food and other needs? All his life he is used to someone taking care of him. Have you not noticed how absent-minded he has grown ever since his wife left? I honestly do not understand how she could ever think of going away leaving him alone.'

Binodini had turned her face away from Rajlakshmi when she was speaking. 'What is bothering you, Binodini?' she asked. 'There is no harm in doing what I am asking you to do. You are not a stranger in our home, whatever others may say.'

Binodini demurred. 'I do not think it will be right, *Pishima*.' Rajlakshmi sighed. 'Well, in that case you do not have to do anything. I will see what I can do myself.' She was about to climb to Mahendra's room when Binodini stopped her. 'No, please. You must not go up the stairs. You are not yet fully fit. Forgive me, I will go up and do whatever you ask me to.'

Rajlakshmi had scant regard for what people said when it suited her. After her husband's death, her whole life and world revolved round her son Mahendra. Mahendra, to her, was a paragon of all virtues, and there was simply no one else to match him. She was, in fact, irritated with Binodini for her refusal to look after Mahendra as she perceived in it a hint of socially unacceptable conduct. As if her son was capable of doing anything wrong! In any case she could not be bothered—she had an inborn hubris to disregard how other people viewed her likes and dislikes.

When Mahendra returned home that afternoon from college a great surprise awaited him. As he opened the door of his room, an agreeable fragrance of incense and sandalwood greeted him. He noticed the mosquito net, trimmed with rose coloured silk valance. The bed sheet was dazzlingly snow white, and instead of the old-fashioned bolsters, he found large square-shaped cushions encased in finely embroidered silk cover. These were the handiwork of Binodini, on which she had spent long and loving hours. When Asha out of curiosity had asked her for whom she was making all those silk cover, Binodini had jokingly replied, 'To be laid on my pyre when I die. Who else other than death can be my loving partner?'

A framed photograph of Mahendra that adorned a wall had now colourful silk bows decorating the four corners. A small table placed below the photograph carried two vases with neat flower arrangements, kind of offerings of devotee. The look of the room had been transformed. The bed had been shifted to divide the room in two sections. The clothes-horse was screened with drapes. The glass cupboard that housed Asha's fancied collections of china and other bric-a-bracs was now curtained off with a red fabric, carefully crimped and gathered. The contents of the cupboard were now not visible, and in this way Binodini attempted to banish all the old tokens, to be replaced by her new decors.

Mahendra, after a tiring day at college, lay down on the snow white bed and when he put his head down on the new cushions, a mild but pleasant aroma rose to his nose. The cotton stuffing of the cushions had sprinklings of flower dust and drops of *attar*. As he relaxed he had the sensation of being caressed by the delicate fingers that had so skilfully embroidered the cushion covers.

A little later a maid walked in carrying a silver platter with refreshments and a tumbler of iced pineapple juice. Nothing was the same, everything had changed, all so different from what he was accustomed to earlier. Mahendra was overwhelmed.

He ate with must relish. Binodini arrived, carrying paan in a silver container. She said with a smile on her face, 'Please forgive me, not being able personally to attend to you at your meals. For heaven's sake, please do not report my neglect of you to my *Chokher Bali*. I do try to do my best, yet I cannot always help as everything in this home has become my responsibility.'

Mahendra took a paan, and even the paan tasted special.

'Well, even the best of care has to have some imperfections,' Mahendra observed cryptically.

Binodini frowned, 'Why so?'

'Because then one can have some scope for complaints, and one can then extract one's dues with interest,' replied Mahendra.

'Aha, I see. So, Mr Banker, how much interest do I owe you?'

Mahendra said, 'As a starter, you were not present when I ate. Your presence thereafter has not fully compensated me. There are still dues outstanding.'

Binodini laughed. 'I had no idea that you are such a severe calculating person. Once in your grip, there is hardly any hope to redeem oneself.'

'Whatever be my dues, I do not appear to have recouped them, have I?' Mahendra ragged her.

Binodini answered, sounding a little desolate, 'Anyway, what have I got with which to pay you back. At any rate, I am still a captive in your home.' She sighed deeply after neatly turning her jocular statement into a serious observation. 'Are we really keeping you in a prison?' Mahendra asked, disturbed.

Before she could answer, a servant walked in with a lamp which he placed on a table. Binodini shaded her eyes with her hand to avoid the sudden glare of light. She said with her eyes down, 'I really do not know. Besides, who can match you in words? But I must fly, there is a lot to do.'

Mahendra, unexpectedly and without any warning, caught hold of her hand and restrained her. 'Since you admit that you are a captive here, how can you then escape?'

Binodini said, 'Shame on you, let me go. What is the point in pinning down one who in any case has nowhere to go.' She forcibly withdrew her hand and left.

Mahendra kept lying in the bed, his head resting on the perfumed cushions, with a violent turmoil raging in his heart. Spring was in the air. The evening was quiet. And Binodini? She had practically surrendered to him. Mahendra doused the lamp, bolted the door and went to bed early. This was not like his old bed to what he was used. With layers of mattress it was considerably more springy, and the capricious aroma—delicate and maddening. He kept tossing in his bed. He was trying to find some old familiar moorings to which he could latch on to, but found none.

Around nine o'clock in the evening there was a knock on the door. Binodini's voice was heard outside. 'I have brought your dinner, please open the door.' Though most eager to do so, he resisted the temptation and refused to open the door. 'I am not hungry. I don't want any dinner,' he said.

'Are you unwell? Shall I get you some water or anything else that you need?' Binodini sounded anxious.

'No, I don't need anything, nothing at all,' Mahendra replied impatiently.

'Don't lie to me. Even if nothing is wrong, do open the door just for a moment.'

'No, I shall not. Please go away.'

Mahendra went back to bed. His guilty mind recalled the sweet memories of the absent Asha, and on his lonesome bed, on this desolate evening, he tossed and turned but sleep eluded him. He sat up to write to Asha. Asha, he wrote, do not leave me alone for much too long now. You are the reigning queen of my heart, and in your absence my desires, free of shackles, drag me down I know not where. I have no light to lead vie in the dark. The light rests in your loving, full of trust, eyes. Come back to me soon, lonestar of my life, my own, my redeemer. Come, shield me with your protective arms, fill my heart, restore my tranquillity. Save me from the slightest of mental aberration that can do injustice to you, from the nightmare of even the momentary lapse of your thought in my heart.

Mahendra pondered long over this letter. He wrote till late at night, as he was straining to focus his mind on Asha, to turn to her. Somewhere in the distant the church clocks chimed the hour of three in the morning; the streets were now empty and noiseless; the city slept. Occupied with the thoughts of Asha, and now having unburdened his heart in his letter, Mahendra was at peace with himself. In no time he fell asleep.

He rose late the next morning. A good sleep had eased his tensions of last night. His eyes then fell on the letter he had written to Asha. He picked it up and read it. He was aghast! What have I done, he mused, it is like a cheap romantic novel. How fortunate that it had not been dispatched. What would poor Asha have made of this letter? She would not have comprehended even half of what was said in that letter. He destroyed the letter, and wrote another, in more simple language.

'How long are you going to be there? If your elder uncle does not wish to return soon, then tell me. I will go and bring you back. I am desolate without you.'

TWENTY-SEVEN

Annapurna was seriously disturbed when Asha reached Kashi soon after Mahendra left her. Had something really gone wrong between the two? She talked to her niece at length and questioned her incisively to elicit information. She asked about Binodini, 'What about your friend, your *Chokher Bali*? According to you, none in this world can match her in either looks or virtues.'

'Absolutely true, *Mashima*, I have not exaggerated at all. In her looks, in her intellect, she really is peerless. She is also extremely capable in managing all household work.'

'As your friend, you naturally think very highly of her, but what do others say?'

'My mother-in-law is full of her. She cannot do without her. She gets most upset whenever *Chokher Bali* talks of going back to her place. She is also so superb in looking after other people. She even takes care of the servants when any of them falls sick, as a mother or a sister does.'

'Mahendra? What does he think of her?'

'You know his nature, *Mashima*. He is uneasy with people other than his near ones. Everyone is fond of my *Chokher Bali* with the exception of my husband. They do not get on well with each other.'

'Why is it so?'

'You see, I did manage with much trouble to introduce them, but they hardly talk to each other. You know well what an introvert my husband is, which people often misunderstand as arrogance. But that is not true; he just cannot get along with anyone except his own family members.'

As Asha said this, her face turned bashfully red, perhaps out of embarrassment. This report both relieved and pleased Annapurna. She smiled and said, 'That must be true, because not even for once did Mahendra talk about her when he was here.'

Asha was sad. 'This is his one major failing. Anyone he does not like ceases to exist as far as he is concerned. He goes on as if he had never known him or met him.'

Annapurna, with a benign smile and a twinkle in her eyes, told Asha, 'At the same time, is it also not true that when Mahendra likes and is fond of a particular person, he has eyes for that person only and no one else? That is how he is, is it not so, Chuni?'

Asha said nothing, just lowered her eyes and smiled. Annapurna's next query concerned Bihari. 'Tell me, Chuni, how is Bihari? Is he not going to get married at all?'

Asha turned instantly pale, and did not know what to say. Asha's silence alarmed Annapurna. She asked anxiously, 'Tell me the truth, Chuni. Is he unwell?'

Bihari, to this childless woman, was like a dear son of whom she was exceedingly fond. Her solitary regret before she renounced her worldly life was that she had not been able to see Bihari settled down with a wife. This was a constant source of unhappiness for her. The thought of Bihari living alone, all on his own, uncared for, troubled her—the only worry that still disturbed her in her otherwise unworldly life.

Asha told her aunt, quite clearly, '*Mashima*, please never talk to me about Bihari-*thakurpo*.'

Annapurna was shocked. 'But why?' she asked.

'I cannot answer that,' replied Asha and abruptly left the room.

Annapurna was now genuinely worried. Bihari was such a wonderful individual. How could he have changed so much that Asha could not even bear his name being taken? Destiny did play tricks with human beings. How else can one account for the fact that Asha who was initially proposed for Bihari was snatched away by Mahendra at the last moment?

It had been a long time since Annapurna had tears in her eyes. If dear Bihari did indeed commit any grievous act that he should not have done, then it must have been done under a great strain of distress and not deliberately. Of that Annapurna was confident. There was a tug in her heart as she contemplated Bihari's agony.

In the evening when Annapurna was engaged in her devotions, a carriage stopped in front of her house. There was a knock on the door. Annapurna shouted from her sanctum, 'Oh, dear. I had totally forgotten that Kunja's mother-in-law and his two nieces were to arrive this evening from Allahabad. Chuni, can you please take a lantern and receive them?'

Asha opened the door, carrying a lantern, and found Bihari on the porch. Surprised to see Asha there, Bihari said, 'How are you, *Bouthan*? I was told that you had dropped your plan to visit Kashi.'

Asha thought she had seen an apparition. The lantern dropped from her hand, and she ran groaning to her aunt to whom she said, '*Mashima*, for heaven's sake, ask him to go away, immediately.'

Annapurna stood up in great dismay abandoning her devotions and asked, 'Ask whom, Chuni?'

'Bihari-*thakurpo* has followed me out here,' spoke Asha in fright and then locked herself in her room.

Bihari heard everything. He was about to go away, when Annapurna arrived. Bihari had almost collapsed, by then, on the floor, all his strength drained away. Annapurna had no lamp with her, so she was hardly able to see Bihari's face, neither could he see her face.

Annapurna said, 'Bihari?' in a stern voice.

Whose sepulchral voice was it? Where was that affectionate and familiar ring? This voice had a veiled judgmental accusation. Why had mother Annapurna turned so vicious against him? Poor Bihari, he had run to her to seek solace at her feet, and was now turned away unceremoniously.

Bihari rose, pulling up his weary body. He cried in deep anguish, 'No, Kakima, you do not have to say anything. I am taking myself away.'

Bihari did not touch her feet, but bent his head to touch the foreground in front of her. He climbed back into his carriage and vanished through the dark night. Annapurna made no gesture of any sort, did not speak to him, did not call him back.

The same evening Asha wrote to her husband, 'Bihari-*thakurpo* unexpectedly called here. I have no idea when my elder uncle plans to return. Please come soon and take me away.'

TWENTY-EIGHT

Following a sleepless night and the emotional turmoil through which he passed, Mahendra woke up drained out in the morning. Nominally though still the season of spring, the weather had been getting warmer. His normal routine would be to sit at his table and work, but he was too listless to do so. Instead, he remained supine on his bed supported by cushions. The day advanced, but he made no move to go for his bath. Down on the streets, vendors passed along crying their wares; endless streams of creaking vehicles carried office goers and con-in-niters; on the roof of a new building coming up in the neighbourhood, women roof beaters kept up their toneless chant. The spring breeze blowing through an open window failed to soothe his ruffled nerves. Such a lazy aimless spring day was not suitable for any serious work or arduous efforts.

Binodini came up. 'I say, *thakurpo*, what is the matter with you this morning? Why are you not up and gone for your bath? Your food is now ready. Not unwell, are you? Not a headache, is it?' She touched Mahendra's brow with her palm to test if he had any fever.

Mahendra mumbled with his eyes half shut, 'I am, perhaps, a little off. I don't think I'll have a bath today.'

'Well, if you do not want a bath, then do not have one,' said Binodini comforting him, 'but do get up and have some food.' Pressed by her he got up, and Binodini fed him with tender care.

Mahendra lay down again after the meal, and Binodini sitting near him gently massaged his temples. With his eyes still shut Mahendra asked, 'Have you had your food yet? If not, please go and eat.' Binodini did not stir.

Warm afternoon breeze rippled through the curtains; rustling coconut trees echoed through the room; Mahendra's heart went beating faster and faster; Binodini's deep sighs continued to deflect Mahendra's forelocks. No one spoke. Mahendra was carried away beyond his conscious self. He had the unusual sensation of floating on an endless sea on a timeless journey. It mattered not a whit to him if his raft ever moored anywhere.

As she kept massaging his temples, the force of her overpowering restless youth with all its pent up desires drew her face closer to Mahendra's, when her unruly loose tresses brushed against his cheeks. That soft touch of her tresses, disarranged by the breeze, charged his whole being with torrid fire. He could hardly breathe. Then, suddenly, his reverie snapped and he sat up. 'I have to go to college, I am already late,' he stood up as he spoke without looking at Binodini.

'Don't fret. I will go and get your things ready,' Binodini told him and went away. Mahendra pushed off to college, but he was on edge all the time he was there. He found it difficult to concentrate on his work, and returned home early.

As Mahendra entered his room he found Binodini lying prone on the carpet clutching a cushion—her thick black tresses fanned out. She was engrossed in a book. She exhaled a deep sigh as Mahendra tip-toed in.

Mahendra said, 'I say, dear kind hearted lady, do not expend your pity needlessly on fictitious characters. May I ask what is it that you are reading?'

Binodini promptly hid the book under her sari. Mahendra tried to grab the book, and after a tussle he succeeded in beating Binodini down. The book turned out to be Bankimchandra's *Bishabriksa*. Binodini was left fuming with rage.

Mahendra's heart pounded wildly. When the excitement subsided, he smiled and said, 'That was a rotten trick. I was hoping to catch you with some highly intimate secret of yours, and all this labour ended with nothing but *Bishabriksa*!'

'What intimate secrets do you think I can possibly have?' Binodini asked archly.

Mahendra blurted out thoughtlessly, 'For example, it could be a letter from Bihari.'

In an instant the expression in Binodini's face changed, her eyes blazing with fire. She stood up shaking with fury. Mahendra, alarmed by her incensed mood, took hold of her hand and said, 'Please forgive me and overlook my taunt.'

Binodini wrenched her hand back and berated him. 'Taunt? Do you realize who the object of your taunt is? If you were fit to be his friend, I could have overlooked your mean jibe. But you are not fit to be his friend, you are small minded person, and yet you dare mock him.'

As Binodini was about to leave, Mahendra stopped her by clasping her legs with his arms. Just about then a shadow fell, and Binodini after extricating herself, was shocked to see Bihari standing there.

Bihari cast a blistering look at both of them, and after he had composed himself, said, 'My apologies, I appear to have come at a rather inconvenient moment, but I won't detain you. I just came to tell you that I had been to Kashi, but I had no idea that *Bouthan* was also there. I may have offended her unwittingly, but unfortunately, I did not have any opportunity to beg for her pardon. I am here to tender my apologies to you instead. It is also my submission to you that she should not suffer for my sins, which I may have committed unknown to me.'

That Bihari had caught him in an extremely vulnerable situation turned Mahendra nastily vicious towards Bihari. It was not the time, he decided, to treat Bihari with any generosity.

He mocked Bihari, 'I have neither asked you to confess your sins nor have I asked you to deny their. What is the point then of posing as a man of great virtue by asking for my forgiveness?'

This remark froze Bihari stiff, he could hardly speak, when Binodini intervened, 'Bihari-*thakurpo*, do not pay any heed to him. The infamy of what he said will stick to him, but will not touch you.'

Whether Bihari had heard her or not was not clear, as he walked out in a daze and started going down the stairs. Binodini followed him, 'Have you nothing to tell me?' she asked. 'If you wish to censure me, by all means do so.' Bihari ignored her and continued to climb down, when Binodini overtaking him tried to stop him. Bihari, with acute aversion, pushed her away, and went out without looking back. Binodini fell down by this impact, but Bihari was unaware of what he had done.

Mahendra came running to Binodini's aid, when he noticed that she had a cut below her left elbow. He tried to staunch the blood with a bandage, but Binodini waved him away, 'Don't do anything. Let the cut bleed.'

Mahendra protested, 'That will not be right. Let me put some medicine and bandage the cut. It will soon heal and you will have no pain.'

Binodini detached herself from Mahendra and told him firmly, 'I do not want this pain to heal. I want this wound to remain as a permanent mark.'

Mahendra moaned, 'In my impetuosity I misbehaved with you and brought you dishonour, which Bihari has seen. Can you ever forgive my lapse?' He was now truly penitent.

Binodini's reply took Mahendra by surprise. 'Forgive you for what? I have no problem with what you did. What others think do not bother me, neither do I care for them. Who are they to me, who push me away and hurt me? On the other hand, surely they, who wish me to stay even going to the extent of physically stopping me, are my true friends.'

Inflamed by Binodini's sentiments Mahendra spoke ecstatically, 'Binodini, you will not then repudiate my love for you?'

'On the other hand, I will heartily welcome it,' said Binodini. 'Love is a commodity that I had not been showered with in my life, so why should I deny any offer of love?'

Thus encouraged Mahendra held Binodini in his arms, and said, 'Come to my room. We have hurt each other, and until and unless we both can wash off our mutual pain, I shall not find peace.' Binodini declined. 'Not tonight. Let me go now. And, forgive me if I have caused you pain.'

'So must you also forgive me, or else I will go sleepless.' Mahendra was truly contrite.

'I do,' Binodini said quietly.

Mahendra was impatient to receive some instant tokens of Binodini's love and exoneration, but one look at her held him back. Binodini went down the steps, and Mahendra climbed up to the roof.

As he strolled on the roof he experienced a great sense of exhilaration. That he was found out by Bihari brought a strange sensation of liberation. There was an element of ignobility in clandestine affairs. Mahendra had no intention to create a false image of himself as a saint to the outside world. On the other hand, he wanted to be truthful and honest to himself and admit that he was in love! As this forbidden love intensified, he rejoiced in the hubris of being a rake. On that silent night, standing under a starry sky, the whole world ceased to exist for him. He had no care for anybody, anything. He told himself, however ill the others might think of me, the truth is that I am in love. Binodini's image had, at that moment, dislodged everything else from his heart—the whole world, the starry sky, his life, his obligations—Binodini had obliterated them all!

TWENTY-NINE

Mahendra woke up in the morning much refreshed and in a high spirit. The morning sun, as it were, gilded all his dreams and desires. The world outside, the azure sky, the balmy spring air—they all seemed so fabulous this morning.

A mendicant *vaishnav* on his day's round had started to sing with his cymbals outside the gate, and the security guard was about to shoo him away, when Mahendra administering a mild rebuke to the guard magnanimously threw a rupee coin to the mendicant, to the utter amazement of the guard. A servant accidentally dropped and broke a lamp and froze to death when he saw Mahendra. Mahendra smiled benignly at the servant, and told him, almost stupefying him, 'Brush that place carefully not to leave any broken piece which may hurt someone.' He was in the most generous of moods.

His unconscious love that lay hidden until now in some private recess of his heart had now come out in the open, dismissing the make belief fig leaf. He viewed everything around him in a new perspective. The whole world stood out so magnificently pellucid. The mundane trivialities of life ceased to matter. The trees, the birds, the crowds on the streets, the bustling city—every prospect was now so pleasing!

Mahendra avidly looked forward to his assignation with Binodini. This assignation, he had decided, was not going to be anything like their earlier meetings. Mundane prose would be inadequate for communication. Their sentiments could be expressed fittingly only through the language of a poet. Mahendra's ardour aimed to create an ambience of the Arabian Night tales, imbuing it with a wealth of splendour, which would be real, yet dream-like. This fancied world of theirs would be free from all restrictions, all taboos, all obligations, all humdrum concerns.

Mahendra was far too restive since early morning. He skipped college, deliberately; after all, how would he know when the precious moment of their tryst might arrive. No almanacs spell out the propitious confluence of stars for such dalliance to guide him!

From time to time he could hear Binodini's voice floating through either the kitchen or the pantry where she was probably engaged in her chores. Mahendra frowned on her involvement in such routines, for had he not already situated her far above a life of domesticity? He was getting increasingly unsettled as the day advanced. He had his bath and meal in due course, and suffered the boredom of a dull afternoon. Restlessly, Mahendra went through turns of anticipation and frustration.

It was around five o'clock in the evening when Binodini finally showed up, with refreshments for Mahendra. 'What are you up to, *Thakurpo*?' she asked. 'Still in bed at five in the evening?'

A shocking jolt for Mahendra. How could she ask what was wrong with him? She should know why. Was this day like any other day? Afraid that the spell might be broken, he thought it better not to talk about yesterday's affair.

Setting the food down before Mahendra, Binodini went to the roof to collect the day's washings from the clothesline. She started to fold them neatly before storing them in the wardrobe.

'Give me a minute, I'll come and give you a hand,' Mahendra offered.

'Spare me please,' Binodini appealed to him. 'Whatever else you may do, just don't come in my way.'

Mahendra got up and said, 'Aha, you think I am thoroughly useless. Come, test me,' he bragged. He applied himself then to folding the clothes, with disastrous results. In the end he gave up, and magnanimously told Binodini, 'Well, carry on. I will watch you and learn.' He parked himself in front of the wardrobe, and Binodini playfully hit him with the clothes on the pretext of shaking them before putting them in the wardrobe.

Thus began their very first tryst. This was not the love feast that Mahendra had earlier fancied. There was no trace of any excitement, none whatever. Such prosaic unions were clearly not the stuff of romantic literature or of love lyrics. Nevertheless, Mahendra was not too disappointed. On the contrary, he was to an extent relieved. He had, in reality, little or no clue how to lead up to his highly colourful visions. This play acting in a down to earth domestic chore, in a sense, rescued him from the improbable task of creating his fairy tale dream world.

Rajlakshmi came in, unexpectedly. She was surprised to see her son there. 'Binodini is doing the clothes, but what are you doing here?' she asked her son.

'*Pishima*, he is just wasting my time by interfering with my work,' Binodini said by way of a complaint.

'Not at all. I was lending her a helping hand,' Mahendra ponderously observed.

Rajlakshmi beamed fondly. 'What? You, lending a helping hand? Do you know what, Binodini, he has been so incorrigibly spoilt by both his mother and aunt that he is totally incapable of fending for himself in any way,' she said casting an adoring look at her son.

The sole mission in Rajlakshmi's life was how to surround her hopelessly dependant-on-mother grown-up son with every comfort, and for this Binodini was her prime aide. She was presently very happy and relaxed with Binodini now taking over complete charge of looking after her son. It also pleased her that Mahendra had developed some regard for Binodini and was not so hostile to her.

She told Binodini, for Mahendra's benefit, 'It was good that you aired Mahendra's winter clothes and stored them. You will now need to stitch his initials on the new bunch of his handkerchiefs. I feel so very bad that ever since you came to us I have only worked you to death, and hardly done anything for you.'

Binodini protested, '*Pishima*, if you keep talking in this fashion, I would then feel that I do not belong here.'

Rajlakshmi looked fondly at her and said, 'No child, where would we get anyone as dear as you are?'

After Binodini finished her work of arranging the clothes, Rajlakshmi suggested, 'Shall we now go and boil the syrup for the sweetmeats, unless you have anything else to do?'

'No, I have nothing else at the moment. Let us go make the sweets,' Binodini said.

'Mother, only a minute ago you moaned that you were working her to death, and now you are proposing to take her away for more work to do,' grumbled Mahendra.

Rajlakshmi fondled Binodini by her chin and said, 'This angelic girl of our lives only for her work.'

Mahendra made a last try, 'I have not much to do this evening, so I thought Bali and I could read a book together.'

Binodini said saucily, 'A great idea. *Pishima*, we will both come and listen to *Thakurpo* reading to us. Right, *Pishima*?'

From all this talk Rajlakshmi concluded that her son was lonely in the absence of his wife and so needed company. She readily assented to Binodini's suggestion and said, 'Yes, we shall, after we finish our cooking. What do you say to that, Mohin?'

Binodini gave an oblique look at Mahendra who, not exactly leaping to the idea, had no option but to agree. Binodini and Rajlakshmi went away together, with Mahendra left fuming. He decided he would go out and return late. He did change into street clothes, but eventually did not go out. Up on the roof he often kept glancing at the staircase with fervent anticipation if anyone was coming up. Finally, in great disgust, he returned to his room, and vowed not to touch the sweets tonight just to give his mother the message that any syrup that took so long to boil could not possibly remain sweet.

Because of her breathing trouble Rajlakshmi normally avoided climbing up the stairs, but tonight Binodini persuaded her to go up for Mahendra's meal. Mahendra sat down to eat in a surly mood. Binodini teasingly asked him, 'Anything wrong with the food? You are hardly eating.'

The mother, rising to the bait, said anxiously, 'Not unwell, are you?'

Binodini added with a sly grin, 'We took so much trouble in making the sweets. You must at least taste them. Oh, you do not like them, then leave them out. No point in eating something, which you do not want to, just because someone insists.'

Mahendra said, 'Very strange. I was particularly looking forward to the sweets that you both made. I do like them, yet you wish to stop me from eating them.' He ate two of them, with relish, to the last crumb.

When the meal was over, they all went to Mahendra's room. Mahendra intentionally did not raise the issue of reading, but his mother remembered. She said, 'You talked about reading a book, so why do you not begin?'

'Mother, you will not enjoy it,' Mahendra said quickly, 'this is not a spiritual book, it does not have anything on your gods and goddesses.'

How could her son ever think that she would not like what her son read to her? She was determined to appreciate whatever the son read, even if it was in the Turkish language! Poor boy, he was so lonely in the absence of his wife. He must be humoured, and so she must fall in line with his wishes.

Binodini piped in, 'I have a suggestion. *Pishima* has a religious book, *Shantishatak*. Why do you not read from it? *Pishima* will love it, and we will all have an enjoyable evening.'

Mahendra looked venomously at Binodini. A maid came in to tell Rajlakshmi that her old friend Kayet-*thakrun* had arrived and was waiting to meet her. This lady was a close friend of Rajlakshmi, and they met invariably each evening. Rajlakshmi found it difficult to resist the temptation to go and talk to her. Nevertheless, she instructed the maid to go and tell Kayetthakrun that she was tied up with her son on an important matter and so she could not see her this evening, but that the *thakrun* must not forget to be back tomorrow.

Mahendra said impatiently, 'But, mother, why don't you go yourself and see her, even if briefly?'

Biriodini chipped in once again. 'No, *Pishima*, you stay on. I will go instead and take care of Kayet-*thakrun*.'

By then Rajlakshmi was dying to see her friend. She stopped Binodini. 'No, you wait here. Let me go and see her, and try to cut her visit short. Let Mahendra start his reading meanwhile. I will join you later.'

As soon as Rajlakshmi left, Mahendra could not contain himself and fumed at Binodini, 'Why do you deliberately torture me in this fashion?'

'Torture You? I? Why, what did I do?' Binodini turned most innocent. 'Should I have not come here then? If that be so, let me go.'

'That is precisely how you go on scorching me.'

'Really, I was never aware that I was such an arsonist person,' she continued as innocent as ever, 'but, frankly, I see no burn marks on you at all. You must have an iron physique to withstand my inflammatory arrows.'

'No, you will not find any mark there, but here...' He pulled her hand with force and placed it on his heart.

Binodini shrieked, 'Ouch!' when Mahendra let go her hand. 'Did I hurt you?' he asked.

He found the spot near her elbow she had cut the day before had started bleeding. 'I am sorry,' Mahendra was apologetic, 'I had forgotten about your cut. Let me apply some medicine there—I insist.'

Binodini refused, 'It is nothing really. I don't need any medicine.'

'Why not?'

'Thank you very much. You need not doctor me. Let my cut alone,' she said waving him away.

Mahendra was once again baffled; there was no accounting for women's whims!

Binodini rose to leave. Mahendra did not try to stop her but asked, 'Where are you off to?'

'Oh, I have a lot of pending work,' she said and left.

He thought of going down and getting her back, but changed his mind. Instead, he went up to the roof and paced up and down restlessly. He realized that he had become a captive to Binodini's charms, but she hardly gave him any encouragement. It had always been his boast that no one could win his heart, but at this point of time he was not all that confident. What, however, peeved him the most was the severe blow to his vanity that he could capture the heart of any woman he wished to win over. He was clearly the loser this evening, because he could not crush her. He regarded no one his peer in matters of heart, and yet he was now humbled. What had he gained in lieu? He was left empty-handed like a supplicant waiting vainly in front of a door that had been shut in his face.

Each year, towards the end of the spring season, Bihari regularly sent Rajlakshmi a supply of mustard flower honey that came from his estate. This year was no exception either, and it was Binodini, who carried the gift to Rajlakshmi when it arrived. 'Bihari-*thakurpo* has, as usual, sent you this mustard flower honey.'

After complying with Rajlakshmi's instruction of where and how to store the honey, Binodini remarked, 'It is really wonderful the way Bihari-*thakurpo* keeps in regular touch with you. Having lost his mother he now looks upon you as his mother.'

In reality, Bihari hardly ever featured in Rajlakshmi's mind. She had always taken him for granted as a most devoted shadow of Mahendra, and a loyal friend of the family. A chord in her motherly heart was touched when Binodini reminded her how Bihari looked upon her as his mother. True, she admitted to herself, Bihari had always regarded her as his mother. She then recalled the numerous instances when Bihari on his own came to her help, at times of sickness, during family crises, unasked for and then looked after her with selfless devotion. Rajlakshmi had always accepted his services at face value, and never had felt the need to have any sense of gratitude to him. Nor did she ever bother much about him. Annapurna did, but she had always treated Annapurna's concern for Bihari with a grain of salt—a pretense, a show off, just to win him to her side.

She now conceded that Bihari truly was like her own son. And, it immediately occurred to her that Bihari, in fact, was much more to her than her own son. He had remained steadfastly devoted to her without any expectations. Bihari suddenly loomed large in her heart.

Binodini nudged her, 'Bihari-*thakurpo* is exceedingly fond of your cooking.'

Rising to the bait Rajlakshmi proudly remarked, 'For him no one can match my fish preparations.' Bihari had been missing for a long time. Why, she wondered. She asked Binodini, 'How is it that we rarely see him these days?'

'The same thought had also occurred to me,' said Binodini. 'You see, after his marriage your son is so besotted with his wife that his friends do not feel like calling.'

A very apt observation according to Rajlakshmi. Absorbed in his wife Mahendra had alienated his friends. It was only but natural for Bihari to take umbrage and opt to stay away. Assuming Bihari to be on her side, her sympathy for him intensified. She recounted the many tales of Bihari's early days, how he had selflessly helped Mahendra on many occasions, the enormous trouble he had courted for his sake. In fact, her own grievances against her own son found an outlet through her newly found appreciation for Bihari. No excuses could justify Mahendra's neglect of his old friends for the sake of his wife who had only recently appeared in his life.

Binodini dropped a hint. 'Tomorrow is a Sunday. I am quite sure Bihari-*thakurpo* will be no end delighted if you invite him for lunch tomorrow.'

'You are quite right,' readily agreed Rajlakshmi, 'Let me ask Mohin to invite him.'

'No, *Pishima*, you must invite him,' Binodini insisted.

Rajlakshmi was alarmed, 'But how can I? I cannot read and write like you.'

'Have no worry, *Pishima*. I shall write on your behalf.'

Which Binodini did and had the letter dispatched to Bihari.

Mahendra always looked forward to his Sundays, for which he used to make advance plans the evenings before. Not necessarily did his plans always work out. At any rate, he woke up this Sunday with pleasurable anticipations. The world outside looked to him most benign. But, apparently, something was in the air. His mother seemed to be unusually busy. Normally, she depended on Binodini for all work at home, so what was she so occupied with? Was she observing any special religious occasion?

The day wore on, but no Binodini was in sight. For diversion he tried to read but could not concentrate. He scanned the newspaper, needlessly focusing on an advertisement, eventually gave up. His patience finally wearing him down, he could not hold himself any longer and went down. He found his mother in the verandah, cooking on a portable oven, and Binodini, her sari tightly wrapped round her waist, lending a helping hand.

'What is on? Why this great show?' he asked mystified.

'Did not Binodini tell you that I have asked Bihari for lunch today?' replied Rajlakshmi.

Invited? Bihari? Mahendra almost blew his top. His immediate sullen reaction was, 'But, I am afraid, I shan't be here.'

'Why not?' Rajlakshmi was most despondent.

'I have some other engagement.'

'Go there after lunch. Lunch would not take much time,'

she suggested.

'Not possible. I have also been invited for lunch,' Mahendra said in a deadpan voice.

With a mischievous glance at Mahendra, Binodini said, '*Pishima*, if he has an invitation, let him go then. Bihari-*thakurpo* will have to eat all by himself, and that is that.'

The thought that Mahendra would be deprived of the food that she had cooked with so much care and trouble made Rajlakshmi utterly miserable. The more she pressed Mahendra to cancel his engagement, the more recalcitrant Mahendra proved. He kept insisting that his engagement was most urgent and no way could he skip it. He was also aggrieved. 'You should have spoken to me before you decided to invite Bihari,' he said.

This was Mahendra's way of venting his wrath on his mother. Poor Rajlakshmi had lost all her interest in the affair. She wished to call it off, but Binodini surprised her. '*Pishima*, do not get needlessly worked up. All *Thakurpo's* protest is mere bluff. He is not going anywhere.'

Rajlakshmi shook her head. 'No child, you do not know him. He does not budge when he makes up his mind.'

It eventually turned out that Binodini knew Mahendra no less well than his mother. Mahendra had correctly guessed that the invitation to Bihari was at Binodini's instigation, and this inflamed his sense of jealousy so acutely that he found it most difficult to be away when Bihari arrived. Regardless of how very aggravating Bihari's presence might be, he decided he must be there, if only to see what plot the two of them were hatching together.

Bihari arrived, after a long absence, and on this occasion as an invitee. He did not enter the house immediately. He stood outside for a few minutes in a pensive mood. It was a house, each nook and corner of which was so familiar to him, where he had unhindered access since his young days, where he had played so many mischievous pranks. The influx of these memories stalled him momentarily. He recovered soon enough to go in and greet Rajlakshmi. He touched her feet more ceremoniously than usual. These courtesies were not normally observed when Bihari was a regular visitor, but this morning he felt that he had, as it were, returned home after a long sojourn away. Rajlakshmi also with more than usual tenderness welcomed him.

Perhaps, because of his long absence, Rajlakshmi was demonstrably more effusive with her expression of love and affection for Bihari. She lamented, 'My son, why did you keep yourself away for so long? Each passing day I expected you to come and see me, but you never did. I thought of you everyday.'

Bihari smiled and said, 'There you are, Ma. You would have not thought of me everyday if I did come everyday. In any case, where is Mohin?'

Rajlakshmi replied, dejected, 'He said he had to go out to some invitation, so he could not stay.'

Bihari's earlier keenness lost a little edge. Was it the final lid, he pondered, on the coffin of their lifelong friendship? In an attempt to shake off his disappointment, he asked Rajlakshmi, 'Tell me what have you been cooking for me this morning?' He started talking about all his favourite dishes. Whenever he came to Rajlakshmi to be fed, it was his usual practice to display excessive craving for her cooking, thus endearing himself even more to Rajlakshmi. This morning was no exception and Rajlakshmi, with equal energy, assured her gourmet guest of the delectable feast that awaited him.

Mahendra, surprising everyone, came in unexpectedly. He spoke to Bihari in a very formal tone, 'Hello, Bihari, how are you?'

'But, Mohin, are you not supposed to go out?' Rajlakshmi asked.

Mahendra smiled weakly to cover his discomfiture, 'Well, I managed to get out of it.'

When a little later Binodini returned after her bath, Bihari felt uneasy in her presence. The scene between her and Mahendra that he had witnessed was still fresh in his mind.

It was Binodini who spoke to Bihari, 'How is it Bihari-*thakurpo* that you do not seem to recognize me?'

Bihar replied, offhand, 'There are times when one forgets to do so.'

'With a little effort one can always do so,' remarked Binodini and then turning to Rajlakshmi told her that lunch was ready.

Mahendra and Bihari sat down to eat. Rajlakshmi kept an eye and Binodini served. Mahendra had little interest in the food, but he kept watching like a hawk if Binodini betrayed any partisanship while serving. The thought crossed Mahendra's mind that Binodini took particular pleasure in looking after Bihari. Bihari, indeed, did receive some special attention, but that was to be expected. After all, he was a guest and Mahendra was the family.

With some effort, out-of-season *Topse* fish had been procured, and this fish when fat with roe inside was considered a particular delicacy. Binodini was about to serve one such fish to Bihari when he raised his hand to stop her. He said, 'Give it to Mohin. He is very fond of them.' Mahendra, his hackles clearly rising, protested, 'No, let Bihari have it. I don't want it.' Binodini, paying no heed to either, dropped the fish on Bihari's plate.

After the meal was over, Binodini invited Bihari to go up and rest. Bihari asked her, 'Are you not going to have your food?' Binodini shook her head, 'No, it is *ekadasi* today, a fast day for us.'

A thin unkind smile rose to Bihari's lips, implying all pretences were in place, including the traditional fasting by widows on *ekadasis*. This sarcastic gesture did not escape Binodini's eyes, but she ignored it. She repeated her request, 'Let us go up.'

Taking unreasonable exception to Binodini's invitation to Bihari, Mahendra spoke up savagely. 'I can never make you out. You have no sense of discretion at all. He may or may not be free, he may not be inclined at all to stay on, and yet you must insist that he should stay back. This over-zealous attention is so pointless.'

Binodini laughed rather loudly, and said, 'Bihari-*thakurpo*, just listen to your friend,' and then turning to Mahendra she said, 'do admit that no one can appreciate what you call overzealous attention more than you do, of which you have been a beneficiary ever since you were born.'

'I must talk to you, Mohin,' Bihari quickly cut in, and went out with Mahendra, unceremoniously denying Binodini the merest courtesy of a formal farewell. Bihari asked Mahendra, 'Is it the end of the road of our friendship?'

By then, Mahendra was burning with fury, fanned by Binodini's banter, her mock-serious barbs at him. In an irascible mood he bluntly told Bihari, 'A reconciliation may suit you, but I don't desire it. I do not particularly want outsiders to have access to our inner sanctum—the inner sanctum has to remain private.'

Bihari looked at Mahendra with intense pain in his eyes, and left without any comment. Driven by a violent impact of jealousy Mahendra swore that he would have nothing more to do with Binodini. But he remained on edge throughout the day, impatiently wandering round the house in the hope of a chance meeting with Binodini.

THIRTY

At Kashi, Asha asked Annapurna, 'Tell me, *Mashima*, can you recollect your husband at all?'

Annapurna replied, 'I was widowed when I was merely eleven years old. I have only a blurred image of my husband.'

'On whom then do you meditate?' asked Asha.

Her aunt replied, 'On my God, in whose arms my husband now rests.'

'And, does that give you any peace of mind?'

Running her fingers affectionately on Asha's head, Annapurna said, 'It will not be easy for you to comprehend what goes on in my heart. Only I know it, and perhaps my God may.'

It set Asha thinking. The person who occupies my heart constantly, Asha nursed, apparently has little time for me. He has even stopped writing me because I cannot write well enough.

Indeed, Asha moped, she had not heard from her husband for a long time. Perhaps, if her *Chokher Bali* were with her, she could have adequately expressed her thoughts.

Asha had little incentive to write to her husband as she was afraid he would hardly appreciate her ill-composed letters. However much she tried, her writing became scrawls, and she could never put in words what were in her mind. Asha wished her husband was gifted with the vision to read her sentiments and emotions though not spelt out in words. In that case, she could just write, 'Dearest husband' and sign off, and leave the rest of the letter blank for Mahendra to interpret. Poor Asha, the good Lord had sent her with an enormous reservoir of love, but denied her the gift of language.

After they returned from the temple one evening, Asha asked her aunt, 'You keep telling me that it is the moral duty of a wife to look after her husband devotedly, as it were, he was her God. But if a woman who is ignorant, has little intelligence, has no idea how to look after her husband, what can such a woman do?'

Annapurna looked apprehensively at Asha, and then with a deep sigh said, 'I am also an ignorant woman, but I try to serve my God in my own way.'

'Well, He knows you, and so He is pleased with your devotion,' said Asha. 'But assume a case where the husband is not happy with the care of an ignorant wife, what happens then?'

Annapurna tried to comfort her niece. She told her, 'Look, it is not possible for any single individual to please everyone. If a wife devotedly and sincerely attends to her husband, then God himself will reward the wife, even if the husband disdains her care.'

Asha was not quite convinced. To her it made little sense to be rewarded by God but ignored by the husband.

Annapurna observed her niece intently for some time, then drawing her close, fondly kissed her forehead. In her quiet way she then told Asha, 'What you learn in the hard school of life cannot be taught through words of mouth. When I was your age I had assumed that all relationships in life were of mutual give and take. I proceeded on the assumption of due returns. If I do someone a good turn, why should this not be reciprocated? If I do render some service, why should the receiver of my service not be thankful to me? In reality, I found that was not the way of the world. When I discovered that whatever I had done had been all in vain, I decided I could take it no longer. It was then that I resolved to renounce the domestic life. Looking back, however, it has occurred to me that perhaps it has not all been futile. What I had not realized then that all my dealings were really with one and one person only, and that person was none other than my God. Had I clearly known this then, I would not have been so frustrated, but I know better now.'

In her bed, late at night, Asha pondered deeply over what her aunt had said, though she still had no clear comprehension. Since she regarded her aunt so highly, that even without fully grasping what she had said, she accepted them as gospel truth. She prayed to the same God that her aunt regarded as the ultimate being. In her prayers she said, 'Dear God, I am a young ignorant girl. I cannot claim really to know you. I only know my husband, so please on that score do not take offence with me. Please God, see to it that my husband accepts what I can offer him. I will not be able to survive if he rejects me. I am not a virtuous woman like my aunt, and I won't find redemption clinging only to you.'

Asha's elder uncle was ready to return to Calcutta. On the eve of her departure, Annapurna told her, 'Chuni, I have not the power to protect you against the rough passages of life. All I can tell you is that regardless of your pains remain unflinching in your faith, in your piety, in your devotion.'

Asha touched her aunt's feet and said, considerably moved, 'Yes, *Mashima*, let that be your benediction.'

THIRTY-ONE

At their their first meeting after Asha's return, Binodini, giving the impression of being much hurt, charged her, 'Not one, not a single letter to me, all the time you were away.'

Somewhat abashed Asha countercharged, 'But neither did you?'

'Surely, yours was the first turn to write,' complained Binodini.

It did not take them long to make up. Asha admitted that she was remiss. 'You know I do not write well at all, and the very thought of writing to so educated a person as yourself puts me off.'

They started exchanging notes. Binodini admonished her, 'You have completely spoilt your husband, being constantly at his side, like his shadow. He now demands someone to be with him all the time.'

'That is why I left him in your hands,' said Asha. 'You are far more gifted in the art of companionship than I can ever be.'

'Well, the mornings were not too problematic,' Binodini continued, 'I was free once I managed to pack him off to college. But come the evenings, and no respite for me. I have to talk to him, read to him, just no end to his demands.'

'There you are, rightly served,' said Asha with an innocent smile. 'Since you are so adept in diverting people, naturally they won't leave you alone.'

'Take care, though, I warn you,' Binodini teased Asha, 'the way *Thakurpo* goes overboard, I sometimes suspect that I may have the gift of casting spells.'

Asha laughed, 'Of course, you do, and I would love to have some of that particular gift of yours.'

'Why, whom are you scheming to ruin?' said Binodini. 'Do not try that game, much too risky. Much better to keep an eye on your own man who is, in any case, yours.'

Asha said, in mock remonstration, 'Come, stop it, don't talk rot.'

Mahendra's comment at his first meeting with his wife after her return was, 'Great. Kashi seems to have done wonders for you. You have gained some weight.'

How mortifying! In her husband's absence she should have pined away, and not gained in health. The poor girl, what could she have done, nothing ever went right for her. How could she have gained weight when, in fact, she did mope for her absent husband? As it was, she could not adequately express her thoughts, and on top of that, her wretched health had to carry the wrong message.

Thus put down, Asha asked mildly, 'How had you been?'

In normal times Mahendra would have replied, half in jest and half seriously, that in her absence he felt as if he was dead. He could not do that truthfully, so came out with a laconic response, 'Not bad, fairly well.'

To Asha, Mahendra appeared to have lost weight. He looked pale, and his eyes had some sort of a hungry look. She felt very bad for her husband. She condemned herself for leaving him alone. Her health had improved, while her husband's had declined. What an awful contretemps!

Both of their appeared to be lost for words. After a pause, Mahendra asked about his aunt, and on being told that she was fine he could think of nothing more to say. He suddenly discovered much interest in an old newspaper, while Asha sat there, weighed down with anxieties. They met after such a long gap, but her husband hardly at all looked at her. What had gone wrong, the poor girl racked her brain. Was he annoyed with her because she did not write him often enough, or did he resent her staying on a little longer at her aunt's request? She searched in vain her distressed heart in what way she could have offended him.

Asha met him with refreshments when Mahendra returned from college. Rajlakshmi was also there. She looked at her son with some anxiety, and asked, 'Are you not well?'

'I am fine,' Mahendra sounded irritated.

'Then, why are you not eating?'

'What do you think I am doing then?' he said with some more heat in his voice.

Mahendra went up to the roof, pacing impatiently up and down. He had been hoping against all odds that Binodini would arrive to continue their usual reading together. They had almost reached the end of *Anandamath*, only a few chapters remained. Surely, she would not be so inconsiderate as not to finish the remaining chapters. Time passed, but she did not appear. A disheartened Mahendra went back to his room.

Late at night Asha went to their bedroom, and found Mahendra already asleep. Re-union after a long separation is usually marked with a sense of inhibition; there is an expectation of a fresh and fond approach. Asha was in a quandary. How could she climb on to the bed unless she was asked? She waited for some time, but there was no response from Mahendra. She tip-toed silently not to disturb her husband. At that moment her careful toilet in anticipation of an intimate meeting with her husband after this long interval stood out like a foolish charade. She thought of running away and sleep somewhere else.

Had Mahendra been truly asleep, even her silent movements would have wakened him up. Since he was merely feigning sleep, he deliberately did not open his eyes. Asha took her usual place in the bed. Mahendra knew well that she was weeping, silently. His own apathy disturbed him, but he found it difficult to break the ice. I will make amends in the morning, he decided, and fell asleep.

Asha saved Mahendra from this predicament. She rose very early in the morning and left the room. She had no desire to confront Mahendra.

THIRTY-TWO

Asha's mind was in turmoil. What had gone wrong? What had she done? Poor Asha. Innocent as she was, she could have never put her finger on the real source of her threat. That Mahendra could fall in love with Binodini was beyond her wildest imagination. The image of Mahendra that was engraved in her heart was so inflexible that to Asha the possibility of a delinquent Mahendra was just absurd.

It was time for Mahendra to get ready for his college. The usual drill was for Asha to stand at the bedroom window and watch Mahendra get into the carriage, when Mahendra would look up and they would exchange glances. Following this routine, as soon as Asha heard the carriage rolling in, she rushed to the window. Though as a matter of habit Mahendra did look up, it was only for a brief instant, and he immediately turned his attention to a book. Mahendra, however, did not fail to observe that by then Asha had not had her bath, neither had she changed into fresh clothes, her hair was unkempt, and she looked jaded and weary. Missing was that silent but pregnant communication, and the smile that earlier spoke volumes.

As Mahendra's carriage rolled away, life for Asha ceased to have any significance. The time was ten-thirty in the morning, the busiest hour of the city. Carriages moved along the streets carrying commuters to their work, tram cars cued up one behind another, and in the midst of this bustling city life, a crushed heart and a benumbed soul laden with pain seemed so incongruous.

Asha's restless mind kept churning trying to get to the root of Mahendra's indifference to her. Suddenly, it occurred to her that the source of Mahendra's resentment could probably be the unexpected visit of Bihari to Kashi. She could not think of any other unpleasant incidents to explain Mahendra's attitude. In what way could she be held culpable for this occurrence? Her heart stopped beating for a moment when she recalled Bihari's visit. Did Mahendra suspect any collusion between them? Oh, how awful, if he indeed, did so! Bihari's name being linked with her was bad enough, but if on top of that

Mahendra had misgivings about her, how could she then live on with this obloquy? What prevented Mahendra to come out in the open and punish her? At the core of her heart Asha believed that Mahendra did actually harbour no such suspicion, but he was too ashamed to admit it to her. What else could account for his furtive looks, or why should he vacillate in this fashion if he had no real grounds to take offence?

All through the day Mahendra was troubled by the thought of the tragic face of Asha that he saw very briefly when he was leaving. The sight of Asha, standing by the window, sad and forlorn, with pain-stricken eyes, kept haunting him.

Mahendra did not return home immediately after college gave over. Instead, he went for a long walk brooding over his dilemma. He was undecided how he ought to deal with Asha. Should he resort to well-intentioned deception, or should be opt for candid candour? There was, of course, no question of giving up Binodini, but the impasse was—could he cope with the claims of his heart as well as his sense of fairness? Mahendra began to rationalize his dilemma in his own mind. He was still very fond of his wife, and, indeed, few wives were so fortunate. There was no earthly reason why Asha should not be happy with what she had. His heart was spacious enough to have room for both Asha and Binodini. His pure and platonic love for Binodini would in no way interfere with his sentiments for his wife.

Persuaded by his own logic Mahendra was now comparatively easy in his mind. He returned home elated by the thought that he would spend all his life without the need for abandoning either of them. He resolved to make amends to Asha tonight when they were in bed, and with his love and tenderness erase all her misery.

Asha was not present during his dinner, but he was sure she would join him later. Lying on his bed his thoughts swung between two poles. He was simultaneously absorbed in the pleasurable anticipation of his re-union with Asha, as well as in the image of another young woman, bright and lively, whose radiance dimmed the mellow lustre of his wife. He recalled their fight for the possession of the book *Bishabriksa*; he recalled their reading together till late at night when everyone else had gone to bed, until her rhapsodic voice would go softer and softer. His whole being experienced an ecstatic thrill as he remembered those rapturous moments. He did not wish Asha to intrude on his amorous thoughts by her sudden arrival. Asha in any case did not turn up at all, and so he was able to absolve himself of his feeling of guilt. What could he do if Asha chose not to come to him when he was prepared for a rapprochement. He felt he had now been set free to dwell on his reverie for Binodini!

Still sleepless well past midnight Mahendra sprang impatiently from his bed and went up to the roof. The city was bathed in bright moonlight. A seductive breeze swirling round its many edifices had lulled the city to sleep. The bewitching ambience inflamed Mahendra's suppressed ardour almost to a breaking point.

Since Asha's return from Kashi, Binodini had assiduously kept herself aloof from Mahendra, and in the process driving him to desperation. The mischievous moon cast a hypnotic spell on him and propelled him towards Binodini. He walked down the steps, as if in a trance, and went to her room. He found the door open, pushed into the room, but she was not there.

Binodini and Rajlakshmi had decided to sleep on the adjoining verandah to escape the summer heat. Woken up by the sound of Mahendra's footsteps Binodini cried out, 'Who is there?'

Mahendra, charged with emotion, said, 'It is I, Binodini,' and came out to the verandah. Rajlakshmi had also got up, and surprised to see her son there, she asked, 'What are you doing here so late at night?'

Binodini scowled at him murderously. Without saying a word Mahendra quickly melted away.

THIRTY-THREE

The next day dawned overcast, promising some relief after the last few days of intense heat. Mahendra had left for college earlier than usual. Asha was listing his soiled clothes to be given to the dhobi, the laundryman. By his nature Mahendra was absent minded, and that was why he had instructed Asha to look carefully in his pockets for anything left behind by mistake. While doing so this morning, Asha discovered a letter in one of the pockets.

The letter was open, it was in Binodini's writing. Asha turned pale. She went to another room and started reading. It said:

'Had you not had enough after last night's foolishness of yours? How could you send me a letter through Khemi? For shame, what do you think she made of it? Are you determined that I shall not be able to show my face publicly to anyone?

'Please, what do you expect from me? Love? That is something that you do not lack. All your life you had a surfeit of it from your dear and near ones. Why is this mendacity then? Is your desire insatiable?

'I have no one to love, and no one to love me. Since I have been denied this happiness, I contrive my satisfaction through play-acting. You joined in the game when you were free to do so. But games cannot go on forever, and presently you are not also free. There are now demands on you. So, why do you peep into the romping room to continue your game? Clean yourself, go back to your sanctum. I have no sanctum of my own, I will be alone, devising my own games. I will not need you there.

'There was a time when you thought you loved Asha. That was a lie. Now you think you love me. That is also a lie. In truth, you are in love with yourself.

'My heart had been arid thirsting for love, but you have no wherewithal to quench my thirst. I know that well enough. I have told you this before, and I repeat, do not run after me. Being without shame yourself, do not put me to shame. I have lost interest in playing games, and I will not respond to your call. You said in your letter that

I am heartless. Perhaps I am, but I am also of compassionate nature, and out of my consideration for you, I am severing my tie with you. If you still write to me, I will have to run away from you, or else I will not find my redemption.'

By the time Asha finished reading this letter she had no strength left in her. She could not breathe, she could not see, all was dark around her. Her nerves, her muscles, ceased to function. She tried to balance herself against the wall, clutching on to the shelves and chairs, and finally collapsed on the floor. She tried once again to read the letter but gave up. Her confused mind could make no sense out of it.

How did this come about, this unthinkable calamity of her life? Why? To whom could she go for help? She sought out for support, as a sinking person clings to a straw. She thought of her aunt. '*Mashima*,' her wail rang out, and she broke into a flood of tears. By the time she came round, her worry was how to dispose of the letter. She would be in an awful fix if her husband came to know that she had read that letter. The best solution, she decided, would be to restore it to Mahendra's shirt pocket and not send it for wash.

She returned to the bedroom and was about to put the letter back when Binodini came in. She quickly threw the letter and the shirt on the bed and sat upon them. Binodini told her, 'The dhobi is misplacing clothes. Let me collect the clothes not yet marked and mark them.'

Not wishing to betray herself to Binodini, Asha turned her face to the window, with her lips compressed to stem the gushing tears. Looking at Asha, Binodini inferred that Asha might have come to know about the last night's episode and was embittered in the belief that Binodini must have been the guilty party. She made no effort to talk to Asha, and collecting some of the clothes left the room.

Until now Asha was confident that Binodini was a genuine and sincere friend of hers, and even in her present distressed predicament she found it difficult to repudiate these sentiments. She decided to read the letter again, at least to check how this letter stood up to her faith in her friend. As she was about to do so, Mahendra walked in unexpectedly. Asha smartly hid the letter. Mahendra fumbled when he saw Asha. His eyes darted searchingly, and Asha knew what he was looking for. Asha wondered if she could get away by restoring the letter to its original spot, but when she observed Mahendra frantically combing through his discarded clothes, she flung his shirt and the letter at him. Mahendra swiftly picked up the letter and, after one look at Asha, ran out of the room.

THIRTY-FOUR

Rajlakshmi did not seek out Binodini at all this morning, which was unusual. When Binodini routinely went to the pantry, she found Rajlakshmi there, but Rajlakshmi ignored her. Binodini noticed this and asked, 'Are you not well, *Pishima*? Indeed, how can you after what *Thakurpo* did last night? Rushed in like a bull. I could hardly sleep after he left.'

Rajlakshmi sat there with a long drawn face, and paid no heed to Binodini.

Binodini continued, 'I guess the husband and wife must have had again some minor tiff, and he wanted me, perhaps, to mediate immediately. Whatever may be the virtues of your precious son, patience is not one of them, and that is why both of us fight so much.'

Rajlakshmi now opened her mouth. 'Will you shut up? All your talk is rubbish. I have no interest in listening to you.'

Binodini spoke calmly, 'That is mutual, *Pishima*. Neither do I have any interest in all this. I was merely trying to find excuses for your son to spare you needless pain. Anyway, it has already gone too far, and difficult to keep it under lid.'

Rajlakshmi, highly irritated, promptly intervened, 'I am well aware of my son's faults and virtues. What I did not know was that you were such a temptress.'

Binodini was about to give a sharp riposte, but held herself. She said, 'You are right, *Pishima*, none of us knows what others are. Did you not intend to use this temptress to divert your son away from his wife because you were not well disposed towards his wife? Think over it, ponder.'

Thus challenged, Rajlakshmi flared up and screamed at Binodini. 'Wretched woman, how can you accuse a mother scheming against her own son? Your tongue will shrivel for such blasphemy.'

Binodini was unperturbed. She said, '*Pishima*, let us not forget that we are the tribe of witches. Neither of us knows what spells we are capable of casting, but both of us set our traps, partly deliberately and partly without realizing the consequences. We both acted according to our nature and that was that.'

Rajlakshmi, unable to take Binodini's impertinence, flounced out of the room in a foul temper.

Later in the day Rajlakshmi sent for her son. Mahendra realized that his mother wished to talk to him about the last night's episode. By then, Binodini's letter had considerably disoriented him, and this shock had the effect of driving him with growing yearning towards Binodini. He was not keen at all to get into an argument with his mother just now. If his mother censured him about his affair with Binodini, he knew he would rebel and tell her truthfully what his feelings were, which would lead to a fight between them. He thought it would be better to be out of the home and engage in some clear thinking. He sent word to the mother that he had some urgent matter at the college and that he would see her on his return. He slunk out, like a fugitive, without even bothering to change his clothes. In the process, he left behind Binodini's letter in the pocket of his discarded shirt.

After a sharp shower the day continued cloudy. It had been a most irritating day for Binodini, and whenever she was unsettled it was her practice of drowning herself in loads of work. This she did by marking clothes with indelible ink. Asha's attitude this morning had also aggravated her annoyance. It was fine to be condemned as a wrongdoer, why must then one be denounced for the sins but deprived of the pleasures?

It had started raining again. Binodini sat facing a heap of clothes. The maid Khemi handed her each piece one by one and she marked them with ink. Suddenly, without any advance warning, Mahendra walked into the room. Khemi hastily covered her head and ran out.

Binodini sprang up and severely frowned at Mahendra. 'What are you doing in my room? Leave me, leave my room immediately.'

'Why? What have I done?' asked Mahendra.

Binodini's voice rang out. 'What have you done? Mean and cowardly, a worthless creature is what you are. Not only are you incapable of giving your love, you are incompetent as well in discharging your obligations. In the midst of all this you are also giving me a bad name.'

Mahendra was mortified. 'How could you ever say that I do not love you.'

'Yes, that is exactly what I am telling you,' Binodini said firmly, 'this hide and seek game, the undercover assignments, the stealthy approaches like thieves have soured me. I can't take it any longer. Please leave me.'

Mahendra was dazed. 'Did you say you hate me?'

'I did, yes.'

Mahendra tried to get himself together. He said, quite firmly, 'We can still make amends, Binodini. If I do not vacillate and am prepared to leave everything behind, will you agree to walk out with me?'

Mahendra grabbed and pulled Binodini to himself. She groaned, 'Let me go. It hurts.'

'Let it hurt. Just tell me if you are prepared to come with me.'

'No, never.'

'But why not?' Mahendra spoke with some force. 'It is you who has driven me to my present desperate situation, how can you then desert me now? You have to come with me.'

Mahendra now held her tightly in his arms, and said with deep feelings, 'Your aversion will not deter me, and I am determined to take you away with me. You will come to love me.'

Binodini extricated herself from his grip. Mahendra warned her, 'You have created an inferno around you, and you can neither douse it nor escape it.'

Mahendra's voice had now climbed to a crescendo. 'Why did you at all engage yourself in this game? There is now no release for you. If we sink, we sink together.'

Rajlakshmi walked into the room and, surprised to see them locked together, shouted at her son, 'What do you think you are doing?'

By now, Mahendra was seized with frenzy. With a defiant look at his mother, he turned to Binodini. 'I am renouncing everything for you. Tell me that you will come away with me.'

Binodini raised her eyes to a devastated Rajlakshmi, and then taking hold of Mahendra's hand, said calmly, 'Yes, I will.'

'Then, wait for me until tomorrow,' Mahendra said. 'From tomorrow you and I will live for each other and no one else.' Mahendra then left.

Meanwhile, the dhobi grumbled. He had been waiting too long, if the lady was not ready, should he return tomorrow?

The maid Khemi came with the message that the ostler wanted replenishment of grains for the horse. Binodini normally rationed out grains for seven days' consumption.

Another servant reported that Jharu, the cleaner, had a row with Sadhucharan and did not wish to continue. He wanted his accounts settled.

Normal life went on, regardless.

THIRTY-FIVE

Bihari was also studying medicine to qualify as a doctor, but he abandoned it just before the final examinations. When asked why he did so, his standard reply was, 'Let me first look after my own health. Taking care of others can come later.'

Oddly enough, Bihari was an extremely enterprising character. He was always involved with something or the other, but had no appetite for money or fame. He, of course, had no need to earn his livelihood. After he earned his Bachelor's degree, he had entered the Shibpore engineering college, and having learned as much as he needed to and having acquired the needed technical skills, he lost any further interest there. Mahendra was a year senior to Bihari in the medical college, but as he failed last year, they were together now in the same class. They were well known in the college for their close friendship; in fact their colleagues often teased them as 'Siamese twins'. Suddenly the friendship snapped, and this baffled their fellow-students and bothered Bihari as well. He found it difficult to cope with the situation when they would meet in the college, and yet avoid each other. It was the general belief that Bihari was sure to come out tops in the final examinations with all the honours, and then he gave it all up.

Bihari had adopted an eight-year-old boy of an impoverished neighbour. He promised the father that he would take care of the boy and educate him. For the poor father it was god sent. He happily agreed to leave his son Basanta in Bihari's hands.

Bihari had formulated his own method of teaching. It would he entirely oral until the boy was ten years old, and no books till then. Bihari devised instructive games in which he engaged the boy, took him on visits to the Maidan, the Museum, the Zoo, and the botanical gardens at Shibpore. He sought to hone the child's faculties through oral coaching in many subjects English language, History, Natural Sciences, etc.

It had been raining the whole day and there was no way they could go out. He took the boy to the upstairs room and evolved a fresh set of games. 'Now, Basanta, how many beams are there in this room? No, you cannot look up.'

'Twenty,' guessed Basanta.

'Wrong. Only eighteen.' He then pulled the lever of the venetian blinds up and shut it immediately. 'Tell me, how many slats this blind has?' he asked Basanta.

Basanta guessed again and answered, 'Six.'

'Absolutely right.' This process of education was carried on with various objects with the idea of invigorating the boy's mind. While this course of instruction was on, a servant announced the arrival of a lady. And, immediately behind him walked in Binodini.

'What are you doing here, *Bouthun*?' asked Bihari shocked.

'Have you any female relation in this home of yours?' asked Binodini.

'No females, either related or unrelated. I have an aunt who lives in her village.'

'Then take me to her.'

Bihari asked, 'Telling her what?'

'That you got a maid to help her,' Binodini replied.

Bihari was intrigued. 'My aunt never asked me to find a maid servant for her. But tell me, what is behind all this madness of yours? Basanta, it is time for you to go to bed.'

After Basanta left, Binodini said, 'Even if I tell you, you will still not grasp the truth.'

'I may not, perhaps I may get you wrong, but does it really matter?'

'So be it then,' Binodini said. 'Mahendra has fallen in love with me.'

Said Bihari, 'Nothing new there. Hardly bears repetition.'

Binodini agreed. 'Yes, and neither do I have any desire to harp on it. I have come to you seeking shelter.'

'Oh, so you have no desire to talk about it,' Bihari observed in mock surprise. 'Then, pray, who caused this calamity? Who led Mahendra astray?'

'I did, I admit. There is no point in lying to you,' Binodini said, 'but even so, regardless of my sins, you ought to perceive what goes on inside me. My anguish, my tormented heart drove me to destroy Mahendra's home. I had once assumed, wrongly I find, that I was in love with Mahendra.'

'How does true love incinerate everything into ashes as you have done?' remarked Bihari.

'That is your holy scriptures talking,' said Binodini, 'and I am sorry I am in no mood to listen to your sermons. For a change, leave aside your books and try to look deep into my heart. I wish to tell you candidly all about myself.'

'No, I cannot dispense with my books, *Bouthan*,' Bihari said. 'It is the Almighty who alone can take measure of one's heart, and we mortals need to refer to our books for guidance, or else we cannot find our moorings.'

'Listen to me, *Thakurpo*,' Binodini spoke in a firm voice, 'if you wished you could have stopped me. I do admit that shamelessly Mahendra may love me, but he is so foolishly blind that he does not really know me. I have a feeling that you came to understand me. There was also a time when you had some respect for me. Is it or is it not true?'

Bihari nodded. 'Yes, quite true. I did cherish some respect for you in the past.'

'If that were so,' Binodini moaned, 'if you, indeed, had some respect for me, some feelings for me, why did you stop there? What inhibited you from loving me? I know well that I am being brazen-faced—I am asking you why did you not fall in love with me? I was, once again, a victim of my wretched destiny. Why else will you be besotted with Asha? No, do not get cross with me. You will have to listen to me, and I shall be open with you. Let me tell you, I knew even before you realized it that you were in love with Asha. Honestly, I could never understand what you men see in Asha. What has she to attract men? Do not men possess any insight to see through things? What beguiles you, what fools you, only you can tell. To me you are all blind and muddleheaded.'

Bihari had kept quiet for some time, and then stood up, clearly disturbed. 'I am prepared to listen to you, to whatever you wish to tell me, with the exception of certain issues, which I do not want raised here. Please, I beseech you.'

'I know where it pinches you, *Thakurpo*,' Binodini was unrelenting, 'but do have some consideration as well for my feelings, my miseries. Try to appreciate what intense desolation drove me to come to you tonight, notwithstanding the disgrace and ignominy I may suffer. You did say that you had once some regard for me, but had you been able to offer me your love, my life would have taken a turn for the better. I confess that had you not been so fond of Asha, I would not have ruined her life.'

Bihari turned pale and asked in alarm, 'Why? What have you done to Asha?'

'Mahendra proposes to leave his home tomorrow and walk out with me,' Binodini informed Bihari.

'No, never, this cannot be allowed,' Bihari almost shrieked.

'Really? You think this should be prevented? Who is going to stop Mahendra? Are You?'

'No, you,' said Bihari unexpectedly.

Binodini did not speak for a while. Then, she looked steadily at Bihari and said, 'And, why should I do this? For your Asha? I must forgo my life so that your Asha may live happily ever after and that your friend Mahendra's home remains inviolate. Sorry, I cannot oblige you. I am not all that a nice person—I am not steeped like you in holy scriptures. What do I stand to gain by my sacrifices?'

There was a perceptible change in Bihari's attitude. He turned stern when he spoke to Binodini. 'Well, you have been open with me, and now let me be candid with you. All that you have done today, all that you are saying now, are artificial—borrowed from the literature you read, your novels, the dramatic works.'

'That is what you think, do you?'

'Yes, I do, and let me also add—borrowed from cheap literature. These are not your own thoughts—merely mirrors of printed stuff. If you really happened to be a simple-minded and unlettered girl, you might have found genuine love. The heroine of a play is only good on a stage, not in the home.'

All Binodini's spirit and vanity collapsed like a deflated balloon. She became docile as a charmed snake. When she spoke, her voice was very low, and she did not look at Bihari. 'What do you advise that I should do now?'

Bihari said, 'Do not attempt anything unusual. I suggest you return to your old village.'

'How do I go there?'

'By train. I will place you in a ladies' compartment, and travel on the same train to escort you to your home station,' Bihari told her.

'Can you not put me up for the night here?' Binodini asked.

'I am afraid not,' Bihari said. 'I cannot trust myself.'

Binodini rose from her seat and sat down at Bihari's feet. Grasping his knees with her arms, she pleaded, 'You do not have to be so hard-hearted. A little softness will do you a whole lot of good. Sin a little by loving a sinner.'

She then did something startling. She commenced showering kisses on Bihari's feet. For a moment he was distracted by this extraordinary conduct of Binodini's. His whole body went limp. Binodini observed his bewildered look. She knelt before him, and locking her arms round Bihari's neck, spoke tenderly to him. 'My dearest, I know you will never belong to me, but tonight do inundate me with your love, even if it be for a brief instant. I will thereafter vanish into my wilderness, with no claims on anybody. All I want is a token to remind me of you.'

Binodini shut her eyes and ecstatically raised her full and inviting lips, vibrant with desire, towards Bihari's. Momentarily, they were both frozen and an eerie silence descended in the room. Bihari recovered to wake up, as if from a trance, released himself from Binodini's embrace, and contriving to make his voice sound normal, informed Binodini, 'There is a slow train early in the morning.'

Binodini seemed lost for a while, and then collecting herself, said, 'Yes, I will take that train.'

Basanta reappeared unexpectedly—fair, comely and small. He went and stood near Bihari and kept looking at Binodini.

'Why are you not in bed?' asked Bihari but received no reply. Binodini extended an arm to the child, and after an initial hesitation, he went over to her. She clasped the boy in her arms and broke down in a torrent of tears.

THIRTY-SIX

With all the turmoil in Mahendra's home, that fateful night was finally over. The morning post had brought a letter for Binodini from Mahendra, asking her to be prepared to leave. The servant showed the letter to Asha who noted that it was for Binodini in Mahendra's writing. Asha went numb, and returned the letter to the servant, and when the servant asked to whom he should give the letter, Asha said she did not know.

Around eight o'clock the same evening Mahendra came looking for Binodini. She was not in her room, neither were her belongings. Surprised, Mahendra looked around, calling her by her name, but received no response.

'What a fool I have been. I should have taken her away yesterday. My mother must have abused her so much that she could not stick here,' so inferred Mahendra.

He went to look for his mother in her room. The room was dark and he found her in bed. He immediately charged her, 'What did you say to Binodini?'

Rajlakshmi denied having spoken to Binodini at all.

'Then where is she?' asked Mahendra.

'How would I know?' the mother said.

Mahendra clearly did not believe her. 'Aha, so you do not know. Anyway, I am going to look for her, and I will find her wherever she is.'

As Mahendra left her room, she got up from her bed and called him back. 'Mohin, please do not go. Listen to me for once.'

Mahendra did not wait, and as he went out, he asked the doorman, 'Do you have any idea where *bohurnnee* has gone to?' *bohuranee* being Binodini.

'No, Sir, we do not. She did not tell us,' the doorman replied.

Mahendra was sure that they were all creatures of his mother and parroting her instructions.

The city, now lit by gas-lamps, was full of life, with street vendors hawking ices and other tasty bits. Mahendra walked through the throng and vanished.

THIRTY-SEVEN

Bihari seldom brooded by himself. He liked to have people around him. He was always busy, if not deep in his studies, with a host of other engagements and friends. He attached no importance to his private life; public engagements were his priorities. An unexpected blow now had demolished his world around him. He found himself isolated, as it were, on the summit of his congealed mount of pain. For once, he was afraid of being with himself; solitude frightened him.

Tonight, however, he could not keep himself away from himself. He saw Binodini to her village last night, and since then, amidst all his work, his anguish-torn heart was constantly pushing him to seek solitude, to be with himself. By nine in the evening, he yielded to this pressure and went up to the roof. It was a dark, moonless night.

He let his young protege, Basanta, off from lessons, having packed him off to bed early. His whole being, on this lonely flight, was searching fervently for some comfort sources to clutch on to, yearning for his former friends, longing for those happy old days, bountiful with love and grace, to which he was so accustomed. He felt abandoned, forlorn. What happened to his firm resolves and iron disciplines? Thoughts of all those whom he had decided to banish from his mind came crowding in and crushing his heart. He had not the strength to resist them.

Memories of his long and sustained friendship with Mahendra—etched in many colours, crammed with many incidents, rent with upheavals and reconciliations—which had so long remained locked in his heart now gushed out and deluged Bihari. What ill-starred events overtook and smashed his small and comfortable world? Who fired the first shot? He recalled the shy and diffident features of Asha, lit by the rays of the dying sun, on that fateful evening when he and Mahendra had gone to see her, followed soon by the happy event of his friend's marriage with her. Before he knew what struck him, from nowhere floated in a dark cloud of misfortune, so intensely agonising, so utterly unimaginable. Yet, this separation, this agony was in some way strangely tempered with a tinge of delicate but inexplicable harmony in their midst.

Unexpectedly, without any warning, appeared an evil star—unleashing ruination all over—driving a wedge between friends, breaking up a happy marriage, vitiating the peace and sanctity of a home. Bihari with all the animosity in his heart had tried hard to exorcise the memory of this evil creature, Binodini, but there was a surprising transformation. The earlier shock tapered off and no longer touched him. Instead, the image of that exquisitely beautiful vision, with all her air of mystery, on this dark night, rose before Bihari, looking intently at him with her intense and steady eyes. The southern breeze of the summertime wafted round him, deep sighs of this tortured soul. Slowly, the bright glare of her eyes thawed and mellowed, and the same eyes that were earlier hard and dry were flooded with a surge of tears and reduced her to an ordinary creature of emotions. In no time she genuflected and embraced his knees with her arms. Like a rare magic creeper she blossomed into bouquet of fragrant flowers, and extended her eager lips for a union with his. Bihari closed his eyes and tried to expunge the image of this vision, but he no longer had the heart to insult her memory. The vision of her lips, slightly parted and amorously lifted, eager for a token of love but spurned, remained transfixed in his eyes. An unusual exhilaration enraptured him.

Bihari could no longer endure this loneliness. He had to do something to take his mind off his boredom. He went down to his bedroom. On a small table stood a framed picture covered with a silk screen. He picked up the picture, removed the cover, and looked intently at it. It was a photograph of Asha and Mahendra taken immediately after their marriage. The photograph had caught for all times the first tender moments of the newly married couple. Mahendra and Asha had both inscribed their names in their own hands at the back of the picture. At the insistence of the photographer, Asha had removed her veil, but the photographer's skill ensured that the coy and blissful aspect of a bride was not lost. Sadly, the same Mahendra had now decided to desert that same Asha, but the inanimate portrait, retaining every aspect of that first love, appeared to defy this cruel turn of fate.

With this picture in his hand, Bihari wished once again contemptuously to banish the thought of Binodini, but she refused to go away. She remained there, still clutching his knees, with all the fervour of a love-inspired youth! Bihari cursed her—how could she destroy such a lovely home? It was still the vision of Binodini's upraised face, ravenous for love that captured his mind, with her unspoken silent message—I love you, I want you for myself.

Rather, a strange response to his curse, was it not? Was it good enough to cover the sins of laying waste a happy family? You are a monster, Binodini, that is what you are! Monster, Bihari called her, but did he really mean it seriously? Was there not somewhere a touch of tenderness also in this rebuke? Denied, and deprived of his first love, Bihari was now destitute and starved of love. Just then, when an unsolicited gift of abundant love came to him, how could he disdain and decline that offer? What had he got so far that can match this offer? Until now he was merely scrounging for morsels of love, but if a gift of love was handed to him on a gold platter to assuage his hungry soul, why should he deprive himself of this feast?

Such were the many thoughts that passed through Bihari's mind, while he kept holding on to the wedding picture of Asha and Mahendra. Sounds of footsteps alerted him, and he was startled to find Mahendra calling on him. He got up, but failed to notice that the photograph had slipped out of his hand and fallen on the floor.

Without any greeting or ceremony Mahendra asked, 'Where is Binodini?'

Bihari took hold of Mahendra's hand and spoke to him kindly, 'Please, Mohin, take a seat. I wish to talk to you.'

'But I don't. I have neither the time nor the inclination to talk. Just tell me where Binodini is,' Mahendra said curtly.

'I am sorry I cannot answer you. Nonetheless, you have to listen to me,' Bihari insisted.

'Ah, you wish to reason with me, offer me advice,' Mahendra said, 'but I have had enough of that from the day I was born.'

Bihari tried to soothe him. 'I have no desire to give you any advice. I do not think I am in a position to do so.'

'What do you wish to do, then?' asked Mahendra petulantly. 'Take me to task? I do know that I am an unmitigated rascal, good for nothing or whatever else you wish to call me. I am only interested in Binodini. Do you know where she is?'

'Yes, I do.'

'But won't tell me.'

'Right.'

'You have to tell me. You have stolen her from me and you are hiding her. She is mine, restore her to me.' Mahendra was most aggressive.

Bihari took some time to answer, and then he said firmly, 'She does not belong to you. In any case, I did not entice her away. She came to me on her own.'

Mahendra shouted at him. 'It is a lie, a bitter lie.' Then, he knocked on the door of an adjacent room, calling loudly, 'Binodini, Binodini.'

He heard a voice, someone crying inside the room. Imagining it was Binodini, Mahendra spoke loudly, 'Have no fear, Binodini. It is I, Mahendra. I will get you out of here. No one can keep you locked up.'

He gave a powerful shove and the door gave in. He ran inside. It was very dark there. He dimly saw a figure, crouching with fear and whining. Bihari rushed in, picked up young Basanta in his arms and comforted him, 'Calm down Basanta, there is nothing to be afraid of.'

Mahendra made a thorough but fruitless search of the entire house. When he returned, young Basanta was still passing through spasms of fright and Bihari was trying to put him to sleep.

Impervious to the child's distress, Mahendra asked bluntly, 'Where have you secreted Binodini.

Bihari, by now disgusted with Mahendra, warned him, 'Enough is enough. Don't try to create a rumpus here. For no reason you have put the fear of death in this young child, who may fall sick because of you. In any case, I cannot see how does Binodini concern you?'

Mahendra raged at Bihari. 'How wonderful! Whom do I see in front of me? A saint, a holy man? Do not try to fence me off by building a wall of your moral pretences. Can you tell me what were you doing, sitting up so late at night, with my wife's picture in your hand? Meditating on your favourite deity? A hypocrite, that is what you are.'

Mahendra snatched the photograph, dashed it on the floor and stable it mercilessly with his booted foot. Then, picking up the picture he tore it to strips and flung the pieces at Bihari.

Mahendra's frenzied conduct threw little Basanta into renewed panic. Bihari lost his patience and, pointing his finger towards the door, roared at Mahendra, 'Go, leave this house, immediately.'

Mahendra stormed out without any word.

THIRTY-EIGHT

As Binodini watched the passing landscape from her railway carriage, she rediscovered her past linkages with rural life. She tried to persuade herself that she would find peace at last in the tree shaded village grove away from the scarred memories of her life in the city. Looking at the vast fallow land scorched by the summer sun, she wanted to forget the past and to find an anchor at a quiet corner in the village after her storm-tossed life. A passing mango grove, profusely blossoming, brought home to her the balmy expectation of peace and quiet. She was trying to come to terms with her coming rural existence. She would go back to her old life and live like other village women.

Thus fortified in her resolution, Binodini entered her home. The home was un-swept, tin-cleaned, and the damp air inside almost choked her. Whatever pieces of furniture she had left behind were now moth-eaten and rat-infested. Where, alas, was the peace that she was looking forward to? All around her was emptiness and waste. How was she going to last here at all?

The elderly relative with whom Binodini shared her home was away visiting a married daughter. Binodini decided to call on the neighbours, who were all startled when they saw her. The new Binodini was a revelation to them. She was not conventionally dressed, and was almost as fair complexioned as western women were. The women exchanged meaningful glances. Were there not some rumours involving her? Looking at Binodini, they believed there could be some truth in those rumours.

Binodini realized very clearly that she had moved miles away from her old village days. She found herself a stranger in her new home. There was no tranquillity for her anywhere.

When she went for a bath to the village tank, she met the postman whom she knew from the past. She eagerly asked him if there was any letter for her. When the postman said there wasn't any, she asked him to look again to make sure, but there was none. One of her old acquaintances, looking at her crest-fallen face, poked fun at her, 'I say,

Bindi, whose letter are you so anxiously looking for?' Another saucy woman teased her. 'Well, how many of us are fortunate enough to receive mails through the post? Many of us have husbands and relations working away from home, but no postman is ever so kind to us.'

Over the days the barbs became sharper and comments more spiteful. Binodini had pleaded very humbly with Bihari to write to her, and although there was no question of a letter due so soon from him, her impatience mounted. It seemed she had left Calcutta so long ago!

The gossips linking her name with Mahendra had somehow trickled to the village, and the scandal had well spread. Her neighbours saw to it that Binodini was kept well primed of her infamy. Binodini tried to steer clear from the village people, but this made her even more unpopular. They were deprived of the pleasure of tormenting this fallen woman.

A village was not a place where one can keep oneself aloof. Watchful and inquisitive eyes will ferret the fugitive out. She could not escape the censorious persecution of the neighbours. Their bigotry stifled her to death, and she did not even have the freedom to suffer in isolation.

When another day passed without any letter from Bihari, she decided to write to him. She wrote:

'Don't get alarmed. This is not a love letter. You now sit in judgment over me, and I do respect you. You have punished me severely for my sins, and I have accepted your sentence. Sadly, you are not here to see how hard it is to obey your decree. As it is, I have lost your sympathy. Nevertheless, I try to carry on bearing your thought in my heart. But, my Lord, does not a prisoner in a jail get to eat? Not fancy food I agree, but at least sustenance enough to keep his body and soul together. For me, in my exile, my sustenance is a few lines from you. Deprived of that, my punishment is just not exile, but a sentence to death. Do not test me too hard. I beg of you. In my sinful ways I was once too proud to believe that I would never submit to anybody, but I have learnt my lessons. The victory is yours, my Lord, and I will not protest. Do not deny me your mercy, let me live. Lend me support to sustain my life in this wilderness. If you do, no one can deviate me from the ruling you imposed on me. I thought of telling you of my unhappiness, and there is so much to say. I had promised you that I shall not complain, and this promise I will keep.'

Bouthan

Binodini mailed the letter. As nothing remains secret in a closed village society, the gossip mill was active speculating on the shameless conduct of Binodini, who wrote to whom no one knew, behind closed doors, and then kept chasing the postman to see if she had a reply. How could a woman lose all sense of balance and decorum after just a short stint in the city?

There was no letter for her even the next day. The whole day she was in some sort of a daze. Being constantly hurt and humiliated from every direction hardened her so much that she felt venomously murderous. This violent mood of hers frightened her.

She had nothing from Bihari as a memento, something that she wanted badly at this moment. She wanted to shake off this maddening rage that boiled in her by holding a keepsake of Bihari's close to her heart. She wanted to douse the fire of rebellion with tears, which had also gone dry. She wanted to hold on to Bihari's rigorous sentence of penance as a symbol of his tender love, but her heart remained arid as the drought affected earth, and no tears rose to moisten her eyes.

Binodini was once told that if one wholeheartedly meditated on someone, then that someone would invariably respond. She closed her eyes and concentrated on Bihari. She told him in her prayers, 'My life is empty, my heart is empty, emptiness engulfs me. Come, fill this void, even it be for a brief period you must come to me. I cannot give you up.'

After this deep meditation she regained some strength, some assurance. She believed her prayers would not go in vain; they would be answered. Merely remembering someone was ineffective; strongly desiring someone was different. That was inspiring and comforting.

The darkness outside deepened as Binodini remained embedded in thoughts of Bihari. The village had already retired to bed. Suddenly, there was a knock on the door. Assuming that it was Bihari, who had responded to her intense prayers, she ran eagerly to open the door, and cried out, 'Are you here, my love?'

'Yes, I am here Binodini.' It was Mahendra. Reacting, violently to her disappointment, and outraged by Mahendra's presence, she shouted at him, 'What are you doing here? Go, go away, immediately.'

Mahendra was struck dumb by this reception. An elderly neighbour, a late visitor, who had called to enquire about Binodini's absent relation, covered her head and rushed away as soon as she saw Mahendra.

THIRTY-NINE

The entire village now rose in protest. The elderly brigade decided that the situation had gone out of control. They were not concerned about what happened in Calcutta, but how could she be so shameless as to write to Mahendra, asking him to come to the village? How can they suffer the presence of a woman of such loose moral timbre in their midst?

Binodini had genuinely expected a letter from Bihari, and when she did not she turned hostile to him. What authority has he over me, she asked herself, that I must obey him? Why was I such a fool to give him the impression that I shall abide by his decisions? He just bent me to his wishes, all for the sake of his dearly beloved Asha. Did I not count at all? Was there nothing due to me? Did I have no claims of my own, not even the expectation of a few lines by way of a letter? Am I so insignificant then, a person to be trifled with?

By then, Binodini was fuming, raging with venomous jealousy of Asha. She could have accepted being sacrificed for someone more deserving, but surely not Asha? Her penurious existence, the life in the wilderness, assaulted by people's contempt and abuses—she would have to carry the pernicious load of all this, all in the interest of Asha. Why on earth, did she accept this punishment? She now cursed herself roundly. 'I was a fool not to consummate my evil designs. I should have done that. My love for Bihari has been wasted.'

Binodini's absent elderly relative returned from visiting her daughter. She straightaway confronted her. 'Wretched woman, what is this scandalous tale that I hear about you?'

'What you heard is all true,' Binodini confirmed.

'Why did you have to bring your ignominy to us?' whined the relative.

Binodini said nothing. The relative went on, 'I have had my share of sorrows and bereavements, all of which I had borne with patience, but I will not tolerate your depravity. You have put all of us to shame, and you must go.'

'Yes, I will,' Binodini assented.

Mahendra walked in, unexpectedly, harried and tired. He looked haggard from lack of sleep. He had originally planned to return early in the morning and try once again to persuade Binodini to leave, but the thought of her rude refusal last night deterred him. Later, as the day advanced, he decided to shake off his hesitation and, abandoning the shelter of the railway waiting room, he hired a carriage and made straight for Binodini's place. To defy openly, shedding any sense of guilt and shame, has its own thrill, and Mahendra presently was armed with such an excitement. His earlier fatigue and inertia troubled him no more, and the reaction of the village people ceased to matter to him.

Upon reaching Binodini, he told her, 'I really cannot abandon you to this climate of aspersion and obloquy. You may think so, but I am not that sort of a cad. I am sorry, you cannot continue here, you will have to come with me. If you wish to dissociate from me thereafter, by all means, do so. I will not stop you. I am prepared to give you my word that I shall not go against your wishes. If you can see your way to forgive me, I will feel relieved. If not, I shall remove myself from your path. I admit I have committed many unworthy acts, but for the present do have faith in me. We are facing a crisis, and it is not the time for us to play games.'

Binodini well understood the predicament she was in, so she said without hesitation, 'Yes, do take me with you. Do you have, by the way, a carriage with you?'

'I have, yes,' said Mahendra.

Binodini's relation came out and spoke to Mahendra, 'You may not know me but we are not unrelated. Your mother is a daughter of this village, and I am a sort of an aunt of hers. May I ask you, what has gone wrong with you? You have a wife at home, your mother is still alive, and yet you have chosen to carry on in this mad and shameless manner. How can you ever show your face to your people?'

Mahendra, who was in a state of trance, received a sharp jolt. That he had a mother and a wife, and that he belonged to the upper crust of the society—all these suddenly came alive as if something new. To Mahendra it sounded absurd that he would be reminded of all this in a far away village by someone unknown to him. He was himself well aware that what he was doing violated the social mores. Even so, the old woman's statement disturbed him.

Mahendra did not reply. The old woman told him, 'If you are leaving, do so now. Do not remain here, not even for a minute.' She went in and banged the door shut in their face. Binodini climbed onto the carriage and told Mahendra, 'I suggest you walk to the railway station. It is not too far.'

'But all the people in the village will see me,' Mahendra protested in horror.

Binodini said, 'I do not know what bothers you. What more have you to lose?' She shut the door of the carriage, and asked the coachman to drive her to the railway station.

Mahendra had no option but to accept. When the carriage rolled off, he avoided the main road and took a circuitous route to the railway station. It was well past midday by then. The village tank was almost deserted except for a few straggling elderly women, who could not catch up with their domestic chores in time.

FORTY

Rajlakshmi was desolated by Mahendra's absence. Where was he? Sadhucharan searched high and low for him but could not trace him.

Mahendra, meanwhile, returned to Calcutta along with Binodini. He left her in a house in Pataldanga, and went home. He made straight for his mother's room, which he found almost in darkness. Rajlakshmi was in bed, like a sick person. Asha was with her. Apparently, the mother-in-law no longer nursed her earlier hostile attitude to the daughter-in-law.

Asha left the room as soon as Mahendra entered. He told his mother, 'I find it difficult to concentrate on my studies in this house. I have rented an apartment near my college. I will shift there for the time being.'

Rajlakshmi asked her son to sit down, which Mahendra did with some qualms. The mother told him, 'Live wherever you wish to, but see to it that your wife does not suffer for that.'

Mahendra kept quiet. Rajlakshmi continued, 'It is my misfortune that I gave no recognition for a long time to such a fine daughter-in-law that I have.' She nearly broke down when she said thus. 'You had known her so long, you loved her to distraction, so how could you condemn her to her present dire distress?' Rajlakshmi started weeping.

Mahendra's first inclination was to run away, but he held on. Eventually, Rajlakshmi asked him, 'Will you be staying here tonight?'

'No. I will leave almost immediately,' Mahendra told her.

Rajlakshmi sat up with some difficulty. 'Almost immediately? Are you not going to see your wife and have a word with her?' she asked.

Mahendra chose not to answer. Rajlakshmi spoke in great anguish. 'It is a pity you will never know how stricken she had been all these days. Have you lost all sense of shame? Your heartlessness to her is killing me.' Exhausted, she lay down on her bed.

Mahendra left his mother's room, and treading softly went up to his own room. He had no desire to meet Asha. When he reached his room, he found Asha on the roof adjoining his bedroom, lying prostrate on the floor. She stood up when Mahendra came in. Had he called her just once by her name, Chuni, she would have melted and yielded to him, forgetting and forgiving all his sins, as if all the indiscretions were hers. But Mahendra made no such move, he did not call her by that loving name. Mahendra himself was passing through conflicting emotions. He would have loved to be reconciled with his wife, but he felt it would be a mockery to try to get back to the old days. Had he not, by his own actions, barred all roads to give up Binodini?

Asha remained there, troubled at heart. A sense of helplessness froze her. Mahendra said not a word, went on aimlessly walking round the roof. The evening was dark and moonless. A few potted flowers desultorily thrust their heads, the stars shone bright—the same stars that were witness in the past oil many a night to their loving togetherness.

Disturbing thoughts assailed Mahendra. If he could but erase the nightmarish occurrences of the past few days and return to his old days with Asha, sitting side by side on their old corner of the roof! Back to their old love, that uncluttered bliss! Sadly, however, there was no way that he could retrieve that old life. He had forfeited for all times that pleasure of sharing his halcyon days with Asha, on that special roof corner of theirs!

His relationship with Binodini lately had been free and easy. Undeniably, he was madly in love with her, but the tie was not unbreakable. Now that Mahendra himself had uprooted Binodini from her secured place in the society, she had nowhere to go and Mahendra was her sole anchor. He was now wholly responsible for her, and like it or not, it was a disturbing thought. Mahendra's thoughts went back to that peaceful corner on the roof, the cosy togetherness with Asha, the nights of their unbridled love—all of these loomed as most covetable to Mahendra. What had once been his for the asking had now receded as an unattainable dream. There was no way for Mahendra to escape the responsibility for Binodini that he had on his own volition assumed.

Mahendra looked longingly at Asha, who sat there, immobile as a statue, the dark night giving her a cover to hide her pain and agony.

Perhaps wishing to talk to her, Mahendra almost went near Asha, when she closed her eyes with blood rushing to her brain. He was keen to speak to her, but was lost for words. Finally, he blurted out, just to say something, 'Where are the keys?'

Asha went inside the room, Mahendra following her. The bunch of keys was normally kept under the mattress. Asha extracted it and placed it on the bed. Mahendra tried to open his clothes cupboard, but none of the keys fitted the lock. Watching Mahendra's futile attempts, Asha could not restrain herself. She told him, 'The key to that cupboard was never with me.' Asha did not say who had the key, but Mahendra understood. Afraid that she might break down again, Asha left the room.

Asha remembered it was time for Mahendra's dinner. She went down, when Rajlakshmi asked her, 'Where is Mahendra now?'

'In his room.'

'Then, what are you doing here?' Obviously annoyed with the daughter-in-law.

Asha said without looking up, 'To get your son's food.'

'I could have managed that,' said Rajlakshmi. 'Now, go and freshen yourself up. Put on that new Dacca sari and come down. I will dress your hair.'

Asha found it difficult to resist the well-intentioned instructions of her mother-in-law, but at the same time she found the very idea of dressing up for Mahendra most humiliating. Nevertheless, to oblige Rajlakshmi, she went up, but did not find Mahendra either in his room or on the roof. Mahendra had, after collecting his books and clothes, left without telling any one. He did not wait for his dinner.

The following day was *ekadasi*, the day of fast for widows. Rajlakshmi lay on her bed, sick and feeble. Asha brought her some fruits and milk. Asha's unaccustomed efforts to look after her melted Rajlakshmi's heart. She drew Asha close to her and kissed her tear stained cheeks. 'Where is Mahendra now?' she asked.

Hurt and embarrassed, Asha stammered, 'He left last night.'

All Rajlakshmi's earlier love and pity for Asha immediately evaporated. She was exasperated with her useless daughter-in-law. This unspoken indignation did not escape Asha, who left the room quietly.

FORTY-ONE

Binodini was in a reflective frame of mind after Mahendra left her in the Pataldanga house the day they arrived there. It was clear to her that there were not many places, where she could find refuge. Her space was now extremely narrow and limited. The boat on which she now floated was very delicately poised. The slightest tilt could throw her into deep waters. She needed to be careful to ply the boat firmly and rigidly, so that it did not rock. A fearful prospect for any woman! Where was the scope in this limited space to make one's own room? She must, she ruminated bitterly, be prepared for a life with Mahendra at her side. Mahendra, however, had the advantage of returning to his home whenever he wished, but she herself had nowhere else to go.

The more she brooded on this state of her desperation, the more determined she was to find a way out of it. Her patience cracked the day she offered her love to Bihari. She had not withdrawn the offer of her spurned kiss—the offer that was made to the object of her adoration. Binodini did not easily admit of defeat, nor did she readily yield to disappointment. Bihari would surrender and requite her love, she was confident.

Binodini now clung on to her love for Bihari as the route to her emancipation. There was no one else other than Bihari on whom she could depend. She had learnt her lessons well to realize that Mahendra was a fragile vehicle to cling to. He resented being tied down, and would run away at the first hint of any effort to hold him back. He was not the type on whom a woman looking for support could rely upon, but Bihari was.

Binodini was vastly confident that Bihari was sure to respond to her letter that she had written from her village. She so firmly believed in this that she had arranged, through Mahendra, to leave instructions at the village post office to re-direct her mails to her present new address. She decided to wait a little longer, and then think of what next she should do.

Binodini opened her window and stared idly at the bustling gas-lit streets. Bihari's house was a mere few streets away, and one could easily walk there. She vividly recalled his house. You cross a small courtyard, which boasts of a newly laid piped water faucet. You climb up the staircase and reach his tidy sitting room, where Bihari is normally ensconced in his comfortable easy chair. Perhaps, sitting near him will be his young protégé, turning over the pages of a picture book. This very imagination filled her heart with great love and affection for Bihari. She would have loved to rush to him, but she knew she needed to exercise considerable restraint. She would have to sort out the issues involved carefully. The aim presently was not to succumb to whims, but to find a solution to one's problems. She would decide on her course of action after Bihari replied to her letter.

It was quite late in the night when Mahendra returned. He was completely drained out. He had passed through a difficult period the last few days. He had hardly slept, had kept very irregular hours, and after successfully getting Binodini back, he was overcome by acute weariness and lethargy. This weariness was, perhaps, indicative of his prospective life with Binodini as his responsibility.

As he stood in front of the closed door of the house, he was overtaken by a conscience of guilt and shame. He shrank from knocking on the door. The earlier frenzy that had propelled him to ignore the world had apparently had its run. The people on the street passing him by made him uneasy. He had no answer why it was so.

Apparently, the newly engaged servant had already gone to bed, so Mahendra had to wait long before the door was opened. As soon as he entered this new unknown place he felt stifled. Cosseted and petted by an adoring mother, Mahendra was accustomed to a life of luxury, and the bareness of this house with no overhead pulling *punkhas* and no decent furniture hit him acutely. It dawned on him that it was he himself, who would have to take care of such details at this new place. Many changes were needed to make this home habitable, and it was his responsibility to run this home. These added concerns aggravated his weariness.

Before ascending the stairs, Mahendra paused to compose himself. Binodini was now his, what he wanted with all his heart at the cost of sacrificing his whole world. Nothing now could come between

Binodini and himself. The very thought excited him.

Binodini was still on the verandah when Mahendra came in. She went inside and lit a lamp. She then picked up some stitching and concentrated on it. The stitching was nothing but a ruse—to keep her distance from Mahendra.

Mahendra's first remark to her as he entered the room was, 'I presume there are too many inconveniences in this place that must be bothering you.'

'No, none at all,' Binodini said while continuing with her stitching.

'Do have patience for a few more days. I will fix everything by then. I will also get a set of new furniture,' Mahendra assured her.

Binodini protested, 'No, please add no more furniture. I have more than my needs here. No point in loading the place with unnecessary items.'

'Do I also fall under this category of unnecessary items?' Mahendra thought he was cracking a good joke.

Binodini said, pleasantly, 'Do not attach too much importance to self. Try and cultivate a sense of modesty.'

This picture of self composed Binodini, intensely focussed on whatever she was doing, with her head bent low, mesmerised him. In his own home he would have probably run to her impulsively, but felt inhibited at this new place. Here, at this new place, Binodini was under his protection and was otherwise helpless, and to lose his head would be dastardly. Binodini asked him, 'Why have you fetched your books and clothes here?'

'Ah, I regard them as essentials, not as surplus to requirements,' Mahendra teased her.

'Of course, but why bring them here?' asked Binodini again.

'A good question. I assume essentials have no place in this house. So, throw them out, but see to it that I am also not jettisoned with them.'

Without lifting her eyes from her needlework, Binodini solemnly observed, '*Thakurpo*, I am afraid you cannot stay here if that is your intention.'

Mahendra was shocked. He appealed to her, 'Why are you pushing me away, Binodini? Is this the return I get after I sacrificed everything for your sake?'

'Precisely,' Binodini replied, 'I cannot allow you to sacrifice yourself for my sake.'

Mahendra cried in anguish, 'But it is too late for that. It is no longer in our hands. My former world has collapsed around me, and I have only you now, only you, my dearest Binodini.'

Mahendra was now so carried away that he went down, clasped her feet and started showering ardent kisses on them. Binodini swiftly withdrew her feet and told him, 'Do you recall your promises to me?'

With great difficulty Mahendra controlled himself and said, 'Yes, I do remember. I gave you my word that I shall do as you wish. I shall not renege on it. Tell me, what do you wish me to do?'

'You should go back to your home and stay there,' Binodini calmly advised Mahendra.

'It appears I am the only undesirable element in your life,' Mahendra was pathetic. 'If that were so, why did you then drag me with you? Why did you make me your victim if you had no need for me? Do be honest. Did I on my own surrender myself to you? Did you not deliberately set out to capture me? Must I go through this cat and mouse game of yours? Nevertheless, I shall keep my word to you, I swear. I shall return to my old home which I have destroyed by my own folly.'

Apparently still intent on her needlework, Binodini remained quiet. Mahendra silently watched her for some minutes and then cried out in exasperation, 'You are the most heartless creature, Binodini, absolutely heartless. It is my misfortune that I came to love you so much.'

Binodini did not react at all. She deliberately feigned some mistake in her work and went near the lamp to examine it. Mahendra longed to crush this hard-hearted woman and crumble her to dust, to deal a severe blow to her cold-blooded disregard of him and her frigid unkindness.

He went out to return immediately. 'If I am not here, who is going to take care of you?'

Binodini assured him, 'I have taken care of all that. Khemi, the maid at your old place, has been dismissed by your mother. I have engaged her. The two women together will be safe here.'

The more indignant he was the more powerful was his urge to grab her, to squeeze and pulverise her. To save himself from this mad impulse he ran out of the house.

Once out on the street, wandering aimlessly, he decided not to placate Binodini any longer. He would be equally indifferent to her. How dare she spurn Mahendra when she had none but him as her last resort—rejecting him so firmly and fearlessly? No man of any dignity can take such humiliation lying down. Though crushed and humbled, Mahendra would not easily give up. Was he so worthless that she could treat him with such defiance? Who else was there to whom she could run for help?

Yes, there was Bihari, it struck Mahendra. His blood almost congealed when this thought occurred to him. Binodini must be depending on Bihari. That was the only possible answer. He, Mahendra, served merely as the stepping-stone to trample on to reach Bihari. This, no doubt, was at the root of her contempt for him. He suspected Binodini and Bihari to be in regular touch, and she must have received some sort of an assurance from him.

Mahendra turned his steps towards Bihari's house. It was near midnight when he fetched up there. He had a long wait before a servant answered his knocks. His employer was out, the servant informed Mahendra. This gave Mahendra a jolt. He immediately assumed that Bihari had gone to meet Binodini, when he was out on the road. It made sense. Binodini deliberately insulted him to get rid of him, and he foolishly succumbed to it and went out without giving it any further thought.

The servant was an old retainer whom Mahendra had known. He asked him, 'When did Bihari leave home?'

'Must be about four or five days ago. He has gone out of town.' This information vastly relieved Mahendra's mind. By now he was so direly stressed out that all he wanted was to sleep. He went up and settled down on a comfortable sofa, and in no time sleep overtook him.

Bihari decided to leave town after Mahendra's unexpected visit to his home and the rumpus he created. It was a deliberate decision to avoid possible skirmishes with his friend that could turn nasty, leading to a permanent rift between them.

It was fairly late when Mahendra woke up next morning. The first thing that caught his eyes was a letter, addressed to Bihari, in Binodini's handwriting. The letter was still unopened, waiting for the absent Bihari. Mahendra tore open the letter and read it. It was the letter that Binodini had written from her village, to which she never had a reply.

The letter devastated Mahendra. Although Bihari was his childhood friend, he never did count for much with Mahendra. And, that it was this Bihari who was preferred to Mahendra was unequivocally clear from Binodini's letter. The few letters that Mahendra had from Binodini, in contrast, were dull and prosaic. Mahendra recalled the arrangement he had made on behalf of Binodini with the village post office to redirect her letters. He now knew why.

Even though Bihari was away, his old retainer brought tea and breakfast for Mahendra. Binodini's letter to Bihari continued to irk him. He read it a few more times, and then decided to cut off his connection with Binodini. He changed his mind when it occurred to him that Binodini might look up Bihari, and then she would know the truth. This must be avoided at all cost.

Mahendra returned to the Pataldanga house in the evening. Looking at his haggard and drawn face, Binodini felt sorry for him. 'Did you not go home last night?' she asked.

'No,' Mahendra replied

'Meaning that you had nothing to eat since last night?' the caring woman in her anxiously reacted. She was about to get some food for him when Mahendra stopped her, 'There is no need. I already had something to eat.'

'Where?' asked Binodini.

'At Bihari's.'

She was flustered for an instant. 'Is Bihari-*thakurpo* well?' she asked.

'I think so. He has gone out of town.' Mahendra's reply was calculated to give Binodini the false impression that Bihari left just this day.

Binodini turned pale. 'Never known anyone so restless. Perhaps, he had heard about us, which must have upset him.'

'May be, or else why should he travel during this hot summer.'

'Did he at all talk about me?'

'Not really. Here is a letter for you.'

Mahendra looked intently at Binodini when he handed her the letter. She immediately recognized the cover in her own writing. She found the letter open. She took out the letter she had written, and then shook the envelope hoping there could be a reply from Bihari. There was none.

'Have you read this letter?' Binodini asked suspecting him, which alarmed Mahendra. He glibly lied that he had not.

Without saying another word Binodini shredded the letter. Mahendra informed Binodini that he had decided to go home. 'I will do exactly as you wish. I will be in my home for a week, and each day on my way to the college, I will come here and check with the maid if all is well. I will not bother you, I promise.'

Not quite trusting Mahendra, Binodini dispatched the maid the following day to Bihari's house. She returned to confirm that Bihari had indeed, left town.

FORTY-TWO

Rajlakshmi was uncommonly annoyed with Asha when told that Mahendra had left home the previous night. Her immediate inference was that Asha must have been unpleasant to him, which drove him away. She asked ungraciously, 'When did he leave home last night?'

'I have no idea,' was Asha's mild reply.

The wretched girl was sulking, Rajlakshmi assumed. 'If you do not know, who will? Did you have any words with him?'

Asha shook her head, 'No.'

How can that be possible? Rajlakshmi was not prepared to believe Asha at all. She repeated her question, 'At what time did he leave home?'

'I really do not know,' Asha said hurt and mortified.

Rajlakshmi flared up. 'You seen, to know nothing. Are you a little babe? Being crafty, that is what you are doing.'

Rajlakshmi loudly and firmly accused Asha for Mahendra leaving home. Silently accepting the rebuke Asha retired to her room to cry her heart out. Poor girl, she racked her brain endlessly but never found the answer to why her husband did once love her so much and how did she lose that love. Would she be ever able to win back this love? The heart dictates how one should deal with the person who loves you, but of the art of retrieving lost love Asha was totally ignorant. In any case, what could be more humiliating than begging for the love of one whose heart was clearly engaged elsewhere?

The family astrologer-priest arrived in the evening, summoned by Rajlakshmi, to propitiate the evil conjunctions of stars which she believed had turned against her son. She also asked the priest to study Asha's horoscope and read her palm. Asha found it most distasteful that her personal misfortunes would be the subject of discussion with an outsider. When this ritual was going on, Mahendra arrived, sheepishly tip-toeing.

Instead of being elated at her husband's return, Asha was mortified when she noted how embarrassed he looked. How awful that he had to enter his home stealthily like a thief! The presence of the priest added to her distress. So, when Rajlakshmi asked one of the maids to get some food for her son, Asha volunteered to do it herself. Her first concern was to screen Mahendra from the curious eyes of the servants.

The sight of the astrologer-priest terribly upset Mahendra. He assumed that his mother and wife in collusion had invited this illiterate person in order to get him back. He rudely told his mother that he was going up to his room. The doting mother assumed that her son wished to speak privately with his wife, which she read as a good omen. She rushed to the kitchen and instructed Asha to drop what she was doing and go up immediately to meet her husband, who was very keen to speak to her.

The way her mother-in-law spoke to her Asha genuinely believed that Mahendra, indeed, had sent for her. She went up, her heart palpitating, her steps halting. Instead of going straight into Mahendra's room, she paused outside the door. She found him sitting half-inclined on the bed, cushioned by bolsters.

It was the same Mahendra, but how frightfully changed now. That was Asha's thought as she watched him from the door. It was the same room where the two of them had once created their own paradise. If his heart were elsewhere, if he were so restless, so unhappy, then why did he have to come back here? If this room, this bed, did not take him back to those halcyon days when each night was filled with ecstatic bliss, those intimate afternoons, those romantic rainy days, those balmy spring evenings when they had no thoughts other than for each other—then what business had Mahendra to be in this room? There were other spare rooms, and he should have gone to one of them, instead of sullying the happy memories associated with this room.

As Asha kept watching her husband, she was assailed by the nauseating thought that he must have been in the company of Binodini just before he returned here. His whole being was now entwined with Binodini—the feel of her body, her voice in his ears, her image in his eyes, his lust for her. How could Asha then be expected to offer her unflinching love and devotion to someone like Mahendra whose heart had no room for her?

She recalled her aunt's sermons, the dictum of the scriptures, the legends of the *puranas*—but they meant nothing to her now. She found it difficult to put Mahendra on a pedestal as her sole and venerable deity. All that she had cherished so long she sacrificed this evening at the altar of Binodini's infamy. Everything around her—this loveless evening, the silence of the stars, in her bloodstream, the lonely roof, the conjugal bed now forsaken—tolled the knell of her love. Binodini's Mahendra was now a stranger as far as she was concerned. No way could she go into that room.

Mahendra, who had so long continued to stare at the ceiling, now brought his eyes down and was looking at Asha's and his own photographs that hung side by side on the wall. Asha noticed this and wished she had removed her picture and thrown it away. She imagined Mahendra was smiling, in amusement, and probably with him Binodini, who was enthroned in his heart, was simultaneously making fun of her!

Mahendra's dinner was ready, but Rajlakshmi deliberately delayed announcing it, assuming that her son and daughter-in-law must be engaged in intimate togetherness after such a long gap. When she found Asha had come down, it surprised her. She decided to take her son's dinner herself. When Mahendra moved to the dining room, Asha quickly removed her portrait and destroyed it with vengeance.

After his meal Mahendra went back to his room, but Asha was not there. Rajlakshmi found her in the kitchen warming up her milk, which was not her usual task. The maid whose job it was, naturally, resented this intrusion as she would be deprived of her share of the milk which she took by diluting the milk with water.

Rajlakshmi was visibly annoyed. 'What are you doing here, child? Go up to your room.'

Asha, instead, went into her mother-in-law's room. Rajlakshmi was thoroughly disgusted with Asha. Why was she behaving in this peculiar manner? Now that her son was back home away from the clutches of that witch, Asha's truculence was bound to drive her husband away again if Mahendra was enticed by Binodini, it was all Asha's fault. Men were like that, ever ready to stray away, and it was always the duty of the wife to bring the husband back to the straight and narrow.

Rajlakshmi spoke to her daughter-in-law sharply, 'Honestly, I cannot make you out at all. Now that your husband is at home, you sulk and keep hiding from him.'

May be, she was at fault, and this thought drove Asha back once again to her room. With nothing to do Mahendra was trying ineptly to fix the mosquito net, and brooding over Binodini. Binodini had terribly upset him. How did she dare disdain him? Was she so assured of his attachment to her, as her bond slave, that she had no qualms in sending him back to Asha? If he really stood by Asha as was his rightful obligation, to whom would Binodini then turn for help? Was he so spineless that Binodini regarded him incapable of resuming his conjugal obligations? Was that his real image in her eyes? In that case, he had not only lost her respect but had received nothing in return. She had, apparently, no compunctions in humiliating him.

He decided that he must answer Binodini's arrogance by resuming his relationship with his wife. That would be his revenge. As Asha came into the room, he was lost for words how to begin, and then he remarked off hand, 'I find you have resumed your lessons.' A pointless remark that offended Asha. Asha wanted her renewed attempt at education to be kept away from the public eye. She was particularly keen to conceal it from Mahendra for fear of his ridicule. When his first words after such a long gap touched on the very same subject that she wished to keep secret, Asha withdrew within herself and said not a word.

It had also struck Mahendra that his opening words after this long hiatus were not quite appropriate, but he could not think of anything else. Resumption of their earlier intimate exchanges was out of the question. Well, perhaps, once in the bed, he would find it easy to talk. Like a novice actor who rehearses his lines repeatedly from stage fright was precisely how Mahendra felt and moved. Suddenly, he noticed that Asha was not in the room.

FORTY-THREE

The next morning, Mahendra told his mother, 'I need a separate room for myself where I can study undisturbed. My aunt's vacant room suggests itself.'

Rajlakshmi was delighted. This meant that her son was staying in at home. He and Asha must have made up with each other, she assumed. That was only right. How can her dear son remain happy in the clutches of that witch ignoring such a wonderful wife?

Falling in readily with her son's suggestion, a retinue of servants was engaged in doing up the room—cleaning, dusting, making the long unused room fit for her princely son. A new covering for the floor, a new table for Mahendra's use, a new lamp to replace the old one, and various other refurbishing. Mahendra, oblivious of the efforts of the women, lost no time in occupying the room.

After dinner, Mahendra resumed his studies. It was not clear whether he would sleep in his usual bedroom or down in the new room. Rajlakshmi dressed up her daughter-in-law and sent her to find out where Mahendra proposed to sleep. Asha was not clearly very keen to do this, but on the mother-in-law's insistence went near the room but hesitated to go in. Rajlakshmi angrily signalled her that she must, and a desperate Asha eventually did so. Without taking his eyes off his books, Mahendra told Asha, 'I am not ready for bed yet. In any case, I need to resume my studies first thing in the morning. I think I shall sleep in this room.' Asha almost died with shame, as if she came to persuade Mahendra to come to bed with her!

When Rajlakshmi saw Asha coming out of Mahendra's room she asked tartly, 'What happened?' Asha replied, 'He is still busy with his studies and wishes to sleep there.' She led to her own room, but there was no place for her where she could find some solace.

Later at night Rajlakshmi went up to Asha's room and knocked on her door. Asha found her mother-in-law standing there, breathless. Rajlakshmi went in and sat on Asha's bed to rest. After she got back her breath, she admonished Asha, 'Why do you go on like this? Is it the time for you to fight each other? In spite of all that you have suffered, you do not appear to come to your senses. Now, go down to him.'

Asha protested mildly, 'But he said he preferred to be left alone.'

'Oh, he did, did he, and so out of pique you decided to stay away from him. Listen to me. There is no premium in such foolishness. I suggest you go to him, now.'

In times of adversities even the mother-in-law chose to overlook the usual formalities of social decorum. Her sole aim was somehow to pin Mahendra down in the house. This emotional outburst was too much for her, and her asthmatic' trouble aggravated. Asha put the mother-in-law in bed, adjusted the pillows and cushions to make her comfortable, when Rajlakshmi dissuaded her. 'Please, child, you have done enough for now. Ask the maid to be here, and you go to your husband.'

Asha did not dither now, and went straight to Mahendra's room. With an open book in front of him and both his feet up on the table, Mahendra was clearly absorbed in deep thought. Asha's footsteps made him turn back. For an instant, he imagined that the object of his meditation had unexpectedly appeared there. When he saw it was Asha, he put his feet down and picked up the open book.

Asha's demeanour tonight came as a surprise to Mahendra. She hardly ever came to him so openly. These days she usually avoided him. Very strange that so late at night she would come to see him so free and easy. Mahendra did not take his eyes off his book, but it dawned on him that Asha might be there for a purpose. Asha went near him and faced him, when Mahendra could no longer pretend that he was deep into his studies. He looked up, and Asha told him, 'Mother's asthma seems to have gone worse. Perhaps, you should have a look at her.'

'Oh, where is she now?' Mahendra asked.

'In her room. She finds it difficult to sleep.'

'Let's go and see her then,' said Mahendra.

This talk with Asha, though brief, came as some sort of a relief to Mahendra. The impregnable granite wall that apparently came between them Mahendra was unable to breach, but Asha managed to break the barrier on her own.

Mahendra went straight to his mother who was in her bed. Alarmed to see her son in her room at this unusual hour she thought the two must have fought again, and the son was there to tell her that he was once again leaving home!

'Haven't you gone to bed yet?' the mother asked anxiously.

Mahendra said, 'I understand your asthma has taken a turn for the worse.'

It hurt her that it had taken Mahendra such a long time to show any interest in his mother's health. She knew immediately that Asha must have spoken to her husband. Though upset, she managed to say, 'It is nothing really. No need for you to bother. Better get back to bed.'

'Still, let me have a look. Cannot ignore your problem.' Mahendra knew that his mother had a history of heart condition, and the look in her face he found worrying.

'I told you not to bother,' Rajlakshmi grumbled. 'There is no need for you to examine me. This is not a sickness that will easily go away.'

'Well, I will get some sleeping draught for you for tonight. Tomorrow we shall have a good look at you,' Mahendra said.

'I have had enough of drugs by now. Medicines are of no use to me. At any rate, it is already very late now, and I suggest you get back to your bed,' Rajlakshmi was both exhausted and irritated.

'I will, as soon as you feel a little better.'

Proud Rajlakshmi, unhappy with her son, protested to the daughter-in-law who was waiting outside the door. 'Why did you have to drag Mohin down here so late at night? Absolutely unnecessary.' Her breathing got worse as she spoke.

Asha went into the room and spoke firmly to her husband, 'Take yourself off now. I shall look after her.'

Mahendra took Asha aside, and told her that he had sent for the sleeping draught. One dose was to be given immediately, and if she were still sleepless, another dose to be given an hour later. And, to keep him informed if her condition deteriorated.

Mahendra went back to his room, impressed by this new Asha. This Asha was confident, suffered from no complex, assured of her own place—she was no longer a supplicant to her husband. He had neglected her as his wife, but tonight discovered a newly found respect for her as a daughter-in-law of the family.

Though enormously pleased that out of concern for her, Asha got the son to come down and have a look at her, Rajlakshmi nevertheless, pretended to be otherwise. She told Asha, 'I sent you to be with him, but why did you have to get him down here?'

Asha said nothing, and went on plying a hand fan, sitting by her side. Rajlakshmi once again tried to send her back to her husband, to which Asha responded gently, 'My husband has asked me to be with you.' Asha was clever enough to know that it would make the mother's day to believe that her son was so concerned about her that he left his wife behind to nurse her!

FORTY-FOUR

The reality was now clear to Rajlakshmi that Asha was no longer able to keep her husband at home. What held Mahendra back was her sickness, and so she decided to malinger. Unknown to Asha, she did not take her medicines. Asha noted with alarm that her mother-in-law was getting worse and not better. Mahendra, in his absent-minded fashion, had failed to notice this change in his mother's condition. Asha was afraid that Mahendra, being otherwise preoccupied, was not paying sufficient attention to his mother. Perhaps, his selection of drugs was not quite right. His present distractions were apparently so acute that he had little or no time for his mother, which Asha found most contemptible.

When she was in intense pain one day, Rajlakshmi suddenly remembered Bihari. It had been a long time since she last saw him. 'Do you know where Bihari is?' she asked Asha. Bihari had always taken care of Rajlakshmi during her illness, and it was only natural that she would think of Bihari at such difficult times. Asha understood her sentiments clearly. Sadly, that rock-like support of the family had been banished from this house. Bihari was not heartless like her husband. Had he been here now, he could have done so much more for the mother-in-law.

Rajlakshmi asked, 'Did Mohin pick a fight again with Bihari? Very wicked if he did. My son has no better friend than Bihari.' Traces of tears collected in her eyes.

Yes, Asha could now see many things in their proper light. Bihari had tried his best to warn her of the potential threats, but Asha in her ignorance turned hostile to him. She cursed herself for her foolishness. Not surprising that the good God thought fit to punish an ingrate who turned her back on a well-wishing friend, and instead, clasped to her heart someone who turned out to be demonic. Would Bihari, who was such a good friend of the family and who was shown the door so unceremoniously, ever willingly return to this house? After a pause Rajlakshmi observed, 'I am sure if Bihari were here, he would have looked after us in these sad times. He would not have allowed the situation to go out of hand. I am confident if Bihari gets to know about my illness, he would rush here to help me.'

Asha interpreted this as her mother-in-law's wish somehow to send a message to Bihari. The mother was clearly desolate in Bihari's absence.

Mahendra's room was dark, as he had doused the lamp. He stood at the window staring aimlessly out. He was not comfortable at all in his home. He found it difficult to apply his mind seriously to his studies. He was presently not on easy terms with his dear and near ones, but even so it was not possible to dismiss them as if they did not count. Equally, he found it difficult to feel very close to them. He found it trying to visit his mother, because she always looked at him with such pointed anxiety, which affected him. And, when Asha came to see him for any specific purpose, he found it awkward to speak to her. On the other hand, not to say anything was equally awkward. Not the sort of life one looked forward to. He had resolved that he would keep away from Binodini for seven days of which another two days remained, but how would he keep going even for these two days?

Mahendra heard footsteps, which he recognized as Asha's, but deliberately took no notice. Asha saw through it but ignored the affront. 'I just came to tell you something, and I will then leave you alone.'

Mahendra turned his face. 'You don't have to go. Stay on if you wish,' he said.

Asha was cold to this formal politeness; she just told him, 'Bihari-*thakurpo* should be informed about mother's health condition.'

Mahendra reacted sharply to Bihari's name. 'Why? You have no confidence in my treatment, is it?' he asked.

Asha did indeed, believe that mother was not receiving proper treatment, and, in a way, Mahendra's apprehensions were confirmed when she replied, 'But she is getting no better, on the contrary she seems to be worse.'

Mahendra was amazed that Asha could be so candidly critical of him, which hurt. His response was to sneer at her. 'I suppose I shall have to take medical lessons from you.'

It was an unnecessary and cynical response, nasty and painful. Asha had learnt to ignore such barbs. She was not the one to be kept down and spoke with considerable vehemence, 'I cannot comment on medical lessons, but at least you can learn how to care for your mother.'

Asha's words stung Mahendra. Unused to rebukes from Asha he turned ferocious. 'You know very well why your Bihari-*thakurpo* has been denied access to our home. So, what makes you think of him again?'

Asha quickly left the room. She was mortified, not for herself but for her husband. How could a person who was himself absorbed in an illicit affair could utter such infamy about another? He was so infernally shameless.

After Asha left Mahendra realized that he had behaved like a cad. That Asha could denounce him so bitingly was beyond his imagination. His once entrenched throne was now lying on a dust heap, and he feared that Asha's bitterness might turn into great loathing for him.

At the thought of Bihari, Mahendra became very fidgety about Binodini. Had Bihari returned from his travels? Did Binodini come to know about Bihari's whereabouts, in which case it was quite possible that the two of then might have got together? A desperate Mahendra was about to abandon his resolve.

Late the same night Rajlakshmi's heart condition took a turn for the worse. She herself sent for her son and with considerable difficulty was able to tell him, 'Bihari had not been here to see me for a long time. I am very anxious to see him.'

'I understand he is not in town,' Mahendra informed her.

'My instinct tells me that he is in town,' Rajlakshmi said haltingly. 'He does not call because of his unhappiness with you. Please, for my sake, go and look him up tomorrow.'

Mahendra promised to do so. Everyone now wanted Bihari. No one had any time for him.

FORTY-FIVE

The first thing the following morning Mahendra called at Bihari's residence. He was surprised to see a row of bullock-carts in the process of being loaded in front of the house.

Mahendra asked the old retainer, 'What is all this, Bhoju?' Bhoju told him, 'The Master has rented a garden house at Bali across the river. All these cart loads of staff are going there.'

'Is your Master at home?'

Bhoju replied, 'No, he is not. He was here for a couple of days after his return from his travels, but shifted to the new place yesterday.'

This information filled Mahendra with panic. He was convinced that during his absence Binodini and Bihari must have got together. He had a vision of carts getting loaded at Binodini's place as well. He was certain in his mind that Binodini had deliberately planned to keep him out of her way.

He mounted his carriage and told the coachman to take him to the Patalrlanga house. He cursed the coachman for not driving fast enough. On reaching the house, he found no signs of any movement or waiting carts. Surely, she could not have left already. He jumped down from the carriage and knocked violently on the door. Immediately as the door was opened, he asked the servant if all was well there. All was, indeed, well, the servant confirmed.

Somewhat relieved, he went up to Binodini's room. She was not there, having gone for her bath. Mahendra eased himself on her bed, savouring the flavour of her association. How coldblooded can you be, Binodini, how merciless, he murmured to himself.

He paced up and down the room waiting impatiently for her. A Bengali newspaper caught his eye. He picked it up, and while skimming through it his attention was riveted on a small report that concerned Bihari. According to this news item, Bihari had established a centre in a garden house in Bali for the benefit of ill-paid clerical workers who could not afford the cost of medical treatment when they fell ill. There would be room only for five inmates at a time. The address of the centre was also given.

He assumed that Binodini must have read this report, in which case how did she take it? It was possible that she would wish to go and join Bihari there. Mahendra's agitation mounted, not just because of what her intentions could be, but because this selfless charitable project of Bihari's would considerably add to Bihari's glamour in her mind. Mahendra cursed Bihari as a humbug, termed his project a passing fancy. Was not Bihari always inclined even in his young days to get involved in do good activities? Uncharitably, he regarded all this work of Bihari's so-called generosity and self sacrifice as a show to delude people—a form of hypocrisy that Mahendra detested with all his heart. On the other hand, he took great credit for himself that he was, in contrast to Bihari, a sincere and a straightforward individual. Sadly, not many people were aware of this noble aspect of him! With all that, he was afraid that Bihari had once again scored over him.

When Binodini came in, Mahendra quickly folded the paper and hid it. What an amazing change he observed in Binodini. She was slimmer and she had a fresh and alluring glow in her face.

Binodini had given up any hope of receiving a reply from Bihari to her letter. Bihari's apparent contempt for her crushed her. He had, probably, deliberately gone away just to avoid her, so she conjectured. As a woman who was used to a busy life she found her present confinement in this small apartment, with nothing to do, excessively claustrophobic. The thought of living in this loveless, joyless, idle cul-de-sac home repelled her, and she wanted to rebel against her present situation with all her heart, knowing well that it was beyond her control.

Binodini now despised intensely that imbecile Mahendra who had manipulated to block all her roads to freedom and reduced her to this circumscribed existence. What perturbed her most was the fear that she would not be able to keep Mahendra away from her. He would visit her everyday and make advances to her to make her life miserable. She shuddered at the very thought of the daily strifes that were inevitable between them, in this wretched dark hole that was her home now, where she lived as a castaway from the society, trying to hold Mahendra at bay. This viper who with its salivating tongue was lasciviously trying to coil its abominable body round her was her own creation. And, who can now get rid of it for her? And, what an atrocious thought it was that she would have to withstand Mahendra's lustful assaults? Where would all this end? When would she be able to get away from it all?

Mahendra's latent jealousy was re-ignited when he saw Binodini's pale but angelic visage. He wished he had some magical power to expunge all thoughts of Bihari from Binodini's heart. His imagination ran riot. He wished to whisk away Binodini to a faraway hideout, away from the eyes of other people, like the eagle which snatched a young lamb and secreted it at some faraway insurmountable mountain niche. His intense jealousy of Bihari added fuel to the fire of his rabid desire for Binodini. He must, he resolved, keep Binodini away from Bihari at all cost.

Binodini spoke first, 'Have you had any tea, yet?' 'May be I had, but let that not stop you from your bounty of offering me another cup.'

A little later Binodini, probably intentionally to needle Mahendra, asked, 'Do you keep any track of Bihari-*thakurpo*?'

Mahendra, somewhat shaken, said, 'He is out of town.'

'Do you have his address?' Binodini asked.

'He wishes to remain incognito, I believe.'

'Is it not possible to trace him?'

'I don't see any need for that,' Mahendra said tersely.

'Must needs be always the overriding consideration? Does not a lifelong friendship mean anything to you?' Binodini asked.

'True, Bihari and I are very old friends, but you have not known him all that long, yet you seem to be particularly keen to trace him,' was Mahendra's dismissive reply.

'That ought to put you to shame. You should have taken lessons from your friend on how to cultivate friends and keep them,' mocked Binodini.

Said Mahendra, 'I have no feeling of remorse on that score, but I wish I could learn from him the art of how to steal women's heart.'

'This art cannot be taught. It requires some special aptitude.'

'Ah, is that so?' Mahendra was pretty riled by then. 'If you happen to know the address of a competent teacher, do let me know. I will then come back and sit for a test of my aptitude.'

Binodini stiffened. She said, 'Do not talk to me about your love if you are incapable of tracing the whereabouts of an old friend. Who can ever trust you the way you have treated this friend of yours?'

Mahendra haughtily remarked, 'You would have never dared to humiliate me the way you do if you had not the fullest confidence in my love for you. And, that is my tragedy; that is why I suffer so much. Bihari is clever; he knows how not to get caught. He would have done me a friend's turn had he taught me that art.'

'Well, Bihari is a human being, so he cannot be tallied like an animal,' Binodini hurled another shot at Mahendra, and remained standing at the window with her back to him. Mahendra stood up and roared furiously at her. 'How dare you slight me again and again in this manner? Because I do not react adversely to your put-downs, you take me for granted. Do you not believe that I may possess some virtues? If you regard me as a beast, then take me for a ferocious beast. I am not the kind of coward that you take me to be. If wounded, I can hit back.'

Mahendra's violent agitation took some time to subside. When he had sufficiently calmed down, be spoke softly to Binodini, 'Let us go away somewhere—anywhere that takes your fancy—maybe, the hills—just let us get away. We cannot go on like this here. It is killing me.'

Binodini had also considerably mellowed by then. She readily agreed, 'Yes, let us, soon.'

'Where should we go?' Mahendra asked.

'Does it really matter? We will just move around, not get rooted at any particular place,' said Binodini.

Mahendra was all for it. 'Good idea. We shall leave tonight.'

It was clear to Mahendra, much to his relief, that Binodini had not seen that piece on Bihari in the newspaper. Mahendra made sure that she never would.

FORTY-SIX

Rajlakshmi kept waiting for Mahendra, expecting that he would be back home after he had made his enquiries about Bihari. She started fretting when her son was not back even late in the night. Worrying for the son aggravated her sickness. Asha had, by then, discovered that the carriage had returned empty after taking Mahendra, first to Bihari's place and then to the Pataldanga house. Rajlakshmi went numb when told this. She lost all interest in life when she found that in spite of her serious illness, Mahendra's priority was Binodini. She asked no questions, made no comments.

It was evident that Mahendra did not take his mother's health condition seriously. His mother had been ill before and had come round. Mahendra probably regarded her present condition just as a recurrence to cause no particular anxiety. This want of concern for his mother was what hurt Rajlakshmi the most. In his frenzied infatuation for Binodini there was no space for anything else in Mahendra's heart—neither any concern for his mother's health nor his obligations to his family. He deliberately dismissed his mother's condition being grave, or else he might be obliged to be at her side. At the earliest pretext he had gone back to Binodini. Rajlakshmi had now no incentive to get well, to prove how ill-founded was her son's lack of concern for her.

At some point of time Asha reminded her mother-in-law that it was time for her medicine. Rajlakshmi said nothing, but when Asha offered the medicine she protested, 'I have no need for any medicine now. Please leave me alone.' Asha realized how unhappy the mother was, and this made her so miserable that she broke into sobs. Rajlakshmi turned towards Asha, took hold of her hand and spoke with great affection, 'Child, you are still quite young. There is time yet for you to regain your happiness, but I have nothing to look forward to. I have lived long enough, and there is no point in trying to keep me alive.'

In the cheerless sick room, the mother and wife waited with

hopes that Mahendra would return home however late, only to be frustrated. Late at night Asha asked the mother-in-law, 'Shall I send someone to fetch him?' Rajlakshmi firmly rejected this suggestion. 'Promise me, never to tell Mohin about me not being well.' Asha sat there helplessly, with no idea what she should do.

A servant came in later, carrying a letter from Mahendra. Immediately the mother's heart panicked that perhaps her son had suddenly taken ill, and so could not come home. She was full of remorse that she had earlier misjudged her son. She urged Asha to read the letter.

Asha carried the letter near the lamp and started reading. The letter said that he had not been feeling too well of late, and so had decided to leave town for a change of air. He added that there was no need for any concern for the mother's health. He had made arrangements for Dr Navin to visit her regularly. The letter also contained a few instructions for the mother.

Asha was stunned by this heartless letter. How could she tell the mother how inconsiderate the son was? Meanwhile, Rajlakshmi was getting impatient with Asha. 'What does Mahendra say in his letter?' she asked. In her eagerness she even managed to sit up. Asha read over the letter to her. 'Can you read me once again what he says about not feeling well?'

Asha repeated, 'I have not been feeling too well of late, so...'

Rajlakshmi quickly intercepted, 'Yes, yes, I can understand too well. You don't have to read any further. How can I blame him? Here is the old mother who refuses to die, only troubles him with her sickness. Really, child, I do not know what made you tell Mohin about my health. Here he was in his own home, kept to himself, busy with his studies, did not bother anyone. And then, you had to go and tell him about me. It is your ill-judged indiscretion that drove him out of his home. How does it matter to anyone if I am dead or alive? I must say you lack the commonest of sense.'

Booted footsteps were heard outside. A servant announced the visit of Dr Navin. Asha moved away as the doctor stepped inside the room. The doctor asked Rajlakshmi, 'Can you tell me please what troubles you?'

Rajlakshmi said unpleasantly, 'My troubles? Won't you allow a person to die in peace? Will your medicine keep me alive forever?'

The doctor tried to comfort her, 'No, we cannot promise immortality, but we try to provide relief to...'

Rajlakshmi cut in, 'The real relief was when widows were immolated with their husbands. It is now a slow torture to death. Doctor, please leave me now. Don't hassle me.'

The doctor said diffidently, 'May I take your pulse, please?'

'Why?' Rajlakshmi was now very irritable. 'Nothing wrong with my pulse. It is not likely to stop beating soon—I have no such hopes. Now, will you let me alone, please?'

The doctor went out and spoke to Asha, who was able to tell the doctor what Rajlakshmi's problems were. He went back to Rajlakshmi's room and spoke somewhat solemnly, 'Your son Mahendra has placed you in my hands. He may feel aggrieved if you do not allow me to treat you.'

Mahendra getting upset sounded like a joke to her. She said, 'Do not let that worry you. I do not think this is going to affect him all that much. Please, let me sleep now.'

The doctor realized that there was little point in his talking to Rajlakshmi. He left, after leaving certain instructions with Asha. Rajlakshmi told Asha to go and get some rest. 'You have been with me the whole day. Send the maid who can keep a watch.'

Asha knew it would be futile to protest against the mother-in-law's wishes. She was herself fagged out, physically and mentally, to the point of dropping off. She went to her room but could hardly sleep. Somewhere in the neighbourhood a marriage was taking place, and the strains of *shehnai* came floating through. This threw her mind back to her own wedding day. Every incident, all the pomp, the lights, the music, the gathering of friends and relations, the ceremony—all came vividly alive in her mind. The happy memories of that significant day of her life swamped her heart, but with painful reminders. Asha, worn out and desolate, was groping for help. At this critical time of her life she could only think of her aunt Annapurna. She did not wish to drag her aunt to these troublesome times, but in her overpowering helplessness, the aunt was her only guiding light. She wrote to her:

> My dearest aunt, I have no one else to call my own except you. Please come to my rescue. I have no other recourse. My respectful pranams.
>
> Your affectionate
Chuni

FORTY-SEVEN

Annapurna duly arrived from Kashi. She went straight to Rajlakshmi's room, and touched her feet. In spite of the earlier alienation Rajlakshmi welcomed back Annapurna with great sense of relief. She, in fact, had been subconsciously praying for her return. Her unexpected arrival helped considerably to ease Rajlakshmi's accumulated pain and agony. Before Mahendra's birth, the two sisters-in-law had shared the responsibilities of their joint family—in happy times and sad amidst life and deaths. After a long separation that friend and associate of her early days had returned to be at her side when Rajlakshmi needed her the most. The two affectionately greeted each other. Emotionally charged, Rajlakshmi's eyes filled with water, which moved Asha also to tears.

Annapurna deliberately refrained from asking Rajlakshmi and Asha about Mahendra. She spoke instead to Sadhucharan, who told her about Mahendra and Binodini. She then asked about Bihari to be told that he had not been seen for a long time, and that no one knew where he was. She instructed Sadhucharan to visit Bihari's house and get whatever information he could. On his return Sadhucharan reported that Bihari had moved to a garden house in Bali on the other side of the river.

Annapurna's next move was to consult Dr Navin about Rajlakshmi's state of health. The doctor drew a grim picture. Her weak heart, now coupled with dropsy, had made her condition extremely precarious. Death could intervene any day. One evening when Rajlakshmi was particularly bad, Annapurna suggested a call to the doctor. Rajlakshmi stopped her. 'No doctor can do me any good now.'

'Is there anyone you wish to see in particular?' asked Annapurna.

'Yes, Bihari, if you can get him,' Rajlakshmi almost appealed.

Annapurna smarted with pain. She had herself been nursing long an unease that concerned Bihari. She remembered with distress the incident when she had turned Bihari away unceremoniously from her doors in Kashi. How can Bihari now return to her? She had little hope that she would ever be able to make amends for her ill-treatment of Bihari.

Annapurna went up to Mahendra's room. It was once the finest place in the house, but it was now in total disarray—untidy and uncared for. No one now watered the flowerpots on the roof, and the plants had all withered.

Asha followed her aunt to the roof. Annapurna drew her niece close to her. The two sat together. Asha said despondently, 'Dear, *Mashima*, I wish I was strong enough to go through so much vicissitudes. How long, tell me *Mashima*, can I go on like this?'

The presence of her aunt gave Asha a sense of security and tranquillity that she had lacked for a long time. Well, she thought, the gods might not much care for a benighted creature like herself, but surely they would not turn down the prayers o someone so saintly as her aunt.

They both sat there long in each other's company when Asha, now at peace with herself, told Annapurna, 'Why do you not write to Bihari-*thakurpo* to come and see us?'

'No point in writing a letter,' Annapurna observed.

'How can we then send him a message?'

Annapurna said, softly, 'I shall go myself and meet him tomorrow.'

FORTY-EIGHT

During his aimless travels, the thought occurred to Bihari that unless he attached himself to some kind of activity there would be no respite for him. That was when he conceived of the scheme of taking care of impoverished clerical workers, who were unable to meet their medical expenses. He had long been concerned about this tribe of low paid clerks, burdened with large families, dwelling in miserable airless homes in dingy lanes. He founded this garden project for the benefit of these poor creatures.

He started building small cottages with the help of Chinese workmen, but this work did not bring him satisfaction as he had expected. To tell the truth, as the work advanced, his resolution progressively wavered. To him this work was devoid of any charm, any pleasure or joy; it was no more than dry-as-dust obligation. Never before had Bihari regarded work as a cheerless burden.

There was a time when Bihari's needs were few. He found satisfaction even in minor chores. Of late, however, there was some sort of a hunger that gnawed at him. He found it difficult to get involved seriously in any particular task. He toyed with many ideas only to reject them.

The young man in Bihari, to which he never gave any thought, was suddenly animated by the touch of Binodini's gold wand. Like the hungry bird, he was now hunting for sustenance. Bihari was earlier innocent of this hungry creature, which now kept driving him. How can concerns for ill paid clerks satisfy this craving?

It was early monsoon. The Ganges, filled to the brim, flowed ceaselessly; banks of dark clouds engulfed the trees, investing the river stream with the shine of a sword blade, now bright with a golden glow, now dark blue. Whenever Bihari scanned the majestic splendour of the first showers, a vision, emerging all by herself, came knocking at his heart. The vision of a woman standing with her wavy dark tresses, a vision glowing in the spray of shafts of rays escaping through the breaks in the clouds, a vision that looked at him with steadfast but plaintive eyes.

These days, when Bihari looked back, his early life, which to him was till then perfectly ideal, now seemed barren. How many such romantic evenings, heavy with rain clouds or silvery bright with a full moon, had come his way, and how those evenings disdained by him passed him by. In his despondent mood he counted those evenings as lost opportunities that he missed by his own folly. The remembrance of Binodini's inviting lips paled all his past memories, discoloured them, rendered them paltry and insignificant.

Bihari recalled the time when he lived as Mahendra's shadow. What was the point of that existence, pondered Bihari. He had never experienced before the melancholic music of love that assailed him from all directions—the sky, the river, the earth. This was beyond the pale of his imagination. How could he ever forget Binodini, the Binodini who with her magic wand opened up for him that fabulous world of splendour? Binodini was now everything in his life, all-pervading. Recollection of her tender soft touch sent waves through his heart, rejuvenating him.

Why did he then keep himself away from Binodini? Because he was not sure of what kind of a relationship he could build with her that would be appropriate and fitting for her. Besides, she could be a bone of contention between Mahendra and himself. There would be an awful scandal if the two of them fought over Binodini. That was unthinkable. That was why he had secluded himself on the bank of the Ganges, with her image entrenched in his heart. He did not intentionally write to Binodini in case his dreams were wrecked by any inopportune reports.

He sat contemplating under a *jaam* tree, heavy with fruits, on this overcast morning. Later in the day a servant came to ask if he was ready for his food. 'Not yet,' Bihari told him. When some workmen approached him for instruction, he waved them away, 'Later, not now.'

In his contemplative and laid-back mood, he was startled by an unexpected occurrence. Standing before him was Annapurna. He quickly stood up, full of curiosity, and bowed his head down on her feet. With great tenderness Annapurna placed her right hand on Bihari's head. With her eyes moist she asked, 'Son, why have you lost weight?'

'So that I can retrieve your love, Kakima,' Bihari said in a touching reply. These words broke her down completely, and tears gushed from her eyes.

After some pause Bihari said, 'I suppose you have had nothing to eat, yet.'

'No, and it is not yet the time for my food,' Annapurna said. Bihari was not going to be put off. 'Come now, let us go and get everything ready for you to cook. I will be the beneficiary. After a long time I will have the good fortune to taste your cooking.'

Bihari did not raise the topic of Mahendra or Asha. Annapurna herself had blotted that out of Bihari's mind, and Bihari rigidly observed this injunction. After they finished eating, Annapurna told Bihari, 'My boat is ready to leave. Do come with me to Calcutta.'

'Why do I need to go to Calcutta?' asked Bihari.

Annapurna told him, '*Didi*—Mahendra's mother—is seriously ill. She keeps asking for you.'

This staggered Bihari. 'Where is Mahendra?' he asked.

'Not in town,' Annapurna told him.

This information staggered Bihari even more. Annapurna was surprised. 'Do you not know at all what has happened?'

'Not really.'

Annapurna then related the story of Mahendra and Binodini fleeing Calcutta together. Immediately, Bihari's entire world went sour. All his sweet dreams turned bitter. Did the siren Binodini then play a game of deception with him? All her offer of love was then palpably false. Shamelessly she left town in the company of Mahendra. He cursed himself for his foolishness that he had genuinely believed her even for an instant.

The magic world that he had been building round Binodini lay shattered.

FORTY-NINE

The thought that kept bothering Bihari was how he was going to face poor, miserable Asha. When Bihari crossed the threshold of Mahendra's house, the ambience of the whole place appeared permeated with an air of gloom. He was too embarrassed even to face squarely the servants of the house, let alone exchange decencies as he usually did. Mahendra had cast his wife away, openly and shamelessly, to a situation, utterly devastating for any woman, and that also for all the public to witness her humiliation.

Bihari's steps faltered as he went inside the house, but this was not the time to dither. Asha came running to Bihari when she saw him. 'Please, *thakurpo*, come and see mother. She is in such pain.' Asha's voice betrayed her anxiety.

This was the very first occasion that they spoke so openly to each other. In times of adversity, barriers do break down. Strangers become friends when they find shelter on the solitary boat in times of flood.

Asha's deep anxiety, now free of any inhibitions, disturbed Bihari. This was evidence enough, if any evidence was needed at all, to tell him to what utter disorder Mahendra had reduced his home. All around him were signs of negligence. Even the young daughter-in-law of the house had to come out of her veil and abandon the normal modest conduct. Indeed, all discretions had to be thrown to the winds.

Bihari went into Rajlakshmi's room. By then she had rallied somewhat; her spell of breathing trouble had eased for the time being. Bihari touched Rajlakshmi's feet, and she waved him to sit on her bed. In a frail voice she asked, 'How are you, my son? It has been a long time since I last saw you.'

Bihari complained, 'Why did you not let me know earlier that you were not well. I would have rushed to you immediately.'

This made Rajlakshmi happy. She said softly, 'Do I not know that? You were not born out of me, but truly there is no one else in my world closer than you.' She started weeping silently.

Bihari got up and started needlessly fiddling with the medicine bottles on the shelf just to hide his emotions. He returned and was about to take her pulse, when she stopped him. She said, 'Forget about my pulse beats. Tell me, why have you gone so thin?'

'Lacking the nourishment of your cooking, Mother,' Bihari said forcing a weak smile. 'So, get well soon. This wretched body of mine will gain no weight until I taste once again food cooked by you.'

Holding Bihari's hand in hers, Rajkalkshmi said, 'I doubt if I will get well enough for that. You must get married. There is no one to look after you.' She turned to Annapurna, 'Get a bride for Bihari. Look at him. How pulled down he is.' Annapurna said, 'Only you can do this, Didi. Get well, and then we shall all have a celebration at his wedding.'

'No, my sister, no,' Rajlakshmi said, 'I will not be around all that time. I must leave him in your hand. See that he is happy. I will never be able to repay my debts to him. May God look after him.' As she said this, she continued lovingly to run her fingers through Bihari's head.

It was too much for Asha to stay there. She was emotionally overwhelmed. Annapurna also looked at Bihari affectionately through her tearful eyes.

Suddenly, Rajlakshmi called her daughter-in-law. When Asha came in, she asked, 'Have you made any arrangements to feed Bihari?' Bihari said with a wide grin, 'Have no worry, Ma. Everyone here knows well your gluttonous son. As I came in I saw a maid going in with a basket of large koi fish. The message is clear to me that the reputation of this boy of yours still remains intact.' He then glanced at Asha.

For once, Asha did not feel discomfited. She reacted to Bihari's joke with a smile. Until today Asha had no conception how important a person Bihari was in this family. How often had she resented his presence in their home? Her antagonism to Bihari was quite evident in her attitude to him, and Bihari was quite well aware of it. She was now extremely contrite, and presently was full of a new-found admiration for Bihari.

Rajlakshmi spoke to Annapurna, 'Do not depend on the cook. Please, do the cooking yourself. This boy of mine from East Bengal likes his food very spicy and hot.'

Bihari reacted in mock protest, 'How can you say this, Ma? Your mother came from Bikrampur, and you have the gall to call a man from the district of Nadia an East Bengali? No, I shall not stand for it.'

This started a chain of light banters and jokes, which eased the otherwise stricken climate of Mahendra's home. Amidst all this talk no one ever mentioned Mahendra by name. At all their former meetings, Rajlakshmi's major topic was Mahendra, and Mahendra had often been critical of his mother's obsession. It came as a great shock to Bihari that not for once did Rajlakshmi refer to her son.

Bihari later told Annapurna, 'Ma is very severely ill.'

'Yes, I can see that for myself,' said Annapurna. She then went and stood at the window, and after a pause told Bihari, 'Should we not get Mahendra back here? I do not think we should put this off much longer.'

Bihari pondered for a while, and then said, 'I will do as you tell me, but does anyone know where he is now?'

'No one does. We shall have to make enquiries,' Annapurna observed. 'There is something else, Bihari. Have you looked at Asha? If you cannot rescue Mahendra from the clutches of Binodini, then Asha will not live long. A look at her face will tell you that the demon of death is knocking at her door.'

Bihari was most disturbed when told this. Good Lord, he thought to himself, it was always my turn to save others, but who would come to my rescue? He gently reminded Annapurna, 'What means do I have to assure you that I shall be able to extricate Mahendra from Binodini's spell forever? He may hold himself back for a while during his mother's illness, but who can say he will not run back to her?'

Asha came in to join them. Dressed in a crumpled sari, her head half covered, she sat demurely at her aunt's feet. She was under the impression that Annapurna and Bihari were probably talking about her mother-in-law, and she was curious to know what they were saying. Her unspoken grief had endowed Asha with a rare majesty, which Bihari found most touching. Her deprivation, patiently borne and sanctified by her sacrifice, brought about a dignified grace to her, placing her in the ranks of the past legendary chaste women of India. She was no longer an ordinary plain woman. For Bihari this was a revelation, generating a high regard for Asha in his mind.

When Asha left after receiving instructions from Bihari concerning her mother-in-law's medicines and diet, Bihari firmly assured Annapurna, 'I shall find Mahendra.'

His enquiries led him to Mahendra's bank, where he discovered that recently the bank had had transactions with its Allahabad office on Mahendra's account.

FIFTY

At the railway station Binodini climbed into an intermediate class railway compartment reserved for women only. Mahendra protested, 'Why are you there? I am getting a second class ticket for you.'

'There is no need for that,' Binodini said, 'I shall be fine here.'

This took Mahendra by surprise. He knew Binodini had expensive tastes. Recollection of her earlier impoverished life was never pleasant to her. Poverty to her was undignified. The opulence of Mahendra's family, access to abundant luxuries, the standing attached to the family's name, had all proved far too attractive for Binodini. That she could have been the mistress of all this wealth and gracious living had captured her imagination. Now that she had Mahendra under her thumb, when she could luxuriate in his fortunes, she suddenly decided to forgo those privileges and arrogantly opted for austerity. Why she did this, Mahendra could not fathom. It was apparent, she was trying to limit her dependence on Mahendra as much as possible. She did not wish anything from him that could be deemed as extractions of her bargain with the love crazy Mahendra, who had uprooted her from her safe harbour and dragged her away with him. When she was at Mahendra's home, she hardly observed the rigidities prescribed for widows, but now she had resorted to the practice of austerities of a widow, had only one meal a day, wore coarse clothes, and her spontaneous sense of humour and laughter had, so it seemed, dried up. The present Binodini was the image of a gaunt, isolated and unapproachable person. Mahendra had to think twice before forcing his will on her. Mahendra, by now impatient and dissatisfied, wondered how was it that having successfully captured him with her wiles, she did not value her prize at all?

Mahendra asked, 'Tell me, to where should I get the tickets for?'

Displaying no particular interest, Binodini said casually, 'Anywhere. It hardly matters. We might get down at the first stop.'

For Mahendra this was not an attractive proposal at all. He was used to comfort, to orderly arrangements. He would prefer big towns where comfortable accommodations would be available. Looking after nitty-gritties of travel chores was not in his blood. He climbed into his compartment, thoroughly disgusted. He was also nervous in case Binodini impulsively got out somewhere midway without telling him.

Thus their wanderings began—from place to place—not striking roots anywhere—Binodini tirelessly, Mahendra helplessly. Binodini had the gift of making friends easily with strangers. She used to seek their help and ask for information about the places they planned to visit. They would find accommodation at rest houses, and went sight seeing with the new friends. Mahendra's idleness was increasingly evident with each passing day. Besides buying railway tickets he had hardly anything else to do. Rest of the time he wrestled with himself. For a few days initially he used to go out with Binodini, which he later discontinued. It was too much for him. After lunch when Binodini went round sight seeing, Mahendra had his siesta. How could a son whom an adoring mother had showered with all comforts trudge the streets in the wake of a woman? An absurd thought!

One morning, they were waiting to catch a train at Allahabad station. For some reason the train was late. Binodini sauntered on the platform, watching the trains steaming in or steaming off, other waiting passengers and what they were doing everything interested her. She preferred this itinerant existence, exploring new areas each day and experiencing a new lifestyle, to her life in that narrow constricted lane in Calcutta.

During her round of inspection, her eyes fell on a glass-fronted case, which happened to be the repository of undelivered letters. Peeking with curiosity through the glass, she discovered a letter addressed to one Bihari. There were many Biharis, of course, and there was no earthly reason to suspect that this Bihari was their Bihari. Nevertheless, she carefully noted down the address. Mahendra was waiting on a bench, with an extremely unpleasant face, when Binodini declared that she would prefer to remain in Allahabad a little longer.

It was Binodini, who was taking all the decisions, and Mahendra went along with her. He was now thoroughly fed up. Binodini had so far not given him any encouragement, leaving his desire unsatisfied. The man in him was on the point of rebellion. He had no real objection to stay on in Allahabad, in fact he would welcome some respite from these endless travels. But in his current mood of rebellion he refused to oblige her. Angrily, he said, 'Since we had already decided to move, we should move on. I do not wish to turn back now.'

'But I have decided to stay back,' Binodini said.

By then Mahendra was most indignant. 'Fine, if you so wish, but I shall push off,' he said in a huff.

All Binodini said was, 'Fair enough,' and then without another word called a porter and walked out with her luggage.

Nursing his manly pride Mahendra remained sitting on the bench. He watched Binodini going out without even one backward glance at him. Sensing problem, he immediately hired a porter and followed Binodini out. By then, she had already engaged a carriage and was inside it. Mahendra hurriedly placed his luggage on the roof, and went up to sit next to the coachman. He did not wish to sit inside and face Binodini.

Mahendra did not know where they were going. The carriage rolled on and on, and after an hour or so they had almost reached one end of the town. He sat with a glum face unwilling to ask the coachman. Finally, the carriage reached a house with a well kept garden on the bank of the Jamuna. Mahendra was puzzled. Whose house was it, and how did Binodini come to know of it? The house was closed, and after some shouting, an old man, probably the caretaker, came out. He told them that the house belonged to a rich local person whose home was not too far away from this place. He could only allow them in with the owners consent.

Binodini looked at Mahendra, who was also tempted by this delightful house. He was equally looking forward to settle down after all this wandering. 'Let us go then and look up the owner. You can wait in the carriage while I negotiate with him,' he suggested.

Binodini said, 'I am too tired. I suggest you take the carriage, while I wait here. I see no grounds for any risk to me.'

Mahendra went off. Binodini picked up a conversation with the caretaker. She asked him about his family, how many they were, what did his sons do, if his daughters were married, and so on. On being told that he had lost his wife, she sympathised with him. 'So, you live all by yourself here at this advanced age of your life, with no one to look after you. Must be a difficult life for you.'

While talking she casually asked, 'Did not a Bihari-*babu* from Calcutta put up here?'

'Yes, he did, indeed, for some days,' the caretaker confirmed. 'Do you know him?'

'He is a relation of ours,' Binodini told him. From the caretaker's description, Binodini was convinced that it was their friend Bihari, indeed, who had stayed there. She persuaded the caretaker to show her the rooms occupied by Bihari. She now knew which room Bihari used as his bedroom, which room as the sitting room. Although the rooms were kept shut after Bihari left, Binodini fancied that the air in the rooms was still charged with Bihari's association. She inhaled this air deeply. However, she got no further information where Bihari presently was. It was also not clear if he planned to return here.

Mahendra returned, having paid a month's rent and armed with permission to move in.

FIFTY-ONE

From time immemorial, the river Jamuna had been fed by the glacial snows of the Himalayas, and equally timeless have been the hymns sung, down the ages, by poets in praise of the Jamuna. The gamut of romantic passions, sentiments and emotions that this river had inspired over the centuries eternally invests its rippling stream.

Mahendra arrived early in the morning and sat down on the sandy bank of the river, watching the changing panorama of the sky and the river. His intense love coursed through his veins, infiltrated his bones, his eyes, his breath, deepening his ardour. By dusk the dying rays of the sun crafted a celestial music—sad and elegiac. The day ended, the low rain clouds darkened the sky and the night fell. This darkness carried its own mystic. It spoke in a language—strange and unuttered! The almost invisible bank on the other side, the still and dark river, the hush of the lush neem groves, engulfed Mahendra from all sides.

His thoughts drifted to the old love lyrics. The lovelorn heroine waited eternally all alone on the bank of the Jamuna. She was far away, but Mahendra could clearly visualise her. She was ageless, timeless, the eternal milkmaid—companion of Krishna. To Mahendra this was his Binodini. She had travelled an eternity, carrying the pangs of her separation, her heartaches, her riotous youth crying out—celebrated in lyrics and songs. She was there, waiting to be taken.

The clouds parted, revealing a thin sliver of the early moon. In this moonlight, the world around Mahendra appeared to recede; there was no bond with the terra firma; time lost its continuum; the past obliterated; the future extinct. The only reality was Binodini and Mahendra, caught in this transient space of time, illuminated by a silvery moon.

Mahendra was now fiercely intoxicated. It was inconceivable that Binodini would spurn him, and not celebrate this unique moment in their life. He rose and hurried back to the house.

When he reached Binodini's room, he found the air heavy with fragrance of flowers. Binodini had decked herself with strings of flowers round her hair, round her neck, round her waist—an image of a flowering creeper, lying on her bed. Mahendra's desire accentuated. He said in an emotional voice, 'I was waiting for you at the river bank, when the moon sent me the message that you are waiting for me here, so I rushed to you.'

Mahendra advanced to sit on the bed, but was immediately warded off by Binodini. 'No, you cannot sit on this bed.' Mahendra, nonplussed, foundered like a boat going aground midstream. No word escaped from his lips, and Binodini, to make doubly sure, came down herself from the bed.

Speech returned to Mahendra. He asked, 'Why are you decked up like this? For whom? Whom are you expecting to visit you?'

Binodini put her hand on her heart and said, 'The person I am waiting for is deep inside in my heart.'

'Who is it? Is it Bihari?' Mahendra asked.

'You are not fit to take that name,' Binodini replied.

'Did you search out this place looking for him?'

'Yes, for him.'

'And, is it for him that you are waiting tonight?'

'Yes, for him.'

'Do you know his address?' asked Mahendra.

'I do not, but I shall find out,' Binodini said confidently.

'I shall make sure that you never do.'

'Even so, you will not succeed in alienating him from my heart.' Binodini closed her eyes when she said this, perhaps, musing on Bihari.

Mahendra was fascinated by this unusual lovelorn look of Binodini's, waiting vainly for her lover. Provoked by rejection by the same Binodini he almost turned violent. He screamed at her, 'I will excise Bihari's image from your heart with a knife.'

Unmoved, Binodini said, 'Your knife will gain easier entry into my heart than your love.'

'Are you not afraid of me at all? Who else is your protector here?'

'You are my protector. You will save me from yourself,' said Binodini calmly.

'So, even now, I qualify for some trust, some confidence,' Mahendra said humourlessly.

'Absolutely, or else I would have died by my own hands. I would not have come out with you the way I have.'

Mahendra was in tearing rage. 'Why did you not kill yourself? Why did you have to drag me around by the leash of your so called trust in me? Your death would have been beneficial for so many.'

'Yes, I well know that,' observed Binodini, 'but I cannot die as long as my hope for Bihari's return to me lingers in my heart.'

Mahendra was now worked up virulently. He said, 'It is my misfortune that as long as you keep alive, so will my yearning for you. I will now start praying with all my heart for your death. In that case, neither Bihari nor I can have you. Yes, go away, leave me. Let me have my freedom back. My mother, my wife they are all troubled on my account. They are pining for me. Their grief is scorching me, and until you die and bring to end my desires, I will never be free to wipe their tears.' He then ran out.

The dream world that Binodini had earlier been shaping in her mind now lay shattered. She did not stir, just kept looking out through the window. The bright moonlit night, the dark water of the river, the well-tended garden, the sandy bank on the other side—they all appeared to her unreal, arid, pointless. Just like a blank sheet of paper.

Her mind was in turmoil as she recalled the turbulent nature of Mahendra's attraction for her, uprooting her like a stormtossed tree. If she was so irresistible, then how was it that she could not captivate Bihari? Why did he not come ashore like the rolling sea surf on a full moon night and break before her? Why did a love that she scorned came repeatedly knocking at her door, but the love she sought so longingly did not come calling at all to fill her empty heart? There was a raging turbulence in her heart, and she did not know how to tame this turbulence.

She took off and destroyed wantonly the strings of flowers with which she had decked herself and which had so fascinated Mahendra. To her, life had ceased to have any charm, nothing now counted, and the world around her was meaningless. For her all was lost.

But life does not cease to flow. It goes on as usual. The sun will rise tomorrow, and even the smallest of chores will not be overlooked. And Bihari, unshaken, would still keep away from her, busy perhaps training his young protégé. Binodini's eyes swelled with tears; she was trying in vain to dislodge a rock; her heart bled, but the rock moved not an inch.

FIFTY-TWO

Mahendra woke up late the following morning after a fretful and sleepless night. A sense of unconscious grief flitted through his insomnia, but the nature of his pain was very evident to him as he woke up. By then, he had a clear recollection of what happened on the previous night, and this induced in him a sense of desolation.

His guilty conscience now tormented him, tarnished by desertion of a happy home in chasing another woman and a sense of growing remorse for sinking into moral turpitude. Why did he at all opt for this demented, unsettled life? In this mood of despondency he believed that he was now cured of his illicit love for Binodini. It dawned on him that thoughtlessly and pointlessly and at the cost of his self esteem, he had sacrificed his life for the love of a woman who had no time for him. His abating infatuation by now had drained him out. He wanted to purge his mind off Binodini. He still could not explain to himself why he courted such indignity. He was superior to Binodini in all respects, he brooded, and yet he had run after her seeking her favours like a humble supplicant. What devilry drove him to this madness! Binodini, to him, was now like any other ordinary woman, shorn of all her tragic allure. That luminous star, created by the beauteous world around him and shaped by his poetic fancy, had now evaporated like a mirage. A mere flesh and blood woman was left behind, with nothing unique about her!

Rid of his infatuation, Mahendra was anxious to return home. The love and affection, the peace and tranquillity, he had repudiated were now for him the priceless treasure he had lost. His friendship with Bihari since their young days came alive to him as inestimable. People were unable to appreciate the worth of what was profound and stable which provided them with a safe anchor, so ruminated Mahendra. On the other hand, people foolishly ran after what was ephemeral and deceptive which gave one no real contentment—life's most desirable prize!

Mahendra decided to return to Calcutta the same evening, after making some suitable arrangements for Binodini wherever she wished to settle down. He would then be truly free, and this thought brought him a great deal of satisfaction. He, had freed himself from a bondage that obliged him to do what he knew was wrong, and yet could not refute. A magnificent relief from all that!

Mahendra went to see Binodini. He found the door locked from inside. He knocked and asked, 'Are you asleep?'

'No, I am not, but please leave me alone,' Binodini said.

'I just wanted to speak to you about something. This will not take much time.'

'I am in no mood to listen to you,' Binodini sounded most peevish, 'go away, please. Don't disturb me.'

Such dismissals in their earlier days would have considerably upset Mahendra, but today he regarded her only with contempt. How could he have ever sunk so low to be dominated by a mere woman that she had the audacity to ignore him just as she pleased? It was entirely his fault, of course. It was his indulgence that made her bold. It did not matter now, as he had cut himself free from her tie, and he had no feeling of loss.

After his meal Mahendra went to town to get some money from the bank. He had planned to get some gifts for his mother and wife, so he went shopping.

There was another knock on Binodini's door. Rattled, she did not respond, but after repeated knocks, she opened the door and shouted, 'Why do you keep annoying me?' and then she reeled back. It was not Mahendra, but Bihari who stood before her.

Bihari peeped into the room to see if Mahendra was there, but all he saw was a room strewn with discarded flowers, which instantly made him suspect the worst. Not that he had no misgivings of the sort of life Binodini had, yet beyond this thought was the image of a bright and enchanting figure that glowed in his heart. As he entered the house, he was nervous in case he found his imagined beauty mutilated, and sadly, this was precisely the shock that he received when he looked inside the room with visible evidence of a debauched living.

Away from Binodini, Bihari had often thought that he would be, by his love, able to wash away the calumnies that touched Binodini. But, from what he saw, he realized that this task would be too formidable. Why else did he not feel any compassion for her? Instead, an intense loathing for her seized him. Binodini, Bihari noted, looked very depressed.

Bihari shouted for Mahendra by his name, but received no response. Though slighted, Binodini said softly, 'Mahendra is out.' Bihari was about to leave, when Binodini implored him, 'Bihari-*thakurpo*, I entreat you, please do not go away.'

Bihari was determined not to listen to her and to remove himself as soon as he could from this disreputable place. Binodini's pitiful cry arrested his steps.

Binodini told him, 'If you turn your face against me and leave me, I swear I will kill myself.'

Bihari turned back and said, 'Binodini, why are you getting my life entangled with yours? What harm have I done you? I have never interfered with your life, never.'

Binodini said, 'I told you once how much you mean to me, which you did not believe. You never gave me any scope to tell you again. You pushed me away, even so I must tell you that I love you.'

Bihari interrupted her, 'You must never say this. I will never believe you.'

Binodini said, 'What other people may not believe, you will. That is my level of faith in you, and that is why I requested you to come and listen to me.'

'How does it matter whether I believe you or not? This will make no difference to your present way of life,' said Bihari.

Binodini said, 'I know this will not affect you, none at all. My present misfortune also disqualifies me to be in your company, and I will always have to keep faraway from you. The only claim that I beg of you—it is a minor claim—that you should regard me with a degree of tenderness. There was a time when I was able to win your respect, which I shall cherish all my life. Before you go, please condescend to listen to me. That is my humble prayer to you.'

Moved by Binodini's pitiful appeal, Bihari agreed to talk and looked for a place other than Binodini's room to sit. Binodini read his mind. 'Please, come into my room,' she invited him. 'I know what is in your mind. I assure you that this room has not been contaminated by anything sordid. The flowers that you see were my offerings to you, dedicated at your altar, alas! now withered. Do come in and sit down.'

Binodini's words stirred him and he went in. He sat on the bed, and Binodini sat on the floor at his feet. Bihari rose in protest, but Binodini stopped him, 'Do not get up please. I feel honoured that you have allowed me to sit at your feet, and I do not wish to lose that privilege.'

Binodini asked, after a pause, 'Before I forget, have you had anything to eat, yet?'

'Yes, I had some food at the railway station,' Bihari told her.

When they sat down, Binodini asked Bihari, 'Why did you return my letter that I wrote from my village, read but with no reply, through Mahendra?'

Bihari was taken aback. 'But I never saw this letter.'

'Did you see Mahendra recently?' asked Binodini.

'Only the day after I saw you to your village. Not since, as I myself left town,' Bihari informed her.

'Earlier, once again, you had returned my letter, read but with no reply, and through Mahendra.'

Bihari was now perplexed. 'I cannot understand this. I never saw that letter, either.'

His answer left Binodini stunned. 'Hmm, I think I now know the truth. Listen to me please. If you believe what I have to tell you, I shall take it as a sign of my good fortune. If you do not, I shall not blame you, because I have forfeited your trust.'

By then, Bihari's attitude had considerably mellowed. To him now it appeared difficult to affront her by denying her request. He said, '*Bouthan*, you do not have to say anything. I have no malice towards you. I trust you fully.'

Bihari's kindness brought tears to her eyes. She said, 'But I need to unload myself, so please spare me a little time. The day I left for my village armed with your advice, which I had accepted with all my heart and soul. I would have continued to live there regardless of all the contempt and abuses heaped on me by my neighbours, even though I received no reply to my letter to you. I would have stuck to the rigours that you had imposed on me, but I was denied that. Perhaps, the weight of my sins was too ponderous to allow me even that comfort.'

Binodini continued, 'Then, Mahendra suddenly arrived in the village, and my disgrace became public knowledge. It was not—possible to live in the village any longer, and I had to leave with Mahendra. When Mahendra returned with my second letter to you with no reply, it became clear to me that you had abandoned me. Of course, I did not know then that Mahendra had played a game of deception with me. I could have gone astray then, become dissolute, but there is something in you that even though separated from you, you watched over me and protected me. I was sanctified because I had placed you in my heart. I realized how strong you were the day you sent me away from you, and I derived my strength from you to be worthy of you. I swear to you that I have not allowed that worth to be sullied.'

They both remained silent thereafter, in deep thoughts. As the afternoon set in, Mahendra returned. He almost reeled when he saw Bihari. The coolness towards Binodini that was germinating in him suddenly gave way to a feeling of jealousy. His resentment mounted when he saw Binodini sitting peacefully at Bihari's feet, while he himself had been repulsed by her. He was convinced it must have been a pre-arranged meeting fixed through writing to each other. Bihari had himself earlier turned away from Binodini, but if the same Bihari returned and surrendered to Binodini, then there was no way to deter her. Mahendra might well give up his hopes for Binodini, but it was too much for him to lose his grip and allow her to go to someone else.

In his frustrated rage, Mahendra lashed at Binodini, his tongue laced with sarcasm, 'A wonderful scene. Exit Mahendra from the stage, and enter Bihari. A great dramatic denouement—deserving wild applause from the audience. I presume this is the last scene before the curtain comes down.'

Binodini went red in the face. She was unable to give a fitting reply to Mahendra, on whom she was unfortunately still dependent. She was terribly upset, and all she could do was to look at Bihari with appealing eyes.

Bihari rose and answered Mahendra, 'Don't insult her like a coward.

If your sense of decency does not bar you from behaving as a cad, then I have the right to stop you.'

Mahendra laughed and spoke witheringly, 'Aha, so mutual rights have already been established. Most charming. Let me give you a new appellation—Charmer Bihari!'

Bihari perceived that the situation was taking a nasty turn. He was also furious with Mahendra. He decided to act, and told Mahendra, 'Let me tell you that I am proposing to marry Binodini. So, take care and mind your language.'

This declaration devastated Mahendra and bewildered Binodini. A violent tempest now raged in her heart.

It took Bihari sometime to collect himself, which he did. He then addressed Mahendra, 'There is another piece of information for you. Your mother is gravely ill, almost in her last days. There is little hope for her to recover. I came down here specially looking for you to tell you this. I am going back by tonight's train, and I propose to take Binodini with me.'

Binodini cried out in dismay. 'What? *Pishima* seriously ill?'

'Yes, very,' Bihari said sombrely, 'she will not be with us for long.'

Mahendra, who had not spoken at all after he was told about his mother, silently walked out.

Binodini confronted Bihari, 'You said just now something about marrying me. Were you joking?'

'Not at all. I do propose to marry you, and that is the honest truth,' Bihari reiterated.

'Just to rescue a sinner like me?' asked Binodini.

'No, because I love you, respect you.'

'That is reward enough for me, my ultimate desire.' Binodini was overcome with emotion. 'I do not ask for anything more. To do so will be to go against our moral principles.'

'What do you mean?'

'The very thought of our marriage is utterly ridiculous. I am a widow, deemed an accursed creature in our society. You will lose your face in your community if you marry me. I can never allow this. Please, give up this idea.'

'Are you forsaking me?' asked Bihari, very unhappy.

'That I will never do,' Binodini assured him. She continued, 'You do a lot of good work away from the public eye. Let me help you in some such work of yours, which will be my route to serve you. In no way can you marry a widow. Your generosity may make this possible, but if I destroy your image by agreeing to marry you, I shall never be able to hold any head high. This must not be allowed.'

'But Binodini, I do love you.'

'And, on the strength of that love I shall now perpetrate an act of indiscretion.' She sat down at his feet and fervently kissed his toes. She spoke passionately, 'I have no expectation in this life, no more is due to me either. I will pray hard that I may have you for my own in my next life. I have suffered much, I have made you suffer much, and now I have learnt my lesson. It is this lesson that saves me from dragging you down with me. Because you stand tall, I am also able to stand with my head held high. I shall not allow this fortune of mine razed to the ground by our indiscrete action.'

Bihari said not a word, contemplating.

Binodini continued, 'Do not get me wrong, please. You will not be happy if you marry me, on the other hand, you will lose your stature, and with you, I will lose the glory with which you have invested me. You have always remained detached and uninvolved, yet contented. Keep that way. I will keep away from you, but will do whatever you ask me to do.'

FIFTY-THREE

As Mahendra was about to step into his mother's room, Asha stopped him, 'Don't go in there now.'

'Why not?' Mahendra was surprised.

'The doctor has warned us that a sudden shock may precipitate a crisis.'

'I will go quietly and just see her. She won't know.' Mahendra almost pleaded.

Asha still objected. 'The slightest noise convulses her. She will know if you go in.'

'What do want me to do then?' Mahendra asked.

'Let Bihari-*thakurpo* come. We will go by what he says.'

Bihari arrived shortly thereafter. It was Asha who had sent word to him to come as soon as he could.

Bihari asked anxiously, 'You sent for me. Is anything wrong with mother?'

Asha was distinctly relieved to see Bihari. She told him, 'Mother had been increasingly restless since you left town. She keeps repeatedly asking for you. I did tell her that you had to go away on some urgent work but should be back soon. Although she cannot speak very coherently now, she is impatient for you to return. After I received your cable, I was able to tell her that you would be back today. Since then she has been looking forward to see you. She reminded me to make special arrangements for your food and not to forget your preferred dishes. She had gone to the extent of instructing that cooking was to be done in the verandah adjacent to her room so that she can oversee the arrangements. She would not listen to the doctor's injunction. She wants me to cook, and then plans to feed you in her presence.'

Bihari was visibly moved. 'How is she now?' he asked.

'Not too good. Go and have a look.'

Bihari went in. Mahendra, who had been watching Asha and Bihari talking, was astounded. Asha had evidently taken charge of the home, without fuss. She had no compunction in stopping Mahendra going into his mother's room, no hesitation, but displayed no ill feelings towards him. Mahendra was no longer the man of the house, his authority most decidedly curbed.

Even more surprising to Mahendra was the ease with which Asha spoke to Bihari. Bihari had emerged now the accepted guardian of the family, and was the friend and protector of everyone. Nothing got done without asking him. He was free to move anywhere, and it was largely his writ that ran in the house. Upon his return, Mahendra discovered that he had been dislodged as head of the family.

Rajlakshmi looked Bihari with her despairing eyes, and asked in a broken voice; 'Back Bihari? Your work done now?'

'Yes, mother, I am back,' Bihari softly replied, 'and all my work successfully accomplished. I have no worries now.' As he said this, he glanced towards the door.

Rajlakshmi perked up. She told Bihari, 'Asha will cook for you today, and I will guide her from the bed. The doctor tells me not to, but what does it matter at this stage of my life? Am I not to be allowed to feed you before the end comes?'

Bihari feigned keenness. 'Of course, you need to guide her, or how else would she manage? I see no reason for the doctor to discourage you. Since our young days, Mahendra and I grew up on your cooking. Mahendra is now sick and tired of the unfamiliar food that he had during his travels. He will doubtless, find your fish preparations heavenly. We two brothers, as of old, will sit and eat together, scrapping with each other for the best morsel as we used to do. I do trust your daughter-in-law would cook enough for the needs of the two of us.'

Rajlakshmi had some faint hopes that Bihari might have located Mahendra and fetched him back. She almost stopped breathing when Bihari mentioned him. When she recovered, Bihari told her, 'Mahendra's travels have done him a world of good. The journey had fatigued him a little, and a bath and a good feed will restore him.'

Rajlakshmi still dared not to ask for Mahendra. Bihari decided it was time to break the good news. He said 'Ma, Mahendra is waiting outside for your summons, otherwise he feels diffident to face you.'

Rajlakshmi looked at the door, and then gently called Mahendra. 'Do come in, Mohin.'

Mahendra entered the room. Afraid that the sudden shock might stop her heart beating, Rajlakshmi dared not look at her son. She lay on her bed with her eyes shut. A look at his mother, shattered Mahendra. He knelt down and seized her feet with his hands. Her heart pounded, her whole body quivered.

A little later Annapurna told Rajlakshmi, 'Didi, unless you tell him to, Mohin will not get up from your feet.'

Rajlakshmi struggled through to say faintly, 'Mohin, get up, son.' Mahendra rose, profusely shedding tears when he heard his mother calling him by his name after so many days. He knelt by his mother's bedside. Rajlakshmi drew him close to kiss his forehead. Mahendra said, vastly penitent, 'I have caused you much pain and agony. How can you ever forgive me, Mother?'

When the pounding of her heart eased, she said to her son, 'How can I not forgive my own son? How can you ever think so? But, where is my daughter-in-law?'

Asha was in another room, preparing Rajlakshmi's food. Annapurna fetched her from there. Rajlakshmi indicated to Mahendra to rise from the floor and to sit on her bed. She asked Asha to sit next to Mahendra. 'Daughter-in-law, come and sit here. I want to see the two of you together. This is no occasion to be shy,' she told Asha. 'Try and shed all your hurt feelings against your husband. Sit next to him, and allay my pains.'

Asha, with her head covered, haltingly and diffidently, with tremors in her heart, sat next to Mahendra. Rajlakshmi took hold of Asha's right hand and placed it in Mahendra's right hand, and then she said to her son, 'I am leaving my little mother in your hand. Take my word, you will not find another more graceful girl than her. Come Annapurna, give them your blessings. Let your goodness bring them good fortune.'

Annapurna went and stood before them, and both Asha and Mahendra bent down at her feet. She said, 'May God look after you.'

Rajlakshmi then called upon Mahendra and Bihari to make up, and Mahendra joyfully embraced Bihari. Rajlakshmi added, 'It is my prayers for you, Mohin that Bihari may remain your most cherished friend as he always was. This will be your most precious gift.'

Rajlakshmi was worn out by then. She turned Bihari away when he attempted to revive her with a medicine. 'No more medicines for me,' she said wearily. 'I am in my God's hand, he will administer my last medicine to free me from the woes of the world. Now, you two go and get some rest, and Asha, better get on with the cooking.'

In the evening the two friends sat facing Rajlakshmi's bed for their dinner. Asha commenced serving as directed by her mother-in-law. Mahendra was too upset to be able to eat at all. Rajlakshmi noticed that and lamented, 'Why are you not eating properly, Mohin? Let me see you eat well.'

Bihari said in fun, 'But you know this well, Ma, Mohin was always a poor eater. There you are, *Bouthan*, may I have another helping of that excellent vegetable preparation.'

It rejoiced Rajlakshmi's heart. She told Asha, 'I knew Bihari was particularly partial to this item. Let him some more, no, no, a little more.'

Bihari said, once again, in fun, 'This daughter-in-law of yours is rather tight-fisted—not very hospitable!'

Rajlakshmi smiled indulgently. 'Did you see that, child? He eats food cooked by you and then gives you a bad name.'

Asha deliberately dropped a largish helping of this favourite dish on Bihari's plate. Bihari said in mock jest, 'What are you doing? Are you determined to fill me with this one item only, and keep all the other goodies for Mahendra?'

Asha passed a comment, in whispers, 'There is no way to shut up a fault finder,' and Bihari shot back, also in whispers, 'Try with the sweets, and see if he can be shut up.'

The meal was over; Rajlakshmi was at peace with herself; her heart filled with contentment. She asked Asha to go and have her food, and told Mahendra to go to bed.

Mahendra was surprised, 'But why so early?' He had planned to be at his mother's side and look after her, but the mother insisted, 'You must be tired, so go to bed.'

When Asha returned after her meal, Rajlakshmi told her quietly, 'Go and see if Mahendra's bed had been properly laid out.' A sense of shyness overtook her, but in obedience to her mother-in-law, she left the room. Only Annapurna and Bihari were left with Rajlakshmi.

Rajlakshmi spoke to Bihari. 'Bihari, anxiety for Binodini keeps haunting me. Do you know at all where she is and how she is?'

'She is presently at Calcutta,' Bihari told her.

Rajlakshmi looked vacantly at him. He knew what was in her mind. He quickly told her, 'Have no worry on her account, Ma.'

'Although she has caused me a great deal of anguish, I still retain some fondness for her,' Rajlakshmi said.

'And so she is, also fond of you, Ma,' Bihari assured her.

Rajlakshmi said, 'That is what I feel in my bones as well. All individuals are a mix of good and bad, but I do know that she was fond of me. The way she looked after me could not be just for show.'

Bihari said, 'She is keen even now to take care of you.'

Rajlakshmi gave out a deep sigh. She said, 'Mahendra has gone to bed. Is it possible to get her here so late in the night?'

Bihari surprised her when he said, 'Binodini is in this very house, hiding somewhere. I have not been able to persuade her to eat or drink at all the whole day. She says until you send for her and forgive her, she will not have even a drop of water to drink.'

Rajlakshmi was most concerned. 'The poor child has been fasting the whole day. What a shame! Go and get her.'

When Binodini approached her, Rajlakshmi said, 'Why did you refuse to eat the whole day? Just go and eat first, and then we will talk.'

Binodini touched her feet and said, 'Until and unless you forgive this sinner, I cannot eat.'

'I have forgiven you. I have no complaint against anyone now. Let no one suffer because of you, and keep well yourself. That is all that I want.'

Binodini said, '*Pishima*, I will not be the source of any harm to anyone, that I will promise you. Your blessings will not go in vain, so I believe.'

Binodini then paid her respects to Annapurna. Rajlakshmi asked after Binodini had her food, 'Will you be going back now?'

Binodini looked appealingly to Rajlakshmi, '*Pishima*, I really would wish to stay back and look after you. I will cause no harm or disgrace to anyone, so help me God.'

Rajlakshmi looked at Bihari, who pondered for a while before he said, 'Let *Bouthan* remain here and look after you. Nothing will go wrong.'

Annapurna, Binodini and Bihari—the three of them by turn attended to Rajlakshmi. Asha rose early. She was uneasy in her mind that she had abandoned her sick mother-in-law the whole night. She quickly dressed and went down to Rajlakshmi's room. It was still a little dark. What she saw in the mother-in-law's room shook her. Was it a dream?

Binodini was busy making tea for Bihari. She stood up when she saw Asha. She said, 'In spite of all my sins I have come to be under your shelter. No one here will ask me to leave unless you do. If you do tell me to go, I shall immediately leave.'

Asha was utterly bewildered. She did not know what to say. She did not even know her mind.

Binodini continued, 'I know, you will never be able to forgive me. Do not even try to do so, but at the same time do not be afraid of me, not at all. In the few days that are left to *Pishima* I would like to look after her, and then I shall promptly melt away.'

When the previous night, Rajlakshmi put the hands of her son and daughter-in-law together, Asha decided to overlook her past injuries and go back to Mahendra. But Binodini's presence in the house this morning rekindled her misgivings. Mahendra was once in love with Binodini, and he might still be so for all she knew. He would be up soon, and how would he react when he spotted Binodini there? Last night she thought her life would once again flow smoothly, but the first thing this morning that greeted her was the very thorn that had ruined her life.

Asha entered her mother-in-law's room with a heavy heart, and was immediately put to shame to see her aunt still in attendance on Rajlakshmi. She told her aunt, '*Mashima*, you have been up all night. Please go and get some rest.' Annapurna, on the other hand, wanted to speak to Asha privately. She took Asha to her room. There, she told Asha, 'There may be some satisfaction in being able to curse the perpetrators of misdeeds, but nursing unhappy memories of one's sufferings can be worse.'

Asha moaned, 'I would like to forget, but I find it so difficult.'

Annapurna said, 'Yes, Asha, I do appreciate how you feel. It is easy to give advice, but not so easy to give the right guidance. Nevertheless, let me try to help you. You must try hard to expunge from your heart all that happened in the past. Even if you cannot do so, you should not let others see that. If you can successfully manage to do this, then in time you will find those thoughts will no longer trouble you. Remember, if you do not forget, then others would not, either. If you are still unwilling, then it is my advice to you—no, it is my instruction to you that you should conduct yourself with Binodini as if she had done you no harm, and that there is no fear of any further injury from her.'

Asha was miserable. 'Then, what must I do?' she asked.

Annapurna advised her. 'Act normal. Binodini, at this moment, is making tea for Bihari. Carry milk and sugar to her and tell her that you are there to help her.'

Asha got up to do what her aunt told her to, but Annapurna had something more to tell her. 'What I told you is not all that difficult to do, but there is something else that you must also do, and that will be more critical. It will be unavoidable for Mahendra and Binodini to come across each other occasionally. I know this will cause you pain, but you must not show any signs of your resentment. You must remain cool, even if it breaks your heart. Mahendra will be happy that you no longer harbour any doubts concerning them, that you have no fear on that score. They should know that you have no rancour against either of them. To you, your life should be back where it was before this break-up. Chuni, this is not just an advice or a request. Treat it as your Mashima's command to you. When I go back to Kashi, remember each word that I told you and not forget them even for a day.'

Asha reached Binodini, carrying milk and sugar, as directed by her aunt. She asked Binodini, 'Is the tea water boiled? I have here with me some milk and sugar for the tea.'

Binodini looked at Asha, nonplussed, and then told her, 'Bihari-*thakurpo* is in the verandah. Will you please take his tea to him? I will go and see to *Pishima's* needs. She will probably be up soon.'

Binodini deliberately avoided taking the tea herself to Bihari. She did not wish indiscreetly to use the privileges that Bihari, by admission of his love for her, granted her. She appreciated that privileges needed to be used with restraint. Dignity has to be maintained, otherwise the acquired rights degenerate from misuse. She had decided not to go to Bihari on her own unless he wished to meet her.

Mahendra came down, and Asha, extremely nervous, managed to control herself sufficiently to speak to him, 'Up so early? I closed the windows to stop light disturbing your sleep.'

A big load was off Mahendra's mind when he found Asha talking so effortlessly in presence of Binodini. Pleased, he said, 'I came down to see how mother has been. Is she still asleep?'

Asha said, 'Yes, she is, but do not go in now. After a long spell, she slept well last night. Let her sleep. Bihari-*thakurpo* says she is much better this morning.'

Thus comforted, Mahendra asked where Annapurna was. Asha pointed to Annapurna's room. Her unusual firmness and restraint of manner amazed even Binodini.

Mahendra went and knocked at his aunt's door. She was about to sit down for her devotions, but asked him to come in. Mahendra greeted her by touching her feet, and spoke remorsefully, 'As a reprobate, I feel most ashamed even to face you.'

Annapurna stopped him, 'Never say that. Remember, a son, even with all the dust and dirt of the road, has always a place in the arms of the mother.'

'But my sins are too grievous to wash away,' Mahendra moaned.

'Yes, they will, give it time,' Annapurna said. 'What happened, in a sense, was good for you. You were much too vain about your virtues, and you were too full of yourself. The storm through which you just passed has demolished that vanity of yours without doing any serious damage to you.'

Mahendra, feeling a little better now, said, 'Kakima, I will not allow you to go away again. All our misfortune is due to your absence.'

Annapurna smiled indulgently. 'You will not need me now. The ordeal that I could have prevented is already over, and you need have no fear for the future.'

Another knock at her door. 'Are you at your puja now?'

'No, not yet, come in,' Annapurna said.

It was Bihari, who was surprised to see Mahendra up so early. He ragged him. 'This must be the first sunrise ever that you saw in your life.'

Mahendra responded sombrely, 'Yes, my first sunrise, in many ways. Perhaps, Bihari wishes to speak to *Kakima*. Let me leave you then.'

Bihari smiled. 'No, don't go. We will make you a member of our inner cabinet. I have never kept anything secret from you, and neither do I wish to do now—if you have no objection.'

'Object? Who, me?' Mahendra said, 'I have lost the right to make any claim on you. In spite of that, if you still chose not to keep any secret from me, I will regard that as the reinstatement of your esteem for me.'

It was not all that easy to talk in the presence of Mahendra, but Bihari decided to do so regardless. He said, 'There has been some talk of I marrying Binodini, and it is about that that I came to talk to *Kakima*.'

Mahendra was embarrassed and Annapurna stunned. 'Are you sure what you are saying, Bihari?' she asked.

Mahendra observed with some force, 'Surely, there is no need for this marriage, Bihari?'

'Is Binodini herself involved in this proposal?' This was from Annapurna.

'Not in the least,' said Bihari.

'But will Binodini agree to this marriage?' asked Annapurna, quire upset.

Mahendra quickly butted in. 'But why not, Kakima? Binodini worships Bihari, so why should she allow such a safe haven to slip out of her hand?'

Bihari turned to Mahendra. 'It is I who proposed marriage to Binodini, and not she. And, for your information, she has turned down my proposal.'

This left Mahendra speechless.

FIFTY-FOUR

For a few days Rajlakshmi remained see-sawing between life and death. One morning she felt all her pains had gone; she looked calm and at peace. She sent for her son and told him, 'My time in this world is now up. I am going happily, with no worries. When you were a little boy, you were the apple of my eyes, my bundle of joy. A resurgence of that same sense of joy pervades my heart now. I go with a feeling of relief that with me I am taking away all your woes. There is nothing more that I want now.' Mahendra, now too overcome, broke down inconsolably.

Rajlakshmi comforted him, 'Don't grieve for me, son. I leave behind a lakshmi daughter-in-law. Give her my keys. All is well set up here; you will want for nothing. And yes, there is something else that I wish to tell you. In my safe you will find two thousand rupees in notes. Give that to Binodini from me. This ought to be sufficient for her needs as a widow. Do not tell anyone about it until my death. See to it also that Binodini does not continue to live here after I go.'

Later she spoke to Bihari. 'I understand from Mahendra that you have founded a home for the medical treatment of impoverished clerical workers. A noble thought, and I pray that God may preserve you to carry on with your mission. At my marriage, my father-in-law had gifted me a village. I wish to donate this village to your cause. Use its revenues for your good work, which will propitiate the soul of my departed father-in-law.'

FIFTY-FIVE

Rajlakshmi passed away, and after the usual religious rites and observations were over, Mahendra accosted Bihari. He proposed to his friend, 'I wish to join you in your social work. Will you please take me? I have some medical knowledge, which may come in handy, and Asha has now matured into a responsible housewife. She would also be able to help.'

Bihari cautioned him. 'Ponder carefully, Mohin. Will this work really suit you? Do not take a hasty decision in your current mood of renunciation, and accept a long-term responsibility, which you may rue later.'

'I have pondered, carefully,' Mahendra replied. 'In my present transformed life, I can no way go through an existence of idle pleasures. I need to engage myself in meaningful toils, or else I may degenerate into a creature of lassitude and ennui. You have to save me from this pitfall, I beg of you.'

Bihari agreed, and it was all settled.

Time had come for departures and farewells. Annapurna and Bihari were talking, when Binodini approached them, 'Can I sit with you for a while, please?'

Annapurna welcomed her, 'Certainly, child, do come in.'

After a few minutes, Annapurna left Bihari and Binodini together. Binodini asked Bihari, 'Have you any advice or instructions for me?'

'Tell me, what is it that you wish to do?'

Binodini said, 'I understand that you have started a home for the medical treatment of the poor. Can I not be of some help to you there? I can do the cooking if needs be.'

Bihari looked at Binodini with keen intensity. He was disturbed, which was evident. He spoke gently to Binodini, 'I have given this question a great deal of thought. Over the past several months, events have overtaken us taking us through nerve-wracking times and got ourselves entangled into a mesh, tying ourselves down with inextricable knots. It is time now to ponder and try to untangle ourselves from this mesh and undo the knots. I dare not encourage what my heart really wants. Until all the turbulence, all the whirlpools, through which we have passed, subside, there will be no peace for any of us. Had the past favoured me, I would have a fulfilling life with you beside me. This I have now been denied, for the rest of my life. There is little point for me to pursue happiness; all I need to do is to trend this fissured life.'

Annapurna returned. Binodini pleaded with her, 'Can I seek shelter at your feet? Please, do not deny me; do not push me away as a sinner.'

Annapurna understood Binodini's situation, and was fully sympathetic. 'Yes, come with me to Kashi,' she agreed.

Before they parted, Bihari met Binodini alone. He said, 'I wish to have some keepsake of yours.'

'But what have I got that I can give as a keepsake?'

Bihari replied, a little sheepishly, 'You know, the Europeans have a custom of keeping tresses of the loved ones as a memento. If you...'

Binodini intervened sharply, 'What nonsense! What will you do with a bunch of my lifeless tresses? I cannot subscribe to this awful custom. But I can give you something that can be of use to you, in your work. Will you accept it?'

'Yes, I will,' Bihari agreed.

Binodini untied a knot at the end of her sari and took out two thousand rupees in notes, and handed them to Bihari. 'Use it for your good work.'

Bihari was, by now, considerably moved with emotion. 'Can I not give you something in return?' he asked. 'You already have,' Binodini informed him. 'It is now part of me; no one can take it away. There is nothing more that I need from you.' Binodini then showed him the scar below her elbow.

Bihari stared at it, puzzled. Binodini said, 'Perhaps you cannot recall the incident. It is your gift to me, and the most fitting. You cannot take it away from me.'

Despite her aunt's words to her, Asha was still not quite comfortable with Binodini. Her mind continued to be haunted by memories and misgivings. Both of them had nursed Rajlakshmi together, and Asha suffered from tension each occasion she had to face Binodini. She found it difficult to speak with her, share a laugh with her. She shrunk from accepting any help or service from Binodini. Nonetheless, her heart melted for Binodini the day she was going away to Kashi with *Mashima*, who was leaving them for the second time.

Asha knew well that Binodini had been in love with Mahendra. But how can one blame her? She knew from her own life how irresistible her husband was. She was now full of pity for Binodini. Binodini was leaving, never to return and see Mahendra ever. Asha appreciated how unbearable such pain could be. There was a time when she was very attached to Binodini, and this remembrance brought tears to her eyes. She went to Binodini and spoke softly, '*Didi*, so you are going away, forever from us.'

Binodini hugged her and said, 'Yes, my sister, it is time for me to go. Once you had some fondness for me, just retain a little of that fondness for me. That is all I ask, and forget everything else.'

Mahendra came to wish her. He said mournfully, 'Do forgive me.' There were traces of tears at the corners of his eyes.

Binodini said, 'You too must forgive all my wrongs. May God be with both of you.'

GLOSSARY

Babu	A gentleman. Also used as a prefix or suffix corresponding to English, Mr.
Bouthan	Wife of an elder brother or cousin. Respectfully applied to non-related ladies.
Chaitra	Twelfth month of the Bengali calendar.
Didi	Elder sister or an elder female cousin. Term also politely used to address older women.
Ekadasi	Eleventh day of the full moon or new moon. Traditionally observed as fast days by Hindu widows.
Kakima	An aunt, wife of father's younger brother.
Koi	A variety of small fish.
Kurta	A collarless shirt.
Lakshman	Devoted younger brother of Rama of *Ramayana*.
Mashima	Sister or female cousin of mother. Term used to address non-related older women.
Paan	Betel leaf, used as mouth freshener.
Punkha	A fan.
Pishima	An aunt, father's sister or female cousin.
Sefali	An orange autumn flower.
Shehnai	Indian wind instrument, traditionally played at weddings.
Thakur-po	Younger brother or male cousin of the husband.
Topse	A species of small fish.

SHORT STORIES

THE CABULIWALLAH

My five years' old daughter Mini cannot live without chattering. I really believe that in all her life she has not wasted a minute in silence. Her mother is often vexed at this, and would stop her prattle, but I would not. To see Mini quiet is unnatural, and I cannot bear it long. And so my own talk with her is always lively.

One morning, for instance, when I was in the midst of the seventeenth chapter of my new novel, my little Mini stole into the room, and putting her hand into mine, said, 'Father! Ramdayal the door-keeper calls a crow a krow! He doesn't know anything, does he?'

Before I could explain to her the differences of language in this world, she was embarked on the full tide of another subject. 'What do you think, Father? Bhola says there is an elephant in the clouds, blowing water out of his trunk, and that is why it rains!'

And then, darting off anew, while I sat still making ready some reply to this last saying, 'Father! What relation is Mother to you?'

'My dear little sister-in-law!' I murmured involuntarily to myself, but with a grave vase contrived to answer, 'Go and play with Bhola, Mini! I am busy!'

The window of my room overlooks the road. The child had seated herself at my feet near my table, and was playing softly, drumming on her knees. I was hard at work on my seventeenth chapter, where Protap Singh, the hero, had just caught Kanchanlata, the heroine, in his arms, and was about to escape with her by the third storey window of the castle, when all of a sudden Mini left her play, and ran to the window, crying, 'A Cabuliwallah! A Cabuliwallah!' Sure enough in the street below was a Cabuliwallah, passing slowly along. He wore the loose soiled clothing of his people, with a tall turban; there was a bag on his back, and he carried boxes of grapes in his hand.

I cannot tell what were my daughter's feelings at the sight of this man, but she began to call him loudly. 'Ah!' I thought, 'he will come in, and my seventeenth chapter will never be finished!' At which exact moment the Cabuliwallah turned, and looked up at the child. When she saw this, overcome by terror, she fled to her mother's protection, and disappeared. She had a blind belief that inside the bag, which the big man carried, there were perhaps two or three other children like herself. The pedlar meanwhile entered my doorway, and greeted me with a smiling face.

So precarious was the position of my hero and my heroine that my first impulse was to stop and buy something, since the man had been called. I made some small purchases, and a conversation began about Abdurrahman, the Russians, the English, and the Frontier Policy.

As he was about to leave, he asked, 'And where is the little girl, sir?'

And I, thinking that Mini must get rid of her false fear, had her brought out.

She stood by my chair, and looked at the Cabuliwallah and his bag. He offered her nuts and raisins, but she would not be tempted, and only clung the closer to me, with all her doubts increased.

This was their first meeting.

One morning, however, not many days later, as I was leaving the house, I was startled to find Mini, seated on a bench near the door, laughing and talking, with the great Cabuliwallah at her feet. In all her life, it appeared, my small daughter had never found so patient a listener, save her father. And already the corner of her little *sari* was stuffed with almonds and raisins, the gift of her visitor. 'Why did you give her those?' I said, and taking out an eight anna bit, I handed it to him. The man accepted the money without demur, and slipped it into his pocket.

Alas, on my return an hour later, I found the unfortunate coin had made twice its own worth of trouble! For the Cabuliwallah had given it to Mini, and her mother catching sight of the bright round object, had pounced on the child with, 'Where did you get that eight anna bit?'

'The Cabuliwallah gave it me,' said Mini cheerfully.

'The Cabuliwallah gave it you!' cried her mother much shocked. 'O Mini! How could you take it from him?' I, entering at the moment, saved her from impending disaster, and proceeded to make my own inquiries.

It was not the first or second time, I found, that the two had met.

The Cabuliwallah had overcome the child's first terror by a judicious bribery of nuts and almonds, and the two were now great friends.

They had many quaint jokes, which afforded them much amusement. Seated in front of him, looking down on his gigantic frame in all her tiny dignity, Mini would ripple her face with laughter, and begin, 'O Cabuliwallah! Cabuliwallah! What have you got in your bag?'

And he would reply, in the nasal accents of the mountaineer, 'An elephant!' Not much cause for merriment, perhaps; but how they both enjoyed the witticism! And for me, this child's talk with a grown-up man had always in it something strangely fascinating.

Then the Cabuliwallah, not to be behindhand, would take his turn, 'Well, little one, and when are you going to the father-in-law's house?'

Now most small Bengali maidens have heard long ago about the father-in-law's house; but we, being a little new-fangled, had kept these things from our child, and Mini at this question must have been a trifle bewildered. But she would not show it, and with ready tact replied, 'Are you going there?'

Amongst men of the Cabuliwallah's class, however, it is well known that the words *father-in-law's house* have a double meaning. It is a euphemism for *jail*, the place where we are well cared for, at no expense to ourselves. In this sense would the sturdy pedlar take my daughter's question. 'Ah,' he would say, shaking his fist at an invisible policeman, 'I will thrash my father-in-law!' Hearing this, and picturing the poor discomfited relative, Mini would go off into peals of laughter, in which her formidable friend would join.

These were autumn mornings, the very time of year when kings of old went forth to conquest; and I, never stirring from my little corner in Calcutta, would let my mind wander over the whole world. At the very name of another country, my heart would go out to it, and at the sight of a foreigner in the streets, I would fall to weaving a network of dreams—the mountains, the glens, and the forests of his distant home, with his cottage in its setting, and the free and independent life of faraway wilds. Perhaps the scenes of travel conjure themselves up before me, and pass and repass in my imagination all the more vividly, because I lead such a vegetable existence that a call to travel would fall upon me like a thunderbolt. In the presence of this Cabuliwallah,

I was immediately transported to the foot of arid mountain peaks, with narrow little defiles twisting in and out amongst their towering heights. I could see the string of camels bearing the merchandise, and the company of turbaned merchants carrying some of their queer old firearms, and some of their spears, journeying downward towards the plains. I could see—but at some such point Mini's mother would intervene, imploring me to 'beware of that man.'

Mini's mother is unfortunately a very timid lady. Whenever she hears a noise in the street, or sees people coming towards the house, she always jumps to the conclusion that they are either thieves, or drunkards, or snakes, or tigers, or malaria, or cockroaches, or caterpillars, or an English sailor. Even after all these years of experience, she is not able to overcome her terror. So she was full of doubts about the Cabuliwallah, and used to beg me to keep a watchful eye on him.

I tried to laugh her fear gently away, but then she would turn round on me seriously, and ask me solemn questions.

Were children never kidnapped?

Was it, then, not true that there was slavery in Cabul?

Was it so very absurd that this big man should be able to carry off a tiny child?

I urged that, though not impossible, it was highly improbable. But this was not enough, and her dread persisted. As it was indefinite, however, it did not seem right to forbid the man the house, and the intimacy went on unchecked.

Once a year in the middle of January, Rahmun, the Cabuliwallah, was in the habit of returning to his country, and as the time approached he would be very busy, going from house to house collecting his debts. This year, however, he could always find time to come and see Mini. It would have seemed to an outsider that there was some conspiracy between the two, for when he could not come in the morning, he would appear in the evening.

Even to me it was a little startling now and then, in the corner of a dark room, suddenly to surprise this tall, loose-garmented, much bebagged man; but when Mini would run in smiling, with her, 'O Cabuliwallah! Cabuliwallah!' and the two friends, so far apart in age, would subside into their old laughter and their old jokes, I felt reassured.

One morning, a few days before he had made up his mind to go, I was correcting my proof sheets in my study. It was chilly weather. Through the window the rays of the sun touched my feet, and the slight warmth was very welcome. It was almost eight o'clock, and the early pedestrians were returning home with their heads covered. All at once I heard an uproar in the street, and, looking out, saw Rahmun being led away bound between two policemen, and behind them a crowd of curious boys. There were bloodstains on the clothes of the Cabuliwallah, and one of the policemen carried a knife. Hurrying out, I stopped them, and inquired what it all meant. Partly from one, partly from another, I gathered that a certain neighbour had owed the pedlar something for a Rampuri shawl, but had falsely denied having bought it, and that in the course of the quarrel Rahmun had struck him.

Now in the heat of his excitement, the prisoner began calling his enemy all sorts of names, when suddenly in a verandah of my house appeared my little Mini, with her usual exclamation, 'O Cabuliwallah! Cabuliwallah!' Rahmun's face lighted up as he turned to her. He had no bag under his arm today, so she could not discuss the elephant with him. She at once therefore proceeded to the next question, 'Are you going to the father-in-law's house?' Rahmun laughed and said, 'Just where I am going, little one!' Then seeing that the reply did not amuse the child, he held up his fettered hands. 'Ah,' he said, 'I would have thrashed that old father-in-law, but my hands are bound!'

On a charge of murderous assault, Rahmun was sentenced to some years' imprisonment.

Time passed away, and he was not remembered. The accustomed work in the accustomed place was ours, and the thought of the once free mountaineer spending his years in prison seldom or never occurred to us. Even my light-hearted Mini, I am ashamed to say, forgot her old friend. New companions filled her life. As she grew older, she spent more of her time with girls. So much time indeed did she spend with them that she came no more, as she used to do, to her father's room. I was scarcely on speaking terms with her.

Years had passed away. It was once more autumn and we had made arrangement for our Mini's marriage. It was to take place during the Puja Holidays. With Durga returning to Kailas, the light of our home also was to depart to her husband's house, and leave her father's in the shadow.

The morning was bright. After the rains, there was a sense of ablution in the air, and the sun rays looked like pure gold. So bright were they that they gave a beautiful radiance even to the sordid brick walls of our Calcutta lanes. Since early dawn today the wedding-pipes had been sounding, and at each beat my own heart throbbed. The wail of the tune, Bhairavi, seemed to intensify my pain at the approaching separation. My Mini was to be married tonight.

From early morning, noise and bustle had pervaded the house. In the courtyard, the canopy had to be slung on its bamboo poles; the chandeliers with their tinkling sound must be hung in each room and verandah. There was no end of hurry and excitement. I was sitting in my study, looking through the accounts, when someone entered, saluting respectfully, and stood before me. It was Rahmun the Cabuliwallah. At first I did not recognize him. He had no bag, nor the long hair, nor the same vigour that he used to have. But he smiled, and I knew him again.

'When did you come, Rahmun?' I asked him.

'Last evening,' he said, 'I was released from jail.'

The words struck harsh upon my ears. I had never before talked with one who had wounded this fellow, and my heart shrank within itself when I realized this, for I felt that the day would have been better-omened had he not turned up.

'There are ceremonies going on,' I said, 'and I am busy. Could you perhaps come another day?'

At once he turned to go; but as he reached the door he hesitated, and said, 'May I not see the little one, sir, for a moment?' It was his belief that Mini was still the same. He had pictured her running to him as she used, calling, 'O Cabuliwallah! Cabuliwallah!' He had imagined too that they would laugh and talk together, just as of old. In fact, in memory of former days he had brought, carefully wrapped up in paper, a few almonds and raisins and grapes, obtained somehow from a countryman, for his own little fund was dispersed.

I said again, 'There is a ceremony in the house, and you will not be able to see any one today.'

The man's face fell. He looked wistfully at me for a moment, said, 'Good morning,' and went out. I felt a little sorry, and would have called him back, but I found he was returning of his own accord. He came close up to me holding out his offerings, and said, 'I brought these few things, sir, for the little one. Will you give them to her?' I took them and was going to pay him, but he caught my hand and said, 'You are very kind, sir! Keep me in your recollection. Do not offer me money! You have a little girl. I too have one like her in my own home. I think of her, and bring fruits to your child, not to make a profit for myself.'

Saying this, he put his hand inside his big loose robe, and brought out a small and dirty piece of paper. With great care he unfolded this, and smoothed it out with both hands on my table. It bore the impression of a little hand. Not a photograph. Not a drawing. The impression of an ink-smeared hand laid flat on the paper. This touch of his own little daughter had been always on his heart, as he had come year after year to Calcutta to sell his wares in the streets.

Tears came to my eyes. I forgot that he was a poor Cabuli fruit-seller, while I was—but no, what was I more than he? He also was a father.

That impression of the hand of his little *Parbati* in her distant mountain home reminded me of my own little Mini.

I sent for Mini immediately from the inner apartment. Many difficulties were raised, but I would not listen. Clad in the red silk of her wedding day, with the sandal paste on her forehead, and adorned as a young bride, Mini came, and stood bashfully before me.

The Cabuliwallah looked a little staggered at the apparition. He could not revive their old friendship. At last he smiled and said, 'Little one, are you going to your father-in-law's house?'

But Mini now understood the meaning of the word 'father-in-law,' and she could not reply to him as of old. She flushed up at the question, and stood before him with her bride-like face turned down.

I remembered the day when the Cabuliwallah and my Mini had first met, and I felt sad. When she had gone, Rahmun heaved a deep sigh, and sat down on the floor. The idea had suddenly come to him that his daughter too must have grown in this long time, and that he would have to make friends with her, anew. Assuredly he would not find her as he used to know her. And besides, what might not have happened to her in these eight years?

The marriage-pipes sounded, and the mild autumn sun streamed round us. But Rahmun sat in the little Calcutta lane, and saw before him the barren mountains of Afghanistan.

I took out a bank note and gave it to him, saying, 'Go back to your own daughter, Rahmun, in your own country, and may the happiness of your meeting bring good fortune to my child!'

Having made this present, I had to curtail some of the festivities. I could not have the electric lights I had intended, nor the military band, and the ladies of the house were despondent at it. But to me the wedding feast was all the brighter for the thought that in a distant land a long-lost father met again with his only child.

THE HUNGRY STONES

My kinsman and myself were returning to Calcutta from our Puja trip when we met the man in a train. From his dress and bearing we took him at first for an up-country Mahomedan, but we were puzzled as we heard him talk. He discoursed upon all subjects so confidently that you might think the Disposer of All Things consulted him at all times in all that He did. Hitherto we had been perfectly happy, as we did not know that secret and unheard-of forces were at work, that the Russians had advanced close to us, that the English had deep and secret policies, that confusion among the native chiefs had come to a head. But our newly acquired friend said with a sly smile, 'There happen more things in heaven and earth, Horatio, than are reported in your newspapers.' As we had never stirred out of our homes before, the demeanour of the man struck us dumb with wonder. Even on the most trivial topic he would quote science or comment on the Vedas or repeat quatrains from some Persian poet, and as we had no knowledge of science or the Vedas or Persian, our admiration for him increased, and my kinsman, a theosophist, was convinced that our fellow-passenger must have been supernaturally inspired by some strange magnetism or occult power or astral body. He listened with devotional rapture to even the tritest saying of our extraordinary companion, and secretly took notes of the conversation. I think that the man saw this and was pleased by it. When the train reached its junction, we stood in the waiting room for our connection. It was 10 p.m. and since we had heard that the train was likely to be quite late, because of something wrong in the lines, I spread my bed on the table and was about to lie down for a comfortable doze, when this extraordinary person began spinning the following yarn. Of course, I got no sleep that night.

'When, owing to a disagreement about some questions of administrative policy, I quit my post at Junagarh and entered the service of the Nizam of Hyderabad, they appointed me at once, as a strong young man, collector of cotton duties at Barich.

'Barich is a lovely place. The *Susta* chatters over stones and babbles on the pebbles, tripping through the woods like a skilful dancing girl. A flight of 150 steps rises from the river, above which, at the foot of the hills, stands a solitary marble palace. Nobody lives nearby; the village and the cotton market are faraway.

'About 250 years ago, Emperor Mahmud Shah II built this lonely palace for his pleasure and luxury. In those days jets of rose water spurted from its fountains, and on the cold marble floors of its spray-cooled rooms young Persian women sat, their hair dishevelled before bathing, and splashing their soft naked feet in the clear water of the reservoirs, would sing the *ghazals* of their vineyards, to the tune of a guitar.

'The fountains play no longer, the songs have ceased, white feet no longer step gracefully on the snowy marble. It is now the lonely home of men oppressed with solitude and deprived of the society of women. Karim Khan, my old office clerk, repeatedly warned me not to take up my abode there. 'Pass the day there if you like,' said he, 'but never stay the night.' I passed it off with a light laugh. The servants said that they would work till dark and then go away. I gave my assent. The house had such a bad name that even thieves would not venture near it after dark.

'At first the solitude of the deserted palace weighed upon me like a nightmare. I would stay out, and work hard as long as possible, then return home at night, jaded and tired, go to bed and fall asleep.

'Before a week had passed, the place began to exert a weird fascination upon me. It is difficult to describe or to induce people to believe; but I felt as if the whole house was like a living organism slowly and imperceptibly digesting me by the action of some stupefying, gastric juice.

'Perhaps the process had begun as soon as I had set my foot in the house, but I distinctly remember the day on which I first was conscious of it.

'It was the beginning of summer, and the market being dull I had no work to do. A little before sunset, I was sitting in an armchair near the water's edge below the steps. The *Susta* had shrunk and sunk low; a broad patch of sand on the other side glowed with the hues of evening; on this side the pebbles at the bottom of the clear shallow waters were glistening. There was not a breath of wind anywhere, and the still air was laden with an oppressive scent from the spicy shrubs growing on the hills close by.

'As the sun sank behind the hilltops, a long dark curtain fell upon the stage of day, and the intervening hills cut short the time in which light and shade mingle at sunset. I thought of going out for a ride, and was about to get up when I heard a footfall on the steps behind. I looked back, but there was no one.

'As I sat down again, thinking it to be an illusion, I heard many footfalls, as if a large number of persons were rushing down the steps. A strange thrill of delight, slightly tinged with fear, passed through my frame, and though there was not a figure before my eyes, I thought I saw a bevy of joyous maidens coming down the steps to bathe in the *Susta* in that summer evening. Not a sound was in the valley, in the river, or in the palace, to break the silence, but I distinctly heard the maidens' gay and mirthful laugh, like the gurgle of a spring gushing forth in a hundred cascades, as they ran past me, in quick playful pursuit of each other, towards the river, without noticing me at all. As they were invisible to me, so I was, as it were, invisible to them. The river was perfectly calm, but I felt that its still, shallow, and clear waters were stirred suddenly by the splash of many an arm jingling with bracelets, that the girls laughed and dashed and spattered water at one another, that the feet of the fair swimmers tossed the tiny waves up in showers of pearl.

'I felt a thrill at my heart—I cannot say whether the excitement was due to fear or delight or curiosity. I had a strong desire to see them more clearly, but naught was visible before me. I thought I could catch all that they said if I only strained my ears; but however hard I strained them, I heard nothing but the chirping of the cicadas in the woods. It seemed as if a dark curtain of 250 years was hanging before me, and I would fain lift a corner of it tremblingly and peer through, though the assembly on the other side was completely enveloped in darkness.

'The oppressive closeness of the evening was broken by a sudden gust of wind, and the still surface of the *Susta* rippled and curled like the hair of a nymph, and from the woods, wrapt in the evening gloom, there came forth a simultaneous murmur, as though they were awakening from a black dream. Call it reality or dream, the momentary glimpse of that invisible mirage reflected from a far-off world, 250 years old, vanished in a flash. The mystic forms that brushed past me with their quick unbodied steps, and loud, voiceless laughter, and threw themselves into the river, did not go back wringing their dripping robes as they went. Like fragrance wafted away by the wind they were dispersed by a single breath of the spring.

'Then I was filled with a lively fear that it was the Muse that had taken advantage of my solitude and possessed me—the witch had evidently come to ruin a poor devil like myself making a living by collecting cotton duties. I decided to have a good dinner—it is the empty stomach that all sorts of incurable diseases find an easy prey. I sent for my cook and gave orders for a rich, sumptuous *moghlai* dinner, redolent of spices and *ghi*.

'Next morning, the whole affair appeared a queer fantasy. With a light heart I put on a sola hat like the *sahebs,* and drove out to my work. I was to have written my quarterly report that day, and expected to return late; but before it was dark I was strangely drawn to my house—by what I could not say—I felt they were all waiting and that I should delay no longer. Leaving my report unfinished I rose, put on *my sola* hat, and startling the dark, shady, desolate path with the rattle of my carriage, I reached the vast silent palace standing on the gloomy skirts of the hills.

'On the first floor, the stairs led to a very spacious hall, its roof stretching wide over ornamental arches resting on three rows of massive pillars, and groaning day and night under the weight of its own intense solitude. The day had just closed, and the lamps had not yet been lighted. As I pushed the door open a great bustle seemed to follow within, as if a throng of people had broken up in confusion, and rushed out through the doors and windows and corridors and verandas and rooms, to make their hurried escape.

'As I saw no one I stood bewildered, my hair on end in a kind of ecstatic delight, and a faint scent of *attar* and unguents almost effaced by age lingered in my nostrils. Standing in the darkness of that vast desolate hall between the rows of those ancient pillars, I could hear the gurgle of fountains splashing on the marble floor, a strange tune on the guitar, the jingle of ornaments and the tinkle of anklets, the clang of bells tolling the hours, the distant note of *nahabat*, the din of the crystal pendants of chandeliers shaken by the breeze, the song of *bulbuls* from the cages in the corridors, the cackle of storks in the gardens, all creating round me a strange unearthly music.

'Then I came under such a spell that this intangible, inaccessible, unearthly vision appeared to be the only reality in the world and all else a mere dream. That I, that is to say, Srijut so-and-so, the eldest son of so-and-so of blessed memory, should be drawing a monthly salary of Rs 450 by the discharge of my duties as collector of cotton duties, and driving in my dog cart to my office every day in a short coat and *sola* hat, appeared to me to be such an astonishingly ludicrous illusion that I burst into a hoarse laugh, as I stood in the gloom of that vast silent hall.

'At that moment my servant entered with a lighted kerosene lamp in his hand. I do not know whether he thought me mad, but it came back to me at once that I was in very deed Srijut so-and-so, son of so-and-so of blessed memory, and that, while our poets, great and small, alone could say whether inside or outside the earth there was a region where unseen fountains perpetually played and fairy guitars, struck by invisible fingers, sent forth an eternal harmony, this at any rate was certain, that I collected duties at the cotton market at Barich, and earned thereby Rs 450 per mensem as my salary. I laughed in great glee at my curious illusion, as I sat over the newspaper at my camp-table, lighted by the kerosene lamp.

'After I had finished my paper and eaten my *moghlai* dinner, I put out the lamps, and lay down on my bed in a small side-room. Through the open window a radiant star, high above the Avalli hills skirted by the darkness of their woods, was gazing intently from millions and millions of miles away in the sky at Mr Collector lying on a humble camp bedstead. I wondered and felt amused at the idea, and do not know when I fell asleep or how long I slept; but I suddenly awoke with a start, though I heard no sound and saw no intruder, only the steady bright star on the hilltop had set, and the dim light of the new moon was stealthily entering the room through the open window, as if ashamed of its intrusion.

'I saw nobody, but felt as if someone was gently pushing me. As I awoke she said not a word, but beckoned me with her five fingers bedecked with rings to follow her cautiously. I got up noiselessly, and, though not a soul save myself was there in the countless apartments of that deserted palace with its slumbering sounds and waking echoes, I feared at every step lest anyone should wake up. Most of the rooms of the palace were always kept closed, and I had never entered them.

'I followed breathless and with silent steps my invisible guide—I cannot now say where. What endless dark and narrow passages, what long corridors, what silent and solemn audience chambers and close secret cells I crossed!

'Though I could not see my fair guide, her form was not invisible to my mind's eye—an Arab girl, her arms, hard and smooth as marble, visible through her loose sleeves, a thin veil falling on her face from the fringe of her cap, and a curved dagger at her waist! Me thought that one of the *Thousand and One Arabian Nights* had been wafted to me from the world of romance, and that at the dead of night I was wending my way through the dark narrow alleys of slumbering Bagdad to a trysting-place fraught with peril.

'At last my fair guide stopped abruptly before a deep blue screen, and seemed to point to something below. There was nothing there, but a sudden dread froze the blood in my heart—me thought, I saw there on the floor at the foot of the screen a terrible negro eunuch dressed in rich brocade, sitting and dozing with outstretched legs, with a naked sword on his lap. My fair guide lightly tripped over his legs and held up a fringe of the screen. I could catch a glimpse of a part of the room spread with a Persian carpet. Someone was sitting inside on a bed—I could not see her, but only caught a glimpse of two exquisite feet in gold-embroidered slippers, hanging out from loose saffron-coloured *paijamas* and placed idly on the orange-coloured velvet carpet. On one side there was a bluish crystal tray on which a few apples, pears, oranges, and bunches of grapes in plenty, two small cups, and a gold-tinted decanter were evidently awaiting the guest. A fragrant intoxicating vapour, issuing from a strange sort of incense that burned within, almost overpowered my senses.

'As with trembling heart I made an attempt to step across the outstretched legs of the eunuch, he woke up suddenly with a start, and the sword fell from his lap with a sharp clang on the marble floor.

'A terrific scream made me jump, and I saw I was sitting on that camp-bedstead of mine sweating heavily; and the crescent moon looked pale in the morning light like a weary sleepless patient at dawn; and our crazy Meher Ali was crying out, as is his daily custom, 'Stand back! Stand back!' while he went along the lonely road.

'Such was the abrupt close of one of my Arabian Nights; but there were yet a thousand nights left. Then followed a great discord between my days and nights. During the day I would go to my work worn and tired, cursing the bewitching night and her empty dreams, but as night came my daily life with its bonds and shackles of work would appear a petty, false, ludicrous vanity.

'After nightfall I was caught and overwhelmed in the snare of a strange intoxication. I would then be transformed into some unknown personage of a bygone age, playing my part in unwritten history; and my short English coat and tight breeches did not suit me in the least. With a red velvet cap on my head, loose *paijamas,* an embroidered vest, a long flowing silk gown, and coloured handkerchiefs scented with *attar,* I would complete my elaborate toilet, sit on a high cushioned chair, and replace my cigarette with a many-coiled *narghileh* filled with rose water, as if in eager expectation of a strange meeting with the beloved one.

'I have no power to describe the marvellous incidents that unfolded themselves as the gloom of the night deepened. I felt as if in the curious apartments of that vast edifice the fragments of a beautiful story, which I could follow for some distance, but of which I could never see the end, flew about in a sudden gust of the vernal breeze. And all the same I would wander from room to room in pursuit of them the whole night long.

'Amid the eddy of these dream-fragments, amid the smell of *henna* and the twanging of the guitar, amid the waves of air charged with fragrant spray, I would catch like a flash of lightning the momentary glimpse of a fair damsel. She it was who had saffron-coloured *paijamas,* white ruddy soft feet in gold-embroidered slippers with curved toes, a close-fitting bodice wrought with gold, a red cap, from which a golden frill fell on her snowy brow and cheeks.

'She had maddened me. In pursuit of her I wandered from room to room, from path to path among the bewildering maze of alleys in the enchanted dreamland of the nether world of sleep.

'Sometimes in the evening, while arraying myself carefully as a prince of the royal blood before a large mirror, with a candle burning on either side, I would see a sudden reflection of the Persian beauty by the side of my own. A swift turn of her neck, a quick eager glance of intense passion and pain glowing in her large dark eyes, just a suspicion of speech on her dainty red lips, her figure, fair and slim, crowned with youth like a blossoming creeper, quickly uplifted in her graceful tilting gait, a dazzling flash of pain and craving and ecstasy, a smile and a glance and a blaze of jewels and silk, and she melted away. A wild gust of wind, laden with all the fragrance of hills and woods, would put out my light, and I would fling aside my dress and lie down on my bed, my eyes closed and my body thrilling with delight, and there around me in the breeze, amid all the perfume of the woods and hills, floated through the silent gloom many a caress and many a kiss and many a tender touch of hands, and gentle murmurs in my ears, and fragrant breaths on my brow; or a sweetly-perfumed kerchief was wafted again and again on my cheeks. Then slowly a mysterious serpent would twist her stupefying coils about me; and heaving a heavy sigh, I would lapse into insensibility, and then into a profound slumber.

'One evening, I decided to go out on my horse—I do not know who implored me to stay—but I would listen to no entreaties that day. My English hat and coat were resting on a rack, and I was about to take them down when a sudden whirlwind, crested with the sands of the *Susta* and the dead leaves of the Avalli hills, caught them up, and whirled them round and round, while a loud peal of merry laughter rose higher and higher, striking all the chords of mirth till it died away in the land of sunset.

'I could not go out for my ride, and the next day I gave up my queer English coat and hat for good. That day again at the dead of night, I heard the stifled heartbreaking sobs of someone—as if below the bed, below the floor, below the stony foundation of that gigantic palace, from the depths of a dark damp grave, a voice piteously cried and implored me, 'Oh, rescue me! Break through these doors of hard illusion, deathlike slumber and fruitless dreams, place me by your side on the saddle, press me to your heart, and riding through hills and woods and across the river, take me to the warm radiance of your sunny rooms above!'

'Who am I? Oh, how can I rescue thee? What drowning beauty, what incarnate passion shall I drag to the shore from this wild eddy of dreams? O, lovely ethereal apparition! Where didst thou flourish and when? By what cool spring, under the shade of what date groves, wast thou born in the lap of what homeless wanderer in the desert? What Bedouin snatched thee from thy mother's arms, an opening bud plucked from a wild creeper, placed thee on a horse swift as lightning, crossed the burning sands, and took thee to the slave-market of what royal city? And there, what officer of the Badshah, seeing the glory of thy bashful blossoming youth, paid for thee in gold, placed thee in a golden palanquin, and offered thee as a present for the seraglio of his master? And O, the history of that place! The music of the *sareng*,[1] the jingle of anklets, the occasional flash of daggers and the glowing wine of Shiraz poison, and the piercing flashing glance! What infinite grandeur, what endless servitude! The slave girls to thy right and left waved the *chamar*,[2] as diamonds flashed from their bracelets; the Badshah, the king of kings, fell on his knees at thy snowy feet in bejewelled shoes, and outside the terrible Abyssinian eunuch, looking like a messenger of death, but clothed like an angel, stood with a naked sword in his hand! Then, O, thou flower of the desert, swept away by the bloodstained dazzling ocean of grandeur, with its foam of jealousy, its rocks and shoals of intrigue, on what shore of cruel death wast thou cast, or in what other land more splendid and more cruel?

'Suddenly at this moment that crazy Meher Ali screamed out, 'Stand back! Stand back! All is false! All is false!' I opened my eyes and saw that it was already light. My *chaprasi* came and handed me

---

[1] A sort of violin
[2] Chamar: chowrie, yak-tail

my letters, and the cook waited with *a salam* for my orders.

'I said, 'No, I can stay here no longer.' That very day I packed up, and moved to my office. Old Karim Khan smiled a little as he saw me. I felt nettled but said nothing and fell to my work.

'As evening approached I grew absent-minded; I felt as if I had an appointment to keep; and the work of examining the cotton accounts seemed wholly useless; even the *Nizamat*[1] of the Nizam did not appear to be of much worth. Whatever belonged to the present, whatever was moving and acting and working for bread seemed trivial, meaningless, and contemptible.

'I threw my pen down, closed my ledgers, got into my dog cart, and drove away. I noticed that it stopped of itself at the gate of the marble palace just at the hour of twilight. With quick steps I climbed the stairs and entered the room.

'A heavy silence was reigning within. The dark rooms were looking sullen as if they had taken offence. My heart was full of contrition, but there was no one to whom I could lay it bare, or of whom I could ask forgiveness. I wandered about the dark rooms with a vacant mind. I wished I had a guitar to which I could sing to the unknown, 'O fire, the poor moth that made a vain effort to fly away has come back to thee! Forgive it but this once, burn its wings and consume it in thy flame!'

'Suddenly two teardrops fell from overhead on my brow. Dark masses of clouds overcast the top of the Avalli hills that day. The gloomy woods and the sooty waters of the *Susta* were waiting in terrible suspense and in an ominous calm. Suddenly, land, water, and sky shivered, and a wild tempest-blast rushed howling through the distant pathless woods, showing its lightning-teeth like a raving maniac who had broken his chains. The desolate halls of the palace banged their doors, and moaned in the bitterness of anguish.

'The servants were all in the office, and there was no one to light the lamps. The night was cloudy and moonless. In the dense gloom within I could distinctly feel that a woman was lying on her face on the carpet below the bed-clasping and tearing her long dishevelled hair

---

[1] Royalty.

with desperate fingers. Blood was trickling down her fair brow, and she was now laughing a hard, harsh, mirthless laugh, now bursting into violent wringing sobs, now rending her bodice and striking at her bare bosom, as the wind roared in through the open window, and the rain poured in torrents and soaked her through and through.

'All night there was no cessation of the storm or of the passionate cry. I wandered from room to room in the dark, with unavailing sorrow. Whom could I console when no one was by? Whose was this intense agony of sorrow? Whence arose this inconsolable grief?

And the mad man cried out, 'Stand back! Stand back! All is false! All is false!'

'I saw that the day had dawned, and Meher Ali was going round and round the palace with his usual cry in that dreadful weather. Suddenly it came to me that perhaps he also had once lived in that house, and that, though he had gone mad, he came there every day, and went round and round, fascinated by the weird spell cast by the marble demon.

Despite the storm and rain I ran to him and asked, 'Ho, Meher Ali, what is false?'

The man answered nothing, but pushing me aside went round and round with his frantic cry, like a bird flying fascinated about the jaws of a snake, and made a desperate effort to warn himself by repeating. 'Stand back! Stand back! All is false! All is false!'

I ran like a mad man through the pelting rain to my office, and asked Karim Khan, 'Tell me the meaning of all this!'

What I gathered from that old man was this: That at one time countless unrequited passions and unsatisfied longings and lurid flames of wild blazing pleasure raged within that palace, and that the curse of all the heartaches and blasted hopes had made its every stone thirsty and hungry, eager to swallow up like a famished ogress any living man who might chance to approach. Not one of those who lived there for three consecutive nights could escape these cruel jaws, save Meher Ali, who had escaped at the cost of his reason.

I asked, 'Is there no means whatever of my release?' The old man said, 'There is only one means, and that is very difficult. I will tell you what it is, but first you must hear the history of a young Persian girl who once lived in that pleasure dome. A stranger or a more bitterly hearrending tragedy was never enacted on this earth.'

Just at this moment the coolies announced that the train was coming. So soon? We hurriedly packed up our luggage, as the train steamed in. An English gentleman, apparently just aroused from slumber, was looking out of a first class carriage endeavouring to read the name of the station. As soon as he caught sight of our fellow-passenger, he cried, 'Hallo,' and took him into his own compartment. As we got into a second class carriage, we had no chance of finding out who the man was nor what was the end of his story.

I said, 'The man evidently took us for fools and imposed upon us out of fun. The story is pure fabrication from start to finish.' The discussion that followed ended in a lifelong rupture between my theosophist kinsman and myself.

THE VICTORY

She was the Princess Ajita. And the court poet of King Narayan had never seen her. On the day he recited a new poem to the king he would raise his voice just to that pitch which could be heard by unseen hearers in the screened balcony high above the hall. He sent up his song towards the star-land out of his reach, where, circled with light, the planet who ruled his destiny shone unknown and out of ken.

He would espy some shadow moving behind the veil. A tinkling sound would come to his ear from afar, and would set him dreaming of the ankles whose tiny golden bells sang at each step. Ah, the rosy red tender feet that walked the dust of the earth like God's mercy on the fallen! The poet had placed them on the altar of his heart, where he wove his songs to the tune of those golden bells. Doubt never arose in his mind as to whose shadow it was that moved behind the screen, and whose anklets they were that sang to the time of his beating heart.

Manjari, the maid of the princess, passed by the poet's house on her way to the river, and she never missed a day to have a few words with him on the sly. When she found the road deserted, and the shadow of dusk on the land, she would boldly enter his room, and sit at the corner of his carpet. There was a suspicion of an added care in the choice of the colour of her veil, in the setting of the flower in her hair.

People smiled and whispered at this, and they were not to blame. For Shekhar the poet never took the trouble to hide the fact that these meetings were a pure joy to him.

The meaning of her name was the *spray of flowers*. One must confess that for an ordinary mortal it was sufficient in its sweetness. But Shekhar made his own addition to this name, and he called her the Spray of Spring Flowers. And ordinary mortals shook their heads and said, 'Ah, me!'

In the spring songs that the poet sang the praise of the spray of spring flowers was conspicuously reiterated; and the king winked and smiled at him when he heard it, and the poet smiled in answer.

The king would put him the question, 'Is it the business of the bee merely to hum in the court of the spring?'

The poet would answer, 'No, but also to sip the honey of the spray of spring flowers.'

And they all laughed in the king's hall. And it was rumoured that the Princess Ajita also laughed at her maid's accepting the poet's name for her, and Manjari felt glad in her heart.

Thus truth and falsehood mingle in life and to what God builds man adds his own decoration.

Only those were pure truths which were sung by the poet. The theme was Krishna, the lover god, and Radha, the beloved, the Eternal Man and the Eternal Woman, the sorrow that comes from the beginning of time, and the joy without end. The truth of these songs was tested in his inmost heart by everybody from the beggar to the king himself. The poet's songs were on the lips of all. At the merest glimmer of the moon and the faintest whisper of the summer breeze his songs would break forth in the land from windows and courtyards, from sailing boats, from shadows of the wayside trees, in numberless voices.

Thus passed the days happily. The poet recited, the king listened, the hearers applauded, Manjari passed and repassed by the poet's room on her way to the river—the shadow l fitted behind the screened balcony, and the tiny golden bells tinkled from afar.

Just then set forth from his home in the south, a poet on his path of conquest. He came to King Narayan, in the kingdom of Amarapur. He stood before the throne, and uttered a verse in praise of the king. He had challenged all the court poets on his way, and his career of victory had been unbroken.

The king received him with honour, and said, 'Poet, I offer you welcome.'

Pundarik, the poet, proudly replied, 'Sire, I ask for war.'

Shekhar, the court poet of the king did not know how the battle of the muse was to be waged. He had no sleep at night. The mighty figure of the famous Pundarik, his sharp nose curved like a scimitar, and his proud head tilted on one side, haunted the poet's vision in the dark.

With a trembling heart Shekhar entered the arena in the morning. The theatre was filled with crowd.

The poet greeted his rival with a smile and a bow. Pundarik returned it with a slight toss of his head, and turned his face towards his circle of adoring followers with a meaning smile. Shekhar cast his glance towards the screened balcony high above, and saluted his lady in his mind, saying, 'If I am the winner at the combat today, my lady, thy victorious name shall be glorified.'

The trumpet sounded. The great crowd stood up, shouting victory to the king. The king, dressed in an ample robe of white, slowly came into the hall like a floating cloud of autumn, and sat on his throne.

Pundarik stood up, and the vast hall became still. With his head raised high and chest expanded, he began in his thundering voice to recite the praise of King Narayan. His words burst upon the walls of the hall like breakers of the sea, and seemed to rattle against the ribs of the listening crowd. The skill with which he gave varied meanings to the name Narayan, and wove each letter of it through the web of his verses in all manner of combinations, took away the breath of his amazed hearers.

For some minutes after he took his seat his voice continued to vibrate among the numberless pillars of the king's court and in thousands of speechless hearts. The learned professors who had come from distant lands raised their right hands, and cried, 'Bravo!'

The king threw a glance on Shekhar's face, and Shekhar in answer raised for a moment his eyes full of pain towards his master, and then stood up like a stricken deer at bay. His face was pale, his bashfulness was almost that of a woman, his slight youthful figure, delicate in its outline, seemed like a tensely strung *viva* ready to break out in music at the least touch.

His head was bent, his voice was low, when he began. The first few verses were almost inaudible. Then he slowly raised his head, and his clear sweet voice rose into the sky like a quivering flame of fire. He began with the ancient legend of the kingly line lost in the haze of the past, and brought it down through its long course of heroism and matchless generosity to the present age. He fixed his gaze on the king's face, and all the vast and unexpressed love of the people for the royal house rose like incense in his song, and enwreathed the throne on all sides. These were his last words when, trembling, he took his seat, 'My master, I may be beaten in play of words, but not in my love for thee.'

Tears filled the eyes of the hearers, and the stone walls shook with cries of victory.

Mocking this popular outburst of feeling, with an august shake of his head and a contemptuous sneer, Pundarik stood up, and flung this question to the assembly, 'What is there superior to words?' In a moment the hall lapsed into silence again.

Then with a marvellous display of learning, he proved that the Word was in the beginning, that the Word was God. He piled up quotations from scriptures, and built a high altar for the Word to be seated above all that there is in heaven and in earth. He repeated that question in his mighty voice, 'What is there superior to words?'

Proudly he looked around him. None dared to accept his challenge, and he slowly took his seat like a lion who had just made a full meal of its victim. The pandits shouted, Bravo! The king remained silent with wonder, and the poet Shekhar felt himself of no account by the side of this stupendous learning. The assembly broke up for that day.

Next day Shekhar began his song. It was of that day when the pipings of love's flute startled for the first time the hushed air of the Vrinda forest. The shepherd women did not know who was the player or whence came the music. Sometimes it seemed to come from the heart of the south wind, and sometimes from the straying clouds of the hilltops. It came with a message of tryst from the land of the sunrise, and it floated from the verge of sunset with its sigh of sorrow. The stars seemed to be the stops of the instrument that flooded the dreams of the night with melody. The music seemed to burst all at once from all sides, from fields and groves, from the shady lanes and lonely roads, from the melting blue of the sky, from the shimmering green of the grass. They neither knew its meaning nor could they find words to give utterance to the desire of their hearts. Tears filled their eyes, and their life seemed to long for a death that would be its consummation.

Shekhar forgot his audience, forgot the trial of his strength with a rival. He stood alone amid his thoughts that rustled and quivered round him like leaves in a summer breeze, and sang the Song of the

Flute. He had in his mind the vision of an image that had taken its shape from a shadow, and the echo of a faint tinkling sound of a distant footstep.

He took his seat. His hearers trembled with the sadness of an indefinable delight, immense and vague, and they forgot to applaud him. As this feeling died away, Pundarik stood up before the throne and challenged his rival to define who was this Lover and who was the Beloved. He arrogantly looked around him, he smiled at his followers and then put the question again, 'Who is Krishna, the lover, and who is Radha, the beloved?'

Then he began to analyse the roots of those names, and various interpretations of their meanings. He brought before the bewildered audience all the intricacies of the different schools of metaphysics with consummate skill. Each letter of those names he divided from its fellow, and then pursued them with a relentless logic till they fell to the dust in confusion, to be caught up again and restored to a meaning never before imagined by the subtlest of wordmongers.

The pandits were in ecstasy; they applauded vociferously; and the crowd followed them, deluded into the certainty that they had witnessed, that day, the last shred of the curtains of Truth torn to pieces before their eyes by a prodigy of intellect. The performance of his tremendous feat so delighted them that they forgot to ask themselves if there was any truth behind it after all.

The king's mind was overwhelmed with wonder. The atmosphere was completely cleared of all illusion of music, and the vision of the world around seemed to be changed from its freshness of tender green to the solidity of a high road levelled and made hard with crushed stones.

To the assembled people their own poet appeared a mere boy in comparison to this giant, who walked with such ease, knocking down difficulties at each step in the world of words and thoughts. It became evident to them for the first time that the poems Shekhar wrote were absurdly simple, and it must be a mere accident that they did not write them themselves. They were neither new, nor difficult, nor instructive, nor necessary.

The king tried to goad his poet with keen glances, silently inciting him to make a final effort. But Shekhar took no notice, and remained fixed to his seat.

The king in anger came down from his throne, took off his pearl chain and put in on Pundarik's head. Everybody in the hall cheered. From the upper balcony came a slight sound of the movements of rustling robes and waist-chains hung with golden bells. Shekhar rose from his seat and left the hall.

It was a dark night of waning moon. The poet Shekhar took down his MSS from his shelves and heaped them on the floor. Some of them contained his earliest writings, which he had almost forgotten. He turned over the pages, reading passages here and there. They all seemed to him poor and trivial—mere words and childish rhymes!

One by one he tore his books to fragments, and threw them into a vessel containing fire, and said, 'To thee, to thee, O my beauty, my fire! Thou hast been burning in my heart all these futile years. If my life were a piece of gold it would come out of its trial brighter, but it is a trodden turf of grass, and nothing remains of it but this handful of ashes.'

The night wore on. Shekhar opened wide his windows. He spread upon his bed the white flowers that he loved, the jasmines, tuberoses and chrysanthemums, and brought into his bedroom all the lamps he had in his house and lighted them. Then mixing with honey the juice of some poisonous root, he drank it and lay down on his bed.

Golden ankles tinkled in the passage outside the door, and a subtle perfume came into the room with the breeze. The poet, with his eyes shut, said, 'My lady, have you taken pity upon your servant at last and come to see him?'

The answer came in a sweet voice, 'My poet, I have come.'

Shekhar opened his eyes and saw before his bed the figure of a woman. His sight was dim and blurred. And it seemed to him that the image made of a shadow that he had ever kept throned in the secret shrine of his heart had come into the outer world in his last moment to gaze upon his face.

The woman said, 'I am Princess Ajita.'

The poet with a great effort sat up on his bed.

The princess whispered into his ear, 'The king has not done you justice. It was you who won at the combat, my poet, and I have come to crown you with the crown of victory.'

She took the garland of flowers from her own neck, and put it on his hair, and the poet fell down upon his bed stricken by death.

LIVING OR DEAD?

I

The widow in the house of Saradasankar, the Ranihat zemindar, had no kinsmen of her father's family. One after another all had died. Nor had she in her husband's family anyone she could call her own, neither husband nor son. The child of her brother-in-law Saradasankar was her darling. For a long time after his birth, his mother had been very ill, and the widow, his aunt Kadambini, had fostered him. If a woman fosters another's child, her love for him is all the stronger because she has no claim upon him—no claim of kinship, that is, but simply the claim of love. Love cannot prove its claim by any document which society accepts, and does not wish to prove it; it merely worships with double passion its life's uncertain treasure. Thus, all the widow's thwarted love went out towards this little child. One night in *Sraban* Kadambini died suddenly. For some reason her heart stopped beating. Everywhere else the world held on its course; only in this gentle little breast, suffering with love, the watch of time stood still forever.

Lest they should be harassed by the police, four of the zemindar's Brahmin servants took away the body, without ceremony, to be burned. The burning-ground of Ranihat was very far from the village. There was a hut beside a tank, a huge banian near it, and nothing more. Formerly a river, now completely dried up, ran through the ground, and a part of the watercourse had been dug out to make a tank for the performance of funeral rites. The people considered the tank as part of the river and reverenced it as such.

Taking the body into the hut, the four men sat down to wait for the wood. The time seemed so long that two of the four grew restless, and went to see why it did not come. Nitai and Gurucharan being gone, Bidhu and Banamali remained to watch over the body.

It was a dark night of *Sraban*. Heavy clouds hung in starless sky. The two men sat silent in the dark room. Their matches and lamp were useless. The matches were damp, and would not light for all their efforts, and the lantern went out. After a long silence, one said, 'Brother, it would be good if we had a bowl of tobacco. In our hurry we brought none.'

The other answered, 'I can ran and bring all we want.'

Understanding why Banamali wanted to go,[1] Bidhu said, 'I daresay! Meanwhile, I suppose I am to sit here alone!'

Conversation ceased again. Five minutes seemed like an hour. In their minds they cursed the two who had gone to fetch the wood, and they began to suspect that they sat gossiping in some pleasant nook. There was no sound anywhere, except the incessant noise of frogs and crickets from the tank. Then suddenly they fancied that the bed shook slightly, as if the dead body had turned on its side. Bidhu and Banamali trembled, and began muttering, 'Ram, Ram.' A deep sigh was heard in the room. In a moment the watchers leapt out of the hut, and raced for the village.

After running about three miles, they met their colleagues coming back with a lantern. As a matter of fact, they *had* gone to smoke, and knew nothing about the wood. But they declared that a tree had been cut down, and that, when it was split up, it would he brought along at once. Then Bidhu and Banamali told them what had happened in the hut. Nitai and Gurucharan scoffed at the story, and abused Bidhu and Banamali angrily for leaving their duty.

Without delay all four returned to the hut. As they entered, they saw at once that the body was gone; nothing but an empty bed remained. They stared at one another. Could a jackal have taken it? But there was no scrap of clothing anywhere. Going outside, they saw that on the mud that had collected at the door of the hut there were a woman's tiny footprints, newly made. Saradasankar was no fool, and they could hardly persuade him to believe in this ghost story. So after much discussion the four decided that it would be best to say that the body had been burnt.

Towards dawn, when the men with the wood arrived they were told that, owing to their delay, the work had been done without them;

---

[1] From fear of ghosts, the burning-ground being considered haunted.

there had been some wood in the hut after all. No one was likely to question this, since a dead body is not such a valuable property that anyone would steal it.

II

Everyone knows that, even when there is no sign, life is often secretly present, and may begin again in an apparently dead body. Kadambini was not dead; only the machine of her life had for some reason suddenly stopped.

When consciousness returned, she saw dense darkness on all sides. It occurred to her that she was not lying in her usual place. She called out 'Sister,' but no answer came from the darkness. As she sat up, terror-stricken, she remembered her deathbed, the sudden pain at her breast, the beginning of a choking sensation. Her elder sister-in-law was warming some milk for the child, when Kadambini became faint, and fell on the bed, saying with a choking voice, 'Sister, bring the child here. I am worried.' After that everything was black, as when an inkpot is upset over an exercise book. Kadambini's memory and consciousness, all the letters of the world's book, in a moment became formless. The widow could not remember whether the child, in the sweet voice of love, called her 'Auntie,' as if for the last time, or not; she could not remember whether, as she left the world she knew for death's endless unknown journey, she had received a parting gift of affection, love's passage-money for the silent land. At first, I fancy, she thought the lonely dark place was the House of Yama, where there is nothing to see, nothing to hear, nothing to do, only an eternal watch. But when a cold damp wind drove through the open door, and she heard the croaking of frogs, she remembered vividly and in a moment all the rains of her short life, and could feel her kinship with the earth. Then came a flash of lightning, and she saw the tank, the banian, the great plain, the far-off trees. She remembered how at full moon she had sometimes come to bathe in this tank, and how dreadful death had seemed when she saw a corpse on the burning-ground.

Her first thought was to return home. But then she reflected, 'I am dead. How can I return home? That would bring disaster on them. I have left the kingdom of the living; I am my own ghost!' If this were not so, she reasoned, how could she have got out of Sardasankar's well-guarded zenana, and come to this distant burning-ground at midnight? Also, if her funeral rites had not been finished, where had the men gone who should burn her? Recalling her death-moment in Saradasankar's brightly-lit house, she now found herself alone in a distant, deserted, dark burning-ground. Surely she was no member of earthly society! Surely she was a creature of horror, of ill-omen, her own ghost!

At this thought, all the bonds were snapped which bound her to the world. She felt that she had marvellous strength, endless freedom. She could do what she liked, go where she pleased. Mad with the inspiration of this new idea, she rushed from the hut like a gust of wind, and stood upon the burning-ground. All trace of shame or fear had left her.

But as she walked on and on, her feet grew tired, her body weak. The plain stretched on endlessly; here and there were paddy fields; sometimes she found herself standing knee-deep in water.

At the first glimmer of dawn she heard one or two birds cry from the bamboo-clumps by the distant houses. Then terror seized her. She could not tell in what new relation she stood to the earth and to living folk. So long as she had been on the plain, on the burning-ground, covered by the dark night of *Sraban,* so long she had been fearless, a denizen of her own kingdom. By daylight the homes of men filled her with fear. Men and ghosts dread each other, for their tribes inhabit different banks of the river of death.

III

Her clothes were clotted in the mud; strange thoughts and walking by night had given her the aspect of a madwoman; truly, her apparition was such that folk might have been afraid of her, and children might have stoned her or run away. Luckily, the first to catch sight of her was a traveller. He came up, and said, 'Mother, you look a respectable woman. Wherever are you going, alone and in this guise?'

Kadambini, unable to collect her thoughts, stared at him in silence. She could not think that she was still in touch with the world, that she looked like a respectable woman, that a traveller was asking her questions.

Again the man said, 'Come, mother, I will see you home. Tell me where you live.'

Kadambini thought. To return to her father-in-law's house would be absurd, and she had no father's house. Then she remembered a friend of her childhood. She had not seen Jogmaya since the days of her youth, but from time to time they had exchanged letters. Occasionally there had been quarrels between them, as was only right, since Kadambini wished to make it clear that her love for Jogmaya was unbounded, while her friend complained that Kadambini did not return a love equal to her own. They were both sure that, if they once met, they would be inseparable.

Kadambini said to the traveller, 'I will go to Sripati's house at Nisindapur.'

As he was going to Calcutta, Nisindapur, though not near, was on his way. So he took Kadambini to Sripati's house, and the friends met again. At first they did not recognize one another, but gradually each recognized the features of the other's childhood.

'What luck!' said Jogmaya. 'I never dreamt that I should see you again. But how have you come here, sister? Your father-in-law's folk surely didn't let you go!'

Kadambini remained silent, and at last said, 'Sister, do not ask about my father-in-law. Give me a corner, and treat me as a servant. I will do your work.'

'What?' cried Jogmaya. 'Keep you like a servant! Why, you are my closest friend, you are my...' and so on and so on.

Just then Sripati came in. Kadambini stared at him for some time, and then went out very slowly. She kept her head uncovered, and showed not the slightest modesty or respect. Jogmaya, fearing that Sripati would be prejudiced against her friend, began an elaborate explanation. But Sripati, who readily agreed to anything Jogmaya said, cut short her story, and left his wife uneasy in her mind.

Kadambini had come, but she was not at one with her friend: death was between them. She could feel no intimacy for others so long as her existence perplexed her and consciousness remained. Kadambini would look at Jogmaya, and brood. She would think, 'She has her husband and her work, she lives in a world faraway from mine. She shares affection and duty with the people of the world; I am an empty shadow. She is among the living; I am in eternity.'

Jogmaya also was uneasy, but could not explain why. Women do not love mystery, because, though uncertainty may be transmuted into poetry, into heroism, into scholarship, it cannot be turned to account in household work. So, when a woman cannot understand a thing, she either destroys and forgets it, or she shapes it anew for her own use; if she fails to deal with it in one of these ways, she loses her temper with it. The greater Kadambini's abstraction became, the more impatient was Jogmaya with her, wondering what trouble weighed upon her mind.

Then a new danger arose. Kadambini was afraid of herself; yet she could not flee from herself. Those who fear ghosts fear those who are behind them; wherever they cannot see there is fear. But Kadambini's chief terror lay in herself, for she dreaded nothing external. At the dead of night, when alone in her room, she screamed; in the evening, when she saw her shadow in the lamp light, her whole body shook. Watching her fearfulness, the rest of the house fell into a sort of terror. The servants and Jogmaya herself began to see ghosts.

One midnight, Kadambini came out from her bedroom weeping, and wailed at Jogmaya's door, 'Sister, sister, let me lie at your feet! Do not put me by myself!'

Jogmaya's anger was no less than her fear. She would have liked to drive Kadambini from the house that very second. The good-natured Sripati, after much effort, succeeded in quieting their guest, and put her in the next room.

Next day, Sripati was unexpectedly summoned to his wife's apartments. She began to upbraid him, 'You, do you call yourself a man? A woman runs away from her father-in-law, and enters your house; a month passes, and you haven't hinted that she should go away, nor have I heard the slightest protest from you. I should take it as a favour if you would explain yourself. You men are all alike.'

Most men have such an unreasoning fondness for their wives that they willingly allow themselves to be put in the wrong. Although

Sripati was prepared to touch Jogmaya's body, and swear that his kind feeling towards the helpless but beautiful Kadambini was no whit greater than it should be, he could not prove it by his behaviour. He thought that her father-in-law's people must have treated this forlorn widow abominably, if she could bear it no longer, and was driven to take refuge with him. As she had neither father nor mother, how could he desert her? So saying, he let the matter drop, for he had no mind to distress Kadambini by asking her unpleasant questions.

His wife, then, tried other means of attack upon her sluggish lord, until at last he saw that for the sake of peace he must send word to Kadambini's father-in-law. The result of a letter, he thought, might not be satisfactory; so he resolved to go to Ranihat, and act on what he learnt.

So Sripati went, and Jogmaya on her part said to Kadambini, 'Friend, it hardly seems proper for you to stop here any longer. What will people say?'

Kadambini stared solemnly at Jogmaya, and said, 'What have I to do with people?'

Jogmaya was astounded. Then she said sharply, 'If you have nothing to do with people, *we* have. How can we explain the detention of a woman belonging to another house?'

Kadambini said, 'Where is my father-in-law's house?'

'Confound it!' thought Jogmaya. 'What will the wretched woman say next?'

Very slowly Kadambini said, 'What have I to do with you? Am I of the earth? You laugh, weep, love; each grips and holds his own; I merely look. You are human, I a shadow. I cannot understand why God has kept me in this world of yours.'

So strange were her look and speech that Jogmaya understood something of her drift, though not all. Unable either to dismiss her, or to ask her any more questions, she went away, oppressed with thought.

IV

It was nearly ten o'clock at night when Sripati returned from Ranihat. The earth was drowned in torrents of rain. It seemed that the downpour would never stop, that the night would never end.

Jogmaya asked, 'Well?'

'I've lots to say, presently.'

So saying, Sripati changed his clothes, and sat down to supper; then he lay down for a smoke. His mind was perplexed.

His wife stifled her curiosity for a long time; then she came to his couch and demanded, 'What did you hear?'

'That you have certainly made a mistake.'

Jogmaya was nettled. Women never make mistakes, or, if they do, a sensible man never mentions them; it is better to take them on his own shoulders. Jogmaya snapped, 'May I be permitted to hear how?'

Sripati replied, 'The woman you have taken into your house is not your Kadambini.'

Hearing this, she was greatly annoyed, especially since it was her husband who said it. 'What! I don't know my own friend? I must come to you to recognize her! You are clever, indeed!'

Sripati explained that there was no need to quarrel about his cleverness. He could prove what he said. There was no doubt that Jogmaya's Kadambini was dead.

Jogmaya replied, 'Listen! You've certainly made some huge mistake. You've been to the wrong house, or are confused as to what you have heard. Who told you to go yourself? Write a letter, and everything will be cleared up.'

Sripati was hurt by his wife's lack of faith in his executive ability; he produced all sorts of proof, without result. Midnight found them still asserting and contradicting. Although they were both agreed now that Kadambini should be got out of the house, although Sripati believed that their guest had deceived his wife all the time by a pretended acquaintance, and Jogmaya that she was a prostitute, yet in the present discussion neither would acknowledge defeat. By degrees their voices became so loud that they forgot that Kadambini was sleeping in the next room.

The one said, 'We're in a nice fix! I tell you, I heard it with my own ears!' And the other answered angrily, 'What do I care about that? I can see with my own eyes, surely?'

At length Jogmaya said, 'Very well. Tell me when Kadambini died.'

She thought that if she could find a discrepancy between the day of death and the date of some letter from Kadambini, she could prove that Sripati erred.

He told her the date of Kadambini's death, and they both saw that it fell on the very day before she came to their house. Jogmaya's heart trembled, and even Sripati was not unmoved.

Just then the door flew open; a damp wind swept in and blew the lamp out. The darkness rushed after it, and filled the whole house. Kadambini stood in the room. It was nearly one o'clock, and the rain was pelting outside.

Kadambini spoke, 'Friend, I am your Kadambini, but I am no longer living. I am dead.'

Jogmaya screamed with terror; Sripati could not speak.

'But, save in being dead, I have done you no wrong. If I have no place among the living, I have none among the dead. Oh! Whither shall I go?' Crying as if to wake the sleeping Creator in the dense night of rain, she asked again, 'Oh! Whither shall I go?'

So saying, Kadambini left her friend fainting in the dark house, and went out into the world, seeking her own place.

V

It is hard to say how Kadambini reached Ranihat. At first she showed herself to no one, but spent the whole day in a ruined temple, starving. When the untimely afternoon of the rains was pitch-black, and people huddled into their houses for fear of the impending storm, then Kadambini came forth. Her heart trembled as she reached her father-in-law's house; and when, drawing a thick veil over her face, she entered, none of the doorkeepers objected, since they took her for a servant. And the rain was pouring down, and the wind howled.

The mistress, Saradasankar's wife, was playing cards with her widowed sister. A servant was in the kitchen, the sick child was sleeping in the bedroom. Kadambini, escaping everyone's notice, entered this room. I do not know why she had come to her father-in-law's house; she herself did not know; she felt only that she wanted to see her child again. She had no thought where to go next, or what to do.

In the lighted room she saw the child sleeping with his fists clenched, his body wasted with fever. At the sight of him, her heart became parched and thirsty. If only she could press that tortured body to her breast! Immediately the thought followed, I do not exist. Who would see it? His mother loves company, loves gossip and cards. All the time that she left me in charge, she was herself free from anxiety, nor was she troubled about him in the least. Who will look after him now as I did?'

The child turned on his side, and cried, half asleep, 'Auntie, give me water.' Her darling had not yet forgotten his auntie! In a fever of excitement, she poured out some water, and, taking him to her breast, she gave it him.

As long as he was asleep, the child felt no strangeness in taking water from the accustomed hand. But when Kadambini satisfied her long-starved longing, and kissed him and began rocking him asleep again, he awoke and embraced her. 'Did you die, Auntie?' he asked.

'Yes, darling.'

'And you have come back? Do not die again.'

Before she could answer disaster overtook her. One of the maidservants coming in with a cup of sago dropped it, and fell down. At the crash the mistress left her cards, and entered the room. She stood like a pillar of wood, unable to flee or speak. Seeing all this, the child, too, became terrified, and burst out weeping, 'Go away, Auntie,' he said, 'go away!'

Now at last Kadambini understood that she had not died. The old room, the old things, the same child, the same love, all returned to their living state, without change or difference between her and them. In her friend's house she had felt that her childhood's companion was dead. In her child's room she knew that the boy's 'Auntie' was not dead at all. In anguished tones she said, 'Sister, why do you dread me? See, I am as you knew me.'

Her sister-in-law could endure no longer, and fell into a faint. Saradasankar himself entered the zenana. With folded hands, he said piteously, 'Is this right? Satis is my only son. Why do you show yourself to him? Are we not your own kin? Since you went, he has wasted away daily; his fever has been incessant; day and night he cries,

'Auntie, Auntie.' You have left the world; break these bonds of *maya*.[1] We will perform all funeral honours.'

Kadambini could bear no more. She said, 'Oh, I am not dead, I am not dead. Oh, *how* can I persuade you that I am not dead? I am living, living!' She lifted a brass pot from the ground and dashed it against her forehead. The blood ran from her brow. 'Look!' she cried, 'I am *living!*' Saradasankar stood like an image; the child screamed with fear, the two fainting women lay still.

The Kadambini, shouting, 'I am not dead, I am not dead,' went down the steps to the zenana well, and plunged in. From the upper story Saradasankar heard the splash.

All night the rain poured; it poured next day at dawn, was pouring still at noon. By dying, Kadambini had given proof that she was not dead.

---

[1] Illusory affection binding a soul to the world.

THE PARROT'S TRAINING

Once upon a time there was a bird. It was ignorant. It sang all right, but never recited scriptures. It hopped pretty frequently, but lacked manners.

Said the Raja to himself, 'Ignorance is costly in the long run. For fools consume as much food as their betters, and yet give nothing in return.'

He called his nephews to his presence and told them that the bird must have a sound schooling.

The pundits were summoned, and at once went to the root of the matter. They decided that the ignorance of birds was due to their natural habit of living in poor nests. Therefore, according to the pundits, the first thing necessary for this bird's education was a suitable cage.

The pundits had their rewards and went home happy. A golden cage was built with gorgeous decorations. Crowds came to see it from all parts of the world.

'Culture, captured and caged!' exclaimed some, in a rapture of ecstasy, and burst into tears.

Others remarked, 'Even if culture be missed, the cage will remain to the end, a substantial fact. How fortunate for the bird!'

The goldsmith filled his bag with money and lost no time in sailing homewards.

The pundit sat down to educate the bird. With proper deliberation he took his pinch of snuff, as he said, 'Text books can never be too many for our purpose!'

The nephews brought together an enormous crowd of scribes. They copied from books, and copied from copies, till the manuscripts were piled up to an unreachable height.

Men murmured in amazement, 'Oh, the tower of culture, egregiously high! The end of it lost in the clouds!'

The scribes, with light hearts, hurried home, their pockets heavily laden.

The nephews were furiously busy keeping the cage in proper trim.

As their constant scrubbing and polishing went on, the people said with satisfaction, 'This is progress indeed!'

Men were employed in large numbers, and supervisors were still more numerous. These, with their cousins of all different degrees of distance, built a palace for themselves and lived there happily ever after.

Whatever may be its other deficiencies, the world is never in want of fault-finders; and they went about saying that every creature remotely connected with the cage flourished beyond words, excepting only the bird.

When this remark reached the Raja's ears, he summoned his nephews before him and said, 'My dear nephews, what is this that we hear?'

The nephews said in answer, 'Sire, let the testimony of the goldsmiths and the pundits, the scribes and the supervisors, be taken, if the truth is to be known food is scarce with the fault-finders, and that is why their tongues have gained in sharpness.'

The explanation was so luminously satisfactory that the Raja decorated each one of his nephews with his own rare jewels.

The Raja at length, being desirous of seeing with his own eyes how his Education Department busied itself with the little bird, made his appearance one day at the great Hall of Learning.

From the gate rose the sounds of conch-shells and gongs, horns, bugles and trumpets, cymbals, drums and kettle-drums, tomtoms, tambourines, flutes, fifes, barrel-organs and bagpipes. The pundits began chanting *mantras* with their topmost voices, while the goldsmiths, scribes, supervisors, and their numberless cousins of all different degrees of distance, loudly raised a round of cheers.

The nephews smiled and said, 'Sire, what do you think of it all?'

The Raja said, 'It does seem so fearfully like a sound principle of Education!'

Mightily pleased, the Raja was about to remount his elephant, when the fault-finder, from behind some bush, cried out, 'Maharaja, have you seen the bird?'

'Indeed, I have not!' exclaimed the Raja, 'I completely forgot about the bird.'

Turning back, he asked the pundits about the method they followed in instructing the bird.

It was shown to him. He was immensely impressed. The method was so stupendous that the bird looked ridiculously unimportant in comparison. The Raja was satisfied that there was no flaw in the arrangements. As for any complaint from the bird itself, that simply could not be expected. Its throat was so completely choked with the leaves from the books that it could neither whistle nor whisper. It sent a thrill through one's body to watch the process.

This time, while remounting his elephant, the Raja ordered his State Earpuller to give a thorough good pull at both the ears of the fault-finder.

The bird thus crawled on, duly and properly, to the safest verge of inanity. In fact, its progress was satisfactory in the extreme. Nevertheless, nature occasionally triumphed over training, and when the morning light peeped into the bird's cage it sometimes fluttered its wings in a reprehensible manner. And, though it is hard to believe, it pitifully pecked at its bars with its feeble beak.

'What impertinence!' growled the *kotwal*.

The blacksmith, with his forge and hammer, took his place in the Raja's Department of Education. Oh, what resounding blows! The iron chain was soon completed, and the bird's wings were clipped.

The Raja's brothers-in-law looked back, and shook their heads, saying, 'These birds not only lack good sense, but also gratitude!'

With textbook in one hand and baton in the other, the pundits gave the poor bird what may fitly be called lessons!

The *kotwal* was honoured with a title for his watchfulness and the blacksmith for his skill in forging chains.

The bird died.

Nobody had the least notion how long ago this had happened. The fault-finder was the first man to spread the rumour.

The Raja called his nephews and asked them, 'My dear nephews, what is this that we hear?'

The nephews said, 'Sire, the bird's education has been completed.'

'Does it hop?' the Raja enquired.

'Never!' said the nephews.

'Does it fly?'

'No.'

'Bring me the bird,' said the Raja.

The bird was brought to him, guarded by the *kotwal* and the sepoys and the sowars. The Raja poked its body with his finger. Only its inner stuffing of book-leaves rustled.

Outside the window, the murmur of the spring breeze amongst the newly budded *asoka* leaves made the April morning wistful.

GITANJALI

GITANJALI

I

Thou hast made me endless, such is thy pleasure. This frail vessel thou emptiest again and again, and fillest it ever with fresh life.

This little flute of a reed thou hast carried over hills and dales, and hast breathed through it melodies eternally new.

At the immortal touch of thy hands my little heart loses its limits in joy and gives birth to utterance ineffable.

Thy infinite gifts come to me only on these very small hands of mine. Ages pass, and still thou pourest, and still there is room to fill.

II

When thou commandest me to sing, it seems that my heart would break with pride; and I look to thy face, and tears come to my eyes.

All that is harsh and dissonant in my life melts into one sweet harmony—and my adoration spreads wings like a glad bird on its flight across the sea.

I know thou takest pleasure in my singing. I know that only as a singer I come before thy presence.

I touch by the edge of the far-spreading wing of my song thy feet which I could never aspire to reach.

Drunk with the joy of singing I forget myself and call thee friend who art my lord.

III

I know not how thou singest, my master! I ever listen in silent amazement.

The light of thy music illumines the world. The life breath of thy music runs from sky to sky. The holy stream of thy music breaks through all stony obstacles and rushes on.

My heart longs to join in thy song, but vainly struggles for a voice. I would speak, but speech breaks not into song, and I cry out baffled. Ah, thou hast made my heart captive in the endless meshes of thy music, my master!

IV

Life of my life, I shall ever try to keep my body pure, knowing that thy living touch is upon all my limbs.

I shall ever try to keep all untruths out from my thoughts, knowing that thou art that truth which has kindled the light of reason in my mind.

I shall ever try to drive all evils away from my heart and keep my love in flower, knowing that thou hast thy seat in the inmost shrine of my heart.

And it shall be my endeavour to reveal thee in my actions, knowing it is thy power that gives me strength to act.

V

I ask for a moment's indulgence to sit by thy side. The works that I have in hand I will finish afterwards.

Away from the sight of thy face my heart knows no rest nor respite, and my work becomes an endless toil in a shoreless sea of toil.

Today the summer has come at my window with its sighs and murmurs; and the bees are plying their minstrelsy at the court of the flowering grove.

Now it is time to sit quiet, face to face with thee, and to sing dedication of life in this silent and overflowing leisure.

VI

Pluck this little flower and take it. Delay not! I fear lest it droop and drop into the dust.

It may not find a place in thy garland, but honour it with a touch of pain from thy hand and pluck it. I fear lest the day end before I am aware, and the time of offering go by.

Though its colour be not deep and its smell be faint, use this flower in thy service and pluck it while there is time.

VII

My song has put off her adornments. She has no pride of dress and decoration. Ornaments would mar our union; they would come between thee and me; their jingling would drown thy whispers.

My poet's vanity dies in shame before thy sight. O master poet, I have sat down at thy feet. Only let me make my life simple and straight, like a flute of reed for thee to fill with music.

VIII

The child, who is decked with prince's robes and who has jewelled chains round his neck loses all pleasure in his play; his dress hampers him at every step.

In fear that it may be frayed, or stained with dust he keeps himself from the world, and is afraid even to move.

Mother, it is no gain, thy bondage of finery, if it keep one shut off from the healthful dust of the earth, if it rob one of the right of entrance to the great fair of common human life.

IX

O fool, to try to carry thyself upon thy own shoulders! O beggar, to come to beg at thy own door!

Leave all thy burdens on his hands who can bear all, and never look behind in regret.

Thy desire at once puts out the light from the lamp it touches with its breath. It is unholy—take not thy gifts through its unclean hands. Accept only what is offered by sacred love.

X

Here is thy footstool and there rest thy feet where live the poorest, and lowliest, and lost.

When I try to bow to thee, my obeisance cannot reach down to the depth where thy feet rest among the poorest, and lowliest, and lost.

Pride can never approach to where thou walkest in the clothes of the humble among the poorest, and lowliest, and lost.

My heart can never find its way to where thou keepest company with the companionless among the poorest, the lowliest, and the lost.

XI

Leave this chanting and singing and telling of beads! Whom dost thou worship in this lonely dark corner of a temple with doors all shut? Open thine eyes and see thy God is not before thee!

He is there where the tiller is tilling the hard ground and where the pathmaker is breaking stones. He is with them in sun and in shower, and his garment is covered with dust. Put off thy holy mantle and even like him come down on the dusty soil!

Deliverance? Where is this deliverance to be found? Our master himself has joyfully taken upon him the bonds of creation; he is bound with us all forever.

Come out of thy meditations and leave aside thy flowers and incense! What harm is there if thy clothes become tattered and stained? Meet him and stand by him in toil and in sweat of thy brow.

XII

The time that my journey takes is long and the way of it long.

I came out on the chariot of the first gleam of light, and pursued my voyage through the wildernesses of worlds leaving my track on many a star and planet.

It is the most distant course that comes nearest to thyself, and that training is the most intricate which leads to the utter simplicity of a tune.

The traveller has to knock at every alien door to come to his own, and one has to wander through all the outer worlds to reach the innermost shrine at the end.

My eyes strayed far and wide before I shut them and said, 'Here art thou!'

The question and the cry, 'Oh, where?' melt into tears of a thousand streams and deluge the world with the flood of the assurance, 'I am!'

XIII

The song that I came to sing remains unsung to this day.

I have spent my days in stringing and in unstringing my instrument.

The time has not come true, the words have not been rightly set; only there is the agony of wishing in my heart.

The blossom has not opened; only the wind is sighing by.

I have not seen his face, nor have I listened to his voice; only I have heard his gentle footsteps from the road before my house.

The livelong day has passed in spreading his seat on the floor; but the lamp has not been lit and I cannot ask him into my house.

I live in the hope of meeting with him; but this meeting is not yet.

XIV

My desires are many and my cry is pitiful, but ever didst thou save me by hard refusals; and this strong mercy has been wrought into my life through and through.

Day by day thou art making me worthy of the simple, great gifts that thou gavest to me unasked—this sky and the light, this body and the life and the mind—saving me from perils of overmuch desire.

There are times when I languidly linger and times when I awaken and hurry in search of my goal; but cruelly thou hidest thyself from before me.

Day by day thou art making me worthy of thy full acceptance by refusing me ever and anon, saving me from perils of weak, uncertain desire.

XV

I am here to sing thee songs. In this hall of thine I have a corner seat.

In thy world I have no work to do; my useless life can only break out in tunes without a purpose.

When the hour strikes for thy silent worship at the dark temple of midnight, command me, my master, to stand before thee to sing.

When in the morning air the golden harp is tuned, honour me, commanding my presence.

XVI

I have had my invitation to this world's festival, and thus my life has been blessed. My eyes have seen and my ears have heard.

It was my part at this feast to play upon my instrument, and I have done all I could.

Now, I ask, has the time come at last when I may go in and see thy face and offer thee my silent salutation?

XVII

I am only waiting for love to give myself up at last into his hands. That is why it is so late and why I have been guilty of such omissions.

They come with their laws and their codes to bind me fast; but I evade them ever, for I am only waiting for love to give myself up at last into his hands.

People blame me and call me heedless; I doubt not they are right in their blame:

The market day is over and work is all done for the busy. Those who came to call me in vain have gone back in anger. I am only waiting for love to give myself up at last into his hands.

XVIII

Clouds heap upon clouds and it darkens. Ah, love, why dost thou let me wait outside at the door all alone?

In the busy moments of the noontide work I am with the crowd, but on this dark lonely day it is only for thee that I hope.

If thou showest me not thy face, if thou leavest me wholly aside, I know not how I am to pass these long, rainy hours.

I keep gazing on the faraway gloom of the sky, and my heart wanders wailing with the restless wind.

XIX

If thou speakest not I will fill my heart with thy silence and endure it. I will keep still and wait like the night with starry vigil and its head bent low with patience.

The morning will surely come, the darkness will vanish, and thy voice pour down in golden streams breaking through the sky.

Then thy words will take wing in songs from every one of my birds' nests, and thy melodies will break forth in flowers in all any forest groves.

XX

On the day when the lotus bloomed, alas, my mind was straying, and I knew it not. My basket was empty and the flower remained unheeded.

Only now and again a sadness fell upon me, and I started up from my dream and felt a sweet trace of a strange fragrance in the south wind.

That vague sweetness made my heart ache with longing and it seemed to me that it was the eager breath of the summer seeking for its completion.

I knew not then that it was so near, that it was mine, and that this perfect sweetness had blossomed in the depth of my own heart.

XXI

I must launch out my boat. The languid hours pass by on the shore—Alas for me!

The spring has done its flowering and taken leave. And now with the burden of faded futile flowers I wait and linger.

The waves have become clamorous, and upon the bank in the shady lane the yellow leaves flutter and fall.

What emptiness do you gaze upon! Do you not feel a thrill passing through the air with the notes of the faraway song floating from the other shore?

XXII

In the deep shadows of the rainy July, with secret steps, thou walkest, silent as night, eluding all watchers.

Today the morning has closed its eyes, heedless of the insistent calls of the loud east wind, and a thick veil has been drawn over the ever-wakeful blue sky.

The woodlands have hushed their songs, and doors are all shut at every house. Thou art the solitary wayfarer in this deserted street. Oh, my only friend, my best beloved, the gates are open in my house—do not pass by like a dream.

XXIII

Art thou abroad on this stormy night on thy journey of love, my friend? The sky groans like one in despair.

I have no sleep tonight. Ever and again I open my door and look out on the darkness, my friend!

I can see nothing before me. I wonder where lies thy path!

By what dim shore of the ink-black river, by what far edge of the frowning forest, through what mazy depth of gloom art thou threading thy course to come to me, my friend?

XXIV

If the day is done, if birds sing no more, if the wind has flagged tired, then draw the veil of darkness thick upon me, even as thou hast wrapt the earth with the coverlet of sleep and tenderly closed the petals of the drooping lotus at dusk.

From the traveller, whose sack of provisions is empty before the voyage is ended, whose garment is torn and dust-laden, whose strength is exhausted, remove shame and poverty, and renew his life like a flower under the cover of thy kindly night.

XXV

In the night of weariness let me give myself up to sleep without struggle, resting my trust upon thee.

Let me not force my flagging spirit into a poor preparation for thy worship.

It is thou who drawest the veil of night upon the tired eyes of the day to renew its sight in a fresher gladness of awakening.

XXVI

He came and sat by my side but I woke not. What a cursed sleep it was, O miserable me!

He came when the night was still; he had his harp in his hands, and my dreams became resonant with its melodies.

Alas, why are my nights all thus lost? Ah, why do I ever miss his sight whose breath touches my sleep?

XXVII

Light, oh, where is the light? Kindle it with the burning fire of desire!

There is the lamp but never a flicker of a flame,—is such thy fate, my heart? Ah, death were better by far for thee!

Misery knocks at thy door, and her message is that thy lord is wakeful, and he calls thee to the love-tryst through the darkness of night.

The sky is overcast with clouds and the rain is ceaseless. I know not what this is that stirs in me,—I know not its meaning.

A moment's flash of lightning drags down a deeper gloom on my sight, and my heart gropes for the path to where the music of the night calls me.

Light, oh, where is the light? Kindle it with the burning fire of desire! It thunders and the wind rushes screaming through the void. The night is black as a black stone. Let not the hours pass by in the dark. Kindle the lamp of love with thy life.

XXVIII

Obstinate are the trammels, but my heart aches when I try to break them.

Freedom is all I want, but to hope for it I feel ashamed.

I am certain that priceless wealth is in thee, and that thou art my best friend, but I have not the heart to sweep away the tinsel that fills my room.

The shroud that covers me is a shroud of dust and death; I hate it, yet hug it in love.

My debts are large, my failures great, my shame secret and heavy;

yet when I come to ask for my good, I quake in fear lest my prayer be granted.

XXIX

He whom I enclose with my name is weeping in this dungeon. I am ever busy building this wall all around; and as this wall goes up into the sky day by day I lose sight of my true being in its dark shadow.

I take pride in this great wall, and I plaster it with dust and sand lest a least hole should be left in this name; and for all the care I take I lose sight of my true being.

XXX

I came out alone on my way to my tryst. But who is this that follows me in the silent dark?

I move aside to avoid his presence but I escape him not.

He makes the dust rise from the earth with his swagger; he adds his loud voice to every word that I utter.

He is my own little self, my lord, he knows no shame; but I am ashamed to come to thy door in his company.

XXXI

'Prisoner, tell me, who was it that bound you?'

'It was my master,' said the prisoner. 'I thought I could outdo everybody in the world in wealth and power, and I amassed in my own treasure-house the money due to my king. When sleep overcame me I lay upon the bed that was for my lord, and on waking up I found I was a prisoner in my own treasure-house.'

'Prisoner, tell me, who was it that wrought this unbreakable chain?'

'It was I,' said the prisoner, 'who forged this chain very carefully. I thought my invincible power would hold the world captive leaving me in a freedom undisturbed. Thus night and day I worked at the chain with huge fires and cruel hard strokes. When at last the work was done and the links were complete and unbreakable, I found that it held me in its grip.'

XXXII

By all means they try to hold me secure who love me in this world. But it is otherwise with thy love which is greater than theirs, and thou keepest me free.

Lest I forget them they never venture to leave me alone. But day passes by after day and thou art not seen.

If I call not thee in my prayers, if I keep not thee in my heart, thy love for me still waits for my love.

XXXIII

When it was day they came into my house and said, 'We shall only take the smallest room here.'

They said, 'We shall help you in the worship of your God and humbly accept only our own share of his grace;' and then they took their seat in a corner and they sat quiet and meek.

But in the darkness of night I find they break into my sacred shrine, strong and turbulent, and snatch with unholy greed the offerings from God's altar.

XXXIV

Let only that little be left of me whereby I may name thee my all.

Let only that little be left of my will whereby I may feel thee on every side, and come to thee in everything, and offer to thee my love every moment.

Let only that little be left of me whereby I may never hide thee.

Let only that little of my fetters be left whereby I am bound with thy will, and thy purpose is carried out in my life—and that is the fetter of thy love.

XXXV

Where the mind is without fear and the head is held high;

Where knowledge is free;

Where the world has not been broken up into fragments by narrow domestic walls;

Where words come out from the depth of truth;
Where tireless striving stretches its arms towards perfection;
Where the clear stream of reason has not lost its way into the dreary desert sand of dead habit;
Where the mind is led forward by thee into ever widening thought and action—
Into that heaven of freedom, my Father, let my country awake.

XXXVI

This is my prayer to thee, my lord—strike, strike at the root of penury in my heart.
Give me the strength lightly to bear my joys and sorrows.
Give me the strength to make my love fruitful in service.
Give me the strength never to disown the poor or bend my knees before insolent might.
Give me the strength to raise my mind high above daily trifles.
And give me the strength to surrender my strength to thy will with love.

XXXVII

I thought that my voyage had come to its end at the last limit of my power,—that the path before me was closed, that provisions were exhausted and the time come to take shelter in a silent obscurity.
But I find that thy will knows no end in me. And when old words die out on the tongue, new melodies break forth from the heart; and where the old tracks are lost, new country is revealed with its wonders.

XXXVIII

That I want thee, only thee—let my heart repeat without end. All desires that distract me, day and night, are false and empty to the core.
As the night keeps hidden in its gloom the petition for light, even thus in the depth of my unconsciousness rings the cry—'I want thee, only thee'.
As the storm still seeks its end in peace when it strikes against peace with all its might, even thus my rebellion strikes against thy

love and still its cry is—'I want thee, only thee'.

XXXIX

When the heart is hard and parched up, come upon me with a shower of mercy.

When grace is lost from life, come with a burst of song.

When tumultuous work raises its din on all sides shutting me out from beyond, come to me, my lord of silence, with thy peace and rest.

When my beggarly heart sits crouched, shut up in a corner, break open the door, my king, and come with the ceremony of a king.

When desire blinds the mind with delusion and dust, O thou holy one, thou wakeful, come with thy light and thy thunder.

XL

The rain has held back for days and days, my God, in my arid heart. The horizon is fiercely naked—not the thinnest cover of a soft cloud, not the vaguest hint of a distant cool shower.

Send thy angry storm, dark with death, if it is thy wish, and with lashes of lightning startle the sky from end to end.

But call back, my lord, call back this pervading silent heat, still and keen and cruel, burning the heart with dire despair.

Let the cloud of grace bend low from above like the tearful look of the mother on the day of the father's wrath.

XLI

Where dost thou stand behind them all, my lover, hiding thyself in the shadows? They push thee and pass thee by on the dusty road, taking thee for naught. I wait here weary hours spreading my offerings for thee, while passers-by come and take my flowers, one by one, and my basket is nearly empty.

The morning time is past, and the noon. In the shade of evening my eyes are drowsy with sleep. Men going home glance at me and smile and fill me with shame. I sit like a beggar maid, drawing my skirt over my face, and when they ask me what it is I want, I drop my eyes and answer them not.

Oh, how, indeed, could I tell them that for thee I wait, and that thou hast promised to come? How could I utter for shame that I keep for my dowry this poverty? Ah, I hug this pride in the secret of my heart.

I sit on the grass and gaze upon the sky and dream of the sudden splendour of thy coming—all the lights ablaze, golden pennons flying over thy car, and they at the roadside standing agape, when they see thee come down from thy seat to raise me from the dust, and set at thy side this ragged beggar girl a-tremble with shame and pride, like a creeper in a summer breeze.

But time glides on and still no sound of the wheels of thy chariot. Many a procession passes by with noise and shouts and glamour of glory. Is it only thou who wouldst stand in the shadow silent and behind them all? And only I who would wait and weep and wear out my heart in vain longing?

XLII

Early in the day it was whispered that we should sail in a boat, only thou and I, and never a soul in the world would know of this our pilgrimage to no country and to no end.

In that shoreless ocean, at thy silently listening smile my songs would swell in melodies, free as waves, free from all bondage of words.

Is the time not come yet? Are there works still to do? Lo, the evening has come down upon the shore and in the fading light the seabirds come flying to their nests.

Who knows when the chains will be off, and the boat, like the last glimmer of sunset, vanish into the night?

XLIII

The day was when I did not keep myself in readiness for thee; and entering my heart unbidden even as one of the common crowd, unknown to me, my king, thou didst press the signet of eternity upon many a fleeting moment of my life.

And today when by chance I light upon them and see thy signature, I find they have lain scattered in the dust mixed with the memory of joys and sorrows of my trivial days forgotten.

Thou didst not turn in contempt from my childish play among dust, and the steps that I heard in my playroom are the same that are echoing from star to star.

XLIV

This is my delight, thus to wait and watch at the wayside where shadow chases light and the rain comes in the wake of the summer.

Messengers, with tidings from unknown skies, greet me and speed along the road. My heart is glad within, and the breath of the passing breeze is sweet.

From dawn till dusk I sit here before my door, and I know that of a sudden the happy moment will arrive when I shall see.

In the meanwhile I smile and I sing all alone. In the meanwhile the air is filling with the perfume of promise.

XLV

Have you not heard his silent steps? He comes, comes, ever comes.

Every moment and every age, every day and every night he comes, comes, ever comes. Many a song have I sung in many a mood of mind, but all their notes have always proclaimed, 'He comes, comes, ever comes'.

In the fragrant days of sunny April through the forest path he comes, comes, ever comes.

In the rainy gloom of July nights on the thundering chariot of clouds he comes, comes, ever comes.

In sorrow after sorrow it is his steps that press upon my heart, and it is the golden touch of his feet that makes my joy to shine.

XLVI

I know not from what distant time thou art ever coming nearer to meet me. Thy sun and stars can never keep thee hidden from me for aye.

In many a morning and eve thy footsteps have been heard and thy messenger has come within my heart and called me in secret.

I know not why today my life is all astir, and a feeling of tremulous joy is passing through my heart.

It is as if the time were come to wind up my work, and I feel in the air a faint smell of thy sweet presence.

XLVII

The night is nearly spent waiting for him in vain. I fear lest in the morning he suddenly come to my door when I have fallen asleep wearied out. Oh, friends, leave the way open to him—forbid him not.

If the sound of his steps does not wake me, do not try to rouse me, I pray. I wish not to be called from my sleep by the clamorous choir of birds, by the riot of wind at the festival of morning light. Let me sleep undisturbed even if my lord comes of a sudden to my door.

Ah, my sleep, precious sleep, which only waits for his touch to vanish. Ah, my closed eyes that would open their lids only to the light of his smile when he stands before me like a dream emerging from darkness of sleep.

Let him appear before my sight as the first of all lights and all forms. The first thrill of joy to my awakened soul, let it come from his glance. And let my return to myself be immediate return to him.

XLVIII

The morning sea of silence broke into ripples of bird songs; and the flowers were all merry by the roadside; and the wealth of gold was scattered through the rift of the clouds while we busily went on our way and paid no heed. We sang no glad songs nor played; we went not to the village for barter; we spoke not a word nor smiled; we lingered not on the way. We quickened our pace more and more as the time sped by.

The sun rose to the mid sky and doves cooed in the shade. Withered leaves danced and whirled in the hot air of noon. The shepherd boy drowsed and dreamed in the shadow of the banyan tree, and I laid myself down by the water and stretched my tired limbs on the grass.

My companions laughed at me in scorn; they held their heads high and hurried on; they never looked back nor rested; they vanished in the distant blue haze. They crossed many meadows and hills, and passed through strange, faraway countries. All honour to you, heroic host of the interminable path! Mockery and reproach pricked me to rise, but found no response in me. I gave myself up for lost in the depth of a glad humiliation—in the shadow of a dim delight.

The repose of the sun-embroidered green gloom slowly spread over my heart. I forgot for what I had travelled, and I surrendered my mind without struggle to the maze of shadows and songs.

At last, when I woke from my slumber and opened my eyes, I saw thee standing by me, flooding my sleep with thy smile. How I had feared that the path was long and wearisome, and the struggle to reach thee was hard!

XLIX

You came down from your throne and stood at my cottage door.

I was singing all alone in a corner, and the melody caught your ear. You came down and stood at my cottage door.

Masters are many in your hall, and songs are sung there at all hours. But the simple carol of this novice struck at your love. One plaintive little strain mingled with the great music of the world, and with a flower for a prize you came down and stopped at my cottage door.

L

I had gone a-begging from door to door in the village path, when thy golden chariot appeared in the distance like a gorgeous dream and I wondered who was this King of all kings!

My hopes rose high and methought my evil days were at an end, and I stood waiting for alms to be given unasked and for wealth scattered on all sides in the dust.

The chariot stopped where I stood. Thy glance fell on me and thou camest down with a smile. I felt that the luck of my life had come at last. Then of a sudden thou didst hold out thy right hand and say, 'What hast thou to give to me?'

Ah, what a kingly jest was it to open thy palm to a beggar to beg! I was confused and stood undecided, and then from my wallet I slowly took out the least little grain of corn and gave it to thee.

But how great my surprise when at the day's end I emptied my bag on the floor to find a least little grain of gold among the poor heap! I bitterly wept and wished that I had had the heart to give thee my all.

LI

The night darkened. Our day's works had been done. We thought that the last guest had arrived for the night and the doors in the village were all shut. Only some said the King was to come. We laughed and said, 'No, it cannot be!'

It seemed there were knocks at the door and we said it was nothing but the wind. We put out the lamps and lay down to sleep. Only some said, 'It is the messenger!' We laughed and said, 'No, it must be the wind!'

There came a sound in the dead of the night. We sleepily thought it was the distant thunder. The earth shook, the walls rocked, and it troubled us in our sleep. Only some said it was the sound of wheels. We said in a drowsy murmur, 'No, it must be the rumbling of clouds!'

The night was still dark when the drum sounded. The voice came, 'Wake up! Delay not!' We pressed our hands on our hearts and shuddered with fear. Some said, 'Lo, there is the King's flag!' We stood up on our feet and cried 'There is no time for delay!'

The King has come—but where are lights, where are wreaths? Where is the throne to seat him? Oh, shame! Oh utter shame! Where is the hall, the decorations? Someone has said, 'Vain is this cry! Greet him with empty hands, lead him into thy rooms all bare!'

Open the doors, let the conch-shells be sounded! In the depth of the night has come the King of our dark, dreary house. The thunder roars in the sky. The darkness shudders with lightning. Bring out thy tattered piece of mat and spread it in the courtyard. With the storm has came of a sudden our King of the fearful night.

LII

I thought I should ask of thee—but I dared not—the rose wreath thou hadst on thy neck. Thus I waited for the morning, when thou didst depart, to find a few fragments on the bed. And like a beggar

I searched in the dawn only for a stray petal or two.

Ah me, what is it I find? What token left of thy love? It is no flower, no spices, no vase of perfumed water. It is thy mighty sword, flashing as a flame, heavy as a bolt of thunder. The young light of morning comes through the window and spreads itself upon thy bed. The morning bird twitters and asks, 'Woman, what hast thou got?' No, it is no flower, nor spices, nor vase of perfumed water—it is thy dreadful sword.

I sit and muse in wonder, what gift is this of thine. I can find no place where to hide it. I am ashamed to wear it, frail as I am, and it hurts me when I press it to my bosom. Yet shall I bear in my heart this honour of the burden of pain, this gift of thine.

From now there shall be no fear left for me in this world, and thou shalt be victorious in all my strife. Thou hast left death for my companion and I shall crown him with my life. Thy sword is with me to cut asunder my bonds, and there shall be no fear left for me in the world.

From now I leave off all petty decorations. Lord of my heart, no more shall there be for me waiting and weeping in corners, no more coyness and sweetness of demeanour. Thou hast given me thy sword for adornment. No more doll's decorations for me!

LIII

Beautiful is thy wristlet, decked with stars and cunningly wrought in myriad-coloured jewels. But more beautiful to me thy sword with its curve of lightning like the outspread wings of the divine bird of Vishnu, perfectly poised in the angry red light of the sunset.

It quivers like the one last response of life in ecstasy of pain at the final stroke of death; it shines like the pure flame of being burning up earthly sense with one fierce flash.

Beautiful is thy wristlet, decked with starry gems; but thy sword, O lord of thunder, is wrought with uttermost beauty, terrible to behold or to think of.

LIV

I asked nothing from thee; I uttered not my name to thine ear. When thou took'st thy leave I stood silent. I was alone by the well where the shadow of the tree fell aslant, and the women had gone home with their brown earthen pitchers full to the brim. They called me and shouted, 'Come with us, the morning is wearing on to noon.' But I languidly lingered awhile lost in the midst of vague musings.

I heard not thy steps as thou camest. Thine eyes were sad when they fell on me; thy voice was tired as thou spokest low—'Ah, I am a thirsty traveller.' I started up from my day-dreams and poured water from my jar on thy joined palms. The leaves rustled overhead; the cuckoo sang from the unseen dark, and perfume of babla flowers came from the bend of the road.

I stood speechless with shame when my name thou didst ask. Indeed, what had I done for thee to keep me in remembrance? But the memory that I could give water to thee to allay thy thirst will cling to my heart and enfold it in sweetness. The morning hour is late, the bird sings in weary notes, neem leaves rustle overhead and I sit and think and think.

LV

Languors upon your heart and the slumber is still on your eyes.

Has not the word come to you that the flower is reigning in splendour among thorns? Wake, oh, awaken! Let not the time pass in vain!

At the end of the stony path, in the country of virgin solitude, my friend is sitting all alone. Deceive him not. Wake, oh, awaken!

What if the sky pants and trembles with the heat of the midday sun—what if the burning sand spreads its mantle of thirst

Is there no joy in the deep of your heart? At every footfall of yours, will not the harp of the road break out in sweet music of pain?

LVI

Thus it is that thy joy in me is so full. Thus it is that thou hast come down to me. O thou lord of all heavens, where would be thy love if I were not?

Thou hast taken me as thy partner of all this wealth. In my heart is the endless play of thy delight. In my life thy will is ever taking shape.

And for this, thou who art the King of kings hast decked thyself in beauty to captivate my heart. And for this thy love loses itself in the love of thy lover, and there art thou seen in the perfect union of two.

LVII

Light, my light, the world-filling light, the eye-kissing light, heart-sweetening light!

Ah, the light dances, my darling, at the centre of my life; the light strikes, my darling, the chords of my love; the sky opens, the wind runs wild, laughter passes over the earth.

The butterflies spread their sails on the sea of light. Lilies and jasmines surge up on the crest of the waves of light.

The light is shattered into gold, on every cloud, my darling, and it scatters gems in profusion.

Mirth spreads from leaf to leaf, my darling, and gladness without measure. The heaven's river has drowned its banks and the flood of joy is abroad.

LVIII

Let all the strains of joy mingle in my last song—the joy that makes the earth flow over in the riotous excess of the grass, the joy that sets the twin brothers, life and death, dancing over the wide world, the joy that sweeps in with the tempest, shaking and waking all life with laughter, the joy that sits still with its tears on the open red lotus of pain, and the joy that throws everything it has upon the dust, and knows not a word.

LIX

Yes, I know, this is nothing but thy love, O beloved of my heart—this golden light that dances upon the leaves, these idle clouds sailing across the sky, this passing breeze leaving its coolness upon my forehead.

The morning light has flooded my eyes—this is thy message to my heart. Thy face is bent from above, thy eyes look down on my eyes, and my heart has touched thy feet.

LX

On the seashore of endless worlds children meet. The infinite sky is motionless overhead and the restless water is boisterous. On the seashore of endless worlds the children meet with shouts and dances.

They build their houses with sand and they play with empty shells. With withered leaves they weave their boats and smilingly float them on the vast deep. Children have their play on the seashore of worlds.

They know not how to swim, they know not how to cast nets. Pearl fishers dive for pearls, merchants sail in their ships, while children gather pebbles and scatter them again. They seek not for hidden treasures, they know not how to cast nets.

The sea surges up with laughter and pale gleams the smile of the sea beach. Death-dealing waves sing meaningless ballads to the children, even like a mother while rocking her baby's cradle. The sea plays with children, and pale gleams the smile of the sea beach.

On the seashore of endless worlds children meet. Tempest roams in the pathless sky, ships get wrecked in the trackless water, death is abroad and children play. On the seashore of endless worlds is the great meeting of children.

LXI

The sleep that flits on baby's eyes—does anybody know from where it comes? Yes, there is a rumour that it has its dwelling where, in the fairy village among shadows of the forest dimly lit with glow-worms, there hang two timid buds of enchantment. From there it comes to kiss baby's eyes.

The smile that flickers on baby's lips when he sleeps—does anybody know where it was born? Yes there is a rumour that a young pale beam of a crescent moon touched the edge of a vanishing autumn cloud, and there the smile was first born in the dream of a dew-washed morning—the smile that flickers on baby's lips when he sleeps.

The sweet, soft freshness that blooms on baby's limbs—does anybody know where it was hidden so long? Yes, when the mother was a young girl it lay pervading her heart in tender and silent mystery of love—the sweet, soft freshness that has bloomed on baby's limbs.

LXII

When I bring to you coloured toys, my child, I understand why there is such a play of colours on clouds, on water, and why flowers are painted, in tints—when I give coloured toys to you, my child.

When I sing to make you dance I truly know why there is music in leaves, and why waves send their chorus of voices to the heart of the listening earth—when I sing to make you dance.

When I bring sweet things to your greedy hands I know why there is honey in the cup of the flower and why fruits are secretly filled with sweet juice—when I bring sweet things to your greedy hands.

When I kiss your face to make you smile, my darling, I surely understand what the pleasure is that streams from the sky in morning light, and what delight that is which the summer breeze brings to my body—when I kiss you to make you smile.

LXIII

Thou hast made me known to friends whom I knew not. Thou hast given me seats in homes not my own. Thou hast brought the distant near and made a brother of the stranger.

I am uneasy at heart when I have to leave my accustomed shelter; I forget that there abides the old in the new, and that there also thou abidest.

Through birth and death, in this world or in others, wherever thou leadest me it is thou, the same, the one companion of my endless life whoever linkest my heart with bonds of joy to the unfamiliar.

When one knows thee, then alien there is none, then no door is shut. Oh, grant me my prayer that I may never lose the bliss of the touch of the one in the play of the many.

LXIV

On the slope of the desolate river among tall grasses I asked her, 'Maiden, where do you go, shading your lamp with your mantle? My house is all dark and lonesome, lend me your light!' She raised her dark eyes for a moment and looked at my face through the dusk. 'I have come to the river,' she said, 'to float my lamp on the stream when the daylight wanes in the west.' I stood alone among tall grasses and watched the timid flame of her lamp uselessly drifting in the tide.

In the silence of gathering night I asked her, 'Maiden, your lights are all lit—then where do you go with your lamp? My house is all dark and lonesome,—lend me your light.' She raised her dark eyes on my face and stood for a moment doubtful. 'I have come,' she said at last, 'to dedicate my lamp to the sky.' I stood and watched her light uselessly burning in the void.

In the moonless gloom of midnight I asked her, 'Maiden, what is your quest, holding the lamp near your heart? My house is all dark and lonesome,—lend me your light.' She stopped for a minute and thought and gazed at my face in the dark. 'I have brought my light,' she said, 'to join the carnival of lamps.' I stood and watched her little lamp uselessly lost among lights.

LXV

What divine drink wouldst thou have, my God, from this overflowing cup of my life?

My poet, is it thy delight to see thy creation through my eyes and to stand at the portals of my ears silently to listen to thine own eternal harmony?

Thy world is weaving words in my mind and thy joy is adding music to them. Thou givest thyself to me in love and then feelest thine own entire sweetness in me.

LXVI

She who ever had remained in the depth of my being, in the twilight of gleams and of glimpses; she who never opened her veils in the morning light, will be my last gift to thee, my God, folded in my final song.

Words have wooed yet failed to win her; persuasion has stretched to her its eager arms in vain.

I have roamed from country to country keeping her in the core of my heart, and around her have risen and fallen the growth and decay of my life.

Over my thoughts and actions, my slumbers and dreams, she reigned yet dwelled alone and apart.

Many a man knocked at my door and asked for her and turned away in despair.

There was none in the world who ever saw her face to face, and she remained in her loneliness waiting for thy recognition.

LXVII

Thou art the sky and thou art the nest as well. O thou beautiful, there in the nest it is thy love that encloses the soul with colours and sounds and odours. There comes the morning with the golden basket in her right hand bearing the wreath of beauty, silently to crown the earth.

And there comes the evening over the lonely meadows deserted by herds, through trackless paths, carrying cool draughts of peace in her golden pitcher from the western ocean of rest.

But there, where spreads the infinite sky for the soul to take her flight in, reigns the stainless white radiance. There is no day nor night, nor form nor colour, and never, never a word.

LXVIII

Thy sunbeam comes upon this earth of mine with arms outstretched and stands at my door the livelong day to carry back to thy feet clouds made of my tears and sighs and songs.

With fond delight thou wrappest about thy starry breast that mantle of misty cloud, turning it into numberless shapes and folds and colouring it with hues everchanging.

It is so light and so fleeting, tender and tearful and dark, that is why thou lovest it, O thou spotless and serene. And that is why it may cover thy awful white light with its pathetic shadows.

LXIX

The same stream of life that runs through my veins night and day runs through the world and dances in rhythmic measures.

It is the same life that shoots in joy through the dust of the earth in numberless blades of grass and breaks into tumultuous waves of leaves and flowers.

It is the same life that is rocked in the ocean-cradle of birth and of death, in ebb and in flow. I feel my limbs are made glorious by the touch of this world of life. And my pride is from the life-throb of ages dancing in my blood this moment.

LXX

Is it beyond thee to be glad with the gladness of this rhythm? To be tossed and lost and broken in the whirl of this fearful joy?

All things rush on, they stop not, they look not behind, no power can hold them back, they rush on.

Keeping steps with that restless, rapid music, seasons come dancing and pass away—colours, tunes, and perfumes pour in endless cascades in the abounding joy that scatters and gives up and dies every moment.

LXXI

That I should make much of myself and turn it on all sides, thus casting coloured shadows on thy radiance—such is thy maya. Thou settest a barrier in thine own being and then callest thy severed self in myriad notes. This thy self separation has taken body in me.

The poignant song is echoed through all the sky in many-coloured teirs and smiles, alarms and hopes; waves rise up and sink again, dreams break and form. In me is thy own defeat of self.

This screen that thou hast raised is painted with innumerable figures with the brush of the night and the day. Behind it thy seat is woven in wondrous mysteries of curves, casting away all barren lines of straightness.

The great pageant of thee and me has overspread the sky. With the tune of thee and me all the air is vibrant, and all ages pass with the hiding and seeking of thee and me.

LXXII

He it is, the innermost one, who awakens my being with his deep hidden touches.

He it is who puts his enchantment upon these eyes and joyfully plays on the chords of my heart in varied cadence of pleasure and pain.

He it is who weaves the web of this maya in evanescent hues of gold and silver, blue and green, and lets peep out through the folds his feet, at whose touch I forget myself.

Days come and ages pass, and it is ever he who moves my heart in many a name, in many a guise, in many a rapture of joy and of sorrow.

LXXIII

Deliverance is not for me in renunciation. I feel the embrace of freedom in a thousand bonds of delight.

Thou ever pourest for me the fresh draught of thy wine of various colours and fragrance, filling this earthen vessel to the brim.

My world will light its hundred different lamps with thy flame and place them before the altar of thy temple.

No, I will never shut the doors of my senses. The delights of sight and hearing and touch will bear thy delight.

Yes, all my illusions will burn into illumination of joy, and all my desires ripen into fruits of love.

LXXIV

The day is no more, the shadow is upon the earth. It is time that I go to the stream to fill my pitcher.

The evening air is eager with the sad music of the water. Ah, it calls me out into the dusk. In the lonely lane there is no passer-by, the wind is up, the ripples are rampant in the river.

I know not if I shall come back home. I know not whom I shall chance to meet. There at the fording in the little boat the unknown man plays upon his lute.

LXXV

Thy gifts to us mortals fulfil all our needs and yet run back to thee undiminished.

The river has its everyday work to do and hastens through fields and hamlets; yet its incessant stream winds towards the washing of thy feet.

The flower sweetens the air with its perfume; yet its last service is to offer itself to thee.

Thy worship does not impoverish the world. From the words of the poet men take what meanings please them; yet their last meaning points to thee.

LXXVI

Day after day, O lord of my life, shall I stand before thee face to face. With folded hands, O lord of all worlds, shall I stand before thee face to face.

Under thy great sky in solitude and silence, with humble heart shall I stand before thee face to face.

In this laborious world of thine, tumultuous with toil and with struggle, among hurrying crowds shall I stand before thee face to face.

And when my work shall be done in this world, O King of kings, alone and speechless shall I stand before thee face to face.

LXXVII

I know thee as my God and stand apart—I do not know thee as my own and come closer. I know thee as my father and bow before thy feet—I do not grasp thy hand as my friend's.

I stand not where thou comest down and ownest thyself as mine, there to clasp thee to my heart and take thee as my comrade.

Thou art the Brother amongst my brothers, but I heed them not; I divide not my earnings with them, thus sharing my all with thee.

In pleasure and in pain I stand not by the side of men, and thus stand by thee. I shrink to give up my life, and thus do not plunge into the great waters of life.

LXXVIII

When the creation was new and all the stars shone in their first splendour, the gods held their assembly in the sky and sang, 'Oh, the picture of perfection! The joy unalloyed!'

But one cried of a sudden—'It seems that somewhere there is a break in the chain of light and one of the stars has been lost.'

The golden string of their harp snapped, their song stopped, and they cried in dismay—'Yes, that lost star was the best, she was the glory of all heavens!'

From that day the search is unceasing for her, and the cry goes on from one to the other that in her the world has lost its one joy!

Only in the deepest silence of night the stars smile and whisper among themselves—"Vain is this seeking! Unbroken perfection is over all!"

LXXIX

If it is not my portion to meet thee in this my life then let me ever feel that I have missed thy sight—let me not forget for a moment, let me carry the pangs of this sorrow in my dreams and in my wakeful hours.

As my days pass in the crowded market of this world and my hands grow full with the daily profits, let me ever feel that I have gained nothing—let me not forget for a moment, let me carry the pangs of this sorrow in my dreams and in my wakeful hours.

When I sit by the roadside, tired and panting, when I spread my bed low in the dust, let me ever feel that the long journey is still before me—let me not forget for a moment, let me carry the pangs of this sorrow in my dreams and in my wakeful hours.

When my rooms have been decked out and the flutes sound and the laughter there is loud, let me ever feel that I have not invited thee to my house—let me not forget for a moment, let me carry the pangs of this sorrow in my dreams and in my wakeful hours.

LXXX

I am like a remnant of a cloud of autumn uselessly roaming in the sky, O my sun ever-glorious! Thy touch has not yet melted my vapour, making me one with thy light, and thus I count months and years separated from thee.

If this be thy wish and if this be thy play, then take this fleeting emptiness of mine, paint it with colours, gild it with gold, float it on the wanton wind and spread it in varied wonders.

And again when it shall be thy wish to end this play at night, I shall melt and vanish away in the dark, or it may be in a smile of the white morning, in a coolness of purity transparent.

LXXXI

On many an idle day have I grieved over lost time. But it is never lost, my lord. Thou hast taken every moment of my life in thine own hands.

Hidden in the heart of things thou art nourishing seeds into sprouts, buds into blossoms, and ripening flowers into fruitfulness.

I was tired and sleeping on my idle bed and imagined all work had ceased. In the morning I woke up and found my garden full with wonders of flowers.

LXXXII

Time is endless in thy hands, my lord. There is none to count thy minutes.

Days and nights pass and ages bloom and fade like flowers. Thou knowest how to wait.

Thy centuries follow each other perfecting a small wild flower.

We have no time to lose, and having no time we must scramble for our chances. We are too poor to be late.

And thus it is that time goes by while I give it to every querulous man who claims it, and thine altar is empty of all offerings to the last.

At the end of the day I hasten in fear lest thy gate be shut; but I find that yet there is time.

LXXXIII

Mother, I shall weave a chain of pearls for thy neck with my tears of sorrow.

The stars have wrought their anklets of light to deck thy feet, but mine will hang upon thy breast.

Wealth and fame come from thee and it is for thee to give or to withhold them. But this my sorrow is absolutely mine own, and when I bring it to thee as my offering thou rewardest me with thy grace.

LXXXIV

It is the pang of separation that spreads throughout the world and gives birth to shapes innumerable in the infinite sky.

It is this sorrow of separation that gazes in silence all night from star to star and becomes lyric among rustling leaves in rainy darkness of July.

It is this overspreading pain that deepens into loves and desires, into sufferings and joys in human homes; and this it is that ever melts and flows in songs through my poet's heart.

LXXXV

When the warriors came out first from their master's hall, where had they hid their power? Where were their armour and their arms?

They looked poor and helpless, and the arrows were showered upon them on the day they came out from their master's hall.

When the warriors marched back again to their master's hall, where did they hide their power?

They had dropped the sword and dropped the bow and the arrow; peace was on their foreheads, and they had left the fruits of their life behind them on the day they marched back again to their master's hall.

LXXXVI

Death, thy servant, is at my door. He has crossed the unknown sea and brought thy call to my home.

The night is dark and my heart is fearful—yet I will take up the lamp, open my gates and bow to him my welcome. It is thy messenger who stands at my door.

I will worship him with folded hands, and with tears. I will worship him placing at his feet the treasure of my heart.

He will go back with his errand done, leaving a dark shadow on my morning; and in my desolate home only my forlorn self will remain as my last offering to thee.

LXXXVII

In desperate hope I go and search for her in all the corners of my room; I find her not.

My house is small and what once has gone from it can never be regained.

But infinite is thy mansion, my lord, and seeking her I have come to thy door.

I stand under the golden canopy of thine evening sky and I lift my eager eyes to thy face.

I have come to the brink of eternity from which nothing can vanish—no hope, no happiness, no vision of a face seen through tears.

Oh, dip my emptied life into that ocean, plunge it into the deepest fullness. Let me for once feel that lost sweet touch in the allness of the universe.

LXXXVIII

Deity of the ruined temple! The broken strings of Vina sing no more your praise. The bells in the evening proclaim not your time of worship. The air is still and silent about you.

In your desolate dwelling comes the vagrant spring breeze. It brings the tidings of flowers—the flowers that for your worship are offered no more.

Your worshipper of old wanders ever longing for favour still refused. In the eventide, when fires and shadows mingle with the gloom of dust, he wearily comes back to the ruined temple with hunger in his heart.

Many a festival day comes to you in silence, deity of the ruined temple. Many a night of worship goes away with lamp unlit.

Many new images are built by masters of cunning art and carried to the holy stream of oblivion when their time is come.

Only the deity of the ruined temple remains unworshipped in deathless neglect.

LXXXIX

No more noisy, loud words from me—such is my master's will. Henceforth I deal in whispers. The speech of my heart will lie carried on in murmurings of a song.

Men hasten to the King's market. All the buyers and sellers are there. But I have my untimely leave in the middle of the day, in the thick of work.

Let then the flowers come out in my garden, though it is not their time; and let the midday bees strike up their lazy hum.

Full many an hour have I spent in the strife of the good and the evil, but now it is the pleasure of my playmate of the empty days to draw my heart on to him; and I know not why is this sudden call to what useless inconsequence!

XC

On the day when death will knock at thy door what wilt thou offer to him?

Oh, I will set before my guest the full vessel of my life—I will never let him go with empty hands.

All the sweet vintage of all my autumn days and summer nights, all the earnings and gleanings of my busy life will I place before him at the close of my days when death will knock at my door.

XCI

O thou the last fulfilment of life, Death, my death, come and whisper to me!

Day after day have I kept watch for thee; for thee have I borne the joys and pangs of life.

All that I am, that I have, that I hope, and all my love have ever flowed towards thee in depth of secrecy. One final glance from thine eyes and my life will be ever thine own.

The flowers have been woven and the garland is ready for the bridegroom. After the wedding the bride shall leave her home and meet her lord alone in the solitude of night.

XCII

I know that the day will come when my sight of this earth shall be lost, and life will take its leave in silence, drawing the last curtain over my eyes.

Yet stars will watch at night, and morning rise as before, and hours heave like sea waves casting up pleasures and pains.

When I think of this end of my moments, the barrier of the moments breaks and I see by the light of death thy world with its careless treasures. Rare is its lowliest seat, rare is its meanest of lives.

Things that I longed for in vain and things that I got—let them pass. Let me but truly possess the things that I ever spurned and overlooked.

XCIII

I have got my leave. Bid me farewell, my brothers! I bow to you all and take my departure.

Here I give back the keys of my door—and I give up all claims to my house. I only ask for last kind words from you.

We were neighbours for long, but I received more than I could give. Now the day has dawned and the lamp that lit my dark corner is out. A summons has come and I am ready for my journey.

XCIV

At this time of my parting, wish me good luck, my friends! The sky is flushed with the dawn and my path lies beautiful.

Ask not what I have with me to take there. I start on my journey with empty hands and expectant heart. I shall put on my wedding garland. Mine is not the red-brown dress of the traveller, and though there are dangers on the way I have no fear in my mind.

The evening star will come out when my voyage is done and the plaintive notes of the twilight melodies be struck up from the King's gateway.

XCV

I was not aware of the moment when I first crossed the threshold of this life.

What was the power that made me open out into this vast mystery like a bud in the forest at—midnight?

When in the morning I looked upon the light I felt in a moment that I was no stranger in this world, that the inscrutable without name and form had taken me in its arms in the form of my own mother.

Even so, in death the same unknown will appear as ever known to me. And because I love this life, I know I shall love death as well.

The child cries out when from the right breast the mother takes it away, in the very next moment to find in the left one its consolation.

XCVI

When I go from hence let this be my parting word, that what I have seen is unsurpassable.

I have tasted of the hidden honey of this lotus that expands on the ocean of light, and thus am I blessed—let this be my parting word.

In this playhouse of infinite forms I have had my play and here have I caught sight of him that is formless.

My whole body and my limbs have thrilled with his touch who is beyond touch; and if the end comes here, let it come—let this be my parting word.

XCVII

When my play was with thee I never questioned who thou wert. I knew nor shyness nor fear, my life was boisterous.

In the early morning thou wouldst call me from my sleep like my own comrade and lead me running from glade to glade.

On those days I never cared to know the meaning of songs thou sangest to me. Only my voice took up the tunes, and my heart danced in their cadence.

Now, when the playtime is over, what is this sudden sight that is come upon me? The world with eyes bent upon thy feet stands in awe with all its silent stars.

XCVIII

I will deck thee with trophies, garlands of my defeat. It is never in my power to escape unconquered.

I surely know my pride will go to the wall, my life will burst its bonds in exceeding pain, and my empty heart will sob out in music like a hollow reed, and the stone will melt in tears.

I surely know the hundred petals of a lotus will not remain closed forever and the secret recess of its honey will be bared.

From the blue sky an eye shall gaze upon me and summon me in silence. Nothing will be left for me, nothing whatever, and utter death shall I receive at thy feet.

XCIX

When I give up the helm I know that the time has come for thee to take it. What there is to do will be instantly done. Vain is this struggle.

Then take away your hands and silently put up with your defeat, my heart, and think it your good fortune to sit perfectly still where you are placed.

These my lamps are blown out at every little puff of wind, and trying to light them I forget all else again and again.

But I shall be wise this time and wait in the dark, spreading my mat on the floor; and whenever it is thy pleasure, my lord, come silently and take thy seat here.

C

I dive down into the depth of the ocean of forms, hoping to gain the perfect pearl of the formless.

No more sailing from harbour to harbour with this my weather-beaten boat. The days are long past when my sport was to be tossed on waves.

And now I am eager to die into the deathless.

Into the audience hall by the fathomless abyss where swells up the music of toneless strings I shall take this harp of my life.

I shall tune it to the notes of forever, and, when it has sobbed out its last utterance, lay down my silent harp at the feet of the silent.

CL

Ever in my life have I sought thee with my songs. It was they who led me from door to door, and with them have I felt about me, searching and touching my world.

It was my songs that taught me all the lessons I ever learnt; they showed me secret paths, they brought before my sight many a star on the horizon of my heart.

They guided me all the day long to the mysteries of the country of pleasure and pain, and, at last, to what palace gate have they brought me in the evening at the end of my journey?

CLI

I boasted among men that I had known you. They see your pictures in all works of mine. They come and ask me, 'Who is he?' I know not how to answer them. I say, 'Indeed, I cannot tell.' They blame me and they go away in scorn. And you sit there smiling.

I put my tales of you into lasting songs. The secret gushes out from my heart. They come and ask me 'Tell me all your meanings.' I know not how to answer them. I say, 'Ah, who knows what they mean!' They smile and go away in utter scorn. And you sit there smiling.

CLII

In one salutation to thee, my God, let all my sense spread out and touch this world at thy feet.

Like a rain-cloud of July hung low with its burden of unshed showers let all my mind bend down at thy door in one salutation to thee.

Let all my songs gather together their diverse strains into a single current and flow to a sea of silence in one salutation to thee.

Like a flock of homesick cranes flying night and day back to their mountain nests let all my life take its voyage to its eternal home in one salutation to thee.

HOME AND THE WORLD

CHAPTER ONE

BIMALA'S STORY

I

Mother, today there comes back to mind the vermilion mark[1] at the parting of your hair, the sari[2] which you used to wear, with its wide red border, and those wonderful eyes of yours, full of depth and peace. They came at the start of my life's journey, like the first streak of dawn, giving me golden provision to carry me on my way.

The sky which gives light is blue, and my mother's face was dark, but she had the radiance of holiness, and her beauty would put to shame all the vanity of the beautiful.

Everyone says that I resemble my mother. In my childhood I used to resent this. It made me angry with my mirror. I thought that it was God's unfairness which was wrapped round my limbs—that my dark features were not my due, but had come to me by some misunderstanding. All that remained for me to ask of my God in reparation was, that I might grow up to be a model of what woman should be, as one reads it in some epic poem.

When the proposal came for my marriage, an astrologer was sent, who consulted my palm and said, 'This girl has good signs. She will become an ideal wife.'

And all the women who heard it said, 'No wonder, for she resembles her mother.'

I was married into a Rajah's house. When I was a child, I was quite familiar with the description of the Prince of the fairy story. But my husband's face was not of a kind that one's imagination would place

---

[1] The mark of Hindu wifehood and the symbol of all the devotion that it implies.

[2] The sari is the dress of the Hindu woman.

in fairyland. It was dark, even as mine was. The feeling of shrinking, which I had about my own lack of physical beauty, was lifted a little; at the same time a touch of regret was left lingering in my heart.

But when the physical appearance evades the scrutiny of our senses and enters the sanctuary of our hearts, then it can forget itself. I know, from my childhood's experience, how devotion is beauty itself, in its inner aspect. When my mother arranged the different fruits, carefully peeled by her own loving hands, on the white stone plate, and gently waved her fan to drive away the flies while my father sat down to his meals, her service would lose itself in a beauty which passed beyond outward forms. Even in my infancy I could feel its power. It transcended all debates, or doubts, or calculations, it was pure music.

I distinctly remember after my marriage, when, early in the morning, I would cautiously and silently get up and take the dust[1] of my husband's feet without waking him, how at such moments I could feel the vermilion mark upon my forehead shining out like the morning star.

One day, he happened to awake, and smiled as he asked me, 'What is that, Bimala? What...*are*...you doing?'

I can never forget the shame of being detected by him. He might possibly have thought that I was trying to earn merit secretly. But no, no! That had nothing to do with merit. It was my woman's heart, which must worship in order to love.

My father-in-law's house was old in dignity from the days of the *Badshahs*. Some of its manners were of the Moguls and Pathans, some of its customs of Manu and Parashar. But my husband was absolutely modern. He was the first of the house to go through a college course and take his M.A. degree. His elder brother had died young, of drink, and had left no children. My husband did not drink and was not given to dissipation. So foreign to the family was this abstinence, that to many it hardly seemed decent! Purity, they imagined, was only becoming in those on whom fortune had not smiled. It is the moon which has room for stains, not the stars.

---

[1] Taking the dust of the feet is a formal offering of reverence and is done by lightly touching the feet of the revered one and then one's own head with the same hand. The wife does not ordinarily do this to the husband.

My husband's parents had died long ago, and his old grandmother was mistress of the house. My husband was the apple of her eye, the jewel on her bosom. And so he never met with much difficulty in overstepping any of the ancient usages. When he brought in Miss Gilby, to teach me and be my companion, he stuck to his resolve in spite of the poison secreted by all the wagging tongues at home and outside.

My husband had then just got through his B.A. examination and was reading for his M.A. degree; so he had to stay in Calcutta to attend college. He used to write to me almost every day, a few lines only, and simple words, but his bold, round handwriting would look up into my face, oh, so tenderly! I kept his letters in a sandalwood box and covered them every day with the flowers I gathered in the garden.

At that time the Prince of the fairy tale had faded, like the moon in the morning light. I had the Prince of my real world enthroned in my heart. I was his queen. I had my seat by his side. But my real joy was, that my true place was at his feet.

Since then, I have been educated, and introduced to the modern age in its own language, and therefore these words that I write seem to blush with shame in their prose setting. Except for my acquaintance with this modern standard of life, I should know, quite naturally, that just as my being born a woman was not in my own hands, so the element of devotion in woman's love is not like a hackneyed passage quoted from a romantic poem to be piously written down in round hand in a school girl's copy-book.

But my husband would not give me any opportunity for worship. That was his greatness. They are cowards who claim absolute devotion from their wives as their right; that is a humiliation for both.

His love for me seemed to overflow my limits by its flood of wealth and service. But my necessity was more for giving than for receiving; for love is a vagabond, who can make his flowers bloom in the wayside dust, better than in the crystal jars kept in the drawing room.

My husband could not break completely with the old time traditions which prevailed in our family. It was difficult, therefore, for us to meet at any hour of the day we pleased.[1] I knew exactly the time

---

[1] It would not be reckoned good form for the husband to be continually going

that he could come to me, and therefore our meeting had all the care of loving preparation. It was like the rhyming of a poem; it had to come through the path of the metre.

After finishing the day's work and taking my afternoon bath, I would do up my hair and renew my vermilion mark and put on my sari, carefully crinkled; and then, bringing back my body and mind from all distractions of household duties, I would dedicate it at this special hour, with special ceremonies, to one individual. That time, each day, with him was short; but it was infinite.

My husband used to say, that man and wife are equal in love because of their equal claim on each other. I never argued the point with him, but my heart said that devotion never stands in the way of true equality; it only raises the level of the ground of meeting. Therefore, the joy of the higher equality remains permanent; it never slides down to the vulgar level of triviality.

My beloved, it was worthy of you that you never expected worship from me. But if you had accepted it, you would have done me a real service. You showed your love by decorating me, by educating me, by giving me what I asked for, and what I did not. I have seen what depth of love there was in your eyes when you gazed at me. I have known the secret sigh of pain you suppressed in your love for me. You loved my body as if it were a flower of paradise. You loved my whole nature as if it had been given you by some rare providence.

Such lavish devotion made me proud to think that the wealth was all my own which drove you to my gate. But vanity such as this only checks the flow of free surrender in a woman's love. When I sit on the queen's throne and claim homage, then the claim only goes on magnifying itself; it is never satisfied. Can there be any real happiness for a woman in merely feeling that she has power over a man? To surrender one's pride in devotion is woman's only salvation.

It comes back to me today how, in the days of our happiness, the fires of envy sprung up all around us. That was only natural, for had I not stepped into my good fortune by a mere chance, and without deserving it? But providence does not allow a run of luck to last

---

into the zenana, except at particular hours for meals or rest.

forever, unless its debt of honour be fully paid, day by day, through many a long day, and thus made secure. God may grant us gifts, but the merit of being able to take and hold them must be our own. Alas for the boons that slip through unworthy hands!

My husband's grandmother and mother were both renowned for their beauty. And my widowed sister-in-law was also of a beauty rarely to be seen. When, in turn, fate left them desolate, the grandmother vowed she would not insist on having beauty for her remaining grandson when he married. Only the auspicious marks with which I was endowed gained me an entry into this family—otherwise, I had no claim to be here.

In this house of luxury, but few of its ladies had received their meed of respect. They had, however, got used to the ways of the family, and managed to keep their heads above water, buoyed up by their dignity as Ranis of an ancient house, in spite of their daily tears being drowned in the foam of wine, and by the tinkle of the 'dancing girls' anklets. Was the credit due to me that my husband did not touch liquor, nor squander his manhood in the markets of woman's flesh? What charm did I know to soothe the wild and wandering mind of men? It was my good luck, nothing else. For fate proved utterly callous to my sister-in-law. Her festivity died out, while yet the evening was early, leaving the light of her beauty shining in vain over empty halls—burning and burning, with no accompanying music!

His sister-in-law affected a contempt for my husband's modern notions. How absurd to keep the family ship, laden with all the weight of its time-honoured glory, sailing under the colours of his slip of a girl-wife alone! Often have I felt the lash of scorn. 'A thief who had stolen a husband's love!' 'A sham hidden in the shamelessness of her new-fangled finery!' The many-coloured garments of modern fashion with which my husband loved to adorn me roused jealous wrath. 'Is not she ashamed to make a show-window of herself—and with her looks, too!'

My husband was aware of all this, but his gentleness knew no bounds. He used to implore me to forgive her.

I remember I once told him, 'Women's minds are so petty, so crooked!' 'Like the feet of Chinese women,' he replied. 'Has not the pressure of society cramped them into pettiness and crookedness? They are but pawns of the fate which gambles with them. What responsibility have they of their own?'

My sister-in-law never failed to get from my husband whatever she wanted. He did not stop to consider whether her requests were right or reasonable. But what exasperated me most was that she was not grateful for this. I had promised my husband that I would not talk back at her, but this set me raging all the more, inwardly. I used to feel that goodness has a limit, which, if passed, somehow seems to make men cowardly. Shall I tell the whole truth? I have often wished that my husband had the manliness to be a little less good.

My sister-in-law, the Bara Rani,[1] was still young and had no pretensions to saintliness. Rather, her talk and jest and laugh inclined to be forward. The young maids with whom she surrounded herself were also impudent to a degree. But there was none to gainsay her—for was not this the custom of the house? It seemed to me that my good fortune in having a stainless husband was a special eyesore to her. He, however, felt more the sorrow of her lot than the defects of her character.

II

My husband was very eager to take me out of purdah.[2]

One day I said to him, 'What do I want with the outside world?'

'The outside world may want you,' he replied.

'If the outside world has got on so long without me, it may go on for some time longer. It need not pine to death for want of me.'

'Let it perish, for all I care! That is not troubling me. I am thinking

---

[1] *Bara* = Senior; *Chota* = Junior. In joint families of rank, though the widows remain entitled only to a life-interest in their husbands' share, their rank remains to them according to seniority, and the titles 'Senior' and 'Junior' continue to distinguish the elder and younger branches, even though the junior branch be the one in power.

[2] The seclusion of the zenana, and all the customs peculiar to it, are designated by the general term 'Purdah', which means Screen.

about myself.'

'Oh, indeed. Tell me what about yourself?'

My husband was silent, with a smile.

I knew his way, and protested at once, 'No, no, you are not going to run away from me like that! I want to have this out with you.'

'Can one ever finish a subject with words?'

'Do stop speaking in riddles. Tell me...'

'What I want is, that I should have you, and you should have me, more fully in the outside world. That is where we are still in debt to each other.'

'Is anything wanting, then, in the love we have here at home?'

'Here you are wrapped up in me. You know neither what you have, nor what you want.'

'I cannot bear to hear you talk like this.'

'I would have you come into the heart of the outer world and meet reality. Merely going on with your household duties, living all your life in the world of household conventions and the drudgery of household tasks—you were not made for that! If we meet, and recognize each other, in the real world, then only will our love be true.'

'If there be any drawback here to our full recognition of each other, then I have nothing to say. But as for myself, I feel no want.'

'Well, even if the drawback is only on my side, why shouldn't you help to remove it?'

Such discussions repeatedly occurred. One day he said, 'The greedy man who is fond of his fish stew has no compunction in cutting up the fish according to his need. But the man who loves the fish wants to enjoy it in the water; and if that is impossible he waits on the bank; and even if he comes back home without a sight of it he has the consolation of knowing that the fish is all right. Perfect gain is the best of all; but if that is impossible, then the next best gain is perfect losing.'

I never liked the way my husband had of talking on this subject, but that is not the reason why I refused to leave the zenana. His grandmother was still alive. My husband had filled more than a hundred and twenty per cent of the house with the twentieth century, against her taste; but she had borne it uncomplaining. She would have borne it, likewise, if the daughter-in-law[1] of the Rajah's house had left its seclusion. She was even prepared for this happening. But I did not consider it important enough to give her the pain of it. I have read in books that we are called 'caged birds'. I cannot speak for others, but I had so much in this cage of mine that there was not room for it in the universe—at least that is what I then felt.

The grandmother, in her old age, was very fond of me. At the bottom of her fondness was the thought that, with the conspiracy of favourable stars which attended me, I had been able to attract my husband's love. Were not men naturally inclined to plunge downwards? None of the others, for all their beauty, had been able to prevent their husbands going headlong into the burning depths which consumed and destroyed them. She believed that I had been the means of extinguishing this fire, so deadly to the men of the family. So she kept me in the shelter of her bosom, and trembled if I was in the least bit unwell.

His grandmother did not like the dresses and ornaments my husband brought from European shops to deck me with. But she reflected, 'Men will have some absurd hobby or other, which is sure to be expensive. It is no use trying to check their extravagance; one is glad enough if they stop short of ruin. If my Nikhil had not been busy dressing up his wife there is no knowing whom else he might have spent his money on!' So whenever any new dress of mine arrived, she used to send for my husband and make merry over it.

Thus it came about that it was her taste which changed. The influence of the modern age fell so strongly upon her, that her evenings refused to pass if I did not tell her stories out of English books.

After his grandmother's death, my husband wanted me to go and live with him in Calcutta. But I could not bring myself to do that. Was not this our House, which she had kept under her sheltering care through all her trials and troubles? Would not a curse come upon me if I deserted it and went off to town? This was the thought that kept me back, as her empty seat reproachfully looked up at me. That noble lady had come into this house at the age of eight, and had died in her

---

[1]The prestige of the daughter-in-law is of the first importance in a Hindu household of rank [Trans.].

seventy-ninth year. She had not spent a happy life. Fate had hurled shaft after shaft at her breast, only to draw out more and more the imperishable spirit within. This great house was hallowed with her tears. What should I do in the dust of Calcutta, away from it?

My husband's idea was that this would be a good opportunity for leaving to my sister-in-law the consolation of ruling over the household, giving our life, at the same time, more room to branch out in Calcutta. That is just where my difficulty came in. She had worried my life out, she ill brooked my husband's happiness, and for this she was to be rewarded! And what of the day when we should have to come back here? Should I then get back my seat at the head?

'What do you want with that seat?' my husband would say. 'Are there not more precious things in life?'

Men never understand these things. They have their nests in the outside world; they little know the whole of what the household stands for. In these matters they ought to follow womanly guidance. Such were my thoughts at that time.

I felt the real point was, that one ought to stand up for one's rights. To go away, and leave everything in the hands of the enemy, would be nothing short of owning defeat.

But why did not my husband compel me to go with him to Calcutta? I know the reason. He did not use his power, just because he had it.

III

If one had to fill in, little by little, the gap between day and night, it would take an eternity to do it. But the sun rises and the darkness is dispelled—a moment is sufficient to overcome an infinite distance.

One day there came the new era of *Swadeshi*[1] in Bengal; but as to how it happened, we had no distinct vision. There was no gradual slope connecting the past with the present. For that reason, I imagine, the new epoch came in like a flood, breaking down the dykes and

---

[1] The Nationalist movement, which began more as an economic than a political one, having as its main object the encouragement of indigenous industries [Trans.].

sweeping all our prudence and fear before it. We had no time even to think about, or understand, what had happened, or what was about to happen.

My sight and my mind, my hopes and my desires, became red with the passion of this new age. Though, up to this time, the walls of the home—which was the ultimate world to my mind—remained unbroken, yet I stood looking over into the distance, and I heard a voice from the far horizon, whose meaning was not perfectly clear to me, but whose call went straight to my heart.

From the time my husband had been a college student he had been trying to get the things required by our people produced in our own country. There are plenty of date trees in our district. He tried to invent an apparatus for extracting the juice and boiling it into sugar and treacle. I heard that it was a great success, only it extracted more money than juice. After a while he came to the conclusion that our attempts at reviving our industries were not succeeding for want of a bank of our own. He was, at the time, trying to teach me political economy. This alone would not have done much harm, but he also took it into his head to teach his countrymen ideas of thrift, so as to pave the way for a bank; and then he actually started a small bank. Its high rate of interest, which made the villagers flock so enthusiastically to put in their money, ended by swamping the bank altogether.

The old officers of the estate felt troubled and frightened. There was jubilation in the enemy's camp. Of all the family, only my husband's grandmother remained unmoved. She would scold me, saying, 'Why are you all plaguing him so? Is it the fate of the estate that is worrying you? How many times have I seen this estate in the hands of the court receiver! Are men like women? Men are born spendthrifts and only know how to waste. Look here, child, count yourself fortunate that your husband is not wasting himself as well!'

My husband's list of charities was a long one. He would assist to the bitter end of utter failure anyone who wanted to invent a new loom or rice-husking machine. But what annoyed me most was the way that Sandip Babu[1] used to fleece him on the pretext of *Swadeshi* work. Whenever he wanted to start a newspaper, or travel about preaching the Cause, or take a change of air by the advice of his doctor, my husband would unquestioningly supply him with the money. This was over and above the regular living allowance which Sandip Babu also received from him. The strangest part of it was that my husband and Sandip Babu did not agree in their opinions.

As soon as the Swadeshi storm reached my blood, I said to my husband, 'I must burn all my foreign clothes.'

'Why burn them?' said he. 'You need not wear them as long as you please.'

'As long as I please! Not in this life...'

'Very well, do not wear them for the rest of your life, then. But why this bonfire business?'

'Would you thwart me in my resolve?'

'What I want to say is this, why not try to build up something? You should not waste even a tenth part of your energies in this destructive excitement.'

'Such excitement will give us the energy to build.'

'That is as much as to say, that you cannot light the house unless you set fire to it.'

Then there came another trouble. When Miss Gilby first came to our house there was a great flutter, which afterwards calmed down when they got used to her. Now the whole thing was stirred up afresh. I had never bothered myself before as to whether Miss Gilby was European or Indian, but I began to do so now. I said to my husband, 'We must get rid of Miss Gilby.'

He kept silent.

I talked to him wildly, and he went away sad at heart.

After a fit of weeping, I felt in a more reasonable mood when we met at night. 'I cannot,' my husband said, 'look upon Miss Gilby through a mist of abstraction, just because she is English. Cannot you get over the barrier of her name after such a long acquaintance?

---

[1] 'Babu' is a term of respect, like 'Father' or 'Mister,' but has also meant in colonial days a person who understands some English. [on-line ed.]

Cannot you realize that she loves you?'

I felt a little ashamed and replied with some sharpness, 'Let her remain. I am not over anxious to send her away.' And Miss Gilby remained.

But one day I was told that she had been insulted by a young fellow on her way to church. This was a boy whom we were supporting. My husband turned him out of the house. There was not a single soul, that day, who could forgive my husband for that act—not even I. This time Miss Gilby left of her own accord. She shed tears when she came to say goodbye, but my mood would not melt. To slander the poor boy so—and such a fine boy, too, who would forget his daily bath and food in his enthusiasm for Swadeshi.

My husband escorted Miss Gilby to the railway station in his own carriage. I was sure he was going too far. When exaggerated accounts of the incident gave rise to a public scandal, which found its way to the newspapers, I felt he had been rightly served.

I had often become anxious at my husband's doings, but had never before been ashamed; yet now I had to blush for him! I did not know exactly, nor did I care, what wrong poor Noren might, or might not, have done to Miss Gilby, but the idea of sitting in judgement on such a matter at such a time! I should have refused to damp the spirit which prompted young Noren to defy the Englishwoman. I could not but look upon it as a sign of cowardice in my husband that he should fail to understand this simple thing. And so I blushed for him.

And yet it was not that my husband refused to support Swadeshi, or was in any way against the Cause. Only he had not been able whole-heartedly to accept the spirit of *Bande Mataram*.[1]

'I am willing,' he said, 'to serve my country; but my worship I reserve for Right which is far greater than my country. To worship my country as a god is to bring a curse upon it.'

---

[1] Lit., 'Hail Mother'; the opening words of a song by Bankim Chatterjee, the famous Bengali novelist. The song has now become the national anthem, and *Bande Mataram* the national cry, since the days of the Swadeshi movement [Trans.].

CHAPTER TWO

BIMALA'S STORY

IV

This was the time when Sandip Babu with his followers came to our neighbourhood to preach Swadeshi.

There is to be a big meeting in our temple pavilion. We women are sitting there, on one side, behind a screen. Triumphant shouts of *Bande Mataram* come nearer, and to them I am thrilling through and through. Suddenly a stream of barefooted youths in turbans, clad in ascetic ochre, rushes into the quadrangle, like a silt-reddened freshet into a dry riverbed at the first burst of the rains. The whole place is filled with an immense crowd, through which Sandip Babu is borne, seated in a big chair hoisted on the shoulders of ten or twelve of the youths.

Bande Mataram! *Bande Mataram*! *Bande Mataram*! It seems as though the skies would be rent and scattered into a thousand fragments.

I had seen Sandip Babu's photograph before. There was something in his features which I did not quite like. Not that he was bad looking—far from it, he had a splendidly handsome face. Yet, I know not why, it seemed to me, in spite of all its brilliance, that too much of base alloy had gone into its making. The light in his eyes somehow did not shine true. That was why I did not like it when my husband unquestioningly gave in to all his demands. I could bear the waste of money; but it vexed me to think that he was imposing on my husband, taking advantage of friendship. His bearing was not that of an ascetic, nor even of a person of moderate means, but foppish all over. Love of comfort seemed to...any number of such reflections come back to me today, but let them be.

When, however, Sandip Babu began to speak that afternoon, and the hearts of the crowd swayed and surged to his words, as though they would break all bounds, I saw him wonderfully transformed. Especially when his features were suddenly lit up by a shaft of light from the slowly setting sun, as it sunk below the roof-line of the pavilion, he seemed to me to be marked out by the gods as their messenger to mortal men and women.

From beginning to end of his speech, each one of his utterances was a stormy outburst. There was no limit to the confidence of his assurance. I do not know how it happened, but I found I had impatiently pushed away the screen from before me and had fixed my gaze upon him. Yet there was none in that crowd who paid any heed to my doings. Only once, I noticed, his eyes, like stars in fateful Orion, flashed full on my face.

I was utterly unconscious of myself. I was no longer the lady of the Rajah's house, but the sole representative of Bengal's womanhood. And he was the champion of Bengal. As the sky had shed its light over him, so he must receive the consecration of a woman's benediction...

It seemed clear to me that, since he had caught sight of me, the fire in his words had flamed up more fiercely. Indra's[1] steed refused to be reined in, and there came the roar of thunder and the flash of lightning. I said within myself that his language had caught fire from my eyes; for we women are not only the deities of the household fire, but the flame of the soul itself.

I returned home that evening radiant with a new pride and joy. The storm within me had shifted my whole being from one centre to another. Like the Greek maidens of old, I fain would cut off my long, resplendent tresses to make a bowstring for my hero. Had my outward ornaments been connected with my inner feelings, then my necklet, my armlets, my bracelets, would all have burst their bonds and flung themselves over that assembly like a shower of meteors. Only some personal sacrifice, I felt, could help me to bear the tumult of my exaltation.

When my husband came home later, I was trembling lest he should utter a sound out of tune with the triumphant paean which was still ringing in my ears, lest his fanaticism for truth should lead him to

---

[1]The Jupiter Pluvius of Hindu mythology.

express disapproval of anything that had been said that afternoon. For then I should have openly defied and humiliated him. But he did not say a word...which I did not like either.

He should have said, 'Sandip has brought me to my senses. I now realize how mistaken I have been all this time.'

I somehow felt that he was spitefully silent, that he obstinately refused to be enthusiastic. I asked how long Sandip Babu was going to be with us.

'He is off to Rangpur early tomorrow morning,' said my husband.

'Must it be tomorrow?'

'Yes, he is already engaged to speak there.'

I was silent for a while and then asked again, 'Could he not possibly stay a day longer?'

'That may hardly be possible, but why?'

'I want to invite him to dinner and attend on him myself.'

My husband was surprised. He had often entreated me to be present when he had particular friends to dinner, but I had never let myself be persuaded. He gazed at me curiously, in silence, with a look I did not quite understand.

I was suddenly overcome with a sense of shame. 'No, no,' I exclaimed, 'that would never do!'

'Why not!' said he. 'I will ask him myself, and if it is at all possible he will surely stay on for tomorrow.'

It turned out to be quite possible.

I will tell the exact truth. That day I reproached my Creator because he had not made me surpassingly beautiful—not to steal any heart away, but because beauty is glory. In this great day the men of the country should realize its goddess in its womanhood. But, alas, the eyes of men fail to discern the goddess, if outward beauty be lacking. Would Sandip Babu find the Shakti of the Motherland manifest in me? Or would he simply take me to be an ordinary, domestic woman?

That morning I scented my flowing hair and tied it in a loose knot, bound by a cunningly intertwined red silk ribbon. Dinner, you see, was to be served at midday, and there was no time to dry my hair after my bath and do it up plaited in the ordinary way. I put on a gold-bordered white sari, and my short-sleeve muslin jacket was also gold-bordered.

I felt that there was a certain restraint about my costume and that nothing could well have been simpler. But my sister-in-law, who happened to be passing by, stopped dead before me, surveyed me from head to foot and with compressed lips smiled a meaning smile. When I asked her the reason, 'I am admiring your get-up!' she said.

'What is there so entertaining about it?' I enquired, considerably annoyed.

'It's superb,' she said. 'I was only thinking that one of those low-necked English bodices would have made it perfect.' Not only her mouth and eyes, but her whole body seemed to ripple with suppressed laughter as she left the room.

I was very, very angry, and wanted to change everything and put on my everyday clothes. But I cannot tell exactly why I could not carry out my impulse. Women are the ornaments of society—thus I reasoned with myself—and my husband would never like it, if I appeared before Sandip Babu unworthily clad.

My idea had been to make my appearance after they had sat down to dinner. In the bustle of looking after the serving the first awkwardness would have passed off. But dinner was not ready in time, and it was getting late. Meanwhile my husband had sent for me to introduce the guest.

I was feeling horribly shy about looking Sandip Babu in the face. However, I managed to recover myself enough to say, 'I am so sorry dinner is getting late.'

He boldly came and sat right beside me as he replied, 'I get a dinner of some kind every day, but the Goddess of Plenty keeps behind the scenes. Now that the goddess herself has appeared, it matters little if the dinner lags behind.'

He was just as emphatic in his manners as he was in his public speaking. He had no hesitation and seemed to be accustomed to occupy, unchallenged, his chosen seat. He claimed the right to intimacy so confidently, that the blame would seem to belong to those who should dispute it.

I was in terror lest Sandip Babu should take me for a shrinking, old-fashioned bundle of inanity. But, for the life of me, I could not sparkle in repartees such as might charm or dazzle him. What could have possessed me, I angrily wondered, to appear before him in such an absurd way?

I was about to retire when dinner was over, but Sandip Babu, as bold as ever, placed himself in my way.

'You must not,' he said, 'think me greedy. It was not the dinner that kept me staying on, it was your invitation. If you were to run away now, that would not be playing fair with your guest.'

If he had not said these words with a careless ease, they would have been out of tune. But, after all, he was such a great friend of my husband that I was like his sister.

While I was struggling to climb up this high wave of intimacy, my husband came to the rescue, saying, 'Why not come back to us after you have taken your dinner?'

'But you must give your word,' said Sandip Babu, 'before we let you off.'

'I will come,' said I, with a slight smile.

'Let me tell you,' continued Sandip Babu, 'why I cannot trust you. Nikhil has been married these nine years, and all this while you have eluded me. If you do this again for another nine years, we shall never meet again.'

I took up the spirit of his remark as I dropped my voice to reply, 'Why even then should we not meet?'

'My horoscope tells me I am to die early. None of my forefathers have survived their thirtieth year. I am now twenty-seven.'

He knew this would go home. This time there must have been a shade of concern in my low voice as I said, 'The blessings of the whole country are sure to avert the evil influence of the stars.'

'Then the blessings of the country must be voiced by its goddess. This is the reason for my anxiety that you should return, so that my talisman may begin to work from today.'

Sandip Babu had such a way of taking things by storm that I got no opportunity of resenting what I never should have permitted in another.

'So,' he concluded with a laugh, 'I am going to hold this husband of yours as a hostage till you come back.'

As I was coming away, he exclaimed, 'May I trouble you for a trifle?'

I started and turned round.

'Don't be alarmed,' he said. 'It's merely a glass of water. You might have noticed that I did not drink any water with my dinner. I take it a little later.'

Upon this I had to make a show of interest and ask him the reason. He began to give the history of his dyspepsia. I was told how he had been a martyr to it for seven months, and how, after the usual course of nuisances, which included different allopathic and homoeopathic misadventures, he had obtained the most wonderful results by indigenous methods.

'Do you know,' he added, with a smile, 'God has built even my infirmities in such a manner that they yield only under the bombardment of Swadeshi pills.'

My husband, at this, broke his silence. 'You must confess,' said he, 'that you have as immense an attraction for foreign medicine as the earth has for meteors. You have three shelves in your sitting room full of...'

Sandip Babu broke in, 'Do you know what they are? They are the punitive police. They come, not because they are wanted, but because they are imposed on us by the rule of this modern age, exacting fines and inflicting injuries.'

My husband could not bear exaggerations, and I could see he disliked this. But all ornaments are exaggerations. They are not made by God, but by man. Once I remember in defence of some untruth of mine I said to my husband, 'Only the trees and beasts and birds tell unmitigated truths, because these poor things have not the power to invent. In this men show their superiority to the lower creatures, and women beat even men. Neither is a profusion of ornament unbecoming for a woman, nor a profusion of untruth.'

As I came out into the passage leading to the zenana I found my sister-in-law, standing near a window overlooking the reception rooms, peeping through the venetian shutter.

'You here?' I asked in surprise.

'Eavesdropping!' she replied.

V

When I returned, Sandip Babu was tenderly apologetic. 'I am afraid we have spoilt your appetite,' he said.

I felt greatly ashamed. Indeed, I had been too indecently quick over my dinner. With a little calculation, it would become quite evident that my non-eating had surpassed the eating. But I had no idea that anyone could have been deliberately calculating.

I suppose Sandip Babu detected my feeling of shame, which only augmented it. 'I was sure,' he said, 'that you had the impulse of the wild deer to run away, but it is a great boon that you took the trouble to keep your promise with me.'

I could not think of any suitable reply and so I sat down, blushing and uncomfortable, at one end of the sofa. The vision that I had of myself, as the Shakti of Womanhood, incarnate, crowning Sandip Babu simply with my presence, majestic and unashamed, failed me altogether.

Sandip Babu deliberately started a discussion with my husband. He knew that his keen wit flashed to the best effect in an argument. I have often since observed, that he never lost an opportunity for a passage at arms whenever I happened to be present.

He was familiar with my husband's views on the cult of *Bande Mataram*, and began in a provoking way, 'So you do not allow that there is room for an appeal to the imagination in patriotic work?'

'It has its place, Sandip, I admit, but I do not believe in giving it the whole place. I would know my country in its frank reality, and for this I am both afraid and ashamed to make use of hypnotic texts of patriotism.'

'What you call hypnotic texts I call truth. I truly believe my country to be my God. I worship Humanity. God manifests Himself both in man and in his country.'

'If that is what you really believe, there should be no difference for you between man and man, and so between country and country.'

'Quite true. But my powers are limited, so my worship of Humanity is continued in the worship of my country.'

'I have nothing against your worship as such, but how is it you propose to conduct your worship of God by hating other countries in which He is equally manifest?'

'Hate is also an adjunct of worship. Arjuna won Mahadeva's favour by wrestling with him. God will be with us in the end, if we are prepared to give Him battle.'

'If that be so, then those who are serving and those who are harming the country are both His devotees. Why, then, trouble to preach patriotism?'

'In the case of one's own country, it is different. There the heart clearly demands worship.'

'If you push the same argument further you can say that since God is manifested in us, our self has to be worshipped before all else; because our natural instinct claims it.'

'Look here, Nikhil, this is all merely dry logic. Can't you recognize that there is such a thing as feeling?'

'I tell you the truth, Sandip,' my husband replied. 'It is my feelings that are outraged, whenever you try to pass off injustice as a duty, and unrighteousness as a moral ideal. The fact, that I am incapable of stealing, is not due to my possessing logical faculties, but to my having some feeling of respect for myself and love for ideals.'

I was raging inwardly. At last I could keep silent no longer. 'Is not the history of every country,' I cried, 'whether England, France, Germany, or Russia, the history of stealing for the sake of one's own country?'

'They have to answer for these thefts; they are doing so even now; their history is not yet ended.'

'At any rate,' interposed Sandip Babu, 'why should we not follow suit? Let us first fill our country's coffers with stolen goods and then take centuries, like these other countries, to answer for them, if we must. But, I ask you, where do you find this 'answering' in history?'

'When Rome was answering for her sin no one knew it. All that time, there was apparently no limit to her prosperity. But do you not see one thing, how these political bags of theirs are bursting with lies and treacheries, breaking their backs under their weight?'

Never before had I had any opportunity of being present at a discussion between my husband and his men friends. Whenever he argued with me I could feel his reluctance to push me into a corner.

This arose out of the very love he bore me. Today for the first time I saw his fencer's skill in debate.

Nevertheless, my heart refused to accept my husband's position. I was struggling to find some answer, but it would not come. When the word 'righteousness' comes into an argument, it sounds ugly to say that a thing can be too good to be useful.

All of a sudden Sandip Babu turned to me with the question, 'What do you say to this?'

'I do not care about fine distinctions,' I broke out. 'I will tell you broadly what I feel. I am only human. I am covetous. I would have good things for my country. If I am obliged, I would snatch them and filch them. I have anger. I would be angry for my country's sake. If necessary, I would smite and slay to avenge her insults. I have my desire to be fascinated, and fascination must be supplied to me in bodily shape by my country. She must have some visible symbol casting its spell upon my mind. I would make my country a Person, and call her Mother, Goddess, Durga—for whom I would redden the earth with sacrificial offerings. I am human, not divine.'

Sandip Babu leapt to his feet with uplifted arms and shouted 'Hurrah!'—The next moment he corrected himself and cried, '*Bande Mataram.*'

A shadow of pain passed over the face of my husband. He said to me in a very gentle voice, 'Neither am I divine, I am human. And therefore I dare not permit the evil which is in me to be exaggerated into an image of my country—never, never!'

Sandip Babu cried out, 'See, Nikhil, how in the heart of a woman Truth takes flesh and blood. Woman knows how to be cruel, her virulence is like a blind storm. It is beautifully fearful. In man it is ugly, because it harbours in its centre the gnawing worms of reason and thought. I tell you, Nikhil, it is our women who will save the country. This is not the time for nice scruples. We must be unswervingly, unreasoningly brutal. We must sin. We must give our women red sandal paste with which to anoint and enthrone our sin. Don't you remember what the poet says,

'Come, Sin, O beautiful Sin, Let thy stinging red kisses pour down fiery red wine into our blood. Sound the trumpet of imperious evil and cross our forehead with the wreath of exulting lawlessness, O Deity of Desecration, Smear our breasts with the blackest mud of disrepute, unashamed.

Down with that righteousness, which cannot smilingly bring rack and ruin.'

When Sandip Babu, standing with his head high, insulted at a moment's impulse all that men have cherished as their highest, in all countries and in all times, a shiver went right through my body.

But, with a stamp of his foot, he continued his declamation, 'I can see that you are that beautiful spirit of fire, which burns the home to ashes and lights up the larger world with its flame. Give to us the indomitable courage to go to the bottom of ruin itself. Impart grace to all that is baneful.'

It was not clear to whom Sandip Babu addressed his last appeal. It might have been She whom he worshipped with his *Bande Mataram*. It might have been the Womanhood of his country. Or it might have been its representative, the woman before him. He would have gone further in the same strain, but my husband suddenly rose from his seat and touched him lightly on the shoulder saying, 'Sandip, Chandranath Babu is here.'

I started and turned round, to find an aged gentleman at the door, calm and dignified, in doubt as to whether he should come in or retire. His face was touched with a gentle light like that of the setting sun.

My husband came up to me and whispered, 'This is my master, of whom I have so often told you. Make your obeisance to him.'

I bent reverently and took the dust of his feet. He gave me his blessing saying, 'May God protect you always, my little mother.' I was sorely in need of such a blessing at that moment.

NIKHIL'S STORY

I

One day, I had the faith to believe that I should be able to bear whatever came from my God. I never had the trial. Now I think it has come.

I used to test my strength of mind by imagining all kinds of evil which might happen to me—poverty, imprisonment, dishonour, death—even Bimala's. And when I said to myself that I should be able to receive these with firmness, I am sure I did not exaggerate. Only I could never even imagine one thing, and today it is that of which I am thinking, and wondering whether I can really bear it. There is a thorn somewhere pricking in my heart, constantly giving me pain while I am about my daily work. It seems to persist even when I am asleep. The very moment I wake up in the morning, I find that the bloom has gone from the face of the sky. What is it? What has happened?

My mind has become so sensitive, that even my past life, which came to me in the disguise of happiness, seems to wring my very heart with its falsehood; and the shame and sorrow which are coming close to me are losing their cover of privacy, all the more because they try to veil their faces. My heart has become all eyes. The things that should not be seen, the things I do not want to see—these I must see.

The day has come at last when my ill-starred life has to reveal its destitution in a long-drawn series of exposures. This penury, all unexpected, has taken its seat in the heart where plenitude seemed to reign. The fees which I paid to delusion for just nine years of my youth have now to be returned with interest to Truth till the end of my days.

What is the use of straining to keep up my pride? What harm if I confess that I have something lacking in me? Possibly it is that unreasoning forcefulness which women love to find in men. But is strength mere display of muscularity? Must strength have no scruples in treading the weak underfoot?

But why all these arguments? Worthiness cannot be earned merely by disputing about it. And I am unworthy, unworthy, unworthy.

What if I am unworthy? The true value of love is this, that it can ever bless the unworthy with its own prodigality. For the worthy there are many rewards on God's earth, but God has specially reserved love for the unworthy.

Up till now Bimala was my home-made Bimala, the product of the confined space and the daily routine of small duties. Did the love which I received from her, I asked myself, come from the deep spring of her heart, or was it merely like the daily provision of pipe water pumped up by the municipal steam engine of society?

I longed to find Bimala blossoming fully in all her truth and power. But the thing I forgot to calculate was, that one must give up all claims based on conventional rights, if one would find a person freely revealed in truth.

Why did I fail to think of this? Was it because of the husband's pride of possession over his wife? No. It was because I placed the fullest trust upon love. I was vain enough to think that I had the power in me to bear the sight of truth in its awful nakedness. It was tempting Providence, but still I clung to my proud determination to come out victorious in the trial.

Bimala had failed to understand me in one thing. She could not fully realize that I held as weakness all imposition of force. Only the weak dare not be just. They shirk their responsibility of fairness and try quickly to get at results through the short cuts of injustice. Bimala has no patience with patience. She loves to find in men the turbulent, the angry, the unjust. Her respect must have its element of fear.

I had hoped that when Bimala found herself free in the outer world she would be rescued from her infatuation for tyranny. But now I feel sure that this infatuation is deep down in her nature. Her love is for the boisterous. From the tip of her tongue to the pit of her stomach she must tingle with red pepper in order to enjoy the simple fare of life. But my determination was, never to do my duty with frantic impetuosity, helped on by the fiery liquor of excitement. I know Bimala finds it difficult to respect me for this, taking my scruples for feebleness—and she is quite angry with me because I am not running amuck crying *Bande Mataram*.

For the matter of that, I have become unpopular with all my countrymen because I have not joined them in their carousals. They are certain that either I have a longing for some title, or else that I am afraid of the police. The police on their side suspect me of harbouring some hidden design and protesting too much in my mildness.

What I really feel is this, that those who cannot find food for their enthusiasm in a knowledge of their country as it actually is, or those who cannot love men just because they are men—who needs must shout and deify their country in order to keep up their excitement—these love excitement more than their country.

To try to give our infatuation a higher place than Truth is a sign of inherent slavishness. Where our minds are free we find ourselves lost. Our moribund vitality must have for its rider either some fantasy, or someone in authority, or a sanction from the pundits, in order to make it move. So long as we are impervious to truth and have to be moved by some hypnotic stimulus, we must know that we lack the capacity for self-government. Whatever may be our condition, we shall either need some imaginary ghost or some actual medicine man to terrorize over us.

The other day when Sandip accused me of lack of imagination, saying that this prevented me from realizing my country in a visible image, Bimala agreed with him. I did not say anything in my defence, because to win in argument does not lead to happiness. Her difference of opinion is not due to any inequality of intelligence, but rather to dissimilarity of nature.

They accuse me of being unimaginative—that is, according to them, I may have oil in my lamp, but no flame. Now this is exactly the accusation which I bring against them. I would say to them, 'You are dark, even as the flints are. You must come to violent conflicts and make a noise in order to produce your sparks. But their disconnected flashes merely assist your pride, and not your clear vision.'

I have been noticing for some time that there is a gross cupidity about Sandip. His fleshly feelings make him harbour delusions about his religion and impel him into a tyrannical attitude in his patriotism. His intellect is keen, but his nature is coarse, and so he glorifies his selfish lusts under high-sounding names. The cheap consolations of hatred are as urgently necessary for him as the satisfaction of his appetites. Bimala has often warned me, in the old days, of his hankering after money. I understood this, but I could not bring myself to haggle with Sandip. I felt ashamed even to own to myself that he was trying to take advantage of me.

It will, however, be difficult to explain to Bimala today that Sandip's love of country is but a different phase of his covetous self-love. Bimala's hero-worship of Sandip makes me hesitate all the more to talk to her about him, lest some touch of jealousy may lead me unwittingly into exaggeration. It may be that the pain at my heart is already making me see a distorted picture of Sandip. And yet it is better perhaps to speak out than to keep my feelings gnawing within me.

II

I have known my master these thirty years. Neither calumny, nor disaster, nor death itself has any terrors for him. Nothing could have saved me, born as I was into the traditions of this family of ours, but that he has established his own life in the centre of mine, with its peace and truth and spiritual vision, thus making it possible for me to realize goodness in its truth.

My master came to me that day and said, 'Is it necessary to detain Sandip here any longer?'

His nature was so sensitive to all omens of evil that he had at once understood. He was not easily moved, but that day he felt the dark shadow of trouble ahead. Do I not know how well he loves me?

At tea-time I said to Sandip, 'I have just had a letter from Rangpur. They are complaining that I am selfishly detaining you. When will you be going there?'

Bimala was pouring out the tea. Her face fell at once. She threw just one enquiring glance at Sandip.

'I have been thinking,' said Sandip, 'that this wandering up and down means a tremendous waste of energy. I feel that if I could work from a centre I could achieve more permanent results.'

With this he looked up at Bimala and asked, 'Do you not think so too?'

Bimala hesitated for a reply and then said, 'Both ways seem good—to do the work from a centre, as well as by travelling about. That in which you find greater satisfaction is the way for you.'

'Then let me speak out my mind,' said Sandip. 'I have never yet found any one source of inspiration suffice me for good. That is why I have been constantly moving about, rousing enthusiasm in the people, from which in turn I draw my own store of energy. Today you have given me the message of my country. Such fire I have never beheld in any man. I shall be able to spread the fire of enthusiasm in my country by borrowing it from you. No, do not be ashamed. You are far above all modesty and diffidence. You are the Queen Bee of our hive, and we the workers shall rally around you. You shall be our centre, our inspiration.'

Bimala flushed all over with bashful pride and her hand shook as she went on pouring out the tea.

Another day my master came to me and said, 'Why don't you two go up to Darjeeling for a change? You are not looking well. Have you been getting enough sleep?'

I asked Bimala in the evening whether she would care to have a trip to the Hills. I knew she had a great longing to see the Himalayas. But she refused... The country's Cause, I suppose!

I must not lose my faith, I shall wait. The passage from the narrow to the larger world is stormy. When she is familiar with this freedom, then I shall know where my place is. If I discover that I do not fit in with the arrangement of the outer world, then I shall not quarrel with my fate, but silently take my leave...use force? But for what? Can force prevail against Truth?

SANDIP'S STORY

I

The impotent man says, 'That which has come to my share is mine.' And the weak man assents. But the lesson of the whole world is, 'That is really mine which I can snatch away.' My country does not become mine simply because it is the country of my birth. It becomes mine on the day when I am able to win it by force.

Every man has a natural right to possess, and therefore greed is natural. It is not in the wisdom of nature that we should be content to be deprived. What my mind covets, my surroundings must supply. This is the only true understanding between our inner and outer nature in this world. Let moral ideals remain merely for those poor anaemic creatures of starved desire whose grasp is weak. Those who can desire with all their soul and enjoy with all their heart, those who have no hesitation or scruple, it is they who are the anointed of Providence. Nature spreads out her riches and loveliest treasures for their benefit. They swim across streams, leap over walls, kick open doors, to help themselves to whatever is worth taking. In such a getting one can rejoice; such wresting as this gives value to the thing taken.

Nature surrenders herself, but only to the robber. For she delights in this forceful desire, this forceful abduction. And so she does not put the garland of her acceptance round the lean, scraggy neck of the ascetic. The music of the wedding march is struck. The time of the wedding I must not let pass. My heart therefore is eager. For, who is the bridegroom? It is I. The bridegroom's place belongs to him who, torch in hand, can come in time. The bridegroom in Nature's wedding hall comes unexpected and uninvited.

Ashamed? No, I am never ashamed! I ask for whatever I want, and I do not always wait to ask before I take it. Those who are deprived by their own diffidence dignify their privation by the name of modesty. The world into which we are born is the world of reality. When a man goes away from the market of real things with empty hands and empty stomach, merely filling his bag with big sounding words, I wonder why he ever came into this hard world at all. Did these men get their appointment from the epicures of the religious world, to play set tunes on sweet, pious texts in that pleasure garden where blossom airy nothings? I neither affect those tunes nor do I find any sustenance in those blossoms.

What I desire, I desire positively, superlatively. I want to knead it with both my hands and both my feet; I want to smear it all over my body; I want to gorge myself with it to the full. The scrannel pipes of those who have worn themselves out by their moral fastings, till they have become flat and pale like starved vermin infesting a long-deserted bed, will never reach my ear.

I would conceal nothing, because that would be cowardly. But if I cannot bring myself to conceal when concealment is needful, that also is cowardly. Because you have your greed, you build your walls. Because I have my greed, I break through them. You use your power, I use my craft. These are the realities of life. On these depend kingdoms and empires and all the great enterprises of men.

As for those avatars who come down from their paradise to talk to us in some holy jargon—their words are not real. Therefore, in spite of all the applause they get, these sayings of theirs only find a place in the hiding corners of the weak.

They are despised by those who are strong, the rulers of the world. Those who have had the courage to see this have won success, while those poor wretches who are dragged one way by nature and the other way by these avatars, they set one foot in the boat of the real and the other in the boat of the unreal, and thus are in a pitiable plight, able neither to advance nor to keep their place.

There are many men who seem to have been born only with an obsession to die. Possibly there is a beauty, like that of a sunset, in this lingering death in life which seems to fascinate them. Nikhil lives this kind of life, if life it may be called. Years ago, I had a great argument with him on this point.

'It is true,' he said, 'that you cannot get anything except by force. But then what is this force? And then also, what is this getting? The strength I believe in is the strength of renouncing.'

'So you,' I exclaimed, 'are infatuated with the glory of bankruptcy.'

'Just as desperately as the chick is infatuated about the bankruptcy of its shell,' he replied. 'The shell is real enough, yet it is given up in exchange for intangible light and air. A sorry exchange, I suppose you would call it?'

When once Nikhil gets on to metaphor, there is no hope of making him see that he is merely dealing with words, not with realities. Well, well, let him be happy with his metaphors. We are the flesh-eaters of the world; we have teeth and nails; we pursue and grab and tear. We are not satisfied with chewing in the evening the cud of the grass we have eaten in the morning. Anyhow, we cannot allow your metaphor-mongers to bar the door to our sustenance. In that case we shall simply steal or rob, for we must live.

People will say that I am starting some novel theory just because those who are moving in this world are in the habit of talking differently though they are really acting up to it all the time. Therefore they fail to understand, as I do, that this is the only working moral principle.

In point of fact, I know that my idea is not an empty theory at all, for it has been proved in practical life. I have found that my way always wins over the hearts of women, who are creatures of this world of reality and do not roam about in cloud-land, as men do, in idea-filled balloons.

Women find in my features, my manner, my gait, my speech, a masterful passion—not a passion dried thin with the heat of asceticism, not a passion with its face turned back at every step in doubt and debate, but a full-blooded passion. It roars and rolls on, like a flood, with the cry, 'I want, I want, I want.' Women feel, in their own heart of hearts, that this indomitable passion is the lifeblood of the world, acknowledging no law but itself, and therefore victorious. For this reason they have so often abandoned themselves to be swept away on the flood-tide of my passion, recking naught as to whether it takes them to life or to death. This power which wins these women is the power of mighty men, the power which wins the world of reality.

Those who imagine the greater desirability of another world merely shift their desires from the earth to the skies. It remains to be seen how high their gushing fountain will play, and for how long. But this much is certain, women were not created for these pale creatures—these lotus-eaters of idealism.

'Affinity!' When it suited my need, I have often said that God has created special pairs of men and women, and that the union of such is the only legitimate union, higher than all unions made by law. The reason of it is, that though man wants to follow nature, he can find no pleasure in it unless he screens himself with some phrase—and that is why this world is so overflowing with lies.

'Affinity!' Why should there be only one? There may be affinity with thousands. It was never in my agreement with nature that I should overlook all my innumerable affinities for the sake of only one. I have discovered many in my own life up to now, yet that has not closed the door to one more—and that one is clearly visible to my eyes. She has also discovered her own affinity to me.

And then?

Then, if I do not win I am a coward.

CHAPTER THREE

BIMALA'S STORY

VI

I wonder what could have happened to my feeling of shame. The fact is, I had no time to think about myself. My days and nights were passing in a whirl, like an eddy with myself in the centre. No gap was left for hesitation or delicacy to enter.

One day my sister-in-law remarked to my husband, 'Up to now the women of this house have been kept weeping. Here comes the men's turn.'

'We must see that they do not miss it,' she continued, turning to me. 'I see you are out for the fray, Chota[1] Rani! Hurl your shafts straight at their hearts.'

Her keen eyes looked me up and down. Not one of the colours into which my toilet, my dress, my manners, my speech, had blossomed out had escaped her. I am ashamed to speak of it today, but I felt no shame then. Something within me was at work of which I was not even conscious. I used to overdress, it is true, but more like an automaton, with no particular design. No doubt I knew which effort of mine would prove specially pleasing to Sandip Babu, but that required no intuition, for he would discuss it openly before all of them.

One day he said to my husband, 'Do you know, Nikhil, when I first saw our Queen Bee, she was sitting there so demurely in her gold-bordered sari. Her eyes were gazing inquiringly into space, like stars which had lost their way, just as if she had been for ages standing on the edge of some darkness, looking out for something unknown. But when I saw her, I felt a quiver run through me. It seemed to me that the gold border of her sari was her own inner fire flaming out

---

[1] Bimala. the younger brother's wife, was the Chota or Junior Rani.

and twining round her. That is the flame we want, visible fire! Look here, Queen Bee, you really must do us the favour of dressing once more as a living flame.'

So long I had been like a small river at the border of a village. My rhythm and my language were different from what they are now. But the tide came up from the sea, and my breast heaved; my banks gave way and the great drumbeats of the sea waves echoed in my mad current. I could not understand the meaning of that sound in my blood. Where was that former self of mine? Whence came foaming into me this surging flood of glory? Sandip's hungry eyes burnt like the lamps of worship before my shrine. All his gaze proclaimed that I was a wonder in beauty and power; and the loudness of his praise, spoken and unspoken, drowned all other voices in my world. Had the Creator created me afresh, I wondered? Did he wish to make up now for neglecting me so long? I who before was plain had become suddenly beautiful. I who before had been of no account now felt in myself all the splendour of Bengal itself.

For Sandip Babu was not a mere individual. In him was the confluence of millions of minds of the country. When he called me the Queen Bee of the hive, I was acclaimed with a chorus of praise by all our patriot workers. After that, the loud jests of my sister-in-law could not touch me any longer. My relations with all the world underwent a change. Sandip Babu made it clear how all the country was in need of me. I had no difficulty in believing this at the time, for I felt that I had the power to do everything. Divine strength had come to me. It was something which I had never felt before, which was beyond myself. I had no time to question it to find out what was its nature. It seemed to belong to me, and yet to transcend me. It comprehended the whole of Bengal.

Sandip Babu would consult me about every little thing touching the Cause. At first I felt very awkward and would hang back, but that soon wore off. Whatever I suggested seemed to astonish him. He would go into raptures and say, 'Men can only think. You women have a way of understanding without thinking. Woman was created out of God's own fancy. Man, he had to hammer into shape.'

Letters used to come to Sandip Babu from all parts of the country which were submitted to me for my opinion. Occasionally he disagreed with me. But I would not argue with him. Then after a day or two—as if a new light had suddenly dawned upon him—he would send for me and say, 'It was my mistake. Your suggestion was the correct one.' He would often confess to me that wherever he had taken steps contrary to my advice he had gone wrong. Thus I gradually came to be convinced that behind whatever was taking place was Sandip Babu, and behind Sandip Babu was the plain common sense of a woman. The glory of a great responsibility filled my being.

My husband had no place in our counsels. Sandip Babu treated him as a younger brother, of whom personally one may be very fond and yet have no use for his business advice. He would tenderly and smilingly talk about my husband's childlike innocence, saying that his curious doctrine and perversities of mind had a flavour of humour which made them all the more lovable. It was seemingly this very affection for Nikhil which led Sandip Babu to forbear from troubling him with the burden of the country.

Nature has many anodynes in her pharmacy, which she secretly administers when vital relations are being insidiously severed, so that none may know of the operation, till at last one awakes to know what a great rent has been made. When the knife was busy with my life's most intimate tie, my mind was so clouded with fumes of intoxicating gas that I was not in the least aware of what a cruel thing was happening. Possibly this is woman's nature. When her passion is roused she loses her sensibility for all that is outside it. When, like the river, we women keep to our banks, we give nourishment with all that we have, when we overflow them we destroy with all that we are.

SANDIP'S STORY

II

I can see that something has gone wrong. I got an inkling of it the other day.

Ever since my arrival, Nikhil's sitting-room had become a thing amphibious—half women's apartment, half men's, Bimala had access to it from the zenana, it was not barred to me from the outer side. If we had only gone slow, and made use of our privileges with some restraint, we might not have fallen foul of other people. But we went ahead so vehemently that we could not think of the consequences.

Whenever Bee comes into Nikhil's room, I somehow get to know of it from mine. There are the tinkle of bangles and other little sounds; the door is perhaps shut with a shade of unnecessary vehemence; the bookcase is a trifle stiff and creaks if jerked open. When I enter I find Bee, with her back to the door, ever so busy selecting a book from the shelves. And as I offer to assist her in this difficult task she starts and protests; and then we naturally get on to other topics.

The other day, on an inauspicious[1] Thursday afternoon, I sallied forth from my room at the call of these same sounds. There was a man on guard in the passage. I walked on without so much as glancing at him, but as I approached the door he put himself in my way saying, 'Not that way, sir.'

'Not that way! Why?'

'The Rani Mother is there.'

'Oh, very well. Tell your Rani Mother that Sandip Babu wants to see her.'

'That cannot be, sir. It is against orders.'

I felt highly indignant. 'I order you!' I said in a raised voice. 'Go and announce me.'

The fellow was somewhat taken aback at my attitude. In the meantime I had neared the door. I was on the point of reaching it, when he followed after me and took me by the arm saying, 'No, sir, you must not.'

What! To be touched by a flunkey! I snatched away my arm and gave the man a sounding blow. At this moment Bee came out of the room to find the man about to insult me.

I shall never forget the picture of her wrath! That Bee is beautiful is a discovery of my own. Most of our people would see nothing in her. Her tall, slim figure these boors would call 'lanky'. But it is just this lithesomeness of hers that I admire—like an up-leaping fountain

---

[1] According to the Hindu calendar [Trans.].

of life, coming direct out of the depths of the Creator's heart. Her complexion is dark, but it is the lustrous darkness of a sword-blade, keen and scintillating.

'Nanku!' she commanded, as she stood in the doorway, pointing with her finger, 'leave us.'

'Do not be angry with him,' said I. 'If it is against orders, it is I who should retire.'

Bee's voice was still trembling as she replied, 'You must not go. Come in.'

It was not a request, but again a command! I followed her in, and taking a chair fanned myself with a fan which was on the table. Bee scribbled something with a pencil on a sheet of paper and, summoning a servant, handed it to him saying, 'Take this to the Maharaja.'

'Forgive me,' I resumed. 'I was unable to control myself, and hit that man of yours.'

'You served him right,' said Bee.

'But it was not the poor fellow's fault, after all. He was only obeying his orders.'

Here Nikhil came in, and as he did so I left my seat with a rapid movement and went and stood near the window with my back to the room.

'Nanku, the guard, has insulted Sandip Babu,' said Bee to Nikhil.

Nikhil seemed to be so genuinely surprised that I had to turn round and stare at him. Even an outrageously good man fails in keeping up his pride of truthfulness before his wife—if she be the proper kind of woman.

'He insolently stood in the way when Sandip Babu was coming in here,' continued Bee. 'He said he had orders...'

'Whose orders?' asked Nikhil.

'How am I to know?' exclaimed Bee impatiently, her eyes brimming over with mortification.

Nikhil sent for the man and questioned him. 'It was not my fault,' Nanku repeated sullenly. 'I had my orders.'

'Who gave you the order?'

'The Bara Rani Mother.'

We were all silent for a while. After the man had left, Bee said,

'Nanku must go!'

Nikhil remained silent. I could see that his sense of justice would not allow this. There was no end to his qualms. But this time he was up against a tough problem. Bee was not the woman to take things lying down. She would have to get even with her sister-in-law by punishing this fellow. And as Nikhil remained silent, her eyes flashed fire. She knew not how to pour her scorn upon her husband's feebleness of spirit. Nikhil left the room after a while without another word.

The next day Nanku was not to be seen. On inquiry, I learnt that he had been sent off to some other part of the estates, and that his wages had not suffered by such transfer.

I could catch glimpses of the ravages of the storm raging over this, behind the scenes. All I can say is, that Nikhil is a curious creature, quite out of the common.

The upshot was, that after this Bee began to send for me to the sitting-room, for a chat, without any contrivance, or pretence of its being an accident. Thus from bare suggestion we came to broad hint, the implied came to be expressed. The daughter-in-law of a princely house lives in a starry region so remote from the ordinary outsider that there is not even a regular road for his approach. What a triumphal progress of Truth was this which, gradually but persistently, thrust aside veil after veil of obscuring custom, till at length Nature herself was laid bare.

Truth? Of course it was the truth! The attraction of man and woman for each other is fundamental. The whole world of matter, from the speck of dust upwards, is ranged on its side. And yet men would keep it hidden away out of sight, behind a tissue of words; and with home-made sanctions and prohibitions make of it a domestic utensil. Why, it's as absurd as melting down the solar system to make a watch-chain for one's son-in-law![1]

When, in spite of all, reality awakes at the call of what is but naked truth, what a gnashing of teeth and beating of breasts is there! But can one carry on a quarrel with a storm? It never takes the trouble to reply, it only gives a shaking.

---

[1] The son-in-law is the pet of a Hindu household.

I am enjoying the sight of this truth, as it gradually reveals itself. These tremblings of steps, these turnings of the face, are sweet to me, and sweet are the deceptions which deceive not only others, but also Bee herself. When Reality has to meet the unreal, deception is its principal weapon; for its enemies always try to shame Reality by calling it gross, and so it needs must hide itself, or else put on some disguise. The circumstances are such that it dare not frankly avow, 'Yes, I am gross, because I am true. I am flesh. I am passion. I am hunger, unashamed and cruel.'

All is now clear to me. The curtain flaps, and through it I can see the preparations for the catastrophe. The little red ribbon, which peeps through the luxuriant masses of her hair, with its flush of secret longing, it is the lolling tongue of the red storm cloud. I feel the warmth of each turn of her sari, each suggestion of her raiment, of which even the wearer may not be fully conscious.

Bee was not conscious, because she was ashamed of the reality; to which men have given a bad name, calling it Satan; and so it has to steal into the garden of paradise in the guise of a snake, and whisper secrets into the ears of man's chosen consort and make her rebellious; then farewell to all ease; and after that comes death!

My poor little Queen Bee is living in a dream. She knows not which way she is treading. It would not be safe to awaken her before the time. It is best for me to pretend to be equally unconscious.

The other day, at dinner, she was gazing at me in a curious sort of way, little realizing what such glances mean! As my eyes met hers, she turned away with a flush. 'You are surprised at my appetite,' I remarked. 'I can hide everything, except that I am greedy! Anyhow, why trouble to blush for me, since I am shameless?'

This only made her colour more furiously, as she stammered, 'No, no, I was only...'

'I know,' I interrupted. 'Women have a weakness for greedy men; for it is this greed of ours which gives them the upper hand. The indulgence which I have always received at their hands has made me all the more shameless. I do not mind your watching the good things disappear, not one bit. I mean to enjoy every one of them.'

The other day I was reading an English book in which sex-problems were treated in an audaciously realistic manner. I had left it lying in the sitting-room. As I went there the next afternoon, for something or other, I found Bee seated with this book in her hand. When she heard my footsteps she hurriedly put it down and placed another book over it—a volume of Mrs Hemans's poems.

'I have never been able to make out,' I began, 'why women are so shy about being caught reading poetry. We men—lawyers, mechanics, or what not—may well feel ashamed. If we must read poetry, it should be at dead of night, within closed doors. But you women are so akin to poesy. The Creator Himself is a lyric poet, and Jayadeva[1] must have practised the divine art seated at His feet.'

Bee made no reply, but only blushed uncomfortably. She made as if she would leave the room. Whereupon I protested, 'No, no, pray read on. I will just take a book I left here, and run away.' With which I took up my book from the table. 'Lucky you did not think of glancing over its pages,' I continued, 'or you would have wanted to chastise me.'

'Indeed! Why?' asked Bee.

'Because it is not poetry,' said I. 'Only blunt things, bluntly put, without any finicking niceness. I wish Nikhil would read it.'

Bee frowned a little as she murmured, 'What makes you wish that?'

'He is a man, you see, one of us. My only quarrel with him is that he delights in a misty vision of this world. Have you not observed how this trait of his makes him look on Swadeshi as if it was some poem of which the metre must be kept correct at every step? We, with the clubs of our prose, are the iconoclasts of metre.'

'What has your book to do with Swadeshi?'

'You would know if you only read it. Nikhil wants to go by made-up maxims, in Swadeshi as in everything else; so he knocks up against human nature at every turn, and then falls to abusing it. He never will realize that human nature was created long before phrases were, and will survive them too.'

Bee was silent for a while and then gravely said, 'Is it not a part

---

[1] A Vaishnava poet (Sanskrit) whose lyrics of the adoration of the Divinity serve as well to express all shades of human passion [Trans.].

of human nature to try and rise superior to itself?'

I smiled inwardly. 'These are not your words', I thought to myself. 'You have learnt them from Nikhil. You are a healthy human being. Your flesh and blood have responded to the call of reality. You are burning in every vein with life-fire—do I not know it? How long should they keep you cool with the wet towel of moral precepts?'

'The weak are in the majority,' I said aloud. 'They are continually poisoning the ears of men by repeating these shibboleths. Nature has denied them strength—it is thus that they try to enfeeble others.'

'We women are weak,' replied Bimala. 'So I suppose we must join in the conspiracy of the weak.'

'Women weak!' I exclaimed with a laugh. 'Men belaud you as delicate and fragile, so as to delude you into thinking yourselves weak. But it is you women who are strong. Men make a great outward show of their so-called freedom, but those who know their inner minds are aware of their bondage. They have manufactured scriptures with their own hands to bind themselves; with their very idealism they have made golden fetters of women to wind round their body and mind. If men had not that extraordinary faculty of entangling themselves in meshes of their own contriving, nothing could have kept them bound. But as for you women, you have desired to conceive reality with body and soul. You have given birth to reality. You have suckled reality at your breasts.'

Bee was well read for a woman, and would not easily give in to my arguments. 'If that were true,' she objected, 'men would not have found women attractive.'

'Women realize the danger,' I replied. 'They know that men love delusions, so they give them full measure by borrowing their own phrases. They know that man, the drunkard, values intoxication more than food, and so they try to pass themselves off as an intoxicant. As a matter of fact, but for the sake of man, woman has no need for any make-believe.'

'Why, then, are you troubling to destroy the illusion?'

'For freedom. I want the country to be free. I want human relations to be free.'

III

I was aware that it is unsafe suddenly to awake a sleep-walker. But I am so impetuous by nature, a halting gait does not suit me. I knew I was overbold that day. I knew that the first shock of such ideas is apt to be almost intolerable. But with women it is always audacity that wins.

Just as we were getting on nicely, who should walk in but Nikhil's old tutor Chandranath Babu. The world would have been not half a bad place to live in but for these schoolmasters, who make one want to quit in disgust. The Nikhil type wants to keep the world always a school. This incarnation of a school turned up that afternoon at the psychological moment.

We all remain schoolboys in some corner of our hearts, and I, even I, felt somewhat pulled up. As for poor Bee, she at once took her place solemnly, like the topmost girl of the class on the front bench. All of a sudden she seemed to remember that she had to face her examination.

Some people are so like eternal pointsmen lying in wait by the line, to shunt one's train of thought from one rail to another.

Chandranath Babu had no sooner come in than he cast about for some excuse to retire, mumbling, 'I beg your pardon, I...'

Before he could finish, Bee went up to him and made a profound obeisance, saying, 'Pray do not leave us, sir. Will you not take a seat?' She looked like a drowning person clutching at him for support—the little coward!

But possibly I was mistaken. It is quite likely that there was a touch of womanly wile in it. She wanted, perhaps, to raise her value in my eyes. She might have been pointedly saying to me, 'Please don't imagine for a moment that I am entirely overcome by you. My respect for Chandranath Babu is even greater.'

Well, indulge in your respect by all means! Schoolmasters thrive on it. But not being one of them, I have no use for that empty compliment.

Chandranath Babu began to talk about Swadeshi. I thought I would let him go on with his monologues. There is nothing like letting an old man talk himself out. It makes him feel that he is winding up the world, forgetting all the while how far away the real world is from his wagging tongue.

But even my worst enemy would not accuse me of patience. And when Chandranath Babu went on to say, 'If we expect to gather fruit where we have sown no seed, then we...' I had to interrupt him.

'Who wants fruit?' I cried. 'We go by the Author of the Gita who says that we are concerned only with the doing, not with the fruit of our deeds.'

'What is it then that you do want?' asked Chandranath Babu.

'Thorns!' I exclaimed, 'which cost nothing to plant.'

'Thorns do not obstruct others only,' he replied. 'They have a way of hurting one's own feet.'

'That is all right for a copy-book,' I retorted. 'But the real thing is that we have this burning at heart. Now we have only to cultivate thorns for other's soles; afterwards when they hurt us we shall find leisure to repent. But why be frightened even of that? When, at last, we have to die it will be time enough to get cold. While we are on fire let us seethe and boil.'

Chandranath Babu smiled. 'Seethe by all means,' he said, 'but do not mistake it for work, or heroism. Nations which have got on in the world have done so by action, not by ebullition. Those who have always lain in dread of work, when with a start they awake to their sorry plight, they look to short-cuts and scamping for their deliverance.'

I was girding up my loins to deliver a crushing reply, when Nikhil came back. Chandranath Babu rose, and looking towards Bee, said, 'Let me go now, my little mother, I have some work to attend to.'

As he left, I showed Nikhil the book in my hand. 'I was telling Queen Bee about this book,' I said.

Ninety-nine per cent of people have to be deluded with lies, but it is easier to delude this perpetual pupil of the schoolmaster with the truth. He is best cheated openly. So, in playing with him, the simplest course was to lay my cards on the table.

Nikhil read the title on the cover, but said nothing. 'These writers,' I continued, 'are busy with their brooms, sweeping away the dust of epithets with which men have covered up this world of ours. So, as

I was saying, I wish you would read it.'

'I have read it,' said Nikhil.

'Well, what do you say?'

'It is all very well for those who really care to think, but poison for those who shirk thought.'

'What do you mean?'

'Those who preach 'Equal Rights of Property' should not be thieves. For, if they are, they would be preaching lies. When passion is in the ascendant, this kind of book is not rightly understood.'

'Passion,' I replied, 'is the street lamp which guides us. To call it untrue is as hopeless as to expect to see better by plucking out our natural eyes.'

Nikhil was visibly growing excited. 'I accept the truth of passion,' he said, 'only when I recognize the truth of restraint. By pressing what we want to see right into our eyes we only injure them, we do not see. So does the violence of passion, which would leave no space between the mind and its object, defeat its purpose.'

'It is simply your intellectual foppery,' I replied, 'which makes you indulge in moral delicacy, ignoring the savage side of truth. This merely helps you to mystify things, and so you fail to do your work with any degree of strength.'

'The intrusion of strength,' said Nikhil impatiently, 'where strength is out of place, does not help you in your work... But why are we arguing about these things? Vain arguments only brush off the fresh bloom of truth.'

I wanted Bee to join in the discussion, but she had not said a word up to now. Could I have given her too rude a shock, leaving her assailed with doubts and wanting to learn her lesson afresh from the schoolmaster? Still, a thorough shaking-up is essential. One must begin by realizing that things supposed to be unshakeable can be shaken.

'I am glad I had this talk with you,' I said to Nikhil, 'for I was on the point of lending this book to Queen Bee to read.'

'What harm?' said Nikhil. 'If I could read the book, why not Bimala too? All I want to say is, that in Europe people look at everything from the viewpoint of science. But man is neither mere physiology, nor biology, nor psychology, nor even sociology. For God's sake don't forget that. Man is infinitely more than the natural science of himself. You laugh at me, calling me the schoolmaster's pupil, but that is what you are, not I. You want to find the truth of man from your science teachers, and not from your own inner being.'

'But why all this excitement?' I mocked.

'Because I see you are bent on insulting man and making him petty.'

'Where on earth do you see all that?'

'In the air, in my outraged feelings. You would go on wounding the great, the unselfish, the beautiful in man.'

'What mad idea is this of yours?'

Nikhil suddenly stood up. 'I tell you plainly, Sandip,' he said, 'man may be wounded unto death, but he will not die. This is the reason why I am ready to suffer all, knowing all, with eyes open.'

With these words he hurriedly left the room.

I was staring blankly at his retreating figure, when the sound of a book, falling from the table, made me turn to find Bee following him with quick, nervous steps, making a detour to avoid passing too near me.

A curious creature, that Nikhil! He feels the danger threatening his home, and yet why does he not turn me out? I know, he is waiting for Bimala to give him the cue. If Bimala tells him that their mating has been a misfit, he will bow his head and admit that it may have been a blunder! He has not the strength of mind to understand that to acknowledge a mistake is the greatest of all mistakes. He is a typical example of how ideas make for weakness. I have not seen another like him—so whimsical a product of nature! He would hardly do as a character in a novel or drama, to say nothing of real life.

And Bee? I am afraid her dream-life is over from today. She has at length understood the nature of the current which is bearing her along. Now she must either advance or retreat, open-eyed. The chances are she will now advance a step, and then retreat a step. But that does not disturb me. When one is on fire, this rushing to and fro makes the blaze all the fiercer. The fright she has got will only fan her passion.

Perhaps I had better not say much to her, but simply select some modern books for her to read. Let her gradually come to the conviction that to acknowledge and respect passion as the supreme reality, is to be modern—not to be ashamed of it, not to glorify restraint. If she finds shelter in some such word as 'modern', she will find strength.

Be that as it may, I must see this out to the end of the Fifth Act. I cannot, unfortunately, boast of being merely a spectator, seated in the royal box, applauding now and again. There is a wrench at my heart, a pang in every nerve. When I have put out the light and am in my bed, little touches, little glances, little words flit about and fill the darkness. When I get up in the morning, I thrill with lively anticipations, my blood seems to course through me to the strains of music...

There was a double photo-frame on the table with Bee's photograph by the side of Nikhil's. I had taken out hers. Yesterday I showed Bee the empty side and said, 'Theft becomes necessary only because of miserliness, so its sin must be divided between the miser and the thief. Do you not think so?'

'It was not a good one,' observed Bee simply, with a little smile.

'What is to be done?' said I. 'A portrait cannot be better than a portrait. I must be content with it, such as it is.'

Bee took up a book and began to turn over the pages. 'If you are annoyed,' I went on, 'I must make a shift to fill up the vacancy.'

Today I have filled it up. This photograph of mine was taken in my early youth. My face was then fresher, and so was my mind. Then I still cherished some illusions about this world and the next. Faith deceives men, but it has one great merit, it imparts a radiance to the features.

My portrait now reposes next to Nikhil's, for are not the two of us old friends?

CHAPTER FOUR

NIKHIL'S STORY

III

I was never self-conscious. But nowadays I often try to take an outside view—to see myself as Bimala sees me. What a dismally solemn picture it makes, my habit of taking things too seriously!

Better, surely, to laugh away the world than flood it with tears. That is, in fact, how the world gets on. We relish our food and rest, only because we can dismiss, as so many empty shadows, the sorrows scattered everywhere, both in the home and in the outer world. If we took them as true, even for a moment, where would be our appetite, our sleep?

But I cannot dismiss myself as one of these shadows, and so the load of my sorrow lies eternally heavy on the heart of my world.

Why not stand out aloof in the highway of the universe, and feel yourself to be part of the all? In the midst of the immense, age-long concourse of humanity, what is Bimala to you? Your wife? What is a wife? A bubble of a name blown big with your own breath, so carefully guarded night and day, yet ready to burst at any pin-prick from outside.

My wife—and so, forsooth, my very own! If she says, 'No, I am myself'—am I to reply, 'How can that be? Are you not mine?'

'My wife'—Does that amount to an argument, much less the truth? Can one imprison a whole personality within that name?

My wife!—Have I not cherished in this little world all that is purest and sweetest in my life, never for a moment letting it down from my bosom to the dust? What incense of worship, what music of passion, what flowers of my spring and of my autumn, have I not offered up at its shrine? If, like a toy paper-boat, she be swept along into the muddy waters of the gutter—would I not also...?

There it is again, my incorrigible solemnity! Why 'muddy'? What 'gutter' names, called in a fit of jealousy, do not change the facts of the world. If Bimal is not mine, she is not; and no fuming, or fretting, or arguing will serve to prove that she is. If my heart is breaking—let it break! That will not make the world bankrupt—nor even me; for man is so much greater than the things he loses in this life. The very ocean of tears has its other shore, else none would have ever wept.

But then there is Society to be considered...which let Society consider! If I weep it is for myself, not for Society. If Bimala should say she is not mine, what care I where my Society wife may be?

Suffering there must be; but I must save myself, by any means in my power, from one form of self-torture, I must never think that my life loses its value because of any neglect it may suffer. The full value of my life does not all go to buy my narrow domestic world; its great commerce does not stand or fall with some petty success or failure in the bartering of my personal joys and sorrows.

The time has come when I must divest Bimala of all the ideal decorations with which I decked her. It was owing to my own weakness that I indulged in such idolatry. I was too greedy. I created an angel of Bimala, in order to exaggerate my own enjoyment. But Bimala is what she is. It is preposterous to expect that she should assume the rôle of an angel for my pleasure. The Creator is under no obligation to supply me with angels, just because I have an avidity for imaginary perfection.

I must acknowledge that I have merely been an accident in Bimala's life. Her nature, perhaps, can only find true union with one like Sandip. At the same time, I must not, in false modesty, accept my rejection as my desert. Sandip certainly has attractive qualities, which had their sway also upon myself; but yet, I feel sure, he is not a greater man than I. If the wreath of victory falls to his lot today, and I am overlooked, then the dispenser of the wreath will be called to judgement.

I say this in no spirit of boasting. Sheer necessity has driven me to the pass, that to secure myself from utter desolation I must recognize all the value that I truly possess. Therefore, through the, terrible experience of suffering let there come upon me the joy of deliverance—deliverance from self-distrust.

I have come to distinguish what is really in me from what I foolishly imagined to be there. The profit and loss account has been settled, and that which remains is myself—not a crippled self, dressed in rags and tatters, not a sick self to be nursed on invalid diet, but a spirit which has gone through the worst, and has survived.

My master passed through my room a moment ago and said with his hand on my shoulder. 'Get away to bed, Nikhil, the night is far advanced.'

The fact is, it has become so difficult for me to go to bed till late—till Bimala is fast asleep. In the day-time we meet, and even converse, but what am I to say when we are alone together, in the silence of the night?—so ashamed do I feel in mind and body.

'How is it, sir, you have not yet retired?' I asked in my turn. My master smiled a little, as he left me, saying, 'My sleeping days are over. I have now attained the waking age.'

I had written thus far, and was about to rise to go off bedwards when, through the window before me, I saw the heavy pall of July cloud suddenly part a little, and a big star shine through. It seemed to say to me, 'Dreamland ties are made, and dreamland ties are broken, but I am here forever—the everlasting lamp of the bridal night.'

All at once my heart was full with the thought that my Eternal Love was steadfastly waiting for me through the ages, behind the veil of material things. Through many a life, in many a mirror, have I seen her image—broken mirrors, crooked mirrors, dusty mirrors. Whenever I have sought to make the mirror my very own, and shut it up within my box, I have lost sight of the image. But what of that. What have I to do with the mirror, or even the image?

My beloved, your smile shall never fade, and every dawn there shall appear fresh for me the vermilion mark on your forehead!

'What childish cajolery of self-deception,' mocks some devil from his dark corner—'silly prattle to make children quiet!'

That may be. But millions and millions of children, with their million cries, have to be kept quiet. Can it be that all this multitude is quieted with only a lie? No, my Eternal Love cannot deceive me, for she is true!

She is true; that is why I have seen her and shall see her so often, even in my mistakes, even through the thickest mist of tears. I have seen her and lost her in the crowd of life's marketplace, and found her again; and I shall find her once more when I have escaped through the loophole of death.

Ah, cruel one, play with me no longer! If I have failed to track you by the marks of your footsteps on the way, by the scent of your tresses lingering in the air, make me not weep for that forever. The unveiled star tells me not to fear. That which is eternal must always be there.

Now let me go and see my Bimala. She must have spread her tired limbs on the bed, limp after her struggles, and be asleep. I will leave a kiss on her forehead without waking her—that shall be the flower-offering of my worship. I believe I could forget everything after death—all my mistakes, all my sufferings—but some vibration of the memory of that kiss would remain; for the wreath which is being woven out of the kisses of many a successive birth is to crown the Eternal Beloved.

As the gong of the watch rang out, sounding the hour of two, my sister-in-law came into the room. 'Whatever are you doing, brother dear?'[1] she cried. 'For pity's sake go to bed and stop worrying so. I cannot bear to look on that awful shadow of pain on your face.' Tears welled up in her eyes and overflowed as she entreated me thus.

I could not utter a word, but took the dust of her feet, as I went off to bed.

BIMALA'S STORY

VII

At first I suspected nothing, feared nothing; I simply felt dedicated to my country. What a stupendous joy there was in this unquestioning surrender. Verily had I realized how, in thoroughness of self-destruction, man can find supreme bliss.

---

[1]When a relationship is established by marriage, or by mutual understanding arising out of special friendship or affection, the persons so related call each other in terms of such relationship, and not by name. [Trans.].

For aught I know, this frenzy of mine might have come to a gradual, natural end. But Sandip Babu would not have it so, he would insist on revealing himself. The tone of his voice became as intimate as a touch, every look flung itself on its knees in beggary. And, through it all, there burned a passion which in its violence made as though it would tear me up by the roots, and drag me along by the hair.

I will not shirk the truth. This cataclysmal desire drew me by day and by night. It seemed desperately alluring—this making havoc of myself. What a shame it seemed, how terrible, and yet how sweet! Then there was my overpowering curiosity, to which there seemed no limit. He of whom I knew but little, who never could assuredly be mine, whose youth flared so vigorously in a hundred points of flame—oh, the mystery of his seething passions, so immense, so tumultuous!

I began with a feeling of worship, but that soon passed away. I ceased even to respect Sandip; on the contrary, I began to look down upon him. Nevertheless this flesh-and-blood lute of mine, fashioned with my feeling and fancy, found in him a master-player. What though I shrank from his touch, and even came to loathe the lute itself; its music was conjured up all the same.

I must confess there was something in me which...what shall I say?...which makes me wish I could have died!

Chandranath Babu, when he finds leisure, comes to me. He has the power to lift my mind up to an eminence from where I can see in a moment the boundary of my life extended on all sides and so realize that the lines, which I took from my bounds, were merely imaginary.

But what is the use of it all? Do I really desire emancipation? Let suffering come to our house; let the best in me shrivel up and become black; but let this infatuation not leave me—such seems to be my prayer.

When, before my marriage, I used to see a brother-in-law of mine, now dead, mad with drink—beating his wife in his frenzy, and then sobbing and howling in maudlin repentance, vowing never to touch liquor again, and yet, the very same evening, sitting down to drink and drink—it would fill me with disgust. But my intoxication today is still more fearful. The stuff has not to be procured or poured out, it springs within my veins, and I know not how to resist it.

Must this continue to the end of my days? Now and again I start and look upon myself, and think my life to be a nightmare which will vanish all of a sudden with all its untruth. It has become so frightfully incongruous. It has no connection with its past. What it is, how it could have come to this pass, I cannot understand.

One day my sister-in-law remarked with a cutting laugh, 'What a wonderfully hospitable Chota Rani we have! Her guest absolutely will not budge. In our time there used to be guests, too; but they had not such lavish looking after—we were so absurdly taken up with our husbands. Poor brother Nikhil is paying the penalty of being born too modern. He should have come as a guest if he wanted to stay on. Now it looks as if it were time for him to quit... O you little demon, do your glances never fall, by chance, on his agonized face?'

This sarcasm did not touch me; for I knew that these women had it not in them to understand the nature of the cause of my devotion. I was then wrapped in the protecting armour of the exaltation of sacrifice, through which such shafts were powerless to reach and shame me.

VIII

For some time all talk of the country's cause has been dropped. Our conversation nowadays has become full of modern sex-problems, and various other matters, with a sprinkling of poetry, both old Vaishnava and modern English, accompanied by a running undertone of melody, low down in the bass, such as I have never in my life heard before, which seems to me to sound the true manly note, the note of power.

The day had come when all cover was gone. There was no longer even the pretence of a reason why Sandip Babu should linger on, or why I should have confidential talks with him every now and then. I felt thoroughly vexed with myself, with my sister-in-law, with the ways of the world, and I vowed I would never again go to the outer apartments, not if I were to die for it.

For two whole days I did not stir out. Then, for the first time, I discovered how far I had travelled. My life felt utterly tasteless. Whatever I touched I wanted to thrust away. I felt myself waiting—from the crown of my head to the tips of my toes—waiting for something, somebody; my blood kept tingling with some expectation.

I tried busying myself with extra work. The bedroom floor was clean enough but I insisted on its being scrubbed over again under my eyes. Things were arranged in the cabinets in one kind of order; I pulled them all out and rearranged them in a different way. I found no time that afternoon even to do up my hair; I hurriedly tied it into a loose knot, and went and worried everybody, fussing about the store-room. The stores seemed short, and pilfering must have been going on of late, but I could not muster up the courage to take any particular person to task—for might not the thought have crossed somebody's mind, 'Where were your eyes all these days!'

In short, I behaved that day as one possessed. The next day I tried to do some reading. What I read I have no idea, but after a spell of absentmindedness I found I had wandered away, book in hand, along the passage leading towards the outer apartments, and was standing by a window looking out upon the verandah running along the row of rooms on the opposite side of the quadrangle. One of these rooms, I felt, had crossed over to another shore, and the ferry had ceased to ply. I felt like the ghost of myself of two days ago, doomed to remain where I was, and yet not really there, blankly looking out forever.

As I stood there, I saw Sandip come out of his room into the verandah, a newspaper in his hand. I could see that he looked extraordinarily disturbed. The courtyard, the railings, in front, seemed to rouse his wrath. He flung away his newspaper with a gesture which seemed to want to rend the space before him.

I felt I could no longer keep my vow. I was about to move on towards the sitting-room, when I found my sister-in-law behind me. 'O Lord, this beats everything!' she ejaculated, as she glided away. I could not proceed to the outer apartments.

The next morning when my maid came calling, 'Rani Mother, it is getting late for giving out the stores,' I flung the keys to her, saying, 'Tell Harimati to see to it,' and went on with some embroidery of English pattern on which I was engaged, seated near the window.

Then came a servant with a letter. 'From Sandip Babu,' said he. What unbounded boldness! What must the messenger have thought? There was a tremor within my breast as I opened the envelope. There was no address on the letter, only the words, An urgent matter—touching the Cause. Sandip.

I flung aside the embroidery. I was up on my feet in a moment, giving a touch or two to my hair by the mirror. I kept the sari I had on, changing only my jacket—for one of my jackets had its associations.

I had to pass through one of the verandahs, where my sister-in-law used to sit in the morning slicing betel-nut. I refused to feel awkward. 'Whither away, Chota Rani?' she cried.

'To the sitting-room outside.'

'So early! A matinée, eh?'

And, as I passed on without further reply, she hummed after me a flippant song.

IX

When I was about to enter the sitting-room, I saw Sandip immersed in an illustrated catalogue of British Academy pictures, with his back to the door. He has a great notion of himself as an expert in matters of Art.

One day my husband said to him, 'If the artists ever want a teacher, they need never lack for one so long as you are there.' It had not been my husband's habit to speak cuttingly, but latterly there has been a change and he never spares Sandip.

'What makes you suppose that artists need no teachers?' Sandip retorted.

'Art is a creation,' my husband replied. 'So we should humbly be content to receive our lessons about Art from the work of the artist.'

Sandip laughed at this modesty, saying, 'You think that meekness is a kind of capital which increases your wealth the more you use it. It is my conviction that those who lack pride only float about like water reeds which have no roots in the soil.'

My mind used to be full of contradictions when they talked thus. On the one hand I was eager that my husband should win in argument and that Sandip's pride should be shamed. Yet, on the other, it was Sandip's unabashed pride which attracted me so. It shone like a precious diamond, which knows no diffidence, and sparkles in the face of the sun itself.

I entered the room. I knew Sandip could hear my footsteps as I went forward, but he pretended not to, and kept his eyes on the book.

I dreaded his Art talks, for I could not overcome my delicacy about the pictures he talked of, and the things he said, and had much ado in putting on an air of overdone insensibility to hide my qualms. So, I was almost on the point of retracing my steps, when, with a deep sigh, Sandip raised his eyes, and affected to be startled at the sight of me. 'Ah, you have come!' he said.

In his words, in his tone, in his eyes, there was a world of suppressed reproach, as if the claims he had acquired over me made my absence, even for these two or three days, a grievous wrong. I knew this attitude was an insult to me, but, alas, I had not the power to resent it.

I made no reply, but though I was looking another way, I could not help feeling that Sandip's plaintive gaze had planted itself right on my face, and would take no denial. I did so wish he would say something, so that I could shelter myself behind his words. I cannot tell how long this went on, but at last I could stand it no longer. 'What is this matter,' I asked, 'you are wanting to tell me about?'

Sandip again affected surprise as he said, 'Must there always be some matter? Is friendship by itself a crime? Oh, Queen Bee, to think that you should make so light of the greatest thing on earth! Is the heart's worship to be shut out like a stray cur?'

There was again that tremor within me. I could feel the crisis coming, too importunate to be put off. Joy and fear struggled for the mastery. Would my shoulders, I wondered, be broad enough to stand its shock, or would it not leave me overthrown, with my face in the dust?

I was trembling all over. Steadying myself with an effort I repeated, 'You summoned me for something touching the Cause, so I have left my household duties to attend to it.'

'That is just what I was trying to explain,' he said, with a dry laugh. 'Do you not know that I come to worship? Have I not told you that, in you, I visualize the Shakti of our country? The geography of a country is not the whole truth. No one can give up his life for a map! When I see you before me, then only do I realize how lovely my country is. When you have anointed me with your own hands, then shall I know I have the sanction of my country; and if, with that in my heart, I fall fighting, it shall not be on the dust of some map-made land, but on a lovingly spread skirt—do you know what kind of skirt?—like that of the earthen-red sari you wore the other day, with a broad blood-red border. Can I ever forget it? Such are the visions which give vigour to life, and joy to death!'

Sandip's eyes took fire as he went on, but whether it was the fire of worship, or of passion, I could not tell. I was reminded of the day on which I first heard him speak, when I could not be sure whether he was a person, or just a living flame.

I had not the power to utter a word. You cannot take shelter behind the walls of decorum when in a moment the fire leaps up and, with the flash of its sword and the roar of its laughter, destroys all the miser's stores. I was in terror lest he should forget himself and take me by the hand. For he shook like a quivering tongue of fire; his eyes showered scorching sparks on me.

'Are you forever determined,' he cried after a pause, 'to make gods of your petty household duties—you who have it in you to send us to life or to death? Is this power of yours to be kept veiled in a zenana? Cast away all false shame, I pray you; snap your fingers at the whispering around. Take your plunge today into the freedom of the outer world.'

When, in Sandip's appeals, his worship of the country gets to be subtly interwoven with his worship of me, then does my blood dance, indeed, and the barriers of my hesitation totter. His talks about Art and Sex, his distinctions between Real and Unreal, had but clogged my attempts at response with some revolting nastiness. This, however, now burst again into a glow before which my repugnance faded away. I felt that my resplendent womanhood made me indeed a goddess. Why should not its glory flash from my forehead with visible brilliance? Why does not my voice find a word, some audible cry, which would be like a sacred spell to my country for its fire initiation?

All of a sudden my maid Khema rushed into the room, dishevelled. 'Give me my wages and let me go,' she screamed. 'Never in all my life have I been so...' The rest of her speech was drowned in sobs.

'What is the matter?'

Thako, the Bara Rani's maid, it appeared, had for no rhyme or reason reviled her in unmeasured terms. She was in such a state, it was no manner of use trying to pacify her by saying I would look into the matter afterwards.

The slime of domestic life that lay beneath the lotus bank of womanhood came to the surface. Rather than allow Sandip a prolonged vision of it, I had to hurry back within.

X

My sister-in-law was absorbed in her betel-nuts, the suspicion of a smile playing about her lips, as if nothing untoward had happened. She was still humming the same song.

'Why has your Thako been calling poor Khema names?' I burst out.

'Indeed? The wretch! I will have her broomed out of the house. What a shame to spoil your morning out like this! As for Khema, where are the hussy's manners to go and disturb you when you are engaged? Anyhow, Chota Rani, don't you worry yourself with these domestic squabbles. Leave them to me, and return to your friend.'

How suddenly the wind in the sails of our mind veers round! This going to meet Sandip outside seemed, in the light of the zenana code, such an extraordinarily out-of-the-way thing to do that I went off to my own room, at a loss for a reply. I knew this was my sister-in-law's doing and that she had egged her maid on to contrive this scene. But I had brought myself to such an unstable poise that I dared not have my fling.

Why, it was only the other day that I found I could not keep up to the last the unbending hauteur with which I had demanded from my husband the dismissal of the man Nanku. I felt suddenly abashed when the Bara Rani came up and said, 'It is really all my fault, brother dear. We are old-fashioned folk, and I did not quite like the ways of your Sandip Babu, so I only told the guard...but how was I to know that our Chota Rani would take this as an insult?—I thought it would be the other way about! Just my incorrigible silliness!'

The thing which seems so glorious when viewed from the heights of the country's cause, looks so muddy when seen from the bottom. One begins by getting angry, and then feels disgusted.

I shut myself into my room, sitting by the window, thinking how easy life would be if only one could keep in harmony with one's surroundings. How simply the senior Rani sits in her verandah with her betel-nuts and how inaccessible to me has become my natural seat beside my daily duties! Where will it all end, I asked myself? Shall I ever recover, as from a delirium, and forget it all; or am I to be dragged to depths from which there can be no escape in this life? How on earth did I manage to let my good fortune escape me, and spoil my life so? Every wall of this bedroom of mine, which I first entered nine years ago as a bride, stares at me in dismay.

When my husband came home, after his M.A. examination, he brought for me this orchid belonging to some faraway land beyond the seas. From beneath these few little leaves sprang such a cascade of blossoms, it looked as if they were pouring forth from some overturned urn of Beauty. We decided, together, to hang it here, over this window. It flowered only that once, but we have always been in hope of its doing so once more. Curiously enough I have kept on watering it these days, from force of habit, and it is still green.

It is now four years since I framed a photograph of my husband in ivory and put it in the niche over there. If I happen to look that way I have to lower my eyes. Up to last week I used regularly to put there the flowers of my worship, every morning after my bath. My husband has often chided me over this.

'It shames me to see you place me on a height to which I do not belong,' he said one day.

'What nonsense!'

'I am not only ashamed, but also jealous!'

'Just hear him! Jealous of whom, pray?'

'Of that false me. It only shows that I am too petty for you, that you want some extraordinary man who can overpower you with his superiority, and so you needs must take refuge in making for yourself another "me".'

'This kind of talk only makes me angry,' said I.

'What is the use of being angry with me?' he replied. 'Blame your fate which allowed you no choice, but made you take me blindfold. This keeps you trying to retrieve its blunder by making me out a paragon.'

I felt so hurt at the bare idea that tears started to my eyes that day. And whenever I think of that now, I cannot raise my eyes to the niche.

For now there is another photograph in my jewel case. The other day, when arranging the sitting-room, I brought away that double photo frame, the one in which Sandip's portrait was next to my husband's. To this portrait I have no flowers of worship to offer, but it remains hidden away under my gems. It has all the greater fascination because kept secret. I look at it now and then with doors closed. At night I turn up the lamp, and sit with it in my hand, gazing and gazing. And every night I think of burning it in the flame of the lamp, to be done with it forever; but every night I heave a sigh and smother it again in my pearls and diamonds.

Ah, wretched woman! What a wealth of love was twined round each one of those jewels! Oh, why am I not dead?

Sandip had impressed it on me that hesitation is not in the nature of woman. For her, neither right nor left has any existence—she only moves forward. When the women of our country wake up, he repeatedly insisted, their voice will be unmistakably confident in its utterance of the cry, 'I want.'

'I want!' Sandip went on one day—this was the primal word at the root of all creation. It had no maxim to guide it, but it became fire and wrought itself into suns and stars. Its partiality is terrible. Because it had a desire for man, it ruthlessly sacrificed millions of beasts for millions of years to achieve that desire. That terrible word 'I want' has taken flesh in woman, and therefore men, who are cowards, try with all their might to keep back this primeval flood with their earthen dykes. They are afraid lest, laughing and dancing as it goes, it should wash away all the hedges and props of their pumpkin field. Men, in every age, flatter themselves that they have secured this force within the bounds of their convenience, but it gathers and grows. Now it is calm and deep like a lake, but gradually its pressure will increase, the dykes will give way, and the force which has so long been dumb will rush forward with the roar, 'I want!'

These words of Sandip echo in my heart-beats like a war-drum. They shame into silence all my conflicts with myself. What do I care what people may think of me? Of what value are that orchid and that niche in my bedroom? What power have they to belittle me, to put me to shame? The primal fire of creation burns in me.

I felt a strong desire to snatch down the orchid and fling it out of the window, to denude the niche of its picture, to lay bare and naked the unashamed spirit of destruction that raged within me. My arm was raised to do it, but a sudden pang passed through my breast, tears started to my eyes. I threw myself down and sobbed, 'What is the end of all this, what is the end?'

SANDIP'S STORY

IV

When I read these pages of the story of my life I seriously question myself, Is this Sandip? Am I made of words? Am I merely a book with a covering of flesh and blood?

The earth is not a dead thing like the moon. She breathes. Her rivers and oceans send up vapours in which she is clothed. She is covered with a mantle of her own dust which flies about the air. The onlooker, gazing upon the earth from the outside, can see only the light reflected from this vapour and this dust. The tracks of the mighty continents are not distinctly visible.

The man, who is alive as this earth is, is likewise always enveloped in the mist of the ideas which he is breathing out. His real land and water remain hidden, and he appears to be made of only lights and shadows.

It seems to me, in this story of my life, that, like a living plant, I am displaying the picture of an ideal world. But I am not merely what I want, what I think I am also what I do not love, what I do not wish to be. My creation had begun before I was born. I had no choice in regard to my surroundings and so must make the best of such material as comes to my hand.

My theory of life makes me certain that the Great is cruel. To be just is for ordinary men—it is reserved for the great to be unjust. The surface of the earth was even. The volcano butted it with its fiery horn and found its own eminence—its justice was not towards its obstacle, but towards itself. Successful injustice and genuine cruelty have been the only forces by which individual or nation has become millionaire or monarch.

That is why I preach the great discipline of Injustice. I say to everyone, Deliverance is based upon injustice. Injustice is the fire which must keep on burning something in order to save itself from becoming ashes. Whenever an individual or nation becomes incapable of perpetrating injustice it is swept into the dustbin of the world.

As yet this is only my idea—it is not completely myself. There are rifts in the armour through which something peeps out which is extremely soft and sensitive. Because, as I say, the best part of myself was created before I came to this stage of existence.

From time to time I try my followers in their lesson of cruelty. One day we went on a picnic. A goat was grazing by. I asked them, 'Who is there among you that can cut off a leg of that goat, alive, with this knife, and bring it to me?' While they all hesitated, I went myself and did it. One of them fainted at the sight. But when they saw me unmoved they took the dust of my feet, saying that I was above all human weaknesses. That is to say, they saw that day the vaporous envelope which was my idea, but failed to perceive the inner me, which by a curious freak of fate has been created tender and merciful.

In the present chapter of my life, which is growing in interest every day round Bimala and Nikhil, there is also much that remains hidden underneath. This malady of ideas which afflicts me is shaping my life within, nevertheless a great part of my life remains outside its influence; and so there is set up a discrepancy between my outward life and its inner design which I try my best to keep concealed even from myself; otherwise it may wreck not only my plans, but my very life.

Life is indefinite—a bundle of contradictions. We men, with our ideas, strive to give it a particular shape by melting it into a particular mould—into the definiteness of success. All the world-conquerors, from Alexander down to the American millionaires, mould themselves into a sword or a mint, and thus find that distinct image of themselves which is the source of their success.

The chief controversy between Nikhil and myself arises from this, that though I say 'know thyself', and Nikhil also says 'know thyself', his interpretation makes this 'knowing' tantamount to 'not knowing'.

'Winning your kind of success,' Nikhil once objected, 'is success gained at the cost of the soul, but the soul is greater than success.'

I simply said in answer, 'Your words are too vague.'

'That I cannot help,' Nikhil replied. 'A machine is distinct enough, but not so life. If to gain distinctness you try to know life as a machine, then such mere distinctness cannot stand for truth. The soul is not as distinct as success, and so you only lose your soul if you seek it in your success.'

'Where, then, is this wonderful soul?'

'Where it knows itself in the infinite and transcends its success.'

'But how does all this apply to our work for the country?'

'It is the same thing. Where our country makes itself the final object, it gains success at the cost of the soul. Where it recognizes the Greatest as greater than all, there it may miss success, but gains its soul.'

'Is there any example of this in history?'

'Man is so great that he can despise not only the success, but also the example. Possibly example is lacking, just as there is no example of the flower in the seed. But there is the urgency of the flower in the seed all the same.'

It is not that I do not at all understand Nikhil's point of view; that is rather where my danger lies. I was born in India and the poison of its spirituality runs in my blood. However loudly I may proclaim the madness of walking in the path of self-abnegation, I cannot avoid it altogether.

This is exactly how such curious anomalies happen nowadays in our country. We must have our religion and also our nationalism; our Bhagavad Gita and also our *Bande Mataram*. The result is that both of them suffer. It is like performing with an English military band, side by side with our Indian festive pipes. I must make it the purpose of my life to put an end to this hideous confusion.

I want the western military style to prevail, not the Indian. We shall then not be ashamed of the flag of our passion, which Mother

Nature has sent with us as our standard into the battlefield of life. Passion is beautiful and pure—pure as the lily that comes out of the slimy soil. It rises superior to its defilement and needs no Pears' soap to wash it clean.

V

A question has been worrying me the last few days. Why am I allowing my life to become entangled with Bimala's? Am I a drifting log to be caught up at any and every obstacle?

Not that I have any false shame at Bimala becoming an object of my desire. It is only too clear how she wants me, and so I look on her as quite legitimately mine. The fruit hangs on the branch by the stem, but that is no reason why the claim of the stem should be eternal. Ripe fruit cannot forever swear by its slackening stem-hold. All its sweetness has been accumulated for me; to surrender itself to my hand is the reason of its existence, its very nature, its true morality. So I must pluck it, for it becomes me not to make it futile.

But what is teasing me is that I am getting entangled. Am I not born to rule?—to bestride my proper steed, the crowd, and drive it as I will; the reins in my hand, the destination known only to me, and for it the thorns, the mire, on the road? This steed now awaits me at the door, pawing and champing its bit, its neighing filling the skies. But where am I, and what am I about, letting day after day of golden opportunity slip by?

I used to think I was like a storm—that the torn flowers with which I strewed my path would not impede my progress. But I am only wandering round and round a flower like a bee—not a storm. So, as I was saying, the colouring of ideas which man gives himself is only superficial. The inner man remains as ordinary as ever. If someone, who could see right into me, were to write my biography, he would make me out to be no different from that lout of a Panchu, or even from Nikhil!

Last night I was turning over the pages of my old diary... I had just graduated, and my brain was bursting with philosophy. Even so early I had vowed not to harbour any illusions, whether of my own or other's imagining, but to build my life on a solid basis of reality. But what has since been its actual story? Where is its solidity? It has rather been a network, where, though the thread be continuous, more space is taken up by the holes. Fight as I may, these will not own defeat. Just as I was congratulating myself on steadily following the thread, here I am badly caught in a hole! For I have become susceptible to compunctions.

'I want it; it is here; let me take it'—This is a clear-cut, straightforward policy. Those who can pursue its course with vigour needs must win through in the end. But the gods would not have it that such journey should be easy, so they have deputed the siren Sympathy to distract the wayfarer, to dim his vision with her tearful mist.

I can see that poor Bimala is struggling like a snared deer. What a piteous alarm there is in her eyes! How she is torn with straining at her bonds! This sight, of course, should gladden the heart of a true hunter. And so do I rejoice; but, then, I am also touched; and therefore I dally, and standing on the brink I am hesitating to pull the noose fast.

There have been moments, I know, when I could have bounded up to her, clasped her hands and folded her to my breast, unresisting. Had I done so, she would not have said one word. She was aware that some crisis was impending, which in a moment would change the meaning of the whole world. Standing before that cavern of the incalculable but yet expected, her face went pale and her eyes glowed with a fearful ecstasy. Within that moment, when it arrives, an eternity will take shape, which our destiny awaits, holding its breath.

But I have let this moment slip by. I did not, with uncompromising strength, press the almost certain into the absolutely assured. I now see clearly that some hidden elements in my nature have openly ranged themselves as obstacles in my path.

That is exactly how Ravana, whom I look upon as the real hero of the Ramayana, met with his doom. He kept Sita in his Asoka garden, awaiting her pleasure, instead of taking her straight into his harem. This weak spot in his otherwise grand character made the whole of the abduction episode futile. Another such touch of compunction made him disregard, and be lenient to, his traitorous brother Bibhisan, only to get himself killed for his pains.

Thus does the tragic in life come by its own. In the beginning it lies, a little thing, in some dark under-vault, and ends by overthrowing the whole superstructure. The real tragedy is, that man does not know himself for what he really is.

VI

Then again there is Nikhil. Crank though he be, laugh at him as I may, I cannot get rid of the idea that he is my friend. At first I gave no thought to his point of view, but of late it has begun to shame and hurt me. Therefore I have been trying to talk and argue with him in the same enthusiastic way as of old, but it does not ring true. It is even leading me at times into such a length of unnaturalness as to pretend to agree with him. But such hypocrisy is not in my nature, nor in that of Nikhil either. This, at least, is something we have in common. That is why, nowadays, I would rather not come across him, and have taken to fighting shy of his presence.

All these are signs of weakness. No sooner is the possibility of a wrong admitted than it becomes actual, and clutches you by the throat, however you may then try to shake off all belief in it. What I should like to be able to tell Nikhil frankly is, that happenings such as these must be looked in the face—as great Realities—and that which is the Truth should not be allowed to stand between true friends.

There is no denying that I have really weakened. It was not this weakness which won over Bimala; she burnt her wings in the blaze of the full strength of my unhesitating manliness. Whenever smoke obscures its lustre she also becomes confused, and draws back. Then comes a thorough revulsion of feeling, and she fain would take back the garland she has put round my neck, but cannot; and so she only closes her eyes, to shut it out of sight.

But all the same I must not swerve from the path I have chalked out. It would never do to abandon the cause of the country, especially at the present time. I shall simply make Bimala one with my country. The turbulent west wind which has swept away the country's veil of conscience, will sweep away the veil of the wife from Bimala's face, and in that uncovering there will be no shame. The ship will rock as it bears the crowd across the ocean, flying the pennant of *Bande Mataram*, and it will serve as the cradle to my power, as well as to my love.

Bimala will see such a majestic vision of deliverance, that her bonds will slip from about her, without shame, without her even being aware of it. Fascinated by the beauty of this terrible wrecking power, she will not hesitate a moment to be cruel. I have seen in Bimala's nature the cruelty which is the inherent force of existence—the cruelty which with its unrelenting might keeps the world beautiful.

If only women could be set free from the artificial fetters put round them by men, we could see on earth the living image of Kali, the shameless, pitiless goddess. I am a worshipper of Kali, and one day I shall truly worship her, setting Bimala on her altar of Destruction. For this let me get ready.

The way of retreat is absolutely closed for both of us. We shall despoil each other, get to hate each other, but never more be free.

CHAPTER FIVE

NIKHIL'S STORY

IV

Everything is rippling and waving with the flood of August. The young shoots of rice have the sheen of an infant's limbs. The water has invaded the garden next to our house. The morning light, like the love of the blue sky, is lavished upon the earth... Why cannot I sing? The water of the distant river is shimmering with light; the leaves are glistening; the ricefields with their fitful shivers, break into gleams of gold; and in this symphony of Autumn, only I remain voiceless. The sunshine of the world strikes my heart, but is not reflected back.

When I realize the lack of expressiveness in myself, I know why I am deprived. Who could bear my company day and night without a break? Bimala is full of the energy of life, and so she has never become stale to me for a moment, in all these nine years of our wedded life.

My life has only its dumb depths; but no murmuring rush. I can only receive, not impart movement. And therefore my company is like fasting. I recognize clearly today that Bimala has been languishing because of a famine of companionship.

Then whom shall I blame? Like Vidyapati I can only lament,

'It is August, the sky breaks into a passionate rain; Alas, empty is my house.'

My house, I now see, was built to remain empty, because its doors cannot open. But I never knew till now that its divinity had been sitting outside. I had fondly believed that she had accepted my sacrifice, and granted in return her boon. But, alas, my house has all along been empty.

Every year, about this time, it was our practice to go in a houseboat over the broads of Samalda. I used to tell Bimala that a song must come back to its refrain over and over again. The original refrain of every song is in Nature, where the rain laden wind passes over the rippling stream, where the green earth, drawing its shadow-veil over its face, keeps its ear close to the speaking water. There, at the beginning of time, a man and a woman first met—not within walls. And therefore we two must come back to Nature, at least once a year, to tune our love anew to the first pure note of the meeting of hearts.

The first two anniversaries of our married life I spent in Calcutta, where I went through my examinations. But from the next year onwards, for seven years without a break, we have celebrated our union among the blossoming water-lilies. Now begins the next octave of my life.

It was difficult for me to ignore the fact that the same month of August had come round again this year. Does Bimala remember it, I wonder?—she has given me no reminder. Everything is mute about me.

'It is August, the sky breaks into a passionate rain; Alas, empty is my house.'

The house which becomes empty through the parting of lovers, still has music left in the heart of its emptiness. But the house that is empty because hearts are asunder, is awful in its silence. Even the cry of pain is out of place there.

This cry of pain must be silenced in me. So long as I continue to suffer, Bimala will never have true freedom. I must free her completely, otherwise I shall never gain my freedom from untruth...

I think I have come to the verge of understanding one thing. Man has so fanned the flame of the loves of men and women, as to make it overpass its rightful domain, and now, even in the name of humanity itself, he cannot bring it back under control. Man's worship has idolized his passion. But there must be no more human sacrifices at its shrine...

I went into my bedroom this morning, to fetch a book. It is long since I have been there in the daytime. A pang passed through me as I looked round it today, in the morning light. On the clothes rack was hanging a sari of Bimala's, crinkled ready for wear. On the dressing-table were her perfumes, her comb, her hair-pins, and with them, still, her vermilion box! Underneath were her tiny gold-embroidered slippers.

Once, in the old days, when Bimala had not yet overcome her objections to shoes, I had got these out from Lucknow, to tempt her. The first time she was ready to drop for very shame, to go in them even from the room to the verandah. Since then she has worn out many shoes, but has treasured up this pair. When first showing her the slippers, I chaffed her over a curious practice of hers; 'I have caught you taking the dust of my feet, thinking me asleep! These are the offerings of my worship to ward the dust off the feet of my wakeful divinity.' 'You must not say such things,' she protested, 'or I will never wear your shoes!'

This bedroom of mine—it has a subtle atmosphere which goes straight to my heart. I was never aware, as I am today, how my thirsting heart has been sending out its roots to cling round each and every familiar object. The severing of the main root, I see, is not enough to set life free. Even these little slippers serve to hold one back.

My wandering eyes fall on the niche. My portrait there is looking the same as ever, in spite of the flowers scattered round it having been withered black! Of all the things in the room their greeting strikes me as sincere. They are still here simply because it was not felt worthwhile even to remove them. Never mind; let me welcome truth, albeit in such sere and sorry garb, and look forward to the time when I shall be able to do so unmoved, as does my photograph.

As I stood there, Bimal came in from behind. I hastily turned my eyes from the niche to the shelves as I muttered, 'I came to get Amiel's Journal.' What need had I to volunteer an explanation? I felt like a wrong-doer, a trespasser, prying into a secret not meant for me. I could not look Bimal in the face, but hurried away.

V

I had just made the discovery that it was useless to keep up a pretence of reading in my room outside, and also that it was equally beyond me to busy myself attending to anything at all—so that all the days of my future bid fair to congeal into one solid mass and settle heavily on my breast for good—when Panchu, the tenant of a neighbouring zamindar, came up to me with a basketful of cocoa-nuts and greeted me with a profound obeisance.

'Well, Panchu,' said I. 'What is all this for?'

I had got to know Panchu through my master. He was extremely poor, nor was I in a position to do anything for him; so I supposed this present was intended to procure a tip to help the poor fellow to make both ends meet. I took some money from my purse and held it out towards him, but with folded hands he protested, 'I cannot take that, sir!'

'Why, what is the matter?'

'Let me make a clean breast of it, sir. Once, when I was hard pressed, I stole some cocoa-nuts from the garden here. I am getting old, and may die any day, so I have come to pay them back.'

Amiel's Journal could not have done me any good that day. But these words of Panchu lightened my heart. There are more things in life than the union or separation of man and woman. The great world stretches far beyond, and one can truly measure one's joys and sorrows when standing in its midst.

Panchu was devoted to my master. I know well enough how he manages to eke out a livelihood. He is up before dawn every day, and with a basket of paan leaves, twists of tobacco, coloured cotton yarn, little combs, looking-glasses, and other trinkets beloved of the village women, he wades through the knee-deep water of the marsh and goes over to the Namasudra quarters. There he barters his goods for rice, which fetches him a little more than their price in money. If he can get back soon enough he goes out again, after a hurried meal, to the sweetmeat seller's, where he assists in beating sugar for wafers. As soon as he comes home he sits at his shell-bangle making, plodding on often till midnight. All this cruel toil does not earn, for himself and his family, a bare two meals a day during much more than half the year. His method of eating is to begin with a good filling draught of water, and his staple food is the cheapest kind of seedy banana. And yet the family has to go with only one meal a day for the rest of the year.

At one time I had an idea of making him a charity allowance. 'But,' said my master, 'your gift may destroy the man, it cannot destroy the hardship of his lot. Mother Bengal has not only this one Panchu. If the milk in her breasts has run dry, that cannot be supplied from the outside.'

These are thoughts which give one pause, and I decided to devote myself to working it out. That very day I said to Bimala, 'Let us dedicate our lives to removing the root of this sorrow in our country.'

'You are my Prince Siddharta,[1] I see,' she replied with a smile. 'But do not let the torrent of your feelings end by sweeping me away also!'

'Siddharta took his vows alone. I want ours to be a joint arrangement.'

The idea passed away in talk. The fact is, Bimala is at heart what is called a 'lady'. Though her own people are not well off, she was born a Rani. She has no doubts in her mind that there is a lower unit of measure for the trials and troubles of the 'lower classes'. Want is, of course, a permanent feature of their lives, but does not necessarily mean 'want' to them. Their very smallness protects them, as the banks protect the pool; by widening bounds only the slime is exposed.

The real fact is that Bimala has only come into my home, not into my life. I had magnified her so, leaving her such a large place, that when I lost her, my whole way of life became narrow and confined. I had thrust aside all other objects into a corner to make room for Bimala—taken up as I was with decorating her and dressing her and educating her and moving round her day and night; forgetting how great is humanity and how nobly precious is man's life. When the actualities of everyday things get the better of the man, then is Truth lost sight of and freedom missed. So painfully important did Bimala make the mere actualities, that the truth remained concealed from me. That is why I find no gap in my misery, and spread this minute point of my emptiness over all the world. And so, for hours on this Autumn morning, the refrain has been humming in my ears,

'It is the month of August, and the sky breaks into a passionate rain; Alas, my house is empty.'

---

[1] The name by which Buddha was known when a Prince, before renouncing the world.

BIMALA'S STORY

XI

The change which had, in a moment, come over the mind of Bengal was tremendous. It was as if the Ganges had touched the ashes of the sixty thousand sons of Sagar[1] which no fire could enkindle, no other water knead again into living clay. The ashes of lifeless Bengal suddenly spoke up, 'Here am I.'

I have read somewhere that in ancient Greece a sculptor had the good fortune to impart life to the image made by his own hand. Even in that miracle, however, there was the process of form preceding life. But where was the unity in this heap of barren ashes? Had they been hard like stone, we might have had hopes of some form emerging, even as Ahalya, though turned to stone, at last won back her humanity. But these scattered ashes must have dropped to the dust through gaps in the Creator's fingers, to be blown hither and thither by the wind. They had become heaped up, but were never before united. Yet in this day which had come to Bengal, even this collection of looseness had taken shape, and proclaimed in a thundering voice, at our very door, 'Here I am.'

How could we help thinking that it was all supernatural? This moment of our history seemed to have dropped into our hand like a jewel from the crown of some drunken god. It had no resemblance to our past; and so we were led to hope that all our wants and miseries would disappear by the spell of some magic charm, that for us there was no longer any boundary line between the possible and the impossible. Everything seemed to be saying to us, 'It is coming; it has come!'

Thus we came to cherish the belief that our history needed no steed, but that like heaven's chariot it would move with its own inherent power—At least no wages would have to be paid to the charioteer; only his wine cup would have to be filled again and again. And then

---

[1] The condition of the curse which had reduced them to ashes was such that they could only be restored to life if the stream of the Ganges was brought down to them. [Trans.].

in some impossible paradise the goal of our hopes would be reached.

My husband was not altogether unmoved, but through all our excitement it was the strain of sadness in him which deepened and deepened. He seemed to have a vision of something beyond the surging present.

I remember one day, in the course of the arguments he continually had with Sandip, he said, 'Good fortune comes to our gate and announces itself, only to prove that we have not the power to receive it—that we have not kept things ready to be able to invite it into our house.'

'No,' was Sandip's answer. 'You talk like an atheist because you do not believe in our gods. To us it has been made quite visible that the Goddess has come with her boon, yet you distrust the obvious signs of her presence.'

'It is because I strongly believe in my God,' said my husband, 'that I feel so certain that our preparations for his worship are lacking. God has power to give the boon, but we must have power to accept it.'

This kind of talk from my husband would only annoy me. I could not keep from joining in, 'You think this excitement is only a fire of drunkenness, but does not drunkenness, up to a point, give strength?'

'Yes,' my husband replied. 'It may give strength, but not weapons.'

'But strength is the gift of God,' I went on. 'Weapons can be supplied by mere mechanics.'

My husband smiled. 'The mechanics will claim their wages before they deliver their supplies,' he said.

Sandip swelled his chest as he retorted, 'Don't you trouble about that. Their wages shall be paid.'

'I shall bespeak the festive music when the payment has been made, not before,' my husband answered.

'You needn't imagine that we are depending on your bounty for the music,' said Sandip scornfully. 'Our festival is above all money payments.'

And in his thick voice he began to sing,

'My lover of the unpriced love, spurning payments, Plays upon the simple pipe, bought for nothing, Drawing my heart away.'

Then with a smile he turned to me and said, 'If I sing, Queen Bee, it is only to prove that when music comes into one's life, the lack of a good voice is no matter. When we sing merely on the strength of our tunefulness, the song is belittled. Now that a full flood of music has swept over our country, let Nikhil practise his scales, while we rouse the land with our cracked voices,

'My house cries to me, Why go out to lose your all? My life says, All that you have, fling to the winds! If we must lose our all, let us lose it, what is it worth after all? If I must court ruin, let me do it smilingly; For my quest is the death-draught of immortality.

'The truth is, Nikhil, that we have all lost our hearts. None can hold us any longer within the bounds of the easily possible, in our forward rush to the hopelessly impossible.

'Those who would draw us back, They know not the fearful joy of recklessness. They know not that we have had our call From the end of the crooked path. All that is good and straight and trim—Let it topple over in the dust.'

I thought that my husband was going to continue the discussion, but he rose silently from his seat and left us.

The thing that was agitating me within was merely a variation of the stormy passion outside, which swept the country from one end to the other. The car of the wielder of my destiny was fast approaching, and the sound of its wheels reverberated in my being. I had a constant feeling that something extraordinary might happen any moment, for which, however, the responsibility would not be mine. Was I not removed from the plane in which right and wrong, and the feelings of others, have to be considered? Had I ever wanted this—had I ever been waiting or hoping for any such thing? Look at my whole life and tell me then, if I was in any way accountable.

Through all my past I had been consistent in my devotion—but when at length it came to receiving the boon, a different god appeared! And just as the awakened country, with its *Bande Mataram*, thrills in salutation to the unrealized future before it, so do all my veins and nerves send forth shocks of welcome to the unthought-of, the unknown, the importunate Stranger.

One night I left my bed and slipped out of my room on to the open terrace. Beyond our garden wall are fields of ripening rice.

Through the gaps in the village groves to the North, glimpses of the river are seen. The whole scene slept in the darkness like the vague embryo of some future creation.

In that future I saw my country, a woman like myself, standing expectant. She has been drawn forth from her home corner by the sudden call of some Unknown. She has had no time to pause or ponder, or to light herself a torch, as she rushes forward into the darkness ahead. I know well how her very soul responds to the distant flute-strains which call her; how her breast rises and falls; how she feels she nears it, nay it is already hers, so that it matters not even if she run blindfold. She is no mother. There is no call to her of children in their hunger, no home to be lighted of an evening, no household work to be done. So; she hies to her tryst, for this is the land of the Vaishnava Poets. She has left home, forgotten domestic duties; she has nothing but an unfathomable yearning which hurries her on—by what road, to what goal, she recks not.

I, also, am possessed of just such a yearning. I likewise have lost my home and also lost my way. Both the end and the means have become equally shadowy to me. There remain only the yearning and the hurrying on. Ah! wretched wanderer through the night, when the dawn reddens you will see no trace of a way to return. But why return? Death will serve as well. If the Dark which sounded the flute should lead to destruction, why trouble about the hereafter? When I am merged in its blackness, neither I, nor good and bad, nor laughter, nor tears, shall be any more!

XII

In Bengal the machinery of time being thus suddenly run at full pressure, things which were difficult became easy, one following soon after another. Nothing could be held back anymore, even in our corner of the country. In the beginning our district was backward, for my husband was unwilling to put any compulsion on the villagers. 'Those who make sacrifices for their country's sake are indeed her servants,' he would say, 'but those who compel others to make them in her name are her enemies. They would cut freedom at the root, to gain it at the top.'

But when Sandip came and settled here, and his followers began to move about the country, speaking in towns and market-places, waves of excitement came rolling up to us as well. A band of young fellows of the locality attached themselves to him, some even who had been known as a disgrace to the village. But the glow of their genuine enthusiasm lighted them up, within as well as without. It became quite clear that when the pure breezes of a great joy and hope sweep through the land, all dirt and decay are cleansed away. It is hard, indeed, for men to be frank and straight and healthy, when their country is in the throes of dejection.

Then were all eyes turned on my husband, from whose estates alone foreign sugar and salt and cloths had not been banished. Even the estate officers began to feel awkward and ashamed over it. And yet, some time ago, when my husband began to import country-made articles into our village, he had been secretly and openly twitted for his folly, by old and young alike. When Swadeshi had not yet become a boast, we had despised it with all our hearts.

My husband still sharpens his Indian-made pencils with his Indian-made knife, does his writing with reed pens, drinks his water out of a bell-metal vessel, and works at night in the light of an old-fashioned castor oil lamp. But this dull, milk-and-water Swadeshi of his never appealed to us. Rather, we had always felt ashamed of the inelegant, unfashionable furniture of his reception-rooms, especially when he had the magistrate, or any other European, as his guest.

My husband used to make light of my protests. 'Why allow such trifles to upset you?' he would say with a smile.

'They will think us barbarians, or at all events wanting in refinement.'

'If they do, I will pay them back by thinking that their refinement does not go deeper than their white skins.'

My husband had an ordinary brass pot on his writing-table which he used as a flower-vase. It has often happened that, when I had news of some European guest, I would steal into his room and put in its place a crystal vase of European make. 'Look here, Bimala,' he objected at length, 'that brass pot is as unconscious of itself as those blossoms are; but this thing protests its purpose so loudly, it is only fit for artificial flowers.'

The Bara Rani, alone, pandered to my husband's whims. Once she comes panting to say, 'Oh, brother, have you heard? Such lovely Indian soaps have come out! My days of luxury are gone by; still, if they contain no animal fat, I should like to try some.'

This sort of thing makes my husband beam all over, and the house is deluged with Indian scents and soaps. Soaps indeed! They are more like lumps of caustic soda. And do I not know that what my sister-in-law uses on herself are the European soaps of old, while these are made over to the maids for washing clothes?

Another time it is, 'Oh, brother dear, do get me some of these new Indian pen-holders.'

Her 'brother' bubbles up as usual, and the Bara Rani's room becomes littered with all kinds of awful sticks that go by the name of Swadeshi pen-holders. Not that it makes any difference to her, for reading and writing are out of her line. Still, in her writing-case, lies the selfsame ivory pen-holder, the only one ever handled.

The fact is, all this was intended as a hit at me, because I would not keep my husband company in his vagaries. It was no good trying to show up my sister-in-law's insincerity; my husband's face would set so hard, if I barely touched on it. One only gets into trouble, trying to save such people from being imposed upon!

The Bara Rani loves sewing. One day I could not help blurting out, 'What a humbug you are, sister! When your "brother" is present, your mouth waters at the very mention of Swadeshi scissors, but it is the English-made article every time when you work.'

'What harm?' she replied. 'Do you not see what pleasure it gives him? We have grown up together in this house, since he was a boy. I simply cannot bear, as you can, the sight of the smile leaving his face. Poor dear, he has no amusement except this playing at shop-keeping. You are his only dissipation, and you will yet be his ruin!'

'Whatever you may say, it is not right to be double-faced,' I retorted.

My sister-in-law laughed out in my face. 'Oh, our artless little Chota Rani!—straight as a schoolmaster's rod, eh? But a woman is not built that way. She is soft and supple, so that she may bend without being crooked.'

I could not forget those words, 'You are his dissipation, and will be his ruin!' Today I feel—if a man needs must have some intoxicant, let it not be a woman.

XIII

Suksar, within our estates, is one of the biggest trade centres in the district. On one side of a stretch of water there is held a daily bazar; on the other, a weekly market. During the rains when this piece of water gets connected with the river, and boats can come through, great quantities of cotton yarns, and woollen stuffs for the coming winter, are brought in for sale.

At the height of our enthusiasm, Sandip laid it down that all foreign articles, together with the demon of foreign influence, must be driven out of our territory.

'Of course!' said I, girding myself up for a fight.

'I have had words with Nikhil about it,' said Sandip. 'He tells me, he does not mind speechifying, but he will not have coercion.'

'I will see to that,' I said, with a proud sense of power. I knew how deep was my husband's love for me. Had I been in my senses I should have allowed myself to be torn to pieces rather than assert my claim to that, at such a time. But Sandip had to be impressed with the full strength of my Shakti.

Sandip had brought home to me, in his irresistible way, how the cosmic Energy was revealed for each individual in the shape of some special affinity. Vaishnava Philosophy, he said, speaks of the Shakti of Delight that dwells in the heart of creation, ever attracting the heart of her Eternal Lover. Men have a perpetual longing to bring out this Shakti from the hidden depths of their own nature, and those of us who succeed in doing so at once clearly understand the meaning of the music coming to us from the Dark. He broke out singing,

'My flute, that was busy with its song, Is silent now when we stand face to face. My call went seeking you from sky to sky When you lay hidden; But now all my cry finds its smile In the face of my beloved.'

Listening to his allegories, I had forgotten that I was plain and simple Bimala. I was Shakti; also an embodiment of universal joy. Nothing could fetter me, nothing was impossible for me; whatever I touched would gain new life. The world around me was a fresh creation of mine; for behold, before my heart's response had touched it, there had not been this wealth of gold in the Autumn sky! And this hero, this true servant of the country, this devotee of mine—this flaming intelligence, this burning energy, this shining genius—him also was I creating from moment to moment. Have I not seen how my presence pours fresh life into him time after time?

The other day Sandip begged me to receive a young lad, Amulya, an ardent disciple of his. In a moment I could see a new light flash out from the boy's eyes, and knew that he, too, had a vision of Shakti manifest, that my creative force had begun its work in his blood. 'What sorcery is this of yours!' exclaimed Sandip next day. 'Amulya is a boy no longer, the wick of his life is all ablaze. Who can hide your fire under your home-roof? Every one of them must be touched up by it, sooner or later, and when every lamp is alight what a grand carnival of a Dewali we shall have in the country!'

Blinded with the brilliance of my own glory I had decided to grant my devotee this boon. I was overweeningly confident that none could baulk me of what I really wanted. When I returned to my room after my talk with Sandip, I loosed my hair and tied it up over again. Miss Gilby had taught me a way of brushing it up from the neck and piling it in a knot over my head. This style was a favourite one with my husband. 'It is a pity,' he once said, 'that Providence should have chosen poor me, instead of poet Kalidas, for revealing all the wonders of a woman's neck. The poet would probably have likened it to a flower-stem; but I feel it to be a torch, holding aloft the black flame of your hair.' With which he...but why, oh why, do I go back to all that?

I sent for my husband. In the old days I could contrive a hundred and one excuses, good or bad, to get him to come to me. Now that all this had stopped for days I had lost the art of contriving.

NIKHIL'S STORY

VI

Panchu's wife has just died of a lingering consumption. Panchu must undergo a purification ceremony to cleanse himself of sin and to propitiate his community. The community has calculated and informed him that it will cost one hundred and twenty-three rupees.

'How absurd!' I cried, highly indignant. 'Don't submit to this, Panchu. What can they do to you?'

Raising to me his patient eyes like those of a tired-out beast of burden, he said, 'There is my eldest girl, sir, she will have to be married. And my poor wife's last rites have to be put through.'

'Even if the sin were yours, Panchu,' I mused aloud, 'you have surely suffered enough for it already.'

'That is so, sir,' he naïvely assented. 'I had to sell part of my land and mortgage the rest to meet the doctor's bills. But there is no escape from the offerings I have to make to the Brahmins.'

What was the use of arguing? When will come the time, I wondered, for the purification of the Brahmins themselves who can accept such offerings?

After his wife's illness and funeral, Panchu, who had been tottering on the brink of starvation, went altogether beyond his depth. In a desperate attempt to gain consolation of some sort he took to sitting at the feet of a wandering ascetic, and succeeded in acquiring philosophy enough to forget that his children went hungry. He kept himself steeped for a time in the idea that the world is vanity, and if of pleasure it has none, pain also is a delusion. Then, at last, one night he left his little ones in their tumble-down hovel, and started off wandering on his own account.

I knew nothing of this at the time, for just then a veritable ocean-churning by gods and demons was going on in my mind. Nor did my master tell me that he had taken Panchu's deserted children under his own roof and was caring for them, though alone in the house, with his school to attend to the whole day.

After a month Panchu came back, his ascetic fervour considerably worn off. His eldest boy and girl nestled up to him, crying, 'Where have you been all this time, father?' His youngest boy filled his lap; his second girl leant over his back with her arms around his neck; and they all wept together. 'O sir!' sobbed Panchu, at length, to my master. 'I have not the power to give these little ones enough to eat—I am not free to run away from them. What has been my sin that I should be scourged so, bound hand and foot?'

In the meantime the thread of Panchu's little trade connections had snapped and he found he could not resume them. He clung on to the shelter of my master's roof, which had first received him on his return, and said not a word of going back home. 'Look here, Panchu,' my master was at last driven to say. 'If you don't take care of your cottage, it will tumble down altogether. I will lend you some money with which you can do a bit of peddling and return it me little by little.'

Panchu was not excessively pleased—was there then no such thing as charity on earth? And when my master asked him to write out a receipt for the money, he felt that this favour, demanding a return, was hardly worth having. My master, however, did not care to make an outward gift which would leave an inward obligation. To destroy self-respect is to destroy caste, was his idea.

After signing the note, Panchu's obeisance to my master fell off considerably in its reverence—the dust-taking was left out. It made my master smile; he asked nothing better than that courtesy should stoop less low. 'Respect given and taken truly balances the account between man and man,' was the way he put it, 'but veneration is overpayment.'

Panchu began to buy cloth at the market and peddle it about the village. He did not get much of cash payment, it is true, but what he could realize in kind, in the way of rice, jute, and other field produce, went towards settlement of his account. In two month's time he was able to pay back an instalment of my master's debt, and with it there was a corresponding reduction in the depth of his bow. He must have begun to feel that he had been revering as a saint a mere man, who had not even risen superior to the lure of lucre.

While Panchu was thus engaged, the full shock of the Swadeshi flood fell on him.

VII

It was vacation time, and many youths of our village and its neighbourhood had come home from their schools and colleges. They attached themselves to Sandip's leadership with enthusiasm, and some, in their excess of zeal, gave up their studies altogether. Many of the boys had been free pupils of my school here, and some held college scholarships from me in Calcutta. They came up in a body, and demanded that I should banish foreign goods from my Suksar market.

I told them I could not do it.

They were sarcastic, 'Why, Maharaja, will the loss be too much for you?'

I took no notice of the insult in their tone, and was about to reply that the loss would fall on the poor traders and their customers, not on me, when my master, who was present, interposed.

'Yes, the loss will be his—not yours, that is clear enough,' he said.

'But for one's country.'

'The country does not mean the soil, but the men on it,' interrupted my master again. 'Have you yet wasted so much as a glance on what was happening to them? But now you would dictate what salt they shall eat, what clothes they shall wear. Why should they put up with such tyranny, and why should we let them?'

'But we have taken to Indian salt and sugar and cloth ourselves.'

'You may do as you please to work off your irritation, to keep up your fanaticism. You are well off, you need not mind the cost. The poor do not want to stand in your way, but you insist on their submitting to your compulsion. As it is, every moment of theirs is a life-and-death struggle for a bare living; you cannot even imagine the difference a few pice means to them—so little have you in common. You have spent your whole past in a superior compartment, and now you come down to use them as tools for the wreaking of your wrath. I call it cowardly.'

They were all old pupils of my master, so they did not venture to be disrespectful, though they were quivering with indignation. They turned to me. 'Will you then be the only one, Maharaja, to put obstacles in the way of what the country would achieve?'

'Who am I, that I should dare do such a thing? Would I not rather lay down my life to help it?'

The M.A. student smiled a crooked smile, as he asked, 'May we enquire what you are actually doing to help?'

'I have imported Indian mill-made yarn and kept it for sale in my Suksar market, and also sent bales of it to markets belonging to neighbouring zamindars.'

'But we have been to your market, Maharaja,' the same student exclaimed, 'and found nobody buying this yarn.'

'That is neither my fault nor the fault of my market. It only shows the whole country has not taken your vow.'

'That is not all,' my master went on. 'It shows that what you have pledged yourselves to do is only to pester others. You want dealers, who have not taken your vow, to buy that yarn; weavers, who have not taken your vow, to make it up; then their wares eventually to be foisted on to consumers who, also, have not taken your vow. The method? Your clamour, and the zamindars' oppression. The result, all righteousness yours, all privations theirs!'

'And may we venture to ask, further, what your share of the privation has been?' pursued a science student.

'You want to know, do you?' replied my master. 'It is Nikhil himself who has to buy up that Indian mill yarn; he has had to start a weaving school to get it woven; and to judge by his past brilliant business exploits, by the time his cotton fabrics leave the loom their cost will be that of cloth-of-gold; so they will only find a use, perhaps, as curtains for his drawing-room, even though their flimsiness may fail to screen him. When you get tired of your vow, you will laugh the loudest at their artistic effect. And if their workmanship is ever truly appreciated at all, it will be by foreigners.'

I have known my master all my life, but have never seen him so agitated. I could see that the pain had been silently accumulating in his heart for some time, because of his surpassing love for me, and that his habitual self-possession had become secretly undermined to the breaking point.

'You are our elders,' said the medical student. 'It is unseemly that we should bandy words with you. But tell us, pray, finally, are you determined not to oust foreign articles from your market?'

'I will not,' I said, 'because they are not mine.'

'Because that will cause you a loss!' smiled the M.A. student.

'Because he, whose is the loss, is the best judge,' retorted my master.

With a shout of *Bande Mataram* they left us.

CHAPTER SIX

NIKHIL'S STORY

VIII

A few days later, my master brought Panchu round to me. His zamindar, it appeared, had fined him a hundred rupees, and was threatening him with ejectment.

'For what fault?' I enquired.

'Because,' I was told, 'he has been found selling foreign cloths. He begged and prayed Harish Kundu, his zamindar, to let him sell off his stock, bought with borrowed money, promising faithfully never to do it again; but the zamindar would not hear of it, and insisted on his burning the foreign stuff there and then, if he wanted to be let off. Panchu in his desperation blurted out defiantly, 'I can't afford it! You are rich; why not buy it up and burn it?' This only made Harish Kundu red in the face as he shouted, 'The scoundrel must be taught manners, give him a shoe-beating!' So poor Panchu got insulted as well as fined.

'What happened to the cloth?'

'The whole bale was burnt.'

'Who else was there?'

'Any number of people, who all kept shouting *Bande Mataram*. Sandip was also there. He took up some of the ashes, crying, 'Brothers! This is the first funeral pyre lighted by your village in celebration of the last rites of foreign commerce. These are sacred ashes. Smear yourselves with them in token of your Swadeshi vow."

'Panchu,' said I, turning to him, 'you must lodge a complaint.'

'No one will bear me witness,' he replied.

'None bear witness? —Sandip! Sandip!'

Sandip came out of his room at my call. 'What is the matter?' he asked.

'Won't you bear witness to the burning of this man's cloth?'

Sandip smiled. 'Of course I shall be a witness in the case,' he said. 'But I shall be on the opposite side.'

'What do you mean,' I exclaimed, 'by being a witness on this or that side? Will you not bear witness to the truth?'

'Is the thing which happens the only truth?'

'What other truths can there be?'

'The things that ought to happen! The truth we must build up will require a great deal of untruth in the process. Those who have made their way in the world have created truth, not blindly followed it.'

'And so—'

'And so I will bear what you people are pleased to call false witness, as they have done who have created empires, built up social systems, founded religious organizations. Those who would rule do not dread untruths; the shackles of truth are reserved for those who will fall under their sway. Have you not read history? Do you not know that in the immense cauldrons, where vast political developments are simmering, untruths are the main ingredients?'

'Political cookery on a large scale is doubtless going on, but—'

'Oh, I know! You, of course, will never do any of the cooking. You prefer to be one of those down whose throats the hotchpotch which is being cooked will be crammed. They will partition Bengal and say it is for your benefit. They will seal the doors of education and call it raising the standard. But you will always remain good boys, snivelling in your corners. We bad men, however, must see whether we cannot erect a defensive fortification of untruth.'

'It is no use arguing about these things, Nikhil,' my master interposed. 'How can they who do not feel the truth within them, realize that to bring it out from its obscurity into the light is man's highest aim—not to keep on heaping material outside?'

Sandip laughed. 'Right, sir!' said he. 'Quite a correct speech for a schoolmaster. That is the kind of stuff I have read in books; but in the real world I have seen that man's chief business is the accumulation of outside material. Those who are masters in the art, advertise the biggest lies in their business, enter false accounts in their political ledgers with their broadest-pointed pens, launch their newspapers daily laden with untruths, and send preachers abroad to disseminate falsehood like flies carrying pestilential germs. I am a humble follower of these great ones. When I was attached to the Congress party I never hesitated to dilute ten per cent of truth with ninety per cent of untruth. And now, merely because I have ceased to belong to that party, I have not forgotten the basic fact that man's goal is not truth but success.'

'True success,' corrected my master.

'Maybe,' replied Sandip, 'but the fruit of true success ripens only by cultivating the field of untruth, after tearing up the soil and pounding it into dust. Truth grows up by itself like weeds and thorns, and only worms can expect to get fruit from it!' With this he flung out of the room.

My master smiled as he looked towards me. 'Do you know, Nikhil,' he said, 'I believe Sandip is not irreligious—his religion is of the obverse side of truth, like the dark moon, which is still a moon, for all that its light has gone over to the wrong side.'

'That is why,' I assented, 'I have always had an affection for him, though we have never been able to agree. I cannot condemn him, even now; though he has hurt me sorely, and may yet hurt me more.'

'I have begun to realize that,' said my master. 'I have long wondered how you could go on putting up with him. I have, at times, even suspected you of weakness. I now see that though you two do not rhyme, your rhythm is the same.'

'Fate seems bent on writing Paradise Lost in blank verse, in my case, and so has no use for a rhyming friend!' I remarked, pursuing his conceit.

'But what of Panchu?' resumed my master.

'You say Harish Kundu wants to eject him from his ancestral holding. Supposing I buy it up and then keep him on as my tenant?'

'And his fine?'

'How can the zamindar realize that if he becomes my tenant?'

'His burnt bale of cloth?'

'I will procure him another. I should like to see anyone interfering with a tenant of mine, for trading as he pleases!'

'I am afraid, sir,' interposed Panchu despondently, 'while you big folk are doing the fighting, the police and the law vultures will merrily gather round, and the crowd will enjoy the fun, but when it comes to getting killed, it will be the turn of only poor me!'

'Why, what harm can come to you?'

'They will burn down my house, sir, children and all!'

'Very well, I will take charge of your children,' said my master. 'You may go on with any trade you like. They shan't touch you.'

That very day I bought up Panchu's holding and entered into formal possession. Then the trouble began.

Panchu had inherited the holding of his grandfather as his sole surviving heir. Everybody knew this. But at this juncture an aunt turned up from somewhere, with her boxes and bundles, her rosary, and a widowed niece. She ensconced herself in Panchu's home and laid claim to a life interest in all he had.

Panchu was dumbfounded. 'My aunt died long ago,' he protested.

In reply he was told that he was thinking of his uncle's first wife, but that the former had lost no time in taking to himself a second.

'But my uncle died before my aunt,' exclaimed Panchu, still more mystified. 'Where was the time for him to marry again?'

This was not denied. But Panchu was reminded that it had never been asserted that the second wife had come after the death of the first, but the former had been married by his uncle during the latter's lifetime. Not relishing the idea of living with a co-wife she had remained in her father's house till her husband's death, after which she had got religion and retired to holy Brindaban, whence she was now coming. These facts were well known to the officers of Harish Kundu, as well as to some of his tenants. And if the zamindar's summons should be peremptory enough, even some of those who had partaken of the marriage feast would be forthcoming!

IX

One afternoon, when I happened to be specially busy, word came to my office room that Bimala had sent for me. I was startled.

'Who did you say had sent for me?' I asked the messenger.

'The Rani Mother.'

'The Bara Rani?'

'No, sir, the Chota Rani Mother.'

The Chota Rani! It seemed a century since I had been sent for by her. I kept them all waiting there, and went off into the inner apartments. When I stepped into our room I had another shock of surprise to find Bimala there with a distinct suggestion of being dressed up. The room, which from persistent neglect had latterly acquired an air of having grown absent-minded, had regained something of its old order this afternoon. I stood there silently, looking enquiringly at Bimala.

She flushed a little and the fingers of her right hand toyed for a time with the bangles on her left arm. Then she abruptly broke the silence. 'Look here! Is it right that ours should be the only market in all Bengal which allows foreign goods?'

'What, then, would be the right thing to do?' I asked.

'Order them to be cleared out!'

'But the goods are not mine.'

'Is not the market yours?'

'It is much more theirs who use it for trade.'

'Let them trade in Indian goods, then.'

'Nothing would please me better. But suppose they do not?'

'Nonsense! How dare they be so insolent? Are you not...'

'I am very busy this afternoon and cannot stop to argue it out. But I must refuse to tyrannize.'

'It would not be tyranny for selfish gain, but for the sake of the country.'

'To tyrannize for the country is to tyrannize over the country. But that I am afraid you will never understand.' With this I came away.

All of a sudden the world shone out for me with a fresh clearness. I seemed to feel it in my blood, that the Earth had lost the weight of its earthiness, and its daily task of sustaining life no longer appeared a burden, as with a wonderful access of power it whirled through space telling its beads of days and nights. What endless work, and withal what illimitable energy of freedom! None shall check it, oh, none can ever check it! From the depths of my being an uprush of joy, like a waterspout, sprang high to storm the skies.

I repeatedly asked myself the meaning of this outburst of feeling. At first there was no intelligible answer. Then it became clear that the bond against which I had been fretting inwardly, night and day, had broken. To my surprise I discovered that my mind was freed from all mistiness. I could see everything relating to Bimala as if vividly pictured on a camera screen. It was palpable that she had specially dressed herself up to coax that order out of me. Till that moment, I had never viewed Bimala's adornment as a thing apart from herself. But today the elaborate manner in which she had done up her hair, in the English fashion, made it appear a mere decoration. That which before had the mystery of her personality about it, and was priceless to me, was now out to sell itself cheap.

As I came away from that broken cage of a bedroom, out into the golden sunlight of the open, there was the avenue of bauhinias, along the gravelled path in front of my verandah, suffusing the sky with a rosy flush. A group of starlings beneath the trees were noisily chattering away. In the distance an empty bullock cart, with its nose on the ground, held up its tail aloft—one of its unharnessed bullocks grazing, the other resting on the grass, its eyes dropping for very comfort, while a crow on its back was pecking away at the insects on its body.

I seemed to have come closer to the heartbeats of the great earth in all the simplicity of its daily life; its warm breath fell on me with the perfume of the bauhinia blossoms; and an anthem, inexpressibly sweet, seemed to peal forth from this world, where I, in my freedom, live in the freedom of all else.

We, men, are knights whose quest is that freedom to which our ideals call us. She who makes for us the banner under which we fare forth is the true Woman for us. We must tear away the disguise of her who weaves our net of enchantment at home, and know her for what she is. We must beware of clothing her in the witchery of our own longings and imaginings, and thus allow her to distract us from our true quest.

Today I feel that I shall win through. I have come to the gateway of the simple; I am now content to see things as they are. I have gained freedom myself; I shall allow freedom to others. In my work will be my salvation.

I know that, time and again, my heart will ache, but now that

I understand its pain in all its truth, I can disregard it. Now that I know it concerns only me, what after all can be its value? The suffering which belongs to all mankind shall be my crown.

Save me, Truth! Never again let me hanker after the false paradise of Illusion. If I must walk alone, let me at least tread your path. Let the drum-beats of Truth lead me to Victory.

SANDIP'S STORY

VII

Bimala sent for me that day, but for a time she could not utter a word; her eyes kept brimming up to the verge of overflowing. I could see at once that she had been unsuccessful with Nikhil. She had been so proudly confident that she would have her own way—but I had never shared her confidence. Woman knows man well enough where he is weak, but she is quite unable to fathom him where he is strong. The fact is that man is as much a mystery to woman as woman is to man. If that were not so, the separation of the sexes would only have been a waste of Nature's energy.

Ah pride, pride! The trouble was, not that the necessary thing had failed of accomplishment, but that the entreaty, which had cost her such a struggle to make, should have been refused. What a wealth of colour and movement, suggestion and deception, group themselves round this 'me' and 'mine' in woman. That is just where her beauty lies—she is ever so much more personal than man. When man was being made, the Creator was a schoolmaster—His bag full of commandments and principles; but when He came to woman, He resigned His headmastership and turned artist, with only His brush and paint-box.

When Bimala stood silently there, flushed and tearful in her broken pride, like a storm-cloud, laden with rain and charged with lightning, lowering over the horizon, she looked so absolutely sweet that I had to go right up to her and take her by the hand. It was trembling, but she did not snatch it away.

'Bee,' said I, 'we two are colleagues, for our aims are one. Let us sit down and talk it over.'

I led her, unresisting, to a seat. But strange! At that very point the rush of my impetuosity suffered an unaccountable check—just as the current of the mighty Padma, roaring on in its irresistible course, all of a sudden gets turned away from the bank it is crumbling by some trifling obstacle beneath the surface. When I pressed Bimala's hand my nerves rang music, like tuned-up strings; but the symphony stopped short at the first movement.

What stood in the way? Nothing singly; it was a tangle of a multitude of things—nothing definitely palpable, but only that unaccountable sense of obstruction. Anyhow, this much has become plain to me, that I cannot swear to what I really am. It is because I am such a mystery to my own mind that my attraction for myself is so strong! If once the whole of myself should become known to me, I would then fling it all away—and reach beatitude!

As she sat down, Bimala went ashy pale. She, too, must have realized what a crisis had come and gone, leaving her unscathed. The comet had passed by, but the brush of its burning tail had overcome her. To help her to recover herself I said, 'Obstacles there will be, but let us fight them through, and not be down-hearted. Is not that best, Queen?'

Bimala cleared her throat with a little cough, but simply to murmur, 'Yes.'

'Let us sketch out our plan of action,' I continued, as I drew a piece of paper and a pencil from my pocket.

I began to make a list of the workers who had joined us from Calcutta and to assign their duties to each. Bimala interrupted me before I was through, saying wearily, 'Leave it now; I will join you again this evening,' and then she hurried out of the room. It was evident she was not in a state to attend to anything. She must be alone with herself for a while—perhaps lie down on her bed and have a good cry!

When she left me, my intoxication began to deepen, as the cloud colours grow richer after the sun is down. I felt I had let the moment of moments slip by. What an awful coward I had been! She must have left me in sheer disgust at my qualms—and she was right!

While I was tingling all over with these reflections, a servant came in and announced Amulya, one of our boys. I felt like sending him away for the time, but he stepped in before I could make up my mind. Then we fell to discussing the news of the fights which were raging in different quarters over cloth and sugar and salt; and the air was soon clear of all fumes of intoxication. I felt as if awakened from a dream. I leapt to my feet feeling quite ready for the fray—*Bande Mataram*!

The news was various. Most of the traders who were tenants of Harish Kundu had come over to us. Many of Nikhil's officials were also secretly on our side, pulling the wires in our interest. The Marwari shopkeepers were offering to pay a penalty, if only allowed to clear their present stocks. Only some Mahomedan traders were still obdurate.

One of them was taking home some German-made shawls for his family. These were confiscated and burnt by one of our village boys. This had given rise to trouble. We offered to buy him Indian woollen stuffs in their place. But where were cheap Indian woollens to be had? We could not very well indulge him in Cashmere shawls! He came and complained to Nikhil, who advised him to go to law. Of course Nikhil's men saw to it that the trial should come to nothing, even his law-agent being on our side!

The point is, if we have to replace burnt foreign clothes with Indian cloth every time, and on the top of that fight through a law-suit, where is the money to come from? And the beauty of it is that this destruction of foreign goods is increasing their demand and sending up the foreigner's profits—very like what happened to the fortunate shopkeeper whose chandeliers the nabob delighted in smashing, tickled by the tinkle of the breaking glass.

The next problem is—since there is no such thing as cheap and gaudy Indian woollen stuff, should we be rigorous in our boycott of foreign flannels and memos, or make an exception in their favour?

'Look here!' said I at length on the first point, 'we are not going to keep on making presents of Indian stuff to those who have got their foreign purchases confiscated. The penalty is intended to fall on them, not on us. If they go to law, we must retaliate by burning down their granaries!—What startles you, Amulya? It is not the prospect of a grand illumination that delights me! You must remember, this is War. If you are afraid of causing suffering, go in for love-making, you will never do for this work!'

The second problem I solved by deciding to allow no compromise with foreign articles, in any circumstance whatever. In the good old days, when these gaily coloured foreign shawls were unknown, our peasantry used to manage well enough with plain cotton quilts—they must learn to do so again. They may not look as gorgeous, but this is not the time to think of looks.

Most of the boatmen had been won over to refuse to carry foreign goods, but the chief of them, Mirjan, was still insubordinate.

'Could you not get his boat sunk?' I asked our manager here.

'Nothing easier, sir,' he replied. 'But what if afterwards I am held responsible?'

'Why be so clumsy as to leave any loophole for responsibility? However, if there must be any, my shoulders will be there to bear it.'

Mirjan's boat was tied near the landing-place after its freight had been taken over to the market-place. There was no one on it, for the manager had arranged for some entertainment to which all had been invited. After dusk the boat, loaded with rubbish, was holed and set adrift. It sank in mid-stream.

Mirjan understood the whole thing. He came to me in tears to beg for mercy. 'I was wrong, sir—' he began.

'What makes you realize that all of a sudden?' I sneered.

He made no direct reply. 'The boat was worth two thousand rupees,' he said. 'I now see my mistake, and if excused this time I will never...' with which he threw himself at my feet.

I asked him to come ten days later. If only we could pay him that two thousand rupees at once, we could buy him up body and soul. This is just the sort of man who could render us immense service, if won over. We shall never be able to make any headway unless we can lay our hands on plenty of money.

As soon as Bimala came into the sitting-room, in the evening, I said as I rose up to receive her, 'Queen! Everything is ready, success is at hand, but we must have money.'

'Money? How much money?'

'Not so very much, but by hook or by crook we must have it!'

'But how much?'

'A mere fifty thousand rupees will do for the present.'

Bimala blenched inwardly at the figure, but tried not to show it. How could she again admit defeat?

'Queen!' said I, 'you only can make the impossible possible. Indeed you have already done so. Oh, that I could show you the extent of your achievement—then you would know it. But the time for that is not now. Now we want money!'

'You shall have it,' she said.

I could see that the thought of selling her jewels had occurred to her. So I said, 'Your jewels must remain in reserve. One can never tell when they may be wanted.' And then, as Bimala stared blankly at me in silence, I went on, 'This money must come from your husband's treasury.'

Bimala was still more taken aback. After a long pause she said, 'But how am I to get his money?'

'Is not his money yours as well?'

'Ah, no!' she said, her wounded pride hurt afresh.

'If not,' I cried, 'neither is it his, but his country's, whom he has deprived of it, in her time of need!'

'But how am I to get it?' she repeated.

'Get it you shall and must. You know best how. You must get it for Her to whom it rightfully belongs. *Bande Mataram* ! These are the magic words which will open the door of his iron safe, break through the walls of his strong-room, and confound the hearts of those who are disloyal to its call. Say *Bande Mataram*, Bee!'

'*Bande Mataram!*'

CHAPTER SEVEN

SANDIP'S STORY

VIII

We are men, we are kings, we must have our tribute. Ever since we have come upon the Earth we have been plundering her; and the more we claimed, the more she submitted. From primeval days have we men been plucking fruits, cutting down trees, digging up the soil, killing beast, bird and fish. From the bottom of the sea, from underneath the ground, from the very jaws of death, it has all been grabbing and grabbing and grabbing—no strong-box in Nature's store-room has been respected or left unrifled. The one delight of this Earth is to fulfil the claims of those who are men. She has been made fertile and beautiful and complete through her endless sacrifices to them. But for this, she would be lost in the wilderness, not knowing herself, the doors of her heart shut, her diamonds and pearls never seeing the light.

Likewise, by sheer force of our claims, we men have opened up all the latent possibilities of women. In the process of surrendering themselves to us, they have ever gained their true greatness. Because they had to bring all the diamonds of their happiness and the pearls of their sorrow into our royal treasury, they have found their true wealth. So for men to accept is truly to give, for women to give is truly to gain.

The demand I have just made from Bimala, however, is indeed a large one! At first I felt scruples; for is it not the habit of man's mind to be in purposeless conflict with itself? I thought I had imposed too hard a task. My first impulse was to call her back, and tell her I would rather not make her life wretched by dragging her into all these troubles. I forgot, for the moment, that it was the mission of man to be aggressive, to make woman's existence fruitful by stirring up disquiet in the depth of her passivity, to make the whole world blessed by churning up the immeasurable abyss of suffering! This is why man's hands are so strong, his grip so firm. Bimala had been longing with all her heart that I, Sandip, should demand of her some great sacrifice—should call her to her death. How else could she be happy? Had she not waited all these weary years only for an opportunity to weep out her heart—so satiated was she with the monotony of her placid happiness? And therefore, at the very sight of me, her heart's horizon darkened with the rain clouds of her impending days of anguish. If I pity her and save her from her sorrows, what then was the purpose of my being born a man?

The real reason of my qualms is that my demand happens to be for money. That savours of beggary, for money is man's, not woman's. That is why I had to make it a big figure. A thousand or two would have the air of petty theft. Fifty thousand has all the expanse of romantic brigandage. Ah, but riches should really have been mine! So many of my desires have had to halt, again and again, on the road to accomplishment simply for want of money. This does not become me! Had my fate been merely unjust, it could be forgiven—but its bad taste is unpardonable. It is not simply a hardship that a man like me should be at his wit's end to pay his house rent, or should have to carefully count out the coins for an Intermediate Class railway ticket—it is vulgar!

It is equally clear that Nikhil's paternal estates are a superfluity to him. For him it would not have been at all unbecoming to be poor. He would have cheerfully pulled in the double harness of indigent mediocrity with that precious master of his. I should love to have, just for once, the chance to fling about fifty thousand rupees in the service of my country and to the satisfaction of myself. I am a nabob born, and it is a great dream of mine to get rid of this disguise of poverty, though it be for a day only, and to see myself in my true character. I have grave misgivings, however, as to Bimala ever getting that fifty thousand rupees within her reach, and it will probably be only a thousand or two which will actually come to hand. Be it so. The wise man is content with half a loaf, or any fraction for that matter, rather than no bread. I must return to these personal reflections of mine later.

News comes that I am wanted at once. Something has gone wrong...

It seems that the police have got a clue to the man who sank Mirjan's boat for us. He was an old offender. They are on his trail, but he should be too practised a hand to be caught blabbing. However, one never knows. Nikhil's back is up, and his manager may not be able to have things his own way.

'If I get into trouble, sir,' said the manager when I saw him, 'I shall have to drag you in!'

'Where is the noose with which you can catch me?' I asked.

'I have a letter of yours, and several of Amulya Babu's.' I could not see that the letter marked 'urgent' to which I had been hurried into writing a reply was wanted urgently for this purpose only! I am getting to learn quite a number of things.

The point now is, that the police must be bribed and hush-money paid to Mirjan for his boat. It is also becoming evident that much of the cost of this patriotic venture of ours will find its way as profit into the pockets of Nikhil's manager. However, I must shut my eyes to that for the present, for is he not shouting *Bande Mataram* as lustily as I am?

This kind of work has always to be carried on with leaky vessels which let as much through as they fetch in. We all have a hidden fund of moral judgement stored away within us, and so I was about to wax indignant with the manager, and enter in my diary a tirade against the unreliability of our countrymen. But, if there be a god, I must acknowledge with gratitude to him that he has given me a clear-seeing mind, which allows nothing inside or outside it to remain vague. I may delude others, but never myself. So I was unable to continue angry.

Whatever is true is neither good nor bad, but simply true, and that is Science. A lake is only the remnant of water which has not been sucked into the ground. Underneath the cult of *Bande Mataram*, as indeed at the bottom of all mundane affairs, there is a region of slime, whose absorbing power must be reckoned with. The manager will take what he wants; I also have my own wants. These lesser wants form a part of the wants of the great Cause—the horse must be fed and the wheels must be oiled if the best progress is to be made.

The long and short of it is that money we must have, and that soon. We must take whatever comes the readiest, for we cannot afford to wait. I know that the immediate often swallows up the ultimate; that the five thousand rupees of today may nip in the bud the fifty thousand rupees of tomorrow. But I must accept the penalty. Have I not often twitted Nikhil that they who walk in the paths of restraint have never known what sacrifice is? It is we greedy folk who have to sacrifice our greed at every step!

Of the cardinal sins of man, Desire is for men who are men—but Delusion, which is only for cowards, hampers them. Because delusion keeps them wrapped up in past and future, but is the very deuce for confounding their footsteps in the present. Those who are always straining their ears for the call of the remote, to the neglect of the call of the imminent, are like Sakuntala[1] absorbed in the memories of her lover. The guest comes unheeded, and the curse descends, depriving them of the very object of their desire.

The other day I pressed Bimala's hand, and that touch still stirs her mind, as it vibrates in mine. Its thrill must not be deadened by repetition, for then what is now music will descend to mere argument. There is at present no room in her mind for the question 'why?' So I must not deprive Bimala, who is one of those creatures for whom illusion is necessary, of her full supply of it.

As for me, I have so much else to do that I shall have to be content for the present with the foam of the wine cup of passion. O man of desire! Curb your greed, and practise your hand on the harp of illusion till you can bring out all the delicate nuances of suggestion. This is not the time to drain the cup to the dregs.

IX

Our work proceeds apace. But though we have shouted ourselves hoarse,

---

[1] Sakuntala, after the king, her lover, went back to his kingdom, promising to send for her, was so lost in thoughts of him, that she failed to hear the call of her hermit guest who thereupon cursed her, saying that the object of her love would forget all about her. [Trans.].

proclaiming the Mussulmans to be our brethren, we have come to realize that we shall never be able to bring them wholly round to our side. So they must be suppressed altogether and made to understand that we are the masters. They are now showing their teeth, but one day they shall dance like tame bears to the tune we play.

'If the idea of a United India is a true one,' objects Nikhil, 'Mussulmans are a necessary part of it.'

'Quite so,' said I, 'but we must know their place and keep them there, otherwise they will constantly be giving trouble.'

'So you want to make trouble to prevent trouble?'

'What, then, is your plan?'

'There is only one well known way of avoiding quarrels,' said Nikhil meaningly.

I know that, like tales written by good people, Nikhil's discourse always ends in a moral. The strange part of it is that with all his familiarity with moral precepts, he still believes in them! He is an incorrigible schoolboy. His only merit is his sincerity. The mischief with people like him is that they will not admit the finality even of death, but keep their eyes always fixed on a hereafter.

I have long been nursing a plan which, if only I could carry it out, would set fire to the whole country. True patriotism will never be roused in our countrymen unless they can visualize the motherland. We must make a goddess of her. My colleagues saw the point at once. 'Let us devise an appropriate image!' they exclaimed. 'It will not do if you devise it,' I admonished them. 'We must get one of the current images accepted as representing the country—the worship of the people must flow towards it along the deep-cut grooves of custom.'

But Nikhil's needs must argue even about this. 'We must not seek the help of illusions,' he said to me some time ago, 'for what we believe to be the true cause.'

'Illusions are necessary for lesser minds,' I said, 'and to this class the greater portion of the world belongs. That is why divinities are set up in every country to keep up the illusions of the people, for men are only too well aware of their weakness.'

'No,' he replied. 'God is necessary to clear away our illusions. The divinities which keep them alive are false gods.'

'What of that? If need be, even false gods must be invoked, rather than let the work suffer. Unfortunately for us, our illusions are alive enough, but we do not know how to make them serve our purpose. Look at the Brahmins. In spite of our treating them as demi-gods, and untiringly taking the dust of their feet, they are a force going to waste.

'There will always be a large class of people, given to grovelling, who can never be made to do anything unless they are bespattered with the dust of somebody's feet, be it on their heads or on their backs! What a pity if after keeping Brahmins saved up in our armoury for all these ages—keen and serviceable—they cannot be utilized to urge on this rabble in the time of our need.'

But it is impossible to drive all this into Nikhil's head. He has such a prejudice in favour of truth—as though there exists such an objective reality! How often have I tried to explain to him that where untruth truly exists, there it is indeed the truth. This was understood in our country in the old days, and so they had the courage to declare that for those of little understanding untruth is the truth. For them, who can truly believe their country to be a goddess, her image will do duty for the truth. With our nature and our traditions we are unable to realize our country as she is, but we can easily bring ourselves to believe in her image. Those who want to do real work must not ignore this fact.

Nikhil only got excited. 'Because you have lost the power of walking in the path of truth's attainment,' he cried, 'you keep waiting for some miraculous boon to drop from the skies! That is why when your service to the country has fallen centuries into arrears all you can think of is, to make of it an image and stretch out your hands in expectation of gratuitous favours.'

'We want to perform the impossible,' I said. 'So our country needs must be made into a god.'

'You mean you have no heart for possible tasks,' replied Nikhil. 'Whatever is already there is to be left undisturbed; yet there must be a supernatural result,'

'Look here, Nikhil,' I said at length, thoroughly exasperated. 'The things you have been saying are good enough as moral lessons. These ideas have served their purpose, as milk for babes, at one stage of man's evolution, but will no longer do, now that man has cut his teeth.

'Do we not see before our very eyes how things, of which we never even dreamt of sowing the seed, are sprouting up on every side? By what power? That of the deity in our country who is becoming manifest. It is for the genius of the age to give that deity its image. Genius does not argue, it creates. I only give form to what the country imagines.

'I will spread it abroad that the goddess has vouchsafed me a dream. I will tell the Brahmins that they have been appointed her priests, and that their downfall has been due to their dereliction of duty in not seeing to the proper performance of her worship. Do you say I shall be uttering lies? No, say I, it is the truth—nay more, the truth which the country has so long been waiting to learn from my lips. If only I could get the opportunity to deliver my message, you would see the stupendous result.'

'What I am afraid of,' said Nikhil, 'is, that my lifetime is limited and the result you speak of is not the final result. It will have after-effects which may not be immediately apparent.'

'I only seek the result,' said I, 'which belongs to today.'

'The result I seek,' answered Nikhil, 'belongs to all time.'

Nikhil may have had his share of Bengal's greatest gift—imagination, but he has allowed it to be overshadowed and nearly killed by an exotic conscientiousness. Just look at the worship of Durga which Bengal has carried to such heights. That is one of her greatest achievements. I can swear that Durga is a political goddess and was conceived as the image of the Shakti of patriotism in the days when Bengal was praying to be delivered from Mussulman domination. What other province of India has succeeded in giving such wonderful visual expression to the ideal of its quest?

Nothing betrayed Nikhil's loss of the divine gift of imagination more conclusively than his reply to me. 'During the Mussulman domination,' he said, 'the Maratha and the Sikh asked for fruit from the arms which they themselves took up. The Bengali contented himself with placing weapons in the hands of his goddess and muttering incantations to her; and as his country did not really happen to be a goddess the only fruit he got was the lopped-off heads of the goats and buffaloes of the sacrifice. The day that we seek the good of the country along the path of righteousness, He who is greater than our country will grant us true fruition.'

The unfortunate part of it is that Nikhil's words sound so fine when put down on paper. My words, however, are not meant to be scribbled on paper, but to be scored into the heart of the country. The Pandit records his Treatise on Agriculture in printer's ink; but the cultivator at the point of his plough impresses his endeavour deep in the soil.

X

When I next saw Bimala I pitched my key high without further ado. 'Have we been able,' I began, 'to believe with all our heart in the god for whose worship we have been born all these millions of years, until he actually made himself visible to us?'

'How often have I told you,' I continued, 'that had I not seen you I never would have known all my country as One. I know not yet whether you rightly understand me. The gods are invisible only in their heaven—on earth they show themselves to mortal men.'

Bimala looked at me in a strange kind of way as she gravely replied, 'Indeed I understand you, Sandip.' This was the first time she called me plain Sandip.

'Krishna,' I continued, 'whom Arjuna ordinarily knew only as the driver of his chariot, had also His universal aspect, of which, too, Arjuna had a vision one day, and that day he saw the Truth. I have seen your Universal Aspect in my country. The Ganges and the Brahmaputra are the chains of gold that wind round and round your neck; in the woodland fringes on the distant banks of the dark waters of the river, I have seen your collyrium-darkened eyelashes; the changeful sheen of your sari moves for me in the play of light and shade amongst the swaying shoots of green corn; and the blazing summer heat, which makes the whole sky lie gasping like a red-tongued lion in the desert, is nothing but your cruel radiance.

'Since the goddess has vouchsafed her presence to her votary in such wonderful guise, it is for me to proclaim her worship throughout our land, and then shall the country gain new life. 'Your image make we in temple after temple.'[1] But this our people have not yet fully realized. So I would call on them in your name and offer for their worship an image from which none shall be able to withhold belief. Oh give me this boon, this power.'

Bimala's eyelids drooped and she became rigid in her seat like a figure of stone. Had I continued she would have gone off into a trance. When I ceased speaking she opened wide her eyes, and murmured with fixed gaze, as though still dazed, 'O Traveller in the path of Destruction! Who is there that can stay your progress? Do I not see that none shall stand in the way of your desires? Kings shall lay their crowns at your feet; the wealthy shall hasten to throw open their treasure for your acceptance; those who have nothing else shall beg to be allowed to offer their lives. O my king, my god! What you have seen in me I know not, but I have seen the immensity of your grandeur in my heart. Who am I, what am I, in its presence? Ah, the awful power of Devastation! Never shall I truly live till it kills me utterly! I can bear it no longer, my heart is breaking!'

Bimala slid down from her seat and fell at my feet, which she clasped, and then she sobbed and sobbed and sobbed.

This is hypnotism indeed—the charm which can subdue the world! No materials, no weapons—but just the delusion of irresistible suggestion. Who says 'Truth shall Triumph'?[2] Delusion shall win in the end. The Bengali understood this when he conceived the image of the ten-handed goddess astride her lion, and spread her worship in the land. Bengal must now create a new image to enchant and conquer the world. *Bande Mataram*!

I gently lifted Bimala back into her chair, and lest reaction should set in, I began again without losing time, 'Queen! The Divine Mother has laid on me the duty of establishing her worship in the land. But, alas, I am poor!'

Bimala was still flushed, her eyes clouded, her accents thick, as she replied, 'You poor? Is not all that each one has yours? What are my caskets full of jewellery for? Drag away from me all my gold and

---

[1] A line from Bankim Chatterjee's national song *Bande Mataram*.
[2] A quotation from the Upanishads.

gems for your worship. I have no use for them!'

Once before Bimala had offered up her ornaments. I am not usually in the habit of drawing lines, but I felt I had to draw the line there.[1] I know why I feel this hesitation. It is for man to give ornaments to woman; to take them from her wounds his manliness.

But I must forget myself. Am I taking them? They are for the Divine Mother, to be poured in worship at her feet. Oh, but it must be a grand ceremony of worship such as the country has never beheld before. It must be a landmark in our history. It shall be my supreme legacy to the Nation. Ignorant men worship gods. I, Sandip, shall create them.

But all this is a far cry. What about the urgent immediate? At least three thousand is indispensably necessary—five thousand would do roundly and nicely. But how on earth am I to mention money after the high flight we have just taken? And yet time is precious!

I crushed all hesitation under foot as I jumped up and made my plunge, 'Queen! Our purse is empty, our work about to stop!'

Bimala winced. I could see she was thinking of that impossible fifty thousand rupees. What a load she must have been carrying within her bosom, struggling under it, perhaps, through sleepless nights! What else had she with which to express her loving worship? Debarred from offering her heart at my feet, she hankers to make this sum of money, so hopelessly large for her, the bearer of her imprisoned feelings. The thought of what she must have gone through gives me a twinge of pain; for she is now wholly mine. The wrench of plucking up the plant by the roots is over. It is now only careful tending and nurture that is needed.

'Queen!' said I, 'that fifty thousand rupees is not particularly wanted just now. I calculate that, for the present, five thousand or even three will serve.'

The relief made her heart rebound. 'I shall fetch you five thousand,' she said in tones which seemed like an outburst of song—the song which Radhika of the Vaishnava lyrics sang,

---

[1] There is a world of sentiment attached to the ornaments worn by women in Bengal.

'For my lover will I bind in my hair, The flower which has no equal in the three worlds!'—it is the same tune, the same song, five thousand will I bring! That flower will I bind in my hair!

The narrow restraint of the flute brings out this quality of song. I must not allow the pressure of too much greed to flatten out the reed, for then, as I fear, music will give place to the questions 'Why?' 'What is the use of so much?' 'How am I to get it?'—not a word of which will rhyme with what Radhika sang! So, as I was saying, illusion alone is real—it is the flute itself; while truth is but its empty hollow. Nikhil has of late got a taste of that pure emptiness—one can see it in his face, which pains even me. But it was Nikhil's boast that he wanted the Truth, while mine was that I would never let go illusion from my grasp. Each has been suited to his taste, so why complain?

To keep Bimala's heart in the rarefied air of idealism, I cut short all further discussion over the five thousand rupees. I reverted to the demon-destroying goddess and her worship. When was the ceremony to be held and where? There is a great annual fair at Ruimari, within Nikhil's estates, where hundreds of thousands of pilgrims assemble. That would be a grand place to inaugurate the worship of our goddess!

Bimala waxed intensely enthusiastic. This was not the burning of foreign cloth or the people's granaries, so even Nikhil could have no objection—so thought she. But I smiled inwardly. How little these two persons, who have been together, day and night, for nine whole years, know of each other! They know something perhaps of their home life, but when it comes to outside concerns they are entirely at sea. They had cherished the belief that the harmony of the home with the outside was perfect. Today they realize to their cost that it is too late to repair their neglect of years, and seek to harmonize them now.

What does it matter? Let those who have made the mistake learn their error by knocking against the world. Why need I bother about their plight? For the present I find it wearisome to keep Bimala soaring much longer, like a captive balloon, in regions ethereal. I had better get quite through with the matter in hand.

When Bimala rose to depart and had neared the door I remarked in my most casual manner, 'So, about the money...'

Bimala halted and faced back as she said, 'On the expiry of the month, when our personal allowances become due…'

'That, I am afraid, would be much too late.'

'When do you want it then?'

'Tomorrow.'

'Tomorrow you shall have it.'

They are not merely indicative of the love and regard of the giver, but the wearing of them symbolizes all that is held best in wifehood—the constant solicitude for her husband's welfare, the successful performance of the material and spiritual duties of the household entrusted to her care. When the husband dies, and the responsibility for the household changes hands, then are all ornaments cast aside as a sign of the widow's renunciation of worldly concerns. At any other time the giving up of ornaments is always a sign of supreme distress and as such appeals acutely to the sense of chivalry of any Bengali who may happen to witness it.

CHAPTER EIGHT

NIKHIL'S STORY

X

Paragraphs and letters against me have begun to come out in the local papers; cartoons and lampoons are to follow, I am told. Jets of wit and humour are being splashed about, and the lies thus scattered are convulsing the whole country. They know that the monopoly of mud-throwing is theirs, and the innocent passer-by cannot escape unsoiled.

They are saying that the residents in my estates, from the highest to the lowest, are in favour of Swadeshi, but they dare not declare themselves, for fear of me. The few who have been brave enough to defy me have felt the full rigour of my persecution. I am in secret league with the police, and in private communication with the magistrate, and these frantic efforts of mine to add a foreign title of my own earning to the one I have inherited, will not, it is opined, go in vain.

On the other hand, the papers are full of praise for those devoted sons of the motherland, the Kundu and the Chakravarti zamindars. If only, say they, the country had a few more of such staunch patriots, the mills of Manchester would have, had to sound their own dirge to the tune of *Bande Mataram*.

Then comes a letter in blood-red ink, giving a list of the traitorous zamindars whose treasuries have been burnt down because of their failing to support the Cause. Holy Fire, it goes on to say, has been aroused to its sacred function of purifying the country; and other agencies are also at work to see that those who are not true sons of the motherland do cease to encumber her lap. The signature is an obvious nom-de-plume.

I could see that this was the doing of our local students. So I sent for some of them and showed them the letter.

The B.A. student gravely informed me that they also had heard that a band of desperate patriots had been formed who would stick at nothing in order to clear away all obstacles to the success of Swadeshi.

'If,' said I, 'even one of our countrymen succumbs to these overbearing desperadoes, that will indeed be a defeat for the country!'

'We fail to follow you, Maharaja,' said the history student. 'Our country,' I tried to explain, 'has been brought to death's door through sheer fear—from fear of the gods down to fear of the police; and if you set up, in the name of freedom, the fear of some other bogey, whatever it may be called; if you would raise your victorious standard on the cowardice of the country by means of downright oppression, then no true lover of the country can bow to your decision.'

'Is there any country, sir,' pursued the history student, 'where submission to Government is not due to fear?'

'The freedom that exists in any country,' I replied, 'may be measured by the extent of this reign of fear. Where its threat is confined to those who would hurt or plunder, there the Government may claim to have freed man from the violence of man. But if fear is to regulate how people are to dress, where they shall trade, or what they must eat, then is man's freedom of will utterly ignored, and manhood destroyed at the root.'

'Is not such coercion of the individual will seen in other countries too?' continued the history student.

'Who denies it?' I exclaimed. 'But in every country man has destroyed himself to the extent that he has permitted slavery to flourish.'

'Does it not rather show,' interposed a Master of Arts, 'that trading in slavery is inherent in man—a fundamental fact of his nature?'

'Sandip Babu made the whole thing clear,' said a graduate. 'He gave us the example of Harish Kundu, your neighbouring zamindar. From his estates you cannot ferret out a single ounce of foreign salt. Why? Because he has always ruled with an iron hand. In the case of those who are slaves by nature, the lack of a strong master is the greatest of all calamities.'

'Why, sir!' chimed in an undergraduate, 'have you not heard of the obstreperous tenant of Chakravarti, the other zamindar close by—how the law was set on him till he was reduced to utter destitution? When at last he was left with nothing to eat, he started out to sell his wife's silver ornaments, but no one dared buy them. Then Chakravarti's manager offered him five rupees for the lot. They were worth over thirty, but he had to accept or starve. After taking over the bundle from him the manager coolly said that those five rupees would be credited towards his rent! We felt like having nothing more to do with Chakravarti or his manager after that, but Sandip Babu told us that if we threw over all the live people, we should have only dead bodies from the burning-grounds to carry on the work with! These live men, he pointed out, know what they want and how to get it—they are born rulers. Those who do not know how to desire for themselves, must live in accordance with, or die by virtue of, the desires of such as these. Sandip Babu contrasted them—Kundu and Chakravarti—with you, Maharaja. You, he said, for all your good intentions, will never succeed in planting Swadeshi within your territory.'

'It is my desire,' I said, 'to plant something greater than Swadeshi. I am not after dead logs but living trees—and these will take time to grow.'

'I am afraid, sir,' sneered the history student, 'that you will get neither log nor tree. Sandip Babu rightly teaches that in order to get, you must snatch. This is taking all of us some time to learn, because it runs counter to what we were taught at school. I have seen with my own eyes that when a rent-collector of Harish Kundu's found one of the tenants with nothing which could be sold up to pay his rent, he was made to sell his young wife! Buyers were not wanting, and the zamindar's demand was satisfied. I tell you, sir, the sight of that man's distress prevented my getting sleep for nights together! But, feel it as I did, this much I realized, that the man who knows how to get the money he is out for, even by selling up his debtor's wife, is a better man than I am. I confess it is beyond me—I am a weakling, my eyes fill with tears. If anybody can save our country it is these Kundus and these Chakravartis and their officials!'

I was shocked beyond words. 'If what you say be true,' I cried, 'I clearly see that it must be the one endeavour of my life to save the country from these same Kundus and Chakravartis and officials. The slavery that has entered into our very bones is breaking out, at this opportunity, as ghastly tyranny. You have been so used to submit to domination through fear, you have come to believe that to make others submit is a kind of religion. My fight shall be against this weakness, this atrocious cruelty!' These things, which are so simple to ordinary folk, get so twisted in the minds of our B.A.'s and M.A.'s, the only purpose of whose historical quibbles seems to be to torture the truth!

XI

I am worried over Panchu's sham aunt. It will be difficult to disprove her, for though witnesses of a real event may be few or even wanting, innumerable proofs of a thing that has not happened can always be marshalled. The object of this move is, evidently, to get the sale of Panchu's holding to me set aside. Being unable to find any other way out of it, I was thinking of allowing Panchu to hold a permanent tenure in my estates and building him a cottage on it. But my master would not have it. I should not give in to these nefarious tactics so easily, he objected, and offered to attend to the matter himself.

'You, sir!' I cried, considerably surprised.

'Yes, I,' he repeated.

I could not see, at all clearly, what my master could do to counteract these legal machinations. That evening, at the time he usually came to me, he did not turn up. On my making inquiries, his servant said he had left home with a few things packed in a small trunk, and some bedding, saying he would be back in a few days. I thought he might have sallied forth to hunt for witnesses in Panchu's uncle's village. In that case, however, I was sure that his would be a hopeless quest...

During the day I forget myself in my work. As the late autumn afternoon wears on, the colours of the sky become turbid, and so do the feelings of my mind. There are many in this world whose minds dwell in brick-built houses—they can afford to ignore the thing called the outside. But my mind lives under the trees in the open, directly receives upon itself the messages borne by the free winds, and responds from the bottom of its heart to all the musical cadences of light and darkness.

While the day is bright and the world in the pursuit of its numberless tasks crowds around, then it seems as if my life wants nothing else. But when the colours of the sky fade away and the blinds are drawn down over the windows of heaven, then my heart tells me that evening falls just for the purpose of shutting out the world, to mark the time when the darkness must be filled with the One. This is the end to which earth, sky, and waters conspire, and I cannot harden myself against accepting its meaning. So when the gloaming deepens over the world, like the gaze of the dark eyes of the beloved, then my whole being tells me that work alone cannot be the truth of life, that work is not the be-all and the end-all of man, for man is not simply a serf—even though the serfdom be of the True and the Good.

Alas, Nikhil, have you for ever parted company with that self of yours who used to be set free under the starlight, to plunge into the infinite depths of the night's darkness after the day's work was done? How terribly alone is he, who misses companionship in the midst of the multitudinousness of life.

The other day, when the afternoon had reached the meeting-point of day and night, I had no work, nor the mind for work, nor was my master there to keep me company. With my empty, drifting heart longing to anchor on to something, I traced my steps towards the inner gardens. I was very fond of chrysanthemums and had rows of them, of all varieties, banked up in pots against one of the garden walls. When they were in flower, it looked like a wave of green breaking into iridescent foam. It was some time since I had been to this part of the grounds, and I was beguiled into a cheerful expectancy at the thought of meeting my chrysanthemums after our long separation.

As I went in, the full moon had just peeped over the wall, her slanting rays leaving its foot in deep shadow. It seemed as if she had come a-tiptoe from behind, and clasped the darkness over the eyes, smiling mischievously. When I came near the bank of chrysanthemums, I saw a figure stretched on the grass in front. My heart gave a sudden thud. The figure also sat up with a start at my footsteps.

What was to be done next? I was wondering whether it would do to beat a precipitate retreat. Bimala, also, was doubtless casting about for some way of escape. But it was as awkward to go as to stay! Before I could make up my mind, Bimala rose, pulled the end of her sari over her head, and walked off towards the inner apartments.

This brief pause had been enough to make real to me the cruel load of Bimala's misery. The plaint of my own life vanished from me in a moment. I called out, 'Bimala!'

She started and stayed her steps, but did not turn back. I went round and stood before her. Her face was in the shade, the moonlight fell on mine. Her eyes were downcast, her hands clenched.

'Bimala,' said I, 'why should I seek to keep you fast in this closed cage of mine? Do I not know that thus you cannot but pine and droop?'

She stood still, without raising her eyes or uttering a word.

'I know,' I continued, 'that if I insist on keeping you shackled my whole life will be reduced to nothing but an iron chain. What pleasure can that be to me?'

She was still silent.

'So,' I concluded, 'I tell you, truly, Bimala, you are free. Whatever I may or may not have been to you, I refuse to be your fetters.' With which I came away towards the outer apartments.

No, no, it was not a generous impulse, nor indifference. I had simply come to understand that never would I be free until I could set free. To try to keep Bimala as a garland round my neck, would have meant keeping a weight hanging over my heart. Have I not been praying with all my strength, that if happiness may not be mine, let it go; if grief needs must be my lot, let it come; but let me not be kept in bondage. To clutch hold of that which is untrue as though it were true, is only to throttle oneself. May I be saved from such self-destruction.

When I entered my room, I found my master waiting there. My agitated feelings were still heaving within me. 'Freedom, sir,' I began unceremoniously, without greeting or inquiry, 'freedom is the biggest thing for man. Nothing can be compared to it—nothing at all!'

Surprised at my outburst, my master looked up at me in silence.

'One can understand nothing from books,' I went on. 'We read in the scriptures that our desires are bonds, fettering us as well as others. But such words, by themselves, are so empty. It is only when we get to the point of letting the bird out of its cage that we can realize how free the bird has set us. Whatever we cage, shackles us with desire whose bonds are stronger than those of iron chains. I tell you, sir, this is just what the world has failed to understand. They all seek to reform something outside themselves. But reform is wanted only in one's own desires, nowhere else, nowhere else!'

'We think,' he said, 'that we are our own masters when we get in our hands the object of our desire—but we are really our own masters only when we are able to cast out our desires from our minds.'

'When we put all this into words, sir,' I went on, 'it sounds like some bald-headed injunction, but when we realize even a little of it we find it to be amrita—which the gods have drunk and become immortal. We cannot see Beauty till we let go our hold of it. It was Buddha who conquered the world, not Alexander—this is untrue when stated in dry prose—oh when shall we be able to sing it? When shall all these most intimate truths of the universe overflow the pages of printed books and leap out in a sacred stream like the Ganges from the Gangotrie?'

I was suddenly reminded of my master's absence during the last few days and of my ignorance as to its reason. I felt somewhat foolish as I asked him, 'And where have you been all this while, sir?'

'Staying with Panchu,' he replied.

'Indeed!' I exclaimed. 'Have you been there all these days?'

'Yes. I wanted to come to an understanding with the woman who calls herself his aunt. She could hardly be induced to believe that there could be such an odd character among the gentlefolk as the one who sought their hospitality. When she found I really meant to stay on, she began to feel rather ashamed of herself. 'Mother,' said I, 'you are not going to get rid of me, even if you abuse me! And so long as I stay, Panchu stays also. For you see, do you not, that I cannot stand by and see his motherless little ones sent out into the streets?'

'She listened to my talks in this strain for a couple of days without saying yes or no. This morning I found her tying up her bundles. 'We are going back to Brindaban,' she said. 'Let us have our expenses for the journey.' I knew she was not going to Brindaban, and also that the cost of her journey would be substantial. So I have come to you.'

'The required cost shall be paid,' I said.

'The old woman is not a bad sort,' my master went on musingly.

'Panchu was not sure of her caste, and would not let her touch the water-jar, or anything at all of his. So they were continually bickering. When she found I had no objection to her touch, she looked after me devotedly. She is a splendid cook!

'But all remnants of Panchu's respect for me vanished! To the last he had thought that I was at least a simple sort of person. But here was I, risking my caste without a qualm to win over the old woman for my purpose. Had I tried to steal a march on her by tutoring a witness for the trial, that would have been a different matter. Tactics must be met by tactics. But stratagem at the expense of orthodoxy is more than he can tolerate!

'Anyhow, I must stay on a few days at Panchu's even after the woman leaves, for Harish Kundu may be up to any kind of devilry. He has been telling his satellites that he was content to have furnished Panchu with an aunt, but I have gone the length of supplying him with a father. He would like to see, now, how many fathers of his can save him!'

'We may or may not be able to save him,' I said; 'but if we should perish in the attempt to save the country from the thousand-and-one snares—of religion, custom and selfishness—which these people are busy spreading, we shall at least die happy.'

BIMALA'S STORY

XIV

Who could have thought that so much would happen in this one life? I feel as if I have passed through a whole series of births, time has been flying so fast, I did not feel it move at all, till the shock came the other day.

I knew there would be words between us when I made up my mind to ask my husband to banish foreign goods from our market. But it was my firm belief that I had no need to meet argument by argument, for there was magic in the very air about me. Had not so tremendous a man as Sandip fallen helplessly at my feet, like a wave of the mighty sea breaking on the shore? Had I called him? No, it was the summons of that magic spell of mine. And Amulya, poor dear boy, when he first came to me—how the current of his life flushed with colour, like the river at dawn! Truly have I realized how a goddess feels when she looks upon the radiant face of her devotee.

With the confidence begotten of these proofs of my power, I was ready to meet my husband like a lightning-charged cloud. But what was it that happened? Never in all these nine years have I seen such a far-away, distraught look in his eyes—like the desert sky—with no merciful moisture of its own, no colour reflected, even, from what it looked upon. I should have been so relieved if his anger had flashed out! But I could find nothing in him which I could touch. I felt as unreal as a dream—a dream which would leave only the blackness of night when it was over.

In the old days I used to be jealous of my sister-in-law for her beauty. Then I used to feel that Providence had given me no power of my own, that my whole strength lay in the love which my husband had bestowed on me. Now that I had drained to the dregs the cup of power and could not do without its intoxication, I suddenly found it dashed to pieces at my feet, leaving me nothing to live for.

How feverishly I had sat to do my hair that day. Oh, shame, shame on me, the utter shame of it! My sister-in-law, when passing by, had exclaimed, 'Aha, Chota Rani! Your hair seems ready to jump off. Don't let it carry your head with it.'

And then, the other day in the garden, how easy my husband found it to tell me that he set me free! But can freedom—empty freedom—be given and taken so easily as all that? It is like setting a fish free in the sky—for how can I move or live outside the atmosphere of loving care which has always sustained me?

When I came to my room today, I saw only furniture—only the bedstead, only the looking-glass, only the clothes-rack—not the all-pervading heart which used to be there, over all. Instead of it there was freedom, only freedom, mere emptiness! A dried-up watercourse with all its rocks and pebbles laid bare. No feeling, only furniture!

When I had arrived at a state of utter bewilderment, wondering whether anything true was left in my life, and whereabouts it could be, I happened to meet Sandip again. Then life struck against life, and the sparks flew in the same old way. Here was truth—impetuous truth—which rushed in and overflowed all bounds, truth which was a thousand times truer than the Bara Rani with her maid, Thako and her silly songs, and all the rest of them who talked and laughed and wandered about...

'Fifty thousand!' Sandip had demanded.

'What is fifty thousand?' cried my intoxicated heart. 'You shall have it!'

How to get it, where to get it, were minor points not worth troubling over. Look at me. Had I not risen, all in one moment, from my nothingness to a height above everything? So shall all things come at my beck and call. I shall get it, get it, get it—there cannot be any doubt.

Thus had I come away from Sandip the other day. Then as I looked about me, where was it—the tree of plenty? Oh, why does this outer world insult the heart so?

And yet get it I must; how, I do not care; for sin there cannot be. Sin taints only the weak; I with my Shakti am beyond its reach. Only a commoner can be a thief, the king conquers and takes his rightful spoil...I must find out where the treasury is; who takes the money in; who guards it.

I spent half the night standing in the outer verandah peering at the row of office buildings. But how to get that fifty thousand rupees out of the clutches of those iron bars? If by some mantram I could have made all those guards fall dead in their places, I would not have hesitated—so pitiless did I feel!

But while a whole gang of robbers seemed dancing a war-dance within the whirling brain of its Rani, the great house of the Rajas slept in peace. The gong of the watch sounded hour after hour, and the sky overhead placidly looked on.

At last I sent for Amulya.

'Money is wanted for the Cause,' I told him. 'Can you not get it out of the treasury?'

'Why not?' said he, with his chest thrown out.

Alas! had I not said 'Why not?' to Sandip just in the same way? The poor lad's confidence could rouse no hopes in my mind.

'How will you do it?' I asked.

The wild plans he began to unfold would hardly bear repetition outside the pages of a penny dreadful.

'No, Amulya,' I said severely, 'you must not be childish.'

'Very well, then,' he said, 'let me bribe those watchmen.'

'Where is the money to come from?'

'I can loot the bazar,' he burst out, without blenching.

'Leave all that alone. I have my ornaments, they will serve.'

'But,' said Amulya, 'it strikes me that the cashier cannot be bribed. Never mind, there is another and simpler way.'

'What is that?'

'Why need you hear it? It is quite simple.'

'Still, I should like to know.'

Amulya fumbled in the pocket of his tunic and pulled out, first a small edition of the Gita, which he placed on the table—and then a little pistol, which he showed me, but said nothing further.

Horror! It did not take him a moment to make up his mind to kill our good old cashier![1] To look at his frank, open face one would not have thought him capable of hurting a fly, but how different were the words which came from his mouth. It was clear that the cashier's place in the world meant nothing real to him; it was a mere vacancy, lifeless, feelingless, with only stock phrases from the Gita—Who kills the body kills naught!

'Whatever do you mean, Amulya?' I exclaimed at length. 'Don't you know that the dear old man has got a wife and children and that he is...'

'Where are we to find men who have no wives and children?' he interrupted. 'Look here, Maharani, the thing we call pity is, at bottom, only pity for ourselves. We cannot bear to wound our own tender instincts, and so we do not strike at all—pity indeed! The height of cowardice!'

---

[1] The cashier is the official who is most in touch with the ladies of a zamindar's household, directly taking their requisitions for household stores and doing their shopping for them, and so he becomes more a member of the family than the others. [Trans.].

To hear Sandip's phrases in the mouth of this mere boy staggered me. So delightfully, lovably immature was he—of that age when the good may still be believed in as good, of that age when one really lives and grows. The Mother in me awoke.

For myself there was no longer good or bad—only death, beautiful alluring death. But to hear this stripling calmly talk of murdering an inoffensive old man as the right thing to do, made me shudder all over. The more clearly I saw that there was no sin in his heart, the more horrible appeared to me the sin of his words. I seemed to see the sin of the parents visited on the innocent child.

The sight of his great big eyes shining with faith and enthusiasm touched me to the quick. He was going, in his fascination, straight to the jaws of the python, from which, once in, there was no return. How was he to be saved? Why does not my country become, for once, a real Mother—clasp him to her bosom and cry out, 'Oh, my child, my child, what profits it that you should save me, if so it be that I should fail to save you?'

I know, I know, that all Power on earth waxes great under compact with Satan. But the Mother is there, alone though she be, to condemn and stand against this devil's progress. The Mother cares not for mere success, however great—she wants to give life, to save life. My very soul, today, stretches out its hands in yearning to save this child.

A while ago I suggested robbery to him. Whatever I may now say against it will be put down to a woman's weakness. They only love our weakness when it drags the world in its toils!

'You need do nothing at all, Amulya, I will see to the money,' I told him finally. When he had almost reached the door, I called him back.

'Amulya,' said I, 'I am your elder sister. Today is not the Brothers' Day[1] according to the calendar, but all the days in the year are really

---

[1] The daughter of the house occupies a place of specially tender affection in a Bengali household (perhaps in Hindu households all over India) because, by dictate of custom, she must be given away in marriage so early. She thus takes corresponding memories with her to her husband's home, where she has to begin as a stranger before she can get into her place. The resulting feeling, of the mistress of her new home for the one she has left, has taken

Brothers' Days. My blessing be with you, may God keep you always.'

These unexpected words from my lips took Amulya by surprise. He stood stock-still for a time. Then, coming to himself, he prostrated himself at my feet in acceptance of the relationship and did me reverence. When he rose his eyes were full of tears...O little brother mine! I am fast going to my death—let me take all your sin away with me. May no taint from me ever tarnish your innocence!

I said to him, 'Let your offering of reverence be that pistol!'

'What do you want with it, sister?'

'I will practise death.'

'Right, sister. Our women, also, must know how to die, to deal death!' with which Amulya handed me the pistol. The radiance of his youthful countenance seemed to tinge my life with the touch of a new dawn. I put away the pistol within my clothes. May this reverence-offering be the last resource in my extremity...

The door to the mother's chamber in my woman's heart once opened, I thought it would always remain open. But this pathway to the supreme good was closed when the mistress took the place of the mother and locked it again. The very next day I saw Sandip; and madness, naked and rampant, danced upon my heart.

What was this? Was this, then, my truer self? Never! I had never before known this shameless, this cruel one within me. The snake-charmer had come, pretending to draw this snake from within the fold of my garment—but it was never there, it was his all the time. Some demon has gained possession of me, and what I am doing today is the play of his activity—it has nothing to do with me.

This demon, in the guise of a god, had come with his ruddy torch to call me that day, saying, 'I am your Country. I am your Sandip. I am more to you than anything else of yours. *Bande Mataram!*' And with folded hands I had responded, 'You are my religion. You are my heaven. Whatever else is mine shall be swept away before my love for

---

ceremonial form as the Brothers' Day, on which the brothers are invited to the married sisters' houses. Where the sister is the elder, she offers her blessing and receives the brother's reverence, and vice versa. Presents, called the offerings of reverence (or blessing), are exchanged.

you. *Bande Mataram!*'

Five thousand is it? Five thousand it shall be! You want it tomorrow? Tomorrow you shall have it! In this desperate orgy, that gift of five thousand shall be as the foam of wine—and then for the riotous revel! The immovable world shall sway under our feet, fire shall flash from our eyes, a storm shall roar in our ears, what is or is not in front shall become equally dim. And then with tottering footsteps we shall plunge to our death—in a moment all fire will be extinguished, the ashes will be scattered, and nothing will remain behind.

CHAPTER NINE

BIMALA'S STORY

XV

For a time I was utterly at a loss to think of any way of getting that money. Then, the other day, in the light of intense excitement, suddenly the whole picture stood out clear before me.

Every year my husband makes a reverence-offering of six thousand rupees to my sister-in-law at the time of the Durga Puja. Every year it is deposited in her account at the bank in Calcutta. This year the offering was made as usual, but it has not yet been sent to the bank, being kept meanwhile in an iron safe, in a corner of the little dressing-room attached to our bedroom.

Every year my husband takes the money to the bank himself. This year he has not yet had an opportunity of going to town. How could I fail to see the hand of Providence in this? The money has been held up because the country wants it—who could have the power to take it away from her to the bank? And how can I have the power to refuse to take the money? The goddess revelling in destruction holds out her blood-cup crying, 'Give me drink. I am thirsty.' I will give her my own heart's blood with that five thousand rupees. Mother, the loser of that money will scarcely feel the loss, but me you will utterly ruin!

Many a time, in the old days, have I inwardly called the Senior Rani a thief, for I charged her with wheedling money out of my trusting husband. After her husband's death, she often used to make away with things belonging to the estate for her own use. This I used to point out to my husband, but he remained silent. I would get angry and say, 'If you feel generous, make gifts by all means, but why allow yourself to be robbed?' Providence must have smiled, then, at these complaints of mine, for tonight I am on the way to rob my husband's safe of my sister-in-law's money. My husband's custom was to let his keys remain in his pockets when he took off his clothes for the night, leaving them in the dressing-room. I picked out the key of the safe and opened it. The slight sound it made seemed to wake the whole world! A sudden chill turned my hands and feet icy cold, and I shivered all over.

There was a drawer inside the safe. On opening this I found the money, not in currency notes, but in gold rolled up in paper. I had no time to count out what I wanted. There were twenty rolls, all of which I took and tied up in a corner of my sari.

What a weight it was. The burden of the theft crushed my heart to the dust. Perhaps notes would have made it seem less like thieving, but this was all gold.

After I had stolen into my room like a thief, it felt like my own room no longer. All the most precious rights which I had over it vanished at the touch of my theft. I began to mutter to myself, as though telling mantrams, *Bande Mataram, Bande Mataram*, my Country, my golden Country, all this gold is for you, for none else!

But in the night the mind is weak. I came back into the bedroom where my husband was asleep, closing my eyes as I passed through, and went off to the open terrace beyond, on which I lay prone, clasping to my breast the end of the sari tied over the gold. And each one of the rolls gave me a shock of pain.

The silent night stood there with forefinger upraised. I could not think of my house as separate from my country, I had robbed my house, I had robbed my country. For this sin my house had ceased to be mine, my country also was estranged from me. Had I died begging for my country, even unsuccessfully, that would have been worship, acceptable to the gods. But theft is never worship—how then can I offer this gold? Ah me! I am doomed to death myself, must I desecrate my country with my impious touch? The way to put the money back is closed to me. I have not the strength to return to the room, take again that key, open once more that safe—I should swoon on the threshold of my husband's door. The only road left now is the road in front. Neither have I the strength deliberately to sit down and count the coins. Let them remain behind their coverings, I cannot calculate.

There was no mist in the winter sky. The stars were shining brightly.

If, thought I to myself, as I lay out there, I had to steal these stars one by one, like golden coins, for my country—these stars so carefully stored up in the bosom of the darkness—then the sky would be blinded, the night widowed for ever, and my theft would rob the whole world. But was not also this very thing I had done a robbing of the whole world—not only of money, but of trust, of righteousness?

I spent the night lying on the terrace. When at last it was morning, and I was sure that my husband had risen and left the room, then only with my shawl pulled over my head, could I retrace my steps towards the bedroom.

My sister-in-law was about, with her brass pot, watering her plants. When she saw me passing in the distance she cried, 'Have you heard the news, Chota Rani?'

I stopped in silence, all in a tremor. It seemed to me that the rolls of sovereigns were bulging through the shawl. I feared they would burst and scatter in a ringing shower, exposing to all the servants of the house the thief who had made herself destitute by robbing her own wealth.

'Your band of robbers,' she went on, 'have sent an anonymous message threatening to loot the treasury.'

I remained as silent as a thief.

'I was advising Brother Nikhil to seek your protection,' she continued banteringly. 'Call off your minions, Robber Queen! We will offer sacrifices to your *Bande Mataram* if you will but save us. What doings there are these days!—but for the Lord's sake, spare our house at least from burglary.'

I hastened into my room without reply. I had put my foot on quicksand, and could not now withdraw it. Struggling would only send me down deeper.

If only the time would arrive when I could hand over the money to Sandip! I could bear it no longer, its weight was breaking through my very ribs.

It was still early when I got word that Sandip was awaiting me. Today I had no thought of adornment. Wrapped as I was in my shawl, I went off to the outer apartments. As I entered the sitting-room I saw Sandip and Amulya there, together. All my dignity, all my honour, seemed to run tingling through my body from head to foot and vanish into the ground. I should have to lay bare a woman's uttermost shame in sight of this boy! Could they have been discussing my deed in their meeting place? Had any vestige of a veil of decency been left for me?

We women shall never understand men. When they are bent on making a road for some achievement, they think nothing of breaking the heart of the world into pieces to pave it for the progress of their chariot. When they are mad with the intoxication of creating, they rejoice in destroying the creation of the Creator. This heart-breaking shame of mine will not attract even a glance from their eyes. They have no feeling for life itself—all their eagerness is for their object. What am I to them but a meadow flower in the path of a torrent in flood?

What good will this extinction of me be to Sandip? Only five thousand rupees? Was not I good for something more than only five thousand rupees? Yes, indeed! Did I not learn that from Sandip himself, and was I not able in the light of this knowledge to despise all else in my world? I was the giver of light, of life, of Shakti, of immortality—in that belief, in that joy, I had burst all my bounds and come into the open. Had anyone then fulfilled for me that joy, I should have lived in my death. I should have lost nothing in the loss of my all. Do they want to tell me now that all this was false? The psalm of my praise which was sung so devotedly, did it bring me down from my heaven, not to make heaven of earth, but only to level heaven itself with the dust?

XVI

'The money, Queen?' said Sandip with his keen glance full on my face.

Amulya also fixed his gaze on me. Though not my own mother's child, yet the dear lad is brother to me; for mother is mother all the world over. With his guileless face, his gentle eyes, his innocent youth, he looked at me. And I, a woman—of his mother's sex—how could I hand him poison, just because he asked for it?

'The money, Queen!' Sandip's insolent demand rang in my ears. For very shame and vexation I felt I wanted to fling that gold at Sandip's head. I could hardly undo the knot of my sari, my fingers trembled so. At last the paper rolls dropped on the table.

Sandip's face grew black... He must have thought that the rolls were of silver... What contempt was in his looks. What utter disgust at incapacity. It was almost as if he could have struck me! He must have suspected that I had come to parley with him, to offer to compound his claim for five thousand rupees with a few hundreds. There was a moment when I thought he would snatch up the rolls and throw them out of the window, declaring that he was no beggar, but a king claiming tribute.

'Is that all?' asked Amulya with such pity welling up in his voice that I wanted to sob out aloud. I kept my heart tightly pressed down, and merely nodded my head. Sandip was speechless. He neither touched the rolls, nor uttered a sound.

My humiliation went straight to the boy's heart. With a sudden, feigned enthusiasm he exclaimed, 'It's plenty. It will do splendidly. You have saved us.' With which he tore open the covering of one of the rolls.

The sovereigns shone out. And in a moment the black covering seemed to be lifted from Sandip's countenance also. His delight beamed forth from his features. Unable to control his sudden revulsion of feeling, he sprang up from his seat towards me. What he intended I know not. I flashed a lightning glance towards Amulya—the colour had left the boy's face as at the stroke of a whip. Then with all my strength I thrust Sandip from me. As he reeled back his head struck the edge of the marble table and he dropped on the floor. There he lay awhile, motionless. Exhausted with my effort, I sank back on my seat.

Amulya's face lightened with a joyful radiance. He did not even turn towards Sandip, but came straight up, took the dust of my feet, and then remained there, sitting on the floor in front of me. O my little brother, my child! This reverence of yours is the last touch of heaven left in my empty world! I could contain myself no longer, and my tears flowed fast. I covered my eyes with the end of my sari, which I pressed to my face with both my hands, and sobbed and sobbed. And every time that I felt on my feet his tender touch trying to comfort me my tears broke out afresh.

After a little, when I had recovered myself and taken my hands from my face, I saw Sandip back at the table, gathering up the sovereigns in his handkerchief, as if nothing had happened. Amulya rose to his seat, from his place near my feet, his wet eyes shining.

Sandip coolly looked up at my face as he remarked, 'It is six thousand.'

'What do we want with so much, Sandip Babu?' cried Amulya. 'Three thousand five hundred is all we need for our work.'

'Our wants are not for this one place only,' Sandip replied. 'We shall want all we can get.'

'That may be,' said Amulya. 'But in future I undertake to get you all you want. Out of this, Sandip Babu, please return the extra two thousand five hundred to the Maharani.'

Sandip glanced enquiringly at me.

'No, no,' I exclaimed. 'I shall never touch that money again. Do with it as you will.'

'Can man ever give as woman can?' said Sandip, looking towards Amulya.

'They are goddesses!' agreed Amulya with enthusiasm.

'We men can at best give of our power,' continued Sandip. 'But women give themselves. Out of their own life they give birth, out of their own life they give sustenance. Such gifts are the only true gifts.' Then turning to me, 'Queen!' said he, 'if what you have given us had been only money I would not have touched it. But you have given that which is more to you than life itself!'

There must be two different persons inside men. One of these in me can understand that Sandip is trying to delude me; the other is content to be deluded. Sandip has power, but no strength of righteousness. The weapon of his which rouses up life smites it again to death. He has the unfailing quiver of the gods, but the shafts in them are of the demons.

Sandip's handkerchief was not large enough to hold all the coins. 'Queen,' he asked, 'can you give me another?' When I gave him mine, he reverently touched his forehead with it, and then suddenly kneeling on the floor he made me an obeisance. 'Goddess!' he said, 'it was to offer my reverence that I had approached you, but you repulsed me, and rolled me in the dust. Be it so, I accept your repulse as your boon to me, I raise it to my head in salutation!' with which he pointed to the place where he had been hurt.

Had I then misunderstood him? Could it be that his outstretched hands had really been directed towards my feet? Yet, surely, even Amulya had seen the passion that flamed out of his eyes, his face. But Sandip is such an adept in setting music to his chant of praise that I cannot argue; I lose my power of seeing truth; my sight is clouded over like an opium-eater's eyes. And so, after all, he gave me back twice as much in return for the blow I had dealt him—the wound on his head ended by making me bleed at heart. When I had received Sandip's obeisance my theft seemed to gain a dignity, and the gold glittering on the table to smile away all fear of disgrace, all stings of conscience.

Like me Amulya also was won back. His devotion to Sandip, which had suffered a momentary check, blazed up anew. The flower-vase of his mind filled once more with offerings for the worship of Sandip and me. His simple faith shone out of his eyes with the pure light of the morning star at dawn.

After I had offered worship and received worship my sin became radiant. And as Amulya looked on my face he raised his folded hands in salutation and cried *Bande Mataram*! I cannot expect to have this adoration surrounding me for ever; and yet this has come to be the only means of keeping alive my self-respect.

I can no longer enter my bedroom. The bedstead seems to thrust out a forbidding hand, the iron safe frowns at me. I want to get away from this continual insult to myself which is rankling within me. I want to keep running to Sandip to hear him sing my praises. There is just this one little altar of worship which has kept its head above the all-pervading depths of my dishonour, and so I want to cleave to it night and day; for on whichever side I step away from it, there is only emptiness.

Praise, praise, I want unceasing praise. I cannot live if my wine-cup be left empty for a single moment. So, as the very price of my life, I want Sandip of all the world, today.

XVII

When my husband nowadays comes in for his meals I feel I cannot sit before him; and yet it is such a shame not to be near him that I feel I cannot do that either. So I seat myself where we cannot look at each other's face. That was how I was sitting the other day when the Bara Rani came and joined us.

'It is all very well for you, brother,' said she, 'to laugh away these threatening letters. But they do frighten me so. Have you sent off that money you gave me to the Calcutta bank?'

'No, I have not yet had the time to get it away,' my husband replied.

'You are so careless, brother dear, you had better look out...'

'But it is in the iron safe right inside the inner dressing-room,' said my husband with a reassuring smile.

'What if they get in there? You can never tell!'

'If they go so far, they might as well carry you off too!'

'Don't you fear, no one will come for poor me. The real attraction is in your room! But joking apart, don't run the risk of keeping money in the room like that.'

'They will be taking along the Government revenue to Calcutta in a few days now; I will send this money to the bank under the same escort.'

'Very well. But see you don't forget all about it, you are so absent-minded.'

'Even if that money gets lost, while in my room, the loss cannot be yours, Sister Rani.'

'Now, now, brother, you will make me very angry if you talk in that way. Was I making any difference between yours and mine? What if your money is lost, does not that hurt me? If Providence has thought fit to take away my all, it has not left me insensible to the value of the most devoted brother known since the days of Lakshman.'[1]

'Well, Junior Rani, are you turned into a wooden doll? You have not spoken a word yet. Do you know, brother, our Junior Rani thinks I try to flatter you. If things came to that pass I should not hesitate to do so, but I know my dear old brother does not need it!'

Thus the Senior Rani chattered on, not forgetting now and then

---

[1] Of the Ramayana. The story of his devotion to his elder brother Rama and his brother's wife Sita, has become a byword.

to draw her brother's attention to this or that special delicacy amongst the dishes that were being served. My head was all the time in a whirl. The crisis was fast coming. Something must be done about replacing that money. And as I kept asking myself what could be done, and how it was to be done, the unceasing patter of my sister-in-law's words seemed more and more intolerable.

What made it all the worse was, that nothing could escape my sister-in-law's keen eyes. Every now and then she was casting side glances towards me. What she could read in my face I do not know, but to me it seemed that everything was written there only too plainly.

Then I did an infinitely rash thing. Affecting an easy, amused laugh I said, 'All the Senior Rani's suspicions, I see, are reserved for me—her fears of thieves and robbers are only a feint.'

The Senior Rani smiled mischievously. 'You are right, sister mine. A woman's theft is the most fatal of all thefts. But how can you elude my watchfulness? Am I a man, that you should hoodwink me?'

'If you fear me so,' I retorted, 'let me keep in your hands all I have, as security. If I cause you loss, you can then repay yourself.'

'Just listen to her, our simple little Junior Rani!' she laughed back, turning to my husband. 'Does she not know that there are losses which no security can make good, either in this world or in the next?'

My husband did not join in our exchange of words. When he had finished, he went off to the outer apartments, for nowadays he does not take his mid-day rest in our room.

All my more valuable jewels were in deposit in the treasury in charge of the cashier. Still what I kept with me must have been worth thirty or forty thousand. I took my jewel-box to the Bara Rani's room and opened it out before her, saying, 'I leave these with you, sister. They will keep you quite safe from all worry.'

The Bara Rani made a gesture of mock despair. 'You positively astound me, Chota Rani!' she said. 'Do you really suppose I spend sleepless nights for fear of being robbed by you?'

'What harm if you did have a wholesome fear of me? Does anybody know anybody else in this world?'

'You want to teach me a lesson by trusting me? No, no! I am bothered enough to know what to do with my own jewels, without keeping watch over yours. Take them away, there's a dear, so many prying servants are about.'

I went straight from my sister-in-law's room to the sitting-room outside, and sent for Amulya. With him Sandip came along too. I was in a great hurry, and said to Sandip, 'If you don't mind, I want to have a word or two with Amulya. Would you...'

Sandip smiled a wry smile. 'So Amulya and I are separate in your eyes? If you have set about to wean him from me, I must confess I have no power to retain him.'

I made no reply, but stood waiting.

'Be it so,' Sandip went on. 'Finish your special talk with Amulya. But then you must give me a special talk all to myself too, or it will mean a defeat for me. I can stand everything, but not defeat. My share must always be the lion's share. This has been my constant quarrel with Providence. I will defeat the Dispenser of my fate, but not take defeat at his hands.' With a crushing look at Amulya, Sandip walked out of the room.

'Amulya, my own little brother, you must do one thing for me,' I said.

'I will stake my life for whatever duty you may lay on me, sister.'

I brought out my jewel-box from the folds of my shawl and placed it before him. 'Sell or pawn these,' I said, 'and get me six thousand rupees as fast as ever you can.'

'No, no, Sister Rani,' said Amulya, touched to the quick. 'Let these jewels be. I will get you six thousand all the same.'

'Oh, don't be silly,' I said impatiently. 'There is no time for any nonsense. Take this box. Get away to Calcutta by the night train. And bring me the money by the day after tomorrow positively.'

Amulya took a diamond necklace out of the box, held it up to the light and put it back gloomily.

'I know,' I told him, 'that you will never get the proper price for these diamonds, so I am giving you jewels worth about thirty thousand. I don't care if they all go, but I must have that six thousand without fail.'

'Do you know, Sister Rani,' said Amulya, 'I have had a quarrel with Sandip Babu over that six thousand rupees he took from you? I cannot tell you how ashamed I felt. But Sandip Babu would have it that we must give up even our shame for the country. That may be so. But this is somehow different. I do not fear to die for the country, to kill for the country—that much Shakti has been given me. But I cannot forget the shame of having taken money from you. There Sandip Babu is ahead of me. He has no regrets or compunctions. He says we must get rid of the idea that the money belongs to the one in whose box it happens to be—if we cannot, where is the magic of *Bande Mataram*?'

Amulya gathered enthusiasm as he talked on. He always warms up when he has me for a listener. 'The Gita tells us,' he continued, 'that no one can kill the soul. Killing is a mere word. So also is the taking away of money. Whose is the money? No one has created it. No one can take it away with him when he departs this life, for it is no part of his soul. Today it is mine, tomorrow my son's, the next day his creditor's. Since, in fact, money belongs to no one, why should any blame attach to our patriots if, instead of leaving it for some worthless son, they take it for their own use?'

When I hear Sandip's words uttered by this boy, I tremble all over. Let those who are snake-charmers play with snakes; if harm comes to them, they are prepared for it. But these boys are so innocent, all the world is ready with its blessing to protect them. They play with a snake not knowing its nature, and when we see them smilingly, trustfully, putting their hands within reach of its fangs, then we understand how terribly dangerous the snake is. Sandip is right when he suspects that though I, for myself, may be ready to die at his hands, this boy I shall wean from him and save.

'So the money is wanted for the use of your patriots?' I questioned with a smile.

'Of course it is!' said Amulya proudly. 'Are they not our kings? Poverty takes away from their regal power. Do you know, we always insist on Sandip Babu travelling First Class? He never shirks kingly honours—he accepts them not for himself, but for the glory of us all. The greatest weapon of those who rule the world, Sandip Babu has told us, is the hypnotism of their display. To take the vow of poverty would be for them not merely a penance—it would mean suicide.'

At this point Sandip noiselessly entered the room. I threw my shawl over the jewel-case with a rapid movement.

'The special-talk business not yet over?' he asked with a sneer in his tone.

'Yes, we've quite finished,' said Amulya apologetically. 'It was nothing much.'

'No, Amulya,' I said, 'we have not quite finished.'

'So exit Sandip for the second time, I suppose?' said Sandip.

'If you please.'

'And as to Sandip's re-entry.'

'Not today. I have no time.'

'I see!' said Sandip as his eyes flashed. 'No time to waste, only for special talks!'

Jealousy! Where the strong man shows weakness, there the weaker sex cannot help beating her drums of victory. So I repeated firmly, 'I really have no time.'

Sandip went away looking black. Amulya was greatly perturbed. 'Sister Rani,' he pleaded, 'Sandip Babu is annoyed.'

'He has neither cause nor right to be annoyed,' I said with some vehemence. 'Let me caution you about one thing, Amulya. Say nothing to Sandip Babu about the sale of my jewels—on your life.'

'No, I will not.'

'Then you had better not delay anymore. You must get away by tonight's train.'

Amulya and I left the room together. As we came out on the verandah Sandip was standing there. I could see he was waiting to waylay Amulya. To prevent that I had to engage him. 'What is it you wanted to tell me, Sandip Babu?' I asked.

'I have nothing special to say—mere small talk. And since you have not the time.'

'I can give you just a little.'

By this time Amulya had left. As we entered the room Sandip asked, 'What was that box Amulya carried away?'

The box had not escaped his eyes. I remained firm. 'If I could have told you, it would have been made over to him in your presence!'

'So you think Amulya will not tell me?'

'No, he will not.'

Sandip could not conceal his anger any longer. 'You think you will gain the mastery over me?' he blazed out. 'That shall never be. Amulya, there, would die a happy death if I deigned to trample him under foot. I will never, so long as I live, allow you to bring him to your feet!'

Oh, the weak! The weak! At last Sandip has realized that he is weak before me! That is why there is this sudden outburst of anger. He has understood that he cannot meet the power that I wield, with mere strength. With a glance I can crumble his strongest fortifications. So he must needs resort to bluster. I simply smiled in contemptuous silence. At last have I come to a level above him. I must never lose this vantage ground; never descend lower again. Amidst all my degradation this bit of dignity must remain to me!

'I know,' said Sandip, after a pause, 'it was your jewel-case.'

'You may guess as you please,' said I, 'but you will get nothing out of me.

'So you trust Amulya more than you trust me? Do you know that the boy is the shadow of my shadow, the echo of my echo—that he is nothing if I am not at his side?'

'Where he is not your echo, he is himself, Amulya. And that is where I trust him more than I can trust your echo!'

'You must not forget that you are under a promise to render up all your ornaments to me for the worship of the Divine Mother. In fact your offering has already been made.'

'Whatever ornaments the gods leave to me will be offered up to the gods. But how can I offer those which have been stolen away from me?'

'Look here, it is no use your trying to give me the slip in that fashion. Now is the time for grim work. Let that work be finished, then you can make a display of your woman's wiles to your heart's content—and I will help you in your game.'

The moment I had stolen my husband's money and paid it to Sandip, the music that was in our relations stopped. Not only did I destroy all my own value by making myself cheap, but Sandip's powers, too, lost scope for their full play. You cannot employ your marksmanship against a thing which is right in your grasp. So Sandip has lost his aspect of the hero; a tone of low quarrelsomeness has come into his words.

Sandip kept his brilliant eyes fixed full on my face till they seemed to blaze with all the thirst of the midday sky. Once or twice he fidgeted with his feet, as though to leave his seat, as if to spring right on me. My whole body seemed to swim, my veins throbbed, the hot blood surged up to my ears; I felt that if I remained there, I should never get up at all. With a supreme effort I tore myself off the chair, and hastened towards the door.

From Sandip's dry throat there came a muffled cry, 'Whither would you flee, Queen?' The next moment he left his seat with a bound to seize hold of me. At the sound of footsteps outside the door, however, he rapidly retreated and fell back into his chair. I checked my steps near the bookshelf, where I stood staring at the names of the books.

As my husband entered the room, Sandip exclaimed, 'I say, Nikhil, don't you keep Browning among your books here? I was just telling Queen Bee of our college club. Do you remember that contest of ours over the translation of those lines from Browning? You don't?

'She should never have looked at me, If she meant I should not love her, There are plenty ... men you call such, I suppose ... she may discover All her soul to, if she pleases, And yet leave much as she found them, But I'm not so, and she knew it When she fixed me, glancing round them.'

'I managed to get together the words to render it into Bengali, somehow, but the result was hardly likely to be a 'joy forever' to the people of Bengal. I really did think at one time that I was on the verge of becoming a poet, but Providence was kind enough to save me from that disaster. Do you remember old Dakshina? If he had not become a Salt Inspector, he would have been a poet. I remember his rendering to this day...

'No, Queen Bee, it is no use rummaging those bookshelves. Nikhil has ceased to read poetry since his marriage—perhaps he has no further need for it. But I suppose 'the fever fit of poesy', as the Sanskrit has it, is about to attack me again.'

'I have come to give you a warning, Sandip,' said my husband.

'About the fever fit of poesy?'

My husband took no notice of this attempt at humour. 'For some time,' he continued, 'Mahomedan preachers have been about stirring up the local Mussulmans. They are all wild with you, and may attack you any moment.'

'Are you come to advise flight?'

'I have come to give you information, not to offer advice.'

'Had these estates been mine, such a warning would have been necessary for the preachers, not for me. If, instead of trying to frighten me, you give them a taste of your intimidation, that would be worthier both of you and me. Do you know that your weakness is weakening your neighbouring zamindars also?'

'I did not offer you my advice, Sandip. I wish you, too, would refrain from giving me yours. Besides, it is useless. And there is another thing I want to tell you. You and your followers have been secretly worrying and oppressing my tenantry. I cannot allow that any longer. So I must ask you to leave my territory.'

'For fear of the Mussulmans, or is there any other fear you have to threaten me with?'

'There are fears the want of which is cowardice. In the name of those fears, I tell you, Sandip, you must go. In five days I shall be starting for Calcutta. I want you to accompany me. You may of course stay in my house there—to that there is no objection.'

'All right, I have still five day's time then. Meanwhile, Queen Bee, let me hum to you my song of parting from your honey-hive. Ah! You poet of modern Bengal! Throw open your doors and let me plunder your words. The theft is really yours, for it is my song which you have made your own—let the name be yours by all means, but the song is mine.' With this Sandip struck up in a deep, husky voice, which threatened to be out of tune, a song in the Bhairavi mode,

'In the springtime of your kingdom, my Queen, Meetings and partings chase each other in their endless hide and seek, And flowers blossom in the wake of those that droop and die in the shade. In the springtime of your kingdom, my Queen, My meeting with you had its own songs, But has not also my leave-taking any gift to offer you? That gift is my secret hope, which I keep hidden in the shadows of your flower garden, That the rains of July may sweetly temper your fiery June.'

His boldness was immense—boldness which had no veil, but was naked as fire. One finds no time to stop it, it is like trying to resist a thunderbolt, the lightning flashes, it laughs at all resistance.

I left the room. As I was passing along the verandah towards the inner apartments, Amulya suddenly made his appearance and came and stood before me.

'Fear nothing, Sister Rani,' he said. 'I am off tonight and shall not return unsuccessful.'

'Amulya,' said I, looking straight into his earnest, youthful face, 'I fear nothing for myself, but may I never cease to fear for you.'

Amulya turned to go, but before he was out of sight I called him back and asked, 'Have you a mother, Amulya?'

'I have.'

'A sister?'

'No, I am the only child of my mother. My father died when I was quite little.'

'Then go back to your mother, Amulya.'

'But, Sister Rani, I have now both mother and sister.'

'Then, Amulya, before you leave tonight, come and have your dinner here.'

'There won't be time for that. Let me take some food for the journey, consecrated with your touch.'

'What do you specially like, Amulya?' 'If I had been with my mother I should have had lots of Poush cakes. Make some for me with your own hands, Sister Rani!'

CHAPTER TEN

NIKHIL'S STORY

XII

I learnt from my master that Sandip had joined forces with Harish Kundu, and there was to be a grand celebration of the worship of the demon-destroying Goddess. Harish Kundu was extorting the expenses from his tenantry. Pandits Kaviratna and Vidyavagish had been commissioned to compose a hymn with a double meaning.

My master has just had a passage at arms with Sandip over this. 'Evolution is at work amongst the gods as well,' says Sandip. 'The grandson has to remodel the gods created by the grandfather to suit his own taste, or else he is left an atheist. It is my mission to modernize the ancient deities. I am born the saviour of the gods, to emancipate them from the thraldom of the past.'

I have seen from our boyhood what a juggler with ideas is Sandip. He has no interest in discovering truth, but to make a quizzical display of it rejoices his heart. Had he been born in the wilds of Africa he would have spent a glorious time inventing argument after argument to prove that cannibalism is the best means of promoting true communion between man and man. But those who deal in delusion end by deluding themselves, and I fully believe that, each time Sandip creates a new fallacy, he persuades himself that he has found the truth, however contradictory his creations may be to one another.

However, I shall not give a helping hand to establish a liquor distillery in my country. The young men, who are ready to offer their services for their country's cause, must not fall into this habit of getting intoxicated. The people who want to exact work by drugging methods set more value on the excitement than on the minds they intoxicate.

I had to tell Sandip, in Bimala's presence, that he must go. Perhaps both will impute to me the wrong motive. But I must free myself also from all fear of being misunderstood. Let even Bimala misunderstand me...

A number of Mahomedan preachers are being sent over from Dacca. The Mussulmans in my territory had come to have almost as much of an aversion to the killing of cows as the Hindus. But now cases of cow-killing are cropping up here and there. I had the news first from some of my Mussulman tenants with expressions of their disapproval. Here was a situation which I could see would be difficult to meet. At the bottom was a pretence of fanaticism, which would cease to be a pretence if obstructed. That is just where the ingenuity of the move came in!

I sent for some of my principal Hindu tenants and tried to get them to see the matter in its proper light. 'We can be staunch in our own convictions,' I said, 'but we have no control over those of others. For all that many of us are Vaishnavas, those of us who are Shaktas go on with their animal sacrifices just the same. That cannot be helped. We must, in the same way, let the Mussulmans do as they think best. So please refrain from all disturbance.'

'Maharaja,' they replied, 'these outrages have been unknown for so long.'

'That was so,' I said, 'because such was their spontaneous desire. Let us behave in such a way that the same may become true, over again. But a breach of the peace is not the way to bring this about.'

'No, Maharaja,' they insisted, 'those good old days are gone. This will never stop unless you put it down with a strong hand.'

'Oppression,' I replied, 'will not only not prevent cow-killing, it may lead to the killing of men as well.'

One of them had had an English education. He had learnt to repeat the phrases of the day. 'It is not only a question of orthodoxy,' he argued. 'Our country is mainly agricultural, and cows are...'

'Buffaloes in this country,' I interrupted, 'likewise give milk and are used for ploughing. And therefore, so long as we dance frantic dances on our temple pavements, smeared with their blood, their severed heads carried on our shoulders, religion will only laugh at us if we quarrel with Mussulmans in her name, and nothing but the quarrel itself will remain true. If the cow alone is to be held sacred from slaughter, and not the buffalo, then that is bigotry, not religion.'

'But are you not aware, sir, of what is behind all this?' pursued the English-knowing tenant. 'This has only become possible because the Mussulman is assured of safety, even if he breaks the law. Have you not heard of the Pachur case?'

'Why is it possible,' I asked, 'to use the Mussulmans thus, as tools against us? Is it not because we have fashioned them into such with our own intolerance? That is how Providence punishes us. Our accumulated sins are being visited on our own heads.'

'Oh, well, if that be so, let them be visited on us. But we shall have our revenge. We have undermined what was the greatest strength of the authorities, their devotion to their own laws. Once they were truly kings, dispensing justice; now they themselves will become law-breakers, and so no better than robbers. This may not go down to history, but we shall carry it in our hearts for all time...'

The evil reports about me which are spreading from paper to paper are making me notorious. News comes that my effigy has been burnt at the river-side burning-ground of the Chakravartis, with due ceremony and enthusiasm; and other insults are in contemplation. The trouble was that they had come to ask me to take shares in a Cotton Mill they wanted to start. I had to tell them that I did not so much mind the loss of my own money, but I would not be a party to causing a loss to so many poor shareholders.

'Are we to understand, Maharaja,' said my visitors, 'that the prosperity of the country does not interest you?'

'Industry may lead to the country's prosperity,' I explained, 'but a mere desire for its prosperity will not make for success in industry. Even when our heads were cool, our industries did not flourish. Why should we suppose that they will do so just because we have become frantic?'

'Why not say plainly that you will not risk your money?'

'I will put in my money when I see that it is industry which prompts you. But, because you have lighted a fire, it does not follow that you have the food to cook over it.'

XIII

What is this? Our Chakua sub-treasury looted! A remittance of seven thousand five hundred rupees was due from there to headquarters. The local cashier had changed the cash at the Government Treasury into small currency notes for convenience in carrying, and had kept them ready in bundles. In the middle of the night an armed band had raided the room, and wounded Kasim, the man on guard. The curious part of it was that they had taken only six thousand rupees and left the rest scattered on the floor, though it would have been as easy to carry that away also. Anyhow, the raid of the dacoits was over; now the police raid would begin. Peace was out of the question.

When I went inside, I found the news had travelled before me. 'What a terrible thing, brother,' exclaimed the Bara Rani. 'Whatever shall we do?'

I made light of the matter to reassure her. 'We still have something left,' I said with a smile. 'We shall manage to get along somehow.'

'Don't joke about it, brother dear. Why are they all so angry with you? Can't you humour them? Why put everybody out?'

'I cannot let the country go to rack and ruin, even if that would please everybody.'

'That was a shocking thing they did at the burning-grounds. It's a horrid shame to treat you so. The Chota Rani has got rid of all her fears by dint of the Englishwoman's teaching, but as for me, I had to send for the priest to avert the omen before I could get any peace of mind. For my sake, dear, do get away to Calcutta. I tremble to think what they may do, if you stay on here.'

My sister-in-law's genuine anxiety touched me deeply.

'And, brother,' she went on, 'did I not warn you, it was not well to keep so much money in your room? They might get wind of it any day. It is not the money—but who knows...'

To calm her I promised to remove the money to the treasury at once, and then get it away to Calcutta with the first escort going. We went together to my bedroom. The dressing-room door was shut. When I knocked, Bimala called out, 'I am dressing.'

'I wonder at the Chota Rani,' exclaimed my sister-in-law, 'dressing so early in the day! One of their *Bande Mataram* meetings, I suppose. Robber Queen!' she called out in jest to Bimala. 'Are you counting your spoils inside?'

'I will attend to the money a little later,' I said, as I came away to my office room outside.

I found the Police Inspector waiting for me. 'Any trace of the dacoits?' I asked.

'I have my suspicions.'

'On whom?'

'Kasim, the guard.'

'Kasim? But was he not wounded?'

'A mere nothing. A flesh wound on the leg. Probably self-inflicted.'

'But I cannot bring myself to believe it. He is such a trusted servant.'

'You may have trusted him, but that does not prevent his being a thief. Have I not seen men trusted for twenty years together, suddenly developing...'

'Even if it were so, I could not send him to gaol. But why should he have left the rest of the money lying about?'

'To put us off the scent. Whatever you may say, Maharaja, he must be an old hand at the game. He mounts guard during his watch, right enough, but I feel sure he has a finger in all the dacoities going on in the neighbourhood.'

With this the Inspector proceeded to recount the various methods by which it was possible to be concerned in a dacoity twenty or thirty miles away, and yet be back in time for duty.

'Have you brought Kasim here?' I asked.

'No,' was the reply, 'he is in the lock-up. The Magistrate is due for the investigation.'

'I want to see him,' I said.

When I went to his cell he fell at my feet, weeping. 'In God's name,' he said, 'I swear I did not do this thing.'

'I do not doubt you, Kasim,' I assured him. 'Fear nothing. They can do nothing to you, if you are innocent.'

Kasim, however, was unable to give a coherent account of the incident. He was obviously exaggerating. Four or five hundred men, big guns, numberless swords, figured in his narrative. It must have been either his disturbed state of mind or a desire to account for his easy defeat. He would have it that this was Harish Kundu's doing; he was even sure he had heard the voice of Ekram, the head retainer of the Kundus.

'Look here, Kasim,' I had to warn him, 'don't you be dragging other people in with your stories. You are not called upon to make out a case against Harish Kundu, or anybody else.'

XIV

On returning home I asked my master to come over. He shook his head gravely. 'I see no good in this,' said he—'this setting aside of conscience and putting the country in its place. All the sins of the country will now break out, hideous and unashamed.'

'Who do you think could have...'

'Don't ask me. But sin is rampant. Send them all away, right away from here.'

'I have given them one more day. They will be leaving the day after tomorrow.'

'And another thing. Take Bimala away to Calcutta. She is getting too narrow a view of the outside world from here, she cannot see men and things in their true proportions. Let her see the world—men and their work—give her abroad vision.'

'That is exactly what I was thinking.'

'Well, don't make any delay about it. I tell you, Nikhil, man's history has to be built by the united effort of all the races in the world, and therefore this selling of conscience for political reasons—this making a fetish of one's country, won't do. I know that Europe does not at heart admit this, but there she has not the right to pose as our teacher. Men who die for the truth become immortal, and, if a whole people can die for the truth, it will also achieve immortality in the history of humanity. Here, in this land of India, amid the mocking laughter of Satan piercing the sky, may the feeling for this truth become real! What a terrible epidemic of sin has been brought into our country from foreign lands...'

The whole day passed in the turmoil of investigation. I was tired out when I retired for the night. I left over sending my sister-in-law's money to the treasury till next morning.

I woke up from my sleep at dead of night. The room was dark. I thought I heard a moaning somewhere. Somebody must have been crying. Sounds of sobbing came heavy with tears like fitful gusts of wind in the rainy night. It seemed to me that the cry rose from the heart of my room itself. I was alone. For some days Bimala had her bed in another room adjoining mine. I rose up and when I went out I found her in the balcony lying prone upon her face on the bare floor.

This is something that cannot be written in words. He only knows it who sits in the bosom of the world and receives all its pangs in His own heart. The sky is dumb, the stars are mute, the night is still, and in the midst of it all that one sleepless cry!

We give these sufferings names, bad or good, according to the classifications of the books, but this agony which is welling up from a torn heart, pouring into the fathomless dark, has it any name? When in that midnight, standing under the silent stars, I looked upon that figure, my mind was struck with awe, and I said to myself, 'Who am I to judge her?' O life, O death, O God of the infinite existence, I bow my head in silence to the mystery which is in you.

Once I thought I should turn back. But I could not. I sat down on the ground near Bimala and placed my hand on her head. At the first touch her whole body seemed to stiffen, but the next moment the hardness gave way, and the tears burst out. I gently passed my fingers over her forehead. Suddenly her hands groping for my feet grasped them and drew them to herself, pressing them against her breast with such force that I thought her heart would break.

BIMALA'S STORY

XVIII

Amulya is due to return from Calcutta this morning. I told the servants to let me know as soon as he arrived, but could not keep still. At last I went outside to await him in the sitting-room.

When I sent him off to sell the jewels I must have been thinking only of myself. It never even crossed my mind that so young a boy, trying to sell such valuable jewellery, would at once be suspected. So helpless are we women, we needs must place on others the burden of our danger. When we go to our death we drag down those who are about us.

I had said with pride that I would save Amulya—as if she who was drowning could save others. But instead of saving him, I have sent him to his doom. My little brother, such a sister have I been to you that Death must have smiled on that Brothers' Day when I gave you my blessing—I, who wander distracted with the burden of my own evil-doing.

I feel today that man is at times attacked with evil as with the plague. Some germ finds its way in from somewhere, and then in the space of one night Death stalks in. Why cannot the stricken one be kept far away from the rest of the world? I, at least, have realized how terrible is the contagion—like a fiery torch which burns that it may set the world on fire.

It struck nine. I could not get rid of the idea that Amulya was in trouble, that he had fallen into the clutches of the police. There must be great excitement in the Police Office—whose are the jewels?—where did he get them? And in the end I shall have to furnish the answer, in public, before all the world.

What is that answer to be? Your day has come at last, Bara Rani, you whom I have so long despised. You, in the shape of the public, the world, will have your revenge. O God, save me this time, and I will cast all my pride at my sister-in-law's feet.

I could bear it no longer. I went straight to the Bara Rani. She was in the verandah, spicing her betel leaves, Thako at her side. The sight of Thako made me shrink back for a moment, but I overcame all hesitation, and making a low obeisance I took the dust of my elder sister-in-law's feet.

'Bless my soul, Chota Rani,' she exclaimed, 'what has come upon you? Why this sudden reverence?'

'It is my birthday, sister,' said I. 'I have caused you pain. Give me your blessing today that I may never do so again. My mind is so small.' I repeated my obeisance and left her hurriedly, but she called me back.

'You never before told me that this was your birthday, Chotie darling! Be sure to come and have lunch with me this afternoon. You positively must.'

O God, let it really be my birthday today. Can I not be born over again? Cleanse me, my God, and purify me and give me one more trial!

I went again to the sitting-room to find Sandip there. A feeling of disgust seemed to poison my very blood. The face of his, which I saw in the morning light, had nothing of the magic radiance of genius.

'Will you leave the room,' I blurted out.

Sandip smiled. 'Since Amulya is not here,' he remarked, 'I should think my turn had come for a special talk.'

My fate was coming back upon me. How was I to take away the right I myself had given. 'I would be alone,' I repeated.

'Queen,' he said, 'the presence of another person does not prevent your being alone. Do not mistake me for one of the crowd. I, Sandip, am always alone, even when surrounded by thousands.'

'Please come some other time. This morning I am...'

'Waiting for Amulya?'

I turned to leave the room for sheer vexation, when Sandip drew out from the folds of his cloak that jewel-casket of mine and banged it down on the marble table. I was thoroughly startled. 'Has not Amulya gone, then?' I exclaimed.

'Gone where?'

'To Calcutta?'

'No,' chuckled Sandip.

Ah, then my blessing had come true, in spite of all. He was saved. Let God's punishment fall on me, the thief, if only Amulya be safe.

The change in my countenance roused Sandip's scorn. 'So pleased, Queen!' sneered he. 'Are these jewels so very precious? How then did you bring yourself to offer them to the Goddess? Your gift was actually made. Would you now take it back?'

Pride dies hard and raises its fangs to the last. It was clear to me I must show Sandip I did not care a rap about these jewels. 'If they have excited your greed,' I said, 'you may have them.'

'My greed today embraces the wealth of all Bengal,' replied Sandip. 'Is there a greater force than greed? It is the steed of the great ones of the earth, as is the elephant, Airauat, the steed of Indra. So then these jewels are mine?'

As Sandip took up and replaced the casket under his cloak, Amulya rushed in. There were dark rings under his eyes, his lips were dry, his hair tumbled, the freshness of his youth seemed to have withered in a single day. Pangs gripped my heart as I looked on him.

'My box!' he cried, as he went straight up to Sandip without a glance at me. 'Have you taken that jewel-box from my trunk?'

'Your jewel-box?' mocked Sandip.

'It was my trunk!' Sandip burst out into a laugh. 'Your distinctions between mine and yours are getting rather thin, Amulya,' he cried. 'You will die a religious preacher yet, I see.'

Amulya sank on a chair with his face in his hands. I went up to him and placing my hand on his head asked him, 'What is your trouble, Amulya?'

He stood straight up as he replied, 'I had set my heart, Sister Rani, on returning your jewels to you with my own hand. Sandip Babu knew this, but he forestalled me.'

'What do I care for my jewels?' I said. 'Let them go. No harm is done.

'Go? Where?' asked the mystified boy.

'The jewels are mine,' said Sandip. 'Insignia bestowed on me by my Queen!'

'No, no, no,' broke out Amulya wildly. 'Never, Sister Rani! I brought them back for you. You shall not give them away to anybody else.'

'I accept your gift, my little brother,' said I. 'But let him, who hankers after them, satisfy his greed.'

Amulya glared at Sandip like a beast of prey, as he growled, 'Look here, Sandip Babu, you know that even hanging has no terrors for me. If you dare take away that box of jewels...'

With an attempt at a sarcastic laugh Sandip said, 'You also ought to know by this time, Amulya, that I am not the man to be afraid of you.'

'Queen Bee,' he went on, turning to me, 'I did not come here today to take these jewels, I came to give them to you. You would have done wrong to take my gift at Amulya's hands. In order to prevent it,

I had first to make them clearly mine. Now these my jewels are my gift to you. Here they are! Patch up any understanding with this boy you like. I must go. You have been at your special talks all these days together, leaving me out of them. If special happenings now come to pass, don't blame me.

'Amulya,' he continued, 'I have sent on your trunks and things to your lodgings. Don't you be keeping any belongings of yours in my room any longer.' With this parting shot, Sandip flung out of the room.

XIX

'I have had no peace of mind, Amulya,' I said to him, 'ever since I sent you off to sell my jewels.'

'Why, Sister Rani?'

'I was afraid lest you should get into trouble with them, lest they should suspect you for a thief. I would rather go without that six thousand. You must now do another thing for me—go home at once, home to your mother.'

Amulya produced a small bundle and said, 'But, sister, I have got the six thousand.'

'Where from?'

'I tried hard to get gold,' he went on, without replying to my question, 'but could not. So I had to bring it in notes.'

'Tell me truly, Amulya, swear by me, where did you get this money?'

'That I will not tell you.'

Everything seemed to grow dark before my eyes. 'What terrible thing have you done, Amulya?' I cried. 'Is it then...'

'I know you will say I got this money wrongly. Very well, I admit it. But I have paid the full price for my wrong-doing. So now the money is mine.'

I no longer had any desire to learn more about it. My very blood-vessels contracted, making my whole body shrink within itself.

'Take it away, Amulya,' I implored. 'Put it back where you got it from.'

'That would be hard indeed!'

'It is not hard, brother dear. It was an evil moment when you first came to me. Even Sandip has not been able to harm you as I have done.'

Sandip's name seemed to stab him.

'Sandip!' he cried. 'It was you alone who made me come to know that man for what he is. Do you know, sister, he has not spent a pice out of those sovereigns he took from you? He shut himself into his room, after he left you, and gloated over the gold, pouring it out in a heap on the floor. 'This is not money,' he exclaimed, 'but the petals of the divine lotus of power; crystallized strains of music from the pipes that play in the paradise of wealth! I cannot find it in my heart to change them, for they seem longing to fulfil their destiny of adorning the neck of Beauty. Amulya, my boy, don't you look at these with your fleshly eye, they are Lakshmi's smile, the gracious radiance of Indra's queen. No, no, I can't give them up to that boor of a manager. I am sure, Amulya, he was telling us lies. The police haven't traced the man who sank that boat. It's the manager who wants to make something out of it. We must get those letters back from him.'

'I asked him how we were to do this; he told me to use force or threats. I offered to do so if he would return the gold. That, he said, we could consider later. I will not trouble you, sister, with all I did to frighten the man into giving up those letters and burn them—it is a long story. That very night I came to Sandip and said, "We are now safe. Let me have the sovereigns to return them tomorrow to my sister, the Maharani." But he cried, "What infatuation is this of yours? Your precious sister's skirt bids fair to hide the whole country from you. Say *Bande Mataram* and exorcize the evil spirit."

'You know, Sister Rani, the power of Sandip's magic. The gold remained with him. And I spent the whole dark night on the bathing-steps of the lake muttering *Bande Mataram*.

'Then when you gave me your jewels to sell, I went again to Sandip. I could see he was angry with me. But he tried not to show it. 'If I still have them hoarded up in any box of mine you may take them,' said he, as he flung me his keys. They were nowhere to be seen. 'Tell me where they are,' I said. 'I will do so,' he replied, 'when I find your infatuation has left you. Not now.'

'When I found I could not move him, I had to employ other

methods. Then I tried to get the sovereigns from him in exchange for my currency notes for six thousand rupees. 'You shall have them,' he said, and disappeared into his bedroom, leaving me waiting outside. There he broke open my trunk and came straight to you with your casket through some other passage. He would not let me bring it, and now he dares call it his gift. How can I tell how much he has deprived me of? I shall never forgive him.

'But, oh sister, his power over me has been utterly broken. And it is you who have broken it!'

'Brother dear,' said I, 'if that is so, then my life is justified. But more remains to be done, Amulya. It is not enough that the spell has been destroyed. Its stains must be washed away. Don't delay any longer, go at once and put back the money where you took it from. Can you not do it, dear?'

'With your blessing everything is possible, Sister Rani.'

'Remember, it will not be your expiation alone, but mine also. I am a woman; the outside world is closed to me, else I would have gone myself. My hardest punishment is that I must put on you the burden of my sin.'

'Don't say that, sister. The path I was treading was not your path. It attracted me because of its dangers and difficulties. Now that your path calls me, let it be a thousand times more difficult and dangerous, the dust of your feet will help me to win through. Is it then your command that this money be replaced?'

'Not my command, brother mine, but a command from above.'

'Of that I know nothing. It is enough for me that this command from above comes from your lips. And, sister, I thought I had an invitation here. I must not lose that. You must give me your prasad[1] before I go. Then, if I can possibly manage it, I will finish my duty in the evening.'

Tears came to my eyes when I tried to smile as I said, 'So be it.'

---

[1] Food consecrated by the touch of a revered person.

CHAPTER ELEVEN

BIMALA'S STORY

XX

With Amulya's departure my heart sank within me. On what perilous adventure had I sent this only son of his mother? O God, why need my expiation have such pomp and circumstance? Could I not be allowed to suffer alone without inviting all this multitude to share my punishment? Oh, let not this innocent child fall victim to Your wrath.

I called him back—'Amulya!'

My voice sounded so feebly, it failed to reach him.

I went up to the door and called again, 'Amulya!'

He had gone.

'Who is there?'

'Rani Mother!'

'Go and tell Amulya Babu that I want him.'

What exactly happened I could not make out—the man, perhaps, was not familiar with Amulya's name—but he returned almost at once followed by Sandip.

'The very moment you sent me away,' he said as he came in, 'I had a presentiment that you would call me back. The attraction of the same moon causes both ebb and flow. I was so sure of being sent for, that I was actually waiting out in the passage. As soon as I caught sight of your man, coming from your room, I said, 'Yes, yes, I am coming, I am coming at once!'—before he could utter a word. That up-country lout was surprised, I can tell you! He stared at me, open-mouthed, as if he thought I knew magic.

'All the fights in the world, Queen Bee,' Sandip rambled on, 'are really fights between hypnotic forces. Spell cast against spell —noiseless weapons which reach even invisible targets. At last I have met in you my match. Your quiver is full, I know, you artful warrior Queen! You are the only one in the world who has been able to turn Sandip out and call Sandip back, at your sweet will. Well, your quarry is at your feet. What will you do with him now? Will you give him the coup de grâce, or keep him in your cage? Let me warn you beforehand, Queen, you will find the beast as difficult to kill outright as to keep in bondage. Anyway, why lose time in trying your magic weapons?'

Sandip must have felt the shadow of approaching defeat, and this made him try to gain time by chattering away without waiting for a reply. I believe he knew that I had sent the messenger for Amulya, whose name the man must have mentioned. In spite of that he had deliberately played this trick. He was now trying to avoid giving me any opening to tell him that it was Amulya I wanted, not him. But his stratagem was futile, for I could see his weakness through it. I must not yield up a pin's point of the ground I had gained.

'Sandip Babu,' I said, 'I wonder how you can go on making these endless speeches, without a stop. Do you get them up by heart, beforehand?'

Sandip's face flushed instantly.

'I have heard,' I continued, 'that our professional reciters keep a book full of all kinds of ready-made discourses, which can be fitted into any subject. Have you also a book?'

Sandip ground out his reply through his teeth. 'God has given you women a plentiful supply of coquetry to start with, and on the top of that you have the milliner and the jeweller to help you; but do not think we men are so helpless...'

'You had better go back and look up your book, Sandip Babu. You are getting your words all wrong. That's just the trouble with trying to repeat things by rote.'

'You!' shouted Sandip, losing all control over himself. 'You to insult me thus! What is there left of you that I do not know to the very bottom? What...' He became speechless.

Sandip, the wielder of magic spells, is reduced to utter powerlessness, whenever his spell refuses to work. From a king he fell to the level of a boor. Oh, the joy of witnessing his weakness! The harsher he became in his rudeness, the more did this joy well up within me. His snaky coils, with which he used to snare me, are exhausted—I am free. I am saved, saved. Be rude to me, insult me, for that shows you in your truth; but spare me your songs of praise, which were false.

My husband came in at this juncture. Sandip had not the elasticity to recover himself in a moment, as he used to do before. My husband looked at him for a while in surprise. Had this happened some days ago I should have felt ashamed. But today I was pleased—whatever my husband might think. I wanted to have it out to the finish with my weakening adversary.

Finding us both silent and constrained, my husband hesitated a little, and then took a chair. 'Sandip,' he said, 'I have been looking for you, and was told you were here.'

'I am here,' said Sandip with some emphasis. 'Queen Bee sent for me early this morning. And I, the humble worker of the hive, left all else to attend her summons.'

'I am going to Calcutta tomorrow. You will come with me.'

'And why, pray? Do you take me for one of your retinue?'

'Oh, very well, take it that you are going to Calcutta, and that I am your follower.'

'I have no business there.'

'All the more reason for going. You have too much business here.'

'I don't propose to stir.'

'Then I propose to shift you.'

'Forcibly?'

'Forcibly.'

'Very well, then, I will make a move. But the world is not divided between Calcutta and your estates. There are other places on the map.'

'From the way you have been going on, one would hardly have thought that there was any other place in the world except my estates.'

Sandip stood up. 'It does happen at times,' he said, 'that a man's whole world is reduced to a single spot. I have realized my universe in this sitting-room of yours, that is why I have been a fixture here.'

Then he turned to me. 'None but you, Queen Bee,' he said, 'will understand my words—perhaps not even you. I salute you. With worship in my heart I leave you. My watchword has changed since you have come across my vision. It is no longer *Bande Mataram* (Hail

Mother), but Hail Beloved, Hail Enchantress. The mother protects, the mistress leads to destruction—but sweet is that destruction. You have made the anklet sounds of the dance of death tinkle in my heart. You have changed for me, your devotee, the picture I had of this Bengal of ours—'the soft breeze-cooled land of pure water and sweet fruit.'[1] You have no pity, my beloved. You have come to me with your poison cup and I shall drain it, either to die in agony or live triumphing over death.

'Yes,' he continued. 'The mother's day is past. O love, my love, you have made as naught for me the truth and right and heaven itself. All duties have become as shadows, all rules and restraints have snapped their bonds. O love, my love, I could set fire to all the world outside this land on which you have set your dainty feet, and dance in mad revel over the ashes… These are mild men. These are good men. They would do good to all—as if this all were a reality! No, no! There is no reality in the world save this one real love of mine. I do you reverence. My devotion to you has made me cruel; my worship of you has lighted the raging flame of destruction within me. I am not righteous. I have no beliefs, I only believe in her whom, above all else in the world, I have been able to realize.'

Wonderful! It was wonderful, indeed. Only a minute ago I had despised this man with all my heart. But what I had thought to be dead ashes now glowed with living fire. The fire in him is true, that is beyond doubt. Oh why has God made man such a mixed creature? Was it only to show his supernatural sleight of hand? Only a few minutes ago I had thought that Sandip, whom I had once taken to be a hero, was only the stage hero of melodrama. But that is not so, not so. Even behind the trappings of the theatre, a true hero may sometimes be lurking.

There is much in Sandip that is coarse, that is sensuous, that is false, much that is overlaid with layer after layer of fleshly covering. Yet—yet it is best to confess that there is a great deal in the depths of him which we do not, cannot understand—much in ourselves too. A wonderful thing is man. What great mysterious purpose he

---

[1] Quotation from the National song—*Bande Mataram*.

is working out only the Terrible One[1] knows—meanwhile we groan under the brunt of it. Shiva is the Lord of Chaos. He is all Joy. He will destroy our bonds.

I cannot but feel, again and again, that there are two persons in me. One recoils from Sandip in his terrible aspect of Chaos—the other feels that very vision to be sweetly alluring. The sinking ship drags down all who are swimming round it. Sandip is just such a force of destruction. His immense attraction gets hold of one before fear can come to the rescue, and then, in the twinkling of an eye, one is drawn away, irresistibly, from all light, all good, all freedom of the sky, all air that can be breathed—from lifelong accumulations, from everyday cares—right to the bottom of dissolution.

From some realm of calamity has Sandip come as its messenger; and as he stalks the land, muttering unholy incantations, to him flock all the boys and youths. The mother, seated in the lotus-heart of the Country, is wailing her heart out; for they have broken open her store-room, there to hold their drunken revelry. Her vintage of the draught for the immortals they would pour out on the dust; her time-honoured vessels they would smash to pieces. True, I feel with her; but, at the same time, I cannot help being infected with their excitement.

Truth itself has sent us this temptation to test our trustiness in upholding its commandments. Intoxication masquerades in heavenly garb, and dances before the pilgrims saying, 'Fools you are that pursue the fruitless path of renunciation. Its way is long, its time passing slow. So the Wielder of the Thunderbolt has sent me to you. Behold, I the beautiful, the passionate, I will accept you—in my embrace you shall find fulfilment.'

After a pause Sandip addressed me again, 'Goddess, the time has come for me to leave you. It is well. The work of your nearness has been done. By lingering longer it would only become undone again, little by little. All is lost, if in our greed we try to cheapen that which is the greatest thing on earth. That which is eternal within the moment only becomes shallow if spread out in time. We were about

---

[1] Rudra, the Terrible, a name of Shiva. [Trans.].

to spoil our infinite moment, when it was your uplifted thunderbolt which came to the rescue. You intervened to save the purity of your own worship—and in so doing you also saved your worshipper. In my leave-taking today your worship stands out the biggest thing. Goddess, I, also, set you free today. My earthen temple could hold you no longer—every moment it was on the point of breaking apart. Today I depart to worship your larger image in a larger temple. I can gain you more truly only at a distance from yourself. Here I had only your favour, there I shall be vouchsafed your boon.'

My jewel-casket was lying on the table. I held it up aloft as I said, 'I charge you to convey these my jewels to the object of my worship—to whom I have dedicated them through you.'

My husband remained silent. Sandip left the room.

XXI

I had just sat down to make some cakes for Amulya when the Bara Rani came upon the scene. 'Oh dear,' she exclaimed, 'has it come to this that you must make cakes for your own birthday?'

'Is there no one else for whom I could be making them?' I asked.

'But this is not the day when you should think of feasting others. It is for us to feast you. I was just thinking of making something up[1] when I heard the staggering news which completely upset me. A gang of five or six hundred men, they say, has raided one of our treasuries and made off with six thousand rupees. Our house will be looted next, they expect.'

I felt greatly relieved. So it was our own money after all. I wanted to send for Amulya at once and tell him that he need only hand over those notes to my husband and leave the explanations to me.

'You are a wonderful creature!' my sister-in-law broke out, at the change in my countenance. 'Have you then really no such thing as fear?'

'I cannot believe it,' I said. 'Why should they loot our house?'

'Not believe it, indeed! Who could have believed that they would

---

[1] Any dainties to be offered ceremonially should be made by the lady of the house herself. [Trans.].

attack our treasury, either?'

I made no reply, but bent over my cakes, putting in the coconut stuffing.

'Well, I'm off,' said the Bara Rani after a prolonged stare at me. 'I must see Brother Nikhil and get something done about sending off my money to Calcutta, before it's too late.'

She was no sooner gone than I left the cakes to take care of themselves and rushed to my dressing-room, shutting myself inside. My husband's tunic with the keys in its pocket was still hanging there—so forgetful was he. I took the key of the iron safe off the ring and kept it by me, hidden in the folds of my dress.

Then there came a knocking at the door. 'I am dressing,' I called out. I could hear the Bara Rani saying, 'Only a minute ago I saw her making cakes and now she is busy dressing up. What next, I wonder! One of their *Bande Mataram* meetings is on, I suppose. I say, Robber Queen,' she called out to me, 'are you taking stock of your loot?'

When they went away I hardly know what made me open the safe. Perhaps there was a lurking hope that it might all be a dream. What if, on pulling out the inside drawer, I should find the rolls of gold there, just as before?... Alas, everything was empty as the trust which had been betrayed.

I had to go through the farce of dressing. I had to do my hair up all over again, quite unnecessarily. When I came out my sister-in-law railed at me, 'How many times are you going to dress today?'

'My birthday!' I said.

'Oh, any pretext seems good enough,' she went on. 'Many vain people have I seen in my day, but you beat them all hollow.'

I was about to summon a servant to send after Amulya, when one of the men came up with a little note, which he handed to me. It was from Amulya. 'Sister,' he wrote, 'you invited me this afternoon, but I thought I should not wait. Let me first execute your bidding and then come for my prasad. I may be a little late.'

To whom could he be going to return that money? Into what fresh entanglement was the poor boy rushing? O miserable woman, you can only send him off like an arrow, but not recall him if you miss your aim.

I should have declared at once that I was at the bottom of this robbery. But women live on the trust of their surroundings—this is their whole world. If once it is out that this trust has been secretly betrayed, their place in their world is lost. They have then to stand upon the fragments of the thing they have broken, and its jagged edges keep on wounding them at every turn. To sin is easy enough, but to make up for it is above all difficult for a woman.

For some time past all easy approaches for communion with my husband have been closed to me. How then could I burst on him with this stupendous news? He was very late in coming for his meal today—nearly two o'clock. He was absent-minded and hardly touched any food. I had lost even the right to press him to take a little more. I had to avert my face to wipe away my tears.

I wanted so badly to say to him, 'Do come into our room and rest awhile; you look so tired.' I had just cleared my throat with a little cough, when a servant hurried in to say that the Police Inspector had brought Panchu up to the palace. My husband, with the shadow on his face deepened, left his meal unfinished and went out.

A little later the Bara Rani appeared. 'Why did you not send me word when Brother Nikhil came in?' she complained. 'As he was late I thought I might as well finish my bath in the meantime. However did he manage to get through his meal so soon?'

'Why, did you want him for anything?'

'What is this about both of you going off to Calcutta tomorrow? All I can say is, I am not going to be left here alone. I should get startled out of my life at every sound, with all these dacoits about. Is it quite settled about your going tomorrow?'

'Yes,' said I, though I had only just now heard it; and though, moreover, I was not at all sure that before tomorrow our history might not take such a turn as to make it all one whether we went or stayed. After that, what our home, our life would be like, was utterly beyond my ken—it seemed so misty and phantom-like.

In a very few hours now my unseen fate would become visible. Was there no one who could keep on postponing the flight of these hours, from day to day, and so make them long enough for me to set things right, so far as lay in my power? The time during which the seed lies underground is long—so long indeed that one forgets that there is any danger of its sprouting. But once its shoot shows up above the surface, it grows and grows so fast, there is no time to cover it up, neither with skirt, nor body, nor even life itself.

I will try to think of it no more, but sit quiet—passive and callous—let the crash come when it may. By the day after tomorrow all will be over—publicity, laughter, bewailing, questions, explanations—everything.

But I cannot forget the face of Amulya—beautiful, radiant with devotion. He did not wait, despairing, for the blow of fate to fall, but rushed into the thick of danger. In my misery I do him reverence. He is my boy-god. Under the pretext of his playfulness he took from me the weight of my burden. He would save me by taking the punishment meant for me on his own head. But how am I to bear this terrible mercy of my God?

Oh, my child, my child, I do you reverence. Little brother mine, I do you reverence. Pure are you, beautiful are you, I do you reverence. May you come to my arms, in the next birth, as my own child—that is my prayer.

XXII

Rumour became busy on every side. The police were continually in and out. The servants of the house were in a great flurry.

Khema, my maid, came up to me and said, 'Oh, Rani Mother! for goodness' sake put away my gold necklace and armlets in your iron safe.' To whom was I to explain that the Rani herself had been weaving all this network of trouble, and had got caught in it, too? I had to play the benign protector and take charge of Khema's ornaments and Thako's savings. The milk-woman, in her turn, brought along and kept in my room a box in which were a Benares sari and some other of her valued possessions. 'I got these at your wedding,' she told me.

When, tomorrow, my iron safe will be opened in the presence of these—Khema, Thako, the milk-woman and all the rest... Let me not think of it! Let me rather try to think what it will be like when this third day of Magh comes round again after a year has passed.

Will all the wounds of my home life then be still as fresh as ever?...

Amulya writes that he will come later in the evening. I cannot remain alone with my thoughts, doing nothing. So I sit down again to make cakes for him. I have finished making quite a quantity, but still I must go on. Who will eat them? I shall distribute them amongst the servants. I must do so this very night. Tonight is my limit. Tomorrow will not be in my hands.

I went on untiringly, frying cake after cake. Every now and then it seemed to me that there was some noise in the direction of my rooms, upstairs. Could it be that my husband had missed the key of the safe, and the Bara Rani had assembled all the servants to help him to hunt for it? No, I must not pay heed to these sounds. Let me shut the door.

I rose to do so, when Thako came panting in, 'Rani Mother, oh, Rani Mother!'

'Oh get away!' I snapped out, cutting her short. 'Don't come bothering me.'

'The Bara Rani Mother wants you,' she went on. 'Her nephew has brought such a wonderful machine from Calcutta. It talks like a man. Do come and hear it!'

I did not know whether to laugh or to cry. So, of all things, a gramophone needs must come on the scene at such a time, repeating at every winding the nasal twang of its theatrical songs! What a fearsome thing results when a machine apes a man.

The shades of evening began to fall. I knew that Amulya would not delay to announce himself—yet I could not wait. I summoned a servant and said, 'Go and tell Amulya Babu to come straight in here.' The man came back after a while to say that Amulya was not in—he had not come back since he had gone.

'Gone!' The last word struck my ears like a wail in the gathering darkness. Amulya gone! Had he then come like a streak of light from the setting sun, only to be gone for ever? All kinds of possible and impossible dangers flitted through my mind. It was I who had sent him to his death. What if he was fearless? That only showed his own greatness of heart. But after this how was I to go on living all by myself?

I had no memento of Amulya save that pistol—his reverence-offering.

It seemed to me that this was a sign given by Providence. This guilt which had contaminated my life at its very root—my God in the form of a child had left with me the means of wiping it away, and then vanished. Oh the loving gift—the saving grave that lay hidden within it!

I opened my box and took out the pistol, lifting it reverently to my forehead. At that moment the gongs clanged out from the temple attached to our house. I prostrated myself in salutation.

In the evening I feasted the whole household with my cakes. 'You have managed a wonderful birthday feast—and all by yourself too!' exclaimed my sister-in-law. 'But you must leave something for us to do.' With this she turned on her gramophone and let loose the shrill treble of the Calcutta actresses all over the place. It seemed like a stable full of neighing fillies.

It got quite late before the feasting was over. I had a sudden longing to end my birthday celebration by taking the dust of my husband's feet. I went up to the bedroom and found him fast asleep. He had had such a worrying, trying day. I raised the edge of the mosquito curtain very very gently, and laid my head near his feet. My hair must have touched him, for he moved his legs in his sleep and pushed my head away.

I then went out and sat in the west verandah. A silk-cotton tree, which had shed all its leaves, stood there in the distance, like a skeleton. Behind it the crescent moon was setting. All of a sudden I had the feeling that the very stars in the sky were afraid of me—that the whole of the night world was looking askance at me. Why? Because I was alone.

There is nothing so strange in creation as the man who is alone. Even he whose near ones have all died, one by one, is not alone—companionship comes for him from behind the screen of death. But he, whose kin are there, yet no longer near, who has dropped out of all the varied companionship of a full home—the starry universe itself seems to bristle to look on him in his darkness.

Where I am, I am not. I am far away from those who are around me. I live and move upon a world-wide chasm of separation, unstable as the dew-drop upon the lotus leaf.

Why do not men change wholly when they change? When I look into my heart, I find everything that was there, still there—only they are topsy-turvy. Things that were well-ordered have become jumbled up. The gems that were strung into a necklace are now rolling in the dust. And so my heart is breaking.

I feel I want to die. Yet in my heart everything still lives—nor even in death can I see the end of it all, rather, in death there seems to be ever so much more of repining. What is to be ended must be ended in this life—there is no other way out.

Oh forgive me just once, only this time, Lord! All that you gave into my hands as the wealth of my life, I have made into my burden. I can neither bear it longer, nor give it up. O Lord, sound once again those flute strains which you played for me, long ago, standing at the rosy edge of my morning sky—and let all my complexities become simple and easy. Nothing save the music of your flute can make whole that which has been broken, and pure that which has been sullied. Create my home anew with your music. No other way can I see.

I threw myself prone on the ground and sobbed aloud. It was for mercy that I prayed—some little mercy from somewhere, some shelter, some sign of forgiveness, some hope that might bring about the end. 'Lord,' I vowed to myself, 'I will lie here, waiting and waiting, touching neither food nor drink, so long as your blessing does not reach me.'

I heard the sound of footsteps. Who says that the gods do not show themselves to mortal men? I did not raise my face to look up, lest the sight of it should break the spell. Come, oh come, come and let your feet touch my head. Come, Lord, and set your foot upon my throbbing heart, and at that moment let me die.

He came and sat near my head. Who? My husband! At the first touch of his presence I felt that I should swoon. And then the pain at my heart burst its way out in an overwhelming flood of tears, tearing through all my obstructing veins and nerves. I strained his feet to my bosom—oh, why could not their impress remain there forever?

He tenderly stroked my head. I received his blessing. Now I shall be able to take up the penalty of public humiliation which will be mine tomorrow, and offer it, in all sincerity, at the feet of my God.

But what keeps crushing my heart is the thought that the festive flutes which were played at my wedding, nine years ago, welcoming me to this house, will never sound for me again in this life. What rigour of penance is there which can serve to bring me once more, as a bride adorned for her husband, to my place upon that same bridal seat? How many years, how many ages, aeons, must pass before I can find my way back to that day of nine years ago?

God can create new things, but has even He the power to create afresh that which has been destroyed?

CHAPTER TWELVE

NIKHIL'S STORY

XV

Today we are going to Calcutta. Our joys and sorrows lie heavy on us if we merely go on accumulating them. Keeping them and accumulating them alike are false. As master of the house I am in an artificial position—in reality I am a wayfarer on the path of life. That is why the true Master of the House gets hurt at every step and at last there comes the supreme hurt of death.

My union with you, my love, was only of the wayside; it was well enough so long as we followed the same road; it will only hamper us if we try to preserve it further. We are now leaving its bonds behind. We are started on our journey beyond, and it will be enough if we can throw each other a glance, or feel the touch of each other's hands in passing. After that? After that there is the larger world-path, the endless current of universal life.

How little can you deprive me of, my love, after all? Whenever I set my ear to it, I can hear the flute which is playing, its fountain of melody gushing forth from the flute-stops of separation. The immortal draught of the goddess is never exhausted. She sometimes breaks the bowl from which we drink it, only to smile at seeing us so disconsolate over the trifling loss. I will not stop to pick up my broken bowl. I will march forward, albeit with unsatisfied heart.

The Bara Rani came and asked me, 'What is the meaning, brother, of all these books being packed up and sent off in box-loads?'

'It only means,' I replied, 'that I have not yet been able to get over my fondness for them.'

'I only wish you would keep your fondness for some other things as well! Do you mean you are never coming back home?'

'I shall be coming and going, but shall not immure myself here any more.'

'Oh indeed! Then just come along to my room and see how many things I have been unable to shake off my fondness for.' With this she took me by the hand and marched me off.

In my sister-in-law's rooms I found numberless boxes and bundles ready packed. She opened one of the boxes and said, 'See, brother, look at all my paan-making things. In this bottle I have catechu powder scented with the pollen of screw-pine blossoms. These little tin boxes are all for different kinds of spices. I have not forgotten my playing cards and draught-board either. If you two are over-busy, I shall manage to make other friends there, who will give me a game. Do you remember this comb? It was one of the Swadeshi combs you brought for me...'

'But what is all this for, Sister Rani? Why have you been packing up all these things?'

'Do you think I am not going with you?'

'What an extraordinary idea!'

'Don't you be afraid! I am not going there to flirt with you, nor to quarrel with the Chota Rani! One must die sooner or later, and it is just as well to be on the bank of the holy Ganges before it is too late. It is too horrible to think of being cremated in your wretched burning-ground here, under that stumpy banian tree—that is why I have been refusing to die, and have plagued you all this time.'

At last I could hear the true voice of home. The Bara Rani came into our house as its bride, when I was only six years old. We have played together, through the drowsy afternoons, in a corner of the roof-terrace. I have thrown down to her green amras from the tree-top, to be made into deliciously indigestible chutneys by slicing them up with mustard, salt and fragrant herbs. It was my part to gather for her all the forbidden things from the store-room to be used in the marriage celebration of her doll; for, in the penal code of my grandmother, I alone was exempt from punishment. And I used to be appointed her messenger to my brother, whenever she wanted to coax something special out of him, because he could not resist my importunity. I also remember how, when I suffered under the rigorous régime of the doctors of those days—who would not allow anything except warm water and sugared cardamom seeds during feverish attacks—my sister-in-law could not bear my privation and used to bring me delicacies on the sly. What a scolding she got one day when she was caught!

And then, as we grew up, our mutual joys and sorrows took on deeper tones of intimacy. How we quarrelled! Sometimes conflicts of worldly interests roused suspicions and jealousies, making breaches in our love; and when the Chota Rani came in between us, these breaches seemed as if they would never be mended, but it always turned out that the healing forces at bottom proved more powerful than the wounds on the surface.

So has a true relationship grown up between us, from our childhood up till now, and its branching foliage has spread and broadened over every room and verandah and terrace of this great house. When I saw the Bara Rani make ready, with all her belongings, to depart from this house of ours, all the ties that bound us, to their wide-spreading ends, felt the shock.

The reason was clear to me, why she had made up her mind to drift away towards the unknown, cutting asunder all her lifelong bonds of daily habit, and of the house itself, which she had never left for a day since she first entered it at the age of nine. And yet it was this real reason which she could not allow to escape her lips, preferring rather to put forward any other paltry excuse.

She had only this one relationship left in all the world, and the poor, unfortunate, widowed and childless woman had cherished it with all the tenderness hoarded in her heart. How deeply she had felt our proposed separation I never realized so keenly as when I stood amongst her scattered boxes and bundles.

I could see at once that the little differences she used to have with Bimala, about money matters, did not proceed from any sordid worldliness, but because she felt that her claims in regard to this one relationship of her life had been overridden and its ties weakened for her by the coming in between of this other woman from goodness knows where! She had been hurt at every turn and yet had not the right to complain.

And Bimala? She also had felt that the Senior Rani's claim over me was not based merely on our social connection, but went much deeper; and she was jealous of these ties between us, reaching back to our childhood.

Today my heart knocked heavily against the doors of my breast. I sank down upon one of the boxes as I said, 'How I should love, Sister Rani, to go back to the days when we first met in this old house of ours.'

'No, brother dear,' she replied with a sigh, 'I would not live my life again—not as a woman! Let what I have had to bear end with this one birth. I could not bear it over again.'

I said to her, 'The freedom to which we pass through sorrow is greater than the sorrow.'

'That may be so for you men. Freedom is for you. But we women would keep others bound. We would rather be put into bondage ourselves. No, no, brother, you will never get free from our toils. If you needs must spread your wings, you will have to take us with you; we refuse to be left behind. That is why I have gathered together all this weight of luggage. It would never do to allow men to run too light.'

'I can feel the weight of your words,' I said laughing, 'and if we men do not complain of your burdens, it is because women pay us so handsomely for what they make us carry.'

'You carry it,' she said, 'because it is made up of many small things. Whichever one you think of rejecting pleads that it is so light. And so with much lightness we weigh you down... When do we start?'

'The train leaves at half past eleven tonight. There will be lots of time.'

'Look here, do be good for once and listen to just one word of mine. Take a good nap this afternoon. You know you never get any sleep in the train. You look so pulled down, you might go to pieces any moment. Come along, get through your bath first.'

As we went towards my room, Khema, the maid, came up and with an ultra-modest pull at her veil told us, in deprecatingly low tones, that the Police Inspector had arrived with a prisoner and wanted to see the Maharaja.

'Is the Maharaja a thief, or a robber,' the Bara Rani flared up, 'that he should be set upon so by the police? Go and tell the Inspector that the Maharaja is at his bath.'

'Let me just go and see what is the matter,' I pleaded. 'It may be something urgent.'

'No, no,' my sister-in-law insisted. 'Our Chota Rani was making a heap of cakes last night. I'll send some to the Inspector, to keep him quiet till you're ready.' With this she pushed me into my room and shut the door on me.

I had not the power to resist such tyranny—so rare is it in this world. Let the Inspector while away the time eating cakes. What if business is a bit neglected?

The police had been in great form these last few days arresting now this one, now that. Each day some innocent person or other would be brought along to enliven the assembly in my office-room. One more such unfortunate, I supposed, must have been brought in that day. But why should the Inspector alone be regaled with cakes? That would not do at all. I thumped vigorously on the door.

'If you are going mad, be quick and pour some water over your head—that will keep you cool,' said my sister-in-law from the passage.

'Send down cakes for two,' I shouted. 'The person who has been brought in as the thief probably deserves them better. Tell the man to give him a good big helping.'

I hurried through my bath. When I came out, I found Bimala sitting on the floor outside.[1] Could this be my Bimala of old, my proud, sensitive Bimala?

What favour could she be wanting to beg, seated like this at my door?

As I stopped short, she stood up and said gently with downcast eyes, 'I would have a word with you.'

'Come inside then,' I said.

'But are you going out on any particular business?'

'I was, but let that be. I want to hear...'

'No, finish your business first. We will have our talk after you have had your dinner.'

I went off to my sitting-room, to find the Police Inspector's plate

---

[1] Sitting on the bare floor is a sign of mourning, and so, by association of ideas, of an abject attitude of mind. [Trans.].

quite empty. The person he had brought with him, however, was still busy eating.

'Hullo!' I ejaculated in surprise. 'You, Amulya?'

'It is I, sir,' said Amulya with his mouth full of cake. 'I've had quite a feast. And if you don't mind, I'll take the rest with me.' With this he proceeded to tie up the remaining cakes in his handkerchief.

'What does this mean?' I asked, staring at the Inspector.

The man laughed. 'We are no nearer, sir,' he said, 'to solving the problem of the thief, meanwhile the mystery of the theft deepens.' He then produced something tied up in a rag, which when untied disclosed a bundle of currency notes. 'This, Maharaja,' said the Inspector, 'is your six thousand rupees!'

'Where was it found?'

'In Amulya Babu's hands. He went last evening to the manager of your Chakna sub-office to tell him that the money had been found. The manager seemed to be in a greater state of trepidation at the recovery than he had been at the robbery. He was afraid he would be suspected of having made away with the notes and of now making up a cock-and-bull story for fear of being found out. He asked Amulya to wait, on the pretext of getting him some refreshment, and came straight over to the Police Office. I rode off at once, kept Amulya with me, and have been busy with him the whole morning. He refuses to tell us where he got the money from. I warned him he would be kept under restraint till he did so. In that case, he informed me he would have to lie. Very well, I said, he might do so if he pleased. Then he stated that he had found the money under a bush. I pointed out to him that it was not quite so easy to lie as all that. Under what bush? Where was the place? Why was he there?—All this would have to be stated as well. 'Don't you worry,' he said, 'there is plenty of time to invent all that.'

'But, Inspector,' I said, 'why are you badgering a respectable young gentleman like Amulya Babu?'

'I have no desire to harass him,' said the Inspector. 'He is not only a gentleman, but the son of Nibaran Babu, my school-fellow. Let me tell you, Maharaja, exactly what must have happened. Amulya knows the thief, but wants to shield him by drawing suspicion on himself. That is just the sort of bravado he loves to indulge in.' The Inspector turned to Amulya. 'Look here, young man,' he continued, 'I also was eighteen once upon a time, and a student in the Ripon College. I nearly got into gaol trying to rescue a hack driver from a police constable. It was a near shave.' Then he turned again to me and said, 'Maharaja, the real thief will now probably escape, but I think I can tell you who is at the bottom of it all.'

'Who is it, then?' I asked.

'The manager, in collusion with the guard, Kasim.'

When the Inspector, having argued out his theory to his own satisfaction, at last departed, I said to Amulya, 'If you will tell me who took the money, I promise you no one shall be hurt.'

'I did,' said he.

'But how can that be? What about the gang of armed men?...'

'It was I, by myself, alone!'

What Amulya then told me was indeed extraordinary. The manager had just finished his supper and was on the verandah rinsing out his mouth. The place was somewhat dark. Amulya had a revolver in each pocket, one loaded with blank cartridges, the other with ball. He had a mask over his face. He flashed a bull's-eye lantern in the manager's face and fired a blank shot. The man swooned away. Some of the guards, who were off duty, came running up, but when Amulya fired another blank shot at them they lost no time in taking cover. Then Kasim, who was on duty, came up whirling a quarterstaff. This time Amulya aimed a bullet at his legs, and finding himself hit, Kasim collapsed on the floor. Amulya then made the trembling manager, who had come to his senses, open the safe and deliver up six thousand rupees. Finally, he took one of the estate horses and galloped off a few miles, there let the animal loose, and quietly walked up here, to our place.

'What made you do all this, Amulya?' I asked.

'There was a grave reason, Maharaja,' he replied.

'But why, then, did you try to return the money?'

'Let her come, at whose command I did so. In her presence I shall make a clean breast of it.'

'And who may 'she' be?'

'My sister, the Chota Rani!'

I sent for Bimala. She came hesitatingly, barefoot, with a white shawl over her head. I had never seen my Bimala like this before. She seemed to have wrapped herself in a morning light.

Amulya prostrated himself in salutation and took the dust of her feet. Then, as he rose, he said, 'Your command has been executed, sister. The money is returned.'

'You have saved me, my little brother,' said Bimal.

'With your image in my mind, I have not uttered a single lie,' Amulya continued. 'My watchword *Bande Mataram* has been cast away at your feet for good. I have also received my reward, your prasad, as soon as I came to the palace.'

Bimala looked at him blankly, unable to follow his last words. Amulya brought out his handkerchief, and untying it showed her the cakes put away inside. 'I did not eat them all,' he said. 'I have kept these to eat after you have helped me with your own hands.'

I could see that I was not wanted here. I went out of the room. I could only preach and preach, so I mused, and get my effigy burnt for my pains. I had not yet been able to bring back a single soul from the path of death. They who have the power, can do so by a mere sign. My words have not that ineffable meaning. I am not a flame, only a black coal, which has gone out. I can light no lamp. That is what the story of my life shows—my row of lamps has remained unlit.

XVI

I returned slowly towards the inner apartments. The Bara Rani's room must have been drawing me again. It had become an absolute necessity for me, that day, to feel that this life of mine had been able to strike some real, some responsive chord in some other harp of life. One cannot realize one's own existence by remaining within oneself—it has to be sought outside.

As I passed in front of my sister-in-law's room, she came out saying, 'I was afraid you would be late again this afternoon. However, I ordered your dinner as soon as I heard you coming. It will be served in a minute.'

'Meanwhile,' I said; 'let me take out that money of yours and have it kept ready to take with us.'

As we walked on towards my room she asked me if the Police Inspector had made any report about the robbery. I somehow did not feel inclined to tell her all the details of how that six thousand had come back. 'That's just what all the fuss is about,' I said evasively.

When I went into my dressing-room and took out my bunch of keys, I did not find the key of the iron safe on the ring. What an absurdly absent-minded fellow I was, to be sure! Only this morning I had been opening so many boxes and things, and never noticed that this key was not there.

'What has happened to your key?' she asked me.

I went on fumbling in this pocket and that, but could give her no answer. I hunted in the same place over and over again. It dawned on both of us that it could not be a case of the key being mislaid. Someone must have taken it off the ring. Who could it be? Who else could have come into this room?

'Don't you worry about it,' she said to me. 'Get through your dinner first. The Chota Rani must have kept it herself, seeing how absent-minded you are getting.'

I was, however, greatly disturbed. It was never Bimala's habit to take any key of mine without telling me about it. Bimala was not present at my meal-time that day, she was busy feasting Amulya in her own room. My sister-in-law wanted to send for her, but I asked her not to do so.

I had just finished my dinner when Bimala came in. I would have preferred not to discuss the matter of the key in the Bara Rani's presence, but as soon as she saw Bimala, she asked her, 'Do you know, dear, where the key of the safe is?'

'I have it,' was the reply.

'Didn't I say so!' exclaimed my sister-in-law triumphantly. 'Our Chota Rani pretends not to care about these robberies, but she takes precautions on the sly, all the same.'

The look on Bimala's face made my mind misgive me. 'Let the key be, now,' I said. 'I will take out that money in the evening.'

'There you go again, putting it off,' said the Bara Rani. 'Why not take it out and send it to the treasury while you have it in mind?'

'I have taken it out already,' said Bimala.

I was startled.

'Where have you kept it, then?' asked my sister-in-law.

'I have spent it.'

'Just listen to her! Whatever did you spend all that money on?'

Bimala made no reply. I asked her nothing further. The Bara Rani seemed about to make some further remark to Bimala, but checked herself. 'Well, that is all right, anyway,' she said at length, as she looked towards me. 'Just what I used to do with my husband's loose cash. I knew it was no use leaving it with him—his hundred and one hangers-on would be sure to get hold of it. You are much the same, dear! What a number of ways you men know of getting through money. We can only save it from you by stealing it ourselves! Come along now. Off with you to bed.'

The Bara Rani led me to my room, but I hardly knew where I was going. She sat by my bed after I was stretched on it, and smiled at Bimala as she said, 'Give me one of your paans, Chotie darling—what? You have none! You have become a regular mem-sahib. Then send for some from my room.'

'But have you had your dinner yet?' I anxiously enquired.

'Oh long ago,' she replied—clearly a fib.

She kept on chattering away there at my bedside, on all manner of things. The maid came and told Bimala that her dinner had been served and was getting cold, but she gave no sign of having heard it. 'Not had your dinner yet? What nonsense! It's fearfully late.' With this the Bara Rani took Bimala away with her.

I could divine that there was some connection between the taking out of this six thousand and the robbing of the other. But I have no curiosity to learn the nature of it. I shall never ask.

Providence leaves our life moulded in the rough—its object being that we ourselves should put the finishing touches, shaping it into its final form to our taste. There has always been the hankering within me to express some great idea in the process of giving shape to my life on the lines suggested by the Creator. In this endeavour I have spent all my days. How severely I have curbed my desires, repressed myself at every step, only the Searcher of the Heart knows.

But the difficulty is, that one's life is not solely one's own. He who would create it must do so with the help of his surroundings, or he will fail. So it was my constant dream to draw Bimala to join me in this work of creating myself. I loved her with all my soul; on the strength of that, I could not but succeed in winning her to my purpose—that was my firm belief.

Then I discovered that those who could simply and naturally draw their environment into the process of their self-creation belonged to one species of the genus 'man',—and I to another. I had received the vital spark, but could not impart it. Those to whom I have surrendered my all have taken my all, but not myself with it.

My trial is hard indeed. Just when I want a helpmate most, I am thrown back on myself alone. Nevertheless, I record my vow that even in this trial I shall win through. Alone, then, shall I tread my thorny path to the end of this life's journey...

I have begun to suspect that there has all along been a vein of tyranny in me. There was a despotism in my desire to mould my relations with Bimala in a hard, clear-cut, perfect form. But man's life was not meant to be cast in a mould. And if we try to shape the good, as so much mere material, it takes a terrible revenge by losing its life.

I did not realize all this while that it must have been this unconscious tyranny of mine which made us gradually drift apart. Bimala's life, not finding its true level by reason of my pressure from above, has had to find an outlet by undermining its banks at the bottom. She has had to steal this six thousand rupees because she could not be open with me, because she felt that, in certain things, I despotically differed from her.

Men, such as I, possessed with one idea, are indeed at one with those who can manage to agree with us; but those who do not, can only get on with us by cheating us. It is our unyielding obstinacy, which drives even the simplest to tortuous ways. In trying to manufacture a helpmate, we spoil a wife.

Could I not go back to the beginning? Then, indeed, I should follow the path of the simple. I should not try to fetter my life's companion with my ideas, but play the joyous pipes of my love and say, 'Do you love me? Then may you grow true to yourself in the light of your love. Let my suggestions be suppressed, let God's design, which is in you, triumph, and my ideas retire abashed.'

But can even Nature's nursing heal the open wound, into which our accumulated differences have broken out? The covering veil, beneath the privacy of which Nature's silent forces alone can work, has been torn asunder. Wounds must be bandaged—can we not bandage our wound with our love, so that the day may come when its scar will no longer be visible? It is not too late? So much time has been lost in misunderstanding; it has taken right up to now to come to an understanding; how much more time will it take for the correcting? What if the wound does eventually heal?—can the devastation it has wrought ever be made good?

There was a slight sound near the door. As I turned over I saw Bimala's retreating figure through the open doorway. She must have been waiting by the door, hesitating whether to come in or not, and at last have decided to go back. I jumped up and bounded to the door, calling, 'Bimal.'

She stopped on her way. She had her back to me. I went and took her by the hand and led her into our room. She threw herself face downwards on a pillow, and sobbed and sobbed. I said nothing, but held her hand as I sat by her head.

When her storm of grief had abated she sat up. I tried to draw her to my breast, but she pushed my arms away and knelt at my feet, touching them repeatedly with her head, in obeisance. I hastily drew my feet back, but she clasped them in her arms, saying in a choking voice, 'No, no, no, you must not take away your feet. Let me do my worship.'

I kept still. Who was I to stop her? Was I the god of her worship that I should have any qualms?

BIMALA'S STORY

XXIII

Come, come! Now is the time to set sail towards that great confluence, where the river of love meets the sea of worship. In that pure blue all the weight of its muddiness sinks and disappears.

I now fear nothing—neither myself, nor anybody else. I have passed through fire. What was inflammable has been burnt to ashes; what is left is deathless. I have dedicated myself to the feet of him, who has received all my sin into the depths of his own pain.

Tonight we go to Calcutta. My inward troubles have so long prevented my looking after my things. Now let me arrange and pack them.

After a while I found my husband had come in and was taking a hand in the packing.

'This won't do,' I said. 'Did you not promise me you would have a sleep?'

'I might have made the promise,' he replied, 'but my sleep did not, and it was nowhere to be found.'

'No, no,' I repeated, 'this will never do. Lie down for a while, at least.'

'But how can you get through all this alone?'

'Of course I can.'

'Well, you may boast of being able to do without me. But frankly I can't do without you. Even sleep refused to come to me, alone, in that room.' Then he set to work again.

But there was an interruption, in the shape of a servant, who came and said that Sandip Babu had called and had asked to be announced. I did not dare to ask whom he wanted. The light of the sky seemed suddenly to be shut down, like the leaves of a sensitive plant.

'Come, Bimal,' said my husband. 'Let us go and hear what Sandip has to tell us. Since he has come back again, after taking his leave, he must have something special to say.'

I went, simply because it would have been still more embarrassing to stay. Sandip was staring at a picture on the wall. As we entered he said, 'You must be wondering why the fellow has returned. But you know the ghost is never laid till all the rites are complete.' With these words he brought out of his pocket something tied in his handkerchief, and laying it on the table, undid the knot. It was those sovereigns.

'Don't you mistake me, Nikhil,' he said. 'You must not imagine that the contagion of your company has suddenly turned me honest;

I am not the man to come back in slobbering repentance to return ill-gotten money. But...'

He left his speech unfinished. After a pause he turned towards Nikhil, but said to me, 'After all these days, Queen Bee, the ghost of compunction has found an entry into my hitherto untroubled conscience. As I have to wrestle with it every night, after my first sleep is over, I cannot call it a phantom of my imagination. There is no escape even for me till its debt is paid. Into the hands of that spirit, therefore, let me make restitution. Goddess! From you, alone, of all the world, I shall not be able to take away anything. I shall not be rid of you till I am destitute. Take these back!'

He took out at the same time the jewel-casket from under his tunic and put it down, and then left us with hasty steps.

'Listen to me, Sandip,' my husband called after him.

'I have not the time, Nikhil,' said Sandip as he paused near the door. 'The Mussulmans, I am told, have taken me for an invaluable gem, and are conspiring to loot me and hide me away in their graveyard. But I feel that it is necessary that I should live. I have just twenty-five minutes to catch the North-bound train. So, for the present, I must be gone. We shall have our talk out at the next convenient opportunity. If you take my advice, don't you delay in getting away either. I salute you, Queen Bee, Queen of the bleeding hearts, Queen of desolation!'

Sandip then left almost at a run. I stood stock-still; I had never realized in such a manner before, how trivial, how paltry, this gold and these jewels were. Only a short while ago I was so busy thinking what I should take with me, and how I should pack it. Now I felt that there was no need to take anything at all. To set out and go forth was the important thing.

My husband left his seat and came up and took me by the hand. 'It is getting late,' he said. 'There is not much time left to complete our preparations for the journey.'

At this point Chandranath Babu suddenly came in. Finding us both together, he fell back for a moment. Then he said, 'Forgive me, my little mother, if I intrude. Nikhil, the Mussulmans are out of hand. They are looting Harish Kundu's treasury. That does not so much matter. But what is intolerable is the violence that is being done to the women of their house.'

'I am off,' said my husband.

'What can you do there?' I pleaded, as I held him by the hand. 'Oh, sir,' I appealed to his master. 'Will you not tell him not to go?'

'My little mother,' he replied, 'there is no time to do anything else.'

'Don't be alarmed, Bimal,' said my husband, as he left us.

When I went to the window I saw my husband galloping away on horseback, with not a weapon in his hands.

In another minute the Bara Rani came running in. 'What have you done, Chotie darling,' she cried. 'How could you let him go?'

'Call the Dewan at once,' she said, turning to a servant.

The Ranis never appeared before the Dewan, but the Bara Rani had no thought that day for appearances.

'Send a mounted man to bring back the Maharaja at once,' she said, as soon as the Dewan came up.

'We have all entreated him to stay, Rani Mother,' said the Dewan, 'but he refused to turn back.'

'Send word to him that the Bara Rani is ill, that she is on her death-bed,' cried my sister-in-law wildly.

When the Dewan had left she turned on me with a furious outburst. 'Oh, you witch, you ogress, you could not die yourself, but needs must send him to his death!...'

The light of the day began to fade. The sun set behind the feathery foliage of the blossoming Sajna tree. I can see every different shade of that sunset even today. Two masses of cloud on either side of the sinking orb made it look like a great bird with fiery-feathered wings outspread. It seemed to me that this fateful day was taking its flight, to cross the ocean of night.

It became darker and darker. Like the flames of a distant village on fire, leaping up every now and then above the horizon, a distant din swelled up in recurring waves into the darkness.

The bells of the evening worship rang out from our temple. I knew the Bara Rani was sitting there, with palms joined in silent prayer. But I could not move a step from the window.

The roads, the village beyond, and the still more distant fringe of trees, grew more and more vague. The lake in our grounds looked up into the sky with a dull lustre, like a blind man's eye. On the left the tower seemed to be craning its neck to catch sight of something that was happening.

The sounds of night take on all manner of disguises. A twig snaps, and one thinks that somebody is running for his life. A door slams, and one feels it to be the sudden heart-thump of a startled world.

Lights would suddenly flicker under the shade of the distant trees, and then go out again. Horses' hoofs would clatter, now and again, only to turn out to be riders leaving the palace gates.

I continually had the feeling that, if only I could die, all this turmoil would come to an end. So long as I was alive my sins would remain rampant, scattering destruction on every side. I remembered the pistol in my box. But my feet refused to leave the window in quest of it. Was I not awaiting my fate?

The gong of the watch solemnly struck ten. A little later, groups of lights appeared in the distance and a great crowd wound its way, like some great serpent, along the roads in the darkness, towards the palace gates.

The Dewan rushed to the gate at the sound. Just then a rider came galloping in. 'What's the news, Jata?' asked the Dewan.

'Not good,' was the reply.

I could hear these words distinctly from my window. But something was next whispered which I could not catch.

Then came a palanquin, followed by a litter. The doctor was walking alongside the palanquin.

'What do you think, doctor?' asked the Dewan.

'Can't say yet,' the doctor replied. 'The wound in the head is a serious one.'

'And Amulya Babu?'

'He has a bullet through the heart. He is done for.'

NATIONALISM IN INDIA

NATIONALISM IN INDIA

Our real problem in India is not political. It is social. This is a condition not only prevailing in India, but among all nations. I do not believe in an exclusive political interest. Politics in the West have dominated Western ideals, and we in India are trying to imitate you. We have to remember that in Europe, where peoples had their racial unity from the beginning, and where natural resources were insufficient for the inhabitants, the civilization has naturally taken the character of political and commercial aggressiveness. For, on the one hand, they had no internal complications, and on the other, they had to deal with neighbours who were strong and rapacious. To have perfect combination among themselves and a watchful attitude of animosity against others was taken as the solution of their problems. In former days they organized and plundered, in the present age the same spirit continues—and they organize and exploit the whole world.

But from the earliest beginnings of history, India has had her own problem constantly before her—it is the race problem. Each nation must be conscious of its mission, and we, in India, must realize that we cut a poor figure when we are trying to be political, simply because we have not yet been finally able to accomplish what was set before us by our providence.

This problem of race unity which we have been trying to solve for so many years has likewise to be faced by you here in America. Many people in this country ask me what is happening as to the caste distinctions in India. But when this question is asked me, it is usually done with a superior air. And I feel tempted to put the same question to our American critics with a slight modification, 'What have you done with the Red Indian and the Negro?' For you have not got over your attitude of caste toward them. You have used violent methods to keep aloof from other races, but until you have solved the question here in America, you have no right to question India.

In spite of our great difficulty, however, India has done something. She has tried to make an adjustment of races, to acknowledge the real differences between them where these exist, and yet seek for some basis of unity. This basis has come through our saints like Nanak, Kabir, Chaitnaya and others, preaching one God to all races of India.

In finding the solution of our problem we shall have helped to solve the world problem as well. What India has been, the whole world is now. The whole world is becoming one country through scientific facility. And the moment is arriving when you also must find a basis of unity which is not political. If India can offer to the world her solution, it will be a contribution to humanity. There is only one history—the history of man. All national histories are merely chapters in the larger one. And we are content in India to suffer for such a great cause.

Each individual has his self-love. Therefore, his brute instinct leads him to fight with others in the sole pursuit of his self-interest. But man has also his higher instincts of sympathy and mutual help. The people who are lacking in this higher moral power and who, therefore, cannot combine in fellowship with one another must perish or live in a state of degradation. Only those peoples have survived and achieved civilization who have this spirit of cooperation strong in them. So we find that from the beginning of history men had to choose between fighting with one another and combining, between serving their own interest or the common interest of all.

In our early history, when the geographical limits of each country and also the facilities of communication were small, this problem was comparatively small in dimension. It was sufficient for men to develop their sense of unity within their area of segregation. In those days they combined among themselves and fought against others. But it was this moral spirit of combination which was the true basis of their greatness, and this fostered their art, science and religion. At that early time the most important fact that man had to take count of was the fact of the members of one particular race of men coming in close contact with one another. Those who truly grasped this fact through their higher nature made their mark in history.

The most important fact of the present age is that all the different races of men have come close together. And again we are confronted with two alternatives. The problem is whether the different groups of peoples shall go on fighting with one another or find out some true basis of reconciliation and mutual help; whether it will be interminable competition or cooperation.

I have no hesitation in saying that those who are gifted with the moral power of love and vision of spiritual unity, who have the least feeling of enmity against aliens, and the sympathetic insight to place themselves in the position of others, will be the fittest to take their permanent place in the age that is lying before us, and those who are constantly developing their instinct of fight and intolerance of aliens will be eliminated. For this is the problem before us, and we have to prove our humanity by solving it through the help of our higher nature. The gigantic organizations for hurting others and warding off their blows, for making money by dragging others back, will not help us. On the contrary, by their crushing weight, their enormous cost and their deadening effect upon living humanity, they will seriously impede our freedom in the larger life of a higher civilization.

During the evolution of the Nation, the moral culture of brotherhood was limited by geographical boundaries, because at that time those boundaries were true. Now they have become imaginary lines of tradition divested of the qualities of real obstacles. So the time has come when man's moral nature must deal with this great fact with all seriousness or perish. The first impulse of this change of circumstance has been the churning up of man's baser passions of greed and cruel hatred. If this persists indefinitely, and armaments go on exaggerating themselves to unimaginable absurdities, and machines and storehouses envelop this fair earth with their dirt and smoke and ugliness, then it will end in a conflagration of suicide. Therefore, man will have to exert all his power of love and clarity of vision to make another great moral adjustment which will comprehend the whole world of men and not merely the fractional groups of nationality. The call has come to every individual in the present age to prepare himself and his surroundings for this dawn of a new era, when man shall discover his soul in the spiritual unity of all human beings.

If it is given at all to the West to struggle out of these tangles of the lower slopes to the spiritual summit of humanity then I cannot but think that it is the special mission of America to fulfil this hope of

God and man. You are the country of expectation, desiring something else than what is. Europe has her subtle habits of mind and her conventions. But America, as yet, has come to no conclusions. I realize how much America is untrammelled by the traditions of the past, and I can appreciate that experimentalism is a sign of America's youth. The foundation of her glory is in the future, rather than in the past; and if one is gifted with the power of clairvoyance, one will be able to love the America that is to be.

America is destined to justify Western civilization to the East. Europe has lost faith in humanity, and has become distrustful and sickly. America, on the other hand, is not pessimistic or blasé. You know, as a people, that there is such a thing as a better and a best; and that knowledge drives you on. There are habits that are not merely passive but aggressively arrogant. They are not like mere walls, but are like hedges of stinging nettles. Europe has been cultivating these hedges of habits for long years, till they have grown round her dense, strong and high. The pride of her traditions has sent its roots deep into her heart. I do not wish to contend that it is unreasonable. But pride in every form breeds blindness at the end. Like all artificial stimulants its first effect is a heightening of consciousness, and then with the increasing dose it muddles it and brings an exultation that is misleading. Europe has gradually grown hardened in her pride in all her outer and inner habits. She not only cannot forget that she is Western, but she takes every opportunity to hurl this fact against others to humiliate them. This is why she is growing incapable of imparting to the East what is best in herself, and of accepting in a right spirit the wisdom that the East has stored for centuries.

In America, national habits and traditions have not had time to spread their clutching roots round your hearts. You have constantly felt and complained of your disadvantages when you compared your nomadic restlessness with the settled traditions of Europe—which can show her picture of greatness to the best advantage because she can fix it against the background of the Past. But in this present age of transition, when a new era of civilization is sending its trumpet-call to all peoples of the world across an unlimited future, this very freedom of detachment will enable you to accept its invitation and to achieve the goal for which Europe began her journey but lost herself midway. For she was tempted out of her path by her pride of power and greed of possession.

Not merely your freedom from habits of mind in individuals, but also the freedom of your history from all unclean entanglements, fits you in your career of holding the banner of civilization of the future. All the great nations of Europe have their victims in other parts of the world. This not only deadens their moral sympathy but also their intellectual sympathy, which is so necessary for the understanding of races which are different from one's own. Englishmen can never truly understand India, because their minds are not disinterested with regard to that country. If you compare England with Germany or France you will find she has produced the smallest number of scholars who have studied Indian literature and philosophy with any amount of sympathetic insight or thoroughness. This attitude of apathy and contempt is natural where the relationship is abnormal and founded upon national selfishness and pride. But your history has been disinterested, and that is why you have been able to help Japan in her lessons in Western civilization, and that is why China can look upon you with her best confidence in this her darkest period of danger. In fact, you are carrying all the responsibility of a great future because you are untrammelled by the grasping miserliness of a past. Therefore of all countries of the earth, America has to be fully conscious of this future, her vision must not be obscured and her faith in humanity must be strong with the strength of youth.

A parallelism exists between America and India—the parallelism of welding together into one body various races.

In my country, we have been seeking to find out something common to all races, which will prove their real unity. No nation looking for a mere political or commercial basis of unity will find such a solution sufficient. Men of thought and power will discover the spiritual unity, will realize it, and preach it.

India has never had a real sense of nationalism. Even though from childhood I had been taught that idolatry of the Nation is almost better than reverence for God and humanity, I believe I have outgrown that teaching, and it is my conviction that my countrymen will truly gain their India by fighting against the education which teaches them that a country is greater than the ideals of humanity.

The educated Indian, at present, is trying to absorb some lessons from history contrary to the lessons of our ancestors. The East, in fact, is attempting to take unto itself a history which is not the outcome of its own living. Japan, for example, thinks she is getting powerful through adopting Western methods, but, after she has exhausted her inheritance, only the borrowed weapons of civilization will remain to her. She will not have developed herself from within.

Europe has her past. Europe's strength therefore lies in her history. We, in India, must make up our minds that we cannot borrow other people's history, and that if we stifle our own we are committing suicide. When you borrow things that do not belong to your life, they only serve to crush your life.

And therefore I believe that it does India no good to compete with Western civilization in its own field. But we shall be more than compensated if, in spite of the insults heaped upon us, we follow our own destiny.

There are lessons which impart information or train our minds for intellectual pursuits. These are simple and can be acquired and used with advantage. But there are others which affect our deeper nature and change our direction of life. Before we accept them and pay their value by selling our own inheritance, we must pause and think deeply. In man's history there come ages of fireworks which dazzle us by their force and movement. They laugh not only at our modest household lamps but also at the eternal stars. But let us not for that provocation be precipitate in our desire to dismiss our lamps. Let us patiently bear our present insult and realize that these fireworks have splendour but not permanence, because of the extreme explosiveness which is the cause of their power, and also of their exhaustion. They are spending a fatal quantity of energy and substance compared to their gain and production.

Anyhow, our ideals have been evolved through our own history, and even if we wished we could only make poor fireworks of them, because their materials are different from yours, as is also their moral purpose. If we cherish the desire of paying our all to buy a political nationality it will be as absurd as if Switzerland had staked her existence on her ambition to build up a navy powerful enough to compete with that of England. The mistake that we make is in thinking that man's channel of greatness is only one—which has made itself painfully evident for the time being by its depth of insolence.

We must know for certain that there is a future before us and that future is waiting for those who are rich in moral ideals and not in mere things. And it is the privilege of man to work for fruits that are beyond his immediate reach, and to adjust his life not in slavish conformity to the examples of some present success or even to his own prudent past, limited in its aspiration, but to an infinite future bearing in its heart the ideals of our highest expectations.

We must recognize that it is providential that the West has come to India. And yet someone must show the East to the West, and convince the West that the East has her contribution to make to the history of civilization. India is no beggar of the West. And yet even though the West may think she is, I am not for thrusting off Western civilization and becoming segregated in our independence. Let us have a deep association. If Providence wants England to be the channel of that communication, of that deeper association, I am willing to accept it with all humility. I have great faith in human nature, and I think the West will find its true mission. I speak bitterly of Western civilization when I am conscious that it is betraying its trust and thwarting its own purpose. The West must not make herself a curse to the world by using her power for her own selfish needs, but, by teaching the ignorant and helping the weak, she should save herself from the worst danger that the strong is liable to incur by making the feeble acquire power enough to resist her intrusion. And also she must not make her materialism to be the final thing, but must realize that she is doing a service in freeing the spiritual being from the tyranny of matter.

I am not against one nation in particular, but against the general idea of all nations. What is the Nation?

It is the aspect of a whole people as an organized power. This organization incessantly keeps up the insistence of the population on becoming strong and efficient. But this strenuous effort after strength and efficiency drains man's energy from his higher nature where he is self-sacrificing and creative. For thereby man's power of sacrifice is diverted from his ultimate object, which is moral, to the maintenance of this organization, which is mechanical. Yet, in this, he feels all the satisfaction of moral exaltation and therefore becomes supremely dangerous to humanity. He feels relieved of the urging of his conscience when he can transfer his responsibility to this machine which is the creation of his intellect and not of his complete moral personality. By this device the people who love freedom perpetuate slavery in a large portion of the world with the comfortable feeling of pride of having done their duty; men who are naturally just can be cruelly unjust both in their act and their thought, accompanied by a feeling that they are helping the world to receive its deserts; men who are honest can blindly go on robbing others of their human rights for self-aggrandizement, all the while abusing the deprived for not deserving better treatment. We have seen in our everyday life even small organizations of business and profession produce callousness of feeling in men who are not naturally bad, and we can well imagine what a moral havoc it is causing in a world where whole peoples are furiously organizing themselves for gaining wealth and power.

Nationalism is a great menace. It is the particular thing which for years has been at the bottom of India's troubles. And inasmuch as we have been ruled and dominated by a nation that is strictly political in its attitude, we have tried to develop within ourselves, despite our inheritance from the past, a belief in our eventual political destiny.

There are different parties in India, with different ideals. Some are struggling for political independence. Others think that the time has not arrived for that, and yet believe that India should have the rights that the English colonies have. They wish to gain autonomy as far as possible.

In the beginning of the history of political agitation in India there was not the conflict between parties which there is today. At that time there was a party known as the Indian Congress; it had no real programme. They had a few grievances for redress by the authorities. They wanted larger representation in the Council House, and more freedom in municipal government. They wanted scraps of things, but they had no constructive ideal. Therefore, I was lacking in enthusiasm for their methods. It was my conviction that what India most needed was constructive work coming from within herself. In this work we must take all risks and go on doing the duties which by right are ours, though in the teeth of persecution; winning moral victory at every step, by our failure and suffering. We must show those who are over us that we have in ourselves the strength of moral power, the power to suffer for truth. Where we have nothing to show, we have only to beg. It would be mischievous if the gifts we wish for were granted to us at once, and I have told my countrymen, time and again, to combine for the work of creating opportunities to give vent to our spirit of self-sacrifice, and not for the purpose of begging.

The party, however, lost power because the people soon came to realize how futile was the half policy adopted by them. The party split, and there arrived the Extremists, who advocated independence of action, and discarded the begging method—the easiest method of relieving one's mind from his responsibility towards his country. Their ideals were based on Western history. They had no sympathy with the special problems of India. They did not recognize the patent fact that there were causes in our social organization which made the Indians incapable of coping with the alien. What should we do if, for any reason, England was driven away? We should simply be victims for other nations. The same social weaknesses would prevail. The thing we in India have to think of is this—to remove those social customs and ideals which have generated a want of self-respect and a complete dependence on those above us—a state of affairs which has been brought about entirely by the domination in India of the caste system, and the blind and lazy habit of relying upon the authority of traditions that are incongruous anachronisms in the present age.

Once again I draw your attention to the difficulties India has had to encounter and her struggle to overcome them. Her problem was the problem of the world in miniature. India is too vast in its area and too diverse in its races. It is many countries packed in one geographical receptacle. It is just the opposite of what Europe truly is, namely, one country made into many. Thus, Europe in its culture and growth has had the advantage of the strength of the many as well as the strength of the one. India, on the contrary, being naturally many, yet adventitiously one, has all along suffered from the looseness of its diversity and the feebleness of its unity. A true unity is like a round globe, it rolls on, carrying its burden easily; but diversity is a many-cornered thing which has to be dragged and pushed with all force. Be it said to the credit of India that this diversity was not her own creation; she has had to accept it as a fact from the beginning of her history. In America and Australia, Europe has simplified her problem by almost exterminating the original population. Even in the present age this spirit of extermination is making itself manifest, in the inhospitable shutting out of aliens, by those who themselves were aliens in the lands they now occupy. But India tolerated difference of races from the first, and that spirit of toleration has acted all through her history.

Her caste system is the outcome of this spirit of toleration. For India has all along been trying experiments in evolving a social unity within which all the different peoples could be held together, while fully enjoying the freedom of maintaining their own differences. The tie has been as loose as possible, yet as close as the circumstances permitted. This has produced something like a United States of a social federation, whose common name is Hinduism.

India had felt that diversity of races there must be and should be, whatever may be its drawback, and you can never coerce nature into your narrow limits of convenience without paying one day very dearly for it. In this India was right; but what she failed to realize was that in human beings differences are not like the physical barriers of mountains, fixed forever—they are fluid with life's flow, they are changing their courses and their shapes and volume.

Therefore in her caste regulations India recognized differences, but not the mutability which is the law of life. In trying to avoid collisions she set up boundaries of immovable walls, thus giving to her numerous races the negative benefit of peace and order but not the positive opportunity of expansion and movement. She accepted nature where it produces diversity, but ignored it where it uses that diversity for its world-game of infinite permutations and combinations. She treated life in all truth where it is manifold, but insulted it where it is ever moving. Therefore, life departed from her social system and in its place she is worshipping with all ceremony the magnificent cage of countless compartments that she has manufactured.

The same thing happened where she tried to ward off the collisions of trade interests. She associated different trades and professions with different castes. This had the effect of allaying for good the interminable jealousy and hatred of competition—which breeds cruelty and makes the atmosphere thick with lies and deception. In this also India laid all her emphasis upon the law of heredity, ignoring the law of mutation, and thus gradually reduced arts into crafts and genius into skill.

However, what Western observers fail to discern is that in her caste system India in all seriousness accepted her responsibility to solve the race problem in such a manner as to avoid all friction, and yet to afford each race freedom within its boundaries. Let us admit India has not in this achieved a full measure of success. But this you must also concede, that the West, being more favourably situated as to homogeneity of races, has never given her attention to this problem, and whenever confronted with it she has tried to make it easy by ignoring it altogether. And this is the source of her anti-Asiatic agitations for depriving aliens of their right to earn their honest living on these shores. In most of your colonies, you only admit them on condition of their accepting the menial position of hewers of wood and drawers of water. Either you shut your doors against the aliens or reduce them into slavery. And this is your solution of the problem of race-conflict. Whatever may be its merits you will have to admit that it does not spring from the higher impulses of civilization, but from the lower passions of greed and hatred. You say this is human nature—and India also thought she knew human nature when she strongly barricaded her race distinctions by the fixed barriers of social gradations. But we have found out to our cost that human nature is not what it seems, but what it is in truth; which is in its infinite possibilities. And when we in our blindness insult humanity for its ragged appearance it sheds its disguise to disclose to us that we have insulted our God. The degradation which we cast upon others in our pride or self-interest degrades our own humanity—and this is the punishment which is most terrible, because we do not detect it till it is too late.

Not only in your relation with aliens but with the different sections of your own society you have not achieved harmony of reconciliation. The spirit of conflict and competition is allowed the full freedom of its reckless career. And because its genesis is the greed of wealth and power it can never come to any other end but to a violent death. In India the production of commodities was brought under the law of social adjustments. Its basis was cooperation, having for its object the perfect satisfaction of social needs. But in the West it is guided by the impulse of competition, whose end is the gain of wealth for individuals. But the individual is like the geometrical line; it is length without breadth. It has not got the depth to be able to hold anything permanently. Therefore its greed or gain can never come to finality. In its lengthening process of growth it can cross other lines and cause entanglements, but will ever go on missing the ideal of completeness in its thinness of isolation.

In all our physical appetites we recognize a limit. We know that to exceed that limit is to exceed the limit of health. But has this lust for wealth and power no bounds beyond which is death's dominion? In these national carnivals of materialism are not the Western peoples spending most of their vital energy in merely producing things and neglecting the creation of ideals? And can a civilization ignore the law of moral health and go on in its endless process of inflation by gorging upon material things? Man in his social ideals naturally tries to regulate his appetites, subordinating them to the higher purpose of his nature. But in the economic world our appetites follow no other restrictions but those of supply and demand which can be artificially fostered, affording individuals opportunities for indulgence in an endless feast of grossness. In India our social instincts imposed restrictions upon our appetites—maybe it went to the extreme of repression—but in the West the spirit of economic organization with no moral purpose goads the people into the perpetual pursuit of wealth; but has this no wholesome limit?

The ideals that strive to take form in social institutions have two objects. One is to regulate our passions and appetites for the harmonious development of man, and the other is to help him to cultivate disinterested love for his fellow creatures. Therefore, society is the expression of those moral and spiritual aspirations of man which belong to his higher nature.

Our food is creative, it builds our body; but not so wine, which stimulates. Our social ideals create the human world, but when our mind is diverted from them to greed of power then in that state of intoxication we live in a world of abnormality where our strength is not health and our liberty is not freedom. Therefore, political freedom does not give us freedom when our mind is not free. An automobile does not create freedom of movement, because it is a mere machine. When I myself am free I can use the automobile for the purpose of my freedom.

We must never forget in the present day that those people who have got their political freedom are not necessarily free, they are merely powerful. The passions which are unbridled in them are creating huge organizations of slavery in the disguise of freedom. Those who have made the gain of money their highest end are unconsciously selling their life and soul to rich persons or to the combinations that represent money. Those who are enamoured of their political power and gloat over their extension of dominion over foreign races gradually surrender their own freedom and humanity to the organizations necessary for holding other peoples in slavery. In the so-called free countries the majority of the people are not free, they are driven by the minority to a goal which is not even known to them. This becomes possible only because people do not acknowledge moral and spiritual freedom as their object. They create huge eddies with their passions, and they feel dizzily inebriated with the mere velocity of their whirling movement, taking that to be freedom. But the doom which is waiting to overtake them is as certain as death—for man's truth is moral truth and his emancipation is in the spiritual life.

The general opinion of the majority of the present-day nationalists in India is that we have come to a final completeness in our social and spiritual ideals, the task of the constructive work of society having been done several thousand years before we were born, and that now we are free to employ all our activities in the political direction. We never dream of blaming our social inadequacy as the origin of our present helplessness, for we have accepted as the creed of our nationalism that this social system has been perfected for all time to come by our ancestors, who had the superhuman vision of all eternity and supernatural power for making infinite provision for future ages. Therefore, for all our miseries and shortcomings, we hold responsible the historical surprises that burst upon us from outside. This is the reason why we think that our one task is to build a political miracle of freedom upon the quicksand of social slavery. In fact we want to dam up the true course of our own historical stream, and only borrow power from the sources of other peoples' history.

Those of us in India who have come under the delusion that mere political freedom will make us free have accepted their lessons from the West as the gospel truth and lost their faith in humanity. We must remember whatever weakness we cherish in our society will become the source of danger in politics. The same inertia which leads us to our idolatry of dead forms in social institutions will create in our politics prison-houses with immovable walls. The narrowness of sympathy which makes it possible for us to impose upon a considerable portion of humanity the galling yoke of inferiority will assert itself in our politics in creating the tyranny of injustice.

When our nationalists talk about ideals they forget that the basis of nationalism is wanting. The very people who are upholding these ideals are themselves the most conservative in their social practice. Nationalists say, for example, look at Switzerland where, in spite of race differences, the peoples have solidified into a nation. Yet, remember that in Switzerland the races can mingle, they can intermarry, because they are of the same blood. In India there is no common birthright. And when we talk of Western Nationality we forget that the nations there do not have that physical repulsion, one for the other, that we have between different castes. Have we an instance in the whole world where a people who are not allowed to mingle their blood shed their blood for one another except by coercion or for mercenary purposes? And can we ever hope that these moral barriers against our race amalgamation will not stand in the way of our political unity?

Then again we must give full recognition to this fact that our social restrictions are still tyrannical, so much so as to make men cowards. If a man tells me he has heterodox ideas, but that he cannot follow them because he would be socially ostracized, I excuse him for having to live a life of untruth, in order to live at all. The social habit of mind which impels us to make the life of our fellow-beings a burden to them where they differ from us even in such a thing as their choice of food, is sure to persist in our political organization and result in creating engines of coercion to crush every rational difference which is the sign of life. And tyranny will only add to the inevitable lies and hypocrisy in our political life. Is the mere name of freedom so valuable that we should be willing to sacrifice for its sake our moral freedom?

The intemperance of our habits does not immediately show its effects when we are in the vigour of our youth. But it gradually consumes that vigour, and when the period of decline sets in then we have to settle accounts and pay off our debts, which leads us to insolvency. In the West you are still able to carry your head high, though your humanity is suffering every moment from its dipsomania of organizing power. India also in the heyday of her youth could carry in her vital organs the dead weight of her social organizations stiffened to rigid perfection, but it has been fatal to her, and has produced a gradual paralysis of her living nature. And this is the reason why the educated community of India has become insensible of her social needs. They are taking the very immobility of our social structures as the sign of their perfection—and because the healthy feeling of pain is dead in the limbs of our social organism they delude themselves into thinking that it needs no ministration. Therefore, they think that all their energies need their only scope in the political field. It is like a man whose legs have become shrivelled and useless, trying to delude himself that these limbs have grown still because they have attained their ultimate salvation, and all that is wrong about him is the shortness of his sticks.

So much for the social and the political regeneration of India. Now we come to her industries, and I am very often asked whether there is in India any industrial regeneration since the advent of the British Government. It must be remembered that at the beginning of the British rule in India our industries were suppressed, and since then we have not met with any real help or encouragement to enable us to make a stand against the monster commercial organizations of the world. The nations have decreed that we must remain purely an agricultural people, even forgetting the use of arms for all time to come. Thus India is being turned into so many predigested morsels of food ready to be swallowed at any moment by any nation which has even the most rudimentary set of teeth in its head.

India, therefore, has very little outlet for her industrial originality. I personally do not believe in the unwieldy organizations of the present-day. The very fact that they are ugly, shows that they are in discordance with the whole creation. The vast powers of nature do not reveal their truth in hideousness, but in beauty. Beauty is the signature which the Creator stamps upon His works when He is satisfied with them. All our products that insolently ignore the laws of perfection and are unashamed in their display of ungainliness bear the perpetual weight of God's displeasure. So far as your commerce lacks the dignity of grace it is untrue. Beauty and her twin brother Truth require leisure and self-control for their growth. But the greed of gain has no time or limit to its capaciousness. Its one object is to produce and consume. It has pity neither for beautiful nature nor for living human beings. It is ruthlessly ready without a moment's hesitation to crush beauty and life out of them, moulding them into money. It is this ugly vulgarity of commerce which brought upon it the censure of contempt in our earlier days, when men had leisure to have an unclouded vision of perfection in humanity. Men in those times were rightly ashamed of the instinct of mere money-making. But in this scientific age money, by its very abnormal bulk, has won its throne. And when from its eminence of piled-up things it insults the higher instincts of man, banishing beauty and noble sentiments from its surroundings, we submit. For we in our meanness have accepted bribes from its hands and our imagination has grovelled in the dust before its immensity of flesh.

But its very unwieldiness and its endless complexities are its true signs of failure. The swimmer who is an expert does not exhibit his muscular force by violent movements, but exhibits some power which is invisible and which shows itself in perfect grace and reposefulness. The true distinction of man from animals is in his power and worth which are inner and invisible. But the present-day commercial civilization of man is not only taking too much time and space but killing time and space. Its movements are violent, its noise is discordantly loud. It is carrying its own damnation because it is trampling into distortion the humanity upon which it stands. It is strenuously turning out money at the cost of happiness. Man is reducing himself to his minimum in order to be able to make amplest room for his organizations. He is deriding his human sentiments into shame because they are apt to stand in the way of his machines.

In our mythology, we have the legend that the man who performs penances for attaining immortality has to meet with temptations sent by Indra, the Lord of the immortals. If he is lured by them he is lost. The West has been striving for centuries after its goal of immortality. Indra has sent her the temptation to try her. It is the gorgeous temptation of wealth. She has accepted it, and her civilization of humanity has lost its path in the wilderness of machinery.

This commercialism with its barbarity of ugly decorations is a terrible menace to all humanity, because it is setting up the ideal of power over that of perfection. It is making the cult of self-seeking exult in its naked shamelessness. Our nerves are more delicate than our muscles. Things that are the most precious in us are helpless as babes when we take away from them the careful protection which they claim from us for their very preciousness. Therefore, when the callous rudeness of power runs amuck in the broadway of humanity it scares away by its grossness the ideals which we have cherished with the martyrdom of centuries.

The temptation which is fatal for the strong is still more so for the weak. And I do not welcome it in our Indian life, even though it be sent by the lord of the Immortals. Let our life be simple in its outer aspect and rich in its inner gain. Let our civilization take its firm stand upon its basis of social cooperation and not upon that of economic exploitation and conflict. How to do it in the teeth of the drainage of our life-blood by the economic dragons is the task set before the thinkers of all oriental nations who have faith in the human soul. It is a sign of laziness and impotency to accept conditions imposed upon us by others who have other ideals than ours. We should actively try to adapt the world powers to guide our history to its own perfect end.

From the above you will know that I am not an economist. I am willing to acknowledge that there is a law of demand and supply and an infatuation of man for more things than are good for him. And yet I will persist in believing that there is such a thing as the harmony of completeness in humanity, where poverty does not take away his riches, where defeat may lead him to victory, death to immortality, and where in the compensation of Eternal Justice those who are the last may yet have their insult transmuted into a golden triumph.

GLIMPSES OF BENGAL

INTRODUCTION

The letters translated in this book span the most productive period of my literary life, when, owing to great good fortune, I was young and less known.

Youth being exuberant and leisure ample, I felt the writing of letters other than business ones to be a delightful necessity. This is a form of literary extravagance only possible when a surplus of thought and emotion accumulates. Other forms of literature remain the author's and are made public for his good; letters that have been given to private individuals once for all, are therefore characterized by the more generous abandonment.

It so happened that selected extracts from a large number of such letters found their way back to me years after they had been written. It had been rightly conjectured that they would delight me by bringing to mind the memory of days when, under the shelter of obscurity, I enjoyed the greatest freedom my life has ever known.

Since these letters synchronize with a considerable part of my published writings, I thought their parallel course would broaden my readers' understanding of my poems as a track is widened by retreading the same ground. Such was my justification for publishing them in a book for my countrymen. Hoping that the descriptions of village scenes in Bengal contained in these letters would also be of interest to English readers, the translation of a selection of that selection has been entrusted to one who, among all those whom I know, was best fitted to carry it out.

RABINDRANATH TAGORE
20 June 1920

BANDORA, BY THE SEA,
October 1885.

The unsheltered sea heaves and heaves and blanches into foam. It sets me thinking of some tied-up monster straining at its bonds, in front of whose gaping jaws we build our homes on the shore and watch it lashing its tail. What immense strength, with waves swelling like the muscles of a giant!

From the beginning of creation there has been this feud between land and water: the dry earth slowly and silently adding to its domain and spreading a broader and broader lap for its children; the ocean receding step by step, heaving and sobbing and beating its breast in despair. Remember the sea was once sole monarch, utterly free.

Land rose from its womb, usurped its throne, and ever since the maddened old creature, with hoary crest of foam, wails and laments continually, like King Lear exposed to the fury of the elements.

July 1887

I am in my twenty-seventh year. This event keeps thrusting itself before my mind—nothing else seems to have happened of late.

But to reach twenty-seven—is that a trifling thing? To pass the meridian of the twenties on one's progress towards thirty? Thirty—that is to say maturity—the age at which people expect fruit rather than fresh foliage. But, alas, where is the promise of fruit? As I shake my head, it still feels brimful of luscious frivolity, with not a trace of philosophy.

Folk are beginning to complain: 'Where is that which we expected of you—that in hope of which we admired the soft green of the shoot? Are we to put up with immaturity forever? It is high time for us to know what we shall gain from you. We want an estimate of the proportion of oil which the blindfold, mill-turning, unbiased critic can squeeze out of you.'

It has ceased to be possible to delude these people into waiting expectantly any longer. While I was under age they trustfully gave me credit; it is sad to disappoint them now that I am on the verge of thirty. But what am I to do? Words of wisdom will not come! I am utterly incompetent to provide things that may profit the multitude. Beyond a snatch of song, some tittle-tattle, a little merry fooling, I have been unable to advance. And as the result, those who held high hopes will turn their wrath on me; but did anyone ever beg them to nurse these expectations?

Such are the thoughts which assail me since one fine Bysakh morning I awoke amidst fresh breeze and light, new leaf and flower, to find that I had stepped into my twenty-seventh year.

SHELIDAH, 1888

Our houseboat is moored to a sand-bank on the farther side of the river. A vast expanse of sand stretches away out of sight on every side, with here and there a streak, as of water, running across, though sometimes what gleams like water is only sand.

Not a village, not a human being, not a tree, not a blade of grass—the only breaks in the monotonous whiteness are gaping cracks which in places show the layer of moist, black clay underneath.

Looking towards the East, there is endless blue above, endless white beneath. Sky empty, earth empty too—the emptiness below hard and barren, that overhead arched and ethereal—one could hardly find elsewhere such a picture of stark desolation.

But on turning to the West, there is water, the currentless bend of the river, fringed with its high bank, up to which spread the village groves with cottages peeping through—all like an enchanting dream in the evening light. I say 'the evening light,' because in the evening we wander out, and so that aspect is impressed on my mind.

SHAZADPUR, 1890.

The magistrate was sitting in the verandah of his tent dispensing justice to the crowd awaiting their turns under the shade of a tree. They set my palanquin down right under his nose, and the young Englishman received me courteously. He had very light hair, with darker patches here and there, and a moustache just beginning to show. One might have taken him for a white-haired old man but for his extremely youthful face. I asked him over to dinner, but he said he was due elsewhere to arrange for a pig-sticking party.

As I returned home, great black clouds came up and there was a terrific storm with torrents of rain. I could not touch a book, it was impossible to write, so in the I-know-not-what mood I wandered about from room to room. It had become quite dark, the thunder was continually pealing, the lightning gleaming flash after flash, and every now and then sudden gusts of wind would get hold of the big lichi tree by the neck and give its shaggy top a thorough shaking. The hollow in front of the house soon filled with water, and as I paced about, it suddenly struck me that I ought to offer the shelter of the house to the magistrate.

I sent off an invitation; then after investigation I found the only spare room encumbered with a platform of planks hanging from the beams, piled with dirty old quilts and bolsters. Servants' belongings, an excessively grimy mat, hubble-bubble pipes, tobacco, tinder, and two wooden chests littered the floor, besides sundry packing-cases full of useless odds and ends, such as a rusty kettle lid, a bottomless iron stove, a discoloured old nickel teapot, a soup-plate full of treacle blackened with dust. In a corner was a tub for washing dishes, and from nails in the wall hung moist dish-clouts and the cook's livery and skull-cap. The only piece of furniture was a rickety dressing table with water stains, oil stains, milk stains, black, brown, and white stains, and all kinds of mixed stains. The mirror, detached from it, rested against another wall, and the drawers were receptacles for a miscellaneous assortment of articles from soiled napkins down to bottle wires and dust.

For a moment I was overwhelmed with dismay; then it was a case of—send for the manager, send for the storekeeper, call up all the servants, get hold of extra men, fetch water, put up ladders, unfasten ropes, pull down planks, take away bedding, pick up broken glass bit by bit, wrench nails from the wall one by one. The chandelier falls and its pieces strew the floor; pick them up again piece by piece.—I myself whisk the dirty mat off the floor and out of the window, dislodging a horde of cockroaches, messmates, who dine off my bread, my treacle, and the polish on my shoes.

The magistrate's reply is brought back; his tent is in an awful state and he is coming at once. Hurry up! Hurry up! Presently comes the shout, 'The sahib has arrived.' All in a flurry I brush the dust off my hair, beard, and the rest of myself, and as I go to receive him in the drawing room, I try to look as respectable as if I had been reposing there comfortably all the afternoon.

I went through the shaking of hands and conversed with the magistrate outwardly serene; still, misgivings about his accommodation would now and then well up within. When at length I had to show my guest to his room, I found it passable, and if the homeless cockroaches do not tickle the soles of his feet, he may manage to get a night's rest.

SHAZADPUR,
February 1891

Just in front of my window, on the other side of the stream, a band of gypsies have ensconced themselves, putting up bamboo frameworks covered over with split-bamboo mats and pieces of cloth. There are only three of these little structures, so low that you cannot stand upright inside. Their life is lived in the open, and they only creep under these shelters at night, to sleep huddled together.

That is always the gypsies' way: no home anywhere, no landlord to pay rent to, wandering about as it pleases them with their children, their pigs, and a dog or two; and on them the police keep a vigilant eye.

I frequently watch the doings of the family nearest me. They are dark but good-looking, with fine, strongly-built bodies, like northwest country folk. Their women are handsome, and have tall, slim, well-knit figures; and with their free and easy movements, and natural independent airs, they look to me like swarthy Englishwomen.

The man has just put the cooking-pot on the fire, and is now splitting bamboos and weaving baskets. The woman first holds up a little mirror to her face, then puts a deal of pains into wiping and rubbing it, over and over again, with a moist piece of cloth; and then, the folds of her upper garment adjusted and tidied, she goes, all spick and span, up to her man and sits beside him, helping him now and then in his work.

These are truly children of the soil, born on it somewhere, bred by the wayside, here, there, and everywhere, dying anywhere. Night and day under the open sky, in the open air, on the bare ground, they lead a unique kind of life; and yet work, love, children, and household duties—everything is there.

They are not idle for a moment, but always doing something. Her own particular task over, one woman plumps herself down behind another, unties the knot of her hair and cleans and arranges it for her; and whether at the same time they fall to talking over the domestic affairs of the three little mat-covered households, I cannot say for certain from this distance, but shrewdly suspect it.

This morning a great disturbance invaded the peaceful gypsy settlement. It was about half past eight or nine. They were spreading out over the mat roofs tattered quilts and sundry other rags, which serve them for beds, in order to sun and air them. The pigs with their litters, lying in a hollow all of a heap and looking like a dab of mud, had been routed out by the two canine members of the family, who fell upon them and sent them roaming in search of their breakfasts, squealing their annoyance at being interrupted in enjoyment of the sun after the cold night. I was writing my letter and absently looking out now and then when the hubbub suddenly commenced.

I rose and went to the window, and found a crowd gathered round the gypsy hermitage. A superior-looking personage was flourishing a stick and indulging in the strongest language. The headman of the gypsies, cowed and nervous, was apparently trying to offer explanations. I gathered that some suspicious happenings in the locality had led to this visitation by a police officer.

The woman, so far, had remained sitting, busily scraping lengths of split bamboo as serenely as if she had been alone and no sort of row going on. Suddenly, however, she sprang to her feet, advanced on the police officer, gesticulated violently with her arms right in his face, and gave him, in strident tones, a piece of her mind. In the twinkling of an eye three-quarters of the officer's excitement had subsided; he tried to put in a word or two of mild protest but did not get a chance, and so departed crestfallen, a different man.

After he had retreated to a safe distance, he turned and shouted back, 'All I say is, you'll have to clear out from here!'

I thought my neighbours opposite would forthwith pack up their mats and bamboos and move away with their bundles, pigs, and children. But there is no sign of it yet. They are still nonchalantly engaged in splitting bamboos, cooking food, or completing a toilet.

SHAZADPUR
February 1891

The post office is in a part of our estate office building,—this is very convenient, for we get our letters as soon as they arrive. Some evenings, the post-master comes up to have a chat with me. I enjoy listening to his yarns.

He talks of the most impossible things in the gravest possible manner.

Yesterday, he was telling me in what great reverence people of this locality hold the sacred river Ganges. If one of their relatives dies, he said, and they have not the means of taking the ashes to the Ganges, they powder a piece of bone from his funeral pyre and keep it till they come across someone who, sometime or other, has drunk of the Ganges. To him they administer some of this powder, hidden in the usual offering of *pán*,[1] and thus are content to imagine that a portion of the remains of their deceased relative has gained purifying contact with the sacred water.

I smiled as I remarked, 'This surely must be an invention.'

He pondered deeply before he admitted after a pause, 'Yes, it may be.'

ON THE WAY,
February 1891

We have got past the big rivers and just turned into a little one.

The village women are standing in the water, bathing or washing clothes; and some, in their dripping saris, with veils pulled well over their faces, move homeward with their water vessels filled and clasped against the left flank, the right arm swinging free. Children, covered all over with clay, are sporting boisterously, splashing water on each other, while one of them shouts a song, regardless of the tune.

Over the high banks, the cottage roofs and the tops of the bamboo clumps are visible. The sky has cleared and the sun is shining. Remnants of clouds cling to the horizon like fluffs of cotton wool. The breeze is warmer.

There are not many boats in this little river; only a few dinghies, laden with dry branches and twigs, are moving leisurely along to the

---

[1] Spices wrapped in betel leaf.

tired plash! Plash! of their oars. At the river's edge the fishermen's nets are hung out to dry between bamboo poles. And work everywhere seems to be over for the day.

CHUHALI,
June 1891

I had been sitting out on the deck for more than a quarter of an hour when heavy clouds rose in the west. They came up, black, tumbled, and tattered, with streaks of lurid light showing through here and there. The little boats scurried off into the smaller arm of the river and clung with their anchors safely to its banks. The reapers took up the cut sheaves on their heads and hurried homewards; the cows followed, and behind them frisked the calves waving their tails.

Then came an angry roar. Torn-off scraps of cloud hurried up from the west, like panting messengers of evil tidings. Finally, lightning and thunder, rain and storm, came on altogether and executed a mad dervish dance. The bamboo clumps seemed to howl as the raging wind swept the ground with them, now to the east, now to the west. Over all, the storm droned like a giant snake-charmer's pipe, and to its rhythm swayed hundreds and thousands of crested waves, like so many hooded snakes. The thunder was incessant, as though a whole world was being pounded to pieces away there behind the clouds.

With my chin resting on the ledge of an open window facing away from the wind, I allowed my thoughts to take part in this terrible revelry; they leapt into the open like a pack of school boys suddenly set free. When, however, I got a thorough drenching from the spray of the rain, I had to shut up the window and my poetising, and retire quietly into the darkness inside, like a caged bird.

SHAZADPUR,
June 1891

From the bank to which the boat is tied a kind of scent rises out of the grass, and the heat of the ground, given off in gasps, actually touches my body. I feel that the warm, living Earth is breathing upon me, and that she, also, must feel my breath.

The young shoots of rice are waving in the breeze, and the ducks are in turn thrusting their heads beneath the water and preening their feathers. There is no sound save the faint, mournful creaking of the gangway against the boat, as she imperceptibly swings to and fro in the current.

Not far off there is a ferry. A motley crowd has assembled under the banyan tree awaiting the boat's return; and as soon as it arrives, they eagerly scramble in. I enjoy watching this for hours together. It is market-day in the village on the other bank; that is why the ferry is so busy. Some carry bundles of hay, some baskets, some sacks; some are going to the market, others coming from it. Thus, in this silent noonday, the stream of human activity slowly flows across the river between two villages.

I sat wondering: Why is there always this deep shade of melancholy over the fields and river banks, the sky and the sunshine of our country? And I came to the conclusion that it is because with us Nature is obviously the more important thing. The sky is free, the fields limitless; and the sun merges them into one blazing whole. In the midst of this, man seems so trivial. He comes and goes, like the ferry-boat, from this shore to the other; the babbling hum of his talk, the fitful echo of his song, is heard; the slight movement of his pursuit of his own petty desires is seen in the world's market-places: but how feeble, how temporary, how tragically meaningless it all seems amidst the immense aloofness of the Universe!

The contrast between the beautiful, broad, unalloyed peace of Nature—calm, passive, silent, unfathomable,—and our own everyday worries—paltry, sorrow-laden, strife-tormented, puts me beside myself as I keep staring at the hazy, distant, blue line of trees which fringe the fields across the river.

Where Nature is ever hidden, and cowers under mist and cloud, snow and darkness, there man feels himself master; he regards his desires, his works, as permanent; he wants to perpetuate them, he looks towards posterity, he raises monuments, he writes biographies; he even goes the length of erecting tombstones over the dead. So busy is he that he has not time to consider how many monuments crumble, how often names are forgotten!

SHAZADPUR,
June 1891

The schoolmasters of this place paid me a visit yesterday. They stayed on and on, while for the life of me I could not find a word to say. I managed a question or so every five minutes, to which they offered the briefest replies; and then I sat vacantly, twirling my pen, and scratching my head.

At last I ventured on a question about the crops, but being schoolmasters they knew nothing whatever about crops.

About their pupils I had already asked them everything I could think of, so I had to start over again: How many boys had they in the school? One said eighty, another said a hundred and seventy-five. I hoped that this might lead to an argument, but no, they made up their difference.

Why, after an hour and a half, they should have thought of taking leave, I cannot tell. They might have done so with as good a reason an hour earlier, or, for the matter of that, twelve hours later! Their decision was clearly arrived at empirically, entirely without method.

SHELIDAH,
October 1891

Boat after boat touches at the landing-place, and after a whole year exiles are returning home from distant fields of work for the Poojah vacation, their boxes, baskets, and bundles loaded with presents. I notice one who, as his boat nears the shore, changes into a freshly folded and crinkled muslin dhoti, dons over his cotton tunic a China silk coat, carefully adjusts round his neck a neatly twisted scarf, and walks off towards the village, umbrella held aloft.

Rustling waves pass over the rice fields. Mango and coconut treetops rise into the sky, and beyond them there are fluffy clouds on the horizon. The fringes of the palm leaves wave in the breeze. The reeds on the sand-bank are on the point of flowering. It is altogether an exhilarating scene.

The feelings of the man who has just arrived home, the eager expectancy of his folk awaiting him, this autumn sky, this world, the gentle morning breeze, the universal responsive tremor in tree and shrub and in the wavelets on the river, conspire to overwhelm this lonely youth, gazing from his window, with unutterable joys and sorrows.

Glimpses of the world received from wayside windows bring new desires, or rather, make old desires take on new forms. The day before yesterday, as I was sitting at the window of the boat, a little fisher-dinghy floated past, the boatman singing a song—not a very tuneful song. But it reminded me of a night, years ago, when I was a child. We were going along the Padma in a boat. I awoke one night at about 2 o'clock, and, on raising the window and putting out my head, I saw the waters without a ripple, gleaming in the moonlight, and a youth in a little dinghy paddling along all by himself and singing, oh so sweetly,—such sweet melody I had never heard before.

A sudden longing came upon me to go back to the day of that song; to be allowed to make another essay at life, this time not to leave it thus empty and unsatisfied; but with a poet's song on my lips to float about the world on the crest of the rising tide, to sing it to men and subdue their hearts; to see for myself what the world holds and where; to let men know me, to get to know them; to burst forth through the world in life and youth like the eager rushing breezes; and then return home to a fulfilled and fruitful old age to spend it as a poet should.

Not a very lofty ideal, is it? To benefit the world would have been much higher, no doubt; but being on the whole what I am, that ambition does not even occur to me. I cannot make up my mind to sacrifice this precious gift of life in a self-wrought famine, and disappoint the world and the hearts of men by fasts and meditations and constant argument. I count it enough to live and die as a man, loving and trusting the world, unable to look on it either as a delusion of the Creator or a snare of the Devil. It is not for me to strive to be wafted away into the airiness of an Angel.

SHELIDAH,
2 Kartik (October) 1891

When I come to the country I cease to view man as separate from the rest. As the river runs through many a clime, so does the stream of men babble on, winding through woods and villages and towns. It is not a true contrast that men may come and *men may go, but I go on forever*. Humanity, with all its confluent streams, big and small, flows on and on, just as does the river, from its source in birth to its sea of death;—two dark mysteries at either end, and between them various play and work and chatter unceasing.

Over there the cultivators sing in the fields: here the fishing-boats float by. The day wears on and the heat of the sun increases. Some bathers are still in the river, others are finished and are taking home their filled water-vessels. Thus, past both banks of the river, hundreds of years have hummed their way, while the refrain rises in a mournful chorus: *I go on forever!*

Amid the noonday silence some youthful cowherd is heard calling at the top of his voice for his companion; some boat splashes its way homewards; the ripples lap against the empty jar which some village woman rests on the water before dipping it; and with these mingle several other less definite sounds,—the twittering of birds, the humming of bees, the plaintive creaking of the houseboat as it gently swings to and fro,—the whole making a tender lullaby, as of a mother trying to quiet a suffering child. 'Fret not,' she sings, as she soothingly pats its fevered forehead. 'Worry not; weep no more. Let be your strugglings and grabbings and fightings; forget a while, sleep a while.'

SHELIDAH,
3 Kartik (October) 1891

It was the *Kojagar* full moon, and I was slowly pacing the riverside conversing with myself. It could hardly be called a conversation, as I was doing all the talking and my imaginary companion all the listening. The poor fellow had no chance of speaking up for himself, for was not mine the power to compel him helplessly to answer like a fool?

But what a night it was! How often have I tried to write of such, but never got it done! There was not a line of ripple on the river; and from away over there, where the farthest shore of the distant main stream is seen beyond the other edge of the midway belt of sand, right up to this shore, glimmers a broad band of moonlight. Not a human being, not a boat in sight; not a tree, nor blade of grass on the fresh-formed island sand-bank.

It seemed as though a desolate moon was rising upon a devastated earth; a random river wandering through a lifeless solitude; a long-drawn fairy tale coming to a close over a deserted world,—all the kings and the princesses, their ministers and friends and their golden castles vanished, leaving the Seven Seas and Thirteen Rivers and the Unending Moor, over which the adventurous princes fared forth, wanly gleaming in the pale moonlight. I was pacing up and down like the last pulse-beats of this dying world. Everyone else seemed to be on the opposite shore—the shore of life—where the British Government and the Nineteenth Century hold sway, and tea and cigarettes.

BOLPUR,
2 May 1892

There are many paradoxes in the world and one of them is this, that wherever the landscape is immense, the sky unlimited, clouds intimately dense, feelings unfathomable—that is to say where infinitude is manifest—its fit companion is one solitary person; a multitude there seems so petty, so distracting.

An individual and the infinite are on equal terms, worthy to gaze on one another, each from his own throne. But where many men are, how small both humanity and infinitude become, how much they have to knock off each other, in order to fit in together! Each soul wants so much room to expand that in a crowd it needs must wait for gaps through which to thrust a little craning piece of a head from time to time.

So, the only result of our endeavour to assemble is that we become unable to fill our joined hands, our outstretched arms, with this endless, fathomless expanse.

BOLPUR,
8 Jaistha (May) 1892

Women who try to be witty, but only succeed in being pert, are insufferable; and as for attempts to be comic they are disgraceful in women whether they succeed or fail. The comic is ungainly and exaggerated, and so is in some sort related to the sublime. The elephant is comic, the camel and the giraffe are comic, all overgrowth is comic.

It is rather keenness that is akin to beauty, as the thorn to the flower. So sarcasm is not unbecoming in woman, though coming from her it hurts. But ridicule which savours of bulkiness, woman had better leave to our sublime sex. The masculine Falstaff makes our sides split, but a feminine Falstaff would only rack our nerves.

BOLPUR,
12 Jaistha (May) 1892

I usually pace the roof-terrace, alone, of an evening. Yesterday afternoon I felt it my duty to show my visitors the beauties of the local scenery, so I strolled out with them, taking Aghore as a guide.

On the verge of the horizon, where the distant fringe of trees was blue, a thin line of dark blue cloud had risen over them and was looking particularly beautiful. I tried to be poetical and said it was like blue collyrium on the fringe of lashes enhancing a beautiful blue eye. Of my companions one did not hear the remark, another did not understand, while the third dismissed it with the reply, 'Yes, very pretty.' I did not feel encouraged to attempt a second poetical flight.

After walking about a mile we came to a dam, and along the pool of water there was a row of tâl (fan palm) trees, under which was a natural spring. While we stood there looking at this, we found that the line of cloud which we had seen in the North was making for us, swollen and grown darker, flashes of lightning gleaming the while.

We unanimously came to the conclusion that viewing the beauties of nature could be better done from within the shelter of the house, but no sooner had we turned homewards than a storm, making giant strides over the open moorland, was on us with an angry roar. I had no idea, while I was admiring the collyrium on the eyelashes of beauteous dame Nature that she would fly at us like an irate housewife, threatening so tremendous a slap!

It became so dark with the dust that we could not see beyond a few paces. The fury of the storm increased, and flying stony particles of the rubbly soil stung our bodies like shot, as the wind took us by the scruff of the neck and thrust us along, to the whipping of drops of rain which had begun to fall.

Run! Run! But the ground was not level, being deeply scarred with watercourses, and not easy to cross at any time, much less in a storm. I managed to get entangled in a thorny shrub, and was nearly thrown on my face by the force of the wind as I stopped to free myself.

When we had almost reached the house, a host of servants came hurrying towards us, shouting and gesticulating, and fell upon us like another storm. Some took us by the arms, some bewailed our plight, some were eager to show the way, others hung on our backs as if fearing that the storm might carry us off altogether. We evaded their attentions with some difficulty and managed at length to get into the house, panting, with wet clothes, dusty bodies, and tumbled hair.

One thing I had learnt; and will never again write in novel or story the lie that the hero with the picture of his lady-love in his mind can pass unruffled through wind and rain. No one could keep any face in mind, however lovely, in such a storm,—he has enough to do to keep the sand out of his eyes!

The Vaishnava poets have sung ravishingly of Radha going to her tryst with Krishna through a stormy night. Did they ever pause to consider, I wonder, in what condition she must have reached him? The kind of tangle her hair got into is easily imaginable, and also the state of the rest of her toilet. When she arrived in her bower[1] with the dust on her body soaked by the rain into a coating of mud, she must have been a sight!

But when we read the Vaishnava poems, these thoughts do not occur. We only see on the canvas of our mind the picture of a beautiful woman, passing under the shelter of the flowering kadambas in the darkness of a stormy Shravan[2] night, towards the bank of the Jumna, forgetful of wind or rain, as in a dream, drawn by her surpassing love. She has tied up her anklets lest they should tinkle; she is clad in dark blue raiment lest she be discovered; but she holds no umbrella lest she get wet, carries no lantern lest she fall!

Alas for useful things—how necessary in practical life, how neglected in poetry! But poetry strives in vain to free us from their bondage—they

---

[1] Bower: A woman's private chamber in a medieval castle; a boudoir.
[2] July-August, the rainy season.

will be with us always; so much so, we are told, that with the march of civilisation it is poetry that will become extinct, but patent after patent will continue to be taken out for the improvement of shoes and umbrellas.

BOLPUR,
16 Jaistha (May) 1892

No church tower clock chimes here, and there being no other human habitation nearby, complete silence falls with the evening, as soon as the birds have ceased their song. There is not much difference between early night and midnight. A sleepless night in Calcutta flows like a huge, slow river of darkness; one can count the varied sounds of its passing, lying on one's back in bed. But here the night is like a vast, still lake, placidly reposing, with no sign of movement. And as I tossed from side to side last night I felt enveloped within a dense stagnation.

This morning I left my bed a little later than usual and, coming downstairs to my room, leant back on a bolster, one leg resting over the other knee. There, with a slate on my chest, I began to write a poem to the accompaniment of the morning breeze and the singing birds. I was getting along splendidly—a smile playing over my lips, my eyes half closed, my head swaying to the rhythm, the thing I hummed gradually taking shape—when the post arrived.

There was a letter, the last number of the Sadhana Magazine, one of the Monist, and some proof-sheets. I read the letter, raced my eyes over the uncut pages of the Sadhana, and then again fell to nodding and humming through my poem. I did not do another thing till I had finished it.

I wonder why the writing of pages of prose does not give one anything like the joy of completing a single poem. One's emotions take on such perfection of form in a poem; they can, as it were, be taken up by the fingers. But prose is like a sackful of loose material, heavy and unwieldy, incapable of being lifted as you please.

If I could finish writing one poem a day, my life would pass in a kind of joy; but though I have been busy tending poetry for many a year it has not been tamed yet, and is not the kind of winged steed to allow me to bridle it whenever I like! The joy of art is in freedom to take a distant flight as fancy will; then, even after return within the prison world, an echo lingers in the ear, an exaltation in the mind.

Short poems keep coming to me unsought, and so prevent my getting on with the play. Had it not been for these, I could have let in ideas for two or three plays which have been knocking at the door. I am afraid I must wait for the cold weather. All my plays except 'Chitra' were written in the winter. In that season lyrical fervour is apt to grow cold, and one gets the leisure to write drama.

BOLPUR,
31 May 1892

It is not yet five o'clock, but the light has dawned, there is a delightful breeze, and all the birds in the garden are awake and have started singing. The koel seems beside itself. It is difficult to understand why it should keep on cooing so untiringly. Certainly not to entertain us, nor to distract the pining lover[1]—it must have some personal purpose of its own. But, sadly enough, that purpose never seems to get fulfilled. Yet it is not down-hearted, and its Coo-oo! Coo-oo! keeps going, with now and then an ultra-fervent trill. What can it mean?

And then in the distance there is some other bird with only a faint chuck-chuck that has no energy or enthusiasm, as if all hope were lost; nonetheless, from within some shady nook it cannot resist uttering this little plaint: chuck, chuck, chuck.

How little we really know of the household affairs of these innocent winged creatures, with their soft breasts and necks and their many-coloured feathers! Why on earth do they find it necessary to sing so persistently?

SHELIDAH,
31 Jaistha (June) 1892

I hate these polite formalities. Nowadays I keep repeating the line: 'Much rather would I be an Arab Bedouin!' A fine, healthy, strong, and free barbarity.

I feel I want to quit this constant ageing of mind and body, with

---

[1] A favourite conceit of the old Sanskrit poets.

incessant argument and nicety concerning ancient decaying things, and to feel the joy of a free and vigorous life; to have,—be they good or bad,—broad, unhesitating, unfettered ideas and aspirations, free from everlasting friction between custom and sense, sense and desire, desire and action.

If only I could set utterly and boundlessly free this hampered life of mine, I would storm the four quarters and raise wave upon wave of tumult all round; I would career away madly, like a wild horse, for very joy of my own speed! But I am a Bengali, not a Bedouin! I go on sitting in my corner, and mope and worry and argue. I turn my mind now this way up, now the other—as a fish is fried—and the boiling oil blisters first this side, then that.

Let it pass. Since I cannot be thoroughly wild, it is but proper that I should make an endeavour to be thoroughly civil. Why foment a quarrel between the two?

SHELIDAH,
16 June 1892

The more one lives alone on the river or in the open country, the clearer it becomes that nothing is more beautiful or great than to perform the ordinary duties of one's daily life simply and naturally. From the grasses in the field to the stars in the sky, each one is doing just that; and there is such profound peace and surpassing beauty in nature because none of these tries forcibly to transgress its limitations.

Yet what each one does is by no means of little moment. The grass has to put forth all its energy to draw sustenance from the uttermost tips of its rootlets simply to grow where it is as grass; it does not vainly strive to become a banyan tree; and so the earth gains a lovely carpet of green. And, indeed, what little of beauty and peace is to be found in the societies of men is owing to the daily performance of small duties, not to big doings and fine talk. Perhaps because the whole of our life is not vividly present at each moment, some imaginary hope may lure, some glowing picture of a future, untrammelled with everyday burdens, may tempt us; but these are illusory.

SHELIDAH,
2 Asarh (June) 1892

Yesterday, the first day of Asarh,[1] the enthronement of the rainy season was celebrated with due pomp and circumstance. It was very hot the whole day, but in the afternoon dense clouds rolled up in stupendous masses.

I thought to myself, this first day of the rains, I would rather risk getting wet than remain confined in my dungeon of a cabin.

The year 1293[2] will not come again in my life, and, for the matter of that, how many more even of these first days of Asarh will come? My life would be sufficiently long could it number thirty of these first days of Asarh to which the poet of the Meghaduta[3] has, for me at least, given special distinction.

It sometimes strikes me how immensely fortunate I am that each day should take its place in my life, either reddened with the rising and setting sun, or refreshingly cool with deep, dark clouds, or blooming like a white flower in the moonlight. What untold wealth!

A thousand years ago Kalidas welcomed that first day of Asarh; and once in every year of my life that same day of Asarh dawns in all its glory—that self-same day of the poet of old Ujjain, which has brought to countless men and women their joys of union, their pangs of separation.

Every year one such great, time-hallowed day drops out of my life; and the time will come when this day of Kalidas, this day of the Meghaduta, this eternal first day of the Rains in Hindustan, shall come no more for me. When I realize this I feel I want to take a good look at nature, to offer a conscious welcome to each day's sunrise, to say farewell to each day's setting sun, as to an intimate friend.

What a grand festival, what a vast theatre of festivity! And we cannot even fully respond to it, so far away do we live from the world! The

---

[1] June-July, the commencement of the rainy season.
[2] Of the Bengal era.
[3] In the *Meghaduta* (Cloud Messenger) of Kalidas a famous description of the burst of the Monsoon begins with the words: *On the first day of Asarh.*

light of the stars travels millions of miles to reach the earth, but it cannot reach our hearts—so many millions of miles further off are we!

The world into which I have tumbled is peopled with strange beings. They are always busy erecting walls and rules round themselves, and how careful they are with their curtains lest they should see! It is a wonder to me they have not made drab covers for flowering plants and put up a canopy to ward off the moon. If the next life is determined by the desires of this, then I should be reborn from our enshrouded planet into some free and open realm of joy.

Only those who cannot steep themselves in beauty to the full, despise it as an object of the senses. But those who have tasted of its inexpressibility know how far it is beyond the highest powers of mere eye or ear—nay, even the heart is powerless to attain the end of its yearning.

P.S.—I have left out the very thing I started to tell of. Don't be afraid, it won't take four more sheets. It is this, that on the evening of the first day of Asarh it came on to rain very heavily, in great lance-like showers. That is all.

ON THE WAY TO GOALUNDA
June 1892

Pictures in an endless variety, of sand-banks, fields and their crops, and villages, glide into view on either hand—of clouds floating in the sky, of colours blossoming when day meets night. Boats steal by, fishermen catch fish; the waters make liquid caressing sounds throughout the livelong[1] day; their broad expanse calms down in the evening stillness, like a child lulled to sleep, over whom all the stars in the boundless sky keep watch—then, as I sit up on wakeful nights, with sleeping banks on either side, the silence is broken only by an occasional cry of a jackal in the woods near some village, or by fragments undermined by the keen current of the Padma, that tumble from the high cliff-like bank into the water.

Not that the prospect is always of particular interest—a yellowish sand-bank, innocent of grass or tree, stretches away; an empty boat is

---

[1] Livelong: Of time long or seemingly long, especially in a tedious way.

tied to its edge; the bluish water, of the same shade as the hazy sky, flows past; yet I cannot tell how it moves me. I suspect that the old desires and longings of my servant-ridden childhood—when in the solitary imprisonment of my room I pored over the Arabian Nights, and shared with *Sinbad the Sailor* his adventures in many a strange land—are not yet dead within me, but are roused at the sight of any empty boat tied to a sand-bank.

If I had not heard fairy tales and read the *Arabian Nights* and *Robinson Crusoe* in childhood, I am sure views of distant banks, or the farther side of wide fields, would not have stirred me so—the whole world, in fact, would have had for me a different appeal.

What a maze of fancy and fact becomes tangled up within the mind of man! The different strands—petty and great—of story and event and picture, how they get knotted together!

SHELIDAH,
22 June 1892

Early this morning, while still lying in bed, I heard the women at the bathing-place sending forth joyous peals of Ulu! Ulu![1] The sound moved me curiously, though it is difficult to say why.

Perhaps such joyful outbursts put one in mind of the great stream of festive activity which goes on in this world, with most of which the individual man has no connection. The world is so immense, the concourse of men so vast, yet with how few has one any tie! Distant sounds of life, wafted near, bearing tidings from unknown homes, make the individual realize that the greater part of the world of men does not, cannot own or know him; then he feels deserted, loosely attached to the world, and a vague sadness creeps over him.

Thus these cries of Ulu! Ulu! made my life, past and future, seem like a long, long road, from the very ends of which they come to me. And this feeling colours for me the beginning of my day.

As soon as the manager with his staff, and the ryots[2] seeking audience, come upon the scene, this faint vista of past and future

---

[1] A peculiar shrill cheer given by women on auspicious or festive occasions.
[2] Ryot: An Indian peasant or tenant farmer.

will be promptly elbowed out, and a very robust present will salute and stand before me.

SHAZADPUR,
25 June 1892

In today's letters there was a touch about A—'s singing which made my heart yearn with a nameless longing. Each of the little joys of life, which remain unappreciated amid the hubbub of the town, send in their claims to the heart when far from home. I love music, and there is no dearth of voices and instruments in Calcutta, yet I turn a deaf ear to them. But, though I may fail to realize it at the time, this needs must leave the heart athirst.

As I read today's letters, I felt such a poignant desire to hear A—'s sweet song, I was at once sure that one of the many suppressed longings of creation which cry after fulfilment is for neglected joys within reach; while we are busy pursuing chimerical impossibilities, we famish our lives...

The emptiness left by easy joys, untasted, is ever growing in my life. And the day may come when I shall feel that, could I but have the past back, I would strive no more after the unattainable, but drain to the full these little, unsought, everyday joys which life offers.

SHAZADPUR,
27 June 1892

Yesterday, in the afternoon, it clouded over so threateningly, I felt a sense of dread. I do not remember ever to have seen before such angry-looking clouds.

Swollen masses of the deepest indigo blue were piled, one on top of the other, just above the horizon, looking like the puffed-out moustaches of some raging demon.

Under the jagged lower edges of the clouds there shone forth a blood-red glare, as through the eyes of a monstrous, sky-filling bison, with tossing mane and with head lowered to strike the earth in fury.

The crops in the fields and the leaves of the trees trembled with fear of the impending disaster; shudder after shudder ran across the waters; the crows flew wildly about, distractedly cawing.

SHAZADPUR,
29 June 1892

I wrote yesterday that I had an engagement with Kalidas, the poet, for this evening. As I lit a candle, drew my chair up to the table, and made ready, not Kalidas, but the postmaster, walked in. A live postmaster cannot but claim precedence over a dead poet, so I could not very well tell him to make way for Kalidas, who was due by appointment,—he would not have understood me! Therefore, I offered him a chair and gave old Kalidas the go-by.

There is a kind of bond between this postmaster and me. When the post office was in a part of this estate building, I used to meet him every day. I wrote my story of 'The Postmaster' one afternoon in this very room. And when the story was out in the *Hitabadi*, he came to me with a succession of bashful smiles, as he deprecatingly touched on the subject. Anyhow, I like the man. He has a fund of anecdote which I enjoy listening to. He has also a sense of humour.

Though it was late when the postmaster left, I started at once on the Raghuvansa,[1] and read all about the swayamuara[2] of Indumati.

The handsome, gaily adorned princes are seated on rows of thrones in the assembly hall. Suddenly a blast of conch-shell and trumpet resounds, as Indumati, in bridal robes, supported by Sunanda, is ushered in and stands in the walk left between them. It was delightful to dwell on the picture.

Then as Sunanda introduces to her each one of the suitors, Indumati bows low in loveless salutation, and passes on. How beautiful is this humble courtesy! They are all princes. They are all her seniors. For she is a mere girl. Had she not atoned for the inevitable rudeness of her rejection by the grace of her humility, the scene would have lost its beauty.

---

[1] Book of poems by Kalidas, who is perhaps best known to European readers as the author of *Sakuntala*.
[2] An old Indian custom, according to which a princess chooses among assembled rival suitors for her hand by placing a garland round the neck of the one whose love she returns.

SHELIDAH,
20 August 1892

'If only I could live there!' is often thought when looking at a beautiful landscape painting. That is the kind of longing which is satisfied here, where one feels alive in a brilliantly coloured picture, with none of the hardness of reality. When I was a child, illustrations of woodland and sea, in Paul and Virginia, or Robinson Crusoe, would waft me away from the everyday world; and the sunshine here brings back to my mind the feeling with which I used to gaze on those pictures.

I cannot account for this exactly, or explain definitely what kind of longing it is which is roused within me. It seems like the throb of some current flowing through the artery connecting me with the larger world. I feel as if dim, distant memories come to me of the time when I was one with the rest of the earth; when on me grew the green grass, and on me fell the autumn light; when a warm scent of youth would rise from every pore of my vast, soft, green body at the touch of the rays of the mellow sun, and a fresh life, a sweet joy, would be half-consciously secreted and inarticulately poured forth from all the immensity of my being, as it lay dumbly stretched, with its varied countries and seas and mountains, under the bright blue sky.

My feelings seem to be those of our ancient earth in the daily ecstasy of its sun-kissed life; my own consciousness seems to stream through each blade of grass, each sucking root, to rise with the sap through the trees, to break out with joyous thrills in the waving fields of corn, in the rustling palm leaves.

I feel impelled to give expression to my blood-tie with the earth, my kinsman's love for her; but I am afraid I shall not be understood.

BOALIA,
18 November 1892

I am wondering where your train has got to by now. This is the time for the sun to rise over the ups and downs of the treeless, rocky region near Nawadih station. The scene around there must be brightened by the fresh sunlight, through which distant, blue hills are beginning to be faintly visible.

Cultivated fields are scarcely to be seen, except where the primitive tribesmen have done a little ploughing with their buffaloes; on each side of the railway cutting there are the heaped-up black rocks—the boulder-marked footprints of dried-up streams—and the fidgety, black wagtails, perched along the telegraph wires. A wild, seamed, and scarred nature lies there in the sun, as though tamed at the touch of some soft, bright, cherubic hand.

Do you know the picture which this calls up for me? In the Sakuntala of Kalidas there is a scene where Bharat, the infant son of King Dushyanta, is playing with a lion cub. The child is lovingly passing his delicate, rosy fingers through the rough mane of the great beast, which lies quietly stretched in trustful repose, now and then casting affectionate glances out of the corner of its eyes at its little human friend.

And shall I tell you what those dry, boulder-strewn watercourses put me in mind of? We read in the English fairy tale of the Babes in the Wood, how the little brother and sister left a trace of their wanderings, through the unknown forest into which their stepmother had turned them out, by dropping pebbles as they went. These streamlets are like lost babes in the great world into which they are sent adrift, and that is why they leave stones, as they go forth, to mark their course, so as not to lose their way when they may be returning. But for them there is no return journey!

NATORE,
2 December 1892

There is a depth of feeling and breadth of peace in a Bengal sunset behind the trees which fringe the endless solitary fields, spreading away to the horizon.

Lovingly, yet sadly withal,[1] does our evening sky bend over and meet the earth in the distance. It casts a mournful light on the earth it leaves behind—a light which gives us a taste of the divine grief of the Eternal Separation;[2] and eloquent is the silence which then broods

---

[1] Withal: Despite that; nevertheless.
[2] I.e. between Purusha (God) and *Prakriti* (Creation).

over earth, sky, and waters.

As I gaze on in rapt motionlessness, I fall to wondering.—If ever this silence should fail to contain itself, if the expression for which this hour has been seeking from the beginning of time should break forth, would a profoundly solemn, poignantly moving music rise from earth to star-land?

With a little steadfast concentration of effort we can, for ourselves, translate the grand harmony of light and colour which permeates the universe into music. We have only to close our eyes and receive with the ear of the mind the vibration of this ever-flowing panorama.

But how often shall I write of these sunsets and sunrises? I feel their renewed freshness every time; yet how am I to attain such renewed freshness in my attempts at expression?

SHELIDAH,
9 December 1892

I am feeling weak and relaxed after my painful illness, and in this state the ministrations of nature are sweet indeed. I feel as if, like the rest, I too am lazily glittering out my delight at the rays of the sun, and my letter-writing progresses but absent-mindedly.

The world is ever new to me; like an old friend loved through this and former lives, the acquaintance between us is both long and deep.

I can well realize how, in ages past, when the earth in her first youth came forth from her sea-bath and saluted the sun in prayer, I must have been one of the trees sprung from her new-formed soil, spreading my foliage in all the freshness of a primal impulse.

The great sea was rocking and swaying and smothering, like a foolishly fond mother, its first-born land with repeated caresses; while I was drinking in the sunlight with the whole of my being, quivering under the blue sky with the unreasoning rapture of the new born, holding fast and sucking away at my mother earth with all my roots. In blind joy my leaves burst forth and my flowers bloomed; and when the dark clouds gathered, their grateful shade would comfort me with a tender touch.

From age to age, thereafter, have I been diversely reborn on this earth. So whenever we now sit face to face, alone together, various ancient memories, gradually, one after another, come back to me.

My mother earth sits today in the cornfields by the riverside, in her raiment¹ of sunlit gold; and near her feet, her knees, her lap, I roll about and play. Mother of a multitude of children, she attends but absently to their constant calls on her, with an immense patience, but also with a certain aloofness. She is seated there, with her faraway look fastened on the verge of the afternoon sky, while I keep chattering on untiringly.

BALIA,
Tuesday, February 1893

I do not want to wander about any more. I am pining for a corner in which to nestle down snugly, away from the crowd.

India has two aspects—in one she is a householder, in the other a wandering ascetic. The former refuses to budge from the home corner, the latter has no home at all. I find both these within me. I want to roam about and see all the wide world, yet I also yearn for a little sheltered nook; like a bird with its tiny nest for a dwelling, and the vast sky for flight.

I hanker after a corner because it serves to bring calmness to my mind. My mind really wants to be busy, but in making the attempt it knocks so repeatedly against the crowd as to become utterly frenzied and to keep buffeting me, its cage, from within. If only it is allowed a little leisurely solitude, and can look about and think to its heart's content, it will express its feelings to its own satisfaction.

This freedom of solitude is what my mind is fretting for; it would be alone with its imaginings, as the Creator broods over His own creation.

CUTTACK,
February 1893

Till we can achieve something, let us live incognito, say I. So long as we are only fit to be looked down upon, on what shall we base our claim to respect? When we have acquired a foothold of our own in the world, when we have had some share in shaping its course, then

---

¹Raiment: Clothing; garments.

we can meet others smilingly. Till then let us keep in the background, attending to our own affairs.

But our countrymen seem to hold the opposite opinion. They set no store by our more modest, intimate wants which have to be met behind the scenes,—the whole of their attention is directed to momentary attitudinizing[1] and display.

Ours is truly a godforsaken[2] country. Difficult, indeed, is it for us to maintain the strength of will to do. We get no help in any real sense. There is no one, within miles of us, in converse with whom we might gain an accession of vitality. No one near seems to be thinking, or feeling, or working. Not a soul has any experience of big striving, or of really and truly living. They all eat and drink, do their office work, smoke and sleep, and chatter nonsensically. When they touch upon emotion they grow sentimental, when they reason they are childish. One yearns for a full-blooded, sturdy, and capable personality; these are all so many shadows, flitting about, out of touch with the world.

CUTTACK,
March 1893

If we begin to attach too much importance to the applause of Englishmen, we shall have to be rid of much in us that is good, and to accept from them much that is bad.

We shall grow ashamed of going about without socks, and cease to feel shame at the sight of their ball dresses. We shall have no compunction in throwing overboard our ancient manners, nor any in emulating their lack of courtesy.

We shall leave off wearing our achgans because they are susceptible of improvement, but think nothing of surrendering our heads to their hats, though no head-gear could well be uglier.

In short, consciously or unconsciously, we shall have to cut our lives down according as they clap their hands or not.

Wherefore I apostrophize myself and say, 'O Earthen Pot! For

---

[1]Attitudinising: To assume an affected attitude; posture.
[2]God-forsaken: Desolate; forlorn.

goodness sake keep away from that Metal Pot! Whether he comes to you in anger or merely to give you a patronizing pat on the back, you are done for, cracked in either case. So pay heed to old Aesop's sage counsel, I pray—and keep your distance.'

Let the metal pot ornament wealthy homes; you have work to do in those of the poor. If you let yourself be broken, you will have no place in either, but merely return to the dust; or, at best, you may secure a corner in a bric-a-brac cabinet—as a curiosity, and it is more glorious far to be used for fetching water by the meanest of village women.

SHELIDAH,
8 May 1893

Poetry is a very old love of mine—I must have been engaged to her when I was only Rathi's[1] age. Long ago the recesses under the old banyan tree beside our tank, the inner gardens, the unknown regions on the ground floor of the house, the whole of the outside world, the nursery rhymes and tales told by the maids, created a wonderful fairyland within me. It is difficult to give a clear idea of all the vague and mysterious happenings of that period, but this much is certain, that my exchange of garlands[2] with Poetic Fancy was already duly celebrated.

I must admit, however, that my betrothed is not an auspicious maiden—whatever else she may bring one, it is not good fortune. I cannot say she has never given me happiness, but peace of mind with her is out of the question. The lover whom she favours may get his fill of bliss, but his heart's blood is wrung out under her relentless embrace. It is not for the unfortunate creature of her choice ever to become a staid and sober householder, comfortably settled down on a social foundation.

Consciously or unconsciously, I may have done many things that were un-true, but I have never uttered anything false in my poetry—that is the sanctuary where the deepest truths of my life find refuge.

---

[1] Rathi, his son, was then five years old.
[2] The betrothal ceremony.

SHELIDAH,
10 May 1893

Here come black, swollen masses of cloud; they soak up the golden sunshine from the scene in front of me like great pads of blotting-paper. Rain must be near, for the breeze feels moist and tearful.

Over there, on the sky-piercing peaks of Simla, you will find it hard to realize exactly what an important event the coming of the clouds is here, or how many are anxiously looking up to the sky, hailing their advent.

I feel a great tenderness for these peasant folk—our ryots—big, helpless, infantile children of Providence, who must have food brought to their very lips, or they are undone. When the breasts of Mother Earth dry up they are at a loss what to do, and can only cry. But no sooner is their hunger satisfied than they forget all their past sufferings.

I know not whether the socialistic ideal of a more equal distribution of wealth is attainable, but if not, the dispensation of Providence is indeed cruel, and man a truly unfortunate creature. For if in this world misery must exist, so be it; but let some little loophole, some glimpse of possibility at least, be left, which may serve to urge the nobler portion of humanity to hope and struggle unceasingly for its alleviation.

They say a terribly hard thing who assert that the division of the world's production to afford each one a mouthful of food, a bit of clothing, is only an Utopian dream. All these social problems are hard indeed! Fate has allowed humanity such a pitifully meagre coverlet, that in pulling it over one part of the world, another has to be left bare. In allaying our poverty we lose our wealth, and with this wealth what a world of grace and beauty and power is lost to us.

But the sun shines forth again, though the clouds are still banked up in the west.

SHELIDAH,
3 July 1893

All last night the wind howled like a stray dog, and the rain still pours on without a break. The water from the fields is rushing in numberless, purling streams to the river. The dripping ryots are crossing the river in the ferry-boat, some with their tokas[1] on, others with yam leaves held over their heads. Big cargo-boats are gliding along, the boatman sitting drenched at his helm, the crew straining at the tow-ropes through the rain. The birds remain gloomily confined to their nests, but sons of men fare forth, for in spite of the weather the world's work must go on.

Two cowherd lads are grazing their cattle just in front of my boat. The cows are munching away with great gusto, their noses plunged into the lush grass, their tails incessantly busy flicking off the flies. The raindrops and the sticks of the cowherd boys fall on their backs with the same unreasonable persistency, and they bear both with equally uncritical resignation, steadily going on with their munch, munch, munch. These cows have such mild, affectionate, mournful eyes; why, I wonder, should Providence have thought fit to impose all the burden of man's work on the submissive shoulders of these great, gentle beasts?

The river is rising daily. What I could see yesterday only from the upper deck, I can now see from my cabin windows. Every morning, I awake to find my field of vision growing larger. Not long since, only the tree-tops near those distant villages used to appear, like dark green clouds. Today the whole of the wood is visible.

Land and water are gradually approaching each other like two bashful lovers. The limit of their shyness has nearly been reached—their arms will soon be round each other's necks. I shall enjoy my trip along this brimful river at the height of the rains. I am fidgeting to give the order to cast off.

SHELIDAH,
4 July 1893

A little gleam of sunlight shows this morning. There was a break in the rains yesterday, but the clouds are banked up so heavily along the skirts of the sky that there is not much hope of the break lasting. It looks as if a heavy carpet of cloud had been rolled up to one side, and at any moment a fussy breeze may come along and spread it over the whole place again, covering every trace of blue sky and golden sunshine.

---

[1] Conical hats of straw or of split bamboo.

What a store of water must have been laid up in the sky this year. The river has already risen over the low chur-lands,[1] threatening to overwhelm all the standing crops. The wretched ryots, in despair, are cutting and bringing away in boats sheaves of half-ripe rice. As they pass my boat I hear them bewailing their fate. It is easy to understand how heart-rending it must be for cultivators to have to cut down their rice on the very eve of its ripening, the only hope left them being that some of the ears may possibly have hardened into grain.

There must be some element of pity in the dispensations of Providence, else how did we get our share of it? But it is so difficult to see where it comes in. The lamentations of these hundreds of thousands of unoffending creatures do not seem to get anywhere. The rain pours on as it lists, the river still rises, and no amount of petitioning seems to have the effect of bringing relief from any quarter. One has to seek consolation by saying that all this is beyond the understanding of man. And yet, it is so vitally necessary for man to understand that there are such things as pity and justice in the world.

However, this is only sulking. Reason tells us that creation never can be perfectly happy. So long as it is incomplete it must put up with imperfection and sorrow. It can only be perfect when it ceases to be creation, and is God. Do our prayers dare go so far?

The more we think over it, the oftener we come back to the starting-point—Why this creation at all? If we cannot make up our minds to object to the thing itself, it is futile complaining about its companion, sorrow.

SHAZADPUR,
7 July 1893

The flow of village life is not too rapid, neither is it stagnant. Work and rest go together, hand in hand. The ferry crosses to and fro, the passers-by with umbrellas up wend their way along the tow-path, women are washing rice on the split-bamboo trays which they dip in the water, the ryots are coming to the market with bundles of jute on their heads. Two men are chopping away at a log of wood with regular,

---

[1] Old sand-banks consolidated by the deposit of a layer of cultivable soil.

ringing blows. The village carpenter is repairing an upturned dinghy under a big aswatha tree. A mongrel dog is prowling aimlessly along the canal bank. Some cows are lying there chewing the cud, after a huge meal off the luxuriant grass, lazily moving their ears backwards and forwards, flicking off flies with their tails, and occasionally giving an impatient toss of their heads when the crows perched on their backs take too much of a liberty.

The monotonous blows of wood-cutter's axe or carpenter's mallet, the splashing of oars, the merry voices of the naked little children at play, the plaintive tune of the ryot's song, the more dominant creaking of the turning oil-mill, all these sounds of activity do not seem out of harmony with murmuring leaves and singing birds, and all combine like moving strains of some grand dream-orchestra, rendering a composition of immense though restrained pathos.

SHAZADPUR,
10 July 1893

All I have to say about the discussion that is going on over 'silent poets' is that, though the strength of feeling may be the same in those who are silent as in those who are vocal, that has nothing to do with poetry. Poetry is not a matter of feeling, it is the creation of form.

Ideas take shape by some hidden, subtle skill at work within the poet. This creative power is the origin of poetry. Perceptions, feelings, or language, are only raw material. One may be gifted with feeling, a second with language, a third with both; but he who has as well a creative genius, alone is a poet.

PATISAR,
13 August 1893

Coming through these *beels*[1] to Kaligram, an idea took shape in

---

[1] Translator's Note.—Sometimes a stream passing through the flat Bengal country encounters a stretch of low land and spreads out into a sheet of water, called a bed, of indefinite extent, ranging from a large pool in the dry season to a shoreless expanse during the rains.
Villages consisting of a cluster of huts, built on mounds, stand out here and

my mind. Not that the thought was new, but sometimes old ideas strike one with new force.

The water loses its beauty when it ceases to be defined by banks and spreads out into a monotonous vagueness. In the case of language, metre[1] serves for banks and gives form and beauty and character.

Just as the banks give each river a distinct personality, so does rhythm make each poem an individual creation; prose is like the featureless, impersonal beel. Again, the waters of the river have movement and progress; those of the beel engulf the country by expanse alone. So, in order to give language power, the narrow bondage of metre[2] becomes necessary; otherwise it spreads and spreads, but cannot advance.

The country people call these beels 'dumb waters'—they have no language, no self-expression. The river ceaselessly babbles; so the words of the poem sing, they are not 'dumb words.' Thus bondage creates beauty of form, motion, and music; bounds make not only for beauty but power.

Poetry gives itself up to the control of metre, not led by blind habit, but because it thus finds the joy of motion. There are foolish persons who think that metre is a species of verbal gymnastics, or legerdemain,[3] of which the object is to win the admiration of the crowd. That is not so. Metre is born as all beauty is born the universe through. The current set up within well-defined bounds gives metrical verse power to move the minds of men as vague and indefinite prose cannot.

This idea became clear to me as I glided on from river to beel and beel to river.

---

there like islands, and boats or round earthen vessels are the only means of getting about from village to village. Where the waters cover cultivated tracts the rice grows through, often from considerable depths, giving to the boats sailing over them the curious appearance of gliding over a cornfield, so clear is the water. Elsewhere these beels have a peculiar flora and fauna of water-lilies and irises and various water-fowl. As a result, they resemble neither a marsh nor a lake, but have a distinct character of their own.

[1] **Metre:** The basic rhythmic structure of a poem.
[2] **Metre:** The basic rhythmic structure of a poem.
[3] **Legerdemain:** Sleight of hand; show of skill or deceitful cleverness.

PATISAR,
26 (Straven) August 1893

For some time it has struck me that man is a rough-hewn and woman a finished product.

There is an unbroken consistency in the manners, customs, speech, and adornment of woman. And the reason is, that for ages Nature has assigned to her the same definite role and has been adapting her to it. No cataclysm, no political revolution, no alteration of social ideal, has yet diverted woman from her particular functions, nor destroyed their inter-relations. She has loved, tended, and caressed, and done nothing else; and the exquisite skill which she has acquired in these, permeates all her being and doing. Her disposition and action have become inseparably one, like the flower and its scent. She has, therefore, no doubts or hesitations.

But the character of man has still many hollows and protuberances; each of the varied circumstances and forces which have contributed to his making has left its mark upon him. That is why the features of one will display an indefinite spread of forehead, of another an irresponsible prominence of nose, of a third an unaccountable hardness about the jaws. Had man but the benefit of continuity and uniformity of purpose, Nature must have succeeded in elaborating a definite mould for him, enabling him to function simply and naturally, without such strenuous effort. He would not have so complicated a code of behaviour; and he would be less liable to deviate from the normal when disturbed by outside influences.

Woman was cast in the mould of mother. Man has no such primal design to go by, and that is why he has been unable to rise to an equal perfection of beauty.

PATISAR,
19 February 1894

We have two elephants which come to graze on this bank of the river. They greatly interest me. They give the ground a few taps with one foot, and then taking hold of the grass with the end of their trunks wrench off an enormous piece of turf, roots, soil, and all. This they go on swinging till all the earth leaves the roots; they then put it into their mouths and eat it up.

Sometimes the whim takes them to draw up the dust into their trunks, and then with a snort they squirt it all over their bodies; this is their elephantine toilet.

I love to look on these overgrown beasts, with their vast bodies, their immense strength, their ungainly proportions, their docile harmlessness. Their very size and clumsiness make me feel a kind of tenderness for them—their unwieldy bulk has something infantile about it. Moreover, they have large hearts. When they get wild they are furious, but when they calm down they are peace itself.

The uncouthness which goes with bigness does not repel, it rather attracts.

PATISAR,
27 February 1894

The sky is every now and then overcast and again clears up. Sudden little puffs of wind make the boat lazily creak and groan in all its seams. Thus the day wears on.

It is now past one o'clock. Steeped in this countryside noonday, with its different sounds—the quacking of ducks, the swirl of passing boats, bathers splashing the clothes they wash, the distant shouts from drovers taking cattle across the ford,—it is difficult even to imagine the chair-and-table, monotonously dismal routine-life of Calcutta.

Calcutta is as ponderously proper as a government office. Each of its days comes forth, like coin from a mint, clear-cut and glittering. Ah! Those dreary, deadly days, so precisely equal in weight, so decently respectable!

Here I am quit of the demands of my circle, and do not feel like a wound-up machine. Each day is my own. And with leisure and my thoughts I walk the fields, unfettered by bounds of space or time. The evening gradually deepens over earth and sky and water, as with bowed head I stroll along.

PATISAR,
22 March 1894

As I was sitting at the window of the boat, looking out on the river, I saw, all of a sudden, an odd-looking bird making its way through the water to the opposite bank, followed by a great commotion. I found it was a domestic fowl which had managed to escape impending doom in the galley by jumping overboard and was now trying frantically to win across. It had almost gained the bank when the clutches of its relentless pursuers closed on it, and it was brought back in triumph, gripped by the neck. I told the cook I would not have any meat for dinner.

I really must give up animal food. We manage to swallow flesh only because we do not think of the cruel and sinful thing we do. There are many crimes which are the creation of man himself, the wrongfulness of which is put down to their divergence from habit, custom, or tradition. But cruelty is not of these. It is a fundamental sin, and admits of no argument or nice distinctions. If only we do not allow our heart to grow callous, its protest against cruelty is always clearly heard; and yet we go on perpetrating cruelties easily, merrily, all of us—in fact, anyone who does not join in is dubbed a crank.

How artificial is our apprehension of sin! I feel that the highest commandment is that of sympathy for all sentient beings. Love is the foundation of all religion. The other day I read in one of the English papers that 50,000 pounds of animal carcasses had been sent to some army station in Africa, but the meat being found to have gone bad on arrival, the consignment was returned and was eventually auctioned off for a few pounds at Portsmouth. What a shocking waste of life! What callousness to its true worth! How many living creatures are sacrificed only to grace the dishes at a dinner party, a large proportion of which will leave the table untouched!

So long as we are unconscious of our cruelty we may not be to blame. But if, after our pity is aroused, we persist in throttling our feelings simply in order to join others in their preying upon life, we insult all that is good in us. I have decided to try a vegetarian diet.

PATISAR,
28 March 1894

It is getting rather warm here, but I do not mind the heat of the sun much. The heated wind whistles on its way, now and then pauses in a whirl, then dances away twirling its skirt of dust and sand and dry leaves and twigs.

This morning, however, it was quite cold—almost like a cold weather morning; in fact, I did not feel over-enthusiastic for my bath. It is so difficult to account for what veritably happens in this big thing called Nature. Some obscure cause turns up in some unknown corner, and all of a sudden things look completely different.

The mind of man works in just the same mysterious fashion as outside Nature—so it struck me yesterday. A wondrous alchemy is being wrought in artery, vein, and nerve, in brain and marrow. The blood stream rushes on, the nerve-strings vibrate, the heart muscle rises and falls, and the seasons in man's being change from one to another.

What kind of breezes will blow next, when and from what quarter—of that we know nothing.

One day I am sure I shall get along splendidly; I feel strong enough to leap over all the obstructing sorrows and trials of the world; and, as if I had a printed programme for the rest of my life tucked safely away in my pocket, I am at ease. The next day there is a nasty wind, sprung up from some unknown inferno, the aspect of the sky is threatening, and I begin to doubt whether I shall ever weather the storm. Merely because something has gone wrong in some blood vessel or nerve-fiber, all my strength and intelligence seem to fail me.

This mystery within frightens me. It makes me diffident about talking of what I shall or shall not do. Why was this tacked on to me—this immense mystery which I can neither understand nor control? I know not where it may lead me or I lead it. I cannot see what is happening, nor am I consulted about what is going to happen, and yet I have to keep up an appearance of mastery and pretend to be the doer...

I feel like a living pianoforte with a vast complication of machinery and wires inside, but with no means of telling who the player is, and with only a guess as to why the player plays at all. I can only know what is being played, whether the mode is merry or mournful, when the notes are sharp or flat, the tune in or out of time, the key high-pitched or low. But do I really know even that?

PATISAR,
30 March 1894

Sometimes when I realize that life's journey is long, and that the sorrows to be encountered are many and inevitable, a supreme effort is required to keep up my strength of mind. Some evenings, as I sit alone staring at the flame of the lamp on the table, I vow I will live as a brave man should—unmoved, silent, uncomplaining. The resolve puffs me up, and for the moment I mistake myself for a very, very brave person indeed. But as soon as the thorns on the road worry my feet, I writhe and begin to feel serious misgivings as to the future. The path of life again seems long, and my strength inadequate.

But this last conclusion cannot be the true one, for it is these petty thorns which are the most difficult to bear. The household of the mind is a thrifty one, and only so much is spent as is necessary. There is no squandering on trifles, and its wealth of strength is saved up with miserly strictness to meet the really big calamities. So any amount of weeping and wailing over the lesser griefs fails to evoke a charitable response. But when sorrow is deepest there is no stint of effort. Then the surface crust is pierced, and consolation wells up, and all the forces of patience and courage are banded together to do their duty. Thus great suffering brings with it the power of great endurance.

One side of man's nature has the desire for pleasure—there is another side which desires self-sacrifice. When the former meets with disappointment, the latter gains strength, and on its thus finding fuller scope a grand enthusiasm fills the soul. So while we are cowards before petty troubles, great sorrows make us brave by rousing our truer manhood. And in these, therefore, there is a joy.

It is not an empty paradox to say that there is joy in sorrow, just as, on the other hand, it is true that there is a dissatisfaction in pleasure. It is not difficult to understand why this should be so.

SHELIDAH,
24 June 1894

I have been only four days here, but, having lost count of the hours, it seems such a long while, I feel that if I were to return to Calcutta today I should find much of it changed—as if I alone had been standing still outside the current of time, unconscious of the gradually changing position of the rest of the world.

The fact is that here, away from Calcutta, I live in my own inner world, where the clocks do not keep ordinary time; where duration is measured only by the intensity of the feelings; where, as the outside world does not count the minutes, moments change into hours and hours into moments. So it seems to me that the subdivisions of time and space are only mental illusions. Every atom is immeasurable and every moment infinite.

There is a Persian story which I was greatly taken with when I read it as a boy—I think I understood, even then, something of the underlying idea, though I was a mere child. To show the illusory character of time, a faquir[1] put some magic water into a tub and asked the King to take a dip. The King no sooner dipped his head in than he found himself in a strange country by the sea, where he spent a good long time going through a variety of happenings and doings. He married, had children, his wife and children died, he lost all his wealth, and as he writhed under his sufferings he suddenly found himself back in the room, surrounded by his courtiers. On his proceeding to revile the faquir for his misfortunes, they said, 'But, sire, you have only just dipped your head in, and raised it out of the water!'

The whole of our life with its pleasures and pains is in the same way enclosed in one moment of time. However long or intense we may feel it to be while it lasts, as soon as we have finished our dip in the tub of the world, we shall find how like a slight, momentary dream the whole thing has been...

SHELIDAH,
9 August 1894

I saw a dead bird floating down the current today. The history of its death may easily be divined. It had a nest in some mango tree at the edge of a village. It returned home in the evening, nestling there against soft-feathered companions, and resting a wearied little body

---

[1] Faquir: A Muslim or Hindu mendicant monk who is regarded as a holy man.

in sleep. All of a sudden, in the night, the mighty Padma tossed slightly in her bed, and the earth was swept away from the roots of the mango tree. The little creature bereft of its nest awoke just for a moment before it went to sleep again for ever.

When I am in the presence of the awful mystery of all-destructive Nature, the difference between myself and the other living things seems trivial. In town, human society is to the fore and looms large; it is cruelly callous to the happiness and misery of other creatures as compared with its own.

In Europe, also, man is so complex and so dominant, that the animal is too merely an animal to him. To Indians the idea of the transmigration of the soul from animal to man, and man to animal, does not seem strange, and so from our scriptures pity for all sentient creatures has not been banished as a sentimental exaggeration.

When I am in close touch with Nature in the country, the Indian in me asserts itself and I cannot remain coldly indifferent to the abounding joy of life throbbing within the soft down-covered breast of a single tiny bird.

SHELIDAH,
10 August 1894

Last night, a rushing sound in the water awoke me—a sudden boisterous disturbance of the river current—probably the onslaught of a freshet[1]: a thing that often happens at this season. One's feet on the planking of the boat become aware of a variety of forces at work beneath it. Slight tremors, little rockings, gentle heaves, and sudden jerks, all keep me in touch with the pulse of the flowing stream.

There must have been some sudden excitement in the night, which sent the current racing away. I rose and sat by the window. A hazy kind of light made the turbulent river look madder than ever. The sky was spotted with clouds. The reflection of a great big star quivered on the waters in a long streak, like a burning gash of pain. Both banks were vague with the dimness of slumber, and between them was this wild, sleepless unrest, running and running regardless of consequences.

---

[1] Freshet: A sudden overflow of a stream resulting from a heavy rain.

To watch a scene like this in the middle of the night makes one feel altogether a different person, and the daylight life an illusion. Then again, this morning, that midnight world faded away into some dreamland, and vanished into thin air. The two are so different, yet both are true for man.

The day-world seems to me like European Music—its concords and discords resolving into each other in a great progression of harmony; the night-world like Indian Music—pure, unfettered melody, grave and poignant. What if their contrast be so striking—both move us. This principle of opposites is at the very root of creation, which is divided between the rule of the King and the Queen; Night and Day; the One and the Varied; the Eternal and the Evolving.

We Indians are under the rule of Night. We are immersed in the Eternal, the One. Our melodies are to be sung alone, to oneself; they take us out of the everyday world into a solitude aloof. European Music is for the multitude and takes them along, dancing, through the ups and downs of the joys and sorrows of men.

SHELIDAH,
13 August 1894

Whatever I truly think, truly feel, truly realize,—its natural destiny is to find true expression. There is some force in me which continually works towards that end, but is not mine alone,—it permeates the universe. When this universal force is manifested within an individual, it is beyond his control and acts according to its own nature; and in surrendering our lives to its power is our greatest joy. It not only gives us expression, but also sensitiveness and love; this makes our feelings so fresh to us every time, so full of wonder.

When my little daughter delights me, she merges into the original mystery of joy which is the Universe; and my loving caresses are called forth like worship. I am sure that all our love is but worship of the Great Mystery, only we perform it unconsciously. Otherwise it is meaningless.

Like universal gravitation, which governs large and small alike in the world of matter, this universal joy exerts its attraction throughout our inner world, and baffles our understanding when we see it in a partial view. The only rational explanation of why we find joy in man and nature is given in the Upanishad:

'For of joy are born all created things.'

SHELIDAH,
19 August 1894

The Vedanta seems to help many to free their minds from all doubt as to the Universe and its First Cause, but my doubts remain undispelled. It is true that the Vedanta is simpler than most other theories. The problem of Creation and its Creator is more complex than appears at first sight; but the Vedanta has certainly simplified it half way, by cutting the Gordian knot and leaving out Creation altogether.

There is only Brahma, and the rest of us merely imagine that we are,—it is wonderful how the human mind should have found room for such a thought. It is still more wonderful to think that the idea is not so inconsistent as it sounds, and the real difficulty is, rather, to prove that anything does exist.

Anyhow, when as now the moon is up, and with half-closed eyes I am stretched beneath it on the upper deck, the soft breeze cooling my problem-vexed head, then the earth, waters, and sky around, the gentle rippling of the river, the casual wayfarer passing along the tow-path, the occasional dinghy gliding by, the trees across the fields, vague in the moonlight, the sleepy village beyond, bounded by the dark shadows of its groves,—verily[1] seem an illusion of Maya; and yet they cling to and draw the mind and heart more truly than truth itself, which is abstraction, and it becomes impossible to realize what kind of salvation there can be in freeing oneself from them.

SHAZADPUR,
5 September 1894

I realize how hungry for space I have become, and take my fill of it in these rooms where I hold my state as sole monarch, with all doors and windows thrown open. Here the desire and power to write are mine as they are nowhere else. The stir of outside life comes into me

---

[1] Verily: In truth; in fact.

in waves of verdure,[1] and with its light and scent and sound stimulated my fancy into story-writing.

The afternoons have a special enchantment of their own. The glare of the sun, the silence, the solitude, the bird cries, especially the cawings of crows, and the delightful, restful leisure—these conspire to carry me away altogether.

Just such noondays seem to have gone to the making of the Arabian Nights,—in Damascus, Bokhara, or Samarkhand, with their desert roadways, files of camels, wandering horsemen, crystal springs, welling up under the shade of feathery date groves; their wilderness of roses, songs of nightingales, wines of Shiraz; their narrow bazaar paths with bright overhanging canopies, the men, in loose robes and multi-coloured turbans, selling dates and nuts and melons; their palaces, fragrant with incense, luxurious with kincob-covered divans and bolsters by the window-side; their Zobedia or Amina or Sufia with gaily decorated jacket, wide trousers, and gold-embroidered slippers, a long narghilah pipe curled up at her feet, with gorgeously liveried[2] eunuchs on guard,—and all the possible and impossible tales of human deeds and desires, and the laughter and wailing, of that distant mysterious region.

ON THE WAY TO DIGHAPATIAYA,
20 September 1894

Big trees are standing in the flood water, their trunks wholly submerged, their branches and foliage bending over the waters. Boats are tied up under shady groves of mango and bo tree, and people bathe screened behind them. Here and there cottages stand out in the current, their inner quadrangles under water.

As my boat rustles its way through standing crops it now and then comes across what was a pool and is still to be distinguished by its clusters of water-lilies, and diver-birds pursuing fish.

The water has penetrated every possible place. I have never before seen such a complete defeat of the land. A little more and the water

---

[1]Verdure: The lush greenness of flourishing vegetation.
[2]Liveried: Wearing distinctive uniforms.

will be right inside the cottages, and their occupants will have to put up machans[1] to live on. The cows will die if they have to remain standing like this in water up to their knees. All the snakes have been flooded out of their holes, and they, with sundry other homeless reptiles and insects, will have to chum with man and take refuge on the thatch of his roof.

The vegetation rotting in the water, refuse of all kinds floating about, naked children with shrivelled limbs and enlarged spleens splashing everywhere, the long-suffering patient housewives exposed in their wet clothes to wind and rain, wading through their daily tasks with tucked-up skirts, and over all a thick pall of mosquitoes hovering in the noxious atmosphere—the sight is hardly pleasing!

Colds and fevers and rheumatism in every home, the malaria-stricken infants constantly crying,—nothing can save them. How is it possible for men to live in such unlovely, unhealthy, squalid, neglected surroundings? The fact is we are so used to bear everything, hands down,—the ravages of Nature, the oppression of rulers, the pressure of our shastras to which we have not a word to say, while they keep eternally grinding us down.

ON THE WAY TO BOALIA,
22 September 1894

It feels strange to be reminded that only thirty-two Autumns have come and gone in my life; for my memory seems to have receded back into the dimness of time immemorial; and when my inner world is flooded with a light, as of an unclouded autumn morning, I feel I am sitting at the window of some magic palace, gazing entranced on a scene of distant reminiscence, soothed with soft breezes laden with the faint perfume of all the Past.

Goethe on his death-bed wanted 'more light.' If I have any desire left at all at such a time, it will be for 'more space' as well; for I dearly love both light and space. Many look down on Bengal as being only a flat country, but that is just what makes me revel in its scenery all the more. Its unobstructed sky is filled to the brim, like an amethyst

---

[1]Machan: A raised platform.

cup, with the descending twilight and peace of the evening; and the golden skirt of the still, silent noonday spreads over the whole of it without let or hindrance.

Where is there another such country for the eye to look on, the mind to take in?

CALCUTTA,
5 October 1894

Tomorrow is the Durga Festival. As I was going to S—'s yesterday, I noticed images being made in almost every big house on the way. It struck me that during these few days of the Poojahs, old and young alike had become children.

When we come to think of it, all preparation for enjoyment is really a playing with toys which are of no consequence in themselves. From outside it may appear wasteful, but can that be called futile which raises such a wave of feeling through and through the country? Even the driest of worldly-wise people are moved out of their self-centred interests by the rush of the pervading emotion.

Thus, once every year there comes a period when all minds are in a melting mood, fit for the springing of love and affection and sympathy. The songs of welcome and farewell to the goddess, the meeting of loved ones, the strains of the festive pipes, the limpid sky and molten gold of autumn, are all parts of one great paean of joy.

Pure joy is the children's joy. They have the power of using any and every trivial thing to create their world of interest, and the ugliest doll is made beautiful with their imagination and lives with their life. He who can retain this faculty of enjoyment after he has grown up, is indeed the true Idealist. For him things are not merely visible to the eye or audible to the ear, but they are also sensible to the heart, and their narrowness and imperfections are lost in the glad music which he himself supplies.

Everyone cannot hope to be an Idealist, but a whole people approaches nearest to this blissful state at such seasons of festivity. And then what may ordinarily appear to be a mere toy loses its limitations and becomes glorified with an ideal radiance.

BOLPUR,
19 October 1894

We know people only in dotted outline, that is to say, with gaps in our knowledge which we have to fill in ourselves, as best we can. Thus, even those we know well are largely made up of our imagination. Sometimes the lines are so broken, with even the guiding dots missing, that a portion of the picture remains darkly confused and uncertain. If, then, our best friends are only pieces of broken outline strung on a thread of imagination, do we really know anybody at all, or does anybody know us except in the same disjointed fashion? But perhaps it is these very loopholes, allowing entrance to each other's imagination, which make for intimacy; otherwise each one, secure in his inviolate individuality, would have been unapproachable to all but the dweller within.

Our own self, too, we know only in bits, and with these scraps of material we have to shape the hero of our life-story,—likewise with the help of our imagination. Providence has, doubtless, deliberately omitted portions so that we may assist in our own creation.

BOLPUR,
31 October 1894

The first of the north winds has begun to blow today, shiveringly. It looks as if there had been a visitation of the tax-gatherer in the Amlaki groves,—everything beside itself, sighing, trembling, withering. The tired impassiveness of the noonday sunshine, with its monotonous cooing of doves in the dense shade of the mango-tops, seems to overcast the drowsy watches of the day with a pang, as of some impending parting.

The ticking of the clock on my table, and the pattering of the squirrels which scamper in and out of my room, are in harmony with all other midday sounds.

It amuses me to watch these soft, grey and black striped, furry squirrels, with their bushy tails, their twinkling bead-like eyes, their gentle yet busily practical demeanour. Everything eatable has to be put away in the wire-gauze cupboard in the corner, safe from these greedy creatures. So, sniffing with an irrepressible eagerness, they come nosing round and round the cupboard, trying to find some hole for entrance. If any grain or crumb has been dropped outside they are sure to find it, and, taking it between their forepaws, nibble away with great industry, turning it over and over to adjust it to their mouths. At the least movement of mine up go their tails over their backs and off they run, only to stop short halfway, sit up on their tails on the doormat, scratching their ears with their hind-paws, and then come back.

Thus little sounds continue all day long—gnawing teeth, scampering feet, and the tinkling of the china on the shelves.

SHELIDAH,
23 February 1895

I grow quite absent-minded when I try to write for the Sadhana magazine.

I raise my eyes to every passing boat and keep staring at the ferry going to and fro. And then on the bank, close to my boat, there are a herd of buffaloes thrusting their massive snouts into the herbage, wrapping their tongues round it to get it into their mouths, and then munching away, blowing hard with great big gasps of contentment, and flicking the flies off their backs with their tails.

All of a sudden a naked weakling of a human cub appears on the scene, makes sundry noises, and pokes one of the patient beasts with a cudgel, whereupon, throwing occasional glances at the human sprig out of a corner of its eye, and snatching at tufts of leaves or grass here and there on the way, the unruffled beast leisurely moves on a few paces, and that imp of a boy seems to feel that his duty as herdsman has been done.

I fail to penetrate this mystery of the boy-cowherd's mind. Whenever a cow or a buffalo has selected a spot to its liking and is comfortably grazing there, I cannot divine what purpose is served by worrying it, as he insists on doing, till it shifts somewhere else. I suppose it is man's masterfulness glorying in triumph over the powerful creature it has tamed. Anyhow, I love to see these buffaloes amongst the lush grass.

But this is not what I started to say. I wanted to tell you how the least thing distracts me nowadays from my duty to the Sadhana. In my last letter[1] I told you of the bumble-bees which hover round me in some fruitless quest, to the tune of a meaningless humming, with tireless assiduity.

They come every day at about nine or ten in the morning, dart up to my table, shoot down under the desk, go bang on to the coloured glass window-pane, and then with a circuit or two round my head are off again with a whizz.

I could easily have thought them to be departed spirits who had left this world unsatisfied, and so keep coming back to it again and again in the guise of bees, paying me an inquiring visit in passing. But I think nothing of the kind. I am sure they are real bees, otherwise known, in Sanskrit, as honey-suckers, or on still rarer occasions as double-proboscideans.

SHELIDAH,
16 (Phalgun) February 1895

We have to tread every single moment of the way as we go on living our life, but when taken as a whole it is such a very small thing, two hours uninterrupted thought can hold all of it.

After thirty years of strenuous living, Shelley could only supply material for two volumes of biography, of which, moreover, a considerable space is taken up by Dowden's chatter. The thirty years of my life would not fill even one volume.

What a to-do there is over this tiny bit of life! To think of the quantity of land and trade and commerce which go to furnish its commissariat alone, the amount of space occupied by each individual throughout the world, though one little chair is large enough to hold the whole of him! Yet, after all is over and done, there remains only material for two hours' thought, some pages of writing!

What a negligible fraction of my few pages would this one lazy day of mine occupy! But then, will not this peaceful day, on the desolate sands by the placid river, leave nevertheless a distinct little gold mark even upon the scroll of my eternal past and eternal future?

---

[1] Not included in this selection.

ON THE WAY TO PABNA,
9 July 1895

I am gliding through this winding little Ichamati, this streamlet of the rainy season. With rows of villages along its banks, its fields of jute and sugarcane, its reed patches, its green bathing slopes, it is like a few lines of a poem, often repeated and as often enjoyed. One cannot commit to memory a big river like the Padma, but this meandering little Ichamati, the flow of whose syllables is regulated by the rhythm of the rains, I am gradually making my very own...

It is dusk, the sky getting dark with clouds. The thunder rumbles fitfully, and the wild casuarina clumps bend in waves to the stormy gusts which pass through them. The depths of bamboo thickets look black as ink. The pallid twilight glimmers over the water like the herald of some weird event.

I am bending over my desk in the dimness, writing this letter. I want to whisper low-toned, intimate talk, in keeping with this penumbra of the dusk. But it is just wishes like these which baffle all effort. They either get fulfilled of themselves, or not at all. That is why it is a simple matter to warm up to a grim battle, but not to an easy, inconsequent talk.

SHEILIDAH,
14 August 1895

One great point about work is that for its sake the individual has to make light of his personal joys and sorrows; indeed, so far as may be, to ignore them. I am reminded of an incident at Shazadpur. My servant was late one morning, and I was greatly annoyed at his delay. He came up and stood before me with his usual salaam, and with a slight catch in his voice explained that his eight-year-old daughter had died last night. Then, with his duster, he set to tidying up my room.

When we look at the field of work, we see some at their trades, some tilling the soil, some carrying burdens, and yet underneath, death, sorrow, and loss are flowing, in an unseen undercurrent, every day,—their privacy not intruded upon. If ever these should break forth beyond control and come to the surface, then all this work would at once come to a stop. Over the individual sorrows, flowing beneath, is a hard stone track, across which the trains of duty, with their human load, thunder their way, stopping for none save at appointed stations. This very cruelty of work proves, perhaps, man's sternest consolation.

KUSHTEA,
5 October 1895

The religion that only comes to us from external scriptures never becomes our own; our only tie with it is that of habit. To gain religion within is man's great lifelong adventure. In the extremity of suffering must it be born; on his life-blood it must live; and then, whether or not it brings him happiness, the man's journey shall end in the joy of fulfilment.

We rarely realize how false for us is that which we hear from other lips, or keep repeating with our own, while all the time the temple of our Truth is building within us, brick by brick, day after day. We fail to understand the mystery of this eternal building when we view our joys and sorrows apart by themselves, in the midst of fleeting time; just as a sentence becomes unintelligible if one has to spell through every word of it.

When once we perceive the unity of the scheme of that creation which is going on in us, we realize our relation to the ever-unfolding universe. We realize that we are in the process of being created in the same way as are the glowing heavenly orbs which revolve in their courses,—our desires, our sufferings, all finding their proper place within the whole.

We may not know exactly what is happening: we do not know exactly even about a speck of dust. But when we feel the flow of life in us to be one with the universal life outside, then all our pleasures and pains are seen strung upon one long thread of joy. The facts: I am, I move, I grow, are seen in all their immensity in connection with the fact that everything else is there along with me, and not the tiniest atom can do without me.

The relation of my soul to this beautiful autumn morning, this vast radiance, is one of intimate kinship; and all this colour, scent, and music is but the outward expression of our secret communion.

This constant communion, whether realized or unrealized, keeps my mind in movement; out of this intercourse between my inner and outer worlds I gain such religion, be it much or little, as my capacity allows: and in its light I have to test scriptures before I can make them really my own.

SHELIDAH,
12 December 1895

The other evening I was reading an English book of criticisms, full of all manner of disputations about Poetry, Art, Beauty, and so forth and so on. As I plodded through these artificial discussions, my tired faculties seemed to have wandered into a region of empty mirage, filled with the presence of a mocking demon.

The night was far advanced. I closed the book with a bang and flung it on the table. Then I blew out the lamp with the idea of turning into bed. No sooner had I done so that through the open windows, the moonlight burst into the room, with a shock of surprise.

That little bit of a lamp had been sneering drily at me, like some Mephistopheles: and that tiniest sneer had screened off this infinite light of joy issuing forth from the deep love which is in all the world. What, forsooth, had I been looking for in the empty wordiness of the book? There was the very thing itself, filling the skies, silently waiting for me outside, all these hours!

If I had gone off to bed leaving the shutters closed, and thus missed this vision, it would have stayed there all the same without any protest against the mocking lamp inside. Even if I had remained blind to it all my life,—letting the lamp triumph to the end,—till for the last time I went darkling to bed,—even then the moon would have still been there, sweetly smiling, unperturbed and unobtrusive, waiting for me as she has throughout the ages.